Hoover Institution Publications 116

Industrial Management in the Soviet Union

INDUSTRIAL MANAGEMENT
IN THE SOVIET UNION

The Role of the CPSU in
Industrial Decision-making, 1917-1970

William J. Conyngham

Hoover Institution Press
Stanford University
Stanford, California

Hoover Institution Publications 116
International Standard Book Number 0-8179-1161-8
Library of Congress Card Number 76-170206

With love to
Margaret and
Bill, Monica, Mike and Maura

Tout commence en mystique et finit en politique—l'intérêt, la question, l'essentiel est que dans chaque ordre, dans chaque système la mystique ne soit point dévorée par la politique à laquelle elle a donné naissance.

Charles Péguy, *Notre Jeunesse*, 1910

Contents

Foreword   xiii
Acknowledgments   xvii
Introduction   xix

Part I: The Legacy of Lenin and Stalin

1. The Leading Role under Lenin   3
2. The Leading Role and the Socialist Offensive   25
3. The Routinization of the Leading Role   43

Part II: The Leading Role under Khrushchev

4. Khrushchev and the Leading Role: The Strategy of Party Reform   65
5. Khrushchev and the Leading Role: The Strategy of Expansion   90

Part III: The Party as Entrepreneur: A Case Study

6. The Decision-making Context of the November Plenum   123
7. The Institutional Effect of the Party Reform   157
8. The Dynamics of Party Reform   187
9. The Economic Impact of the November Plenum   213

Part IV: An Epilogue

10. The Leading Role Since Khruschev   253

Notes   289
Glossary   353
Bibliographical Note   357
Bibliography   359

Foreword

by John N. Hazard

Communists believe in leadership, but how shall that leadership function? That is the question to which Dr. Conyngham devotes his attention, and well he might. It is the key question in analyzing the Soviet system of government, which has been the prototype for variations in Eastern Europe, Asia, Africa, and Latin America. Both Soviet and Chinese leaders have reiterated their position on frequent occasions that the primary distinguishing feature of any governmental system they can approve is that it incorporates the Communist Party as its guiding political force.

At times, as varying types of communist-led systems have proliferated, the question has become important to those trying to anticipate Soviet reaction to variation, to determine whether a given variation will be accepted or whether it will stimulate efforts to initiate greater conformity to the Soviet model. Judging from reactions since Stalin's death in 1953, variation of almost any sort will receive the cachet of Lenin's heirs if the leadership component of the system he devised is retained. It is leadership that determines acceptance or rejection of a system seeking recognition from the oldest of all communist-led systems; all other features of the governmental structure can be accepted, though perhaps not always with good grace.

Since the preeminence of the leadership component has been recognized by all Western authors who write about Marxist-inspired systems of government, all have had much to say about the nature of communist leadership in those systems. Dr. Conyngham has not, therefore, discovered a previously neglected feature of the Soviet system of government when he focuses upon the importance of its leadership. What he has done is to examine exhaustively the nature of that component, especially as it reveals itself in responding to the needs of industrial development. In doing so he has found it necessary, and properly so, to delve into the history of the Communist Party from its inception at the beginning of the twentieth century.

The earliest years of the experience of Russian revolutionaries forming an instrument of revolution were years of hot debate. In those debates Lenin's position seems always to have been clear: he was for a disciplined, centralized, professional revolutionary party, and he was prepared to go to any length to achieve his goal. History gave him the victory, but that victory opened the door to new problems. The first to face him was the need to transform the party from a revolutionary force in the ranks of the opposition into a guiding instrument dedicated to creating an effective administrative apparatus for a great state committed to a system based on state economic entrepreneurship. His pressing task was to determine whether his reorganized party should seek efficiency by immersing itself in the paperwork and the day-to-day economic decision-making of the state bureaucracy, or whether it should remain outside the bureaucracy where it might think out basic policy positions without having to meet the burdensome pressures of administrative duties.

More than fifty years have passed since the Soviet Socialist experiment was initiated. Those years have been replete with varied approaches, sometimes seemingly inspired by a need to meet immediate crises and sometimes stimulated by no more than the selfish desire of an individual to enhance his personal power. There has been the temptation at all times to try to set right the chronically inefficient administrative bureaucracy of the state apparatus by putting matters directly into party hands. That temptation has been yielded to on some occasions and resisted on others. Throughout all such oscillations, the word "leadership" has been on the lips of those who pronounce policy, but it has implied different underlying concepts at different times. Dr. Conyngham examines the record and provides some enlightening and carefully researched conclusions.

Quite properly, Dr. Conyngham sees the fallibility of the research materials available to him. He could not question large numbers of party and non-party people about what they believe "leadership" means, and about what they think are the factors that make for change in meaning. The Soviet Union is not open to behavioral studies of the kind that can be conducted in the West. While other East European states may become theaters for such field surveys in the future, development in that direction is slow. To contemporary political scientists anxious to apply to the study of communist-led states the techniques developed so brilliantly for analysis of Western societies, research in Soviet political institutions is frustrating. The more familiar techinques of documentary analysis have to be used, supplemented by the occasional interview with a disgruntled refugee from the system and stimulated by such inferences as can be drawn from the surface manifestations of the system in operation. Dr. Conyngham has done all that can be done with the material available.

Those who read this book will perhaps reflect upon what may occur in other societies when alienated peoples seek a way out of their dilemmas by installing avant-garde leadership of the Leninist type to meet their formidable problems of organization for development. Admittedly, a leadership claiming special knowledge of the industrial imperative because of its study of the historical materialistic aspects of social events can seem attractive, at least for an experimental period. But what will happen if leadership is installed on such a basis? Will it guide or will it dictate? Will it withdraw if it becomes unpopular? Chileans of liberal persuasion have recently made the choice, and some today give evidence that they did so without understanding fully what type of leadership they had chosen.

Dr. Conyngham poses other fascinating questions arising from the imperatives of industrial decision-making and management. Can a policy-making party remain aloof from the administrative process and leave to administrators the daily decisions required for production? Will there inevitably be a merger between party and state apparatuses to create one mighty bureaucratic monolith with both policy-making and administrative functions? If such a merger occurs, will the party as a separate instrument tend to wither away?

Dr. Conyngham's study is more than an analysis of techniques of government developed by Marxist-oriented politicians in the Soviet Union. It is a study in techniques available to all those who wish to lead ailing societies regardless of what they envision as the philosophical basis for the decision-making process. It is more particularly something of a guidebook, a compendium of "do's" and "don'ts" for those prepared to depart from Jeffersonian principles of democracy for whatever purpose, be it humanitarian or narrowly selfish. It shows what has been happening in one prominent case of one-party government, and, as such, it may help those leaders in developing countries who sometimes deem it necessary to guide without from time to time presenting accounts to the people and seeking new mandates.

Finally, although Marxist concepts are considered fundamental to the functioning of the Soviet government, a similar type of government can function in circumstances where the Marxist component is reduced in great degree. The Soviet system has been a model for development and modernization adapted by many leaders to their own particular situations, and the problems Dr. Conyngham has found seen to emerge wherever it is used. For this reason Dr. Conyngham's work deserves study as a perceptive contribution to the literature concerning one-party avant-garde leadership systems.

Acknowledgments

It is perhaps trite to state that one can never fully acknowledge much less repay the debts accumulated in almost a decade of research. But one should try.

This book originated in the intellectually exciting seminars on the American and Soviet political systems conducted by Zbigniew Brzezinski and Samuel P. Huntington at Columbia University in the early sixties. A major portion of the research was done as a doctoral dissertation under John N. Hazard, without whose knowledge and concern the manuscript might never have been written. Among my colleagues, I am particularly grateful to Peter Juviler of Columbia for his penetrating criticisms of the manuscript at an early stage of its writing. The book's value would not be there without the help of these persons; its faults, of course, are particularly my own.

The manuscript underwent a series of revisions and various retypings in its evolution. I am grateful for the skills and often touching fortitude of Mrs. Mary Hennessy, Mrs. Hilda Macarthur, Mrs. Estrella Dizon, and Miss Eileen Donegan, who typed so many successive drafts.

Finally, I should like to thank Mrs. Carole Norton and the editorial staff of the Hoover Institution Press for making the publication of the book so pleasurable. In this respect, my debt to Mrs. Barbara Pronin for her expert and devoted editing of the book is immeasurable. Whatever order and grace it has is surely hers.

Stanford, California　　　　　　　　　　　　　　　　　　W.J.C.
June, 1972

Introduction

The following study attempts to probe a central relationship in the Soviet political system: the doctrine and practice of the *leading and directing role* of the Communist party, with particular reference to the industrial decision-making process, clearly a matter of importance in an era in which governments assume increasing responsibilities and controls over economic life. The Soviet variant—industrialization under the auspices of a revolutionary political party—is, of course, a significant major alternative of this process. In this respect, the relationship of Party and state encompassed in the Soviet term *rukovodstvo* is fundamental.

Because the transactions between the Communist party apparatus and the Soviet industrial system are immensely complex and multifaceted, approximately one third of this book is devoted to a detailed analysis of the Party's role between November 1962 and Khrushchev's fall in October 1964. The radical structural reorganization and expansion of managerial functions which the Party apparatus underwent during these years to increase its role in industrial management provides a particularly useful vantage point for examining the problem. The Party's extreme involvement in industrial management in 1963–64 revealed not only the inherent strengths and weaknesses of formal Party guidance, but also brought into sharp relief certain informal practices normally underplayed or ignored in Soviet discussion of the leading role in industrial administration. Although unique components were introduced into the leading-role concept by the reorganization of the winter of 1962, the practices actually adopted by the Party apparatus have had a more continuing and generalized application.

In analyzing the impact of the November 1962 reorganization by measuring changes in authority relationships, formal structures, and informal institutional patterns, attention is directed first to a detailed description of the specific institutional qualities of Party *rukovodstvo* in this period. In addition, the study points up a number of significant issues, such as the extent to which the Party's extreme engagement in the operational direction of industrial administration conformed to those operational norms which define its legitimate administrative role. The contemporary Soviet interpretation of these guidelines, which have been in continuous existence since the Civil War, is discussed in part 3 of the Introduction.

More particularly, the drastic quality and far-reaching effects of the November 1962 reforms raised complex questions of basic ideological, political, and institutional significance for the Soviet political system itself. The reform carried profoundly disturbing implications with respect to the leading role and the internal stability of the Party apparatus as well. Caught up in the turbulence of major controversies, the reform proceeded unevenly but with distinct impacts at various levels of the Party's structure. The reorganization of the state industrial apparatus likewise proceeded in a context of strenuous debate—debate which challenged some of the most basic assumptions of the Stalinist administrative system. The outcomes of these various political engagements provided the operational context for both the reforms themselves and for the subsequent interaction of the Party and state mechanisms.

In a broader view, the November 1962 plenum raised challenging problems of perspective extending beyond the more immediate issues of the politics and structures of reform. The dynamics of Party *rukovodstvo* during 1963 and 1964 were related to the major patterns of political and institutional change which proceeded in the Soviet political system following Stalin's death. Underlying these varied, incomplete, and often inconsistent trends was the fundamental question of whether the Party could legitimately represent itself any longer as a revolutionary political force committed to the further basic transformation of Soviet society.

Logically related to this broad question was a narrower one which is the formal subject of this study: the question of the Party's efficiency as an agent of industrial development. In tracing the patterns of institutional reform under Khrushchev, the study attempts not only to link the continuities and changes in the Party and state administrative systems to the November reforms but also to examine these questions in view of the Party's increasingly complex role in a society of maturing social and economic institutions.

The moderate degree of institutional reform actually achieved under Khrushchev's leadership raises the question of the extent to which the leading role had become institutionalized under Lenin and Stalin. Out of the turmoil and crisis of the first ten years of the Party's transformation from a revolutionary to a governing institution, the doctrinal development of the Party's operational role and the institutional characteristics associated with the Party bureaucracy both emerged. The critical point in the evolution of the Party's decision-making role, however, came with the turning toward rapid industrialization in 1928. The assumption by the Party apparatus of a new and demanding managerial role as an agent of industrialization produced serious strains and disequilibria within the apparatus. In the Party's prolonged and often conflict-ridden adjustment to the requirements of guiding a rapidly growing industrial complex, the central parameters framing its decision-making role were set. The Khrushchev reforms appear in this perspective as an attempt to ameliorate the liabilities of the Stalinist system without, however, undertaking a program of radical political reform.

2

This study employs a basically historical approach in order to place the complexities of Party leadership within a specific, limited framework. In dealing with the data, however, certain theoretical assumptions were necessary for purposes of categorization and interpretation. The assumptions and the approach reflect both the problems under investigation and the limitations in access to data. The area of initial interest—the November 1962 plenum and its consequences—was a historical event largely devoted to organizational issues.

Under contemporary conditions of research, the problem of access to data limits the degree of theoretical generality possible in the study of Soviet politics. Alfred Meyer has noted this basic methodological limitation in an excellent article on Communist leadership, in which he declares that "a strictly behavioral approach to the study of authority in communist systems is impossible, because the social scientists' access to necessary data is severely restricted in a variety of ways. The use of the vocabulary of contemporary political sociology in this chapter therefore cannot (and is not meant to) conceal the basic impressionism and intuitivism pervading it."[1] This disclaimer is true for any study of Soviet politics.

Concerning the dimension of Party *rukovodstvo* in the Soviet industrial economy, there are, perhaps, three theoretical assumptions present in both the categorization and interpretation of the data in this study. The first is that Party leadership is basically a decision-making activity. The second, closely related assumption is that decision-making is largely framed within a bureaucratic structure and can best be understood in terms of the interaction of two massive organizations. Finally, there is an assumption that decision-making, structure, and function are themselves part of a larger matrix, which, however elusive and fragmentary its description, nevertheless imposes boundaries and influences on the other, more limited processes. Each will be considered briefly.

Decision-making is used here to mean the processes by which choices among alternative courses of action are framed into policies and implemented. Following the model of Brzezinski and Huntington, it is here assumed that decision-making can be analyzed in terms of the sequential stages in which a policy is initiated, exposed to support and opposition, is either approved or vetoed by an authoritative decision-making body, and finally, if approved, is implemented either in accordance with its original intentions or in a modified form.[2]

In the context of this study, decisions are generally of two basic types, although broader subcategorization is, of course, possible. One type consists of decisions which have been routinized; most of the decisions involved in Soviet planning and plan-implementation structures are of this type. This is not to suggest that such decisions are automatic. There is discretion, bargaining, and compromise in the process; but the actions are specific, repetitive, and task oriented, and innovation is narrowly defined and controlled. In contrast are those decisions in which some degree of innovation *is* involved and in which there is a perceptible shift in goals or methods with implications involving the values or positions of significant actors within the system.

The varying degree of policy generalization is an important factor in the decision-making process. Policy-making, as Talcott Parsons points out, may involve a functional division of labor.[3] At the most general level are policies which commit the resources of the organization as a whole to the decision and which bear the heaviest risks—such as, for example, Khrushchev's decision to reorganize the Party apparatus in 1962. At an intermediate level of generality are the allocative decisions which distribute power, responsibility, human and material resources for achieving goals. Finally, there are coordinative or operational decisions which maintain direction and cohesion through task definition, and motivation through an ancillary structure of sanctions, pressures, and rewards.

These three types of decision-making are interrelated in a complex fashion. Decisions with the most basic implications may be either *ad hoc* or part of a broader strategy. Allocative decisions may integrate or separate the distribution of authority, of responsibility, and of human and material resources. The framework does not require an assumption of cognitive rationality;[4] the decisions may be either routinized or innovative, and they may be staged through the phases smoothly or with great conflict. The Soviet system is distinguished primarily by the degree to which it has centralized all aspects of the decision-making process.

A discussion of the Party's leading role involves a serious consideration of every phase and level of the decision-making process. A specific term used by this leadership may be identified with another basic assumption—that Party *rukovodstvo* proceeds through and is conditioned by bureaucracy. The predominance of organizational issues in Soviet politics gives organizational theory, despite its lack of inner cohesion, a useful heuristic value. More specifically, there are reasonably close correspondences between the ''machine school'' of theory and the structure and practices of the Party and economic agencies seen as large-scale organizations.

The central goal of the ''machine school'' as an ideal type is to reduce random or spontaneous behavior on the part of organization members for the purpose of increasing the security and permanence of the organization and the reliability of its operation.[5] Under the technical and rationalized arrangements inherent in this type of bureaucracy, power and efficiency are central instrumental values in task orientation and are regarded as being essentially harmonious.

The "machine school" model stresses (in Thompson's term) a "monocratic" concept in which authority is hierarchically structured in a pyramidal pattern of superior-subordinate relationships which govern communication as well as direction and accountability.[6] In complex organizations, this basic authority structure may be complicated by the existence of specialized functional and staff groups, a condition evidently true in both the Communist party and the Soviet industrial administration.

Other characteristics of this type of bureaucracy include (1) unity of command and centralized decision-making; (2) a narrow span of control to permit detailed supervision of subordinates; (3) a disciplined response from subordinates; (4) a factoring of general goals and procedures into subgoals emphasizing a formal division of labor and role specialization, (5) the presence of an ideology and a reward system which legitimate, integrate, and motivate those within the organization.[7]

The essentially rationalist and technical premises of the machine model have evoked serious criticism, and a number of these criticisms are of interest in this study. Perhaps the most relevant is by Victor Thompson, who advances the view that there is a basic conflict between power and efficiency inherent in modern organizations. The monocratic model of centralized, hierarchical authority arose during a period of relatively simple technology. But as structure and function differentiate to accommodate increasing technical complexity, knowledge and authority tend likewise to divide, thus producing a condition in which power and efficiency become conflicting values and a decisional dilemma.[8] Khrushchev's intellectual dilemma may be said to lay precisely in this dimension.

Other, more limited aspects of the critique are of interest here as well. One important effect of bureaucracy is to produce through routine performance a "trained incapacity" based upon habits and skills no longer appropriate under changed circumstances. Bureaucratic conservatism, technicism, and timidity may lead to a displacement of energy from ends to means and to a defensive and stereotyped behavior which produces personal conflict in addition to such familiar complaints as red tape, stereotyped application of rules, conflict with clients, and so forth.[9]

Two functional aspects of Soviet bureaucracy seem particularly affected by the authority and structural elements of the system. One important effect has been a perceptible tendency to turn limited subgoals into ends in themselves, thus achieving a certain pluralism, autonomy, and limited discretion within the subunits. In industrial decision-making, however, this tendency may result in institutionalized cleavages exhibiting a clear conflict of interest between the enterprise and the central planning agencies. In other cases, and particularly within the Party apparatus, the divergence of interests from the central authorities may be subtler, the indications more ambiguous and difficult to ascertain. However, the potentiality for divergence and conflict between the whole and the part is here assumed to be omnipresent in the Soviet system.

A second effect is clearly to be discerned in the area of communications. The high degree of centralization in the Soviet system creates massive cognitive and informational problems which directly affect the decision-making process. The size, scope, functional complexity, levels of hierarchy, and detailed social controls of Soviet communications produce problems in the volume and quality of information, which reduce the accuracy, speed, and utility of the information and the ability of the organization to respond to it effectively. This overload along hierarchical channels is in some respects mirrored by the lack of lateral communication.[10] "Departmentalism" has significant consequences for vertical relationships in the Soviet hierarchy, and its tendency to restrict lateral communication within and between organizations likewise produces major coordinative problems.

Where organizations have become legitimatized into institutions, the underlying power-efficiency dilemma creates singular problems for those who would undertake their reform in the interests of greater efficiency. Reform is infinitely more complex than the terrible simplifications of revolution and social violence. Reform through innovation cuts against the obstinate grain of organizational structure and the enveloping social structure which has given it value and meaning. As Samuel P. Huntington has indicated, reform is a political process, and those who undertake it with any success are master politicians.[11] However otherwise one may view Lenin, Stalin, and Khrushchev, it must be concluded that each possessed political skills of a high order.

The power-efficiency dilemma becomes particularly complex in the reform of mature bureaucratic institutions. Michel Crozier has noted that power and dependency relationships underlie bureaucratic structure. Overt conflict, however, is illegitimate.[12] To control conflict and promote stable response, the leadership routinizes activity. Structural alteration, however, involves disrupting routine as a preliminary phase of establishing new relationships. This, in turn, increases uncertainty and thus stimulates a power struggle. Conflict and change are thus inseparable. In the Soviet context, the power struggles around issues requiring structural change have been continuous, and many of them are discussed in this book. While the number of legitimate options has diminished with time, the puzzle of how to maintain organizational power and cohesion while at the same time pressing for environmental transformation and structural adaption remained as enigmatic a problem for Khrushchev as it had been for Lenin and Stalin.

To note a second and more limited aspect of the problem, Victor Thompson has recently called attention to the difficulties of inducing innovation at the lower levels of a bureaucracy which has been heavily programmed. Under conditions (as in the Soviet Union) in which a "production ideology" eliminates slack in an organization by overcommitting its resources and in which there is a centralized and detailed specification of resources, the risks of innovation may be high,[13] and the reform policies of the leadership will be blunted in favor of the status quo. The repeated blunting of Khrushchev's drives to increase efficiency in industry and agriculture may be attributable in part to this fact.

To apply the "machine school" of organizational theory and its critique to the problems under study is not to imply a one-to-one relationship. Soviet reality is a complex and contradictory phenomenon which eludes ensnaring simplicities. The problems under discussion—those of the middle-range—are not without theoretical implication, but neither are they dependent upon a macroscopic theory of Soviet politics. No student, however, can completely ignore the theories of the larger system. Since a study of the Party's role in industrial decision-making involves some overlapping of economic and political processes, each of these will be discussed briefly in turn.

The economic theory most relevant to this study is that of the "command economy" as it has been elaborated by Gregory Grossman and Peter Wiles.[14] In the command economy defined by Grossman, the individual firm employs resources and produces goods primarily by means of specific directives relayed through a bureaucratic structure. In this authoritarian system, economic goals and priorities are set by the political leadership. The planning system involves a high degree of centralized allocative and coordinative decision-making. In such a system the major problem is centralization—or more broadly, the allocation of decision-making power at various levels of the command hierarchy. While centralization allows the setting and enforcing of primary goals and priorities, allowing a degree of resource mobility as well, the command economy also exacts heavy costs.

Under conditions of high pressure for economic growth, the "logic of haste" creates a microimbalance in the economy and produces serious problems in coordination. Also, as Grossman notes elsewhere, economic growth—a primary value of the system—becomes bureaucratized or routinized.[15] Investment, financial controls, research and development, the training of manpower, and the dissemination of information are repeated year after year according to standardized bureaucratic procedures.

The effect is to breed conservatism and to hamper technological growth, both crucial factors in industrial expansion. Coordinative imbalance and the threat of technological stagnation are both assumed in this study to frame the operational environment. The virtually constant reorganizing of the Party and state bureaucracies under Khrushchev was the result of adaptive policies designed, from the efficiency point of view, to cope with these problems.

To conceptualize a political system having the precision and empirical validity of the command economy theory is more difficult. There is, to be sure, the suggestion of a macroscopic model implicit in the Soviet view of the Party's structural-functional role, which is discussed in Part 3.[16] Soviet writers define *rukovodstvo* as those activities which legitimate and integrate Soviet society, control the processes of policy-making and implementation, participate in or indirectly control the selection and recruitment of elite members, and which act to mobilize human and material resources toward Party-selected goals. To have centered this study on primarily Soviet categories is not to suggest that the system is unique, although, of course, unique elements are certainly present. The idea is rather that the use of Soviet concepts provides a useful framework for evaluating concrete events in the system.

The structural-functional approach, however, is insufficient for a reasonable understanding of the Soviet political system. The stability, harmony, and rationality implicit in the Soviet model is a normative rather than empirical design, as even a casual inspection of the power conflicts and disruptive, often cataclysmic movements of Soviet history will reveal. The problems of power, change, and conflict evident in the system indicate the exercise of caution in excessive reliance on either an organizational or functional approach to explaining the system.

The element of coercive power has perhaps been most extensively conceptualized in the totalitarian model, which, although clearly applicable to Stalinism, is questionable as an analytical framework for the post-Stalin period.[17] Still, some basic assessment of power in the Party's leading role is needed. Such dynamic features of the system as those noted by Paul Hollander, for example, are useful in this respect. Hollander attributes to the system an ideologically committed leadership; intense political controls; a concerted drive for industrialization; an absence of legitimate and significant pluralism; and, finally, a deliberately contrived interdependence of all significant societal functions.[18] This list is neither exhaustive nor empirically verifiable in every respect; neither does it suggest that the Party's control over Soviet society's resources and developments is total. It does suggest a set of reality restraints in contrast to the conception of the Soviet power structure as tightly integrated and is for that reason valuable as a model in developing a perspective on the central issue of power.

The system, while relatively closed, has been susceptible to change, and, from the particular view of this study, these processes of change appear to be deeply contingent. Structured into a pattern, however, these changes have been largely in the direction of modernization, a direction compatible with the revolutionary ethos of bolshevism and the power needs of the Soviet state. The commitments to the rationalization of science and technology, industrialization, and urbanization, to a set of modern cultural institutions, and to a social structure capable of supporting these values and institutions have been among the major goals of Soviet leadership.

The achievement of these goals through the leadership of a one-party state dictatorship has raised at least two fundamental questions directly related to the concept of *rukovodstvo*. The first question is whether the Party's political and administrative power is compatible with the highly complex society it has created.[19] The second question—which in the contemporary Soviet context has perhaps even greater urgency—is whether Soviet social, cultural, and economic institutions can function at significantly higher levels of efficiency and growth without qualitative changes in the political system.[20] Although no final answer is suggested here, the data herein collected point (1) to severe stress produced by both the process and results of modernization, and (2) to a need for qualitative reforms, beyond those attempted by Khrushchev, to adapt the political structure to the environmental changes imposed by modernization.

Conflict involving the issues of power and change is considered in this study to be linked at societal as well as at organizational levels. These processes clearly overlap where the scope of political power has no formal or legitimate restraints. Political change is inevitably a conflict-laden process under conditions of modernization—a condition intensified (again as in the Soviet Union) where growth induces differentiation and complexity as it multiplies options and obscures consequences. In the Soviet case, where access to information is restricted and political roles but vaguely defined, both research and conceptualization of political processes are difficult. However illegitimate the process and the pluralism, conflict can be observed both within and between the Party and the economic bureaucracies.[21]

A number of such conflicts generated by Khrushchev's innovative efforts are of interest in this study. The decisions to alter the Party structure, to institute the Liberman proposals, and to establish a Party-State Control Committee, which formed the substance of the November 1962 Central Committee Plenum, were profoundly controversial issues in which personal, policy, and institutional values and interests were inextricably intertwined. The data here are interpreted conservatively where the author has used his own research or has critically incorporated into his own work the work of the Kremlinologists. It is, presumably, reasonable to see Kosygin as the prime mover in the Presidium after the July 1960 plenum, particularly in view of his role in promoting economic reform after Khrushchev's fall.

Identification of Kosygin as the spokesman and advocate of managerial interests between 1960 and 1964, however, should be cautiously approached in light of the conflicts among the economic managers on the issue of reform. There is little evidence of consensus among economists, central planners, financial officials, sovnarkhoz chairmen, or enterprise managers on the nature and problems of reform, or on the procedures which reform should take. In view of this situation and of the lack of direct confirming evidence, the author has preferred a conservative approach to the issue. A number of other examples could as easily have been cited.

This study of Party *rukovodstvo* has been placed in a context of decision-making both within and between large-scale organizations. Since the Party's role is believed to have functional implications for both the political and the economic process, the Soviet view of these relations is of major importance and is treated below.

3

The Soviet conception of the Party's guiding role has been strongly influenced by the traditional political culture and institutional heritage of the Russian past. Etymologically, *rukovodit'* is linked with *vospitat'* ("to bring up") and has the meaning of educating, advising, and aiding youth.[22] "To guide" is a paternalistic, personalistic conception of authority based upon the intellectual and moral superiority of those holding power. Ideally, the interaction of leader and led is achieved through personal example and imitation. This traditional notion of authority is in sharp contrast with the Weberian conception of the explicit and rational exercise of impersonal power contained in the term *upravlenie*, or formal bureaucratic authority legitimately exercised on the basis of law.[23] The distinction between Party leadership and state administration has lost much of its meaning in contemporary Soviet conditions. The traditional concept of authority, however, still holds some interest, since Khrushchev, in his relentless search for solutions to the problems of "bureaupathology" induced by large-scale organization, often reverted to the traditional model.

The historical and institutional concept of *rukovodstvo* is rooted in the legitimacy implied in the Party's revolutionary mission. The claim to an organizational monopoly of power rests upon the premise that only a Marxist-Leninist party can unify revolutionary practice. The *Fundamentals of Marxism-Leninism* has stated this basic assertion of the right to power simply:

> It is the Party, armed with scientific theory and attentively hearing the voice of experience that most fully, comprehensively, and deeply learns the objective tendencies of reality itself and on this basis directs and organizes the constructive, purposeful activities of the broadest masses.[24]

At this most general level, the Party is regarded as the "cement" of Soviet society, directing and coordinating all of its complex and multifaceted activities toward a single goal, the building of communism. In the process, the Party's political role, which was believed to be continually expanding under Khrushchev, would be one in which "the Party more and more acts not only as the collective leader and organizer of the masses but as a collective educator as well."[25]

The distinctive features of the Party's leading role, however, lie not only in its general claim to a monopoly of social truth and authority within Soviet society. Party *rukovodstvo* is also a specific system of political and administrative power designed to translate the abstractions of social theory into concrete social realities. Existing Soviet theory on the leading role consists of a set of general norms rather than of a detailed code providing specific regulation for each situation. Soviet theorists concentrate on two basic and coordinate elements of the Party-state complex. The first deals primarily with internal Party structures and processes (*partiinoe stroitel'stvo*); the second and more complex concerns the related problem of the Party's role in directing subordinate administrative agencies (*rukovodstvo* proper).

The machine is the metaphor ordinarily used to depict the internal structure and dynamics of the Party. In discussing the use of discipline in regulating the Party, two Soviet writers have noted: "In a large machine each part fulfills a definite role. Without well-greased screws and wheels the machine cannot run. So it is with the Party."[26] The centralized, integrated, and hierarchical nature of the Party is stressed as the fundamental construct. In theory, the Party's internal authority structure is a complex blend of vertical centralism and democracy, and monocratic and collective leadership. In practice, however, centralism and the rule of the line secretaries has predominated.

Lazar Slepov, perhaps the most prestigious of contemporary Soviet writers on the Party, has noted:

...The Party is not just an accumulation of individuals or the sum total of its organizations, but a single system of these organizations. The Communist Party represents a single organizational unit, with higher and lower organs of direction with obligatory subordination of the minority to the majority, and with practical decisions which are binding on all members of the Party.[27]

The disavowal of any form of constitutional pluralism within the Party structure is closely related to the emphasis upon the necessity of concentrating unrestricted authority within higher Party organs. In the opinion of one Soviet writer, centralism is the fundamental organizational principle for a successful realization of the Party's mission of destroying the old society and creating the new.[28]

The operational theory defining the Party's external leading role stresses two somewhat incompatible subordinate relationships. The most significant ideological and symbolic expression of Party *rukovodstvo* is the mobilization and integration of the masses by the elite. This relationship, heavily stressed by Lenin and singled out for special emphasis in the literature of totalitarianism,[29] was, however, inadequate for effective control over such an organized center of power and interest as the massive Russian bureaucracy. While Soviet administrative theory continues to emphasize the masses, the more significant relationship lies in the complex transactions between the Party apparatus and the major bureaucracies of Soviet society. *Rukovodstvo* at this level has aimed at retaining a tightly centralized hierarchical political institution which maintains a monopoly of power as it directs an increasingly complex administrative system. Under contemporary Soviet conditions, the power problem competes with an urgent need to maximize the efficiency of the administrative system.

The theory defining the Party's institutional role in relation to the Soviet state attempts to combine the concept of the Party as the highest form of social organization, possessing absolute and unlimited authority, with the practical and limiting requirements of directing the Soviet state as a specialized legislative and executive apparatus. In terms of classic Western theory, the situation is anomalous: two political institutions exercising sovereign power over the same territory and population. This condition has led one European legal scholar to describe the relationship as one in which the Communist party exercises political sovereignty and the Soviet state judicial sovereignty.[30] The concept of dual sovereignty, however, only partially resolves the theoretical difficulty. Some Soviet writers hold the view that Party decisions have the force of a legal command.[31] Soviet writers also make clear that the basic Party-state relationship is instrumental insofar as the state serves as a lever in the realization of Party policy.[32] The relationship has been restated in a recent authoritative work on Soviet ideology.

> How does the Party play its leading role in the conditions of the dictatorship of the proletariat? It acts through the government and mass public organizations, guiding their efforts toward one single goal. But, in guiding all the state and public organizations, it does not supplant them. Party leadership may be compared with the art of the conductor, who strives for harmony in the orchestra but, of course, does not try to play for every musician. The Party ensures the implementation of its policy, acting through its members working in the state apparatus and public organizations.[33]

In traditional theory, Party guidance establishes a relationship in which the individual Party organ is the source of basic political determination; it carries full responsibility for the execution of Party policy but plays a limited, restricted administrative role. Guidance of the state apparatus is indirect, restricted, and supervisory. Decision-making and supervision of execution, however, are channeled through a formal Party structure in which authority is centralized. Then, the Soviet state, under the general leadership of the Communist party, is conceded to have a special technical and executive competence which allows it some degree of autonomy. From these conditions arise two basic, interrelated questions concerning (1) the applicability of the doctrine of the leading role and (2) the division of functions between Party and state organs at the central level.

On the question of applicability, there is significant disagreement among Western specialists concerning the extent of meaningful separation between central Party and state organs.[34] The problem is an extraordinarily difficult one to assess since any judgment involves a large number of variables based upon inadequate information. What contemporary Soviet literature makes clear is that systematic application of the doctrine is most relevant to lower Party and state organs. Understood in these terms, the doctrine of *rukovodstvo* fits logically within the framework of centralization. The separation of functions has the advantage of securing to the central Party and state authorities maximum power over lower governing agencies.

The operational norms which constitute the substance of the theory of *rukovodstvo* concentrate on two major categories in the executive process. The first focuses on the Party's role in the formation of policy; the second, on the Party's legitimate administrative role in supervising and controlling the implementation of decisions.

The Party-state relationship in Soviet theory bears certain legal and institutional distinctions which have symbolic but little operational significance. The Party, for example, is ideologically legitimated, whereas the authority of the state is founded in positive law and limited by it. The Party is a voluntary organization, whereas the Soviet state integrates the whole population. The Party's structure is unitary; the Soviet state is a federation. The fundamental political resources of the Party are moral and persuasive, while the Soviet state operates on the basis of law and a monopoly of violence.[35] In fact, however, the distinction between politics and law as the institutional basis for distinguishing the authority of the Party and the Soviet state has been insignificant, even symbolically, since 1931 when joint Party-state decrees began to be issued.[36]

The Party's substantive role in decision-making is broadly "political," a term which in Soviet usage is susceptible to almost infinite interpretation. The general sense is, nonetheless, clear enough. The Party's executive agencies are responsible for implementing programmatic goals and deciding specific issues which arise in the building of Communist society. At one end of the authority spectrum, the Party's role is unlimited since any issue relevant to ideologically determined goals is within the legitimate frame of decision-making.[37] For local Party organs the range of Party *rukovodstvo* is more restricted. They are essentially administrative instruments of the central will,[38] and their role is clearly coordinative.

Local Party organs are expected to achieve maximum efficiency in executing Party policy. Creative decision-making, in contrast to either mechanical or bureaucratic leadership, involves, first of all, the ability to select from the mass of issues which press on the local Party organ those issues which have "principled" significance[39]—those which affect basic direction and long-range development as a whole. The political decision is therefore long-range rather than immediate: it elaborates basic problems, generalizes concrete experience, exposes trouble spots and proposes effective measures for eliminating them. There are no specific objective criteria for distinguishing the authentic political decision. Correct *rukovodstvo* is arrived at through trained intuition, the result of "political feeling and experience."[40]

The major danger to the local Party organ as a political decision-maker lies in the mass of minor, petty administrative problems which cloud perspective. This does not mean that the Party decision should be indifferent to details. The reverse is true. Decisions should be specific and detailed, particularly in economic decision-making, an area in which the Party decision-making role has been an issue of major concern.[41]

Where fulfillment and overfulfillment of the annual central plan is the major responsibility of Party, state, and economic officials, traditional distinctions between "politics" and "economics" are inevitably obscured. Soviet writers offer little guidance in distinguishing between the two, except to note that they may not be placed in opposition but must be properly joined.[42] There are, however, several relatively clear connotations in the concept. For one thing, the Party organ does not permit itself to ignore the totality of social life in its pursuit of a single activity. *Rukovodstvo* connotes area coordination within specified jurisdictional boundaries, which goes beyond simple functional coordination whether in the economy or elsewhere. For another thing, *rukovodstvo* involves executive method and style. Party political work is directed toward influencing attitudes and motivating behavior through ideological persuasion and influence as well as through organizational methods. Intrinsic in this process is the function of inspiring and mobilizing the masses toward maximum effort in the fulfillment of planned tasks.[43]

The major ambiguity in distinguishing political and economic leadership arises from the joint responsibility of the Party and economic organs for the results of economic activity. This has led to the familiar complaint during virtually every stage of Soviet history of "substitution" or "petty tutelage" over state economy agencies. In the case of Party decision-making in agriculture, such criticism has been far less evident. Here, Party administration and control of the production and procurement of agricultural products has been the rule rather than the exception. In this respect, the Party's role has been that of extracting maximum resources from the peasantry.

The situation in industrial administration, however, has been otherwise, since the technical competence required to direct industrial production efficiently is much higher. Under the twin impact of centralized industrial administration and increasing technical complexity, the meaning of "substitution" has acquired a dual significance. On the one hand, it has meant direct administrative control by local Party organs over specific activities concerned with the production of material goods. It has also meant the services which the local Party organ has performed to insure the uninterrupted flow of production. Activities of the first type were frequent during the first years of total industrialization, and services of the second type were generally encouraged during the operation of the ministerial system.[44]

The doctrine of *rukovodstvo* makes no formal distinction between the making and the administration of policy. Both are aspects of a continuous, interrelated, and mutually reinforcing process. In supervising the carrying out of decisions, traditionalist doctrine has emphasized two key elements in the administrative process: cadres policy and checkup-and-control on adopted decisions.[45] Of these basic administrative levers, "the selection, distribution and upbringing of cadres," to use the Soviet formula, have been of central importance. "In cadre policy," Lesnoi notes, "the Party is guided by the Marxist proposition that the conduct of work depends first of all on who conducts it."[46]

The criteria for political recruitment and socialization have both political and technical implications. These norms, despite their general form, apply in a special sense to Party leaders since political leadership carries responsibilities not present in the same degree among state and economic officials. The concept of the political quality of the official has varied over the years depending on the importance attributed by the Party leadership to social conflict. As the Party grew increasingly bureaucratized, however, there emerged model personality traits characteristic of the ideal political leader. Under Stalin, the model was the Bolshevik, or "positive hero," type, who displayed epic qualities of energy and fidelity in translating revolutionary policies into action against difficulties and opposition.[47] The ideal political leader to emerge under Khrushchev was cut from smaller cloth. His energy, skills, and commitments were those of an organizer possessing managerial ability and sensitive to interpersonal relationships.

The contemporary Soviet version of the political leader contrasts the "organizational" and "bureaucratic" models. Unlike the bureaucratic and routine-ridden individual who lacks initiative, guides according to stereotyped instructions, and relies upon his formal position and administrative power to execute Party decisions, the true political leader accepts personal responsibility, shows initiative, is helpful and accessible, but is also demanding toward those over whom he exercises authority. He is measured politically by his ability to influence people and to serve as an example for emulation. As part of a collective, the leader should know people individually, display tact and patience, and be persuasive rather than coercive.[48] Competence involves a technical mastery of Party tools and work methods in addition to technical and economic knowledge.

Soviet normative theory on the leading role gives little overt attention to the problems of power, complexity, and mobility which are evident in the functioning of the apparatus. The clash of interest and perspective between central and local Party officials and state agencies, for example, is little noted. Yet, within the Party, such informal methods of control as close personal observation and communication, periodic transfer, promotion, and purge have ensured the responsiveness of local Party officials to central priorities. Moreover, complaints are widespread against the deeply rooted practice of forming "family group" enclaves of officials in local areas to provide a measure of personal security against central controls, and for shifting these individuals from post to post regardless of their qualifications or experience.

Similarly, one should note the Party's increasing difficulties in controlling the quality of management within the state structure. Information concerning the size and structure of the appointments list, or *nomenklatura*, is relatively scarce. However, it is reasonable to assume that the growth and differentiation of Soviet institutions has imposed particularly serious strains on the process of personnel control.[49] Size alone indicates the difficulties of carefully evaluating each individual appointment made or approved by a Party organ. In 1956, for example, the Moscow City Party organization had some twenty-two thousand officials on its appointments list, a condition which made for a routinization of cadre work.[50]

The process of *vospitanie*, or socialization of political cadres, has been of prime importance to Party leadership, although modes and objectives have varied through the years. During the final years of his life, Lenin's basic concern involved the transformation of revolutionary politicians into managerial officials. Stalin, on the other hand, appears to have been most troubled by issues of ideological formation, particularly after the Great Purge. Khrushchev was obviously concerned with both, although his repeated reorganization of the Party's higher educational system indicated his determination to emphasize technical competence in Party cadres. All three were committed to creating that ideological unanimity necessary to maintaining the Party's monocratic structure and image. Given the intense stress of Soviet conditions, that this should be an imperfect process is not surprising.

The formation of the professional Party politician is directed toward producing a generalist.[51] It involves, as Armstrong has pointed out, "alternation of intensive training with practical experience" in the development of the apparatus official.[52] The growing economic and technical complexity of the Soviet economy has increasingly required technical expertise in Party cadres at all levels and has aroused a demand that Party officials possess higher technical training. Some Soviet writers, however, continue to emphasize the primacy of personal and practical experience. Practice, it is held, enables natural leaders to emerge and aids cadres in developing a feeling for the contingencies and nuances of specific situations.[53] It is also believed that institutional continuity is best achieved through the proper joining of young and old cadres.[54] The argument over the superiority of formal or practical training is relatively minor, however, because both are acknowledged to be necessary to produce an effective generalist under contemporary conditions.

The Communist party is also instrumental in forming the "organizational personality'' of the Soviet industrial executive. Virtually all industrial management officials in important posts are Party members and subject to Party discipline.[55] Increasingly, both Party and economic officials receive similar educations, and both carry responsibility as line officials in a bureaucratic structure. There are, however, significant differences. Party professionals have predominantly worker and peasant social origins, in contrast to Soviet industrial executives who have largely middle-class backgrounds.[56] There may be motivational differences as well, although lack of information about Party executives makes generalization hazardous.

It seems clear, however, that the industrial manager has been motivated less by political and ideological drives than by career and economic incentives.[57] There may be some significance in the fact that the Party professional deals in the intangibles of political control, whereas the industrial executive deals with a material product in a substantial and predictable environment. Finally, the having different jobs would seem to ensure some difference in outlook and goals between Party and economic officials. Party *vospitanie* produces overlapping but not identical drives and interests.

The second major lever sanctioned by the doctrine of guidance for the realization of Party decisions is the process of "checkup and control." *Proverka i kontrol'* is essentially a political process, different from such concepts as *reviziia, inspektsiia* which describe bureaucratic and technical control functions carried out by trained personnel on the basis of administrative instructions.[58] As a political term, checkup and control means, in the first place, that Party influence is exerted on those having direct responsibility for the execution of decisions. As Leopold Haimson has observed, this is a total process.

> First of all, Soviet leaders do not assume that the executives, technicians, and workers who man their industrial complexes have sufficiently internalized the values of the 'new Soviet man' or are sufficiently self-disciplined, well-trained, and responsive to available incentives to adjust, purely by their own resources, to the functional requirements of the job.[59]

Checkup thus goes beyond the inspection of an assignment to insure its proper completion. It is an active organizational role in which the Party organ specifies clearly the desired objective, indicates the proper means to its achievement, and finally extends direct aid in implementing the decision.[60] This means in the first instance a full mobilization of the aktiv and mass organs in executing the decision. A second function implied in the term checkup involves accepting the need for operational decision-making during the course of execution. *Proverka* in this context means a continuous testing of the human and material framework of the decision to resolve unexpected difficulties or to exploit a policing function. Party organs are expected to represent and enforce national priorities as well as to correct and discipline those who evade or otherwise distort them.[61] Control functions may be exercised positively, as a function of education and persuasion, or negatively, through the uses of administrative power.

The checking and controlling function of both central and local Party organs has in the course of Soviet experience been subject to certain limitations and problems. The first limitation has concerned the proper internal structure and competence of the Party itself. Whether Party competence should extend beyond cadre control and mass agitation to include active supervision of the industrial economy has evoked serious conflict within Party ranks. Consequently, the presence or absence of Party administrative structure has significantly affected the degree of daily Party control which could be exercised over the economy.

A second condition has also limited the authority of local Party organs. The highly centralized management of the Soviet economy has severely circumscribed the authority of local Party organs to intervene in the management of local industrial or construction enterprises under direct central control. In addition, local Party authority has been further reduced by the existence of a number of independent, centrally directed Party and state controlling agencies. Finally, Party cadres have been limited by a lack of formal training and industrial experience to cope with the technical and operational complexity of the Soviet economy.

Bearing full responsibility for results but having limited authority or resources to affect basic situations, local Party organs have been charged, on the one hand, with excessive activism or substitution of economic decision-makers, and, on the other, with partial withdrawal of responsibility through formalism or bureaucratic routine.[62] In the latter situation, *proverka* has been understood to mean a formal and detailed resolution by the responsible Party organ and, in the course of time, a visit by an instructor of the local apparatus. This instructor would have noted the inadequacies of execution, issued a *spravka*, or statement of inquiry, and reported the matter to his superiors. In the course of time, they would issue another formal and stereotyped resolution, portion out Party punishment to the delinquents, and then send out an instructor to investigate the status of the assignment.[63] The cycle was capable of almost infinite extension and was a major (if not the sole) means of reducing the gap between formal and actual power within local Party organs. The relative impotence and bureaucratic inefficiency of the territorial Party apparatus was a central objective of reform under Khrushchev.

PART ONE

THE LEGACY OF LENIN AND STALIN

— 1 —

The Leading Role under Lenin

The doctrine of Party *rukovodstvo* and its institutional development may be largely attributed to Lenin. Historically, the concept derives from Marxism and from the workings of the Russian radical revolutionary intelligentsia within the structures of the czarist state. The doctrine was not, however, a mechanical extension of these; it was forged in the contingencies of the struggle for power, and in the conditions of seizing power, in a society experiencing war and revolution, foreign intervention, and internal social and economic disintegration.

Ideologically, Lenin was deeply committed to the radical transformation of Russia's traditional society. On the fourth anniversary of the Revolution he declared:

> The immediate and direct object of the revolution in Russia was the bourgeois-democratic one, namely to destroy the survivals of medievalism and to eliminate them completely; to purge Russia of this stigma and barbarism and to remove this immense obstacle to all culture and progress in this country.[1]

Cleaning the "Augean stables" of czarist Russia required eliminating the autocracy, the caste system, private land ownership and tenure, the inferior status of women, religion, and national oppression.[2] As a Marxist, Lenin was convinced that social liberation was possible only on the basis of relationships between science and technology and material production. "Socialism," he stated in *Tax in Kind*,

> is inconceivable without the technique of large-scale capitalist industry based on contemporary science. It is inconceivable without planned state organization which subjects tens of millions of people to the strictest observance of a single standard in production and distribution. We Marxists have always insisted on this, and it is not worthwhile wasting two seconds talking to people who do not understand this [anarchists and Social Revolutionaries].[3]

Lenin's commitment to the larger Marxian revolutionary goals, however, raised important questions on the more practical but no less urgent issue of instrumentalities. Before the 1917 Revolution, he identified the Russian Social Democratic party as the basic political instrument for achieving a modern society based on socialist principles. As many have pointed out, current doctrine on the Party's internal structure can be adduced from Lenin's conception of the Party as a political elite of professional revolutionaries working within a hierarchical and rational bureaucratic structure. The insistence on strict hierarchy within the Party and on a military-like discipline binding it together (described in *What Is to Be Done?* and *One Step Forward, Two Steps Back*) was based on an assumption of the inherent intellectual and moral superiority of the elite over its constituency. The vanguard was to the mass what "consciousness" is to "spontaneity." The mass movement, which Lenin recognized as the basis of revolutionary power, was incapable of full political consciousness without the close guidance of the leading core. Paternalistic *rukovodstvo* was evident in Lenin's definition of the elite-mass relationship, made on the eve of the Revolution.

> Marxism educated the vanguard of the proletariat and leads the whole people to socialism, directs and organizes the new structure, is teacher, guide, leader [*vozhd'*] of all workers and exploited in the work of constructing its own life, without the bourgeoisie and against the bourgeoisie.[4]

Consciousness and rationality, however, coexisted with an acutely pragmatic sense of contingency. Both before and after the Revolution, Lenin emphasized that theory must maintain contact with concrete experience. It was "precisely because Marxism is not a lifeless dogma, not a final, finished, and ready-made doctrine but a living guide to action that it was bound to reflect the astonishingly abrupt change in the condition of social life."[5] He also argued for a high degree of organizational flexibility, quoting with approval Napoleon's observation "*On s'engage et puis ... on voit,*" which he translated, "One must first plunge into the big battle and then see what happens."[6] To the charge that the Bolsheviks had made a revolution without knowing its final outcome, Lenin replied: "How could one have made the greatest revolution knowing beforehand how it would go to the end? Could this knowledge have been secured from books? No, our decisions could have been drawn only from the experience of the masses."[7]

Lenin's views concerning the general strategy of the leading role were ambiguous. In both theory and practice, the orthodoxies and rigidities of bolshevism were tempered by a strong dash of flexibility. In the transformation of the Party into a ruling apparatus, this ambiguity persisted. Both Stalin and Khrushchev could quote Lenin on the need for "creative Marxism" and organizational flexibility, but at a lower level it was the rigid orthodoxy and bureaucratic centralism of *What Is to Be Done?* which would become decisive.

This was apparent by 1927 when Lenin's conception of authority and the Party's decision-making role in the Soviet state had emerged as a specific articulated relationship.

1

Lenin's Conception of Authority

The authoritarianism associated with the doctrine of Party *rukovodstvo* was implicit in defining the Party as the rationally organized will of the masses. Although formally committed to democratic values, Lenin rejected them in practice because he claimed they were inefficient as vehicles of revolutionary action.[8] Political elitism seemed the most efficient instrument for political revolution in an autocratic state with minimal resources and a great gap between the intelligentsia and the urban and peasant masses.[9] Expressing a hostility to *kustarnichestvo* in revolution, Lenin demanded a modern technology of revolution which he linked with centralism, discipline, and rational organization.[10]

Lenin was not, however, insensitive to the need for some functional decentralization. The basic problem was to secure the proper specialization without losing control over the movement as a whole; united action was the basic imperative, and unity "is impossible without organization. Organization is impossible without subordinating the minority to the majority."[11]

During the period of internal factional struggle, these views were modified. Before the 1905 Revolution, Lenin's strict centralism had evoked charges of "bureaucratic centralism" and "organized distrust" of local organs of power, which he dismissed by declaring centralism necessary to survival.[12] The mass revolutionary movement and the subsequent formal unification of the Bolshevik and Menshevik factions in 1905 led to the formulation of the principles of democratic centralism at the Tammerfore Conference in 1906.[13] A minority member of the coalition, Lenin insisted that centralism be joined with local autonomy in local conditions and that central interference in local activity be prohibited.[14] In power, Lenin favored centralism and discipline; out of power, he championed decentralization and local autonomy. In either event, the basic tactical determinant was power.[15]

During the Party's transition from an underground, illegal, alienated political force to a ruling party, Lenin's views on centralism, collegiality, and Party-state relations underwent three distinct stages.[16] In the first stage, he was prepared to accept a relatively liberal concept of central-local relations. After Brest-Litovsk, in order to fight economic collapse, then civil war and foreign intervention, he advocated strict centralism and discipline. After the Tenth Congress in 1921 and the introduction of NEP, he adopted still another view (which will be discussed later in considering the development of *rukovodstvo* under NEP).

A combination of revolutionary optimism, bewilderment, and a lack of political resources to fight the political and economic fragmentation brought on by mass action caused Lenin to stress the democratic features of the Revolution in the first phase. As late as March 1918 he disavowed any single superimposed stereotype as the basis of Soviet rule. Basic unity was not disrupted but ensured by the use of multiple methods in working out localized problems.[17] The major issue was the proper joining of centralism and mass energy. Democratic centralism, he stated, excluded both bureaucratic centralism and anarchy and not only did not exclude local autonomy but supposed its necessity.[18]

Under the urgencies of war and revolution, however, this balance disappeared in both the Party and the Soviet state. Power flowed into the center and into the Party as militarization progressed. In 1919 Lenin asserted that the Soviet republic was a single military camp.[19] Centralism and discipline were written into the Party. At the Eighth Congress held in March 1919, Zinoviev rejected a federated structure based on nationality or other grounds, declaring that the Party must be a single, unified, centralized structure with the strictest discipline and a subordination of lower to higher authority.[20] In reply to Osinskii's protest that the Central Committee was run without collective leadership, Lenin declared that-the Party was an executiveagency; it was not a parliament and therefore was not run like one.[21] The concept of a centralized organization of authority and discipline was written into the Twenty-one Conditions for the organization of a Communist party in July 1920.[22] In *Leftwing Communism, an Infantile Disorder*, Lenin noted that "the strictest centralization and discipline are required within the political party of the proletariat in order to counteract this [petit-bourgeois influence] in order that the organizational role of the proletariat (that is its *principal* role) may be exercised correctly, successfully, victoriously."[23]

The issues of *kollegialnost'* and *edinonachalie*, so close to the question of centralization, had not been part of prerevolutionary Bolshevik doctrine.[24] This problem—an inheritance from the czarist administration—arose first within the state structure on the subject of the specific role of the masses and, later, on the role of the trade unions in industrial administration. While accepting the principle of the subordination of the minority to the majority, Lenin made it very clear that the definitions of majority and minority were flexible and contingent.

In the enthusiasm and uncertainty following the Revolution, Lenin accepted, if he did not fully condone, the principle of industrial management by elected factory committees. But spreading chaos soon changed his mind, and in the *Immediate Tasks of Soviet Government* he repudiated mass management in favor of a bureaucratic and mechanistic structure. Expressing admiration for the Taylor system of organization, Lenin held that modern industrial management required for its efficient functioning the absolute subordination of millions of individual wills to a single directing will. The weakness of all previous revolutions, he declared, was their excessive reliance on mass enthusiasm. The change in policy was to be one of "manoeuvre, retreat, wait, build slowly, ruthlessly tighten up, rigorously discipline, smash laxity."[25]

Lenin's emphasis on concentrated authority within administrative organs was basically a practical measure. Collegiality led to endless palaver and conflict, resulted in an evasion of personal responsibility, and interfered with the brisk execution of directives. At his most vehement, Lenin claimed that collegiality led inevitably to chaos and catastrophe. The attempt to join collective discussion with unified action was a simple abstraction. Practice demonstrated that in only one in a hundred cases did the proper union take place.[26]

With the emergence of dictatorial power, however, a broader justification was required from Lenin than this. The concept of the dictatorship of the proletariat provided one powerful support. To Kautskii's charge that he had betrayed the democratic values of the Revolution, Lenin replied that while dictatorship is rule unrestricted by law and terror is inherent in class struggle, unrestricted power was not exercised against the class making the revolution.[27] As the Civil War intensified, the class struggle became a total conflict: "The dictatorship of the proletariat is a persistent struggle—bloody and bloodless, violent and peaceful, military and economic, educational and administrative—against the traditions and forces of the old society."[28] Yet dictatorship and the *edinonachalie* closely associated with it were compatible with socialism, because socialism was based on large-scale machine industry, which in turn demanded the subordination of many wills to a single centralized will.[29]

These views produced an authority crisis which began in the fall of 1919 and increased until the Tenth Congress met in March 1921. The crisis involved a protest against the extreme concentration of power by the Democratic Centralists and the more radical and proletarian Workers' Opposition, which opposed the abandonment of collegiality and the reduced role of the trade unions.[30] The Democratic Centralists, composed of intellectuals like Osinskii and Vladimir Smirnov, argued that the Central Committee was supposed to guide, not administer, local Party organs and that the Party should provide for open elections and the protection of minority views.[31] The Workers' Opposition of Shliapnikov and Mme Aleksandra Kollontai demanded in the name of revolutionary ideals a return to collegiality, mass administration of industry through producer congresses, and the autonomy of the trade unions in relation to the Party.[32]

Lenin regarded the Workers' Opposition as a profound threat for two reasons. Collegiality meant workers' administration, and *edinonachalie*, administration by technically qualified specialists. Under the threat of national starvation, collegiality placed the very survival of Russia in question.[33] The second objection was more serious. As Leonard Schapiro suggests, the proposal for a producers' congress was designed to break the power of the Central Committee and the local Party organs.[34] Aware of the threat, Lenin noted in the *Party Crisis* that syndicalism turns management over to non-Party workers and thus renders the Party unnecessary. "Why have a Party, if industrial management is to be appointed ('mandatory nominations') by the trade unions nine-tenths of whose members are non-Party workers?"[35] This challenge to the Party's power and leadership over industry was formally ended, however, by the Resolutions of the Tenth Congress on Unity and the "Anarchist-Syndicalist Deviation."[36]

At the end of the Civil War, Lenin had developed an authoritarian and oligarchic conception of internal Party authority. After the Civil War, despite his growing dissatisfaction with the administration of the Party and the state, he never reversed this basic conception of power.

Lenin and Party Guidance of the Soviet State

Lenin's conception of what type of authority should prevail in Party-state relations was only vaguely formulated before the Revolution. Again, his general views derived from orthodox Marxism.[37] For Marx, the answer had been the Paris Commune and the substitution of mass administration for a specialized ruling structure, and it was this conception of the state which Lenin expressed in *State and Revolution*.[38] But the antibureaucratic hostility of this work was rapidly superseded by an extreme conception of bureaucratic rule expressed in terms of industrial administration as the presence of a single will and the necessity for competent trained administrators. As an ideal, however, Lenin continued to express confidence in the eventual capacity of the masses for direct and democratic self-rule.

On the whole, Lenin showed a marked reluctance to define Party-state relations. Neither the Soviet Constitution of 1918 nor the Party Program adopted at the Eighth Congress specifically defined the Party's role, and it was not until April 1920 that Lenin agreed to make an extended statement on the issue. The dictatorship of the proletariat, he explained, was exercised by the Party through the soviets. In the state apparatus, the Party served as a general staff. "This, it would appear, is a full-fledged 'oligarchy.' Not a single important political or organizational question is decided by any state institution in our republic without the guiding instructions of the Central Committee."[39] Formally, however, the trade unions were independent of the Party.

Actually, all the directing bodies of the vast majority of the trade unions, and primarily, of course, of the all-Russian general trade union center or bureau [the All-Russian Central Council of Trade Unions] consist of Communists and carry out the directives of the Party. Thus, on the whole, we have a formally non-Communist, flexible, and relatively wide and very powerful proletarian apparatus, by means of which the Party is closely linked up with the class and with the *masses*, and by means of which, under the guidance of the Party, the *dictatorship of the class* is exercised.[40]

This description of the Party's role in the Soviet state expressed toward the end of the Civil War, had been unforeseeable at its beginning when decision-making and administration were functions of the soviets. The Seventh Congress was the watershed, and Jacob Sverdlov, chairman of the Central Executive Committee and Party secretary, announced the shift.

Up to this time in the work, the greatest attention was turned to the Soviet or-ganizations; the work in the Soviets had to consolidate those conquests which had been achieved by the October Revolution.

But now before the Party stand new tasks, before the Party stand the tasks of conducting a significant part of the work which the Soviets conducted up to this time.[41]

The rapid shift in power in the latter half of 1918 produced serious conflicts within the Party and between Party and Soviet Workers. The conflicts were particularly severe in the Petrograd and Moscow organizations, but, as Zinoviev remarked, the city in the Soviet republic which was not torn by some aspect of the Party-state conflict was fortunate.[42] The issue was joined at the Eighth Congress. The Moscow delegation, headed by Osinskii and Sapronov, charged that the Central Committee consisted of Lenin and Sverdlov holding a con-versation and that the Soviet apparatus had become bureaucratic and rigid. The central Soviet institutions were characterized by red tape, departmental autarchy, jurisdictional disputes, duplication of both decision-making and administrative functions. At the local level, the Soviets were guilty of widespread abuses of authority and were immersed in red tape.[43] E. N. Ignatov opposed explicitly the substitution of local soviets by local Party organs and the proliferation of local agents of the central government which were independent of local soviet control.[44]

The theses presented for the Central Committee by Zinoviev could only partially meet these objections. Zinoviev declared that "Basic questions of policy, international and national, must be decided by the Central Committee of our Party, that is, the Party of Communists which then conducts its own decisions through the soviets."[45] At the regional level, however, Zinoviev significantly refused to extend this ascendancy of local Party organs over the soviets. When asked which organ was superior, he replied simply that both were necessary for the proletarian dictatorship.[46]

The Resolution of the Eighth Congress on Party-state relations was essentially an expression of Party *rukovodstvo*. The soviets were mass organs uniting millions of workers and peasants, but the Party united the proletariat vanguard with the poorest peasantry. The Party's task was to establish its own decisive influence in all Soviet institutions by dividing and conquering undivided political power and controlling every aspect of their work. But:

> ...to fuse the functions of the Party collective with the functions of state organs, as the soviets are, is in no case permissible. Such a fusion would give catastrophic results, particularly in military affairs. The Party must conduct its decisions through the Soviet organs, in the bounds of the Soviet constitution. The Party strives to guide [*rukovodit'*] the activity of the soviets but not to replace them.[47]

The Resolution of the Eighth Congress remained a dead letter for the duration of the Civil War. The Orgburo meddled continually in the affairs of Sovnarkom, and direct administration by local Party organs was a general, though deplored, phenomenon.[48]

Particularly at the local level, the Party encountered basic problems of structure, communication, and cadres during the Civil War. While the Eighth Conference affirmed the primacy of the territorial principle, the conflict continued between the central Party and trade union organs over the control of Party factions. The existence of local politotdely for railroads and waterways operating under the direct authority of the Central Committee offered another threat to the authority of local Party organs. Kamenev's solution—of placing the head of the local otdel under the local committee—was an unworkable compromise, and the political otdely began to be liquidated in the summer of 1920.[49]

The creation at the Eighth Congress of the Politburo, the Orgburo, and the Secretariat was an effort to come to grips with the Party's decision-making and administrative functions. The Secretariat was formed to replace Sverdlov (who died in 1919), who had administered the Party with fifteen assistants. Specifically, it was to establish control over local Party organs and to create central otdely to systematize Party work. Of these otdely, two were to become primary instruments of central control—the Account and Assignment Division (Uchraspred) and the Organizational-Instruction Otdel, respectively concerned with cadres and lower Party organization. The central apparat grew rapidly to 602 full-time members by 1921.[50]

Communication between higher and lower Party organs was difficult and irregular during the Civil War. By the Eighth Congress, regular communication had been established with the gubernii and by 1920 with the uezdy. The institution of Central Committee instructors was begun in July 1920, but its full-scale operation began only after NEP. More frequent contact was established through ''plenipotentiaries'' sent out to these localities, who (so the Opposition maintained) simply by-passed local Party organs.[51]

The primary tool of central control during the Civil War was the Orgburo's control of appointments. Although mass transfers for military work remained its chief concern, the Orgburo appointed both Party and state personnel down to the uezd level.[52] Energetic and politically trustworthy cadres were desperately needed. Lenin told the Eighth Congress:

> If some future historian collects data concerning what kind of group ruled Russia for these past seventeen months, what hundreds, thousands of people carried all the work, carried the whole incredible weight of administration of the country—no one will believe how it was possible to achieve this with such a small number of forces.[53]

A permanent personnel crisis arose in the gubernii and uezdy, where there was a continual raiding of personnel by higher organizations.[54]

The Party's lower organs also experienced a disorder arising from intense factional power struggles on personal, ideological, and class bases. Disunity at all levels arose from the growth of conflicting interests in the Party. At the Tenth Congress, Milonov noted the development within the Party at both central and local levels of professional politicians with distinctly conflicting outlooks.[55] The struggles between gubernii and uezdy over personnel and other issues could be equally acute at local levels.

The Party's moral unity, lost during the Civil War, could be replaced only by ideological and institutional structures. Zinoviev noted that the experienced Party worker recruited from the ranks soon acquired the outlook of the *chinovnik* when appointed to an administrative job.[56] Moreover, the mass recruitments of 1919 and 1920 threatened to swamp the elite by dint of their youth, numbers, and generally low education. The moral quality of local cadres was often low. The Sol'ts report of 1921 confirmed many of the Opposition's charges that abuse of power and the use of office for personal gain was so general as to demand a Central Committee investigation.[57]

The Party's moral unity, lost during the Civil War, could be replaced only by ideological and institutional structures. Zinoviev noted that the experienced Party worker recruited from the ranks soon acquired the outlook of the *chinovnik* when appointed to an administrative job.[56] Moreover, the mass recruitments of 1919 and 1920 threatened to swamp the elite by dint of their youth, numbers, and generally low education. The moral quality of local cadres was often low. The Sol'ts report of 1921 confirmed many of the Opposition's charges that abuse of power and the use of office for personal gain was so general as to demand a Central Committee investigation.[57]

Party Guidance of Industrial Administration

Under the pressures of civil war and severe economic disorganization, industrial administration was soon concentrated on the single goal of supplying the Red Army. This was the responsibility of the Supreme Council of the National

Economy, or Vesenkha, a collegiate body directed by a presidium and administered through line departments concerned with planning, supply, statistics, and general coordination. Grouped within the production departments were the glavki and centers which actually supervised specific enterprises. Originally eighteen, the glavki proliferated rapidly and numbered fifty-two by 1920.[58] At the local level, regional councils of the national economy served as the formal instruments of industrial administration. Originally conceived as economic counterparts of the local soviets and subordinate to them (as well as to Vesenkha), they were stripped of all autonomy by 1919 and operated independently of both local Party and state organs of power.

Not all industrial plants were administered by Vesenkha. Severe resource shortages forced a concentration of production, so that of 37,000 nationalized plants, only 6,908 were actually registered with the Supreme Council. These were subdivided into three categories. The largest and most important plants enjoying the highest priority comprised some 2,374 enterprises directly administered from the center. A second category included 3,450 plants of lower priority administered by the glavki. The local sovnarkhozy administered the remaining low-priority industries.[59]

The economic system to emerge from this intense effort to mobilize resources was a virtually complete command economy. The extreme centralization of power which followed nationalization eradicated any meaningful distinction in the levels of decision-making. Most important decisions were concentrated at the top. The result was the production of the barest minimum required to supply the military but at an economic and administrative cost that threatened to bring the economy to a halt.[60]

The extreme vertical centralism was complicated by the continuous multiplication of glavki, which, while permitting more direct contact between Moscow and the operating units, at the same time made coordination next to impossible. The fragmentation of administrative units also produced innumerable jurisdictional disputes which were further complicated by the intervention at every level by trade unions, local sovnarkhozi, and central organs. The attempt to direct the economy from the physical center, and without money, produced further imbalance. Despite the centralization of decision-making and the proliferation of controls, such factors as conflicting orders, poor communication, incomplete information, and the lack of a well-developed administrative apparatus led to "a free life," in Baykov's phrase, and the flow of production into local and black markets.[61]

Party *rukovodstvo* during the Civil War involved not only centralization but also a fusion of Party and state posts at the very top, thus concentrating (as the various oppositions were to charge) policy-making and administration in a small group around Lenin. In November 1918 Lenin became chairman of the Council of Workers' and Peasants' Defense which was set up to direct military production and procurement. Just below the top, however, administrative apparatus remained in the hands of the former czarist bureaucracy. As Professor Azrael has pointed out in his excellent study, Lenin's policy was to turn the managers and technical specialists of the old regime into active collaborators.[62] Against bitter Leftist opposition, he staved off the most direct attacks on the specialists and permitted them a privileged position in Soviet society.[63]

Lenin's dependence on non-Communists was genuine and realistic. According to E. H. Carr, the number of bourgeois specialists in Vesenkha and the glavki rose from 300 in 1918 to 6,000 two years later.[64] Lenin could not, of course, fully trust the specialists. He admitted in 1919 that because of the shortage of qualified Communist personnel and the demands of the military front, the state bureaucracy had to be conquered position by position, and full control had not been achieved.[65] In 1920, Communists made up only 51.4 percent of the glavki and Vesenkha and 63.5 percent of the plant directors.[66]

The supervision of this unwieldy and hostile apparatus was achieved by means of Party factions within each institution and cells in the plants—although the latter, like the trade union committees, were stripped of autonomous power with the decline of collegiality. More important were the Cheka and the Workers' and Peasants' Inspectorate. In October 1919 a Special Revolutionary Tribunal was established to deal with economic crimes. Liberman has noted the formation of a *troika* by the Economic Division of the Cheka, which, he says, watched "my department and all my actions with the greatest possible suspicion."[67] The presence of the Cheka and its frequent arrest of bourgeois specialists on suspicion of sabotage revealed that efficiency often suffered at the hands of excessive concern for security.[68]

The mass power principle which Lenin had fought in 1918 was revived in 1919 as a principle of bureaucratic control. Lenin stressed *letuchii kontrol'* as a method of mass participation in the administration, a means of checkup and uncovering sabotage and theft.[69] Through a series of administrative reorganizations, the state control system of the old regime acquired a bureaucratic structure which encompassed the mass movement. In April 1919 Stalin was appointed head of the Peoples' Commissariat of Workers' and Peasants' Inspectorate. In April 1920 the trade unions were brought into Rabkrin, and the Bolshevik principle of using direct mass participation as a lever of bureaucratic control passed into the tradition of *rukovodstvo*.[70]

During War Communism, the role of the local Party organs in industrial management was fundamentally one of mobilizing resources for the war effort, their specific functions differing according to different conditions. In Smolensk, an agricultural guberniia, the Party was an arm of the center in mass recruiting, overcoming shortages, and quelling banditry and strikes.[71] In Moscow and

Leningrad, both centers of war production, the Party's role was much broader. Both mobilization and command were used in Moscow: to press the nationalization of industry, to enforce labor discipline, to conduct mass campaigns and endless socialist competitions, to procure supplies and organize agricultural collections, to watch production in military plants, to deal with the transport crisis, to fight the Left Oppositions, to counteract the demoralization produced by hunger and war weariness, and to perform countless other activities directed toward reducing the serious imbalances in the political administrative systems.[72]

In another respect, however, the Party's role was relatively weak. The vertical centralism of the administrative structure, the establishment of independent organs of industrial administration, and the decline of collegiality removed major industrial establishments from local Party and soviet control. Regularized decision-making and administrative controls were hampered primarily by disorder at the center. There were also internal structural weaknesses within the Party organs themselves. Shortages of cadres and material resources, poor communications, severe internal conflicts, the lack of an established governing tradition, unremitting demands from the center and from military conflict, economic breakdown, and social antagonisms militated against any regularized system of Party decision-making at the local level.

The Party's single institutional achievement during the Civil War was to bring the local soviets under permanent control. As the documents collected by Antonov-Saratovskii demonstrate, this process was achieved rapidly.[73] But it was accomplished only against stiff local opposition, and as the Zinoviev speech at the Eighth Congress illustrates, it was the policy of central Party leadership to prevent a fusion of local Party and state organs. Although there was some discussion of this issue in Petersburg guberniia at the beginning of 1920, serious opposition kept it at the project stage.[74]

2

Rukovodstvo during NEP

The New Economic Policy which Lenin introduced at the Tenth Congress aimed at reviving and controlling certain old forces of czarist society. NEP was compared to a military retreat required to prevent panic and organizational disintegration.[75] The revival of a market economy, a stable currency, private agriculture, trade, and small-scale industrial production involved no change in basic aims. Large-scale mechanized agriculture and industrialization remained essential for a socialist society.[76] NEP—the result of colossal ruin, the exhaustion of the proletariat, and peasant alienation—meant only an exchange of extreme revolutionism for reformism. The adjustment was necessary because "among the people we are as a drop in the ocean, and we can administer only when we properly express what the people are conscious of. Unless we do this the Communist Party will not lead the proletariat, the proletariat will not lead the masses, and the whole machine will collapse."[77]

The basic problem in creating a socialist society lay in the Party's inappreciable numbers and its inadequacy in governing a culturally backward peasantry, a dispersed proletariat, and a hostile, inefficient bureaucracy. Bureaucratism arose from the bourgeois need for a state apparatus and the "atomized and dispersed character of small production, its poverty, lack of culture, absence of roads, illiteracy, absence of exchange between agriculture and industry, the absence of connection and interconnection between them."[78] The long-range solution lay in industrialization and education. During the post-Civil War period, Lenin reemphasized the Party's educational role, without, however, significantly reducing his concern with its organizational role in the Soviet state.[79]

At the Eleventh Congress in 1922 and later, Lenin expressed concern about the effect of War Communism on the decision-making process. The Politburo was flooded with petty questions and conflicts requiring decisions. Party-state relations were unbalanced. The dominant figure during the Civil War, his absence was causing eccentricity in the Politburo, and it was now necessary to raise the prestige and responsibilities of Sovnarkom and the Central Executive Committee.[80] Lenin's views on centralism were ambiguous. Concerned about central-local tensions, he nevertheless considered them unavoidable under the prevailing low cultural standards.[81] In some respects he remained a thorough centralist. There would be no dual subordination for the Procuracy, he told Stalin, because a single, uniform legal standard was required to overcome the localism he identified with barbarism.[82]

Lenin was particularly distressed by the mediocrity of Soviet administration and by the tenuous control in which the Party held the czarist administrative structure. In 1922 he confessed: "Well, we have lived through a year, the state is in our hands but has it operated the New Economic Policy the way we wanted in the last year? No, but we refuse to admit this. It did not operate in the way we wanted. The machine refused to obey the hand that guided it."[83] A few months later he added:

We now have a vast army of government employees, but we lack sufficient educated forces to exercise real control over them. Actually, it often happens at the top, where we have some political power, the machine functions somehow, but down below, where these state officials are in control, they often function in such a way as to counteract our measures—below these are hundreds of thousands of officials who came over from the old society. They will be there for a long time.[84]

How to transform political intellectuals into competent managers and administrators was a particularly difficult problem for Lenin. The Party official would have to sacrifice his arrogance and learn from the bourgeoisie how to govern. He would have to learn to direct and not try to manage everything himself. Communist officials must seize the apparat and not succumb to bourgeois influences so far as to be seized by it.[85] The only institutional solution that Lenin eventually evolved was to reorganize Rabkrin and fuse it with the Party Control Commission formed at the Ninth Conference. This fusion he justified in terms of the situation in the Commissariat of Foreign Affairs, although this obviously contradicted not only the Eighth Congress resolution but his own analysis at the Eleventh Congress as well.[86]

Reflecting both Lenin's views and the early mood of NEP, the Eleventh Congress affirmed "with special force" the resolution of the Eighth Congress. It prohibited direct interference in economic administration by local Party organs and restricted their functions to indoctrination and the selection of cadres. The basic principles of centralism were affirmed, but the congress also recognized the need for adapting central policy to local conditions. The Party's major internal tasks were ideological indoctrination and raising the cultural standards of its members.[87] The relative liberalism of the Eleventh Congress, however, was partially reversed at the Twelfth Congress in 1923, which was an important initial stage in the struggle of succession between Trotskii and the Stalin, Kamenev, and Zinoviev *troika*. The strong assertion of the Party's right to intervene actively in economic decision-making was thus closely linked to the role of the apparatus as a weapon in the developing intra-Party conflict.[88]

The pressure for a more active expression of Party *rukovodstvo*, however, was challenged at the congress. Leonid Krasin, a veteran Bolshevik business-man, argued forcefully for a shift in the Party's organizational policies to ac-knowledge the need for economic and technical specialists in the central Party organs.[89] The argument was essentially a question of general political direction and specific economic competence. Preobrazhenskii noted the clear political danger of a loss of power by the Party, but it was true nevertheless that the managers received incompetent directives from the political organs.[90] At the local level, Zinoviev admitted, the managers challenged Party officials by de-claring, "Comrades, you are not competent in economic questions."[91]

The challenging of the competence of the Communist economists at the Twelfth Congress was less a call for complete autonomy in the making of basic economic policy than a recognition of the need for freedom in the allocation of resources and coordination of economic activity. It was, in any event, decisively defeated in favor of the activist conception adopted by Stalin, which he discussed with an American labor delegation in 1927. Party guidance, he told the delegation, was achieved, first, by electing Communists to leading positions in the state. Secondly, the Party checked the work of state organs, aided them, and corrected their errors: "Not a single important decision is taken by them without appropriate instructions from the Party." Finally, such instructions defined the character and plan of work for the given period.[92]

According to E. H. Carr, "Lenin never really faced the problem of large-scale administration in modern society."[93] Whereas Stalin accepted the need for large-scale administrative procedures and therefore the need for bureaucratization, Lenin hoped that a rise in the levels of mass culture and a simplification of the apparatus would solve the problem.[94] The systematic bureaucratization of the Party's administrative structure advanced with relentless logic during the NEP under the supervision of Stalin, Molotov, and Kaganovich, who became head of the Orgotdel following Stalin's appointment as General Secretary in April 1922.[95] The essential strategy remained, however, a more methodical extension of the policies begun during the Civil War.

Party Structure during NEP

The Secretariat (with the able assistance of the reorganized Party-state control agency) was the key institution in extending the Party's administrative control over lower Party and state organs. The single major change in the apparat occurred in 1924 when the work with cadres and lower Party organs was united into a single centralized department. Despite its increased power, the size increase of the central apparatus was relatively slow during NEP. From 602 in 1921,[96] the Secretariat reached a high of 767 at the Fourteenth Congress,[97] but in a wave of economy it was cut to 657 in 1927.[98]

The central apparat continued to experience serious problems of structure and function during NEP. These difficulties were attributable in part to the dysfunctions of bureaucracy, in part to the specific adversities under which the apparatus worked. Nogin noted the disorder within the apparatus in the 1922 report of the Central Revision Commission. Each department worked in isolation; the vast quantities of statistical information being collected were unused and badly filed; and the clerical staff of 600 was clearly too small to process the increasing quantities of material.[99]

Administrative efficiency unquestionably improved, but problems of staffing persisted. Particularly serious was the heavy turnover in instructors, which reached 90 percent in 1924–25[100] and remained high through 1927. The coming and going of instructors was roughly equal, and 60 percent of the working staff were temporary employees recruited from worker-trainees at Moscow *vuzy*.[101] Only the long and intense hours of work—which affected the health of many employees—compensated for administrative and personnel weaknesses.[102]

Despite the evident weaknesses of the apparat's administrative structure, political control over local Party organs was complete by 1923, and the Party structure was securely Stalin's by 1926. The Secretariat and the otdely extended the methods of the Civil War—central appointments, regular written and oral reports, the sending out of special commissions, the strengthening of the Central Committee instructor corps, and (after the Twelfth Congress) the use of central and local Control commission-Rabkrin organs to purge Stalin's political opponents and to check on local Party activities.

Communications problems, so acute during the Civil War, virtually disappeared during NEP. By the Eleventh Congress, Molotov reported that 120,000 communications were received yearly, and the number was undoubtedly to grow.[103] Despite turnover and other evident difficulties, the instructor corps increased in authority. Prior to the Edict of 27 March 1927 the roles of instructor and local Party secretary were ambiguous; both submitted joint reports to the Orgburo. In 1927, however, the ascendancy of the instructor was established. He was given rights in the selection of local cadres and was freed from prior submission of his report to the local secretary, reporting directly to the Central Committee.[104]

Politically and technically qualified cadres were essential in establishing effective local instruments of the center. The flow of local Party personnel into soviet and economic work after the Tenth Congress weakened the Party in the early phases of NEP; and there was a serious shortage of qualified personnel during the whole period. The fundamental problem noted in the debate of the Twelfth Congress was the joining of political loyalty with technical competence. During NEP the basic emphasis was on political loyalty, ensured by worker social origins and underground experience. The informal criteria lay in the local Party worker's obedience to the directives of the center. The ideal was never fully realized in securing proletarian secretariats. At the Fifteenth Congress, Kossior reported that about 78 percent of gubkom secretaries were from the underground and 9 percent were from other parties.[105] The educational level could not have been high. According to Leonard Schapiro, as late as 1927 the underground provided 71 percent of the senior secretaries.[106]

The formation in 1923 of a Party-state control commission was a major instrument of the center in purging the Party of the Left Opposition. It also served, together with the Commissariat of Justice and the GPU, to control the state industrial administration. Fiercely resisted by local Party organs in 1921 and 1922, the joint TsKK-RKI committees formed their own staffs, which steadily encroached on the authority of the local Party committees, particularly after 1925.[107] Figures on political expulsions are difficult to estimate. Kuibyshev noted at the Fourteenth Congress that 5 percent of the entire Party, or 46,605 persons, had been brought to responsibility; of these, 25.5 percent were expelled.[108] In spite of its small size, the opposition put up a strong resistance. In Saratov guberniia in 1924, the TsKK-RKI purged the committee, but a year later the gubkom again reported strong Trotskyite opposition.[109]

Structure and internal relationships became clearer during NEP when local

Party committees were small but under constant pressure to expand. At the gubkom level in 1924, the average committee numbered about twenty-seven; by the Fifteenth Congress this figure had almost doubled. There were, however, sharp differences in relative size. The Moscow Committee numbered one hundred forty-one in 1927; but the Odessa and Stalingrad committees, with approximately the same number of Party members, elected only ninety-three and thirty-nine members.[110] During NEP serious efforts were made to proletarianize the local committees. At the end of 1927, the composition of guberniia conferences registered 64.9 percent, but only 25 percent were from the bench. Turnover of local committees was high. In the elections of 1927, there was a 57.1 percent turnover among gubkomy, 61.6 percent among ukomy, and 66.8 percent among city raikomy.[111]

Bureaus tended likewise to increase in size and vary in numbers. By 1927, Ivanovo-Voznesensk had twenty-two members and Kharkov seventeen, although others were smaller.[112] Social composition grew steadily more proletarian, with 63 percent in 1926 and 69.7 percent in 1927 reporting worker origins. As in the local committees, only 10 percent were from the bench and 20 percent were from other parties. As early as 1922, specific instructions regarding the composition of the local bureau were given through the local heads of important institutions. From the Eleventh Congress, the Party secretary was established as the generalist responsible for the territorial unit over which he ruled, and his dominance increased as centralized control was made routine.[113]

The functioning of the apparat was an issue of some concern during NEP. Pressures for a size increase were evident, and turnover was heavy. In 1925–27, turnover among gubkom instructors was reported to be 80 percent.[114] Complaints that the gubkom instructor was insignificant were frequent. Generally he lacked authority and was a mere collector of statistics. The Vladimir Gubkom instructors, for example, were young, inexperienced, isolated from each other, and had little contact with the gubkom secretariat.[115] Other conflicts presented major internal problems for local Party organs during NEP. The Thirteenth Conference noted tensions arising from the inequalities of status and income among Communists, the ideological influence of NEP, and the important fact that Communists tended to identify more strongly with their specific responsibilities than with general Party interest.[116] Kossior pointed out that conflicts also stemmed from ideological differences between workers and the intelligentsia, between Party secretaries and officials of local soviet and other institutions, and between Russians and non-Russian minorities within the national area.[117]

A program for rationalizing the apparat was inaugurated after the Fourteenth Congress. The reform followed four lines: (1) the substitution of paid by unpaid staff; (2) the abolition of multiple Party commissions which had proliferated under NEP; (3) increasing the flow of information to the Party aktiv as a measure of democratization; (4) the abolition of apparat otdely and subotdely and the organization of instructors according to the type of cells they guided. A special effort was made to recruit nonstaff instructors on a voluntary basis.[118] In many of its basic features the reform resembled the program adopted by Khrushchev after Stalin's death. The program appears, however, to have been carried out sporadically and without plan and to have been abandoned by the Sixteenth Congress when the local Party organs became the spearheads of industrialization and collectivization.[119]

The Party in Industrial Administration

Industrial administration underwent a number of changes during NEP. With the introduction of a market economy, administrative controls were reduced through denationalization and economic accounting, or khozraschët. The degree of centralized control varied. Administrative decentralization was begun in 1921–22, but recentralization occurred in 1924, and, with the reorganization of 1927, administrative controls were established on a new and centralized level.[120]

For the state sector, the glavki were reorganized into trusts for the direct administration of plants. In 1922, 430 trusts administering 4,144 enterprises employed 977,000 workers, but trusts varied in size. Of the 61 trusts for the metallurgical industry, 6 employed 143,000; the other 55 employed only 72,000.[121] Originally, trusts were concerned with supply, sales, and production, but these functions were gradually relegated to commercial syndicates which retained their importance until the end of NEP. Under the new system, the regional sovnarkhozy lost their production functions. In 1924, republican sovnarkhozy were formed with otdely for trusts of republican and local industry.[122] The most powerful trusts were retained under the direct administration of Vesenkha. About 25 percent of all industrial production, principally light industry, remained under local subordination. In 1926, Vesenkha was reorganized and chief administrations were formed to administer whole branches of industry. In July 1927 a decree on trusts placed planning, supply, and sales under the chief administrations.[123]

Under the trust system, the enterprise was based on khozrashchët. Under the new division of authority, the trust handled the plant's external relationships; the director was in charge of internal production matters and could engage in limited market operations. Although the director was formally responsible for the operation of the plant, an informal troika comprising the director, the plant Party secretary, and the trade union chairman often exercised authority.[124] Under the growing centralization, the new law stressed the personal authority of the manager and his responsibility before the trust.[125] In February 1928 a Vesenkha decree established the sole authority of the director in the plant.[126]

Industrial management undoubtedly improved in efficiency over War Communism. Even under a limited market economy, the elements of a command economy remained in force. The generic problems of bureaucracy and deep involvement by the central agencies in coordinative decision-making remained in evidence. Sergo Ordzhonikidze, summing up the work of the Party-state control commission, described the system as excessively centralized, with much duplication of effort, paper-ridden, and seriously distorting the execution of decrees and orders. The most insignificant trifles were passed up through the apparat for decision, and the paper work produced by the detailed central control over production he termed "astonishing."[127] One commissariat reported using over 400,000 pounds of paper. Detailed questionnaires often required as many as 27,000 different answers, and the demand for statistical material was such that many managerial and technical personnel were required to quit production to fulfill the requests. Jurisdictional disputes and intense competition among the trusts for raw materials and markets continually ensnarled the decision-making process, which continued to expand despite efforts to check the bureaucracy. After the Fourteenth Congress, a serious effort was made to pare the administrative structure, although a number of speakers questioned the ultimate usefulness of the cuts since they were no sooner made than the staff began to expand again.[128]

The Party's central organs were closely and directly involved in economic decision-making. Economic policy was a major issue for both ideological and practical reasons and both the Politburo and the Orgburo were involved in details of its administration. In April 1924 the Politburo formed an *ad hoc* commission to study consumer credit, and the policy of reequipment of industry, decided in January 1925, was the subject of detailed technical discussion.[129] The Orgburo was particularly involved with questions of cadres and structure. In 1925 the Orgburo established administrative order in the textile industry; in 1926–27 it became deeply involved in the campaigns for lowering wholesale and retail prices and in the rationalizing of production—the latter an outgrowth of Stalin's concern with the program of the Left Opposition.[130]

The major concern of Orgaspred was cadres, particularly those in the central economic agencies. At the Ninth Congress Kamenev sharply criticized the mass mobilization system as chaotic and expressed a necessity for individual selection.[131] But close, methodical control over Party members required a preliminary collection of data on personnel in Party, Soviet, and economic organs. By March 1923 the *kharakteristika* of each Party member to the uezd level was complete, and in December 1922 the accounting of economic officials began.[132] Uchraspred's first report indicated Party weakness. Only 5 percent of more than 5,000 officials of Vesenkha, and only 15 percent of the whole economic apparat were Communists.[133]

By 1925, following an exhaustive analysis of eighteen central institutions, of 3,190 officials investigated, only 27.1 percent were Party members, of which 19.4 percent had worker and 16.9 percent peasant social origins. Among institution heads and deputy heads, over 90 percent were Party members, with over 75 percent from middle-class origins. At the operational level the number dropped sharply: only 43.8 percent of heads and deputy heads of administrations, and 33 percent of heads and deputy heads of functional and production branch otdel, were Communists, and over two-thirds of these had middle-class origins. The Party was weakest among technical specialists. Only 11.2 percent were Party members, and these were concentrated in Gosplan and Tsentrosoiuz. In the other sixteen institutions, Communist technical specialists were either negligible or absent.[134]

This situation improved with time, but the gap between power and administrative and technical competence was never bridged. In 1928, Communists held 71.4 percent of the leading positions in trusts, 84.2 percent of the syndicates, and 68.4 percent of the joint-stock companies. Their education, however, was low. Of Party members in trusts and in syndicates, respectively 62.9 percent and 56.2 percent had lower educations. The situation was similar among plant directors. Although 89.3 percent were Party members, only 2.8 percent had a higher education; among non-Party plant directors, 58 percent had higher educations. Turnover was higher among Communists than among non-Party members. In the trusts, 39.8 percent held their jobs less than a year, as did 43 percent of the Communist plant directors.[135]

The *nomenklatura* was responsible for the selection and distribution of cadres. Set up in October 1923 and repeatedly revised, it placed 5,500 offices within the central Party organs in 1926, most of them controlled by the Secretariat in conjunction with the commissariats and special economic organs. Plant directors were appointed by the chief administrations. After 1924 the major mechanism within the Secretariat was Orgaspred, which mounted special commissions for handling different categories of officials. Because of the intense political struggle during NEP, a special list of 1,640 offices normally handled by the Secretariat was referred to the Politburo in case of conflict, and special Central Committee commissions were appointed for another 1,590 elective offices.[136]

Local Party functions changed during NEP as Stalin's primary concern shifted from agitation and propaganda to cadres selection and checkup in executive agencies. Local Party administration was greater in agriculture than in industry. In agriculture, local Party organs were in continuous conflict with the *kulak* and employed economic measures to shore up the poorer peasantry against him. In addition, local Party organs regularly conducted campaigns for the repair of machinery during planting and harvesting or during elections to local soviets.[137] During NEP, however, the Party remained extremely weak in rural areas.

In industrial administration, the centralization of power in Party and state administrative apparatuses limited the role of local Party organs; the assigning of production trusts to different levels of the administrative hierarchy produced a basic anomaly. Although the local Party was responsible for the performance of all institutions within a given territory, the major administration of plants under all-union subordination was under direct Party and state control in Moscow. The distinction between authority and responsibility either produced conflict and efforts to seize control of the industrial apparatus, or it produced passivity and the formation of mutual interest family groups between Party and economic officials—"*v semeinom poriadke*," as Stalin noted to the Fifteenth Congress.[138]

Both tendencies were in evidence. In 1926, a Central Committee circular prohibited direct interference by Party organs in operational decisions, such as hiring, firing, and the payment of wages.[139] Regarding the second aspect, a *Bol'shevik* article complained that the chief decision-making role of the local organs was in settling conflicts among different local economic agencies. Where these included agencies under the direct administration of the center, the result was to flood the Secretariat with local, often technical, issues. In the absence of conflict, economic decisions were made without Party influence or knowledge.[140]

The cadres situation remained uncertain. Under *nomenklatura*, local Party organs were concerned with local institutions (including cooperatives) where a secretary or orgotdel head often served as council chairman. A major characteristic of the cadres work was the tendency toward centralization within the local Party apparatus. Each level attempted to absorb the offices formally assigned to lower organs. In 1926, for example, the Belorussian republican organization appointed the deputy heads of raion otdely.[141] On the whole, cadres work proceeded unevenly. As late as 1926, the Tula Gubkom had no *nomenklatura*, but conducted its work through mass mobilization.[142] For many other gubkomy the work was largely formal. The selection and placement of cadres was unplanned, given little study, and there were few reserves.[143] After the Fourteenth Congress, the local TsKK-RKI were sufficiently implicated in the selection of cadres to encroach further on the authority of local Party organs.[144] A basic element in cadre policy during NEP was the advancement of workers from the bench to leading industrial posts, although the number of trade union members so advanced was extremely small. Between 1925 and 1927, of 794 advanced, the trade unions supplied only 22.[145]

During the Civil War, the Party fractions in institutions like the soviets were expected to be primary in the formulation of policy and administration. Conflict between the local apparat and the fractions was eliminated during the early part of NEP by the substitution of direct ties between the local Party committee and the institution, and by 1925 the fraction was considered a superfluous institution.[146]

The leadership of Party cells in industry was, on the whole, weak. At the beginning of the New Economic Policy, an official Party statement noted the serious inroads made on the urban and proletarian base by the flight from the cities during War Communism.[147] Repopulating the Party with proletarian elements, which was begun shortly after Lenin's death, helped to strengthen the mass organizations. According to official figures for 1926, 14.4 percent of all workers at the bench were enrolled in the Party, with over 20 percent in three major industries.[148] Throughout the New Economic Policy, however, the Party remained weakest in the largest state enterprises. A plant in Zaloust, for example, reported only 250 Communists in a plant employing 5,000 workers. In this and other cases, the passivity and inertia were attributed to the low standards of the primary Party secretaries.[149]

The cells were a function of the class conflict pervading the NEP. Although primarily agitational, the industrial cells were also involved in the checkup on decisions and mobilization of workers in support of central directives. From the Eleventh Congress, the definition of Party authority at the enterprise level was complex. In nationalized plants, the cells and trade unions shared the task of ensuring industrial managers' compliance with state directives. In enterprises under private management, the cells were denied any formal role and Party control was formally exercised through the factory trade union committees.[150]

While Party cells were forbidden to substitute for either the plant management or the trade unions, the October 1925 plenum of the Central Committee sharply criticized their tendency to take over the functions of the factory committees, and violation of the rights of management were frequent.[151] The conflict between the Party cells and the industrial managers appears to have been particularly acute in privately controlled plants. Direct intervention in the hiring and firing of workers appears to have been frequent.[152] To resolve the numerous quarrels between cells and management, the cells were encouraged in 1924 to submit conflicts to the territorial Party apparatus,[153] thus establishing for the local Party organs the adjudicating role which they perform to the present time.

— 2 —

The Leading Role and the
Socialist Offensive

Stalin's "revolution from above," introduced after the Fifteenth Party Congress, and the basic change in the Party's leading role which followed the collectivization and industrialization drives did more than transform the Party-state relationship: the radical "socialist offensive" would gradually transform the U.S.S.R. into a major industrial nation. Modernization is disruptive and difficult even under conditions of gradual change, but the brutality of Stalin's social revolution greatly augmented human anguish and the waste of resources. By harnessing these resources to rapid industrialization, Stalin produced a totalitarian state.

The initial industrialization and collectivization drives clearly aimed at solving some of the problems raised by NEP. By 1925–26 industry had for the most part been reestablished, and the Party urgently needed large investment resources to expand the industrial plant through new construction.[1] The debate on industrial development, so intimately linked with the succession struggle, presented two alternative strategies. In order to expand infrastructure, production capacity and defense, the Left argued, more of the national product would have to be shifted from consumption to investment. By means of compulsory savings, the monopoly of foreign trade, and price manipulation, the necessary capital for industrial expansion could be obtained.[2] But a policy of compulsory savings directed primarily at the peasant could only be obtained by force.

The Right, opposed to forced rates of investment and growth and compulsory savings at the peasants' expense, argued that expanding agricultural production would in turn stimulate urban industry to provide goods for the countryside. Stalin, reflecting Bukharin's views at the Fourteenth Party Congress, began cautiously moving to the Left during 1926 and 1927. During the 1928 grain crisis, he took a firm Left position, and, since the problems of industry and agriculture were inseparable, he also took the Left's position on industrialization.[3]

The economic issues of NEP were closely tied to both ideology and power, and Stalin's personal stake in the struggle against the Right Opposition was evident once the Left and United Oppositions had been defeated.[4] Apart from personal power, however, the Party was hampered in following ideological

25

directives by the existence of a large, independent peasantry, a relatively small proletariat, and by its dependence upon a non-Party managerial and technical elite. To destroy real or potential opposition and group autonomy and to integrate their resources and support behind Stalin's goals were simply two aspects of the same strategy.

Although Stalinism was perhaps implicit in Lenin's political and ideological structures, Stalin's extremism was something new. Stalin undoubtedly reversed some of the erosion which the Party had undergone during NEP. His sharp definition of goals and intense demand for mobilization of resources increased the Party's instrumental values. The principal effects of Stalinism on *rukovodstvo* however, were varied. The Party and state economic apparatuses both took definitive shape as bureaucratic command structures, and Party and state became increasingly entwined as the Party began to adapt to the new demands of industrialization.

The structural adjustments made in the formal organization and composition of the Party elite, however, were uneven and not altogether satisfactory. As growth induced differentiation and complexity, strains became clearly visible within the bureaucratic structures. Even in the early years of industrialization, power and growth conflicted with efficiency. As Stalin's rule closed, the rationalization and reform of bureaucracy became urgent.

The massive commitment to economic growth was combined in the command economy with a drive toward autarky.[5] Stalin's recipe was to increase investment through a shift in the investment-consumption balance, and in the process the logic of the Left was inexorably worked out. Agricultural collectivization provided the primary resources required for building and staffing the industrial plant. The new investment was concentrated upon heavy industry, and, within heavy industry, on the key sectors of machine building, metallurgy, power, and fuel. Infrastructure, light industry, and agriculture were systematically sacrificed.

To achieve the politically determined investment and growth rates and to maintain motivation required much coercion, resource mobilization, propaganda, and an incentive system based on extreme rewards and penalties. The driving forces were pressure and centralized directives administered through the Party and state bureaucracies. The concentration of basic policy and decision-making in Moscow served, as one Western economist has pointed out, "both as a means of directly concentrating economic efforts on high-priority sectors and as a means of transmitting pressure and urgency to the economy."[6] In this way, the fundamental form of economic pressure—the planned overcommitment of resources—was extended and reinforced through the political and administrative system.

Under the First Five-Year Plan (and in varying degrees under the ministerial system) forced draft industrialization would give economics priority in the perspectives of the leading role.[7] Achievement of the plan was to engage the core of the territorial Party apparatus. In general, the Party was politically responsible for legitimating the policies and justifying the sacrifices required of the Soviet people to meet the goals of industrialization. This involved the apparatus in a communications net in which information, explanation, and inspiration were relentlessly pushed through the media. The mobilization functions also included the recruitment and socialization of cadres.

Finally, the lower Party apparatus was responsible for enforcing central priorities in the localities, a process which required—during the First Five-Year Plan, at least—political struggle against the protests generated by the pace and severity of the industrialization and collectivization drives. To this was added the responsibility of providing regional and functional coordination to correct those microimbalances which the absence of a market, excessive centralization, coercion, and the overcommitment of resources had produced.

Economic results revealed the strengths and weaknesses of the system. The aggregate economic effects of the political mobilization of resources, in Jasny's calculations, would increase Soviet gross industrial output from 1928 to 1950 by 4.7 times in 1926–27 prices.[8] Over the same period, producers' goods increased 8.8 times, and industrial construction fivefold. Agriculture, on the other hand, virtually stagnated. Sectoral allocations give essentially the same picture. The amount of resources available to the state increased some eight times; net investment grew six times, while investment in heavy industry expanded twelve times. Increases in the allocations to defense rose 2,600 percent, but personal incomes increased by only one-third.[9] Not until the final years of Stalin's rule were the 1928 standards of living finally surpassed.[10]

The Stalinist system of industrialization, however, was also characterized by uneven growth rates and a relatively low level of static and dynamic efficiency. Between 1929 and 1933, during the wildly unrealistic planning of the First Five-Year Plan, achievement was about 40 percent of planned levels. Further, the severe shortage of experienced managerial and labor resources caused serious wastage and a sharp decline in the quality of production.[11] The high growth rates between 1934 and 1937 were sharply reversed by the massive purges and the preparations for war. Not until the years following World War II, as a result of reestablishing the war-ravaged economy, did the economy exhibit high and sustained growth rates, reaching by 1950 an increase of 40 percent over 1940 output levels.[12]

The unevenness of the economy, partially the result of external factors, was matched by its relatively low efficiency. As late as 1960, measured by national income per unit of factor inputs, the Soviet economy was essentially on a level with Italy and from 28 to 45 percent of the United States, according to the price weights used.[13] Moreover, although the U.S.S.R. was a relative newcomer to industrialization, its dynamic efficiency (defined in terms of its capacity to exploit new technological knowledge acquired either internally or externally) has been notably low in the civilian sector. The labor theory of value, a price system which failed to measure scarcity, and cost evaluation by average rather than marginal norms have contributed to the relative inefficiency of the economy.[14] The central inefficiency, however, has clearly been managerial.[15]

Under Stalin, the Party's role shifted visibly, although the dynamics of its leadership are difficult to trace. Two related, but not identical, changes are discernible in relation to the great drive for industrialization. The first involved a decline in the Party's policy-making and institutional role as Stalin consolidated his personal dictatorship.[16] In the second, following the massive dislocations and demoralization produced by the First Five-Year Plan, the Party's role as transforming agent was replaced by an emphasis on extensive growth and system maintenance. Both changes led to a further bureaucratization of the Party, to a routinization of its internal processes, and—in the lower Party apparatus—to a routine role in coordinative decision-making.

The decline in the Party's political role should not be exaggerated. Centralization of power within the Party apparatus remained a key feature of decision-making during NEP as earlier. Stalin's power base throughout the First Five-Year Plan was principally within the Party, and it seems reasonably clear, for example, that protests within the Party were primarily responsible for the relative moderation of the economic policies of the Second Five-Year Plan.[17] The crucial change in the Party's decision-making role began with the Terror of the late 1930s, which, by smashing the Old Bolshevik party apparatus, enabled Stalin to redistribute power among the managers, the police, and the military. In the post-purge period, Stalin increasingly relied on the state and economic apparatus as the primary instruments of government.[18]

The effect of this fundamental change in the Party's leading role is discernible in two trends: (1) the Presidium of the Council of Ministers superseded the Politburo and Central Committee as primary decision-making organs, and (2) Stalin signed major decrees as Chairman of the Council of Ministers rather than as General Secretary. Moreover, beginning in 1941, an important symbolic change occurred when the government was placed ahead of the Party in joint decrees. The decline of the Party's institutional role was further indicated by the decline in the number of Party congresses and plena of the Central Committee and the policy of recruiting and co-opting nonapparat industrialists into the highest levels of leadership.[19] The resulting administrative system, with its competing and overlapping bureaucracies, was pervaded by distrust, highly centralized, and dependent upon Stalin for both its legitimacy and direction.[20]

Political decline was accompanied by a further reduction in solidarity. Conflicts based upon loyalties to different leaders and functional differentiation based upon the growing complexity of the Party's tasks as industrialization proceeded produced serious conflict in addition to raising central questions of purpose and structure.[21] The internal rigidities were matched by a shift in external leadership. As the First Five-Year Plan revealed the limitations of totally politicizing economic leadership, economic growth became routinized, and the Party's decision-making functions, largely reduced to this sector, became coordinative in character.

Khrushchev's central problem for reform was thus clear. To expand the power of the Party apparatus over industrial management required revitalizing the apparatus to increase its efficiency. This meant, first, deroutinizing those economic and political developments of the system which had been established under Stalin.

1

Stalin and the Doctrine of the Leading Role

Ideas were perhaps less important to Stalin than the iron will which enabled him to dominate, if never fully to master, the social forces his policies set in motion. In contrast to the subtlety and force of his actions, his ideas were conventional, uncomplicated derivations from Marx and Lenin. His pre-revolutionary views on capitalism, technology and industrialization, and socialism closely followed Lenin,[22] and he was especially attracted to Lenin's brand of revolutionary Marxism. The political revolution he accorded absolute ascendancy, seeing it as a class struggle conducted through a revolutionary, international, and centralized political party.[23]

Stalin also identified himself closely with Lenin's positions in the internecine conflicts which racked the Social Democratic party before the Revolution. His model was Lenin's *What Is to Be Done?*[24]; like Lenin, he was hostile to the bourgeois intelligentsia and distrusted the peasantry. He fought the idea of bourgeois dominance in the democratic revolution, insisting upon proletarian hegemony. In 1910, when the revolutionary movement was at a very low ebb, he continued to oppose an all-class struggle against the autocracy if it meant any weakening of the class struggle against the bourgeoisie.[25] The peasant and the proletarian, he maintained, had ultimately conflicting interests because the peasant supported the democratic revolution only to further his own interest in private property. On every point, Stalin supported the radical over the moderate forces.

Stalin also shared with Lenin a conviction of the primacy of organizational power in the revolutionary movement. Committed to a stringently mechanistic organizational theory, he believed the authority of the Party should be unitary, indivisible, and centralized.[26] In an extensive expression of his views in 1905, he emphasized the Party's elitist and bureaucratic character. As a party of leaders, the formal organization must be smaller than the class and its superior in understanding and experience.[27] The three conditions essential to the success of the revolutionary struggle, Stalin explained, were: (1) the existence of class-conscious leaders organized in a strong, centralized Party unified in program, tactics, and organizational views; (2) impersonal leadership, since the Party was a battle group and not "a hospitable, patriarchal family"; and (3) the formulation of inter-Party relations on the basis of centralized discipline, since the Party was not a chance conglomeration of individuals.[28]

The control of organizational power pervaded virtually every aspect of Stalin's political views, without, however, affecting his basic opportunism. On the national question, which he developed as a specialty before the Revolution, he held steadfastly to the superiority of international and class forms of political organization over national ones.[29] By 1904, in support of Lenin, he had already rejected the concept of a federal party structure based on national identity on the theory that a central party structure would break down national barriers and substitute a single class line for plural national structures.[30] Yet, even on an issue as central as national self-determination, he was basically opportunistic. At the April Conference in 1917, for example, he supported the right of the Finns to self-determination: "Thus, we are at liberty to agitate for or against secession in accordance with the interests of the proletariat, of the proletarian revolution."[31]

This coupling of organizational power with tactical opportunism persisted into the post-revolutionary period. In the initial phase of his thought, from the October Revolution to the Sixteenth Congress in 1930, he followed Lenin. Two major works—*The Foundations of Leninism* in 1924 and *Questions Concerning Leninism*, issued in 1926—established Stalin as a theoretician, the most prominent of Lenin's disciples, and, not least, as a political polemist against the Left and United Oppositions. Despite their limitations, both works have been decisive in defining *rukovodstvo*.

The Foundations of Leninism emphasizes the importance of *What Is to Be Done?* in laying the theoretical foundations for a revolutionary movement in Russia. The Party, Stalin explained, was not an electoral machine for securing votes and maneuvering in parliament, but a General Staff in the vanguard of the Revolution. It was essentially an elite organization; open enrollment would have corrupted it into a "loose, amorphous, disorganized 'formation,' lost in a sea of 'sympathizers' that would have abolished the dividing line between the Party and the class and would have upset the Party's task of raising the unorganized masses to the level of the advanced detachment."[32]

Authority within the Party, Stalin held, excluded any form of pluralism:

But the Party is not merely the sum total of Party organizations. The Party is at the same time a single system of these organizations, their formal union into a single whole, with higher and lower leading bodies, with the subordination of the minority to a majority, with practical decisions binding on all members of the Party. Without these conditions the Party cannot be a single organized whole capable of exercising systematic and organized leadership in the struggle of the working class.[33]

All Party work should be directed from a single center with emphasis on the necessity for solid organization and iron discipline. This discipline, however, should be neither blind nor mechanical. Controversy was permissible until a decision was reached, but at that point, unity of action was required. Factions or groups would lead inevitably to multiple centers and an ultimate splintering of the Party. Stalin also stressed the purge as an organizational means of strengthening the Party.[34]

In terms of the Soviet state, Stalin declared, the Party was the highest form of class organization but not the only one. Other organs were necessary to realize the dictatorship, and this raised a basic problem: "What guarantee is there that this multiplicity will not lead to divergence in leadership?" The Party's basic role was to integrate the specialized mass organizations into a single whole. The relationship between Party and state was that of a motor to its transmission belts.[35] The Party's specific organizational role in the Soviet state involved the issuance of guiding directives, the selection and distribution of cadres, and finally, the checkup of decision.[36]

The struggle for succession did not directly challenge the Party's leading role. Even in defeat, none of the leading contenders for power questioned the inherent superiority of the Party or its ideology. It was the concentration of power in the central Party apparat that led Trotskii, in *The New Course* of December 1923, to formulate the thesis of the degeneration of the Party from a revolutionary to a bureaucratic and conservative machine. This was partly the result, he charged, of the absorption of Party cadres into the still-czarist state apparatus. "The Communist Party is the leading Party of the proletariat, and consequently of its state." Thus, "the whole question is to realize this leadership without merging into the bureaucratic apparatus of the state, in order not to expose itself to bureaucratic degeneration."[37] To the demand that Party and state be separated, the Thirteenth Conference in January 1924 replied that Trotskii's logic "could lead to nothing else than to the emancipation of the state apparatus from Party influence on it."[38] In this regard, Stalin would later remark objectively, "if unconsciously," that Trotskii was a tool of "wavering" and anti-Soviet elements.[39]

In the polemic against Zinoviev, Stalin pursued the reverse line, holding for a distinction between Party and state organs. To Zinoviev's view that the dictatorships of Party and proletariat were equivalent, Stalin replied: "The dictatorship of the proletariat cannot be identified with the dictatorship of the Party since the former concept is a state concept and involves the use of force...."

The Party is at the core of this power, but it is not and cannot be identified with the state power."[40] Admitting that the substitution of Party for state organs was somewhat ambiguous, he attempted to draw a distinction between them.

> "As the ruling Party," says Lenin, "we could not but merge the Soviet 'top leadership' with the Party 'top leadership'—in our country they are merged and will remain so." This is quite true. But by this Lenin by no means wants to imply that our Soviet institutions as a whole, for instance, our army, our transport, our economic institutions, etc., are Party institutions, that the Party can replace the Soviets and their ramifications, that the Party can be identified with State power.[41]

Against the Left Opposition, Stalin maneuvered on the middle ground, arguing against either excessive identification or separation of Party and state. Against the Right Opposition, his polemics were somewhat different because the issues in this case involved problems of power and policy rather than of institution as with the Left.

According to the Right Opposition, the seizure of power had transformed the proletarian dictatorship. The Party had ceased to be a party of civil war, fomenting class division and struggle; it had become the party of civil peace, promoting class struggle on the one hand and interclass cooperation in the peaceful construction of a new society on the other. In both the city and the countryside, the class struggle had changed from a political to an economic matter. Since the preponderance of economic power was in the hands of the state, the victory of socialism over the urban and rural bourgeoisie was assured. The gradual development and dominance of socialist over capitalist forms would ultimately, with the aid of education, transform the peasant into a member of socialist society. Thus, through the mechanisms of the economic struggle, both the class struggle and the proletarian dictatorship would ultimately wither away.[42] The Party's role in such a process was to agitate and educate rather than to administer.

The onset of industrialization and collectivization in 1928, which was the immediate cause of the conflict between Stalin and the Right Opposition, led Stalin to a conception of social transformation which would result in the totalitarian state. In opposition to the doctrine of gradualistic, mechanistic, and apolitical transition to socialism, Stalin advanced an ultraleft conception of social revolution based on shock tempo, voluntarism, and the total politicization of society. Bukharin's ideological defense of NEP in 1925—Stalin told the Sixteenth Congress in 1930—by repudiating these features, had repudiated the leading role.[43] The launching of the "revolution from above" through the Party-state bureaucracy marked a fundamental turn in the leading role without, however, providing a new doctrinal base for the Party's change in roles.

Like other Russian Marxists, Stalin accepted the necessity of large-scale industry as the basis of socialism. His published works give little indication of an interest in industrialization as a specific issue before the Revolution; and during the struggle with the Left Opposition, he could only reply to the charge that Russian technical backwardness made socialism in one country impossible with the countercharge that such a view was capitulationism before the domestic and world bourgeoisie.[44] In 1928, however, Stalin justified the tempo of industrialization and collectivization as a means of eliminating technical lag, and in his familiar address of June 1931, he coupled industrial capacity with national power by noting, "You are backward, you are weak—therefore you are wrong."[45] Stalin did not view backwardness as a national character trait. In his final remarks before the Sixteenth Congress, he castigated Demian Bedny's poem "Get Down from the Oven" as a slander, not a criticism, of the Russian proletariat. Later, in an interview with Emil Ludwig, he denied that the Russian worker was lazy.[46]

In the years following the onset of industrialization, Stalin's twofold task was to legitimate the new technical and industrial order which began to emerge after 1930 and to justify the growth of organized repression and social inequality which the consolidation of his personal power demanded. Under Stalin, as Herbert Marcuse points out, the Soviet state "becomes the Archimedian point from which the world is moved into socialism, the 'basic instrument' for the establishment of socialism and communism."[47] The rationalizations he developed required repudiating Engels' doctrine of the withering away of the state (in *Anti-Duhring*), which Stalin insisted did not apply to a country building socialism while surrounded by hostile capitalist forces.[48]

Stalin also repudiated increasing social equality as part of the transition to socialism. "It is time to understand," he reported to the Seventeenth Congress, "that Marxism is the enemy of equalization." Marxism rejects social leveling and "primitive utopian socialism." Under Soviet conditions: "Equalization in the sphere of requirements is a piece of reactionary petit-bourgeois absurdity worthy of a primitive sect of ascetics, but not of a socialist society organized on Marxian lines."[49]

Buttressed by a theory of organized social inequality and permanent bureaucracy, the growth of the state during the transition from socialism to communism meant a decline in, but not a repudiation of, the primacy of the Party's leading role. The elevation of Stalin to a unique and suprainstitutional role meant the relative decline in status of all institutions. Although he continued to refer to the Party as the decisive force in the Soviet state through the Eighteenth Congress, during the war and postwar period his emphasis changed. In his electoral speech of 9 February 1946 Stalin attributed the military victory to the Soviet social structure, the Soviet state, the Red Army, and the economic base created by Soviet industrialization.[50]

Postwar commentary by Soviet writers and theoreticians continued, on the whole, to stress the Party's traditional role in the Soviet state,[51] although some articles in *Bol'shevik* (principally by such members of the central apparat as Suslov and Pospelov) quoted *The Foundations of Leninism* or *Questions Concerning Leninism* to assert the Party's leading role in the victory over fascism—or, more directly, the right to control the state apparatus.[52] Since Stalin failed in his later years to make any direct, authoritative statement on the relative roles of Party and state, the doctrinal issue was mooted by the inconsistencies of his earlier and later pronouncements.

2

Party Structure under the First
Five-Year Plan

The First Five-Year Plan adopted at the Sixteenth Conference in April 1929 required a massive commitment of human resources to meet its goals. The plan envisaged a capital investment of 64.4 million rubles compared with the 26.5 millions invested in the previous five years. Gross industrial output was slated to rise by 280 percent, with heavy industry to rise by 330 percent. Branches (such as pig iron) were to increase output by 300 percent, electric power by 400 percent, chemicals by over 2,300 percent. The effort to meet such goals placed a severe strain on the Party and state industrial apparatuses. Where political will and mass zeal were supposed to substitute for adequate material and managerial resources, the Party and state administrative systems responded with feverish activity, frequent structural change, and a heavy turnover in cadres.

Initially, the industrialization drive intensified those processes of Party reform which had begun earlier. A 1928 decree of the Central Committee on Party structure ordered a simplification of the Party apparatus, the abolition of sectors and subsectors at the local level, an increase in the role of the aktiv, and an increase in the amount of information to the apparatus at all levels.[53] Vladimirskii reported in 1930 that the staff of the central apparat had been cut to 375.[54] The formation of the rural raion in the summer of 1929 reversed this reductive trend. In less than a year, the raikomy had grown about 20 percent.[55] The increased work load at the center was partially compensated for by the development of nonstaff apparatus, although their proper organization evoked serious conflict in the Orgburo.[56] Approximately 200 nonstaff instructors were engaged to deal with the sharply increased demand for Party and state cadres, but, as Kaganovich testified, the central Party apparatus simply could not cope with the mounting problems of industrialization.[57] In 1930 the Party structure underwent the first of four major reorganizations under Stalin to cope with the problems of industrial decision-making.

The new "functional" system of Party administration involved two basic principles: the first (announced by Stalin) was to divide the Party and state administrative structure into a smaller number of units in order to bring decision-making and administration as close as possible;[58] the second was to assign the selection and distribution of Party and state cadres to two different otdely and to separate the administration of propaganda and mass agitation.

In the Assignment Otdel, which centralized the distribution of all administrative and industrial cadres on the central *nomenklatura*, subdepartments were formed for different sectors of Soviet industrial administration. Internal Party organization and Party cadres were assigned to the Organization-Instruction Otdel, which was divided into regional sectors, each headed by a responsible instructor.[59] Similar structures were set up at the local level. In the obkom, the organizational otdel—the analogue of the Assignment Otdel—had an average of six sectors for industrial cadres, although the number varied. The usual gorkom structure had four otdely, with the orgotdel divided into a variable number of sectors for industry.[60]

During 1931 the industrial tempo increased and the apparat responded with further reorganization. In May 1932, the Organizational-Instruction Otdel was reorganized to increase the grip of the central apparatus over the local Party organs. A new checkup and instruction section was added with regional sub-divisions, and the Otdel for Culture and Propaganda was reorganized. In July 1933, political otdely for railroads were reestablished and placed directly under the Central Committee, with the head of the otdel (as in 1919 and 1920) made a member of the local committee.[61]

The pressure on local Party organs also precipitated the organizing of special industrial branch otdely—as in the Donbass, where a special otdel for coal was formed in 1933. The apparat began to expand as a whole under the increased work load. In 1932 alone, almost 300,000 documents were received in the Secretariat, and this figure was exceeded in the first nine months of 1933. The result was to triple the Party budget between 1930 and 1933 and to increase the number of Party workers by 61 percent. By 1933, 75 percent of all professional Party workers were in the gorkomy and raikomy.[62]

Under the system of *funtsional'shchina*, the apparat worked badly at all levels because of the shock tempo, rapid economic growth, opposition and protest, and the permanent crises in planning, coordination, material shortage, and cadres. The increase in the intensity of control over local Party organs by the Secretariat was characteristic of the period. The new Organization-Instruction Otdel was to exercise direct daily control over the obkomy. Detailed reporting from local Party organs increased rapidly, and a steady flow of representatives from the center tightened centralized control. Increased centralism overloaded the central apparat. The chairman of the Central Control Commission complained about the inefficiency of the central apparat, particularly about the amount of time required for decision-making.[63] The regional and local Party committees seemed permanently disorganized, and the reorganization by the Sixteenth Congress was extremely slow. In May 1931, the Central Black Earth Kraikom had still not begun to convert to the functional system.[64]

Structural disorganization became so acute in the cadre sector that it seemed to threaten the integrity of the apparatus. By 1930, only 15 (or 6.8 percent) of 220 secretaries occupied the posts they had held in 1927. More dramatically, two-thirds of these secretaries had either been purged or had left the Party apparat voluntarily.[65]

The shortage of qualified cadres, which became critical in the latter half of 1931, continued through 1932 and into 1933. Local Party organs beseeched the Secretariat for cadres, which were apparently rationed since a number of local organs pleaded for cadre "advances." According to a report issued in 1932, the lower the Party organ, the greater the instability.[66] The kraikomy and obkomy appeared most stable. The heads of otdely at this level lasted an average of eight months. In 1931 the Central Black Earth Party Committee reported an annual turnover of three heads of the organizational-instruction otdel and three heads of agitprop.

The turnover was higher among gorkom and raikom secretaries. In 100 gorkomy and raikomy of the Northern Caucasus, turnover of secretaries reached 87 percent per year; of these, 24 percent turned over three times. In the Lower Volga and Central Black Earth regions, turnover was 300 to 500 percent.[67] One gorkom reported that in two years it had had two secretaries, three heads of the organizational otdel, six heads of culture and propaganda, five heads of agitprop, and ten newspaper editors. One apparat member held nine different jobs in one year. The turnover of instructors was even more rapid. In the Urals and Nizhnegorod kraikomy, turnover was 150 percent per year; in the Lower Volga, the instructor apparat turnover was 250 percent. Secretaries of primary Party cells were in perpetual motion; they averaged about two months in office although many lasted a week or less.[68] Despite efforts to end the extreme instability, the turnover in cadres continued into 1933.

Administration of Industry under the
First Five-Year Plan

Under the First Five-Year Plan the state industrial apparatus mirrored the institutional patterns and dynamics of the Party administrative structure.[69] At every administrative level over the enterprise, the system underwent a complex and, in some respects, circular change. During 1929 and 1930, Vesenkha's glavki were abolished and replaced by branch and functional otdely specializing in long-range planning and technical control. The direct administrative functions of the glavki were entrusted to a system of "unions" formed like the syndicates, which had gradually been taking over the functions of the trusts.

The highly centralized unions created in the general reorganization of December 1929 exercised operational control over all economic and technical functions of the enterprises, including supply and sale. Their cumbersome size, however, made them difficult to manage, and in 1930 they began to break down into smaller components in line with Stalin's general policy of administrative division announced at the Sixteenth Congress. Finally, on 8 November 1932 the unions were formally liquidated.[70]

Their functions were assumed by the sectors of Vesenkha which, from 1931, began to resemble glavki. In 1931, Vesenkha began to concentrate on heavy industry and allow other commissariats to absorb its additional functions. The Commissariat of Trade absorbed the food industry; the Commissariat of Agriculture, the cotton industry. The trend climaxed in the reorganization of 1932 when Vesenkha was incorporated into three commissariats. Vesenkha itself became the Commissariat of Heavy Industry; the others, the Commissariat of Light Industry and the Commissariat of the Wood-Working Industry. The republican sovnarkhozy became union republic commissariats of light industry, and local sovnarkhozy were turned into krai or oblast light industry administrations.[71]

The trust evolved similarly. In 1929 the major all-union trusts began to be subdivided. By 1932, eighty-two unions administered 190 trusts on the all-union level. With the abolition of unions, the all-union trust passed to the Vesenkha glavki or the all-union commissariats. The enterprise continued to be administered under the statutes of June 1927. In December 1929, however, all production units of the enterprise were placed on *khozrashchët*, and in January 1930 Gosbank acquired direct lending rights over the enterprise, thus adding financial to political, administrative, and social controls.[72]

Despite Party efforts to convince business executives that ordering a boiler was not a routine administrative decision but part of the worldwide struggle against the bourgeoisie, deep-rooted administrative characteristics emerged during the period and were aggravated by the atmosphere of crisis and purge. The Central Committee responded to the extreme shortage of technical cadres by centralizing all functions in a single center,[73] a policy which impelled a flow of local representatives to Moscow. By 1932, it was estimated that their numbers had increased by 50 percent, and in the process, local organs of administration were deprived of virtually any administrative authority.[74]

Competing and conflicting jurisdictions, excessive paperwork, the minute breakdown of administrative units, poor planning, excessive amounts of defective or low-quality production—these were among the complaints raised against the industrial administration. Continuous reorganization was one of the major causes of overlapping authority; another was the relentless interference of Party and

TSKK-RKI inspectors in administration. Yugostal, one of the great iron and steel trusts, was investigated by eight major commissions within a year on the very issue of bureaucratic and mass investigations.[75] The endless investigation aroused deep resentment and disrupted administrative and production processes. In a moving defense of his administration of Yugostal, a competent Austrian Communist named Birman complained that the First Five-Year Plan had had an incredible tempo and that he and his associates had worked frantically to achieve the goals. Reading the inspection reports of the state controllers, he said that he felt like a criminal or an idiot.[76]

Conflicting jurisdictions and ill-defined boundaries delayed decisions by appealing them to the Central Committee, already overwhelmed by the problem of cadres.[77] The paper flow increased the communication problem. Moscow's demands for statistical information continued to grow. In one year, one mine in the Donbass was required to submit sixty-four forms with a total of over 50 thousand indicators[78]—an extreme example, to be sure, but indicative of the general trend. The instructions on the industrial tax issued by Narkomfin in 1929 covered 684 points in 240 pages. Paper work almost certainly accounts in part for the inflation of administrative staffs, which increased in some narkomaty by 15 percent in the wake of the December 1929 reorganization.[79] This was particularly serious in plant administrations suffering shortages of technical cadres, where over 50 percent of the engineering staff spent its time filling out reports.[80] Other complaints were registered against the administration of planning: frequent changes, conflicting orders, late affirmation of plans, and the lengthy, time-consuming, complex process of targeting the annual promfinplan—all were frequent charges.[81] Plan formulation and fulfillment were of critical importance in the area of capital construction.[82]

The cadres issue, with its fundamental political and administrative implications, was industrial administration's greatest problem during the First Five-Year Plan. The bourgeois intelligentsia was a major target in the issues of *kto kogo*, which began with the Shakhty trial of May–July 1928, in which forty-seven German and Russian specialists were tried and five shot for alleged sabotage and wrecking.[83] In December 1930 Molotov told a joint plenum of the Central Committee and the Central Control Commission that the GPU had classified as class enemies both the *Prompartiia* and the Soviet Mensheviks.[84] In December 1930 Professor Ramzin and seven others were tried on charges of economic sabotage and political conspiracy with France, and in March 1931 Professor Groman and thirteen others were tried for counterrevolutionary effort in conjunction with émigré Mensheviks.[85] The trying of economic specialists, which Stalin claimed would have wide educational value, seemed designed to break resistance to Stalin's policies, energize the administration, provide scapegoats for industrial failures, and reestablish Stalin's revolutionary credentials.[86]

The administrative revolution had three strategic aims: to purge the apparatus, to advance workers from the bench, and to create a Soviet technical intelligentsia. The purge carried out by the GPU, the TsKK-RKI and the trade unions eliminated about 17 thousand by the Sixteenth Conference (April 1929) and aimed at purging 100 thousand by the Sixteenth Congress (June–July 1930). Although efforts were made to discriminate, the purge acquired a mass character. In some institutions whole groups of specialists were purged, and since qualified replacements were unavailable, workers were recruited directly from the bench to fill the gap. By the middle of 1929, a total of 14,500 workers had been advanced to executive positions, 75 percent directly from the bench. On the whole, the purge fell unevenly upon the apparat. Some institutions, such as the Ministry of Finance and the Central Union of Cooperatives, were cut in half; others averaged from 12 to 15 percent.[87] Despite the expansion of Soviet higher technical education, the shortage of qualified technical workers remained acute through the Seventeenth Congress.

3

Party Guidance of the Industrial Economy

During the First Five-Year Plan, economic decision-making was concentrated in the Politburo—ultimately in Stalin himself—and established characteristics became intensified here as elsewhere in the Soviet regime. Molotov noted in December 1930 that the Central Committee had taken a number of state institutions under direct control.[88] Direct Central Committee, and even Politburo, control was extended to the major construction and industrial projects and plants.[89] In addition, a number of Politburo commissions were formed to deal with such crucial problems as the transport crisis of January 1931. Alexander Barmine, a high official in the Soviet foreign trade apparat, has given a graphic description of the pace and degree of coordination exercised from the center:

After a year at Stanko-Import, I became familiar at first hand with the workings of the enormous and highly centralized bureaucracy which managed the Soviet state. Naturally, I expected the Politburo to concern itself with the broader aspects of our work at Stanko-Import, which involved tens of millions of rubles in a vital branch of import. But I was astonished at the minuteness of this concern and the interminable red tape which reached to Stalin himself.

As a result of overcentralization so much time was spent on relative trivialities that not enough was left for the consideration of really major problems. I saw the Politburo was hours discussing a small contract made by Stanko-Import....

For this reason among others, the Soviet bureaucracy is a cumbersome and frequently unworkable machine. Initiative on the part of subordinate bureaucrats is stifled. Everyone seeks to avoid responsibility. Everyone looks to the top for a covering order. And since thousands of relatively unimportant, as well as all-important, problems must pass through Stalin's hands for final decision, the top is always jammed. Weeks are spent in waiting; commissars wait in Stalin's office; presidents of companies wait in the offices of the commissars; and so on down the line.... When Stalin got bored or tired, he would go off to one of his villas, giving orders that he was not to be disturbed; the top machinery would practically cease to function, and the whole thing would be in a bottleneck.[90]

Politburo decisions were organized by the Orgburo, which closely controlled the otdely, and by Orgraspred in particular. Beginning in 1931, the Orgburo work plan was reorganized to correspond with that of the Assignment Otdel; it was divided into eight sections which corresponded to the priorities of the economic plan.[91] The major burden of supplying cadres for the expanding economy fell upon Orgraspred, which labored under severe organizational difficulties until the 1930 reorganization.[92] Direct cadre control, often aided by limited mass mobilizations, was a major concern of the Assignment Otdel throughout the period. Daily control over the industrial administrative system was limited by the fact that the apparat lacked parallel industrial branches, although Party organizers and special political otdely set up under the Secretariat partially compensated this lack.

To fulfil the plan was the local Party organs' central task from the beginning of the Five-Year Plan. The extreme politicization of society at both local and central levels encouraged the closest union of Party and state organs. Molotov warned that the elections to the soviets in 1931 should permit no *shchel*, or split, between Party and state, and he told the plenum that there would be no danger of "petty interference" in the fulfillment of the plan.[93] In certain critical industries, such as the coal industry, a Central Committee decree of January 1929 made local Party organs responsible for raising coal production and labor productivity, lowering costs, eliminating labor turnover, and educating the peasants flowing into the factories.[94] These general directives were supplemented from time to time by specific directives to perform special tasks. The responsibility for transferring engineering personnel from administration to production, for example, was delegated by the Secretariat to the Don Obkom, which was required to report monthly on the results.[95]

The effectiveness of the lower Party apparatus was undoubtedly reduced by both the general atmosphere of crisis and the fluidity of Party structure and cadres. The apparatus struggled heroically against mounting disorder in the industrial economy. Throughout the U.S.S.R. it fought repeated efforts by Right Opposition supporters to reduce the tempo, and it quelled the spontaneous, often bitter, and prolonged labor demonstrations against rising production norms and Draconian labor legislation.[96] The territorial Party apparatus also worked assiduously to impose *edinonachalie* within the industrial plants.[97] The frantic search by the local Party organs for cadres met with indifferent success, and the continuous change in *nomenklatura* as well as the heavy turnover of managerial personnel brought charges that the regional secretariats knew very few qualified personnel.[98] The Party apparatus also acted as troubleshooter in the numerous bottlenecks plaguing the production process.[99]

Under pressure from the center, the substitution of local and primary Party organs for enterprise officials appears to have been frequent. The Seventeenth Conference in 1932 brought forth a general complaint that Party officials intervened in the hiring and firing of shop heads, foremen, and technical personnel. Party officials were also, at this early stage, involved in problems of material and technical supply.[100] It is difficult to determine the effectiveness of Stalin's secret order of June 1931 to curb the populist and antimanagerial fervor whipped up by the Party and mass organizations.[101] Yet, its impact was clearly evident until the Seventeenth Congress, when the course toward full bureaucratization was adopted.

That the territorial Party apparatus was integrated into the industrialization drive as a coordinating agent, and, in some degree, to correct the serious microimbalances of the First Five-Year Plan, was evident primarily in its efforts to mobilize human and material resources in behalf of the plan. The formation of operational priorities was an important development to emerge from the initial impact of industrialization. By the end of the plan, the Gorky Obkom had begun to concentrate its effort on the leading plants of the province, giving only passing attention to the lagging smaller plants. More importantly, the obkom had begun to stress the fulfillment of the quantitative indicators of the annual production plan, ignoring the qualitative indicators.[102]

The local Party organs were responsible for mobilizing the masses to fulfill the regime's political and economic goals. The slogan "*litso k proizvodstvu*" ("face to production") would be in Stalin's phrase, an "expression of the creative initiative of the masses."[103] Against the critics of the mass movement, he held that it stimulated a heroic attitude toward labor; he even defended the exaggerations of its success by claiming that gross distortion of fact may be true if it inspires the reader to emulation.[104] The *udarnichestvo*, or shock campaign, directed against Tomskii's followers in the trade unions was intended to unleash mass energy and to pressure workers to a maximum effort to fulfill goals.[105] By 1929, according to official Soviet sources, 63 percent of workers in large enterprises were engaged in some form of socialist emulation, and 26 percent were engaged in shock brigades.[106] Much of this must be discounted, however, since a number of Party committees took an "administrative approach" to the problem. One kraikom committee, ordered to mobilize 50 thousand *udarniki*, simply registered whole shops. When the center checked the results, it was discovered that the workers were unaware of their distinction.[107] The mass movement aroused serious resentment in the plants, both as a method of exploitation and of administration. After the Seventeenth Congress, it would assume an economic and technical form.

— 3 —

The Routinization of the Leading Role

According to Alexander Barmine: "Stalin sought to achieve all the wonders of the Five-Year Plan, not by organization and expert direction, but by working up the masses to ecstatic enthusiasm and superhuman efforts. He did achieve some wonders, but the plan threatened to flounder in a kind of anarchy. Costs increased, wastage of labor and of human energy became enormous."[1] The decisions to strengthen organization, to employ expertise, and to reduce the politicization of the industrial economy fell to the Seventeenth Congress, which met in Moscow in January and February 1934.

Undoubtedly, the degree of depoliticization can be exaggerated. The purges of the middle and late thirties, the war years, and the years of the *zhdanovshchina* increased the diffusion of Soviet political and ideological values. Bureaucratization nevertheless increased markedly after 1934, partly to meet the needs of Party and state officials for personal security. The results were predictable: conservatism, technicism, the turning of subgoals into final goals by the intermediate and lower levels of both hierarchies, and serious problems of both vertical and horizontal communication.

Routinization bred a hostility toward innovation, and as bureaucratization proceeded, devitalization ensued. Stasis was never fully achieved, however. Continuous politicization (and purge) of the administration and the structural expansion and differentiation compelled by the growing complexity in the industrial environment ensured a certain disequilibrium and change within the Party and managerial apparatuses. Moreover, despite the extreme centralization under Stalin, Moscow was unable to impose total allocative and coordinative controls on the lower levels of the hierarchy. The motion underlying the informal structure could mitigate, but not significantly overcome, the rigidity and atrophy developing in the Party and state bureaucracies. As Stalin's rule drew to a close, the imbalance between power and efficiency had reached serious proportions.

1

Party Structure under the
Ministerial System

Under the ministerial system, the Party developed structurally according to the pattern which Stalin had decreed at the Sixteenth Congress. Local Party organs continued to increase in number with a diminishing span of control. By the Eighteenth Congress, seven union republics had become eleven; and there were six kraikomy, 104 obkomy, thirty national okrugov, 212 gorkomy, 336 city and 3,479 rural raikomy, and 113 thousand primary Party organs.[2] At the Nineteenth Congress in 1952, the structure had expanded to include sixteen union republics, eight kraikomy, 167 obkomy, thirty-six okrugov, 544 city and 4,886 rural raikomy. Primary party organs had tripled to 350 thousand.

The increase in general Party membership and the changes in its social and occupational composition reflected the growth of a large-scale bureaucratic organization. Numbering approximately 3.5 million on 1 January 1933, Party membership fell as a result of the purges to about 2.3 million on 1 January 1939. From this low, however, it climbed steadily, reaching over 6.8 millions by 1952. Numerical growth was accompanied by a significant change in the pattern of recruitment. The policy of recruiting workers and peasants directly engaged in production, begun during NEP and intensified during the First Five-Year Plan, gave way to a new policy designed to bring the new administrative and technical intelligentsia under Party influence. In the years 1939–41, approximately 70 percent of the new recruits were from this stratum. Mass recruitment increased during the war, but the Party reverted to a policy of elite recruitment in the postwar period.[3]

Adjusting the central and regional Party apparatuses to the requirements of guiding an increasingly complex economic structure induced the most significant changes in Party structure from the Seventeenth Congress. The functional system set up at the Sixteenth Congress had limited control of the economy, for reasons of departmental structure, to cadres. The Seventeenth Congress created a production-branch structure in which the Central Committee apparatus paralleled the state industrial administration. Controlling functions were concentrated in each branch otdel, and general coordination and supervision were entrusted to the Secretariat.

At the local level, secretariats were abolished; local committees were restricted to two secretaries; the bureaus of republican and oblast committees were limited to eleven members; gorkomy and raikomy, from five to seven. At the regional level, branch otdely were set up to guide industry and agriculture. Party propaganda was concentrated in a Department for the Culture and Propaganda of Leninism, and lower Party organs were supervised through a Department of Leading Party Organs. In the gorkomy and raikomy, all departments were once again liquidated and instructors regrouped by category of enterprise. The previous system of Party-state control was significantly reorganized by the formation of separate Party and state control commissions charged with checkup and control over the fulfillment of Party and state decisions and operating independently of each other.[4]

The 1934 reorganization, however, was only partially stable. Both *Kul'tprop* and the Department of Leading Party Organs were repeatedly reorganized between 1935 and 1938.[5] At the local level, secretariats were reestablished,[6] and by 1936 local departments began to reappear.[7] At the Eighteenth Congress, the system underwent major surgery again. The functional system was reinstituted. The industrial branch departments were abolished, and a Cadres Administration exercised centralized control over all managerial cadres. Internal Party supervision and control remained in a separate organization-instruction otdel; only agriculture retained its branch department. At the regional level, otdely were formed for cadres, propaganda and agitation, organization and instruction, and agriculture, with secretaries for cadres and propaganda. The local Party organs were restricted to departments for cadres, propaganda and agitation, and organization and instruction.[8]

The functional system, emphasizing the political role of the Party, was further modified at the obkom level at the Eighteenth Conference in 1941. Secretaries were authorized for industry and transport, and the territorial Party apparatus won a major victory in the decision to bring the politotdely under local Party control. Finally, the conference ratified the development of branch departments, which had been re-forming as early as 1940,[9] at the obkom level. During the war, the apparatus remained relatively untouched. In 1946, the Organization-Instruction Otdel, which had declined steadily in importance, was replaced by an Administration for Checking Party Organs, which, in turn, evolved into a new Department of Party, Trade-Union, and Komsomol Organs. On Zhdanov's death in 1948, the Party apparatus underwent its final major reorganization, when special branch departments were set up for heavy industry, light industry, transport, and planning-finance-trade.[10] It was this structure, with further refinement and development, that Khrushchev inherited.

To cope with industrialization and its expanded decision-making role, the Party's professional staff increased and evolved into the Stalinist apparatus. At the February–March 1937 plenum, Stalin estimated the total Party apparatus at 133 thousand to 194 thousand full-time Party leaders.[11] On the basis of these figures, Fainsod has estimated the total size of the Party apparat in 1952 at 194 thousand;[12] Schapiro, at 225,000–235,000.[13] A more recent estimate by George Fischer has placed the number of Party executives excluding political officers in the armed forces, at about 240 thousand in 1956.[14] The heavy turnover during the First Five-Year Plan and the purges had decimated the older pre-revolutionary generation and created a new generation of political bureaucrats. At the Eighteenth Congress, both Zhdanov and Andreev noted the emergence of a new middle stratum of Party officials. Of 333 republican and obkom secretaries, 48.9 percent had a secondary to higher education, with 28.6 percent having higher educations. Over 80 percent had entered the Party after 1924; 52.6 percent were of worker origin; 91 percent were under forty and 53.2 percent from thirty-one to thirty-five years of age.[15]

The essential patterns in local Party cadre structure to emerge from the purges of the thirties persisted through Stalin's death. In his intensive study of the postwar Ukrainian apparatus, Armstrong has demonstrated the preponderance of power among those who entered the Party between 1921 and 1930 and assumed executive posts after 1938.[16] Formal education became increasingly important in gaining key offices in the Party or state apparatus.[17] It is also clear that the specialized requirements of industrialization created career specialization within the obkom apparatus. The directing of major industrial oblasti was entrusted to secretaries with higher education and technical training. For a political and administrative elite, however, the Ukrainian first secretaries were men of humble, predominantly peasant backgrounds, whose average tenure of office was two to three years, and who had prospered under the rigors of the Stalinist system.[18]

Internal Party Relationships under the Ministerial System

The frequent reorganizations of Party structure after 1934 were manifestations of certain deep-rooted problems which accompanied the industrial development of the Soviet economy. Extreme vertical centralism had proved only partially effective as a decision-making instrument, particularly at territorial levels. The reorganizations and quarrels behind the façade of totalitarian unity revealed fundamental dilemmas in the organization of authority and the style of Party *rukovodstvo* arising from the Party's extensive involvement in economic and technical decision-making.

Under the ministerial system, certain tensions arose from the twofold necessity of producing a rigid, hierarchical authority structure while, at the same time, mobilizing resources for efficient direction of the economy. The result was a pattern of centralized pressure balanced by widespread deception and the formation of family groups, both of which served in some degree to reduce anxiety and isolation. At the February–March 1937 plenum, Stalin and Zhdanov both denounced attempts by lower Party secretaries to form local groups free from central Party control.[19]

The territorial secretarial corps' unresponsiveness to the demands of the center was a central theme of Malenkov's political report to the Nineteenth Congress fifteen years later. The Party's cadres, he charged, were crammed with arrogant officials who refused criticism and who continuously violated Party and state discipline by elevating local and regional over national interests. Cadre selection on a personal rather than a merit basis led to the appointment of sycophants devoted to pleasing superiors rather than to displaying initiative and competence. The control mechanism of the lower Party apparatus, he noted, was extremely weak.[20]

Local organs imitated the extreme authoritarianism that characterized the relations between Moscow and the provinces. Data from the Smolensk archives and the Soviet press indicate that at the republican and oblast levels, the first secretary's personal responsibility was virtually absolute over the Party apparatus under his control.[21] Although elections of local Party committees and bureaus ceased during the war, they were reinstituted between 1947 and 1949.[22] This, however, appears to have very little modified the essential situation.

The rigid division of authority and status at every level of the Party hierarchy led to frequent complaints about ineffective leadership.[23] Sessions of the regional bureau, for example, which were dominated by the first secretary, were often poorly prepared, included too many questions, were held far too often, and consumed too much time.[24] Decisions were often merely repetitive and too general to provide specific guidance and direction. Within the secretariat, the excessive concentration of authority continued to restrict the administrative apparatus to narrowly defined, principally clerical functions.[25] Department heads were generally without administrative authority, and instructors continued to preoccupy themselves with the collection of data for bureau decisions or to act as *tolkachi* in matters of supply.[26]

The Party's internal administrative structure contributed to the sporadic character of Party *rukovodstvo* under the ministerial system. Information concerning the republic or oblast was tightly restricted to the secretariats. Important documents were often withheld from circulation, or else secretaries made decisions without informing others. Despite the noncirculation of necessary information, the average territorial apparatus was swamped with paper work, and much time was spent at every level in compiling reports, filling requests for information, and responding to a continuous flow of correspondence.[27] A failure to plan ahead further reduced the cohesiveness and internal stability of the local apparatus. The Party moved from situation to situation as passing needs and central requirements dictated.[28] Finally, there was bitter, often destructive competition among the apparatus departments.[29]

The characteristics of authority and style to emerge as industrialization proceeded were already rooted in the dynamics of the Party apparatus before the Fifteenth Congress. An industrial economy, however, raised new problems on the nature of the Party's guiding role and methods of execution. At the policy level, the quarrel over priorities was generally expressed in terms of "politics"

versus "economics," with basic reference, however, to specific observable results and specific methods of *rukovodstvo*. The organizational point of reference
was the functional versus the production-branch system, and the principal
standard-bearers among Stalin's lieutenants were Zhdanov, the ideological
specialist, and Malenkov, the organizational specialist. Although their differences
were only distinctions of priority and emphasis, they were still significant enough
to require different definitions in terms of the Party's organizational role as
the guiding force of Soviet society.

The most serious long-range threat to the Party was that its absorption in
economic and technical issues, together with the purge of old cadres and the
influx of new specialists, would transform it from an elite political organization
into a technocracy. The threat to its elitist nature and political mission had
been of formal concern to the leadership since the Eighth Congress in 1919.
The specific problem of 1939 was a new one, however, and Stalin discussed
it at the Eighteenth Congress.

> There is hardly need to dwell on the cardinal importance of our Party propaganda,
> of the Marxist-Leninist training of our personnel.... The work of regulating the
> composition of the Party and bringing the leading bodies closer to the activities
> of the lower bodies may be organized satisfactorily; the work of promoting, selecting
> and allocating cadres may also be organized satisfactorily; but, with all this, if
> our Party propaganda for some reason or other goes lame, if the Marxist-Leninist
> training of our cadres begins to languish, if our work of raising the political and
> theoretical level of these cadres flags, and the cadres themselves cease on account
> of this to show interest in the progress of our further progress, cease to understand
> the truth of our cause and are transformed into narrow plodders with no outlook,
> blindly and mechanically carrying out instructions from above—then our entire
> state and Party work must inevitably languish. It must be accepted as an axiom
> that the higher the political level and the Marxist-Leninist understanding of the
> workers in any branch of state or Party work, the better and more fruitful will
> be the work itself, and the more effective the results of the work, and vice-versa,
> the lower the political level and the Marxist-Leninist understanding of the workers,
> the greater will be the likelihood of disruption and failure in the work, of the
> workers themselves becoming shallow and deteriorating into paltry plodders, of
> their degenerating altogether.[30]

Stalin held that scientific or technological specialization was required but warned
against a purely technical or apolitical approach.

> For a man who calls himself a Leninist cannot be considered a real Leninist in
> his specialty, in mathematics, botany or chemistry, let us say, and see nothing
> beyond that specialty. A Leninist cannot be just a specialist in his favorite science;
> he must also be a political and public worker, keenly interested in the destinies
> of his country, acquainted with the laws of social development, capable of applying
> these laws, and striving to be an active participant in the political guidance of
> the country. This, of course, will be an additional burden on specialists who are
> Bolsheviks. But it will be a burden more than compensated for by its results.[31]

This concern with unanimity of outlook and ideology was pursued with savage intensity by Zhdanov until his death in August 1948 and formed a principal issue in Malenkov's political report to the Nineteenth Congress. Undoubtedly reflecting Stalin's view, Malenkov accused some Party organs of having become absorbed in economic work to the neglect of political and ideological matters. The reduction of ideological truth to rote and formula, poorly trained propaganda cadres, and low political literacy among Party workers indicated, Malenkov told the Congress, that the Party had become bureaucratic and weakened.[32]

The production-branch system enabled the Party to enter into economic administration far deeper than did the functional system. As administrative systems, each exhibited certain strengths and weaknesses. By decentralizing cadre control, the production-branch system (in Zhdanov's view) provoked competition and conflict and replaced economic organs.[33] Without parallel departments to guide industry, Malenkov told the Eighteenth Conference in February 1941, Party guidance was superficial; decisions were not actively supervised or implemented. Many local Party organs, he added, tended to concentrate on either industry or agriculture, each excluding the other. In his report, he listed fourteen specific responsibilities of the Party organization toward the economy, which, if carried through, would have placed primary responsibility for the operation of every important phase of economic development and operation on the Party.[34]

"Politics" versus "economics",—a serious issue in the November 1962 Party reorganization,—raised the generalist-specialist specter in a particularly acute form for the local Party organization. Generally responsible for operating and coordinating all aspects of the life of its territory, the local Party leadership was judged principally by the results of plan fulfillment within its jurisdiction. When the economic responsibility took priority, the danger to political cohesiveness and dynamism lay not only in the loss of perspective through absorption in current economic issues but also in the possibility that the Party organ would become for all practical purposes an appendage of industrial management.[35] This particular threat to the leading role was omnipresent under the ministerial system.

2

The Industrial Management System
under Stalin

The system of industrial administration that followed the Seventeenth Congress was not new but a rationalization of the 1932 structure. Its basic features were outlined in the directive of the Central Executive Committee and Council of People's Commissars of 15 March 1934. The functional system which had concentrated all aspects of industrial administration within one unit was abolished. The new organ of direct industrial administration would be the production-territorial administration (glavk), which, generally subordinate to an economic commissariat, would administer a single branch of industry for the whole country or for a single region. To safeguard the operational authority of the glavk, all functional organs were required to operate through the administration. Only industrial enterprises of all-union scale were concentrated within the glavk. Unions were finally liquidated and the number of trusts were to be reduced.[36] In July 1936 the glavk was granted the right to conclude direct and general contracts for supply and sale, and it acted as basic coordinator and director of planning, supply, production, and sale activities of subordinate trusts and enterprises until Stalin's death.[37]

The important functional relationships that had remained stable under the ministerial system were subject to frequent reorganization during Stalin's lifetime and after. In 1936, of the eighteen commissariats created under the new constitution, twelve were economic. By 1939, there were thirty-four commissariats, of which twenty-four were economic. The process of administrative subdivision climaxed in 1947 when fifty-nine ministries were created, fifty of them economic. By 1949, a partial reversal had occurred; but new ministries began to re-form after 1949; and in the summer of 1952, the number had again expanded to fifty-one, with forty of these concerned with economic activity.[38]

The ministerial system continued the practice of categorizing branches of industry and individual plants in terms of union, republican, and local significance. The most important branches of heavy and light industry were placed under union control. Vlasov has estimated that in 1952, 70 percent of all industrial production was under the direct administration of Moscow.[39] The most important branches of heavy industry were concentrated in all-union ministries which maintained independent administrative offices at the republican or local level. Light industry and regionally concentrated industries were administered through ministries subordinate to both the various republican councils of ministers and the union ministry. While formal authority for the direct administration of industries within the republic lay with the republican ministry—with the U.S.S.R. Ministry restricted to technical control over standards and quality of output—close administrative supervision by the union-republic ministry seems to have been the rule. Organizing local industry was the responsibility of the local soviets, although republican ministries of communal economy functioned together with the local soviets as general administrative supervisors of local production.[40]

Under the ministerial system, the administrative structure of the enterprise remained virtually unchanged, although the director's personal and legal responsibility was finally consolidated. The plant administration included the director and his deputy, the chief engineer. In larger plants, where a director might have deputy directors for construction or economics, the chief engineer enjoyed operational primacy. The basic production unit within the plant was the shop, or *tsekh*, which was subdivided into *uchastki*, basic processing or assembling aggregates. The shop head (*nachal'nik*), who worked under the central plant administration on the principles of *edinonachalie*, was responsible for output and discipline, and, assisted by deputy shop heads, exercised control over the foreman and shift chiefs.[41]

The Party was rapidly transformed into a managerial and technical elite under the ministerial system. In 1927, there had been only 9 thousand Party members with higher education and 751 with higher technical education. In ten years, 105 thousand members had higher education and 47 thousand higher technical education.[42] The influx into the industrial economy of young technical specialists and their promotion to leading technical and administrative posts was accelerated by the purge of administrative and economic officials in 1936 and 1937. The Old Bolshevik glavki heads were liquidated, and the composition of plant managerial personnel altered significantly with the purge of the Red directors. The total number of purged personnel cannot be ascertained, but the heavy industry commissariats were most heavily decimated. In 1939, 76.1 percent of the personnel in these branches were under forty years of age.[43] The rise of a new administrative and technical intelligentsia created a political indoctrination problem but also reduced the class tensions characteristic of earlier periods. The new personnel, as Armstrong points out, were more professional and homogeneous, emphasizing career and economic rewards over political and ideological goals.[44]

The placement of economic cadres remained problematic. A 1940 survey showed that the majority of engineers and technicians was still absorbed in administration. In the coal industry, for example, only 25.7 percent were in the field; in the oil industry, 34.8 percent; in the electrical industry, only 22.3 percent; in agriculture, only 6 percent.[45] Since technical personnel tended to concentrate in plants within or near the city, distribution was uneven. Some plants lacked engineers, others had too many; and this remained characteristic in the postwar period as well. In 1954, 76 percent of all specialists in the Ministry of Machine Building and Instruments were in administration.

The Functioning of the Ministerial System

Within the limitations imposed by Stalin, the ministerial structure was a reasonably effective administrative mechanism for the rapid industrialization of an agrarian society. By means of centralized political and administrative pressure, economic administration had been institutionalized into a pattern emphasizing a high level of capital investment in heavy industry. Planning and administration took place in an environment of haste, centrally enforced priorities, and chronic shortages and imbalances, the result in part of excessive targets; in part, of ignoring or reducing the importance of economic criteria. But the administration was effective in the early stages of industrialization when the need to marshal scarce resources for a limited number of well-defined objectives was basic.

Increased scale and volume of production created, however, a new administrative environment. Capital became less scarce while the human resources capable of managing the new economy grew. Physical expansion induced a corresponding increase in the number of investment, production, and consumption options open for decision, and each set of decisions had increasingly complex consequences. Whether the system was capable of adjusting to the conditions of industrial complexity was a major issue in the postwar period.[46] Stalin's testament, the conservative *Economic Problems of Socialism*, appealing to law rather than to will, visualized no extensive changes in the transition to communism; but the complex issues of priority and institutional relationships which arose with Stalin's death challenged the industrial administration's competence and efficiency.

The management system which had become institutionalized under Stalin was inadequate to meet the demands of planning and administering a complex, interdependent economy and by 1953 had become a stubborn obstacle to further economic development. As early as the Eighteenth Conference in 1941, Malenkov had noted the major deficiencies which would be so frequently cited in the four years after Stalin's death. In his report, he accused the ministries of an ignorance of cadres and of such administrative practices in the enterprises as excessive meetings, delayed decisions, and the proliferation of decisions which would go unfulfilled. He called attention to the hoarding of excessive raw material stocks, a large amount of unused machinery, serious shortage of supplies, unrhythmic production, and weak technical control. He noted, too, an indifference to technical development, high production costs, a problematic wage structure, and high labor turnover.[47] These reflect the substance of the charges against the ministerial system in the immediate post-Stalin period. In October 1954, the system was characterized as extremely centralized, with an excessive paper flow, inflated staffs, excessive administrative links, and irrational fragmentation.[48]

The intensely centralized administrative processes of industrial management were, in Pervukhin's phrase, "survivals of the old mistrust of local agencies and heads of enterprises."[49] The concentration of decision-making power in Moscow impelled a flow of petty issues to the center and retarded decision-making. In 1954, Zverev (then Minister of Finance) estimated that the average issue required about six months to resolve.[50] The massive paper flow and accounting formally occupied some 30 percent of the administrative staff.[51] In 1953, the Ministry of Construction issued and received an estimated 1.5 million documents. Coordination and cooperation were particularly hampered by the counterthrust of the ministries toward autarky and self-sufficiency, which resulted in an extremely complex, multistaged, and cumbersome formal structure of administration.[52]

The assignment of specific tasks, allocation of resources and responsibilities, and evaluation of performance was basically achieved through the tekhpromfinplan. Planning as a whole emphasized current over long-range planning and industrial branch over regional planning. Reconciling economic targets with available resources was essentially a process of command, mitigated and distorted by informal bargaining, simulation, and illegality. In conditions in which plan fulfillment involved the most intense stretching of resources, the search for security and bonuses was a basic determinant of managerial behavior.[53]

Since plan construction was guided by past performance records of the individual enterprise or ministry, the basic strategy of administrative or operational units involved minimizing production obligations and maximizing resource allocation. Eventually, inflated requests for supply coexisted with the hoarding of raw materials, padding overhead, overstating needs for working capital, and establishing low material utilization norms.

Similarly, manpower and wage needs were usually overstated because this created a production reserve and eased planned targets for labor productivity. Low labor norms were deliberately maintained, labor overstated, workers improperly classified and graded. These practices were not exclusively confined to the enterprises. Since the legal authority for the planning and control of production and supply was concentrated in the glavk and ultimately in the ministry, collusion was necessary and usually forthcoming.[54] At the Twentieth Congress, Saburov noted that the ministries of ferrous metallurgy, coal, and building materials made strenuous efforts to limit both the output plan and the index for labor productivity. In the latter case, the ministries submitted a rise in labor productivity of 4 percent, a figure which the planning officials corrected by doubling.[55]

The production process itself was seriously flawed. During the Fifth Five-Year Plan, more than one-third of all industrial enterprises failed to fulfill the production plan, and in 1953 and 1954, more than 50 percent of all industrial plants under union jurisdiction failed to fulfill their plans for lowering costs, with many operating at a deficit.[56] The losses from the less efficient plants were covered by the profits of the more efficient, a practice which penalized the leading plants and confirmed the status quo. The general quality of production was low, with a high percentage of defective equipment in such industries as radio, light industry, and instruments. Plan fulfillment was often simulated by substituting material inputs or by including unfinished, defective, or otherwise inferior products in the plan. Assortments of product mixes were manipulated, and reports were falsified. In capital construction, investments were dispersed, and the pool of unfinished construction increased yearly. Construction technology was low and the construction costs extremely high.[57] In both industry and construction, the central operational problem was supply, an issue which absorbed major resources of both Party and state apparatuses.

The most serious long-range issues, however, concerned technical progress and economic growth, questions that would become crucial in terms of the Party's leading role in the post-Stalin period. In his important report to the July 1955 plenum on industry, Bulganin stated that industrial technology was lagging in the Soviet Union and becoming increasingly obsolescent. Heavy machinery lagged in productivity behind the best foreign models, and the rise in labor productivity through the mechanization of labor-consuming processes was slight. Industrial research and development were particularly weak under the ministerial system because the thrust toward autarky and its accompanying jurisdictional conflict stilled the development of such interbranch industries as petrochemicals and machine building. Ministerial pluralism also led to irrational transportation costs and low standards of specialization. More than half the spare parts used in the machine-building industry, for example, were produced by hand at a cost fourteen times greater than their mass-produced counterparts.[58]

Industrial administrators were criticized for their indifference to the issues of industrial progress on the basis of three factors, of which the first was fundamentally administrative. Bulganin pointed out that engineering and technical personnel continued to be absorbed into administration rather than into production. Turnover of industrial cadres was high. Many young specialists in research and development lacked industrial experience, and far too few young industrial cadres were being promoted. In addition, the technical preparation of industrial cadres was poor, and the rigid educational system was unresponsive to the changing demands of industry.[59] A second factor in explaining the attachment of the industrial executive to the status quo involved the relationship between centralism and poor communication. An article in *Kommunist* complained:

> Administrative officials are accustomed to dealing with practical matters only on instructions of the chiefs and local officials are accustomed to expecting directives from above on even the simplest questions. Sometimes instructions from ministries are drawn up insufficiently, without knowledge of the actual state of affairs at the enterprise or without consideration for the local conditions and peculiarities of production.[60]

Third, cadres were charged with moral delinquency, and technological lag was attributed to their conservatism, complacency, conceit, and self-satisfaction. In his report to the Twentieth Congress, Khrushchev summarized this view.

> The fact of the matter is that the successes of our industry have turned the heads of some economic and Party officials, have fostered conceit and complacency in them, and in a number of cases have brought about the underestimation of the need for continuous improvement in production, for the introduction of the latest achievements of domestic and foreign science and technology. We still have

officials—"men in mummy cases"—who fear everything that is new and advanced. An old fossil of an official argues: "Why should I become mixed up in all of this? There will be a lot of bother and it might lead to a lot of unpleasantness. They talk about improving production! Is it worthwhile knocking your brains over it? Let the higher-ups worry. Let the top men do the thinking. When a directive comes, we'll see about it." Another official, after he has received instructions, directs his energies largely to evading a vital job or merely going through the motions of tackling it.[61]

There was, however, some recognition of the industrial administrators' anxiety that the introduction of new products and processes would adversely affect labor productivity and the fulfillment of quantitative planned indices. The planners' refusal to lower the planned volume of production during periods of technical changeover or to acknowledge the risks inherent in technical innovation reduced the industrial officials' interest in technological progress because it structured their response to planning and current production. In addressing the problem of technical progress, a major question of reform was how much the system would be modified to meet the conditions of mature industrialization.

Although some basic changes would be introduced to Soviet industrial administration on the eve of the Khrushchev era, a number of important prerevolutionary characteristics would be carried forward as well. Edeen has noted that at least five major characteristics from the czarist past have persisted into the Soviet period: (1) the highly centralized government machinery and state direction of the economy corresponded to previous administrative practice; (2) state administrators under both regimes were dependent, insecure, and relatively powerless; (3) both czarist and Soviet civil servants inclined toward rigid bureaucratic styles with a heavy emphasis on hierarchy and stratification; (4) each system exhibited the ills of bureaucracy, including red tape, excessive paper flow, and corruption; and (5) each experienced, in different degrees of intensity, harsh police repression. Under the Soviet system, however, the abolition of private property and the increased overall efficiency of the structure has had the effect of reducing even the limited autonomy of the czarist officials.[62] The fundamental difference between the two administrative structures was the creation of a parallel political and administrative authority in the Communist party.

3

Party Guidance under the Ministerial System

The Party guided the ministerial system according to general institutional practices which had developed during the previous years of Communist party rule. During the last twenty years of Stalin's dictatorship, however, the Party's involvement in the economy was in many respects unique. Stalin was elevated to a unique position in the political system, and this primary shift changed the balance of power within the Party-state relationship. The Party's decision-making role was reduced and the reduction reinforced by the routinization of planning and plan implementation within the command economy. As the Stalinist system of industrial administration matured, the Party's entrepreneurial role declined, particularly at the territorial level. In a highly selective way, however, it did contribute to the extensive growth of the economy and help to reduce the often severe microimbalances involved in the command economy.

Stalin's dictatorial stance has, of course, raised profound moral and political problems, including the legitimacy of the system itself, for his successors. With respect to industrial decision-making, the available evidence is unclear concerning whether Stalin and his lieutenants remained as deeply involved in the detailed coordination of the economy as they had been during the First Five-Year Plan. Nevertheless, two characteristics are clear. First, Stalin could and frequently did make decisions independently of both the Party and managerial groups. Second, managers and technical specialists had ascendancy over Party officials in the areas of competence Stalin delegated to them.

Stalin's use of his virtually unlimited power to make arbitrary decisions has, of course, been one of the principle charges against him. As the revised Party history pointed out in 1961:

> Following the Seventeenth Congress of the C.P.S.U. (B) Stalin ceased completely to take into account the collective opinion of the Party and Central Committee. The personality cult was creating a favorable atmosphere for such negative practices as arbitrary decisions and abuses of power, self-seeking and servility, suspicion and distrust; in the ideological sphere, it bred dogmatism and led to the separation of theory from practice.[63]

The institutional ascendancy of state over Party organs bespoke a subservient role for the Politburo, which, as Khrushchev bitterly complained, met sporadically and at Stalin's initiative.[64] By forming special Politburo commissions with overlapping jurisdictions and memberships, Stalin protected his own power at the same time that new ideas and policy alternatives were generated. The bitter rivalry, internecine warfare, and intrigue among Stalin's lieutenants for position and influence with the dictator was one result of this practice.

At the Secretariat and Central Committee departments level, as Professor Nemzer has indicated, Party administration functioned as neither brain trust nor controller of the state administration.[65] Under the production-branch system which existed from 1934 to 1939, and again after 1948, daily Party control over planning and plan execution was undoubtedly much greater than under the functional system, which concentrated Party guidance on cadre policy and checkup and control. Before 1948, cadre policy was centralized in the Cadres Administration, which controlled appointments on both its own *nomenklatura* and that of the industrial ministries. Checkup and control was exercised through the Organization-Instruction Department, which linked the center with the local Party organs and served as a central coordinating and executive department by gathering data, raising problems, implementing decisions, and closely supervising the execution of central directives by local Party organs. In the absence of industrial departments, the Central Committee was represented in the major industrial plants by Party organizers.

The return to a production-branch structure after Zhdanov's death in 1948 increased the capacity of the central apparatus for technical operational control. Cadre policy and checkup were again dispersed among specialized production departments. The consequence was presumably to increase the problems of internal Party administration and the tension between the Party and managers. Throughout this period, the central Party apparatus resolved the numerous disputes between local Party and state officials[66] and responded to the numerous requests for resources and support which rose through the hierarchy from the territorial apparatus.

In the guidance of industry, local Party organs tended to preserve previous institutional relationships. Unlike the central apparat, the local Party organs (except for the year after the Eighteenth Congress) maintained industrial departments during the entire period. In fact, many republican and Party committees in the more industrialized areas had deputy secretaries for individual branches of industry. The central plan, its extreme centralization of power, and the competing demands of agriculture in the less industrialized provinces limited local Party direction of industry. The role of the territorial apparatus appears to have been further reduced by the intense bureaucratization within the Party, which restricted the scope and influence of its decision-making activities.

Local Party committees were relatively weak in relation to central Party and state organs.[67] This condition was of long standing and was deeply rooted in the Party-state order. The republican and provincial Party committees remained pivotal points in the translation of central policy into practice, and they carried the basic responsibility for both industry and agriculture. Their relationship with the central state organs contained elements of both latent conflict and cooperation, the conflict reflecting their underlying diversity of interests and responsibilities. The obkom normally assumed a local and predominantly territorial point of view; the ministry and its production glavki were usually integrated on a broader geographical and narrower production basis.

The ministry's authority to allocate capital investment, production assignments, supply, and profits could, under the tight operational margins usually prevailing in Soviet industry, influence the success or failure of the enterprises under the jurisdiction of the regional Party organizations. That the obkom shared formal responsibility with the ministry for planning and production within the enterprise only intensified and complicated the matter. Such conflicts were resolved in favor of the ministry quite simply. The regional Party committee was formally required to execute ministerial, and even glavk, decisions, and the discretion of the obkom was reduced to a minimum: Moscow simply sent down, as it had done in previous periods, specific and detailed instructions which the obkom was required to carry out without substantial change.[68]

The local Party organ's authority and functions in relation to the individual enterprise varied according to the general political line and the subordination of the enterprise. The assumption of direct operational control—in violation of the traditional doctrine on the leading role—occurred between the Seventeenth and Eighteenth Congresses and during the Second World War when the regional Party committees were given direct administrative responsibilities for production and supply. In 1939–40 and after the war, when Party policy emphasized strengthening the political role and reducing the administrative role of the local Party committees, substitutions still occurred but without official central sanction.[69]

The power of the obkom was also conditioned by the formal subordination of the particular plant. In plants of union ministries, the ministry carried full responsibility for their economic and technical functioning. Each of the major industrial plants in 1939 was placed under the supervision of a Central Committee Party Organizer elected by the local committee but reporting directly to the central apparat. The role of the Partorg was ambiguous, and in one student's view, relatively ineffective.[70] Plants of republican ministries were placed under republican committees, and local industry was under obkom control.[71]

The strength of the ministries was particularly felt in those traditional areas of Party competence, cadre supervision and checkup and control. In plants of union subordination, the obkom could not appoint, change, or dismiss a plant director without the ministry's consent. The legislation behind this issue was the June 1938 decree of the Central Committee, which criticized the Yaroslavl Obkom for dismissing a plant director and appointing a new one without the consent of the interested ministry.[72] In the postwar period, the ministry had the initiative in the appointment of plant directors of union ministries. Where the appointment was on the obkom *nomenklatura* for approval, the appointment or dismissal of a director was often a source of tension between ministry and obkom. Under such conditions, the usual recourse was to transfer the dispute to the Central Committee otdel for resolution. In the majority of cases, an authoritative Soviet source makes clear, there was no necessity for the obkom to dispute or even to discuss a ministerial decision.[73]

The relative lack of control over cadres was extended to checkup and control as well. In cases involving high ministerial officials, even a relatively powerful obkom like the Moscow Committee was usually cautious. In 1954, the Ministry of Construction of Metallurgical and Chemical Plants siphoned off enough building materials from state projects to build thirty-nine dachas for high ministerial officials, and according to a Soviet press report, the obkom did not "dare to object" to the illegal action.[74] In another case involving the same ministry, a lagging construction project was put on the bureau agenda of the responsible obkom, but no action was taken. The interested gorkom went so far as to collect data on the lagging project, but the item was not placed on the agenda.[75]

The executive functions of the obkom were still more limited in resolving issues between enterprises or administrative agencies of more than one ministry. Where the obkom was limited in taking direct action, the approved course of action was to signal or otherwise to raise the issue with the ministry or ministries involved. Yet, whether the issue involved capital investment, the annual plan, or more frequently, issues of supply, the warning or the request was frequently lost in the bureaucratic mill of the ministry, with little hope for an early or effective resolution of the problem.[76]

The local Party organ's authority over the plants under its jurisdiction was restricted, first of all, by the centralization in the state administration. Its fundamental principle of operation, however, was determined by the national plan. In general, the obkom seems to have evolved a basic pattern in this regard. Its first concern was territorial: the obkom concentrated on the production quotas for the oblast as a whole, which led to a concentration on major plants producing items of most importance. A second rule was to leave undisturbed those plants which were coping successfully with the production plan.[77] A third rule involved identifying the obkom's interests with the local industrial enterprise in its relations with the center. Under the ministerial system, republican and oblast Party committees would appear as petitioners before the ministries on behalf of their enterprises. This convergence of interests led also to the formation of the ubiquitous "family groups" and the toleration, or even active support, by obkom officials of actions by plant management which were illegal or contrary to state interests in the fulfillment of the plan.[78]

The tendency to elevate local priorities over central interests in the fulfillment of the plan led obkom officials alternately to ignore and to support the efforts of plant officials to secure lower output plans, conceal production capacity, maintain above-norm raw material stocks, or inflate the demands for material inputs.[79] Local Party officials evidently had little interest in correcting distortions in the production plan through insuring high-quality production in the proper amount and assortment.[80] The obkom also lacked either the authority or interest in rationalizing the administration or in reducing excessive personnel in the plant. The obkom seemed generally to accept the figures of the plant management on plan fulfillment without independent check.[81] But it did, on occasion, participate in the distortion or falsification of reports on the fulfillment of plans.[82]

In the interests of preserving a smoothly functioning industrial administration,

the obkom was required to intervene actively in the affairs of the plant management. This intervention—in the Soviet phrase, "substitution"—was most
frequently invoked in the problem of material-technical supply.[83] The central
clearinghouse on problems of supply within the obkom apparat was the industrial-
transport otdel or the branch otdel specializing in a given branch of industry.
The otdel and the secretary for industry performed this service in two general
ways. First, the obkom could mobilize local resources to overcome bottlenecks
in production. This consisted of ordering local plants to produce spare parts
or construction materials to meet the production needs of large enterprises.
The obkom otdel was also important in securing transportation to import or
export raw materials and products as well as in arranging for the transportation
of local plant officials. Second, the otdel served as an alternate channel and
reinforcement of plant management in their dealings with Moscow and with
plants in foreign oblasti.[84] As a means of bringing pressure upon ministerial
supply and marketing organizations as well as direct suppliers, this function
was clearly important. The obkom's role in resolving the problems of material
supply was limited, however, and represented only one of several means by
which the plant management attempted to balance input and output requirements.

Although the republican or oblast apparat was primarily responsible for the
operation of economic enterprises, including agriculture, the gorkom and raikom
were significant in guiding the industry within their jurisdictions. The allocation
of authority between them seems to have followed no single or standard pattern.[85]

In some cases, the obkom completely dominated the gorkom; in others, the
obkom dealt with the plant directors and their immediate subordinates, and
the raikom or gorkom with the shop and its officials. The gorkom had less
influence with the central ministries than the obkom; the gorkom often depended
upon the individual plant director of a union ministry and was virtually powerless
to affect a managerial decision without obkom support. Like the obkom, the
major criteria for judging the performance of gorkomy and raikomy was meeting
state economic plans, and the average gorkom was deeply involved in procuring
material supply. In executing this function, however, the gorkom possessed
few independent resources and depended heavily upon the obkom for leverage
in dealing with administrative and economic organs outside its jurisdiction.[86]

The general political importance of the gorkom was greater than its minimal
authority in the economic sector would suggest. The city was the center of
political, cultural, and administrative activities; it was regarded as the fundamental
basis for the Party's work and its source of strength. While gorkomy of republican
or oblast centers were of decisive importance, all gorkomy were responsible
for guiding primary Party organs within their jurisdictions.

The gorkom or raikom was the territorial Party organ that most directly touched
the life of the average Soviet citizen; in that respect, it was important in shaping
the Party's mass image and relating the average Soviet citizen to its goals.

These political factors were reinforced by the gorkom's special economic responsibilities in public services, including housing, and in local consumer industries. Because these service functions were of low central importance under the ministerial system, the gorkom was frequently charged with neglecting them.[87]

By reinforcing the bureaucratic principle at the expense of the mass principle, the Seventeenth Congress weakened further the authority and control functions of the primary Party organs. The Party's mobilization role continued but with emphasis on the generation of mass energy for the fulfillment of the enterprise plan. The endless variety of socialist competitions, including the Stakhanovite movement, which were continually mounted by the lower Party organs and executed through the plant Party organizations, had a production rather than political orientation, in contrast to the early years of the First Five-Year Plan. The role of the primary Party organization in relation to the enterprise administration appears to have been relatively low notwithstanding the Eighteenth Party Congress decree affirming its rights of control over the managers.[88] For them, as for the superior Party agencies, fulfillment of the enterprise plan was the overriding priority.

The low status of the primary Party organs reflected not only the reigning operational priorities but sociological factors and bureaucratic relationships as well. Sociologically, plant directors in large plants were generally superior in status to plant secretaries. Educationally, Armstrong has noted, 77 percent of factory directors had higher education. The comparable figure for the secretaries was 37.3 percent higher and 22.3 percent secondary.[89] Hierarchical relationships further reduced the authority of the plant secretary. He was frequently bypassed in conferences between obkom or gorkom officials and the plant management, and where strong informal relations existed between the plant and local Party officials, his complaints and signals were often ignored. Again, the manager would often draw the secretary into his private circle or illegally pay him premiums, thus turning him into an adjunct of the administration.[90] This criticism of primary Party secretaries also applied to some Party organizers, who conceived their function less as control over the administration than as securing the fulfillment of the plan.[91]

As Stalin's rule came to an end, the Party had ceased to be an active and transformative element in economic decision-making. It had contributed to extensive growth by mobilizing human and material resources for the industrial system. Its coordinative role, particularly at the local level, had mitigated the serious imbalances which followed from the planning and administrative structures. While useful and perhaps necessary under Soviet working arrangements, the Party was clearly insufficient to expand the economy's efficiency.

The reasons for this were primarily to be found within the apparatus of industrial management rather than the Party. There was, all the same, a widespread conviction that the qualitative performance and technological growth of the economy was a fundamental responsibility of the Party. In the period following Stalin's death, the scrutiny of the Party's role indicated, first, a recognition of the restricted power of the apparatus in relation to the managers. There was, moreover, a more sophisticated grasp of functional defects within the apparatus itself. Going beyond the relatively simple structural debates of the thirties, the expanded analysis of the Party's role stressed the technical competence of cadres and the impact of intense centralization and bureaucratization on the dynamism of the Party as an organization.[92] In attempting to reform the Party as an institution in order to significantly increase economic efficiency, Khrushchev raised a central issue for the political system.

PART TWO

THE LEADING ROLE UNDER KHRUSHCHEV

— 4 —

Khrushchev and the Leading Role: The Strategy of Party Reform

Stalin's death touched virtually every aspect of Soviet political and economic life and was particularly significant with respect to the process of renewal within the Party apparatus. Events at the Nineteenth Congress and afterward indicated a forthcoming change in the Party from its highest to its lowest organs by means of purge and possibly a new wave of terror. But Stalin's death removed the system's most important factor and changed the conditions for invigorating the Party apparatus. In the subsequent vacuum and dispersal of power among his lieutenants, the reform of the Party and expansion of its power over economic decision-making became both a goal of, and an instrument in, the power struggle.

Reforming the Communist party under conditions of power struggle further complicated an already difficult undertaking. Basically, Party renewal meant a thorough debureaucratization of the apparatus. It also implied a readjustment of its authority, structure, functions, and style as a means of dealing effectively with an environment transformed by modernization. These two processes were closely, perhaps inextricably, linked.

Between 1953 and 1962, the rationalization of the Party as an organization fell into three distinct periods corresponding to the basic approaches to the reform and the contingencies of the power struggle.[1] The first period, roughly from Stalin's death to the fall of 1958, was one of relatively conservative and cautious structural adjustment of bureaucratic relationships. The second phase, which had its most forceful initial expression at the Twenty-first Party Congress in 1959, represented a deeper and more intense effort to achieve differently what the first period had failed to do. Khrushchev's radical reorganization of the Party in November 1962 represented a final attempt to reinvigorate the institution toward a significant role in industrial decision-making. His failure may be attributed to the conservative reform policies, to bureaucratic inertia and resistance, and to those conditions of the post-Stalin period which restrained the uses of power.

No one, prior to Khrushchev's victory over the Anti-Party Group in 1957, had had sufficient power to force a radical or unilateral solution to the numerous policy and institutional issues that arose for decision during the period of collective leadership, and the decline of terror after Beria's fall in July 1953 removed a major instrument for resolving conflicting positions and policies.[2] In place of force majeure, certain ambiguous and unstable criteria arose based, presumably, on both ideological-political and pragmatic considerations, which had the effect of expanding the groups and interests involved in policy determination.

None of the participants in the power struggle, including Khrushchev, ever gained Stalin's position as lawgiver. By itself, the word was inadequate. Power, policy, and institutional relationships were judged in terms of specific consequences and were in some degree contingent on them. While there was evidently no mechanism for enforcing responsibility, serious policy failures—such as Khrushchev's failure in Eastern Europe in 1956 or in dealing with the West in 1960 at the time of the U-2 incident—carried political penalties such as were reflected not only in Khrushchev's personal status but in the role of the Party itself.

The alternatives for change were limited by other factors as well, including the growth of strong mediating relationships both within the Party and between the Party and other institutions. All of the candidates for supreme power within the system had been major architects of Stalin's policies and institutions and successful executors of his will. Neither the strength and legitimacy of institutional ties nor the roles of individual actors actually precluded rapid or fundamental change but they reduced its likelihood. As Professor Brzezinski has pointed out, the debate on the great alternatives of historical development was over. Conflicts among the leaders were largely over policy issues which would adjust rather than transform Soviet society.[3]

Finally, there were the public commitments of those who, like Khrushchev, espoused change. The first question, involving the relegation of reform to a series of limited in-system measures, was, in Crankshaw's formulation: "how to liberate the productive forces from the Stalinist ice age without calling into being such a torrential thaw that they themselves would be swept away by it?"[4] The power-efficiency dilemma, however, had greater political overtones. Reform aimed at eliminating certain excesses of Stalin's system implied some weakening in the structure of compulsion. But could change take place without resort to the centralized power and violence at the core of the Stalinist system? Khrushchev's anti-Stalinist position from the Twentieth Party Congress removed the legitimacy of one-man dictatorship and terror as components in the system, but his surrogates were both less forceful and less effective.

To create a "Stalinism without tears"[5] involved major problems, if only because of the intensity of the excesses to be removed. The regime's isolation from the population was an acute political issue. To reduce the alienation of the Soviet people from the regime required basic policy changes directed toward a decline in compulsion and a rise in personal security, a rise in living standards, and some increase in freedom of expression. There was also the need to break out of the dangerous isolation and immobility imposed by Stalin's foreign policy, the emergence of nuclear arms, the decline of Western colonialism and the rise of new states, unrest in Eastern Europe, and the urgent pressures of domestic policy.[6] To move from a coercive posture to one of increased legitimacy and reconciliation, however, required structural change in social and economic orientation.

A forward movement in domestic and foreign policy would place a particularly severe strain on the economic priorities and institutions of Stalin's command economy,[7] and the serious imbalances of agriculture would prove the most difficult and complex to resolve. Although agricultural issues would dominate the Khrushchev era, the issues of the industrial sector were serious enough. The shift to welfare would require a redistribution in allocation, an increase in static and dynamic efficiency, and an improvement in managerial performance—in short, institutional adaptation in both the Party and state bureaucracies to meet the requirements of a partially modernized society.

If general lines and directions were relatively clear, specific structures and processes remained blurred. The Party's goal was to increase its economic and technical decision-making power by expanding its penetration, influence, and control over the administrative and productive sectors of industry and agriculture. To do this raised involved issues concerning organizational foundations and established practice, but no debate like the extensive public discussion of the industrial management structures ever developed, and adaptation followed established doctrinal and structural-functional paths.

The reform of authority relationships within the Party, for example, was critical in reducing the dysfunctional consequences of monocratic organizational extremism, but there was surprisingly little analysis of bureaucracy or its social consequences within the Party. Proposed policy changes were both conceptualized and limited by the doctrine of democratic centralism and collective leadership. Until November 1962, policy on the rationalization of the structures and functions of the Party followed conservative principles without open debate. The Soviet leadership espoused nineteenth-century doctrines of social development and organizational theory, both irrelevant and inadequate to contemporary Soviet conditions.

The influence of the power struggle in inclining internal Party reform toward conservatism is largely obscure, but that it was influential in the Party's adaptation to new policy goals and environmental conditions cannot be doubted. There was one important distinction, however. Before 1958, the Party apparatus was Khrushchev's primary power base in his struggle against his rivals. Alterations in the Party's authority relationships, structures, and functions appear designed not only to enlarge the Party's role vis-à-vis other institutions but also to strengthen the ties of the intermediate and lower echelons to Khrushchev personally.

Beginning in 1958, a change in basic approach to Party reform is evident. Khrushchev began, as Stalin had earlier, to reduce his dependence on the Party apparatus and to expand his formal base of power in the state and other apparatuses.[8] In place of the earlier, primarily administrative, rationalization of the Party bureaucracy, revitalization took a populist, ideological, and mobilizational direction with antiapparat overtones. The shift, it should be emphasized, was only a change of degree but unmistakable nonetheless. In this view, the changes in the 1961 Party statutes and the wholesale reorganization of the Party apparatus in November 1962 were culminations of this second direction. The subsequent erosion of personal support in his primary power base was a significant factor in Khrushchev's fall from power in 1964.

1

Khrushchev's Approach to Reform

Despite the intensity of rhetoric, risk, and conflict accompanying Khrushchev's effort to ameliorate Stalinism and its structures, little authentic change was evident.[9] To explain the inflexibility of the Soviet institutional structure by exclusive reference to objective factors would be to omit the personality, experience, and conviction that Khrushchev brought to the issue. Undoubtedly, there is much justice in Robert Conquest's general judgment that

> Khrushchev was (as some of us remarked) a typical transitional ruler. He saw there was something badly wrong with the system, and he took measures in a whole series of fields to try and find a solution. They were dramatic measures but they were not radical. Looking back, I suppose we would now all agree that the spectacle was that of a leader grasping at a series of "bright ideas" not based on any profound analysis of the requirements and incapable, even in principle, of effecting a cure. They were symptoms rather than treatments.[10]

Khrushchev's failures and successes were undoubtedly owing in large part to his personality, which was quick, energetic, and action-oriented, but lacking in philosophical depth—a dreamer of grandiose dreams given to inadequately calculated action; an authoritarian populist who had the ruthlessness to ascend the heights of the Soviet system without even losing either his earthiness or his peasant shrewdness.[11]

Part of the answer, however, must also be sought in the experience and beliefs he acquired in the system he sought to conserve and to develop. Khrushchev, whose style differed so dramatically from the stereotype of the Party bureaucrat, was nonetheless a product of the apparatus, and his approach to Party reform reflected this. Khrushchev approached reform as a political generalist rather than as an expert administrator. While unquestionably aware of the organizational problems, he took an agitational approach stressing mass mobilization and commitment over bureaucratic rationalization and direction. This preference for direct action may have reflected his lack of formal education and his experience as a line official in the field. In 1934, as second in command to Lazar Kaganovich in the construction of the Moscow metro, Khrushchev gave a convincing demonstration of his conception of an effective Party official. A brochure of the period described his style as follows.

> Comrade Kaganovich's closest assistant in the subway construction was Comrade N. S. Khrushchev. All engineers, all brigadiers, and shock workers on the project know Nikita Sergeyevich. They know him because he visits the construction sites each day, issues daily instructions, checks, criticizes, cheers on, and advises this or that shaft overseer, this or that Party organizer, on all specified and urgent problems.
>
> Comrade Khrushchev's office became indistinguishable from the project manager's office where Party organizers, shaft overseers, engineers, and all individual brigade leaders work out the detailed plans required to fulfill the daring, urgent requirements of their proved leader, L. M. Kaganovich.[12]

Khrushchev's convictions seemed to transcend even his fortuitous combination of temperament and experience. Walter Lippmann's impression was that he had "a basic revolutionary faith that a new history had begun and that a Communist man is a new kind of man."[13] Khrushchev himself, of course, tirelessly reiterated his basic ideological commitments. At the opening of the University of Friendship in November 1960, he stated: "If you want to know my political convictions, I will not hide them from you. I am a Communist and deeply convinced that the most advanced ideology is Marxist-Leninist ideology."[14] This declaration of faith should be distinguished, of course, from the obscure and inarticulate meanings which it may acquire in the specific circumstances of a given life. In Khrushchev's case, deeper penetration is difficult because he appears not to have been a contemplative or elaborately articulate man. He was, of course, a public political figure consciously defending and propagandizing a credo. Despite the political context of most of Khrushchev's pronouncements, there is little reason to doubt the sincerity of his belief in the universality, dynamism, and relevance of Marxism-Leninism as social theory. In the 1960 speech quoted above, for example, he noted that from its origins as a minor political movement in the nineteenth century, Marxism had grown in the twentieth to include one-third of mankind and would ultimately conquer.[15] Like Lenin and the early Stalin, however, he eschewed Marxism-Leninism as dogma. At the Twentieth Congress he echoed both of his predecessors.

> Revolutionary theory is not a collecting of fossilized dogmas and formulas but a militant guide to practical activity for changing the world and building Communism.

Marxism-Leninism teaches that theory divorced from practice is dead, but practice that is not illuminated by revolutionary theory is blind.[16]

On the whole, Khrushchev's basic theoretical approach was in the tradition of voluntarism. The functions of ideology transcended its value as an intellectual guide. Ideology was an educational tool, a consciously forged structure for providing a common political framework and foundation for legitimacy. In addition, Khrushchev recognized the value of ideology as myth in inspiring and mobilizing the masses. The building of communism, he told the Twenty-first Congress, was just such a great and overarching myth.[17]

Ideology defined the social goals of the reform, its expected results, and provided much of its underlying motivation as well, but it could not provide basic policies or specific methods. As it turned out, the general pattern of reform would involve two contrasting but closely related processes which Khrushchev, on one occasion at least, called "dialectical."[18] The first process may be described as de-Stalinization; the second, Communist construction.

Khrushchev's most extensive statement concerning the first set of issues and policies is to be found in the Secret Speech delivered in 1956 at the Twentieth Party Congress. Although this speech provided neither a comprehensive analysis nor a rationale for the larger and more complex process of de-Stalinization, its value is nevertheless great because it sheds some light on the nature of the system and its effect on the Party as an institution.

The critical question was to what extent Stalin could be obliterated as a symbol and institution without seriously damaging the legitimacy of the Party's rule. In the Secret Speech, Khrushchev attempted to resolve the problem by means of the relatively simple device of historical periodization. Dividing Stalin's rule into two distinct periods separated by the Seventeenth Congress had the effect of preserving the Party's monopoly of power, monolithic structure, and ideological primacy at the same time that the justification for politically suppressing the Left, United, and Right oppositions remained intact.[19] (State ownership of the means of production, a centralized planning and executive administrative structure, and a collectivized agriculture were beyond discussion.) The historical division also allowed Khrushchev significant latitude in criticizing the ascendancy of the secret police and the use of mass terror, Stalin's cadre policies, his conduct of the Second World War, and his postwar line in foreign policy.[20] The attack on Stalin was radical but also selective and permitted a great flexibility in defining specific issues and programs within the existing system.

Although the emotional quality of the denunciation of Stalin arose partly from the personal insecurity and humiliation induced by Stalin's capriciousness, Khrushchev was more concerned with Stalin's effect on the Party as an institution. The Stalin cult had lowered Party status and authority; all its activity and achievement was credited to Stalin; and his deification had evoked the attitude that "such a man supposedly knows everything, sees everything, thinks for everyone, can do anything, is infallible in his behavior."[21] Dictatorship had ended collegial rule, created a regime of violence and intrigue, and had damaged moral unity within the Party and reduced its effectiveness. Khrushchev held the cult of personality responsible for the bureaucratization of the Party, its separation from the masses, and its weak political influence among them.[22] The role of central Party organs had declined. Unlike Lenin, who regularly consulted the Party's collective organs, Stalin had failed to call a congress in thirteen years and had frequently ignored both the Central Committee and the Politburo.[23]

Khrushchev singled out two aspects of Stalin's style to have contributed to the bureaucratization of the Party: his indifference to immediate experience and personal impression in making a decision and his failure to evaluate the effect of decisions on people concerned with their execution.[24] To these were added a denunciation of Stalin's reliance on administrative sanctions to eliminate opposition and to execute his will.[25] The demoralizing effect of Stalinism on the Party's authority, institutions, and political methods was particularly felt by the Party apparatchik.

> Comrades! The cult of the individual leader caused the employment of faulty principles in Party work and economic activity; it brought about gross violations of inner-Party democracy and Soviet democracy, sterile administration by fiat, deviations of all sorts, covering of shortcomings and varnishing of reality. Our country gave birth to many flatterers and specialists in false optimism and deceit.[26]

Stalin's authority structure, said Khrushchev, had produced stultification, stagnation, and bureaucratic conservatism and had been counterproductive in terms of the Party's decision-making role. Party and state resolutions "were prepared in a routine manner, often without considering the concrete situation. This went so far that Party workers even during the smallest sessions, read their speeches. All this produced the danger of formalizing Party and Soviet work and of bureaucratizing the whole apparatus."[27]

To characterize the Stalinist generation of Party professionals as one pervaded by fear and timidity, sycophancy, conservatism, and a primary concern for personal security was exaggerated and inadequate. The relationship between Stalin and the apparat was not unilateral but mutually reinforcing, as George Lukacs has pointed out.

> My first reaction to the Twentieth Congress concerned not only the personality but the organization: the apparatus which had produced the cult of personality and which had fixed it in a sort of endless enlarged reproduction. I pictured Stalin to myself as the apex of a pyramid which widened gradually toward the base and was composed of many "little Stalins." They, seen from above, were the objects and, seen from below, the creators and guardians of the "cult of personality." Without the regular and unchallenged functioning of this mechanism the "cult

of personality'' would have remained a subjective dream, a pathological fact, and would not have attained the social effectiveness which it exercised for decades.[28]

As Richard Lowenthal has pointed out, there is both congruence and conflict between modernization and the egalitarian goals of the Marxist-Leninist revolution.[29] If Stalin systematically sacrificed utopian goals to the demands of industrial society, the 1961 Party Program, which Khrushchev publicly sponsored and identified with, was but a partial answer to the maladies it was designed to cure. The Party Program, however, should be judged politically—as a means of securing Soviet ideological supremacy against Yugoslav and Chinese challenges and as a means of providing legitimate goals and effective means of ideological mobilization in the wake of de-Stalinization. In the complex balance between further revolutionary transformation and adaptation to modernization, the program stressed adaptation. According to Robert Tucker, the program was "concerned most of all with the preservation, without radical change, of the existing institutional structure and its associated pattern of power, policy, and privilege.''[30]

The future Communist society which Khrushchev envisioned for the public between 1959 and 1961 retained its traditional emphases on authoritarianism and tight social organization. The commitment to reduce state and bureaucratic power by implementing social and democratic principles of management did not include decentralizing the economy, although its administrative improvement was pledged. Adhering to conservative and traditional organizational principles did not, however, preclude substantial improvements in the living standards of the Soviet people.[31] Khrushchev saw a society of abundance as the principal means of resolving existing political and social tensions within the system—an approach which led him to place extraordinary emphasis on economic growth through technical progress and increasing the productivity of social labor.

This commitment to welfare goals had an important effect on Khrushchev's interpretation of Marxism as social theory and the specific functions of the leading role. He insisted that Marxism-Leninism as social theory be concretely applied to the political economy. During different phases of social construction, he told the Twentieth Congress, different aspects of theory come forward; at the moment, economics was primary.[32] Therefore, the chief task of Party *rukovodstvo* in the Party Program was to be the building of the material-technical base of communism. While the reformulation of the Party's functional role implied no radical shift in existing relationships, it served to legitimate more concrete policies designed to adapt the institutional Party to a more differentiated and complex modern society.

Khrushchev also insisted that the traditional distinction, and opposition, between political and economic work, as it had been defined in the Zhdanov-Malenkov struggle, was now irrelevant. By redefining the substance of politics as essentially economic, Khrushchev initiated the erosion of the Party's distinctive political and ideological role. This position could significantly change formal Party-state relations toward increased cooperation and fusion of functions. Although in 1956 he enjoined against the substituting of Party for economic agencies,[33] the injunction would not often be repeated. In approaching the reform of the Party-state relationship, Khrushchev's overriding practical goal was to increase the efficiency of the apparat. This involved, first of all, a rationalization of the processes of authority, structure, and function within the apparat itself.

2

Khrushchev and the Reform of Authority

The principle of monolithic organization remained intact under Khrushchev. Both before and after the Anti-Party affair in 1957, he decisively rejected any form of factionalism within the Party, stressing that unity within the ranks was fundamental to the Party's strength.[34] Like Stalin before him, he defined the Party structure as essentially a monocratic bureaucracy: "The leading core of the Party is not a group bound together by personal relationships or mutual advantage but a business-like group of leaders whose relations are based on a foundation of principled ideas which permit neither mutual forgiveness nor personal antagonisms."[35] At the Twentieth Congress, he emphasized the close relationship between internal unity and effectiveness: "Any problem is within its powers when it acts as a united force, knowing no fear in battle, no hesitation in its conduct of its policy, and no retreat in the face of difficulties.[36]

But the primacy of monolithism was complicated by the redistribution of authority within the apparat. Although in his Secret Speech Khrushchev had severely indicted Stalin for reducing the role of central Party institutions, principally the Presidium and Central Committee,[37] the reduced role of the local Party apparat had gone unnoticed. During the first phase of reform, the major concern was the central Party organs, but this would change after Malenkov's defeat. From 1955 to 1958 (the most liberal period in this phase of reform), limited but significant measures were introduced to increase the rights of local Party organs. In August 1955, oblast and republican committees were granted increased rights over local Party budgets—within centrally assigned limits—and the right to reassign primary Party secretaries and officials within the local apparat without previous central clearance.[38]

The Twentieth Congress accelerated this process. In March and June of 1956 and in April 1957, the political administrations for railway transport, the militia, and the merchant marine were abolished.[39] In August 1956, the Central Committee Party Organizers for industry, transport, and scientific and educational institutions were eliminated.[40] The reorganization of industrial management was followed by new legislation in May and August 1957 increasing the authority of oblast and republican organs. The May decree affirmed the right of obkomy and republican committees to establish paid secretaries in industrial plants.[41] In August, republican committees (within centrally assigned staff limits) were given the right to affirm staffs of gorkomy, raikomy, and other Party institutions; abolish and create new gorkomy and raikomy; and make minor changes in the staffs of obkomy and republican committees. They were also given greater control over the mass media of communication within their jurisdictions.[42] This was evidently the crest in decentralizing the authority within the apparat, because a decree of September 1958 required republican organs to obtain the agreement of the Administration of Affairs Department of the Central Committee before changing the structure of gorkomy and raikomy.[43]

A review of published Party legislation on the measures of decentralization suggests the depth of detailed control which the central apparat normally exercised over local Party functions; the limited nature of the measures also indicates the caution in this phase of reform. Caution was likewise evident in relation to collective leadership. The attack on Stalinism explicitly invoked collective leadership as the only legitimate alternative to autocracy. But the measures advanced to achieve collective leadership—the regular convention of plena, conferences, and Party congresses—while contributing to internal communications and social integration, did little to resolve the central problem of power and its abuse. Khrushchev was aware of this. Great power, he noted in 1961, belonged to the executive, but it should not be abused; a "situation must not be permitted to arise whereby any authority, even the most deserving one, can cease to heed the opinions of those around him."[44] It had been the Party's tradition, however, to reject any form of constitutional pluralism. In view of Khrushchev's insistence on monolithism and a single line, the institutional safeguards erected to protect oligarchical rule from the threat of dictatorship (not least from Khrushchev himself) could only be temporary.

In the post-Stalin period, the Presidium evolved into "a regularly functioning collective body which keeps within the field of vision all the more important questions of the life of the Party and country."[45] Normally, the Presidium met once a week, and most issues were resolved through unanimity.[46] Some issues were apparently resolved by majority vote,[47] but on issues of fundamental policy conflict, the palace coup continued to restore the necessary consensus in decision-making. Where policy conflicts involved neither fundamental ends nor means, some political development in Party decision-making became evident. A more or less systematic consultation by leading Party officials of expert opinion developed as an alternative to the arbitrary and often uninformed opinions of Stalin.[48] Khrushchev seems to have used the consultation system extensively in matters of domestic and foreign policy. This was a major step in the rationalization of decision-making, but it fell short of providing an institutional safeguard against the emergence of another totalitarian dictator.

To reinvigorate the principles of collective leadership within Party organs below the top was a different problem, because collective leadership and limiting the power of local secretaries had been one device for preserving the power of the central organs. At the Nineteenth Congress, a prime target of Khrushchev's criticism had been those local Party leaders who, by imagining two standards of discipline within the Party, flouted central directives and suppressed criticism.[49] At the Twentieth Congress, Suslov attacked the inefficiency that had resulted from Stalin's abrogation of collective leadership. His argument that dictatorial control led to suppression of initiative, lack of control, irresponsibility, arbitrary, one-sided, and mistaken decisions seems to have been directed primarily against the lower Party organs.[50]

The establishment of collective leadership at lower levels of the Party hierarchy had certain political objectives. The minimum objective was to establish a balance of power within the local bureau to keep the first secretary in check. The maximum was to reduce the rigidity and isolation of the local Party committee by opening up access and communication both within the apparat and between the apparat and the local population. This was especially important at the gorkom and raikom levels, the most frequent point of contact between the Soviet population and the Party. Strengthening the Party's admittedly weak mass influence and extending its day-to-day influence would be accomplished by invigorating the local Party committee.[51] The minimal objective, however, involved reformulating the role of the apparat, principally the secretariat, with respect to the decision and execution of Party decrees; and the adjustment would raise significant political and ideological issues.

Every major political opposition within the Communist party from the Workers' Opposition and the Democratic Centralists had protested Party bureaucratization through the political dominance of the apparat. In post-Stalinist Russia, moreover, any effort to alter seriously the power or status of the Party bureaucracy evoked charges of heresy and revisionism. Through the Twenty-first Congress and presumably thereafter, Khrushchev had a personal stake in the apparat because it was his principal instrument in the struggle for, and retention of, power. At the same time, his antibureaucratic and reformist position precluded any absolute identification with the apparat.

The result was a policy consistent with neither the logic of personal power nor the requirements of reform. At the Nineteenth Congress, Khrushchev proposed that the secretariat to be formed at the oblast level be limited to three secretaries in order to prevent the substitution of the bureau by the secretariat.[52] This measure, however, died in the power struggle between 1953 and 1955. At the Twentieth Congress, Khrushchev noted that the average obkom secretariat had grown to four or five secretaries, and the Party rules were amended to accommodate this development.[53] Throughout the 1953–62 period, the Party bureau was dominated numerically and politically by the professional Party politician at all levels of the hierarchy.

3

The Party and Structural Reform

Khrushchev's failure to alter authority patterns within the apparatus in a meaning-ful way ensured the continuance of the Stalinist Party structure. Centralized decision-making and detailed control by the central over the territorial Party apparatus changed very little between 1954 and 1962. To the extent that the sluggishness of the Party apparatus derived from the conflict between monolithic and hierarchical organization and the Party's need to increase its decision-making resources and expand their uses, measures taken to revitalize the Party in other aspects would be of marginal value.

Nonetheless, such measures were adopted, and, as in November 1962, Party reform was principally structural. From 1954 through 1962, the major components of the Party structure—general membership, representative organs, and executive agencies—evolved continuously toward increased dynamism and effectiveness in the Party's economic leadership. Although rates of change differed and were inconsistent, in general, modification was moderate and none of the fundamentals of the Stalinist structure were changed.

The components of the Party structure varied in importance. Reforming the general membership and its representative organs was politically less sensitive; its purpose was to strengthen the Party's influence among those classes of the economic population relevant to Khrushchev's economic policies. Reforming the Party's executive organs was not only politically sensitive; it was central to increasing the Party's efficiency as a precondition for increasing the leading role in the economy. Here, preserving the power of the first secretary at each level of the hierarchy ensured that the effect of structural change on Party *rukovodstvo* would be minimal.

Reform of the general membership. Structural reform to increase the size and change the quality of Party membership was supposed to increase the Party's relatively slight mass influence and provide a younger, more technically oriented membership capable of carrying out Khrushchev's economic ambitions. But a central issue arose in this regard which was never fully resolved. Party structure had always been characterized by elitism and an expectation of tension between quantitative growth and quality of membership. This view, expressed by Malen-kov at the Nineteenth Congress,[54] was not shared by Khrushchev, who firmly accepted the utility of a mass party[55] without, however, advocating either in-definite expansion or indiscriminate recruitment. His recruitment policies aimed at bringing the most active and influential members of Soviet society into the Party, particularly those employed as scientific, technical, and production specialists.[56]

As T. H. Rigby has pointed out, the shift in recruitment policy associated with Khrushchev actually preceded Stalin's death.[57] The policy of recruiting primarily from the administrative elite had produced in 1948 composition in which workers and collective farmers constituted only 18.8 percent of the membership.[58] In 1951 and the first half of 1952—a period coinciding with Khrushchev's return to Moscow from the Ukraine—the mass recruitment of workers and collective farmers jumped from an average of 40.7 percent to 49.8 percent. Between the Nineteenth Congress and February 1954, recruitment dropped sharply to 1.2 percent. But in February 1954, Khrushchev resumed the policy of mass recruitment, reaching a tempo of 6.6 percent per year through the Twentieth Congress.[59] Between the Twentieth and Twenty-second Congresses, Party membership grew by 2.5 millions.

The increase in the Party's size was accompanied by a change in its composition. Between 1956 and 1961, recruitment of workers increased from 30.4 to 43.1 percent, while recruitment of employees dropped from 46.2 to 34.3 percent. The recruitment of kolhozniki, however, despite Khrushchev's emphasis on the Party's role in agriculture, remained virtually static.[60] The pattern of recruitment stressed not only the industrial sector but also heavy industry and those branches within heavy industry which underlay technological growth. From 30 to 80 percent of the workers in industry were selected from the machine-building, instruments, electronics, chemistry, and wood industries.[61] Among employees, the pattern was designed to increase the flow of fresh forces into the Party from the nonadministrative elite. Among candidates accepted into the Party in this category between 1955 and 1960, engineers, scientists, and economic specialists increased from 53.5 to 65.8 percent.[62]

But Khrushchev's gradualist approach failed to produce a basic shift in the Party's population. Workers still represented only 34.5 percent of the Party, and peasant representation remained as it had been. Those classified as employees, the elite of Soviet society, made up 48 percent of the general membership,[63] and educational levels changed only marginally.[64] Still, the heavy flow of new members did raise the possibility of a new Party generation coming of age.[65]

On the whole, a stronger Party presence was achieved in production. Less clear was the effect of the policy on the rank and file. While the representation and role of those directly concerned with the branches of industry underlying economic growth was increased, the policy of repopulating the Party with youthful, energetic activists capable of extending the Party's influence into every aspect of production was only partially successful.[66]

Reform of representative organs. Apathetic Party committees under Lenin and Stalin had reduced the significance of the aktiv as an instrument of communication and mobilization and contributed to the Party's relatively weak mass influence. But structural reform of the aktiv did not include shifting the traditional balance of power between the representative and executive organs. The more restricted measures of increasing the size, changing the composition, and regulating the turnover of the elected committees, however, were consistent with the patterns of membership recruitment. Both were part of a larger strategy of increasing political and technical resources to cope with new environmental challenges. The change in the Party Rules adopted at the Twenty-second Congress, requiring a minimal turnover of 25 percent in the Central Committee and its Presidium, 33.3 percent in the regional, and 50 percent in the local and primary Party organs, institutionalized this basic policy of reform.[67]

Committees' size increase was everywhere evident. The Central Committee, for example, grew from 235 full and candidate members in 1952 to 330 members in 1961. The territorial committees likewise increased between 1956 and 1961 (by 45 percent) to 306 thousand. At central and lower levels, the size increase was accompanied by a significant turnover in membership.[68] Judged according to occupational status at election time, changes in the composition of Central Committee groups appear to have been marginal between 1952 and 1961. Although their proportion of representation declined, Party apparatchiki continued to dominate, and the major functional groups remained steady and even increased slightly.[69] The crucial change in the Central Committee, however, may have been qualitative. The trend indicates a steadily increasing influx of co-opted officials. The promotion of officials who had made careers in specialized and nonpolitical fields before assuming high Party posts indicated a major structural adjustment by the Party to secure the skills necessary to deal effectively with modernization.[70]

Structural change was similar within the territorial Party committees, any differences arising from their different functions as instruments of communication and mobilization. Data on the city and raion levels indicate a shift away from electing line officials toward increasing the proportion of workers and collective farmers.[71] The trend was similar at higher levels. While the situation varied at the regional and republican levels, a recent study of the Stalingrad Oblast Party Committee suggests the general trend. Between 1954 and 1960, the percentage of Party and soviet officials represented dropped from 64.9 to 51.9 percent. Workers and peasants, unrepresented in 1954, increased to 16.9 percent by 1960. The percentage of managerial officials almost doubled between 1954 and 1956, but, with Khrushchev's ascendancy, declined sharply thereafter. In contrast, the percentage of engineers and technicians declined.[72]

Reform of the Party's decision-making organs. New policies concerning recruitment and representation in Party committees could be but secondary where dominant authority relationships were bureaucratic and changed only minimally. Whether, indeed, any increase in the Party's functional capacities could be expected without a major redistribution of authority is dubious. Changes in the structure and composition of the apparatus and the anticipated increase in efficiency should be judged primarily in this light. Basic institutional reform simply did not occur between 1953 and 1962.

Structural rationalization of the Presidium and Secretariat had less to do with efficiency than with power. Although their various expansions and contractions bespoke the politics of the few, the determination and achievement of goals greatly depended upon the managerial abilities of their members. In examining the Presidium elected at the Twenty-second Congress, certain characteristics stand out. Among the eleven full and five candidate members, the average age was fifty-eight. Of those trained under the Soviet system, nine had an engineering or technical education. All but a few had experience in economic management, but only Kosygin had risen to political power through the industrial administrative system. And, most important for continuity, all but one had held a Central Committee seat in 1952. While the distinction between Party and state officials at the national level is somewhat shadowy, professional Party officials tended to dominate both the Presidium and Secretariat under Khrushchev.[73]

The Secretariat, the object of extensive revision in November 1962, was more sensitive politically to shifts in the Party's decision-making role, particularly in relation to the state and managerial groups. Like the Presidium, the Secretariat grew and diminished repeatedly under Khrushchev.[74] In the Secretariat elected in 1961, four of the eight secretaries were also members of the Presidium. Of the four new members added in 1961, two—Ilychev and Ponomarev—were ideologists. The third, A. N. Shelepin, had headed the Young Communist League and the state security forces before joining the Secretariat. Only P. N. Demichev, a chemical engineer, had made his career within the Party as a line official.[75] Although ideologists were significant, in 1961 the Secretariat conspicuously lacked Party executives with extensive experience in economic guidance. This defect was partially corrected by the Russian Bureau, a central regional Party organ created in 1956 to guide the RSFSR. The bureau, which he headed, was Khrushchev's own contribution to the structural alteration of the central Party apparatus.

Before 1962, the principal focus of rationalization and revitalization was the territorial Party apparatus, the object of Khrushchev's most searing criticism of the Party bureaucracy. But reform failed to disturb either the traditional territorial basis of the Party structure or the dominant role of the apparatchiki on the bureaus.[76] Khrushchev, responsible for expanding the role of the secretariats after 1954, took a forceful but incremental approach before 1962. His principal methods included offering incentives, offering more specialized economic and technical training, and, above all, recruiting better trained and experienced cadres.

One of the more interesting proposals which Khrushchev repeatedly advanced was to adopt the bonus system for Party cadres so that part of their income would depend directly upon the production results of the enterprises under their direction.[77] This might have further strengthened the "localist" direction of the territorial apparatus, but it was strenuously resisted by Party officials and

not implemented above the primary Party level.[78] Khrushchev was more successful in stressing the necessity of more intensive economic and technical training
for Party officials. Party schools, he insisted at the Twentieth Congress, should
offer courses equal to those offered in a technical college.[79] In the 1957 reform
of the Higher Party School, the new four-year curriculum required 3,200 hours
in twenty-two subject fields, with over half to be given over to the study of
technology and applied economics.[80] The reform of the apparatus through
education, however, was a long-range affair, offering only meager short-term
results. Turnover was principally relied upon for increasing the Party's decision-
making resources during this period.

The systematic turnover of Party secretaries and the continuous raising of
their levels of formal education was part of a well-established personnel policy
antedating Khrushchev. While part of the emphasis on formal education reflected
Party bureaucratization, it more immediately indicated Khrushchev's goal of
turning the Party apparatus from generalized to specialized decision-making.
In 1959, none of the obkom department heads in the RSFSR had occupied
their positions over ten years, and only 9.3 percent had held the same position
before 1954.[81] In 1962, Frol Kozlov stated that 70.5 percent of regional Party
secretaries had held their posts less than three years, although 12.5 percent
were in office over five years. At the gorkom and raikom level, 78.8 percent
of these secretaries had been in office for three years or less.[82]

Age and education statistics cannot demonstrate significant differences between
the political attitudes of these officials and their elder colleagues; but the lowering
of age levels and the increase in higher and technical education do suggest
their increased decision-making potential. The age of the obkom secretarial
corps ranged between thirty-five and fifty; at the local level, between thirty
and forty.[83] Over 90 percent of obkom and 75 percent of gorkom secretaries
had higher educations.[84] The higher technical education, however, considered
so essential for more effective economic *rukovodstvo*, was less widespread.
Only 46 percent of obkom secretaries and 32 percent of gorkom secretaries
possessed higher technical training.[85] During this period, the policy was apparently to place at least one technician in a secretariat. By 1962, even in an agricultural
republic like the Turkmen SSR, each gorkom had at least one engineer in
its secretariat.[86]

These data alone only dimly illuminate the direction and effect of change
within the directing core of the Party apparatus. It should be noted, however,
that functional differentiation and specialization between line and staff specialists
within the Party bureaucracy and Party specialization within the industrial and
agricultural sectors undoubtedly added a dimension of competence and sophistication to Party leadership in time.[87] In addition, as a number of excellent Western
studies have shown, the recruitment of first secretaries to head the most important,
largely industrialized Party committees was an important trend to have developed

under Khrushchev.[88] These new officials tended to have higher and, increasingly, technical educations as well as significant experience in economic management before entering the Party apparatus.[89]

This sharp rise in co-opted officials, particularly after the Twentieth Congress, reflects the urgency of Khrushchev's timetable. Neither the recruitment of young specialists nor the retraining and resocialization of experienced Party officials promised the rapid and visible gains in decision-making effectiveness which he demanded. The change in the type of official to head the Party's decision-making organs, however, may reflect a still deeper change, as George Fischer suggests.

In his study of 306 Party executives occupying the most significant line posts of the Party apparatus in 1958 and 1962, Fischer points out the emergence of both political and economic skills.[90] Party officials who lacked technical training and at least four years of white collar work in the economy were being replaced. These officials (categorized as Officials) whose career experience was primarily in political and ideological work, while still 46 percent of sample, tended to have been drawn from the least economically developed republics. In the RSFSR and more economically developed republics, the emerging high-level Party executive had both political and economic skills, indicating a certain degree of in-system adaptability to the challenge of industrialization and the power-efficiency dilemma.[91]

Co-opting, as a short-term device, is difficult to evaluate. The fact that the Stalinist bureaucratic politician was being replaced does not automatically reveal any difference in personal values and attitudes on the part of the replacement; nor can the data, without considerably greater refinement and specification, indicate the relevance of such change to Khrushchev's goals of intensified political and economic entrepreneurship. There is reason to believe that such officials' basic orientation would be toward improving the existing system rather than transforming it.[92] It is also a fact that, even in the accelerated and expanded terms used by Khrushchev and the Soviet leadership, co-opting was itself a long-term measure employed without a corresponding change in the institutional environment.

The most significant change in relation to the November 1962 reorganization was the growing differentiation and specialization between industrialized and agricultural oblasti which co-opting reflected. The distinctions in age, technical training, and nonapparat experience which had developed between first secretaries heading obkomi at different levels of development were given formal acknowledgment in reorganizing the territorial apparatus along functional lines.[93]

Reform of the Party's administrative structure. Increasing Party *rukovodstvo* in economic decision-making meant not only increasing the decision-making capabilities of the secretariats but also improving the processes through which the Party apparatus carried out its supervisory responsibilities. Nevertheless, structural changes, though continuous, were moderate. The monocratic principle and hierarchical status system within the apparatus effectively frustrated any qualitative expansion in the role of the department heads and instructors. Line officials continued to dominate the staff, and the production-branch departmental structure remained the same. But general criticism of the dull ineffectiveness of Party leadership nonetheless evoked a series of measures to rationalize the apparatus.

At all levels of the Party hierarchy efforts were made to cut costs and reduce the number of professional Party workers. Structurally, the Russian Bureau divided the central apparatus into two distinct structures. At the territorial level, structural reform proceeded by phases. Before the Twentieth Congress, major attention was focused on the rural raikom. Between 1956 and 1958, the local urban sector was reorganized. After 1958, the reform of administrative structure was directed toward the recruitment of volunteer and unpaid aktivisty into the Party apparatus. This was consistent with the policies of general recruitment and reform of the Party's representative organs; it was Khrushchev's use of the social principle to break the ice of custom which had limited the Party's mass influence.

After the May 1956 reorganization, the central apparat was composed of some thirty departments organized in three basic groups, two defined according to geography and one according to function. Of the first group, which supervised the non-Russian republics, five were concerned with the supervision of the lower Party, soviet, and educational systems, and seven were structured to administer the basic branches of industry and agriculture. The apparat for the RSFSR—the second group—duplicated that of the union republics, except that industry and transport were concentrated in a single department. The third set of departments supervised the press, the armed forces, relations with Communist parties within and outside the Soviet bloc, and general administrative affairs.[94] Professor Fischer estimates that the total paid personnel at the central level numbered about 3 percent of the total full-time personnel. Between 1956 and 1961, the staff had been cut from 6,000 to 4,500 officials.[95]

Administrative structures at the republican and oblast levels underwent only minimal change before November 1962. Republican and oblast departments ranged from seven to ten, the number of specialized departments for industry depending upon the industrial profile of the republic or region.[96] Reducing the number of specialized departments achieved only limited results. More successful was the cutting of staffs, estimated at about 25 percent between 1956 and 1961. In 1961, the professional staff, comprising about 12.2 percent of the total, numbered about 21 thousand officials.[97]

Between 1953 and 1958, structural reform was concentrated primarily at the local level, where the largest number of professional Party workers were located and where the major part of the Party's transactions with other Soviet institutions were made. Whereas the structure of the rural raikom and the administration of agriculture as a whole were almost continuously reorganized,[98] reform of the urban local Party organs occurred principally between 1956 and 1958. Structural rationalization followed publication of the Central Committee decree of 17 May 1956 which announced the abolition of departments in four gorkomy in Latvia.[99]

The reform was basically directed at the smaller city committees with excessively cumbersome structures, but its effect on their efficiency is ambiguous. Designed to cut staff, to bring the instructor closer to the secretariat, and to end the internal isolation and jurisdictional conflicts associated with departmentalism, the reform did serve to reduce the number of primary Party organs assigned to each instructor.[100] But by making each instructor responsible for all the functions of a given primary organ, functional specialization was ended at this level and accompanied by a loss of concrete controls.

Among the more significant consequences of the rationalization of the Party bureaucracy at this level was the shift in the ratio of paid Party officials to general Party membership. Pigalev notes a threefold decline in this ratio compared with 1941.[101] George Fischer places the number of full-time Party executives at this level at 73 percent of the whole staff, or 132 thousand in 1961.[102] Calculated on the basis of a Party membership of 9.7 million, the ratio would be 1/80 at this level, and in certain gorkomy the ratio was probably much higher. In one of the few explicit comparisons made in Soviet sources, the Sverdlovsk Gorkom listed an increase in Party membership of 150 percent and a staff cut of 25 percent, which raised the ratio of 1/78 in 1950 to 1/173 in 1961.[103] While this figure was undoubtedly high for the Soviet Union as a whole, the general reduction of paid staff, the policy of intensive recruitment, and the increased demands of the Party leadership placed heavy burdens on the urban Party organs.[104]

One solution lay in reviving the social principle, which had declined during the First Five-Year Plan. But the development of voluntarism in staffing the Party apparatus went beyond meeting an urgent practical problem.[105] Ideologically, introducing volunteers into the apparat would provide an answer to charges of bureaucratism and a pledge of the eventual withering away of the apparat. Politically, it was a device for spanning the traditional chasm between the apparatus and the general membership. The social principle also promised to expand the pool of technical expertise available to the decision-making of local Party committees, and, not least, to serve as an instrument for recruiting and training new and competent personnel for the apparatus. Finally, voluntarism was encouraged as a means to aid the apparatus in penetrating the state managerial structures.[106]

The social principle, which was responsible for the rapid proliferation of a wide variety of volunteer Party forms, was formally endorsed in the Central

Committee decree of 30 September 1958, which authorized the use of nonstaff instructors from the union republic to the raikom.[107] Corps of nonstaff instructors had begun forming earlier, however, in the spring of 1958. From the beginning, the republican and oblast Party organs resisted this diluting of the professional bureaucracy, and its implementation was largely confined to the local level.[108] In 1960, there were some 32 thousand nonstaff instructors:[109] by the beginning of 1962, these had increased to 320 thousand activists enrolled in staff work, 80 thousand as nonstaff instructors.[110] In 1962, for the U.S.S.R. as a whole, over 50 percent of all nonstaff instructors had at least incomplete higher educations; 40 percent had specialized technical educations.[111] Wherever possible, instructors were recruited who were not only technically competent but "opinion leaders" as well. Although results varied, some gorkomy did succeed in raising their technical potential.[112]

The increase in nonstaff instructors was accompanied by the formation of a nonstaff apparatus. By mid-1962, there were about 4 thousand nonstaff departments and sectors, and a start had been made toward the formation of nonstaff secretaries. Local Party organs created numerous advisory councils and commissions. At the end of 1961, fifty-six republican and oblast committees and 1,043 local committees set up such groups.[113] In six months the number had jumped to 8,934 councils and commissions enrolling 90 thousand aktivisty.[114] These groups engaged in virtually every phase of Party activity. In addition to economic commissions, there were permanent ideology commissions, commissions on organizational work, special commissions for dealing with the personal affairs of Communists and for entering the Party. Unlike the nonstaff apparatus, the permanent commissions and councils were generally staffed with pensioners and others not fully employed. The councils, in contrast to the commissions, also recruited non-Party members.[115]

Party reform at the primary Party level through the development of the social principle was significant in Khrushchev's strategy of strengthening the leading role.[116] Structural reform of primary organs followed the pattern of the higher organs, the plan being to reduce the number of units and increase the size of the average organ. Between the Twentieth and Twenty-second Congresses, the number of primary Party organs was cut by 55 thousand to 296,444, the majority of changes owing to the amalgamation of kolkhozy and reduction in the number of administrative units. During the same period, the number of primary Party organs having more than 100 members more than doubled to 5 percent, and those with fewer than fifteen members were cut from 62.2 to 42.6 percent. The membership of the primary Party organization in the average industrial enterprise role from thirty-eight to sixty-one in the five years following the Twentieth Congress.[117]

Primary Party organs with committees increased ten times between 1956 and 1961. Shop committees showed a sharp growth of over 300 percent—from

57 thousand to 187 thousand—and Party groups were up by 50 percent to 174 thousand. An effort to extend the Party's penetration could also be observed in the formation of territorial primary Party organs staffed by pensioners and retired military personnel and placed under the authority of the raikom or gorkom. In the report-and-election meetings held before the Twenty-second Congress, an unprecedented 1,151,000 people were elected to office at the primary level, and another 652 thousand at the shop and group level. At all levels, an estimated 21.5 percent of all Party members were elected to some Party office and could therefore be regarded as members of the expanded aktiv.[118]

As part of the general tendency toward renewing Party cadres, the new Party Rule of 1961 prohibited the elected secretaries of primary Party organs from serving more than two terms.[119] This measure, designed to broaden representation, increase competence, and introduce fresh forces at the mass level, was seriously opposed because it threatened to disorganize and weaken primary Party organs by removing experienced secretaries.[120] The projected measure was, however, part of a broader trend to increase the educational qualifications of Party cadres. In the Lugansk Obkom in 1957, 37 percent of the secretaries at this level had an incomplete secondary education. By 1962, 142 of 154 had completed the secondary level.[121] In the major industrial centers, the average was normally high. In Leningrad, for example, 115 of 162 secretaries had a higher education, 88 of them trained as engineers; but 72 (or 44 percent) were over forty-five years of age; only 16 percent were under twenty-five.[122] Primary Party secretaries as a group continued to lag behind the secretaries of territorial Party organizations in educational achievement.

The social principle was extended to the primary Party organs with the Central Committee decree of 26 June 1959 which formed Party control commissions to strengthen the role of Party organs in pressing for the fulfillment of central directives.[123] By 1962, over 600 thousand Party members were enrolled in these commissions.[124] In the Zaporozhe Oblast, for example, more than 750 commissions were formed to supervise such functions as the introduction of new technology, control over the quality of production, the fulfillment of state plans and cooperative deliveries.[125]

Between 1959 and 1962, the Party Control Commission remained a weak and generally ineffective instrument of mass control. The average commission numbered only five or six members and was in many cases dominated by the enterprise management. A *Pravda* editorial of 2 July 1961 noted that after two years of operation, the control commissions had signally failed to exercise serious control over the management of enterprises or to improve the technical performance of the enterprises to which they were attached.[126] They were also accused of interfering in managerial functions, of bureaucratism, of having little influence, and of isolation from other forms of social control.[127] Of particular concern to obkom and gorkom officials was a tendency of plant commissions to bypass them and to register complaints directly in the Party's republican and central organs. One of the major objectives of the 1962 reorganization was to introduce order into the increased activity of the Party at the mass level.[128]

4

Reform: An Evaluation

Since the effect of the reform measures on the internal operation of the Party was one of degree rather than of kind, estimates can only be judged, not demonstrated. In general, its effect was limited, and the allocation of authority between central and local organs and within the bureau was only marginally affected. Structural changes produced different effects at different levels of the institution. The division of the central apparat into two parallel, overlapping administrative organs presumably complicated the problems of authority and coordination within the Secretariat, although evidence in this regard is insufficient to render a firm judgment. The republican and oblast committee structures underwent minimal change; structural experimentation was principally confined to the gorkom and raikom levels. A drastic overhaul of the entire Party structure was not achieved until the November 1962 reorganization.

The mass discussions of important issues, used to communicate Party decisions and as a form of mass consultation, were among the more visible signs of the reactivization of the Party. The New Party Program was discussed in meetings throughout the Soviet Union by over 73 million people, and more than 4.6 million were reported to have spoken at meetings convened for this purpose.[129] From 1953 to 1962, more than 100 all-union, republican, and zonal conferences were held, in which over 120 thousand participated.[130] Bugaev and Leibson have noted the calling of thirty-one plena of the Central Committee during the same period.

The holding of regular plena was equally frequent at the republican level and below.[131] Between the Twentieth Congress and the November 1962 reorganization, the Moldavian Central Committee, for example, met twenty-four times. At the gorkom level in the same republic, the Kishinev City Committee held fourteen plena in eighteen months. *Sovetskaia Rossiia*, on the other hand, complained in both 1958 and 1959 about the number of Party conferences which were not held in the scheduled time.[132] It would appear that discussion at Party conferences and plena continued to be limited in scope and carefully directed. During the series of local conferences held before the Twenty-second Congress, *Pravda* published lengthy criticisms of the methods by which several

Party organs conducted their meetings. Reports were formal and stereotyped; questions from the floor were either ignored or were submitted in writing and answered at the end of the meeting without an opportunity for further questioning or rebuttal.[133]

The decision-making process was little changed at any level. The domination of the bureau by the apparat, and the predominance of the secretariat within the apparat, ensured that major decisions concerning the Soviet Union would be made (at least theoretically) within the Party bureaucracy. To what extent consultation was adopted in decision-making at the local level is obscure. The Russian Bureau's extensive criticism of the Lipetsk Obkom suggests that the concentration of virtually all authority in the oblast first secretary remained the dominant pattern.[134]

There may have been some procedural improvement, however. In 1962, the Perm Obkom conducted forty sessions over a six-month period and discussed an average of only six to eight questions.[135] The Cheliabinsk Obkom, over the period of a year, discussed about 475 questions, for an average per session of eight to ten questions.[136] Reducing the number of questions on the agenda almost certainly improved both their preparation and discussion, but the practice was not universal, and criticism of long, dry, stereotyped resolutions lacking concrete and constructive instructions continued to appear in Party literature.[137]

The administrative structure likewise experienced relatively minor change during this period. Extensive delegation of authority from the secretariat to department heads or instructors remained the exception rather than the rule. Further, Khrushchev's determined effort to reform the Party by placing Party workers in the field rather than in offices met with only indifferent success. The instructor's role in particular seems to have undergone little change in either status or function, despite such efforts as those of the Lugansk Obkom, which categorically forbade holding any meeting within the apparat on four days of the week.[138]

After a protracted scrutiny of his own role, one instructor complained that despite the expectations raised by the reform, his work remained essentially clerical—gathering facts and writing reports. His visits to the field were closely supervised and usually involved dealing with an urgent problem. Public appearances and speeches were still the prerogative of the secretaries and department heads. His opinion on matters affecting his area were ignored, and decisions were made without his participation. Not once in three years had a secretary of the obkom asked his opinion on a single issue.[139] Other instructors filed essentially similar complaints.[140]

Cutting staffs and enlarging Party committees produced severe tensions within the average gorkom and raikom, and voluntarism not only failed to substitute for the reduced staff but created problems of its own, staff resistance not least among them. Nonstaff officials threatened the status and specialized expertise of the regular Party bureaucrat, and the recruitment of highly educated, specialized personnel from outside the apparat probably produced friction and further demoralization, among the instructors particularly. Further, an integrated corps of nonstaff instructors would have access to such data and information as to seriously restrict the discretion of those local Party officials whose power was partially based on secrecy.

The apparat resisted in a variety of ways. One way was to avoid forming nonstaff instructor groups or at least to minimize their number.[141] Another was to recruit nonstaff instructors from secretaries of primary Party organs.[142] A third was to restrict the nonstaff instructor's role to the narrowest possible bounds. The Kalinin Gorkom, which affirmed seven nonstaff instructors, gave them no assignments in two years.[143] When assignments were given, they were usually to relieve the staff instructor of minor clerical duties. Nonstaff instructors participated in collecting data and conducting investigations, and occasionally were used as *tolkachi*.[144]

The rapid proliferation of nonstaff departments and sectors and permanent commissions and councils within the Party structure enormously complicated the problems of coordination and direction.[145] Increasing the span of control might have loosened the organization, creating a greater de facto delegation of authority and opportunities for undirected initiative. But the involved secretariats reacted otherwise. Originally intended to supplement the formal Party structure where the staff otdely had been abolished or were lacking, nonstaff departments would soon duplicate existing staff structures.[146] One gorkom in Lithuania had four different nonstaff organizations working on the problems of construction.[147] Another gorkom went so far as to create a complete nonstaff apparat in competition with the regular staff departments.[148] The creation of parallel staff and nonstaff departments and sections was accompanied by a clear reluctance to define their jurisdictional boundaries and competence, with the result that they overlapped not only with regular Party agencies but also with similar groups in the local soviets.[149]

Another response by the secretariat to the problems of directing and coordinating the work of the nonstaff departments and commissions was to reduce their significance and responsibility. Nonstaff organizations were kept isolated, with little contact permitted between them and the staff otdely.[150] The secretaries devoted most of their time and energy to the staff otdely and provided little direction to the nonstaff otdely.[151] These acted principally as auxiliaries of the instructor in preparing bureau questions or as "checkup brigades" in checking the execution of bureau resolutions.[152] While this was undoubtedly useful in reducing the strain produced by personnel cuts, the social principle had been introduced too rapidly and haphazardly to have produced significant change within the apparat by the time of the November 1962 reorganization.

The overall change in the Party's internal relationships and dynamics was therefore moderate. The Party remained a monocratic structure in which intense centralization, hierarchy, the dominance of line officials over staff personnel, and close control by the apparatchiki over bureaucratic participation by the membership were in full force. The major changes in the apparatus involved recruitment. Khrushchev's determination to transoform the Party into an effective agent of economic efficiency and development led to a discernible shift in patterns of recruitment to senior line posts. In the period between Stalin's death and Khrushchev's victory over the Anti-Party Group, evidence suggests that personal political loyalties were the primary, if not the sole, basis of recruitment to senior Party posts and basically related to the struggle for power.[153] Even before the Twentieth Congress, however, Khrushchev had to go beyond political and personal relationships in his search for competence.

An example is to be found in the case of G. I. Voronov, elected a full member of the Presidium at the Twenty-second Congress. Although a member of the 1952 Central Committee, Voronov had spent his entire career in Siberia. During a visit to Chita in 1954, Khrushchev was favorably impressed with his grasp of agriculture and animal husbandry; a few months later, in February 1955, he was appointed to head the procurement administration in the Ministry of Agriculture.[154] In 1957 Voronov headed the Orenburg Obkom, and in 1961 and 1962, he became deputy chairman, then first deputy chairman of the Russian Bureau in charge of agriculture. There is little evidence to suggest a personal or institutional relationship between Khrushchev and Voronov before 1952; but there is evidence of serious conflict between them in 1962.[155]

The policy of co-opting Party officials with more intensive training and a broader range of experience not only responded to the developmental needs of the system but also coincided in some measure with Khrushchev's own power position, which stressed visible results over the short term. The political risks—to Khrushchev personally as well as to the internal cohesion of the Party—were evident. But even this basic structural adjustment failed to expand those capacities for entrepreneurial leadership and control by the Party which Khrushchev's position and program demanded.

— 5 —

Khrushchev and the Leading Role:
The Strategy of Expansion

To reform the Party as an institution in order to increase its authority over the state industrial administration presented a complex problem after Stalin's death. It involved breaking down those patterns of economic administration inherited from Stalinism and creating new, viable administrative and economic relationships at the same time. To move from one step to the next raised problems of vision and power which Khrushchev would have to define in political terms. Politically, reform involved two closely related issues: the legitimacy of the course of action pursued and the resources available to Khrushchev for change.

Revitalizing the Party was one aspect of this change. Another involved re-defining the nature and role of the Soviet state, rationalizing its structure, and increasing its efficiency. Khrushchev also sought to change the nature of the Party-state relationship which had emerged during Stalin's last years, primarily by means of Party growth and penetration into the decision-making structures of the state bureaucracy. In the conflict that developed, the personal and in-stitutional power of Khrushchev and his group was repeatedly challenged, both from within the Party itself and by the complex, internally divided economic bureaucracy he sought to control.

Khrushchev possessed large but by no means unlimited resources for achieving the cloudy, short-term goals of his vision of a modernized communism. Perhaps his greatest asset was his skill in breaking the political deadlocks which his initiatives repeatedly produced. But constrained power and limited purpose operated against a major breakthrough in reforming the command economy or the Party's guiding role. The enduring quality of Khrushchev's politics of reform lies in the nature of the problems raised rather than in the complex compromises offered by himself and his successors. Khrushchev's measures not only failed to change the Leninist-Stalinist monocratic organizational base, but, by continuous reorganization, further reduced its efficiency.

90

1

*Khrushchev and the Redefinition
of Rukovodstvo*

Khrushchev's search for legitimacy and his restatement of ideological formulas
were part of a more general political thrust to place Party power in a moral
context, a process that would involve reversing the statism at the heart of Stalin's
primitive power theory. Redefining the nature and role of the state was a necessary
stage in legitimating an enhanced role for the Party. But reducing the role
of the state carried strong implications of debureaucratization and would
fundamentally affect the prestige and autonomy of officials in the state bureaucracy, including the managers. Khrushchev's failure to redefine the Party's role
and specific functions in guiding the state apparatus became a serious political
problem in 1962 and 1963.

Here as elsewhere, Khrushchev approached the Party-state relationship
cautiously. In the course of his power struggle with Malenkov, his conservatism
on resource allocation and foreign policy had led him in January 1955 to uphold
the Stalinist doctrine of the maximization of state power.[1] In closed session
at the Twentieth Congress, he attacked Stalin's 1937 doctrine of increasing
class struggle in the transition to socialism;[2] but, in clear contrast to his important
ideological revisions in foreign policy, his public Central Committee report
avoided any discussion of the withering away of the state or the dictatorship
of the proletariat. In preceding years, Khrushchev's political opponents had
repeatedly charged him with pragmatism and utilitarianism.[3] Open discussion
of revising Stalin's political theory (generally disguised as a return to Leninism)
began only with Khrushchev's victory over the Anti-Party Group in 1957.

The intensity of the antirevisionist campaign by conservative ideologists revealed the strenuous opposition of major Party segments to de-Stalinization.
Yugoslavia refused to sign the 1957 Moscow Declaration, and the publication
in April 1958 of the Yugoslav Party Program brought attacks on Yugoslav
charges that the Soviet state had become "bureaucratic-statist" and had dis-
associated the struggle against bureaucratism from the withering away of the
state.[4] In a lengthy article in *Sovetskaia Rossiia*, for example, Chesnokov,
a staunch Stalinist ideologist, called the struggle against "dogmatism" and
"Stalinization" fallacious and reaffirmed the basic Stalinist views concerning
the transition to communism, Soviet democracy, and the role of the state.[5]
Similar, though more moderate, opposition to de-Stalinization continued through
the summer of 1958 and included the publication of a hasty edition of speeches
and articles by Soviet and Eastern European writers opposing revisionism.[6]

Khrushchev, whose personal prestige was deeply involved in improving relations with Yugoslavia, took an ambiguous public stand. On the anniversary of the Revolution, on the one hand, he restated the Stalinist formula that the state would wither away only when the highest phase of communism was reached.[7] On the other hand, he told Henry Shapiro that the process of withering away had already begun in the Soviet Union, but he emphasized its gradualism on the grounds that there would be no "leftist" blunder of excessively weakening the state.[8] He attempted later to underplay the significance of the conservative attack on the Yugoslavs. In December 1957 before the Supreme Soviet, he called Yugoslavia's failure to sign the declaration a "negative" point and predicted that relations would grow stronger.[9] Even after the publication of the Party program, he noted that the Yugoslavs should not be paid more attention than they deserved and reiterated the necessity for practicality in working out Communist construction in concrete terms.[10]

In November 1957 and February 1958, Khrushchev gave two interviews to the foreign press. To Henry Shapiro, he signalled his determination to redefine Party-state relationships by citing Lenin's *State and Revolution* as the basis for his views on the withering away of the state.[11] In a more revealing interview with Iverach McDonald, foreign editor of the *Times* of London, he explicitly identified the rise in the Party's leading role with the process of reducing the status and functions of the state bureaucracy. To McDonald's question: "Does the appointment of a greater number of Party secretaries indicate the growing role of the Central Committee of the Communist party?" Khrushchev replied:

You understand this question correctly. Yes, the changes you have mentioned indicate the continually growing role of the Communist Party in the life of our country, and evidently this role is increasing....

Relations among the peoples of our country are constantly developing. Changes are also taking place in the various functions of the state. The process of change in these functions results from our conception of things, from the theoretical postulates of Marxism-Leninism concerning the state. When the conditions for the transition to communist society are created in our country, many state administrative agencies will gradually wither away. For instance, the army, the court, the prosecutor's office and other agencies will wither away.

The courts are evidently destined to outlive the army and other administrative agencies. The courts will probably continue to exist, naturally in a different form. After all, there will still be various conflicts among people, and there must be some kind of arbitration agency to settle them.

I do not intend to make forecasts of changes in our society over a longer period, but even today social life here is developing exactly along a line that follows from the theoretical principles of Marxism-Leninism. Hence in these conditions the Party's role is increasing so that all our available material and other resources might be utilized as correctly as possible. The Party has a stronger foundation than the government agencies. It has arisen and exists not as a result of duties of a legislative nature. Its development is called forth by circumstances stemming from the political views of people, that is, from principles of the moral factor. And mankind will always need moral factors.[12]

The February 1958 interview, given in the thick of the conservative reaction against the Yugoslavs, the abolition of the machine tractor stations, and the tightening of Party controls over the military, provides an interesting glimpse into Khrushchev's "revisionist" thinking on the nature of the state and the dialectic of Party-state relations. But a year later, he was more cautious, announcing to the Twenty-first Congress a new stage of Communist construction in which he sought, by occupying the ideological center, to avoid the shoals of either "leftism" or Stalinist conservatism. In the new phase of social development, he held, the state would begin to wither away, but "dialectically." There would be no bourgeois democracy or political pluralism. In the long view, the identification of state and society would take the form of increased mass participation in the processes of government and the gradual transferral of functions from governmental to social organizations, particularly in social control. The military (which a year earlier he had predicted would be among the first state institutions to wither away) required strengthening until imperialism was crushed.[13]

Khrushchev's position, even as revised and compromised, did not go unchallenged. At a conference held at the Higher Party School in February 1959, two sharply conflicting views were expressed on the evolution of political institutions in the future Communist society. While there was little disagreement concerning the withering away, the nature of this process and the evolving structural relations of Party and state evoked a major debate. The state-oriented view was expressed by P. S. Romashkin, an editorial board member of *Sovetskoe gosudarstvo i pravo*, who held that in the process of withering away, a new, universal sociopolitical organization would emerge out of a process of fusion in which Party, Soviet, and trade union organs would lose their individual identities. That the Party as well as the state would wither away, however, was unacceptable to many at the conference. N. S. Akhmedov, for example, admitted that if a universal sociopolitical organ should evolve to replace the existing institutional pluralism, that universal organization would in fact be the present Communist party. Both positions accepted the further merging of Party and state, but in the Party-oriented view this meant absorbing governmental functions into the Party.[14]

The debate failed to affirm any new conception of Party-state relations or to alter the traditional doctrine of *rukovodstvo* in any fundamental way. The 1961 Party Program, designed in part to legitimate Khrushchev's program of economic and social development, omitted theoretical innovations in institutional power and declined either to describe the process of withering away or to suggest any change in Party-state relationships. On the issue of mass control, the program supported a fusion of state and social control but excluded any participation by the Party.[15]

As the discussion included in the *Fundamentals of Marxism-Leninism* reveals, however, the 1959 issue remained vital. In the process of withering away, the authors admitted guardedly, "it is quite possible that in the future a new type of social organization will arise which will incorporate the best elements accumulated in the work of the Party, governmental, and trade union organizations."[16] But this possibility was not acknowledged in the author's conservative view of Party-state relations. Although both institutions would undergo "considerable change," there would be no fusion of Party and state functions, nor would the Party's enhanced role be achieved at the expense of state or social organs.[17] Khrushchev's search for a new doctrine defining the nature of Party-state relations was complicated not only by the difficulties inherent in the problem but also by conservative forces sustaining the doctrinal status quo.

In his exposition of the New Party Program to the Twenty-second Congress, Khrushchev closely followed the document's conservative line. In proposing a new state structure for the Soviet Union, he declared an end to the dictatorship of the proletariat and to the application of organized state violence against classes within Soviet society. The withering away of the state would occur over "an entire historical period and only when society had matured for self-government." The soviets would be neither weakened nor fused but democratized by increasing the importance of the representative organs and devices of direct democracy, by rationalization of the state administrative apparatus, and by a transfer of functions from the government to social organizations.[18]

Although both his report and discussion eluded any direct discussion of future Party-state relations, one conflict between his personal policy and the program was evident. Whereas the program endorsed only fused state and social control, Khrushchev called for a fusion of Party, state, and social control.[19] What is clear, at any rate, is that (1) Khrushchev failed to establish a new ideological base for legitimating an increase in the Party's decision-making role; and (2) the preservation of the traditional doctrine of *rukovodstvo* would be a serious political obstacle to further institutional reform.

Khrushchev and the Expansion of Party Leadership

A series of formulas emerged after the Twenty-first Congress which embodied a number of Khrushchev's populist and antibureaucratic conceptions. The 1961 Party Program supported his views on ending the dictatorship of the proletariat, on the growth of Communist self-government, and on the general expansion of the Party's role in the leadership of Soviet society. But while predicting the gradual replacement of apparatchiki by unpaid volunteers and systematic turnover, it remained silent on the relations between the Party bureaucracy and the organs of management,[20] and this failure to confront the problem of permanent, specialized, self-interested bureaucracies confirmed its essential conservatism. Preserving the traditional doctrine on Party-state relations, however, would have more immediate political repercussions. Khrushchev had failed to secure ideological approval for any qualitative power or functional change in the Party's organizational role. Although essentially a secondary issue, this would nevertheless haunt him in the widespread challenge to the legitimacy of the November 1962 reorganization.

The failure to redefine the Party's functional role in terms relevant to maturing industrialization may have been more intellectual than political. There is little evidence that Khrushchev had a systematic, comprehensive critique of the existing system or that he and his advisers had developed coherent, far-ranging alternatives. Personal limitations, his immediate, utilitarian approach, and his protracted experience within the apparatus impelled him toward institutional adjustment rather than transformation. The general strategy of reform and his own power limitations induced conservatism as well. There is therefore a contradiction between Khrushchev's doctrinal pronouncements on the Party's role and the thrust of his policies toward increasing its technical competence and mobilizational power in relation to the economy. The inner complexities and contradictions of his policies were largely the result of attempts to maneuver within these limitations. At both the Twentieth and Twenty-second Congresses, Khrushchev gave clear public expression to the Party's traditional functions, emphasizing mass mobilization, cadres, and the classic paternalism of checkup and control.[21]

There is little doubt, however, that Khrushchev's plans for increasing the Party's role to include technical and economic functions greatly exceeded traditional, legitimate boundaries. In assessing these developments, a distinction should be made between the industrial and agricultural sectors. From 1953 on, Khrushchev gave priority to the Party's managerial role in agriculture. The decision-making authority of the managers was considerably greater in industrial management, and while Khrushchev did not hesitate to press the Party's role in increasing efficiency and technical development, his emphasis, particularly after 1959, was primarily on the control, rather than the direct absorption, of managerial functions.

The conceptualization of this process is complicated by the wall of bureaucratic secrecy behind which the most important events of the period were concealed and by the diversity of factors and differing weights informing the total process. There was, however, a logic to the movement which revolved around the power-efficiency dilemma, and power and efficiency are, for that reason, useful categories in dealing with the organizational aspects of the problem. Increasing the Party's role involved redistributing control between the Party and managerial officials. It called for increased Party penetration into the relatively closed managerial apparatus; and above all, it meant restructuring power and influence in such a way as to increase the responsiveness and efficiency of the managerial elite to Khrushchev and the Party's policy initiatives. This, in turn, required rationalizing the planning and plan implementation system, both to reduce the autonomy of the managers and to increase the flexibility of the administrative structure.

These goals were only partially met before 1962 for a number of reasons. For one thing, political resistance within the Presidium and the managerial apparatus dampened the impact of Khrushchev's reforms over time.[22] For another, Khrushchev had attempted to alter a set of deeply institutionalized relationships, which, however inefficient, had nevertheless acquired a distinctive character of their own. Again, none of Khrushchev's reforms were sufficiently incisive to touch the basic institutional mechanisms of the command economy. His reorganizations of the formal structures of the industrial bureaucracy were blunted by its continuity in personnel and functional relationships. Finally, his relationship with the Party apparatus varied, and the identification of his personal power with the Party apparatus began to change in 1958 with significant consequences for the direction and purpose of Party leadership.

Khrushchev's struggle to expand the Party's role and to increase the efficiency and responsiveness of the industrial managers was contingent until his overthrow in 1964. From 1953, economic policy was closely related to, but not identical with, questions of economic management. Both the priorities and the course of economic development involved continuing conflict on the balance of production and consumption and the sectoral allocation of resources among defense, investment, and welfare claimants. In both the industrial and agricultural sectors, basic developmental policy, closely related to the issues of allocation, further complicated the power-efficiency dilemma.

The initial phase of the conflict between Malenkov, who appears to have won the support of the managers, and Khrushchev and the Party apparatus should not be oversimplified. Cohesiveness was not a characteristic of the early post-Stalin era. The managers were divided along hierarchical, departmental, and factional lines. Enduring cleavages—between the Moscow planners and ministerial officials and the plant directors, between the various ministries and departments for resources and jurisdictional ascendency, and among the high-level managers in their support of various contending Party factions and claimants for power—seriously reduced their potential effect on the policy process.[23] At the same time, factional splits at the apex of the Party had the effect of opening up the decision-making process to key functional groups in the system and also of dividing the Party apparatus along hierarchical and factional lines. These vertical divisions were spiderwebbed with regional and national loyalties and with institutional relationships at the local level that crossed Party-state lines.

The initial confrontation by Khrushchev and the Party apparatus with the industrial managers was indirect, and centered on Khrushchev's initiatives in agriculture. The radical critique of agricultural policy and practice at the

September 1953 Plenum of the Central Committee had revealed Khrushchev's intention of increasing the Party's role and competence in directing agriculture at the expense of the agricultural ministries and of changing the balance of resource flows between industry and agriculture. At that time, his general strategy for solving Soviet administrative difficulties was to separate planning and allocative decisions from coordinative decision-making by means of decentralization. By removing line responsibilities from the Moscow agricultural ministries, Khrushchev reduced the political opposition to his programs at the same time that he transferred the directing functions of agriculture to the republican and provincial Party and state authorities.[24] The assumption of technical and economic functions by the territorial Party apparatus in turn demanded a rationalization of the Party apparatus to increase its technical competence and organizational efficiency.

Even before Malenkov's fall in February 1955, however, Khrushchev had clashed with the central planners on resource allocation to agriculture, particularly with respect to the massive Virgin Lands project which he had initiated in the winter of 1953.[25] His determination to secure the Party's ascendancy over the industrial managers was revealed in August 1954 when the Stalinist practice of placing state agencies before the Party was reversed. The full assault on the managers, however, which would culminate in the 1957 industrial reorganization and the Anti-Party Group crisis, began only in the late spring of 1955.

The national industrial conference of May 1955 and the July 1955 plenum (the first on industry in the post-Stalin period) subjected the Stalinist system of industrial management and the managers themselves to withering criticism for bureaucratism and routinization inhibiting economic efficiency and technological progress. Bulganin's defense of the rationalization and decentralization measures corresponded with Khrushchev's agricultural policies. Despite his harsh criticism of the territorial Party apparatus, Bulganin also echoed Khrushchev in enjoining republican and enterprise officials and local Party organs "to struggle against routine and backwardness."[26]

Whatever Khrushchev's role behind the scenes, his public identification with the criticism of industrial management was circumspect. His discussion of industrial management at the Twentieth Congress was mild, although he approved the criticism of the July plenum and promised further decentralization and rationalization of industrial management.[27] His virulent attack on the ministerial system and Moscow managers came only with the threat to his political survival by the mass upheavals in Poland and Hungary following the public release of his Secret Speech to the Twentieth Congress.

The threat was signalled by the increasing status and visibility of his most staunchly conservative presidial opponents. In early September, Kaganovich rose from the State Committee on Labor and Wages to become minister of construction.[28] In late November, Molotov took over the Ministry of State

Control, indicating a reversal in the trend toward Party control of the economic bureaucracy.[29] The movement against Khrushchev and the ascendancy of the Party bureaucracy culminated in the December 1956 plenum of the Central Committee, in whose proceedings neither Khrushchev nor any other member of the Secretariat played a significant role. The plenum ordered a downward revision of the targets of the Sixth Five-Year Plan and for 1957 in order "to eliminate excessive strain in the plan for some industries and to bring production goals and the volume of investment into line with material resources."[30]

The plenum offered a more serious threat to the expansion of Party *rukovodstvo* by sanctioning the reorganization of the State Economic Commission, the organ for current planning, placing in charge a powerful group of industrial officials headed by Pervukhin and including Kosygin and Malyshev as deputies.[31] They were responsible for the significantly lowered growth goals presented to the February 1957 convocation of the Supreme Soviet.[32] But despite this challenge, the plenum explicitly affirmed earlier criticism of the central planners, ministries, and enterprise officials and pledged further rationalization and decentralization of the economic bureaucracy. Khrushchev notwithstanding, there was a presidial consensus on the need for moderate reform of the industrial management system.

Khrushchev's counterattack was framed at the unannounced Central Committee plenum of 13–14 February 1957. Although the speech was unpublished, the plenum's resolution reflected his objectives. He proposed the reorganization of Molotov's Ministry of State Control, the strengthening of the State Planning Committee at the expense of the State Economic Commission, the return to a policy of maximum pressure to stimulate the growth rate, the abolition of the ministerial system, and its replacement by line agencies structured along the territorial principle.[33]

This proposed reform combined wider political and administrative objectives than his earlier, parallel thrust in agriculture. As Jeremy Azrael has noted, Khrushchev's political objectives indicated a destruction of the institutional base of managerial power; an increase in the political status of the Party apparatus and an extension of its administrative control over the bureaucracy; a further fragmentation of the industrial bureaucracy and intensification of conflict within it; and the possibility of a purge of the managers. Administratively, the reform was an attack on routinization and hypercentralization, an attempt (as Khrushchev stressed) to improve efficiency through regionalization and reduce the military vulnerability of Soviet industry through deconcentration. In Azrael's view, Khrushchev also sought to reduce the attendant risks of administrative disorganization during the transition period.[34]

Khrushchev's intense struggle to mount support for his drastic scheme of reorganization has been carefully studied, and the details need not be repeated here.[35] Basically the evidence suggests that Khrushchev could not have overcome his presidial opposition without the strong support of the Party apparatus and the military in June 1957 and that placing administrative reorganization in the hands of the Party apparatus assured a relatively smooth administrative transition from the ministerial to the sovnarkhoz system. In the year following the June crisis, the power of the Party apparatus crested. In October 1957, Party control over the armed forces was reasserted with the ouster of Marshal Zhukov from the Presidium.[36] By December 1957, the Presidium had grown to fifteen full members, nine of whom were simultaneously members of the Secretariat.

In retrospect, it seems evident that appearances belied the reality of Khrushchev's political authority. Neither the intense political conflict nor the drastic administrative reorganization had basically changed the Party or the industrial bureaucracies. As Robert Conquest has observed: "If the whole government and economic interest were abolished tomorrow, the problems would remain the same."[37] The huge, complex, specialized structures of industrial management required managers and technicians whether within the Party or otherwise. Neither regionalization nor administrative decentralization of coordinative decisions negated the principles of the command economy, and the basic problems remained intact. No purge followed Khrushchev's attack on the central ministerial officials. The staffing of the reorganized State Planning Committee and the sovnarkhozy with high ministerial officials pointed not only to a changing political climate but also to Party recognition of its dependence on the new classes created by modernization.[38]

Khrushchev's struggle before the November 1962 reorganization to resolve the power-efficiency dilemma within a basically Stalinist framework may perhaps be best understood in these terms. His failure to achieve decisive power or significantly to revise the system after his victory over the Anti-Party Group greatly affected his decision-making capacity, his relationships with the Party apparatus, and the role of the Party apparatus in guiding the state. In terms of economic policy, his efforts to change the consumption-production balance and the sectoral allocation of resources were continuously opposed.

As Sidney Ploss has indicated, Khrushchev was forced either to compromise or to accept a deadlock on his agricultural initiatives beginning with the machine tractor station reform in 1958.[39] His public commitments in January 1960 to higher standards of mass welfare at the expense of military expenditures led to a struggle of sporadic intensity with the military and heavy industrial advocates until his ouster in October 1964.[40] These policy conflicts were further entangled by acute budgetary strain and a declining growth rate, attributable in part to his overcommitment of resources.

Frustrations in economic policy and performance may suffice to explain Khrushchev's search for personal power within the political system, but there are at least five other plausible indications of his ambition.[41] In March 1958, he became prime minister, thereby joining in his person the highest offices of Party and state. Secondly, there is evidence of the growth of a Khrushchev personality cult emphasizing his personal leadership within the Presidium. To these may be added his continuing effort to gain additional reprisals against the Anti-Party Group. A fourth factor was Khrushchev's strenuous effort in 1958 to become an acknowledged ideological leader. Perhaps the charges of pragmatism and utilitarianism raised by his presidial opponents in June 1957 had exposed a major flaw in his image. Finally, there was his determination to reduce the political status of the Party bureaucracy. The development of the personality cult, the enlarged plena of the Central Committee, the implementation of the social principle, the ideological pronouncements in the Party Program—all pointed to a widening gap in the hitherto close relationship between Khrushchev and the territorial Party apparatus.

The alienation may have stemmed from inefficiency as well.[42] The evidence points strongly to Khrushchev's growing dissatisfaction with the Party apparatus in meeting his demands for economic efficiency. His support of co-optation and the systematic renewal of cadres reflects this. More personal were his bitter strictures against the alleged moral delinquencies of the Party cadres in 1960 and 1961[43] and his criticism in October 1961 of the "parasites" who fought to cut production quotas and increase investment allocations to their own regions.[44] That the apparatus pursued subgoals at variance with his own did nothing to allay his frustration.

But this alienation, which led to a series of bitter conflicts during 1962, should not obscure two persistent trends after 1959. Khrushchev continued to press for an instrumental role for the Party in agricultural and industrial decision-making, and the managers continued likewise to struggle to maintain autonomy and independence after the industrial reorganization of 1957. A continuous, gradual strengthening of the central managerial officials was evident within a year after the sovnarkhoz reform, and the upper levels of the managerial bureaucracy, which had opposed the 1957 reorganization, fought to restore the structure to its original shape.[45]

The crucial period of the conflict was probably between the June 1959 and July 1960 plena of the Central Committee. The 1959 plenum, the first since the adoption of the Seven-Year Plan, was more sharply critical of the managers' technological conservatism and the inefficiencies of the system of management than at any time since the reorganization. The resolution of the plenum, faithfully reflecting the tenor of Khrushchev's speech, placed the responsibility for technological progress squarely on the Party apparatus:

> Party organizations are obliged to head the struggle for technical progress, to be concerned concretely and purposefully with questions of the complex mechanization and automation of production processes, to support and to introduce staunchly into production everything which is progressive and advanced and to conduct a decisive struggle with appearances of stagnation, a scornful relation to technology and the experience of innovators. The feeling for the new, a permanent concern

for the growth of labor productivity, raising the culture of production must be the dominant quality of each Communist.[46]

At the plenum, Khrushchev demonstrated his determination to control managerial behavior by establishing mass organs of Party control within each enterprise. Protests he dismissed by saying: "The Party organizations have matured and become stronger organizationally and ideologically. In these circumstances we need not fear that the institution of control commissions will serve to supplant the management or violate the principle of one-man command."[47]

The decision to maximize the pressure of the Party apparatus in economic decision-making, however, met such opposition that it was reversed by the July 1960 plenum, which, like the December 1956 plenum, was dominated by state economic officials. Of the thirty-three speakers, only seven were Party officials. Khrushchev, although present, did not speak, and the only active member of the Presidium at the plenum was A. N. Kosygin, a member of the economic bureaucracy who had only been appointed to the Presidium in May 1960.[48] In the resolution of this plenum, Party organs were again admonished to struggle against backwardness and conservatism but were also advised to consult with state officials on Party decisions. Local Party organs were ordered "to decisively eliminate facts of unnecessary tutelage, substitution, petty interferences in the work of economic organs and their leaders."[49] Of more enduring importance was the decision to order an investigation of the problem of success indicators, thus returning the problem of economic growth and efficiency to the managers.[50]

The July 1960 plenum marks a convenient turning point in Party-state relations. The increased role of the state apparatus in economic decision-making became evident and was symbolized at the top of the Party structure by the sharp cut in the Secretariat from ten to five members at the May and July plenums. At the territorial level, the recentralization of industrial management was accompanied by a continuing decline in the authority of the local Party organs.

Underlying the reduced role of local Party organs were a series of problems which the November plenum was designed in part to correct. One such problem was Khrushchev's shifting the territorial Party apparatus to agriculture in 1960 to cope with the stagnation in that sector. Equally important was his failing confidence in the Party apparat. The extensive development of the social principle in the Party structure says much the same thing, and the widespread complicity by the Party apparatus in fraud and deception revealed at the January 1961 plenum undoubtedly further reduced his confidence in the reliability of the local Party organs as executives of central policy.

During the two years preceding the November 1962 plenum, therefore, Khrushchev faced a situation of increasing complexity. The economic decline in the agricultural and industrial sectors seriously threatened his general political strategy and prestige at the same time that it provided a context for reasserting the decision-making role of the state managerial apparatus. This reassertion, however, was complicated by at least two opposing trends within the economic bureaucracy: the conservatives who favored a return to the administrative centralism of Stalin, and a small, increasingly influential group of liberals sharply critical of the existing system. Committed by principle, policy, and personal interest to the Party's institutional supremacy, Khrushchev was nonetheless forced to acknowledge the inadequacy of the Party apparat as an operational instrument of economic development and political control. In the long perspective of Party-state relations, the November 1962 plenum represented the final effort to resolve this aspect of the power-efficiency dilemma.

2

The Rationalization of the Managerial Apparatus

The politics of administrative reform, however dimly seen as part of a larger pattern of adjustment, produced a virtually continuous reorganization. To develop relationships in industrial management capable of raising Russia's industrial economy was obviously a formidable undertaking. Measured against growing complexity and increasing political demands, the reform of industrial administration was conservative. Specific, concrete measures of rationalization were undertaken to remove the most evident Stalinist excesses, but the more basic problems arising from the application of the machine theory and the dynamics of the command economy were left untouched.

Part of the reform's conservatism may be attributed to compromises generated by political and bureaucratic opposition. But another part of the explanation may lie in Khrushchev's determination to keep these basic structures intact. The principles of administrative rationalization were themselves conservative since they made use of the Soviet experience developed during NEP. Finally, there was, perhaps, a central assumption peculiar to Soviet conditions which reflected the labor theory of value: the view that, unlike direct participation in material production, administration is nonproductive of economic value, thus leading to a strategy to reduce the scale of administration and expand the production sphere. The simplicity of this strategy served only to disguise the intricacy of the problem.

The period of administrative reform falls into three phases. The first (from 1953 through 1957) involved moderate decentralization and structural rationalization. Khrushchev's abolition of the ministerial system in 1957 and the creation of regional organs of administration—the second phase—was a major effort to break through the limits on rationality and growth imposed by the ministerial system. Beginning in 1958, the problems arising from the sovnarkhoz reform provoked a conservative reaction—the third phase—which continued into 1962 and 1963, although the return was far from complete. In the interim, liberal Soviet economists offered a fundamental criticism that would challenge the basic assumptions of Stalin's administrative system.

The first phase, 1953–57. During the two years between Stalin's death and Malenkov's resignation as chairman of the Council of Ministers in 1955, the policy of administrative reform was linked with other issues in the power struggle between Malenkov and Khrushchev.[51] Malenkov's close ties with the managers are reflected in the decree of 11 April 1953 which strengthened the power of the ministries over staffs, technical design, construction, distribution of enterprise profits, and material-technical supply.[52] With Malenkov's fall, reorganization gained momentum. In the spring of 1955, current and long-range planning were split, and centralized resource allocation was reorganized. The decentralization of decision-making power also began. The number of centrally planned items was cut from five thousand to about fifteen hundred between 1953 and 1956. Detailed statistical indices in the annual plan were cut by 46 percent and the number of reports by one-third.[53]

The devolution of central authority indicated a corresponding rise in the role of republican organs. Local budgets were placed under republican control. Republican councils of ministers were authorized to exercise complete control over enterprises of republican subordination; and the process of transferring enterprises from union to republican subordination occurred as early as 1954. Over fifteen thousand enterprises were decentralized in this way before 1957. Decentralization was also evident in the transfer of whole industries to republican administration.[54] Following the July 1955 plenum, the legal authority of the enterprise was enlarged by a decree of 9 August 1955, which increased the authority of the plant director.[55] Structural rationalization was also abundantly evident in the four years after Stalin's death. Three decrees in 1954 ordered drastic cuts in the number and staffs of economic organs. The result was the abolition of forty-six ministries and departments, 200 glavki, 147 trusts, as well as hundreds of smaller offices.[56] In 1954 and 1955, over 750 thousand administrative workers were reported to have been dropped; in 1956, another 200 thousand were cut.[57]

The policy of reforming the apparatus was seriously resisted by the state managers in Moscow.[58] At the Twentieth Congress, Bulganin complained about the opposition of the central ministerial officials to decentralization:

It must be noted that the measures to eliminate excessive centralization of economic authority are being opposed by certain officials of all-Union and Union-republic ministries who want to run everything from the center, as though they could see the state affairs more clearly "from the top" than the union-republic leaders can see them.[59]

Central officials also sought to undermine the rights of the plant managers which had been expanded in August 1955. Pervukhin complained in 1956 that the Moscow ministries exercised extremely close control over the enterprises and resisted any attempt to increase their autonomy.[60] Similarly, Zverev, the minister of finance under the general supervision of whose ministry the reforms of 1954 were carried out, complained that the central ministerial officials not only fought the reduction of staffs but attempted to increase them.[61] That they were partially successful in keeping their authority and structure intact is attested by Mrs. Furtseva, who noted that once the pressure for reform had eased, the increase in staffs resumed and the number of glavki created actually exceeded prereform levels.[62]

The sovnarkhoz reform of 1957. The sovnarkhoz reform of May 1957 was an integral element in Khrushchev's thrust to extend his personal power and the authority of the Party apparat and to increase the efficiency of the state apparatus. As a device for raising the efficiency of industrial administration, it was directed first toward eliminating these problems which had brought the criticisms of the July 1955 plenum. As Khrushchev was repeatedly to emphasize, the reorganization was designed to provide a new relationship between centralized planning and decentralization of execution.[63]

The new system, Khrushchev held, would end the ministerial autarky which produced waste, duplication, irrational transport, a low level of regional planning, the braking of the development and introduction of new products, red tape, and local irresponsibility in the management of the economy. Among the benefits, Khrushchev expected an increased role for local Party and trade union organs, an improvement in material-technical supply, a regional integration of science and technology, more effective coordination and cooperation of the intermediate level of administration, more effective use of local economic potentials, and the transfer of more administrative officials into production. The major danger of the reform, Khrushchev felt, was the development of regional autarky, or *mestnichestvo*, in place of ministerial autarky.[64]

In the sovnarkhoz system, the devolution of operational authority was to be accompanied by an increase in the role of the central planning agencies, which Khrushchev linked with a strong technical policy. In the reorganization of planning, the State Economic Commission was abolished, and both long-range and current planning were placed in the State Planning Commission. Gosplan's principal functions included developing technological policy, integrating technology with production, and consolidating sovnarkhoz and republican plans. The State Planning Committee assumed the major responsibility for solving chronic problems of supply by absorbing intact the supply and sale administrations of the former ministries. Not least among the new responsibilities of both the union and republican planning agencies was the coordination of plan fulfillment by the enterprise, a function which involved them deeply in the daily management of the economy.[65]

The new system to emerge between February and September 1957 was a radical administrative alteration in the system of industrial management.[66] In place of the 141 union, union-republican, and republican ministries, 105 councils of the national economy were formed.[67] In each of eleven remaining union republics, republican sovnarkhozy were created. Divided into four basic structural types, the formal structure of the average sovnarkhoz included a chairman and his deputies in a council of about fifteen, a series of line departments formed on the branch principle, and functional departments.[68] The leading posts in the sovnarkhoz were staffed principally by the reassignment of high officials from the abolished ministries. Heads of departments, however, which were on the *nomenklatura* of the regional apparatus, were largely recruited from local sources, principally among former plant directors and Party officials.[69]

The 1957 system underwent frequent but limited structural change. A major power shift occurred in June and July 1960 with the formation of republican sovnarkhozy in the RSFSR, the Ukraine, and Kazakhstan.[70] The new administrative organs, intended in part to relieve the overburdened republican gosplany, culminated a process of recentralization of administrative power. The growth in operational control at the republican level and the subsequent loss of autonomy at the regional level is reflected in the rapid proliferation in 1961 and 1962 of branch departments within the Russian Sovnarkhoz, which increased from seventeen to forty.[71] The major role extended to the planning organs in the 1957 reorganization also resulted in a virtually continuous reorganization in the vital area of planning.[72]

The improvements in authority and structure envisioned by the reform failed to materialize. The administrative structure remained complex, cumbersome, and multistaged. Despite repeated cuts, the sovnarkhoz staffs continued to grow,[73] and the deep-rooted practices of Russian administrative centralism swiftly re-surfaced in a flood of paper and massive red tape characteristic of the ministerial system.[74] As early as 1958, recentralization began in the number of centrally planned products, reaching some 18 thousand products on the eve of the November 1962 reform.[75] In 1958 and 1959, the sovnarkhozy lost their discretion over the distribution of funded materials and of products and equipment produced above-plan.[76] In 1959, decisions on capital investment were returned to the central planning organs.[77] The establishment of the 1960 republican sovnarkhozy further reduced the decision-making role of the regional sovnarkhozy and created its own administrative complications as well.[78] The loss of regional initiative produced overlapping jurisdictions and duplication of functions between union and republican agencies and severe jurisdictional disputes between the republican planning and operational agencies.[79] The gradual reassertion of traditional, conservative practices of industrial administration was fundamental in structuring the *rukovodstvo* of the territorial Party apparatus.

The administration of planning and supply. There is little evidence to suggest that the 1957 reform increased efficiency in planning or reduced microeconomic imbalance. Planning and supply remained deeply routinized, and the initial burden on Gosplan appears to have been great. The substance of planning grew increasingly complex, multiplying the problems of rationality and information processing. A Soviet scholar has estimated, for example, that the composition of the annual plan for the Moscow City Sovnarkhoz alone, in all of its technical-economic indicators, would require about 675 million distinct operations and 3.5 million man-hours, with each operation repeated for each change in plan.[80] The system of "success indicators" continued to dictate the strategy of planning and plan fulfillment of the enterprises and at intermediate levels of industrial administration. The decree of 1959, which made the payment of premiums dependent on the fulfillment of cost reduction norms, proved in many respects counterproductive and, as Bergson pointed out, was irrelevant to the problems of the Soviet economy.[81]

Despite the development of countercycle planning in 1959, the planning process continued to be one of bargaining in which the enterprises understated their production reserves and the sovnarkhozy and planning agencies automatically raised the production quotas by a few percentage points.[82] The reverse process characterized the supply plan, with enterprises and sovnarkhozy overstating supply needs and the central planners usually cutting them.[83]

The defense of the plan remained as administratively complex as it had been under the ministerial system. That the average sovnarkhoz in the Russian Republic was required to coordinate and to secure the approval of the administrative departments in both republican gosplan and sovnarkhoz absorbed major administrative resources.[84] Internal instability provided a further complication. In 1961, for example, the plan for the Kharkov Sovnarkhoz was changed 400 times.[85] Closely related to the problem of planning changes was the issue of supplemental planning by union, republican, and Party organs, which were often uncoordinated with the planning organs.[86] The power of the regional sovnarkhozy to refuse supplemental orders was severely circumscribed.

In terms of the Party's decision-making role, the fundamental difficulty of the sovnarkhoz system was supply.[87] The supply system became increasingly complex with the centralization of planning and distribution, and from 1960, as a consequence, the sovnarkhozy had virtually no control over Group A products.[88] Lack of coordination between the production and supply plans could be attributed primarily to the technical problem of information and of achieving accurate balances. The planning of supply, however, continued to change production plans without corresponding changes in the supply plan, to assign production to plants under construction or without adequate capacity, or to use obsolete norms.[89] These problems were undoubtedly worsened by both the overcommitment of resources and the managerial practice of maintaining excessive stocks as a "reserve."[90] In 1961, for example, Union Gosplan reported a reserve of less than five days in ball bearings.[91] "Frozen" materials continued to grow and the *tolkachi* flourished, absorbing an estimated one billion rubles in 1962 and 1963.[92] The supply problem was also largely responsible for the new practice of *mestnichestvo*, the practice of a sovnarkhoz or republic of fulfilling its own needs while failing to meet the requirements of other republics or regions.[93] Despite the law of 24 April 1958 which made the failure to fulfill deliveries a criminal matter, this practice continued until the November 1962 reform.[94]

The dynamics of plan fulfillment. The reorganization of 1957 affected the individual enterprise least. The basic relationship between the sovnarkhoz and the enterprise was one of close and detailed control by the councils of every phase of the plant's productive activity. A number of plant directors complained that the branch otdely led the enterprises like the former glavki.[95] Sovnarkhoz control was tempered, however. In the period before 1960, the sovnarkhozy actively competed with the republican planners, the Ministry of Finance, and Gosbank for control over the enterprises' resources and activity, a condition which ended with the formation of the republican sovnarkhozy.[96] Conflict arose in determining the enterprise plan and the assignment of supply. But antagonism was moderated by the interest of the sovnarkhozy in fulfilling the assigned plan by imposing limits on the center's demands for increased production indices.[97] From the point of view of economic development, the sovnarkhoz continued the ministerial practice of stressing average regional indices, with emphasis on highly productive units and indifference to lagging plants.

The operational procedures of the enterprise seem to have experienced little modification. The practice of *shturmovshchina* persisted, the result of uneven or inadequate deliveries of supplies,[98] along with those marginal and illegal activities which had been a basic feature of the ministerial system. The use of *tolkachi* in securing supply was supplemented by buying or illegally trading surplus stocks.[99] Plan deception and simulation remained widespread. In the wake of the revelations of the January 1961 Central Committee Plenum, the Soviet press reported many instances of fraud and of unfinished, defective, or improperly assorted products included as finished production.[100] The Orenburg Sovnarkhoz, for example, permitted the enterprises under its jurisdiction to include over 750 thousand rubles of padded production in the figures submitted for the first eight months of 1961.[101]

Managerial incentives to raise the quality of production or to achieve technical progress remained marginal under the sovnarkhoz system. As one engineer explained, the problem raised by the July 1959 decree was that raising production quality meant adding additional inputs which violated the norms for the rise of labor productivity and the reduction of costs and in so doing, threatened bonuses and jobs. To achieve planned goals for costs, managers preferred to "squeeze a little" by substituting inexpensive for expensive materials, replacing simple devices with complex ones, reducing the quality of inputs by thinning the thickness of steel, and so on.[102] In addition, the sovnarkhozy and plant directors actively opposed the introduction of new technology.[103] The existing system of success indicators and the pressure for quick results were partially responsible for this,[104] but the problems of training workers, of supply, of securing additional investment, and fear and distrust of the new equipment also inhibited technological growth.[105] Nonetheless, some advance was made. In 1962, it was claimed that 42 percent of the basic capital stock had been renovated.[106]

Plan fulfillment for capital construction, which Khrushchev in 1961 termed "the question of questions" was in serious arrears.[107] In 1961 there were more than 100 thousand unfinished construction sites in the Soviet Union, over 50 percent of them industrial, and the number growing.[108] Closely related to this was the increasing lag in putting new capacity into operation. In some industries, unfinished construction constituted from 70 to 75 percent of total annual investment.[109] This lag was the more serious because it was most concentrated in those industries which had priority in Khrushchev's strategy for economic growth: the chemical, metallurgical, and power industries.[110] Further, as Kosygin pointed out, construction costs were highest in the chemical and oil refining and automobile industries.[111]

Increased anxiety in capital construction was owing partly to the over-commitment of resources (particularly after 1961, with the increase of defense expenditures) and partly to the administrative factor. The absence of a charge on capital investment encouraged sharp competition among sovnarkhozy and local Party organs for new investment. As Khrushchev described the process, the local organs started new construction projects without sufficient documentation or material resources, thinking that, once begun, the planning organs would have to appropriate further capital to complete them.[112] In reality, however, the planning organs spread inadequately increasing amounts of material to an increasing number of construction sites, which resulted in lengthy periods of unfinished construction. The effect was to "freeze" large amounts of unused capital and to induce technological obsolescence.[113]

Capital construction was also plagued by the poor coordination of construction and supply schedules, particularly in the equipping of new plants.[114] This reflected, in addition to the general problems of supply, a shortage of capital equipment made more acute by the decline in 1961 and 1962 in the growth of metallurgical, chemical, and power industries. The shortage of capital equipment, however, was partially the result of poor organization of the system of deliveries. At the November 1962 plenum of the Central Committee, P. N. Demichev noted that the amount of uninstalled equipment had grown 35 percent in 1962 over 1961. In the U.S.S.R. in 1962, there were over three million square meters of unused production space, but the number of uninstalled cutting machines equalled the total production for these machines in 1962.[115]

3

The Thrust of Rukovodstvo

The role of the Party apparatus in industrial decision-making should be examined in the context of the political and economic relationships underlying Khrushchev's policies. The goal was to achieve a qualitative increase in the efficient exploitation of existing technologies and in the development and diffusion of new technology, and the industrial reorganization of 1957 largely failed to achieve this. Both economic growth and performance remained bureaucratized and routinized processes within the limits of the command economy. The retention of a bureaucratic command structure of decision-making virtually ensured a strong continuity in the Party's functional role.

By increasing Party *rukovodstvo*, the source of so much intraelite conflict, Khrushchev intended to produce an innovative, developmental, and entrepreneurial relationship with the industrial and agricultural economies. Internal Party rationalization and revitalization aimed at expanding the technical and economic resources of the apparatus for the purpose of gaining enough competence to induce and control efficiency and development. The expansion of co-optation and repreparation of cadres, improvement in the process of consultation, and regularization of internal dynamics undoubtedly contributed to a more efficient instrument of leadership. Nevertheless, the Party remained intensely bureaucratic, and this reduced the scope of action and initiative of many of the full-time apparatus officials.

If the Party's role as a transforming force in promoting economic development fell short of Khrushchev's expectations, its role in maintaining existing structures increased. As under the ministerial system, basic economic policy, allocation of resources, and, to a significant degree, coordination were all centralized within the central Party organs. The influence of the lower Party organ on the allocative process was limited, but it continued to contribute to regional and national development.

The basic economic function of the territorial apparatus, however, was to alleviate the serious microimbalances which the sovnarkhoz system shared with the ministerial system. Its involvement in the economic and technical processes of industrial production and distribution was essentially coordinative, designed to correct the imbalances in inputs and outputs which the planning system produced. This contribution to economic performance, castigated in the literature on *rukovodstvo* as substitution, was useful and perhaps necessary. But an overall inspection of the Soviet economy indicates that the power and the capacity of the Party apparatus were insufficient to alter Soviet economic efficiency in a fundamental way.

The Authority and Substance of Party Rukovodstvo

Although the 1957 industrial reorganization succeeded initially in raising the Party's authority and status in relation to the state apparatus, the change in relationship, even before 1960, should not be overestimated. The power of the republican and provincial Party organs was structurally limited in two major ways: one was the continued close vertical supervision exercised by the central Party apparatus; the second (more contingent but never fully absent), the authority of the Party apparatus varied with the degree of centralization of decision-making within the managerial bureaucracy. There were, to be sure, other elements more subtle and difficult to evaluate in structuring the Party's role,[116] among them the ambiguity in interests arising from the local Party organ's dual role of enforcing central directives and simultaneously being judged by the results achieved by those over whom they exercised control. This problem was sharper under the sovnarkhoz system than it had been earlier.

The formation in 1956 of the Russian Bureau significantly narrowed the central Party apparatus' control over the provincial Party organs. K. Gerasimov, the head of the Russian Republic Gosplan, noted that the bureau was intimately involved in every aspect of the work of the Russian planning machine.[117] On its decision, the Urals Machine-Building Plant was expanded.[118] It intervened (although how often it is impossible to say) in the production plans of different enterprises. The bureau ordered, for example, the doubling of production in a crystal plant in the Far East.[119] It also served as a prime instrument in enforcing central policy. After an investigation of the increasing amount of uninstalled equipment, the Russian Bureau in July 1962 ordered the first secretaries of the Cheliabinsk and Sverdlovsk obkomy and the chairmen of the respective sovnarkhozy to report personally in a month on the measures taken to install new equipment in metallurgical enterprises.[120]

Occasionally, as when a high-priority construction project failed to meet its schedule, the Russian Bureau would substitute for local Party and sovnarkhoz organs. An example may be found in the experience of the Sterlitamskii chemical plant in Bashkir, which had failed to meet its schedule under the direction of the Bashkir Committee. The bureau established a special commission from the central apparat which took over every phase of construction, including assuring the construction site of material technical supply and placing a *Pravda* "rabkor" there to issue bulletins.[121] While such detailed involvement was exceptional, it suggests that basic authority lines were essentially unmodified by the industrial reorganization. The heightened role of the local Party organs was relative and circumstantial.

Notwithstanding its limitations, the sovnarkhoz system led to a significant rise in the formal authority of the local Party organs over the Soviet managers at the intermediate level. In 1957, the local Party organs were responsible for the initial structuring and staffing of the new sovnarkhozy. The obkom appointed otdely heads and working officials, although the appointment of chairman and deputy chairman remained on the central *nomenklatura*.[122]

The reform also gave local Party officials greater access to information and decision-making. The sovnarkhoz chairman was normally a member of the oblast bureau; reciprocally, the oblast first secretary, the secretary for industry, or the head of the industrial-transport otdel normally attended sovnarkhoz sessions and decided issues on the spot.[123] Daily contact with the various branch otdely was maintained by assigning an instructor of the industrial-transport otdel or a gorkom secretary to work with individual branch administrations.[124] The obkom and, to a lesser degree, the gorkom gained additional power with the transfer of plants of union and union-republic subordination to the sovnarkhoz. The *nomenklatura* of the obkom and gorkom now included the appointment of plant managers, an issue of intense conflict under the ministerial system. In the case of the Leningrad City Sovnarkhoz, for example, the plants under union jurisdiction were divided between the obkom and gorkom, with the more important enterprises under obkom direction.[125]

Increasing the formal authority of the local Party organs was intended to secure a reliable, effective instrument for executing Khrushchev's economic policies. Local Party organs were expected to use their new power to construct tight investment and production plans, to mobilize hidden reserves, to press for economic and technical rationalization, and, particularly, to enforce central priorities against local deviations or *mestnichestva*.[126] The expectation that a radical reorganization of the administrative machinery would result in a radical shift in the balance of interests of the local Party organs, however, would be disappointed.

The local Party organ retained those interests which had developed under the ministerial system. Its fundamental obligation, which increased when Khrushchev made economics the major field of Party endeavor, was to fulfill its own particular and limited segment of the national plan. The oblast committee, like the sovnarkhoz, therefore had a direct interest in securing a plan which could be fulfilled without excessive regional strain.[127] The obkom was also responsible for assuring the necessary means to achieve those goals. But the essentially local interest of the obkom and gorkom was counterbalanced by continued pressures from the center for higher production and technical progress, which demanded a response from both the Party organs and, to lesser extent, from the sovnarkhozy.

In balancing these requirements, the local Party organs were still dependent on the authority distribution and operational efficiency of the state administrative structure. Their authority, closely linked with that of the sovnarkhozy, was limited by the degree of power centralization on such crucial items as allocations of investment and supply. The operational environment in which they functioned to achieve their goals was determined in large measure by the efficiency of the industrial administrative mechanism. Since the working characteristics of the sovnarkhoz system generally resembled those under the ministerial system, the overall role of the local Party organs between 1957 and 1962 appears to have modified but marginally.

The Role of Local Party Organs
in Planning

The reorganization of industry increased the role of local Party organs in both current and investment planning. The obkom secretariat and departments reviewed the entire sovnarkhoz plan and corrected it, usually by increasing the output or changing the product mix.[128] The obkom also appears to have been responsible for composing the plan for new technology for the sovnarkhoz and for planning the production of agricultural spare parts.[129] Its powers in the planning and disposal of the products of local industry which had been transferred to the local soviets appear to have been much greater than in relation to the sovnarkhozy, but its role in supplemental planning, except in placing orders for agriculture, seems to have been limited. While it did add above-plan production assignments to the basic production plan, these changes usually reflected central needs and were probably directed by central Party organs.[130] A case in point: the Karelian Obkom demanded increased output from the sovnarkhoz of newsprint, an item in critically short supply, despite the protests of the sovnarkhoz officials that the plan could not be met.[131] The system of socialist obligations, introduced in industry and agriculture in 1959 as a propaganda and mobilizing device, was insignificant as a method of planning. Most of the obligations to raise output or to complete production schedules ahead of plan were, as Soviet leadership frequently complained, purely formal.

The reorganization of industry also raised the role of the local Party organs in investment planning. The obkom reviewed the investment plan and introduced correctives in it.[132] In composing the Seven-Year Plan, local Party organs generally raised targets and, as a function of their responsibility for new technology, became deeply immersed in the selection of investment variants.[133] But their ability or interest in establishing central investment policies in the localities appears to have been relatively weak. In August 1958 the Central Committee accused four sovnarkhoz chairmen and the oblast first secretaries of localism for permitting the diversion of planned investment from state projects to local needs.[134]

The lack of local Party control over investment planning and construction was a major cause of the recentralization of decision-making over construction. In 1961, Khrushchev admitted that the placing of construction affairs in the Otdel of Construction was the direct result of the failures of local Party organs and sovnarkhozy.[135] The recentralization of the planning function in 1959 and 1960, however, represented less of a loss of local authority than would superficially appear. The obkom or republican committee was an intermediate, never a final source of plan determination. Their judgments, even during 1957 and 1958, were subject to correction by central Party and state organs.

The Local Party Organs as Executive
Party Organs

The primary purpose of the industrial reform was to increase the Party's operational role in economic decision-making. Under the sovnarkhoz system, the organs of industrial administration could be more deeply penetrated at all levels and were therefore more susceptible to Party influence and control than under the relatively closed ministerial system. The point was to create a more effective instrument in executing central economic policies. But local Party organs responded to their new status without dramatics, and the expectation of an aggressive, new, and dramatic leadership faded within a few years. The sovnarkhoz reform nevertheless opened avenues for Party leadership that had been closed under the ministerial system, and, in that respect, some progress was made.

In the territorial Party apparatus, the basic strategy of plan fulfillment resembled that of the sovnarkhoz: the overfulfillment of production quotas according to average indices laid down for the region as a whole. This differed from the ministerial system where the Party's territorial interests often conflicted with the branch interests of the ministry. In general, where the individual plant or industry met the indicators, the oblast apparatus did not intervene in the production or construction process. Where the plan's success was threatened, however, particularly in priority industrial or construction areas, the obkom tightened its supervision. There are numerous examples of obkomy directly taking over plants or construction sites. The usual methods of intervention included establishing loading and unloading schedules for a lagging coal trust or sending out special obkom brigades to establish construction schedules, secure supply, or to "pump up" the operation by mass agitation or direct pressure.[136]

The emphasis on collective leadership and the growing recognition within the Party apparatus of the need for technical and economic expertise may have reduced administrative *rukovodstvo* by Party organs in favor of consultation, although the extent to which consultation and systematic decision-making developed is difficult to assess. One secretary in the Ukraine wrote that his obkom had abandoned the practice of calling officials of lagging plants into the obkom to explain the lag in production and to issue Party punishment. Instead, technically qualified officials were assigned to investigate the problem, and on the basis of their report the obkom would decide what to do.[137]

City and urban borough committees were only marginally affected by the formation of the sovnarkhozy. The exceptions were the Moscow and Leningrad city committees which directed their own sovnarkhozy and therefore operated with the authority and staffs of large obkomy.[138] On the whole, however, the average gorkom or raikom had little authority in relation to either the center or the sovnarkhoz. Suggestions and appeals to the sovnarkhoz by the gorkom were often either pigeonholed or ignored, and conflict appears to have been frequent.[139] Obkom support was apparently mandatory for the gorkom to influence the sovnarkhoz successfully.

The situation is well-illustrated in an obkom first secretary's account of a conflict between a city committee and sovnarkhoz. New industrial enterprises were being built in the city of Berdiansk.

> The city committee directed all the forces of the collective to the timely completion of the work of construction and reconstruction. But in a series of cases, the gorkom of the Party ran up against difficulties which it could not overcome. At the base of the problem was the poor supply of construction materials, equipment, etc. The administrations and departments of the sovnarkhoz to which the gorkom turned did not react to their requests. The workers of the sovnarkhoz explained that most important for them were the ferrous metallurgy construction sites, not the industry of Berdiansk.
>
> The city committee was obliged to turn to the oblast committee with the request that responsible sovnarkhoz workers come to Berdiansk and examine the problems on the spot.[140]

The obkom sent a team, which included its industrial secretary, the chairman of the sovnarkhoz and his deputies, and a number of technical experts, to Berdiansk, where they spent several days and made a number of decisions which the obkom took under direct control.[141]

The gorkom had more authority in relation to local industry, housing construction, and public services[142] and continued to play its traditional role in resolving disputes and serving as a labor exchange for Communists seeking new jobs.[143] Although responsible for the production quotas of all industrial enterprises within its jurisdiction, it functioned principally as a source of information and cadres for the obkom and in carrying out obkom orders.

Both the obkom and gorkom continued to be absorbed with the issue of material-technical supply. The burdening of local Party organs with secondary concerns, which Kozlov criticized sharply at the Twenty-second Congress, stemmed (as it had under the ministerial system) from the critical problems of supply. An important initial result of the shift to the sovnarkhozy system was the obkom's increased capacity to maneuver above-plan and local production for construction and industrial bottlenecks. The centralization of planning, supply, and distribution in 1959 and 1960 evidently reduced this discretion, with the result that the obkomy and gorkomy intensified their function as *tolkachi*. Serving as an alternative network of pressure and petition, the obkom and, to a lesser degree, the gorkom appealed to foreign Party organs and to the Central Committee for aid in speeding up deliveries or producing additional material.

Less than a year after the reorganization of industrial management, the crucial problems of supply under the new managerial system were revealed by a *Pravda* investigation of the Bashkir Province Party Committee.

One cannot but recall in this connection the incorrect methods of the industrial departments of Party Committees before the reorganization of the management of industry. At that time the Party Committee departments for all practical purposes played the role of intermediate links between the enterprises and the ministries. Administrative and managerial functions were uppermost in their activities.

The facts show that under the new conditions as well the industrial department of the Province Party Committee has retained its former undesirable features. As before, its staff members often play the role of expeditors in business matters. They spend a large part of the day on the telephone. They plead on behalf of some factory directors, beg for others and apply pressure for still others. A great deal of their time is taken up answering telegrams and requests from other areas....

Comrade Ostrovsky, director of the department, said, "We spend 90 percent of our time solving these questions" and added by way of explanation, "But we Party workers cannot brush aside requests from the enterprises...."[144]

In mediating issues of supply, the Central Committee—and after 1958 the Party Control Commission—continued to perform the crucial role. Conflicts between republics or even within a single republic routinely brought complaints and requests to the central Party organs. In pressuring a supplier within the Russian Republic, for example, the Stalinsk City Committee appealed to Central Committee, the Stalinsk Obkom, and the Ukrainian Central Committee to secure deliveries of spare parts for a continuous steel pouring operation.[145] The Saratov Province Committee likewise appealed to the Party Control Commission to investigate a Novosibirsk plant which had failed to meet its delivery schedule.[146] The intense pressure on the economy induced by overcommitment of resources and administrative inefficiency is strikingly revealed in the often petty quantities and types of materials which preoccupied the local Party organs. The Ashkhabad Gorkom, for example, wrote letters to Saratov, Berezniki, Tambov, and Minsk for small quantities of molasses, molding, sand, calcium hypochlorite, and even for 90 cubic meters of second-grade oak planking.[147]

The Local Party Organs and
Technical Progress

The continuous involvement of the local Party organs in the short-run problems of plan fulfillment was little changed from the ministerial system, even though their authority in economic decision-making was increased in the interests of higher growth. In this respect, the sovnarkhoz system may be said to have tested the apparat's relevance and capacity to exercise competent leadership under conditions of mature industrialization. Their consistent failure to reach the plans for technical progress bespeaks the relative ineffectiveness of the Party organs in responding to the massive upsurge in economic modernization. Nonetheless, slow progress was made, and the local Party organs did contribute to the realization of Khrushchev's goals.

The Soviet press and literature provide numerous examples of leadership by oblast committees in reequipping plants or developing new products. The approved procedure was to have the given enterprise or installation surveyed by a group of specialists and, on the basis of their reports, to plan and schedule the operations and often directly to supervise the work. Following such a procedure, in 1958 the Moscow City Committee installed 450 machines and introduced 1,500 new products.[148] The Zaporozhe Obkom directly supervised the reconstruction of a plant and initiated and prepared the experimental model of a new automobile as well.[149] The Kharkov Obkom undertook the production of a new diesel motor and pressured the sovnarkhoz to design and build a new tractor.[150] Other obkomy directed the building of blast furnaces, the installing of semiautomatic lines, or drew up comprehensive plans for developing the chemical industry.[151] Such measures were often limited, however, and directed to specific ends.

But local Party organs were more frequently under attack for their relative indifference to promoting technical change. In 1958 and 1959, the Soviet press directed a campaign against the weak control by local Party organs over technical progress. The most intense criticism was contained in the resolution of the June 1959 plenum of the Central Committee.[152] The plenum of July 1960—dominated by managerial rather than Party officials and emphasizing the political rather than the economic functions of local Party organs—was nonetheless sharply critical of the weak control over the development of technology.[153] The decline in the authority of the Party apparat, which began with the operational centralization in 1960, was reinforced by revelations at the January 1961 plenum of widespread complicity on the part of the lower Party organs in deception and report padding. The Twenty-second Congress in October 1961 was a thinly veiled attack on the Party apparat; its part in developing new technology went unremarked in both Khrushchev's report to the Central Committee and the congress' resolutions. The attack on the apparat, of course, coincided with the declining rates of growth in both industry and agriculture.

Local Party Organs as Controllers

Between the industrial management reform of 1957 and the November 1962 reorganization of the Party structure, highly selective controls were exercised over other aspects of the activity of industrial managers. The obkomy and gorkomy appear not only to have done little to restrict the informal managerial practices that persisted in the new industrial management but demonstrated little concern with the qualitative indicators and hidden reserves, and actively participated in report padding and deception. An examination of some of the more important factors underlying this situation reveals the basic limits operating to reduce the effect of local Party organs.

Local Party organs were generally reluctant to exercise strict and continuous control over the sovnarkhoz and managerial officials partly because of their own interest in fulfilling the plan but also because of their perception of the administrative realities of the system. A prototypical example is the case of V. A. Maiorev, a director of an Astrakhan shipyard. Generally regarded as a successful enterprise director, Maiorev understated his productive capacity, maintained hidden reserves, and requested excessive amounts of supply. He inflated his output by means of price manipulation, reported fictitious work to clients, and included unfinished work as completed. To maintain his position, Maiorev built a family group and bribed oblast officials. Both the Astrakhan Obkom and Gorkom were aware of Maiorev's practices but tolerated them. Asked why, the gorkom second secretary replied, "Suppose you try to run an enterprise such as a shipyard. Do you think you could do it without violating laws?"[154]

Closely associated with this species of pragmatism was the mutuality of interest between the local Party organs and sovnarkhozy. The fact that administrative pressures and sanctions were insufficient to produce strong motivation and commitment and the natural community of interest produced by a common territorial identification apparently served to moderate conflict and reduce the intensity of control from the obkom, particularly in matters affecting the payment of premiums to the managers. That control by Party officials was only part of the job rather than a matter of moral conviction is suggested by the case of Zakharov, the secretary of industry for the Kiev Obkom. In composing the plan for light industry for the sovnarkhoz, Zakharov included the production of electrical goods which the enterprises lacked the capacity to produce. During the course of plan fulfillment, Zakharov was transferred from the obkom to head the light industry otdel of the sovnarkhoz, where he subsequently defended the failure of the enterprises to fulfill the plan that he himself had established.[155] The example, inconclusive in itself, nevertheless suggests the essentially flexible institutional loyalties of even Party officials.

A third factor was the dependence of both Party and managerial officials on the central Party and state organs. Intensive technical development required investment, supply, and trained manpower which could only be secured by influencing the economic decisions of the center. In competing for capital investment, Party organs and sovnarkhozy joined on a regional basis to evolve long-range plans for developing and petitioning the Central Committee or planning organs for favorable consideration. While this might explain the diversion of resources from state construction projects to local needs, it does not explain local Party organs permitting the approval of new construction sites without sufficient planning and resources as the number of unfinished construction sites grew. To start a new facility, however impractical from a national point of view, benefitted the individual oblast because it represented a future resource which probably could not be secured otherwise.

Khrushchev's increased demands on the apparat undoubtedly contributed to the further debilitation of its controlling functions. His relentless demands for a radical increase in agricultural production, particularly after the failures of the fall of 1960, led to a series of reforms in agricultural administration in 1961 and 1962.

Evaluation of Party Reform in Relation to Rukovodstvo

The aggregate measures herein discussed were designed in large part to overcome bureaucratic stagnation and to increase the effectiveness of the Party as the central institution of Soviet life. If their effectiveness is measured by their effect on economic growth and technical innovation, then the Party's role in agriculture may be said to have been relatively ineffective and its role in industry only moderately effective. Evaluating the basic trends of reform within the Party between 1953 and 1962 in relation to raising the leading role in economic decision-making, certain factors become prominent.

To put an end to bureaucratic isolation and stereotyped relations between the Party and the economic institutions and processes of Soviet society, an effort was made to broaden the social base and shift the occupational structure within the Party. Reducing the recruitment of administrative personnel and increasing the selective recruitment of specially skilled workers in industry and agriculture reflected an attempt to increase the Party's influence in areas judged critical to economic growth. This also explains the enlargement of local Party committees, new patterns of recruitment into the elective organs, and the emphasis upon the value of frequent plenums, specific discussions of concrete objectives, the participation of the aktiv in Party assignments, and the need to broaden consultative processes.

Reactivating the Party by broadening its base of involvement, depth of commitment, and participation was largely negated by preserving intact the power structure by which Party policy was defined and executed. The executive and administrative structures of the Party were least changed. At all levels, the bureau was dominated by the apparat and the apparat by the secretarial corps. There is little to suggest that the traditionally dominant role of the first secretary of the bureau was diminished from the republican to the raion level. Within the secretarial corps, an increase in educational qualifications, an age reduction, and the promotion of officials with managerial experience in either industry or agriculture—all were directed toward increasing the competence and energy of the secretaries through specialization. Throughout the period, however, the secretaries remained generalists whose prime responsibility involved coordinating and integrating a variety of cultural, social, and economic functions rather than acting as superior economic managers. That the secretarial corps was heavily burdened by demands for results seems evident.

The Party's administrative organs experienced comparatively little change. Cutting staff to introduce flexibility into the apparat was of dubious value in view of the increased demands upon the apparat. The major experimentation in administrative structure was concentrated at the level of the gorkomy and raikomy within the smaller administrative districts. Abolishing departments had the effect of reducing the number of primary Party organs under the control of any given instructor, at the expense, however, of specialization. At the local Party level, the rapid increase in Party membership, the cutting of staffs, and the abolition of departments produced serious strains on the apparat and served to weaken rather than to strengthen Party control. At the oblast and republican level, where the administrative system retained its basically Stalinist forms, the major fault was the highly restricted role of the instructor, who remained essentially a *tolkachi* and a collector of data.

The social principle provided an attractive solution to the apparat's inadequacies. Theoretically, it promised an end to the conflict between a permanent Party bureaucracy and Soviet society in general and a pledge of ultimate political equality. Practically, the enlistment of unpaid labor was a pledge of moral strength; it also served at the gorkom and raikom levels to relieve some of the pressure on the professional staff, to extend the Party's influence into the enterprises, and to serve as a reservoir for training new cadres. In fact, however, the recruitment, organization and employment of volunteer Party forces created a series of political and administrative problems which reduced their overall effectiveness. Implementing a democratic and populist policy in the period before the November 1962 reorganization was relatively ineffective.

Similarly, the effort to institute a new style of *rukovodstvo* to replace the formal and bureaucratic stereotypes which had (or so it was believed) alienated the Party as an institution from Soviet society as a whole, seems not to have succeeded. The renewed emphasis upon *rukovodstvo* in terms of personal and moral leadership between leaders and led was a revived species of paternalism which, at best, may have had some positive effect in increasing the influence of Party leaders within agriculture. Paternalism failed, however, to cope with the tangled web of economic, technical, and administrative interests which underlay the operational problems of the Soviet economy.

PART THREE

THE PARTY AS ENTREPRENEUR:
A CASE STUDY

— 6 —

The Decision-making Context of the November Plenum

The November 1962 Plenum of the Central Committee, the first industrial plenum since July 1960, was Khrushchev's final and most significant effort to reform the Party and state managerial structures to achieve a breakthrough in the Party's leadership of the economy. In general, it was a more radical administrative response to the problems of economic efficiency and growth stemming from the maturity and complexity of the economy and to the short-term and political problems arising from the declining productivity of industry and agriculture.

Khrushchev's proposals to meet these issues were essentially intensifications of his earlier attempts to increase the Party's decision-making power over the industrial economy by functional specialization and mass mobilization. In the two years to follow, the Party's direct involvement in economic and technical functions and the degree of mass mobilization would reach a crisis pitch. Unlike previous periods, the environment was now too rigid and complex to respond to Khrushchev's effort to mobilize the economy in behalf of his programs and policies. His failure not only signalled political eclipse but introduced a historic new stage in Soviet politics.

The alternatives open to Khrushchev were limited by the resistance of the bureaucratic structures to transformation, by his own previous decisions, and by his restricted power. In the political context of 1962, he was required to deal with the diverse, conflicting forces which had arisen after Stalin's death as elements in the power structure. The politics underlying the reform will not be cast here into an explicit interest group framework. Although data are available, too many ambiguities remain to cloud the issue.

The politics of reform discussed here is fundamentally a bureaucratic politics; from it emerged the intricate and inconsistent compromises which produced the Party, managerial, and control structures of 1963 and 1964. These provide evidence of the limitations of Soviet political leadership after Stalin as well as an illustration of the practical modification by a major functional group in Soviet society of significant policy changes initiated by the Party. The change

123

following the November reorganization was sufficient only to create a modified, essentially unstable, and unsatisfactory balance of administrative forces in the management of the economy.

Whether the process of restructuring the Party, the agencies of industrial management, and the organs of Party and state control is conceived as a single, integrated set of changes or as three distinct but overlapping processes is basically a matter of analytical generalization. Conceived as a concrete, linear, chronological process, it seems clear that the initiation, development of support and opposition, approval, and implementation were all concentrated within the framework of the Presidium and the Secretariat. The sources of initiative, the term of each component's political development, the groups and interests involved, however, all point to a limited pluralism within the bureaucratic context. Moreover, the decisions to emerge from the November plenum suggest a complex pattern of short-range initiatives, compromises, and modifications over the entire process, while, in the case discussed here, implementation was crucial to the success of the enterprise. Overall, the plenum would approve two proposals in significantly modified form and veto one temporarily, and this, in general, is indicative of Khrushchev's limited power resources to achieve change.

1:

The Preludes to the November Plenum

Among the immediate pressures leading to the reorganization of the Party apparatus were the slowdown in the industrial growth rate and the failure of the territorial Party apparatus to respond to the challenges of decision-making and control placed on it by the 1957 industrial reform. The more intense pressure, however, arose from the virtual stagnation of agriculture after 1959, a condition threatening Khrushchev's personal status and his general strategy as well. There were, to be sure, many reasons for the lag in agriculture. Climate, soil, choice of technique, levels of investment, incentives and peasant values, communication—all were involved in Soviet agriculture's "permanent crisis."[1]

The problems stemming from the administration of agriculture, and especially from the Party's administrative role, were paramount.[2] With the January 1961 Plenum of the Central Committee, Khrushchev and the Party apparat turned decisively to agriculture. In 1961 alone, according to a Central Intelligence Agency study, sixteen of thirty-three of Khrushchev's speeches were predominantly devoted to agriculture.[3] The series of reorganizations in agricultural management revealed the same preoccupation.

To strengthen the Party's control over agriculture had induced virtually continuous reorganization since the September 1953 plenum.[4] Khrushchev's basic strategy in the countryside involved gradually whittling down the authority and functions of the central agricultural ministries and strengthening the local institutions of industrial management established during the early phases of collectivization.[5] In February 1958 the machine tractor stations were abolished.[6] The decline in the agricultural growth rate and the exposure at the January 1961 plenum of widespread fraud provided the springboard for a series of new reorganizations in the Party and state administrative structures, which would lead to the November 1962 plenum.

In 1961 the Ministry of Agriculture was stripped of most of its executive functions and transformed into an agricultural service agency. A new system of material-technical supply for agriculture was instituted, and the system of agricultural procurements was revised. At the raion level, an inspectorate with both procurement and executive responsibilities was set up to supervise the conclusion and execution of contracts with each kolkhoz and sovkhoz. To provide centralized, specialized guidance of agriculture, an ultimately abortive all-union committee was formed.[7]

But the 1961 administrative changes had little effect on stagnation in agriculture, and in March 1962, Khrushchev reasserted his intention of rebuilding the apparatus of agricultural management from its foundations. It was necessary, he declared, to set up a system of centralized agricultural management which would exercise direct, continuous control over production.[8] While the new managerial structure would differ significantly from the older form, two organizational principles of the 1961 reorganization would be strengthened: (1) the concept of a single, specialized Party-state agency for planning and coordinating agriculture would be preserved and extended to the republican and oblast levels; and (2) the concept of a single state agency concentrating the functions of agricultural management would find expression in the interdistrict territorial production administrations.

The coexistence of agricultural councils and territorial production administrations produced, as Howard Swearer has described it, a complex system in which a unified state agricultural agency was dominated by a Party-controlled network of committees.[9] The structure of the councils at both the union and regional levels revealed the extent to which Khrushchev had attempted to narrow and concentrate agricultural decision-making. The union council consisted of a deputy chairman of the Council of Ministers, the minister of procurements and of agriculture, the chairman of the union agricultural supply agency (Soiuzsel'khoztekhnika), and the heads of the agricultural departments of the Central Committee and the Gosplan SSSR. The structure of the republican and oblast councils was similar, with one important exception—here the chairman was the first secretary of the corresponding Party committee.[10] While it is perhaps unwarranted to see in the March 1962 agricultural councils the model for the agricultural oblast and republican bureaus created after the November 1962 plenum, there does appear to have been a strong element of continuity.

Most important, with the March agricultural reorganization the raion was abandoned as the local unit of agricultural administration. The average territorial production administration was formed on an interdistrict basis, including three to five raiony within its jurisdiction. In the Russian Republic, for example, 960 production administrations were formed, averaging 3.2 raiony and managing thirty to sixty collective and state farms.[11] The internal structures and composition of the territorial production administrations resembled those of the former machine tractor stations. They were designed to provide a pool of economic and technical expertise for the Soviet countryside. Each administration was composed of from thirty to forty agronomists, engineers, planners, and accountants; and daily guidance of the farms was organized through a corps of inspector-organizers, whose functions included extending technical and managerial assistance to the farm.[12]

The formation of interdistrict production administrations carried fundamental implications for the system of Party leadership of agriculture, which, despite numerous administrative shifts, had remained unchanged since Stalin.[13] The new Party structures were clearly a compromise. The old rural raikom was retained, but direct operational leadership was shifted to the oblast and republican Party committees. To give specific guidance, a new oblast Party official—the Party organizer—was detached along with three or four obkom instructors to each production administration. The oblast Komsomol committee similarly specialized its structure by sending special Komsomol organizers with instructors to the production administrations. The Party organizers were responsible for guiding both the Party and state organs with a view toward increasing the quality of information on conditions within their zones, selecting better cadres, and enforcing central policy.[14] The establishment of oblast Party officials with specialized zonal responsibilities recalled a similar arrangement at the raikom level between 1953 and 1957,[15] but this aspect of the March reorganization would vanish with the November plenum.

The new system of Party-state agricultural administration was in trouble from the start. In an unpublished *zapiska* circulated by Khrushchev in late 1961 or early 1962, the new system was opened for criticism and evaluation by local Party organs.[16] Judging from the criticism revealed in the discussions of the March plenum, the territorial Party apparatus reacted strongly against the new agricultural structures. Strenuous efforts were made to modify the new system. Proposals were advanced, for example, to establish the new production administrations on a district rather than interdistrict basis. Some officials wanted the raion newspaper retained on a district level. Others were opposed to Party organizers, who were removed from local control by being placed on the *nomenklatura* of the republican Central Committee. Efforts were also made to modify the agricultural councils by including an industrial official, the sovnarkhoz chairman, on the committee, or by placing an agricultural secretary rather than the first secretary as chairman of the council.[17] In the stenogram of the March plenum, the strongest critic of the new system was P. E. Shelest, then first secretary of Kiev, who seriously doubted the viability and utility of the whole system.[18]

The modifications pressed by the Party apparat were unheeded. Khrushchev's imposition of an obviously unpopular system of Party-state agricultural management reflected his attempt to solve the agricultural crisis by centralizing and specializing administrative power. In this sense, the March 1962 plenum represented no significant departure from Stalinist orthodoxy. In another respect, however, the plenum was a basic departure since it signified Khrushchev's determination to change the obkom first secretary from a political generalist to an economic specialist. This became apparent in his attempt to justify the formational particularities of the new councils. The appointment of the first secretary rather than an agricultural secretary to head the new councils, he declared, would ensure that the Party apparatus as a whole was concentrated on agriculture, unlike the existing system in which agricultural leadership was part of the general responsibilities of Party guidance.[19] G. I. Voronov expressed a similar preference for specialization in defending his decision to exclude sovnarkhoz chairmen from the new agricultural councils.[20]

During the spring and summer of 1962, the new system provoked serious problems and conflicts, the most prominent among them being the power struggle between the raion secretaries and the Party organization. This conflict became so bitter that a special conference was called in July 1962 to resolve the issue.[21] The July conference was an important stage in the development of the concept on which the November plenum was built. In his speech before the conference, Khrushchev committed the Party to the production, rather than the territorial, principle of agricultural management.[22] The old territorial system, expressed through the raion Party and soviet agencies, was obsolete. Agricultural management must be placed on an industrial basis, where "no one has the right to violate the organization or the technology of the production process."[23] The choice of the term "production administration," Khrushchev told the conference, was deliberate: "The inspector-organizer is the technologist of the production administration. These management agencies must be strengthened with the most highly qualified cadres."[24] In July, Khrushchev regarded the territorial production administration as the agricultural equivalent of the sovnarkhoz.[25]

The July conference produced only a set of temporary compromises for the conflicts of authority and jurisdiction in agriculture. One decision was to deny district Party or state agencies the right to interfere in "production questions." To resolve the conflict between the Party organizers and raikom first secretaries, the latter were subordinated to the organizers. The raion as an administrative unit, Khrushchev indicated, would be abolished. New, expanded territorial units based on the production administration would be formed, and the territorial services of the raion soviet administration were to be transferred to the new districts. Further changes, Khrushchev promised, would be undertaken only after additional discussion and consultation within the Party, but he emphasized that the production principle as the basic principle of management would be strictly maintained.[26]

Khrushchev's determination to specialize the Party apparatus according to economic sectors and to produce a structure of *rukovodstvo* based on the production principle was a logical development of his views on the proper role of the Party in the evolution of Soviet society, but it was deeply unpopular within the apparatus itself and it raised serious new problems. If, as Khrushchev indicated, the republican and oblast Party committees were to be committed to agricultural management, then a question arose concerning the Party's role in industry and construction as well as its control over ideological institutions. To pursue the process to its logical ultimate conclusion would not only vitally affect the decision-making and coordinating roles of the local Party organs but would also free major areas of Soviet life from systematic institutional control by the Party. The dilemmas of authority and function raised in the reform of agricultural management in the spring and summer of 1962 were sufficiently urgent to require further structural adjustment within the Party apparatus; in a major sense, the November 1962 plenum attempted to resolve those dilemmas.

The thrust for the structural reform of the Party at the November plenum was essentially at Khrushchev's initiative and was directed toward resolving the specific problems of agricultural management. The drive to reform the structures of industrial management was more complex and evoked a series of responses and solutions designed to accelerate the growth rate and intensify the rates of economic and technical innovation. There were three discernible, only partially reconcilable, trends, two operating within an orthodox ideological and institutional context. The third trend, which presented a distinctive alternative to the 1961 and 1962 system of management, was more controversial and prevailed only after Khrushchev's fall. The rise of a significant consensus in favor of economic methods of industrial management, however, was a major force in the structural outcomes of the November plenum.

The first, powerful change in 1959–60 was directed toward reimposing bureaucratic and centralist controls on the economy. This is reflected in the sharp increase in the number of centrally planned products; the formation of the republican sovnarkhozy in June and July 1960; the increasing centralization of investment planning and technical guidance of capital construction in October 1961;[27] and the efforts to resolve the critical supply problem through increased central controls, which also occurred in October 1961.[28] Administrative coercion accompanied the process. The laws of 27 May 1961 and 20 February 1962 were among the basic pieces of legislation designed to achieve administrative order through compulsion.[29]

The intensification of administrative controls was accompanied by a wave of arrests for economic crimes and a blatant anti-Semitic campaign only partially mitigated by simultaneous appeals to the social principle and mass orthodoxy. "Comrades' courts" and the "anti-parasite" campaigns were a type of coercive populism designed to mobilize and discipline the whole of Soviet society. A small group of older Bolshevik economists, however, held to the Marxist principle that the problems of economic management should be resolved through political and social methods. Their views were effectively represented by Academician Strumilin who envisioned the complete democratization of economic management through the election of economic officials, their periodic accountability to their constituents, and provisions for their recall.[30]

Although the intensification of traditional democratic centralism was an essentially conservative, orthodox response, the terms framing the discussion of reform were changing. In 1961, as Rush Greenslade has pointed out, the essential premises of a tightly centralized economy were politically acceptable.[31] By November 1962, this was no longer entirely true. The change was largely attributable to the development of an innovative interest group composed of economists and managerial officials who advanced a searching analysis of the existing system and offered a series of alternatives at sharp variance with existing practices.[32]

The July 1960 Plenum of the Central Committee is generally considered to be the turning point in the search for nonadministrative methods of economic management.[33] In March 1961, Gosekonomsovet convened a scientific conference on planning problems. The union conference induced a series of further conferences at the union and local levels in 1961 and 1962 in which the problems of planning and administration were openly and frankly discussed.[34] The momentum generated in 1961 and 1962 did not vanish with the November plenum. While the tempo and edge of criticism were somewhat reduced in 1963, an important conference on the uses of mathematics in planning was held in March 1964.[35] Following the round table discussions of March, the Soviet press again strongly criticized the existing system of management, pressing for those proposals which had been temporarily tabled in the spring of 1963.

The issues and themes developed in the 1961–64 discussions contained elements of both unity and diversity. Proponents of reform were substantially united on the basic proposition that the centralized and bureaucratic system of industrial management was, in some degree, obsolescent in view of the size, scale, specialization, interdependence, and technical sophistication of the present Soviet economy. The growing gap between administrative structure and economic and technical processes was an obstacle to economic growth and efficiency and required qualitative reforms to overcome bureaucratic inertia and managerial delinquency. In his excellent discussion of the debates on managerial reform stimulated by the July 1960 plenum, Professor Birman has noted eight specific issues raised in relation to economic reform, of which the most fundamental was the relative importance which administrative, economic, and social methods of administration would have in the general structure of industrial management.[36] The mass principle was given relatively little formal attention, although *edinonachalie* and collective methods of enterprise management were deeply divisive issues.

The major confrontation was between advocates of the administrative and economic points of view. Those who still held to a totally administered economic mechanism, as one Soviet commentator has pointed out, dreamed of a comprehensive bureaucratic state embracing the largest number of production relations, distributing resources from a single center, and administering the economy through direct, specific administrative orders and commands.[37] Those favoring a reorientation toward economic methods called this fantastic, insisting that under present conditions the only reliable method for ending the conflict of interests in the industrial system was by restructuring economic incentives.[38]

Centralization and decentralization of power, a basic issue of the November plenum, was implicated in the conservative-liberal conflict. To the conservative, the political integrity of the Soviet system of planning and administration demanded a high degree of centralization. Such managerial practices as the search for easy plans, excessive staff and supply, indifference to quality of output or technical progress proceeded from moral delinquency. To the liberal, the problem was a technical one centering on the issues of bureaucratic authority and the relevance of the success indicators in structuring managerial responses.[39]

Solutions ranged from a more extensive use of cybernetics in the planning system to a relatively conservative set of proposals focused on structural reform. Professor Gatovskii stated the case for cybernetics: "It is impossible to conduct planning at the highest degree of precision and effectiveness without mathematical methods."[40] But the March 1964 round table discussion on the use of computers revealed that the use of mathematical methods of planning raised deep ideological cleavages[41] and that state-of-the-art problems prevented any comprehensive adoption of computers in planning in 1962.[42] The more limited structural alternatives operating well within existing boundaries included demands for further reorganization of supply,[43] redefinition of the rights of the sovnarkhozy and the reform of its structure, and a series of proposals to reform the enterprise, including a new legal charter for the socialist enterprise and, above all, the expansion of the production association or "firm."[44]

The most comprehensive proposals for instituting economic methods of management were made by Evsei Liberman, a professor at the Kharkov Engineering

Economics Institute.[45] Liberman suggested profitability as a single, universal index for judging the effectiveness of an enterprise's performance. In place of the detailed production plan which officially guided the economic activity of the enterprise, Liberman advocated a system of central planning in which the enterprise would receive planned assignments for volume, assortment, and dates of delivery. Final determination of the plant's specific production schedule would be left to the plant itself. The radical decentralization of planning and the broad operational autonomy of the enterprise would be measured by profitability calculated as a percentage of fixed capital. The structure of incentives would be linked to profitability because deductions from profits would provide the sole source of funds to the incentive fund. In compiling a scale of incentives, Liberman stressed that a system of planned profits combined with a high degree of decentralization of authority would reduce the perennial search for investment and turnover capital, maximize equipment and resources, and reduce administrative overload. The new system of economic levers, Liberman explained, was designed to produce a qualitatively new administrative environment in Soviet industry.[46]

The practically conceivable alternatives for reforming the administrative structure in the fall of 1962 were therefore of two types: (1) a series of limited and segmental reforms in the tradition of Soviet administrative reform; and (2) the prospect of a qualitative reform through the adoption of economic methods and decentralization. The conflict between central and local officials reflected, of course, both the immediate interests of those officials directly affected and also characteristic habits and values deeply rooted in the czarist and Soviet administrative traditions.[47] To achieve a breakthrough, the supporters of economic methods had to overcome the central officials' profound distrust of the plant managers as a group, whom they regarded as essentially irresponsible and whose responses were therefore conditioned by the degree of external control exercised over them.

The selection of the Liberman proposals or some variant was significant on another level as well. Although omitted from the public polemics on administrative reform, it seems clear that the Liberman reforms were considered and probably extensively debated in the Central Committee for six months prior to the November plenum. While there is little to indicate the course of the debate or to identify the Party officials who opposed or supported, a number of considerations arise nevertheless.[48] In one respect, Liberman's reforms were incompatible with Khrushchev's determination to raise the leading role by increasing the Party's administrative power over the economy. To reduce central decision-making to general planning directives and to grant wide autonomy to the individual enterprise would conflict with this tendency, and the adoption of the production principle for framing the Party's structure in March and July of 1962 would only deepen the conflict. Yet, Khrushchev was not a man for formal logic or theoretical coherence. His concrete single-mindedness did not preclude adopting conflicting principles of Party and state organization.

In the broader relationship of traditional institutional forms of Party *rukovodstvo*, the incompatibility diminishes. The least affected functions of Party leadership would be the ideological and mobilizing functions, which operated for the most part independently of the structure and distribution of administrative power. It was the administrative role that would be most deeply affected by a full implementation of the economic method of administration. Daily interference in the details of administration as well as the traditional Party responsibility for planning and production would probably be reduced. But Liberman's reforms did not necessarily imply a total withdrawal of organized Party authority from economic administration.

Measured against the variants of Party guidance, it is the Malenkov variant of Party structure, with its reliance on production branch departments paralleling the organs of state administration, that was least compatible with Liberman's proposals. More harmonious was the Zhdanov variant, which stressed the distinctions between political and economic leadership and concentrated Party *rukovodstvo* on cadres and checkup and control. Most compatible with a highly decentralized system of economic management was direct guidance by fractions within the production units—most compatible but least likely, however, since this variant allowed the Party apparat only a minimal administrative role and was indistinguishable from revisionism.

In general, therefore, directing Party and managerial reform presented a paradox insofar as establishing the production principle in Party structure and, at the same time, instituting economic methods of management appeared logically incompatible. Curiously, the proponents of a generalist and nonspecialized system of Party *rukovodstvo* could find more harmony in administration by economic methods than those who, like Khrushchev, advocated a deeper and more extensive administrative involvement by Party organs in the daily affairs of economic management. That an alliance existed between Party conservatives and economic liberals seems doubtful. The actual structures to develop from the November plenum were the result of far more complexity than that.

These problems would be further complicated by the radical reorganization of checkup which was instituted at the November plenum. Although a constituent element in the general theory of *rukovodstvo*, the emphasis upon checkup varied during Khrushchev's rule. Generally underplayed in the years before the Twenty-first Congress, it gradually resumed importance in Khrushchev's strategy of raising the leading role until it had become a major instrument for the implementation of his policies. Stalin's separation of Party and state control and his decisive turning to a fundamentally bureaucratic system of *proverka* had sharply reduced the importance of specialized control agencies in the general structure of *rukovodstvo*. After Stalin's death, Goskontrol' emerged as a highly centralized agency with the bulk of its staff in Moscow and a small staff of officials scattered throughout the Soviet Union. This structural weakness of the Ministry of State Control was reflected in its lack of formal authority. Although it possessed some rights over the expenditure of resources by economic institutions, it lacked the right to call economic managers to account, to impose fines, to reprimand them without the authorization of the republican Council of Ministers, to order the managers to cease, or to correct violations.[49] The general impotence of state control, however, was not equally evident in the Party control agency whose powers were expanded at the Nineteenth Party Congress in 1952.[50]

The growth in Party control, however, was sharply reversed at the Twentieth Congress when the Party Control Committee was denied an independent staff in the localities and its formal authority was reduced to control over the personal affairs of Communists.[51] At the same congress, Khrushchev delivered a scathing attack on the USSR Ministry of State Control, scoring its inefficiency and bureaucratism and demanding that this "weakest link in the whole system of checkup" be "radically reorganized."[52] During Khrushchev's political decline in 1956, the Ministry of State Control emerged briefly as an instrument in the power struggle between Khrushchev and his opponents. In November 1956, V. M. Molotov was appointed its minister, and in the ensuing struggle between the Anti-Party Group and Khrushchev it was singled out for an especially sharp attack in March 1957.[53] With the defeat of Molotov and Khrushchev's other opponents in June 1957, the reorganization of the structure of state control proceeded smoothly. In August 1957, the Ministry of State Control was transformed into the Soviet Control Commission.[54] While the new commission would have formally enhanced powers, it would also lose power and status. Khrushchev's determination to implement a system of mass control in the state as well as in the Party apparatuses was an important aspect of this reform.

The failure of the territorial Party apparatus to control the managers stimulated Khrushchev's reliance on nonbureaucratic controls. A gradual but perceptible trend toward reestablishing centralized control was evident in the wake of the revelations of "localism" made known in 1958. Contrary to the Party Rules adopted in 1956, the Party Control Committee expanded its functions in 1958 to include control over economic functions.[55] Party and mass control were further increased by the founding of a specialized Party control mechanism in the enterprises in June 1959.

A similar emphasis was evident in the State Control Commission. In August 1959, the Chairman of the Soviet Control Commission, G. Eniutin, announced an all-out effort to increase control over the economic managers,[56] but this phase of control remained weak between 1959 and 1962. According to a 1959 article in *Partiinaia zhizn'*, the State Control Commission still lacked direction and coordination, permitted excessive duplication of effort, and was isolated from public support.[57]

The tendency toward a more powerful control structure was further stimulated by the revelations in January 1961 of widespread violation of Party and state discipline. In July 1961, as part of the general policy of administrative coercion, the Soviet Control Commission was reorganized and became the State Control Committee with a renewed mandate to impose stringent controls over the managerial bureaucracy.[58] There was continued stress on the social principle, which emphasized the role of nonstaff controllers and the formation of councils of controllers which would include not only state but Party and Komsomol officials as well.[59]

The precise structure of the strengthened system of control and the scope of authority of the control effort, however, aroused deep controversy. One issue involved the merging of the Party and state control structures; another involved the control to be exercised over the territorial Party apparatus. The first issue concerned the direct administrative role to be assumed by the Party in the management of control. One body of opinion, expressed, for example, by the chairman of the Kirgiz Goskontrol', argued for a unified system of state and social control formally independent of the regular Party organs.[60] The counter formula, pressed by Khrushchev, was for a unified system of Party, state, and social control which would include direct Party administration and control.[61] Although neither formula had gained a clear ascendancy at the Twenty-second Congress, the 1961 Party Program carried the formula of state and social control. The resolution of the Twenty-second Congress on this matter, however, included Khrushchev's preference for a combined Party, state, and social control.[62]

Closely related to the problems of structure were the problems of authority of the new control mechanism. Most penetrating was the question of whether the staff Party organs would again be subordinated to an external control agency. The argument for placing the Party agencies under the same external controls as the state bureaucracy was perhaps most forcefully stated by A. I. Boliasnyi, who held that the irregularities in the state apparatus had originated in the Party apparatus. In their efforts to conceal their own weaknesses, Party officials often shielded their counterparts in the state administration. To control the family group phenomenon, Boliasnyi advocated the formation of a joint Party-state control agency under the administrative authority of the Party.[63] Whether Khrushchev personally sought to place the Party organs under external control and thereby reverse the policy of the Twentieth Congress is ambiguous. That he was clearly committed to making the local Party organs formally accountable was made abundantly clear at the Twenty-second Congress.[64] But the precise scope and structure of the unified, centralized control mechanism remained in doubt through 1962.

2

The Formation of the New
Party Structures

The November 1962 plenum was the last major effort which Khrushchev was permitted in his search for institutional reform. But the structural alternatives of the reform were in deep dispute at the plenum. In one sense, the evolution of the new Party, state, and control structures was the result of compromises negotiated in an atmosphere of intense bargaining and struggle among various points of view and interests. In another sense, however, the managerial structures followed a logic consistent with the previous experience of reform in the post-Stalin period.

The radical administrative changes in Party structure which Khrushchev announced at the November plenum stemmed essentially from his vindication of the production principle over the territorial principle in Party structure. In this respect, the new Party organs represented a solution to the conflict which had arisen in agricultural management after the March plenum. The November plenum, however, extended the production principle to the whole Party structure and in so doing resolved the evident problems of Party *rukovodstvo* which had arisen from concentrating the energies of the territorial apparatus on agriculture. In pressing for a Party structure based upon the economic branch, Khrushchev created the structural conditions for full concentration of Party resources on economic development at the same time that he raised profound doubts in the Party apparat of the general legitimacy and specific utility of the reorganization.

In justifying the new Party structures, Khrushchev argued the utility of the reforms in terms of managerial efficiency and largely ignored their implications for the basic traditions of *rukovodstvo*. The implementation of the production principle in reorganizing the apparat, Khrushchev held, had five major advantages: (1) The new structures would permit the concentration of all Party forces on production; (2) they would increase the apparat's capacity to intervene deeper and more concretely into the technical and economic aspects of the production process; (3) they would enhance the Party's entrepreneurial role, particularly in relation to technical progress; (4) specialization would provide an opportunity for more careful, efficient placement of cadres; and (5) the new structures would strengthen the Party's capacity to control the execution of decisions.[65] Above all, he seemed convinced that the reorganization would deal with two specific problems which the development of a mature industrial economy joined with a crisis in agriculture had produced.

The system of general *rukovodstvo* and the territorial principle associated with it—in which the republican and oblast secretariats were responsible for the over-all direction and guidance of the economies within their territorial jurisdictions—had outlived its usefulness. It was no longer possible, he declared, for a single Party agency to guide both industry and agriculture effectively. Under the existing system, the apparat's major attention was directed to either one branch or the other, with the consequence that either one or the other escaped continuous Party control at the oblast or republican levels.[66] This condition Khrushchev implied was largely responsible for the slowdown in industrial growth after 1960.

Beginning in 1960, the Central Committee had concentrated the forces of the republican and oblast committees on agriculture with the result that industry was ignored. In evidence of this, Khrushchev cited 1962. Of the more important 100 questions discussed at the sixty republican plena, only five were on industry. Of the 215 questions discussed at the obkom plena of the twenty-five largest industrial oblasti, only fourteen were directed toward industry.[67] Dividing and specializing the apparat seemed the logical corrolary of recovering de facto Party control over the industrial economy. Another issue which Khrushchev believed the reorganization would resolve was the selection of Party cadres, particularly first secretaries of oblast committees. In oblasti with well-developed industrial and agricultural bases, selecting an industrial or agricultural specialist to head the committee was particularly difficult. Under the new structures this important problem would automatically be resolved.[68]

Khrushchev outlined his views on the new structure in two basic documents. In a *zapiska* to the Presidium, dated 10 September 1962, he presented to the apparat the generalities of the proposed reorganization. Two and one-half months later, following the apparat's strong reaction to the proposals and the Cuban missile crisis, he presented a refined and expanded version of the new structure which was modified only in detail. In examining these proposals, an important continuity with the previous nine years becomes evident. Before November 1962, structural reform was directed principally at the local Party organs. The November plenum's principal targets, however, were the central and regional Party apparatuses, levels of the Party hierarchy which had been only moderately affected in the previous period.

The September memorandum was focused primarily on the oblast and republican committees. As expected, it proposed liquidating the rural raikom.[69] At the oblast level, two Party committees would be formed to lead industry and agriculture. Each Party committee would guide all the agencies of industrial or agricultural production independently of territorial location. Each obkom would remain independent of the other, operating under the direct control of the republican committee.[70] Reorganizing the republican committee was evidently intended to facilitate this control over the branch obkom. At the republican level, a single committee would be retained, but separate bureaus would be established for the guidance of industry and agriculture. To coordinate and direct the republican committee, a presidium for general *rukovodstvo* was proposed. In the special case of the RSFSR, Khrushchev suggested that the Russian Bureau, divided into separate branch bureaus, be subordinated directly to the Presidium of the Central Committee.[71]

Between the September 10 memorandum and the convening of the November plenum, these proposals were further developed and adjusted. Khrushchev proposed that the gorkom be abolished in those cities in which the oblast and republican centers contained an obkom and gorkom with raikomy. More important were his additions and modifications for the management of agriculture.[72] The unwieldy territorial production administrations were to be reduced in size and increased by one-third in number. The rural raion and raikom were finally abolished. The office of oblast Party organizer was dropped and a new, hybrid Party organ formed for the leadership of agriculture. The new Party organ was formed by expanding the structure of the primary Party organ attached to the production territorial administration. Formed on the production principle but given the rights of a raikom, the new structure was headed by a secretary and two deputy secretaries, the latter heading the organizational and ideological otdely of the new committee.[73] To point up their departure from the traditional bureaucratic style of *rukovodstvo*, the lower officials of the apparat were designated "inspector-Party organizers." Since the new rural organs were responsible only for agricultural production and services, a new organ was to be formed for the guidance of industry in rural areas. The new zonal production industrial Party committees were structured much like their agricultural counterparts, although they were not attached to any single state organ and their instructors functioned under the old designation.[74]

The republican and oblast structures proposed in the September memorandum were least altered at the November plenum. In November, Khrushchev added an explosive proposal which was not in the September memorandum: he favored a radical reduction in the number of obkom secretaries from the usual four to two.[75] In addition, but without indicating the nature of the changes he had in mind, Khrushchev declared that the obkom departments, presently inadequate to the tasks of economic management, would be basically reorganized. Khrushchev's determination to emasculate the obkom eludes analysis because of the lack of concrete evidence. It is not certain, for example, whether such a proposal was simply an unexpressed component of the blueprint for the Party reform he had advanced in September or whether it was a vindictive political response to the apparat's opposition to the reform. The proposals, of little practical significance in structuring the new oblast organs, are nonetheless important because they indicate the sharp deterioration in the political relationships of Khrushchev and the obkom first secretaries which would culminate in the events of October 1964.

In his September memorandum and report to the November plenum, Khrushchev was perhaps least candid about the changes to be introduced into the central Party apparat. The new central Party organs were formed in secrecy, with their authority, structures, and functions beclouded and in conflict from the start. In his report to the plenum, Khrushchev revealed the formation of the Central Asian Bureau, under the direct control of the Presidium, for the guidance of the Uzbek, Kirgiz, Turkmen, and Tadzhik republics.[76] In contrast to his determination to form the Russian Bureau along production lines, the Central Asian Bureau would be formed on the territorial principle and would guide both industry and agriculture. Nothing done by Khrushchev at the plenum illustrates so well his willingness to breach a general principle in favor of a specific situation and insight.

More problematical were the three branch bureaus and two internal Party commissions which sprang suddenly from the plenum. Khrushchev's report mentioned briefly, without discussion or amplification, the formation within the Central Committee of two bureaus for industry and construction and for agriculture.[77] It is clear, however, that these bureaus were in addition to the industrial and agricultural bureaus of the Russian Bureau.[78] A basic ambiguity and conflict underlying the formation of these organs was evident, however, by the announcement on the final day of the plenum that not two, but three branch bureaus, each headed by a Central Committee secretary, would be formed. The announcement that the Central Committee would form an Ideological Commission and a Commission for Organizational-Party Questions, to be headed by secretaries of the Central Committee, was also made on the last day of the plenum but without public discussion or even indication that such structures were under consideration.[79]

The absence of hard data reduces judgment of this aspect of the plenum to speculation. The simultaneous broadening, specializing, and collectivizing of the decision-making processes was undoubtedly intended to increase and regularize the processes of consultation. That such organs would also reduce the influence and status of the central apparat seems reasonably clear. The obscure, bitter, and largely successful struggle of the apparatchiki to frustrate the functioning of these organs also testifies to the alienation between Khrushchev and the apparat in the final two years of his rule.

The Reform of Economic Management

In his report to the plenum, Khrushchev admitted that the Soviet industrial economy was lagging in its most basic indicators. This, of course, was not new. Labor productivity was behind the goals set for the Seven-Year Plan, with wages outstripping productivity for whole regions of the country despite the additions of capital, energy, and qualified workers to the economy. Technological progress was also seriously lagging. The production of obsolete products, poor standardization of parts, the growth rather than the decline of universal plants had raised costs, complicated supply, and increased repair. Capital construction presented major difficulties. Investment remained scattered and the number of uncompleted plants was growing in spite of earlier efforts to control these problems. Design and documentation facilities were scattered and still unspecialized. New construction was poorly supplied with documentation and raw materials. Localism was still rife within the construction industry.[80]

Khrushchev searchingly criticized the system of planning, scoring particularly its inefficiency and unresponsiveness to new methods and needs. The officials of the State Planning Commission and the State Scientific-Economic Commission, he intimated, were technical and economic conservatives. They still planned economic growth by mechanically assigning arithmetical increase of existing proportions by branch and region, a procedure containing an inherent bias against new industries, such as the chemical. The central planners, he declared, wore "steel blinders"; they opposed any replacement of metal with synthetic raw materials and met every decision to reduce steel production with a cry for more steel. Yet, they were extravagantly wasteful of metal as well as of other raw materials in short supply. In addition, production plans were poorly coordinated. The chronic tire shortage which rendered many automobiles inoperative was largely due to the fact that their production was planned in a different Gosplan department from that which planned the production of automobiles, and the plans were uncoordinated. Lack of coordination and its results were also reflected in the frequent changes in the annual plan and in the disjunctions of the production and supply plan. Khrushchev agreed that part of the disorder in planning could be traced to the system of success indicators. He was convinced that the index of value of production did not lead to a proper evaluation of the work of the enterprises or to the stimulation necessary for efficient use of capital.[81]

The intermediate and local levels of economic administration were also sharply criticized. Sovnarkhoz administrations were too small. That many more plants within the smaller sovnarkhozy failed in plan fulfillment than in larger sovnarkhozy Khrushchev attributed to the size of the administrative unit; he therefore proposed that the number of sovnarkhozy be reduced and their jurisdictions expanded. Since local industry generally showed higher costs and produced lower quality goods under the soviets than comparable plants under the sovnarkhozy, Khrushchev wanted the control of local industry passed to the enlarged sovnarkhozy. Under the new scheme, the local soviets would be confined to the improvement of public services. Finally, Khrushchev made the numerous small construction trusts, poorly equipped with cadres and resources, basically responsible for the problems of capital construction. Construction trusts would be removed from the jurisdiction of the sovnarkhozy, and industry and construction would be placed under separate administrative structures.[82] By enlarging and specializing local administrative organs, Khrushchev sought (as in the parallel reorganization of agricultural administration) to secure the advantages of centralized direction and concentration of human and technical resources provided by large-scale administration. Less evident was his willingness to sacrifice the advantages of decentralized and small-scale relations.

Placed against the various alternatives for managerial reform which arose in 1961 and 1962, Khrushchev's criticism of the central and local planning and administrative order presents a familiar dualism. While he and the economists agreed on the ills of the existing system, they differed over the prescriptions required to restore its administrative health. Rush Greenslade is probably correct in attributing the difference to a distinction between the intellectual and pragmatic approaches to reform. To Khrushchev, the bad specific practices of economic administration did not require a theoretical construction to resolve.[83] As his proposals for the reform of local administration suggest, he applied this kind of thinking (noted in relation to his proposals to reform the Party structure) to the state administrative system as well. The eclectic, conservative, and often contradictory nature of the reform may therefore be attributed not only to the complexity of the situation itself but to Khrushchev's intellect and political style as well. Nonetheless, a discussion of these measures within such an analytical framework produces useful insights into Khrushchev's approach to institutional reform.

Concerning the administrative, social, and economic methods of management, Khrushchev sought simultaneously to strengthen both the administrative and social levers of control. Administrative centralism, dominant since 1960, was further reinforced. Planning would once again be concentrated in a single organ, the State Planning Committee.[84] Secondly, Khrushchev favored full control of technical policy in the state branch committees situated in Moscow.[85] Tighter centralized administrative controls over capital construction were evident in the strengthened State Construction Affairs Committee.[86] An even more convincing example was the new Council of the National Economy, an organ that would be given full administrative authority and that would relieve Gosplan and the Current Commission of the Council of Ministers of the decision-making related to current plan fulfillment.[87] The trend toward centralization of authority within the administrative hierarchy was equally evident in the creation of the interrepublican Central Asian Sovnarkhoz and other union agencies in Central Asia and the amalgamation of sovnarkhozy in the Russian and Ukrainian republics.

Khrushchev's heavy reliance on administrative methods to correct the administrative structure was not a simple return to administrative Stalinism. His hostility to bureaucratism was expressed in the plenum in a strong commitment to the social principle. Khrushchev's insight that the key to invigorating the administrative structure lay in the formation of strong communal bonds at the grass roots level was revealed in an interesting anecdote. The proper way to secure the cooperation of the workers at the bench was to approach them in a democratic, comradely spirit, not in a formal, impersonal, bureaucratic fashion. He recalled the economic disaster in the Donbass in 1922. Struggling to raise output, he had gone to the workers, explained the country's need for coal, and in response the miners had assumed heavier obligations.[88]

Ideology seems also to have influenced his thinking. The populist, even revisionist, cast of his thought at the Twenty-second Congress was undiminished at the plenum. The belief that the ultimate solution to the problem of the state lay in its withering away and the replacement of specialized bureaucracies with workers' self-administration remained a basic element in his argument for mass participation. He also continued to emphasize the role of the masses in overcoming bureaucratic stagnation. Conservative bureaucrats, embedded in their routines, had to be directly controlled by the masses. Only by relentless, withering criticism could the sluggish bureaucracy be made responsive to the changed conditions and new demands of the economy. As the formation of the new organs of mass control would show, Khrushchev's insistence on the necessity for mass control was more than rhetoric.[89]

The emphasis on strengthened administrative and social methods did not preclude the adoption of economic methods, but Khrushchev reacted cautiously to the debate on the Liberman reforms. Aware of the faults of the system of success indicators, he accepted the need for experimentation to find more effective gauges of enterprise activity.[90] Khrushchev rejected the argument of "several economists" that profitability was incompatible with socialism. Rather, he adopted the moderates' view that while profitability could not be used as the basic index for stimulating society as a whole, it was acceptable if confined to the enterprise.[91] Except for this reservation, Khrushchev seemed to endorse the introduction of some form of economic method in planning:

Recently, in *Pravda, Izvestiia,* and *Ekonomicheskaia gazeta* a serious discussion of a broad circle of questions on economics has developed. Many specialists of industry and construction, managerial personnel, and economic scholars have participated in it. In the course of the discussions and in letters sent directly to the Central Committee, many valuable proposals were introduced. The planning organs, the Institute of Economy of the Academy of Sciences must attentively study these proposals in order to use everything useful, rational for the improvement of planning. On the basis of an analysis of these proposals, recommendations of an economic character should be elaborated which are directed toward the improvement of the planning of production and scientific organization of labor.[92]

Whether this fully endorses the Liberman proposals is unclear since Khrushchev fails to mention the radical decentralization of authority and increase in the discretion of the enterprise which was an integral component of this particular reform. Although the plenum clearly favored further centralization, it was not a direction to which Khrushchev was fully committed. Having proposed strong central administrative organs for planning and administration, he was cautious about the degree of authority and functions which these organs should possess. For Khrushchev to have proposed the unconditional strengthening of union Gosplan, an organ which he described as the center of bureaucratic and conservative opposition to his plans, was inconceivable. He therefore not only divested Gosplan of its supply and operational functions but reduced its authority in relation to the annual plan. The fundamental responsibility for composing and executing the annual plan would be placed on the republican gosplany and sovnarkhozy, with the functions of Union Gosplan limited to aggregating and balancing the plans presented by the republics.[93] Similarly, Khrushchev sought to balance and check the power of the new Council of the National Economy by his emphasis upon the expanded rights and authority of the new, enlarged sovnarkhozy. It seems clear that he relied on these organs to counteract localist tendencies or "the attempt to build a closed economy" by securing excessive investment and material-technical resources.[94]

The plenum, therefore, did not in fact ensure an absolute ascendancy of either centralization over decentralization or of the branch over the territorial principle. A similar lack of precision characterized Khrushchev's discussion of the role and authority of the enterprise in the new managerial system. Concerning the authority of the manager and the production collective, Khrushchev once again indicated his preference for social rather than administrative-coercive methods. Upholding *edinonachalie*, he nonetheless argued that in large plants employing thousands of workers it was physically impossible for the director to decide all questions arising in all the production and social relations of the plant. To achieve such a pervasive control required mass participation. To link the authority of the manager and mass administration, Khrushchev announced still another social organ at the mass level—an elected production committee which would function as a general consultative body to the director.[95]

Khrushchev's adherence to the conventional formula for the distribution of power within the enterprise suggests again his qualified enthusiasm for those aspects of the Liberman reform stressing the autonomy of the enterprise, but this is not certain. Adopting a cardinal point of those advocating an increase in the interdependence and authority of the director, he ordered as part of the overall program of modernization a reexamination of the legal structure and powers of the enterprise. How open Khrushchev was to a fundamental change in internal structure and external authority of the enterprise is unknown since he failed to specify the direction such a law should take. If the new Law on the Socialist Enterprise, however, was framed in consultation with the more liberal scholars and enterprise officials, significant changes in the role of the enterprise seemed in the offing. That such a statute would legislate the Liberman reforms, however, was unlikely in the fall of 1962.

The New Forms of Party and State Control

The whole nature of Party and state structural reform was complicated by the reversion to a system of centrally directed mass control. Replacing bureaucratic by public methods of control was a clear extension of Khrushchev's line at the Twenty-second Congress, but extensive justification was required to establish its legitimacy. The existing system of control was therefore linked with Stalin, the secret police, and the repressions which followed the Seventeenth Congress, which abandoned mass control.[96] The positive sanctions for combining Party and state control in a single mechanism were to be found in Lenin's final writings on public administration. According to Khrushchev, uniting the Workers'-Peasants' Inspectorate and the Central Control Commission had been Lenin's mature solution to the problem of controlling bureaucratism and crime.[97]

But Khrushchev's historical account of the Twelfth Congress and the subsequent activity of the TsKK-RKI skated over some of the acute problems raised by combining Party and state control. The savage conflict between the Party apparatus and the control organs and the encroachments on the authority and jurisdiction of the Party organs by the control agencies, particularly in economic decision-making, were passed over in silence. It was perhaps to be expected that Khrushchev would not mention the use of the Party-state control organs together with the GPU and Commissariat of Justice as instruments for purging the Party apparat of Stalin's opponents. That such a structure might be used to consolidate his own power by purging the territorial apparatus was at least an abstract possibility in the fall of 1962.

There is little evidence, however, that Khrushchev intended a political use of the strengthened control mechanisms. His intention, as he had so frequently stated in the preceding period, appears to have been to mount sufficient mass pressure to force the managerial apparatus into adopting those measures necessary for economic growth. Basically, he charged the existing system of control with ineptitude. The control exercised by the local Party organs, especially at the republican and oblast levels, was generally weak.[98] Restricting the Party Control Committee and its local organs to investigating the personal affairs of Communists had further limited Party control.[99] The state control apparatus functioned even less satisfactorily. It was passive in raising basic questions for decision, and it exercised weak control over such economic crimes as deception, bribery, waste, theft of public property, and graft—crimes which Khrushchev considered to be widespread.[100] Finally, he was impatient with the legal delays in correcting problems uncovered by state control. The inability of state control agencies to take immediate action was a basic weakness of bureaucratic control.

A "single, all-encompassing, permanently acting" system of control would presumably correct these deficiencies. The new organs would be primarily responsible for extirpating and controlling managerial abuses prevalent under both the ministerial and sovnarkhoz administrative systems. Particular emphasis was to be placed on production control over inputs and quality, which Khrushchev admitted was low.[101] The emphasis on external control to eliminate the tenacious abuses of enterprise management provides important additional commentary on Liberman's proposals. Khrushchev obviously rejected the economists' argument that these practices would be eliminated on a wide scale only as a result of self-correction by the managers themselves. Economic self-interest was in his view insufficient motivation in this respect.

In addition to economic control, Khrushchev expected the new agencies of Party-state control to play a major role in controlling inflated staffs, irrational structure, and red tape.[102] They should also open up an alternative line of communication to the center. Despite the massive reporting to Moscow from a variety of agencies at the local level, Khrushchev was dissatisfied with the existing system of communication and bore a residue of distrust from the report-padding and deception scandals of 1961 and 1962.[103] He held that the new agencies should be staffed with "a group of inspectors qualified for the investigation of affairs connected with bribery, pilfering, speculation" and indicated that they should have police powers as well.[104]

Whether the Party-State Control Committee could realize these functions would depend on the authority and structure with which it was endowed. Although it would be a joint Party-state institution, Khrushchev indicated that it would be a Party structure.[105] Two politically sensitive issues arose in connection with the committee's authority: (1) the degree to which the new organs would operate independently of the territorial apparat; and (2) the committee's authority to investigate and control the Party apparat. The authority issue probably presented a serious dilemma to Khrushchev.

A centrally directed structure operating independently of the territorial apparatus would more effectively cut through the tangled web of local interests limiting control of local Party organs. But centralized control would further divide Party authority, further reduce the status of local Party organs, institute serious jurisdictional conflicts between staff and control agencies, heighten central-local tensions, and thereby contribute to a further deterioration in Khrushchev's relations with the territorial apparatus. To place the local agencies of control under the regular Party apparat, however, would nullify their efficiency as instruments of the central will. Similar doubts must have informed his considerations of turning the control agencies against the Party as well as the state agencies.

Insofar as his scattered remarks at the plenum suggest his views, Khrushchev's inclination appears to have been to create a control structure independent of the Party's staff organs. Two clues, inconclusive in themselves, were the joint Party-state sponsorship of the committee and the historical precedent on which it was founded. The implication of centralization was more direct in his statement: "In the republics, kraia, and oblasti, committees of Party-state control should be created, in our opinion, which would be organs of the Committee of Party-State Control in the localities."[106] Although Khrushchev gave no indication of the scope which the new organs should have, only a fully centralized control structure would have had the power to place the local Party organs under permanent observation.

3

The Responses to the November Plenum

As Priscilla Blake has noted, the changes proposed by the November plenum were, on the whole, unpopular.[107] Part of this dissatisfaction can be attributed to the atmosphere of doubt and uncertainty accompanying the campaign against economic crime, with its barely concealed anti-Semitic overtones.[108] The serious blow to Soviet prestige following the Cuban missile crisis and the Sino-Soviet dispute undoubtedly contributed as well. The reorganization itself, unmatched in scope and intensity in the previous nine years, promised far-reaching effects on virtually every function and group within the Soviet administrative system. But many of Khrushchev's proposed reforms were indeterminate and ambiguous in character, and the interstices of the new Party, state, and control structures were loose enough to stimulate intensive bargaining and maneuver within each of the major structures.

Inevitably, the interests of different groups and of individuals within groups were affected in different ways, and divisions of opinion probably cut across Party and state lines. Nevertheless, Khrushchev's initiatives of reform did evoke serious opposition, particularly within the Party apparat and directed against the Party reform. A less public politics was involved in framing the authority and structures of the state and control apparatuses. It seems evident that the framework around which the new organs were created materially affected the quality of their functioning in the next two years.

Responses to the New Party Structures

The Party apparat's hostility to the strategy of transforming the Party into an economic managerial apparatus was a continuation of the earlier hostility to the transformation of Party *rukovodstvo* in agriculture. That such a transformation was the intention of the plenum was made explicit in a *Pravda Ukrainy* editorial noting that, henceforth, the Party official was to be an economist,[109] a role in sharp contrast to the usual view of the apparatchik as a politician. This perception of the fundamental shift in the role of the Party apparat aroused bitter controversy within the Party ranks on the legitimacy of the reform.

Opposition before the plenum was expressed in a variety of ways. In his *zapiska* of 10 September, Khrushchev proposed that the new Party structures be adopted in January or February 1963, after the harvest, at a Party conference.[110] The actual event occurred at an ordinary Central Committee plenum only ten days after the public notice of its convocation. The expansion of the agenda of reform to include the state and control mechanisms suggests that the plenum was a hurried affair and that the anticipated changes had not been fully worked out. Another indication of underlying tension is to be seen in the events which followed Khrushchev's submission of his memorandum of 10 September to the Presidium. On 28 September, *Pravda* unexpectedly published an alleged newly discovered variation of Lenin's March 1918 brochure "Immediate Tasks of Soviet Government," which justified the primacy of "economics over politics."[111] The publication of a new document by Lenin directly legitimating a controversial policy of Khrushchev's two weeks after the submission of his memorandum seems to have been a counterresponse to the initial opposition. Similarly, the publication of Evtushenko's poem "Stalin's Heirs" on 21 October (reportedly on Khrushchev's direct orders) appears to have been a further blow against the conservatives who were, in Evtushenko's view, biding their time and awaiting an opportunity to return to power.[112]

Unlike the March plenum, when apparat opposition was open, the stenographic report of the November plenum is suggestive of general approval and gives little indication of the storm to follow. Expressions of support for Khrushchev, to whom the reforms were freely and personally attributed, ranged from the personally favorable praise of speakers like Voronov and Rashidov to the mechanical, formal statements of D. A. Kunaev, the first secretary of Kazakhstan, who would soon be replaced.[113] A more sensitive indicator of the degree of support for Khrushchev personally was the apparat's response to the denunciation of Stalin and his methods. Only the three Transcaucasion first secretaries made strong, direct attacks on Stalin;[114] and among state officials speaking at the plenum, only A. P. Volkov, the chairman of the State Committee on Labor and Wages, launched an extensive attack on Stalin.[115] For the rest, routine references to the cult of personality were accompanied by assurances that its consequences had been overcome, thereby blocking any extensive attack on the conservatives opposing the reorganization.

Specific plans for reorganizing the Party structure were discussed guardedly. Only Podgorny, then first secretary of the Ukraine and closely associated with

Khrushchev, mentioned in passing the necessity for reforming the central apparat.[116] The formation of interrepublic administrative organs received routine approval among the first secretaries of the Central Asian republics, except that Usubaliev, the Kirgiz first secretary, failed explicitly to approve the formation of the Central Asian Bureau.[117] Extending interrepublican agencies to the Transcaucasus and possibly to the Baltic republics received less support. The suggestion by Akhundov, the first secretary of Azerbaidzhan, to study the Central Asian experience with a view toward adopting it in the Transcaucasus, was not supported by the first secretaries of Georgia or Armenia. To the more limited proposal to unite under one regional administration specific aspects of the economy, such as the electrical power system and the oil industry, V. P. Mzhavanadze of Georgia was more amenable.[118] But Zarobian, the first secretary of Armenia, pointedly ignored any, even the most limited, form of interrepublican cooperation, and the formation of interrepublican organs for the Baltic republics went unmentioned. In an interesting aside, however, P. I. Morozov, the first secretary of Amur, suggested forming a Far Eastern Bureau for guiding the obkomy in the Soviet Far East.[119]

Indirect discussion of the changes in the central apparat also arose in connection with the new republican and oblast structures. But A. P. Liashko, first secretary of the Donetsk Obkom, expressed two problems in relation to the oblast: (1) a fear that the reorganization of the Party structure would seriously reduce the obkom's autonomy relative to the republican committee; and (2) a doubt concerning the new relations between the urban and rural sectors of Soviet society. Specifically, though indirectly, Liashko raised doubts concerning the legitimacy of splitting the guidance of industry and agriculture, citing a 1921 letter of Lenin's instructing the Donbass Party organization to maintain close contact with the countryside. Liashko introduced another note at the plenum which would be heard again later. Calling attention to the competition between the industrial and agricultural obkomy in the struggle for resources, he proposed placing the responsibility for rural construction under the industrial oblast committee.[120] On the issue of abolishing the rural raikom, the source of such serious friction in the spring and summer of 1962, the speakers at the plenum entered no protest.

The stenographic report of the November plenum did not accurately reflect the apparat's opposition to the new Party structure, but it seems clear that the opposition lacked sufficient power to force any abandonment, delay, or serious modification of the proposals. The major exceptions involved the restructuring of the central and obkom secretariats. That the opposition should focus with some degree of success on preserving these structures without fundamental change seems entirely natural in view of their central role in exercising Party *rukovodstvo*. The struggle over the formation and authority of the branch bureaus was evident at the plenum and for two years afterwards. In view of the normally tight control exercised by the central leadership over the proceedings of the Central Committee, it seems reasonable to assume that the question of forming the new secretarial organs had been decided before the plenum. It also appears probable, if not altogether certain, that the Presidium had agreed upon two branch bureaus and had selected one, and probably both, secretaries. Demichev's speech to the plenum, for example—his stress on chemistry and on consumer goods—seems to bespeak his selection as a bureau secretary.[121]

On the last day of the plenum, following Khrushchev's unreported concluding speech, a short statement announced the addition of six members to the Secretariat, including three who were to head the new branch bureaus. From the very beginning, however, the power and status of these organs in the Secretariat's decision-making structure was problematical. In the weeks and months following the plenum, they were shrouded in silence. No public announcement concerning their structure or roles was ever made. Khrushchev himself ignored them after the plenum, notwithstanding that they were almost certainly formed at his initiative and in pursuit of his ends. The most reasonable explanation for their subsequent marginal role apparently lies in the hostility with which they were met at the central levels of the Party leadership.

Khrushchev was also forced to modify his proposed Party structure for the industrial and agricultural secretariats. His key proposal to reduce the obkom secretariats to two members was scrapped. Although there is no information concerning the struggle on this issue, the ultimate formation of four-man secretariats was a decisive defeat for Khrushchev. The conservative opposition's victory was significant because it virtually ensured the secretariat's continued dominance at this reduced but still important level of the Party structure. Fundamentally, therefore, the apparat's largely successful opposition to a qualitative reform of the secretarial structures at the central and oblast levels seriously reduced the overall effect of the reorganization on internal Party relationships and on the role of the new structures in guiding the state managerial apparatus.

Such judgments come with hindsight, but it is clear that the psychological reaction was such that the legitimacy of the reform and Khrushchev's personal authority were challenged. Within a week after the plenum, the most prestigious authorities on Party *stroitel'stvo* began to defend the new Party structure in print, and their defenses revealed both the extent and specific directions of the criticism. Critics charged that the reform lacked legitimacy because it was the subjective, arbitrary act of an individual rather than the result of objective necessity. It was also held that breaking down the traditional wall between Party and economic functions would lead to the substitution of economic organs by the Party apparat.[122] "Dogmatists" charged that ideological work was being thrown overboard,[123] that the split in the obkom Party organization would decelerate the drawing together of town and country, and that the reform pointed to a decline in the leading role.[124] The Chinese charge of revisionism levelled against Khrushchev was unquestionably echoed within the Party apparat.

Much criticism was directed against the reform's inconsistency with institutionalized ideology.[125] Attacking the numerous officials whom he believed to be still infected with Stalinism, E. Bugaev, the editor of *Partiinaia zhizn'*, argued that Party forms were not a procrustean bed into which reality had to be forced. In particular, he emphatically denied the charge that the new structures directly contradicted the Leninist tradition.[126] D. Chesnokov, considered a Stalinist ideologue, justified the new Party and state structures by recalling in *Kommunist* the view that the territorial principle was linked with the exploiter society.[127] Possibly the most interesting defense was offered by V. Stepanov, an official in the Ideological Department, who argued that the new Party organization represented a decisive break with the Stalinist view of the Party as an instrument of command based on military discipline. The new Party structure, he insisted, would transform the Party into an ideological and political leader.[128]

The key issue in the struggle over the reform's legitimacy, however, was the validity of the formula of economics over politics. The publication in September of the document in which Lenin purportedly justified the primacy of economics in Party *rukovodstvo* evidently failed to quell doubts concerning the formula's conformity with Marxism.[129] Another doubt: did the formula conform with Leninism? In the exchange of quotations from Leninist scripture, opponents of the reform cited Lenin's opposition to Trotskii in the 1920 trade union controversy in support of politics over economics.[130] G. I. Glezerman advanced a more sophisticated defense of the fundamentally political role of the Party, arguing that the economic basis for class conflict still existed within Soviet society. While Glezerman did not advocate a return to class dictatorship in the Stalinist or Chinese manner, the implication was clear that the Party's political role in the building of communism could not be abandoned.[131] In rebuttal of this particular criticism, supporters of the reform simply reiterated Khrushchev's basic strategy: the relationship between politics and economics was dialectical. The question of *"kto kogo"* would be fully decided in the area of production; therefore, by heading the struggle for economic growth the Party was creating the necessary foundations for the ultimate victory of communism.[132]

In general, the Party apparat responded to the reform negatively. Khrushchev succeeded only in raising serious doubts concerning his own authority and the legitimacy of his measures. The opposition would deepen the wedge between Khrushchev and the territorial Party apparatus, and an essential link with the institutionalized traditions and practices of *rukovodstvo* would be maintained.

Response to the Reform of
Industrial Management

The response of the Party and state bureaucracies to the new organization of industrial management was likewise complex. In both cases, the falling industrial and agricultural growth rates and the increasing pressures in resource allocation evoked competing measures for managerial reform in the open forum of the press as well as among the highest levels of the Party leadership. Although the exact relation between the March reorganization of agriculture and the subsequent reorganization of industrial administration is not precisely clear, the latter's rapid rise to prominence suggests that the problems were linked rather than independent. And although a reconstruction of the events leading to the plenum must be speculative, there is a sufficient number of threads to indicate the general pattern of events.

Shortly after the close of the March plenum—in March or April—a decision was made, presumably within the Presidium, to start discussing specific alternatives to the reform of industrial management. In a speech in early May, Khrushchev indicated to a conference of railroad workers that such a discussion was under way, without revealing, however, the content of the various proposals under scrutiny.[133] Shortly before the Khrushchev speech, in April, the Institute of Economics of the Academy of Sciences had heard and endorsed a special report by Liberman and had recommended to Gosplan that the Liberman proposals be tested experimentally.[134] At the same time, it appears that the Central Committee was actively considering the reform of planning through the use of the "normative cost of turnover" index, which was under the sponsorship of the Central Statistical Administration. The issue of planning reform was undoubtedly sharpened by the abrupt rise in agricultural prices on 1 June[135] and by Khrushchev's attack on the incompetence of the central planning organs for permitting inflation.[136] The conflict between Khrushchev and Gosplan over resource allocation fanned the flame; shortly thereafter, V. E. Dymshits replaced V. N. Novikov as head of Gosplan.

July 1962 brought at least a temporary resolution of some aspects of the problem. In a little publicized conference on Russian industry presided over by Frol Kozlov and featuring A. P. Kirilenko as the main speaker, a number of important, unpublished decisions were made.[137] One decision was to reform the lower levels of the administrative structure by adopting the "firm" structure;[138] a second was to adopt the normative cost of turnover indicator in the Tatar Republic under the direct control of the Central Committee.[139] The July conference, which selected the more conservative of the variants before the top Party leadership, is important for Khrushchev's absence from its deliberations. Moreover, far from being a limited conference on Russian industry (as *Pravda* labeled it), it appears to have been, in fact, of all-union character and therefore of equal status with the agricultural conference presided over by Khrushchev earlier in the month.

Whether the decision to conduct a large-scale experiment in the Tatar Republic under Central Committee direction was intended to preempt an experiment along Liberman lines is unknown. Unknown as well are the events which led to the publication of Liberman's article, coincident with the circulation of the memorandum on Party structure, which appears to have opened a campaign to legitimate further action on the Liberman proposals. This connection is suggested by an article that appeared in *Pravda Ukrainy* after the plenum stating that a decision had been made to introduce the Liberman proposals on a limited basis in September. On 21 September the chairman of Gosplan SSSR sent letters to both the Ukrainian Gosplan and Sovnarkhoz ordering them to give priority to equipping Liberman's laboratory in Kharkov in order to test his proposals. That this order reflected the initiative and endorsement of the highest Party echelons is indicated by the fact that the Kharkov Obkom informed the Kharkov Sovnarkhoz that such an order had been issued and that the sovnarkhoz should begin to make preparations. The order, however, was not transmitted to Kharkov immediately; it was held up in the republican organs from the end of September until early November. Its release to the Kharkov Sovnarkoz seems to have coincided with the public announcement of the plenum.[140]

Because of the tension and conflict at all levels, the Party officials' discussion of the reform of the industrial administration appears to have been circumspect. Although Khrushchev's proposals met virtually unanimous approval, the basic policy of centralizing economic management was a potential source of tension between the lower Party apparatus and the managers. In general, the apparat's power over the organs of state administration was maximized under the decentralized and basically territorial system of administration. The thrust toward a tightly centralized and branch system of economic administration could only threaten the territorial Party apparatus with a return to conditions resembling those under the ministerial system. On this critical issue, however, the speakers from the republican and oblast committees, with one exception, maintained a discreet silence. Yet, indirect evidence revealed in the plenum speeches suggests little change in perception of the territorial Party officials of their interests.

Khrushchev's sharp attack on the central planning organs was undoubtedly the most popular aspect of his report on the state administration. The republican and oblast Party secretaries unanimously echoed his assault on Gosplan's inefficiency, although they had no suggestions concerning a proper administrative approach to resolving the problems of planning and supply. V. S. Tolstikov, first secretary of the Leningrad Obkom, suggested making Gosplan officials materially responsible for errors in planning for a period of two years,[141] and Liashko suggested establishing direct contacts between suppliers and clients.[142] The creation of a centralized organ for direct administration of the economy evoked little enthusiasm among Party officials at the plenum; both Podgorny of the Ukraine and Mzhavanadze of Georgia stressed the values of the sovnarkhoz system and decentralized administration.[143] Centralizing the powers of the State Committee for Construction Affairs received formal, routine approval. More popular was the centralization of technical policy, which promised to relieve the individual republican or oblast committee of some of the responsibility for generating and executing technical change. The creation of heavy sovnarkhozy was strongly approved by the oblast first secretaries appearing before the plenum, although each was slated to head an oblast in which an enlarged sovnarkhozy was to be placed. No obkom Party official from an oblast in which a sovnarkhoz was to be abolished spoke at the plenum.

Regarding the reform of the enterprise and the adoption of the Liberman proposals, no sharply defined opinion by the territorial Party apparatus is evident in the stenogram. Only P. N. Demichev offered a serious complaint about the conservatism of plant officials, many of whom, he held, were still infected with the spirit of Stalinism.[144] More representative of the opinion of the apparat as a whole, perhaps, were those expressions of support by Podgorny, Akhundov, and others for an increase in the rights of plant directors, although this did not necessarily imply a similar support for economic methods of administration or profitability. Podgorny, in whose republic the Liberman proposals had originated and would presumably be tested, strongly supported the concept of the "firm" while studiously avoiding any commitment to Libermanism.[145] Of the republican secretaries speaking at the plenum, K. T. Mazurov alone gave serious attention to planning indicators, approving both the indicator to measure labor intensity (or the normative cost of turnover index) and the index for output per ruble of fixed capital costs. Also unique among territorial officials was Mazurov's enthusiastic approval of democratic principles in plant administration.[146] Among oblast officials, the single proponent of economic levers in management and an increase in local initiative was B. F. Komiakov, first secretary of Poltava, an agricultural oblast. The first secretaries of industrial oblasti ignored the issue.[147]

The economic bureaucracy, like the territorial apparatus of the Party, generally supported the proposed structures. Unlike the Party officials, however, their views were more clearly identified by the interests which they represented. Dymshits, then serving as chairman of the Gosplan, for example, spoke for the central planners in charging plant officials with continuous and willful violations of plan and state discipline, often failing to meet planning quotas even when supply was sufficient.[148] In contrast, the most articulate of the plant directors speaking at the plenum, V. V. Krotov of the Uralmashzavod, demanded an end to petty tutelage from higher administrative organs and greater rights for the plant and sovnarkhoz.[149] The chairmen of the branch and functional committees, whose roles would be strengthened by the policy of centralizing technical policy, expressed unusually warm support for the reorganization. One speaker, A. I. Kostousov of the State Committee on Automation and Machine Building, used the platform to refute the view that centralization of design meant a cut in the number of design institutes and attacked Demichev, who wanted the design institutes of Moscow placed under a single city agency rather than under the State Committee.[150] Among sovnarkhoz officials at the plenum, the unanimous support for the formation of the new union sovnarkhoz and enlarged sovnarkhozy was compromised only by L. F. Grafov, the chairman of Kemerovo Sovnarkhoz, who insisted on decentralizing authority in planning.[151] No official, directly or otherwise, discussed the problem of planning indicators or the Liberman proposals.

After the plenum, responses to the new structure of industrial management differed markedly from the reaction to the new principles of Party structure and *rukovodstvo*. Unlike the 1957 reorganization of management, the changes within the state administrative apparatus appeared moderate rather than radical and therefore threatened no group (such as the central ministerial officials) with a sudden loss of authority and status. The ambiguities of Khrushchev's proposals also contributed to the relative harmony in which the state reforms were carried through. The proponents of economic reform, for example, undaunted by the evident lack of support for economic methods of management at the plenum, singled out Khrushchev's favorable commentary on the debate on economic reform as specific authorization for further discussion and organization.[152] To summarize the discussion, a special commission was formed, composed of representatives of the Economics Division of the Academy of Sciences, members of the editorial board of *Pravda* and other press organs, as well as members of the industrial bureaucracy. The commission was placed under the Learned Council on the Problem of Cost Accounting and Material Production Incentives, and charged with a coordinating role.[153]

The liberals' conviction that the November plenum signalled a decisive turn toward economic and decentralized methods of management therefore persisted into January 1963, buttressed by a 30 November decision of the Council of Ministers ordering the preparation of a draft statute on the Law of the Socialist Enterprise as well as a new statute on the sovnarkhoz.[154] This was followed shortly thereafter in Leningrad by a conference of plant directors and Party officials under the sponsorship of the "*delovoi klub*" of *Ekonomicheskaia gazeta*. The convening of enterprise officials for the purpose of articulating a common position as an interest group was in itself a remarkable event, and the reportage on the meeting is a valuable record of their values and interests in 1962.

The managers showed considerable diversity of opinion and exhibited very little support for the Liberman proposals,[155] which were presumably as controversial among the plant officials as they were among the Kharkov Sovnarkhoz officials. The Kharkov Sovnarkhoz, having finally received the official order to equip Liberman's laboratory, formed a commission of eleven to investigate the matter. Almost immediately the commission was bitterly divided. In a resolution passed by six members, they announced that the Liberman system removed the enterprise from the general system of planning; that forming the enterprise fund out of profits was wrong; and finally, that if such an event should transpire, all experimental enterprises should be placed under a single branch administration.[156]

The decision to form the USSR Supreme Council of the National Economy in the middle of March 1963 was the decisive turning point in the events following the plenum because it consolidated the thrust toward administrative centralism.[157] Neither the Law on the Socialist Enterprise nor the new statute on the sovnarkhoz were formulated in the following two years. Public advocacy of economic methods of administration diminished in intensity for almost a year after this decision, although it would revive and grow stronger as the inadequacies of the reform were revealed.

The compromised results of the plenum failed to satisfy the Party apparatus, the economic liberals, or Khrushchev himself. The intricate problems and tensions inherent in his own thinking on industrial administration were far from being resolved, and the return to full-blown administrative centralism in March 1963 did not persuade him of its value. In April 1963, having weathered the conservative reaction of the previous winter,[158] he sharply criticized those chairmen of the strengthened state committees—the "old ministers"—who surreptitiously attempted to rebuild the ministerial system by struggling to remove enterprises from the jurisdiction of the enlarged sovnarkhozy.[159] Convinced that it was impossible to manage a whole branch of industry from Moscow, Khrushchev also remained committed to some form of regional planning. He was undoubtedly responsible for proposing the formation of regional planning commissions for Gosplan in each major economic region as well as of a coordinating council for planning in each economic region to be composed of obkom, kraikom, and district Party officials.[160]

This underlying ambiguity concerning the leading role of the central and local Party agencies in the industrial economy would clearly be increased under the reorganization. The Supreme Council of the National Economy was placed under the direct guidance of the Central Committee. Yet Khrushchev's confidence in the apparat and his willingness to accept the consequence of its increased power was limited. This underlay his intention, expressed in April, to centralize the approval of all construction projects in the State Construction Committee since the obkomy and gorkomy did not control localist tendencies in investment. In attempting to increase the role of the apparat while simultaneously attempting to control the negative consequences of this policy, Khrushchev in fact contributed to the rigidity in the established relationships of Party *rukovodstvo*.

The Response to the New Control
Mechanism

The response to the establishment of the new Party-state control mechanism was essentially hostile. At the plenum itself, the general reaction was favorable, but there were few expressions of strong support. Among central Party officials, P. N. Demichev, the only secretary speaking at the plenum and one who had consistently displayed a strong antimanagerial bias, ignored the reorganization of control,[161] although G. I. Voronov warmly approved it.[162] The territorial Party apparatus, against which the threat of the Party-State Control Committee was most clearly directed, responded with acute distrust. Of the fourteen first secretaries of republican committees, including Tolstikov of Leningrad, only three expressed warm approval; five made no reference to the new structures in their speeches. The fifteen obkom secretaries speaking at the plenum were more direct. The expression of warm support was confined to a single secretary, and no fewer than eleven simply ignored it. State officials, particularly those with operational responsibilities, were equally negative. Of the nine sovnarkhoz chairmen and enterprise directors, only one made a routine reference to the Party-State Control Committee. Even among heads of institutions whose interests were presumably served by the new structure, there was no unanimity. V. V. Grishin, the head of the Soviet trade unions, was unenthusiastic, but S. S. Pavlov, head of the Young Communist League, was among the strongest supporters of the new system.[163]

The lack of support for the Party-State Control Committee reflected, in part at least, the general hostility to the reform of the Party structure itself. Underlying this general antagonism, however, was the clash of specific interests, which delayed the formation of local structures, for example, until well into March 1963. The struggle over the specific structures of control was, of course, intimately related to the struggle to define the authority and scope of activity of the new institution. The actual structure of the Party-State Control Committee to emerge from these largely concealed conflicts was essentially a compromise of competing tendencies.[164]

On the issue of the PGK's independence from the staff Party organs, the familiar principle of "dual subordination" was evoked to permit the existence of a separate control apparatus within the localities while retaining direct Party control over it. This compromise, however, extended only to the republican and oblast control committees. Control organs below the oblast level were directly subordinated to the oblast control committees. The attribution of "localism" to the city and raion Party committees, which this arrangement assumed, was, of course, fictitious but useful since it permitted the establishment of independent and centrally controlled agencies below the oblast level while retaining formalized party controls at the regional level.

Equally important, and closely related, was the actual scope of authority which these organs would possess. In relation to control over the Party staffs and individual Communists, the new agency's failure to absorb the Party Control Committee and its powers would seriously limit its authority. Without the right to probe the moral, political, or ideological attitudes of individuals, the PGK lacked an important base for becoming an instrument of political purge. A second limitation on the control agency was the retention by local Party organs of the right to control entrance and expulsion of Party members within the regular staff organs. A third restriction was its lack of a mandate to check up on the local Party organs themselves. Additional limits would be observed in the new organs' role in economic decision-making.[165] If Khrushchev's original intention had been to resurrect the old control structure of the New Economic Policy period as a model—independent of the territorial apparatus and checking it—this intention failed. While the Party-state control apparatus was not simply an aspect of the territorial Party apparatus operating under a different name, it was far from being a simple copy of previous historical patterns.

— 7 —

The Institutional Effect of the
Party Reform

The effect of the structural reorganization of the Party apparatus on the Party bureaucracy was mixed. New forms mingled with old, and new directions of *rukovodstvo* competed with persisting institutional practices. The reorganization was undertaken to strengthen the Party's monocratic structure through specialization and differentiation; but the new limitations imposed on the leading role by Soviet society and the profound doubts of the reform's legitimacy entertained by those entrusted with its implementation blunted any extreme consequences, thus preserving the Party's essential continuity with the past. Bureaucratic resistance, inertia, and the vested interests of the apparatchiki in the existing system braked fundamental change within the apparatus.

The emphasis on tightening centralized bureaucratic discipline and direction, however, should not obscure other significant, only partially anticipated consequences. Comprehensive change in a large-scale organization like the Communist party apparatus, particularly under Khrushchev's conditions, carries major possibilities for disorganization. In the short run, the November plenum would loosen the cohesion and discipline of the Party bureaucracy and introduce conflict and confusion in the Party's authority, political style, and relationships with the industrial administration. In this respect, the reform was an important, unintended step toward debureaucratization. The conflict and confusion within the apparatus induced a major restructuring of bureaucratic relationships. The policies of recruitment and the apparatus' concentration on economic and technical issues tended to strain the Party's structure. But since the measures of reform were only selectively applied and partially implemented, the result was to contain the spontaneous forces set loose by the reorganization within the existing system.

1

The General Profile of the Party

The November plenum continued the earlier trend toward a mass party closely integrated around the economic functions of Soviet society. Between 1 January

157

1963 and 1 January 1965, the Party increased by 1,230,294 persons, or 11 percent.[1] Increasing the number of Party candidates was particularly emphasized. In 1964, 879,428 were accepted as candidates, an increase of 100,000 over 1963. Earlier recruitment patterns were unchanged: over 45 percent of the 1964 candidates were classified as workers, with particular emphasis on those employed in technically sophisticated industries, such as chemistry, electronics, machine building, and instruments manufacture. Recruitment declined slightly in the countryside, although pressure to increase the number of agricultural specialists was intensified. Reducing managerial and administrative personnel also continued as Party policy. Of the total number of Communist employees, the percentage of managers dropped from 10 to 7.8 percent.[2]

The policy of rejuvenating the Party by recruiting energetic, educated youth remained strong. By 1 January 1965, 42.8 percent of the Party had tenure of less than ten years, and for the first time in the post-Stalin period the majority of Communists were under forty years of age. During 1963 and 1964, however, the generation which had entered the Party under Stalin remained firmly established. Those with from ten to thirty years of Party service constituted the majority, and over one-fifth of all Party members were over fifty.[3] The Stalinist generation retreated visibly but slowly.

There is little indication of a general purge of the Party in 1963 and 1964. The number of full members expelled in 1963 rose by 10 percent, largely for "various actions incompatible with the title of Communist," but in 1964 the number dropped below the 1962 levels.[4] Because of the establishment of the Party-State Control Committee the mass purge was not used extensively during this period as an instrument of invigoration and discipline.

As in previous periods, the great influx of new Party members produced strains and distortions in Party policy. Qualitative admission standards suffered for familiar reasons. Investigation and documentation on new Party members was often poor. Recruitment was conducted mechanically according to general quotas, violating specific categories for individual types of workers. In some cases, gorkomy accepted primary Party organ rejects. The Party's increased mass influence, predicated on the careful recruitment of "opinion leaders," was frustrated by the induction of personal friends or of individuals uninterested in joining the aktiv.[5] While the Party's heroic image was undoubtedly served by conferring honorary membership for outstanding achievement,[6] Khrushchev's vision of a massive beehive pressing for economic growth was largely unrealized. If focusing recruitment on economic functions promised a fundamental reorganization of the Party as a political institution in the long run, its short-term effects in 1963 and 1964 were marginal.

The Party's New Elective Organs

More significant were the structural shifts in the number, size, turnover, and composition of the elected Party committees. The most important political measure for renewing the Party committees was the application of the mandatory turnover quotas adopted in the Party Rules in 1961. Almost as controversial was the decision to redistribute the number of committees at the regional and local levels. Dividing seventy-five oblast and krai committees into separate organs for industry and agriculture expanded the number of regional committees, including the union republican committees, to 222. Among local city and urban borough committees, there was a sharp deviation from established policy. The new tendency was toward abolishing city committees with subordinate raikomy in oblast centers. Even providing that the urban raikomy would be enlarged, this meant increased burdens on the already heavily pressed industrial obkomy, and it was therefore strongly resisted.

The proposal was, however, unevenly implemented.[7] In the Russian Republic, for instance, there was a conflict of views between Khrushchev and Voronov. At the November plenum, Voronov advocated retaining all city and borough committees in the Russian Republic and forming an additional fifty-seven city committees to cover the suburbs.[8] Once again, Khrushchev was only partially victorious. The exact number of city committees that were actually dropped in the Russian Republic, however, was never revealed. Some gorkomy, such as the Leningrad City Committee, slated for elimination in November, were finally retained.[9]

Although some objective standard was probably worked out for deciding which city committees would be eliminated or retained, no criteria clearly emerge from the selections actually made.[10] Theoretically, a maximum of fifty-five oblasti and kraia and sixteen autonomous republics could be affected by the decision. The number of city committees actually dropped, however, was far less, perhaps as few as twenty-five for the RSFSR. For the Soviet Union as a whole, the number of gorkomy and raikomy in 1963–64 can be reasonably estimated at 550 and 350. Among local Party bodies, the agricultural area was the most adversely affected. After the abolition of the majority of rural raikomy and the expansion of territorial production units, there were 1,711 Party organs. Representation in the agricultural sector, however, was increased by the addition of 352 industrial-production (zonal) Party committees.[11] The reorganization of local Party organs in agriculture would ultimately cut the number of Party organs to two-thirds of 1962 levels.

The November reorganization also shifted the relative balance in representation between the regional and local Party organs. Representation at the regional level grew from twenty thousand in 1961 to twenty-seven thousand in 1963.[12] The increase of almost one-third at this level is almost wholly attributable to the split in oblast and krai committees. The republican committees' size remained virtually unchanged. The major change was at the local level. In 1963, the membership of city, urban raikomy, territorial production, and zonal committees numbered only 208 thousand, a reduction of 78 thousand from the 1961 level of 286 thousand.[13] The 23 percent reduction which resulted from the reorganization ran directly counter to Khrushchev's earlier strategy of increasing the ties of the local Party organs with the Party masses and of increasing the size of the economic aktiv at the production level.

During 1963 and 1964, the turnover and composition of the committees from the republican to zonal levels sharply altered previous patterns. The 1963 and 1964 elections represented the first large-scale application of the controversial turnover quotas adopted in the Party Rules at the Twenty-second Congress, and the quotas were rigorously enforced over the protests of the territorial apparatus.[14] As a result, the turnover resembled a purge. City raikomy were renewed by 77.4 percent, gorkomy by 75.5 percent. Oblast committees were turned over by 69.2 percent and republican committees by 57 percent.[15]

In some measure, the new committees reflected Khrushchev's priorities.[16] In the industrial-production committees formed in 1963, 67 percent of the members were directly engaged in material production.[17] In the new urban raikomy, 52 percent, and in the gorkomy, 54 percent, were workers, technicians, or enterprise directors.[18] Among industrial obkomy, however, this dropped to 43.2 percent, and in the agricultural oblast committees the number of ordinary kolkhozniki remained extremely low.[19] In the latter, agricultural specialists and Party and state administrators continued to predominate.

The compositional change of the 1963 and 1964 territorial Party committees may be suggested by comparing the Kazakh republican committees elected in 1963 and 1964 with the national averages of the 1961 committees. In 1961, workers and peasants constituted approximately 38 percent; technicians, 17.4 percent; and Party, state, and other administrators, 44.7 percent.[20] In 1963 and 1964 in Kazakhstan, workers and peasants dropped to 34.6 percent, but technicians jumped to over 26 percent; administrative personnel of all categories dropped to under 40 percent.[21] If the Kazakhstan figures can be extrapolated for the Soviet Union as a whole, it appears that the policy of turning the territorial Party apparatus into an economic and technical aktiv was advanced, particularly at the local level, while Party and state administrators remained a diminished but still dominant element.

2

The New Central Party Organs

The November reorganization, directed primarily at the Party's executive and administrative organs, raised questions concerning whether the central and local apparatus could meet the challenges of administrative and technical complexity and institutional resistance to reform. The major shift in executive structure at the central Party levels had been the formation in 1955 and 1956 of the Russian Bureau and the division of the central departments into two sectors serving the RSFSR and the fourteen other union republics. The November reorganization, intended to cut deeper, was an attempt to rationalize and strengthen the Party's role in industry and agriculture. The effect of the new decision-making structures was minimal in many respects, but the significance of the reorganization exceeds its immediate consequences because it represented Khrushchev's final, most drastic attempt to demonstrate the Party's organizational relevance to the mature Soviet economy.

The key measure in the sweeping reorganization of the Secretariat was the creation of six collective organs of decision-making, each under the chairmanship of a Central Committee secretary. One of the new agencies, The Party-State Control Committee under A. N. Shelepin, had its own independent apparatus and was formally subordinate to both the Council of Ministers and the Central Committee. Whether it was an integral part of the Secretariat or whether it should be regarded as a separate agency directly subordinate to the Presidium, however, is a complex question.

The five other collective organs were clearly within the formal structure of the Secretariat. Two of them, the Commission for Organizational-Party Questions and the Ideological Commission, were formed to guide the Party's internal structural and ideological functions. More immediately relevant to the Party's guidance of the economy were the three branch bureaus: the Bureau for Industry and Construction chaired by A. P. Rudakov; the Bureau for the Chemical Industry and Light Industry headed by P. N. Demichev; and the Bureau for Agriculture, of which V. I. Poliakov served as chairman.[22]

With the exception of the Party-State Control Committee, the formal structure and functions of these organs remained shadowy during their two years of existence. That their legitimacy was dubious was demonstrated by their exclusion as central Party organs from the new edition of the Program and Regulations of the Communist party issued in 1964, although they were briefly acknowledged in 1964 by Bugaev and Leibson in their authoritative discussion of the new Party Rules.[23]

In contrast to the usual practice concerning established central Party organs, the memberships of the new commissions and bureaus were never published. At none of the three Central Committee plena held during 1963 and 1964 were they officially alluded to in any way. Although the two commissions' activities were discussed in the daily press, a tight wall of secrecy shrouded the roles of the economic bureaus. Their formal structures can therefore be identified only in part.

The most fully publicized of the new organs was the Ideological Commission, headed by L. F. Ilychev. In addition to the chairman, there were at least eight other members. Three were journalists; two (and probably three) were officials in the Ideological Department; and the others included the first secretary of the Komsomols and the chairman of the State Committee on Cinematography, the latter being the only cultural official of the state apparatus to be publicly identified as a member of the commission.[24] Far fewer officials could be identified in the other bureaus and the Organizational-Party Commission. Two officials were publicly identified as members of the Bureau for Industry and Construction and the Agricultural Bureau, but there were no positive identifications of the memberships of either the Bureau for the Chemical Industry and Light Industry or for the Commission for Organizational-Party Questions.

The absence of even the most elementary information on the new secretarial organs precludes any detailed analysis of their roles and functions within the Party's decision-making apparatus. But since changes of this magnitude in the Secretariat generally involve both political and efficiency factors, it is possible to advance a number of reasonable hypotheses concerning them.

The most hypothetical aspect of the political problem is the degree to which Khrushchev's personal power was enhanced by the November appointments to the Secretariat. Of the eight major appointments to the Secretariat and Russian Bureau, including Iu. Andropov and L. N. Efremov as first deputy vice-chairman of the Russian Bureau, all reached high Party positions under Khrushchev, suggesting that Khrushchev was instrumental in advancing their careers. That they were his lieutenants or part of his personal "tail" is, however, extremely doubtful. Only Rudakov, V. N. Titov, and Demichev, for example, had served with Khrushchev in the Ukrainian or Moscow apparats. His personal relationship with the others is more complex. One case, however—the appointment of V. I. Poliakov (chief editor of *Agricultural Life*, who lacked previous experience in the Party apparatus) to head successively the Agricultural Department and then the Bureau for Agriculture—suggests Khrushchev's strong personal intervention.

To what extent these officials were personally loyal to him is unknown, but their subsequent fates are suggestive. In November 1964, Shelepin and Demichev became respectively full and candidate members of the Presidium. Andropov and Rudakov remained in the Secretariat through the Twenty-third Congress. Of the four who were dropped after Khrushchev's fall, Efremov was posted as first secretary to Stavropol Krai, the careerist graves of A. I. Kirichenko and N. A. Bulganin. In April 1965, Titov was sent as second secretary to Kazakhstan under D. A. Kunaev, ousted by Khrushchev in December 1962 as Kazakh first secretary. Ilychev and Poliakov faded rapidly into obscurity, the former serving as deputy minister of foreign affairs. While the rapid elimination of Ilychev and Poliakov after Khrushchev's fall suggests close personal ties with him, the demotions of Titov and Efremov may have had other implications.[25]

The formation of collective decision-making organs at the secretarial level may also have been intended to blunt and diffuse the power of those Presidium members, principally Kozlov and Suslov, who most probably opposed Khrushchev's reform policies. There is little public evidence to suggest Kozlov's specific opposition to the Party reorganization, although his responsibilities for organizational affairs were most immediately and directly affected; his one major speech on the reform expressed qualified approval of it. Moreover, if the new organs were intended to filter the day-to-day influence of the Presidium on decision-making, they failed to do so. None of the November appointments except Efremov was advanced to the Presidium. Furthermore, four (possibly five) of the men heading the new commissions and bureaus were heads of central departments, serving as administrative specialists in political or economic affairs rather than as political generalists. A direct thrust at the balance of power in presidial-secretarial relations seems more likely to have occurred in June 1963, when Leonid Brezhnev and N. A. Podgorny were posted to the Secretariat.[26] While the greater activity and public visibility of the two commissions for internal Party affairs may have reflected this change, there is little indication of a significant rise in the importance of the economic bureaus after June 1963.

More probably, the new secretarial organs were intended to increase the efficiency of the apparatus and the comprehensiveness and effectiveness of the Party's control of the economy. Judging from the models of the republican economic bureaus and from the identifications at the central level, the presence on the branch bureaus of department heads and first deputy heads intended an association of the individual branch departments under an official Party organ with the power to establish and control interbranch decisions. In part, this reflected Khrushchev's concern with the unwillingness or inability of the central departments to respond adequately to his priorities; it also reflected the difficulties of centralized Party control of a complex economy.

Administrative reorganization would presumably reduce the departmental barriers and parochial loyalties of the departments and open interbranch cooperation on such important and lagging sectors as chemistry, instruments, and machine building. It would also improve communication by widening the formal channels for representation and consultation within the central apparatus. Collective leadership would improve the discussion and resolution of increasingly difficult problems for a longer span of time. Decision implementation would be improved by assigning formal responsibilities for specific results. Finally, the senior secretaries would be freed from the details of day-to-day policy to concentrate on larger problems. Whatever the administrative advantages of the new system, these organs were a radical break with existing traditions; they would reduce the autonomy of the departments, disturb existing relationships outside the apparat, and, finally, they may have promoted policies to which many in the central apparat were opposed.

They seem also to have been intended to increase the specific controls of the central Party apparatus on the state administrative structure. In 1958, Khrushchev had indicated that the Party's growing role was closely related to the increase in the number of secretaries in July 1957.[27] The removal of Aristov, Brezhnev, Furtseva, Ignatov, and Kirichenko in May 1960 significantly reduced the number of Party officials in the Secretariat with economic experience and probably indicated its return to a more generalized decision-making role. The addition of Demichev at the Twenty-second Congress was a partial corrective to this situation, and with the appointment of three new secretaries in November and two more in June 1963, a capacity for more direct, specific intervention in economic decision-making was strengthened. The formation of new bureaus for the chemical industry and light industry and agriculture signaled the economic bureaucracies that Party agencies had been created to enforce Khrushchev's policies. As in previous periods, it may be assumed that increased administrative controls from the Party apparatus encountered opposition from the state administrative apparatus.

The Regional Bureaus

That the November plenum aimed at more explicit, detailed centralized control of the economy by the Presidium and the Secretariat was demonstrated by the reorganization of the Russian Bureau and the formation of the Central Asian and Transcaucasian bureaus. Khrushchev was deeply dissatisfied with the Russian Bureau's guidance of the republic's economy in 1962.[28] The decision to split the bureau, clearly indicated in the September *zapiska* but ambiguous at the plenum, was as controversial as the decision to create specialized structures within the Secretariat. Equally controversial was the formation of regional bureaus under presidial direction for Central Asia and the Transcaucasus.

The formation of interrepublican bureaus, however, went beyond concern with economic policy and efficiency. First, the two non-Russian bureaus can be seen in the context of constitutional reform which, as John Hazard has pointed out, appeared to envision a return to the federal structures of the constitution of 1924.[29] Second, as one specialist has indicated, the centralization of Party policy was a direct response to the growth in cultural nationalism and the resistance to sovietization.[30] Of more immediate importance was the problem, particularly in Central Asia, of widespread deception and corruption at the highest levels of the republican Party and state organizations. Most significant, however, was Khrushchev's determination to promote large-scale specialization and integration of the regional economies, in part to increase centralized controls over the lagging cotton industry, construction, and technical progress. Not least among the objectives of this particular phase of the reform was Moscow's desire to control the economic nationalism and autarky which Ilychev railed against in June 1963.[31]

The November plenum struck hard at the Russian Bureau. Two separate bureaus, for industry and construction and for agriculture, were in fact formed, but neither Kirilenko nor Efremov were ever identified as their chairmen, nor was the list of members ever published. There were no recorded meetings of the Bureau for Agriculture. There were, however, two public meetings of the Bureau for Industry and Construction in February 1964 on the chemical industry. While the Russian Bureau as a whole was deeply involved in specific problems of economic management, the industrial and agricultural bureaus appear to have been dormant.

After the November plenum, the Russian Bureau underwent a sharp reorganization and turnover. Cut from eleven to ten members, the bureau's most important change was the replacement of G. I. Voronov by L. N. Efremov as first deputy chairman in charge of agriculture. As Chairman of the Russian Republic Council of Ministers, Voronov continued to hold an ordinary membership but retained his post as a full member of the Presidium. His superior on the Russian Bureau, however, was advanced only to candidate membership in the Presidium, which offered an interesting problem in status and authority.

Five of the 1962 members of the Russian Bureau were removed but not all were purged. D. S. Polianskii remained in the Presidium. P. F. Lomako and A. V. Romanov assumed important posts in the state apparatus. N. N. Organov became ambassador to Bulgaria, but V. M. Churaev was demoted to deputy chairman of the Russian Republic's Party-State Control Committee. The four new members were N. G. Egorychev, the head of the Moscow Gorkom; G. V. Eniutin, the chairman of the Russian Republic's Party-State Control Committee; V. S. Tolstikov, first secretary of the Leningrad Oblast and the replacement of I. V. Spiridonov; and N. G. Ignatov, the chairman of the ill-fated All-Union Committee of Agriculture abolished in 1962. G. G. Abramov, dropped as first secretary of the Moscow Industrial Obkom to become deputy chairman of the Moscow Oblast Sovnarkhoz, continued to be listed as a member of the Russian Bureau, as was M. A. Iasnov.

In general, these changes would increase the dominance of the Party apparat. Polianskii's departure reduced the presidial representation of the bureau; and the loss of Lomako deprived the bureau of a specialist with heavy industrial and managerial experience. The lack of industrial expertise on the bureau would presumably be compensated by the activity of the Bureau for Industry and Construction.

The structure of the Central Asian Bureau, on the other hand, was fully publicized. Situated in Tashkent, the Central Asian Bureau had twelve members and was headed by a chairman and two deputy chairmen, all Russian. V. G. Lomonosov had been a secretary of the Kalinin Raion Committee in Moscow before his sudden promotion to the chairmanship. Both of his deputies, however, were drawn from posts within Central Asia. The more important of the two was V. K. Akulintsev, a mining engineer who had served as a secretary of the Turkmen Central Committee and as chairman of the Turkmen Sovnarkhoz. The other deputy was S. M. Veselov, who had served the preceding seven years as the second secretary of the Tashkent Obkom. Included in the membership of the new organ were five Party officials: the four first secretaries of the Tadzhik, Turkmen, Kirgiz, and Uzbek republics and the First Secretary of the Chimkent Oblast in Kazakhstan, V. A. Liventsov. The other members of the Central Asian Bureau were the chairman of the Central Asian Sovnarkhoz, and the three chairmen of the interrepublican agencies for cotton growing, irrigation and sovkhozy construction, and general construction.

The structure and composition of the Central Asian Bureau reflected most of the major conceptions underlying its formation. Slavs predominated, five, and probably six, being either Russian or Ukrainian. The selection of Slavs as chairman and deputy chairmen opposed the usual practice of appointing natives to head such organizations. While their selection may have reflected the difficulty of discriminating among the four nationalities, it would appear that nationalism was the more important reason. The structure also reveals the traditional dominance by the Party apparatus. Eight of the twelve posts were held by Party officials, four of the eight by Slavs.

Again, an interesting problem of status arose concerning the relationship between the chairman, chosen from a relatively low position in the Moscow apparat, and Rashidov, a candidate member of the Presidium but an ordinary member of the Central Asian Bureau. Whether choosing a chairman with few personal political resources was a concession to the status of the republican Party officials or an indication of the chairman's dependence upon the Presidium is an interesting, if not wholly answerable, question. Restricting the representation of state institutions to interrepublican and economic organs indicated the predominance of economic issues within the bureau's functions. It also indicated that the representation of local issues within the bureau would be achieved through the Party rather than the Soviet structure.

The Transcaucasian Bureau's structure was much simpler than that of the Central Asian Bureau. It emerged after a considerable delay in February 1963, and only five of its members were ever identified. The chairman, like his counterpart in Central Asia, was a Russian who had been a Moscow raikom secretary before his appointment. The single deputy chairman was a Georgian, O. D. Gotsiridze. A graduate of the Bauman Institute in Moscow, Gotsiridze had served in the central apparat of the Komsomols, the Georgian apparatus, and, immediately prior to his appointment, as the deputy chairman of the Georgian Gosplan. The bureau was completed by the three first secretaries of Armenia, Georgia, and Azerbaidzhan.

The Transcaucasian Bureau therefore differed sharply from the Central Asian Bureau—smaller in size, with only one Russian, the dominant nationality was

Georgian, evidence of the influence of Mzhavanadze, a candidate Presidium member. The bureau was purely a Party structure, without state officials, in which local interests, which were represented through the Party apparatus, were dominant. Although the formal structure does not provide a wholly accurate index to its actual authority or functions, it does indicate certain political concessions made to this region which were not made to the Central Asian republics.

The Central Party Apparatus

To impose a new administrative discipline in the central Party apparatus, the central departments were further specialized by the addition of new, and the reorganization of old, departments. The Secretariat's directing and coordinating role was tightened through the creation of the bureaus for economic guidance. Despite these changes, however, the essential administrative structures of the Stalinist period remained: the production-branch principle of organization was left intact and the 1956 reorganization of the administrative system untouched. The rationalization of the central Party administration was, therefore, limited and even conservative. The reorganization would refine and intensify the traditional system rather than create a new set of relationships.

The most important change in the organizational structure of the departments for the union republics was the regrouping of the individual otdely into five sectors, headed by a secretary and chairman of the respective commission or bureau. In addition, according to the reconstruction of the Jackson Committee, eight departments were directly subordinate to the Secretariat.[32] In the new order, the Bureau for Industry and Construction directed five departments; the Bureau for the Chemical Industry and Light Industry, two; and the Agricultural Bureau directed the agricultural departments. The Department of Party Organs was placed within the jurisdiction of the Commission for Organizational-Party Questions and the Ideological Department, and the related cultural, educational, and press departments were probably subordinated to the Ideological Commission. Among individual departments, the changes were comparatively few. The Department for Science, Higher Education, and Schools was reorganized: the sections for science and higher education were absorbed into the Ideological Department, the section for schools assuming the status of an independent department. The only new department identified for the union republics was the Department for Industries Processing Agricultural Products. A second department for rural construction may also have been formed.

Two major changes distinguished the new structure for the Russian Republic. First, the departments for Party organs and for ideology were split into industrial and agricultural sections and placed under the formal jurisdiction of their respective bureaus. Second, the number of specialized economic departments was expanded, another indication of the determination to increase the specific authority of the central Party apparatus in the daily affairs of economic management.

The Department of Industry and Transport became four departments: the Department of Heavy Industry, Transport, and Communications; the Department of Machine-Building; the Department of Light, Food Industry, and Trade, and a Department for the Chemical Industry. In the RSFSR, there was also added a Department for Industries Processing Agricultural Products.

Thus, for the central administrative apparatus as a whole, at least five new departments were formed, which, calculated on 1961 levels, raised the number of personnel in the apparatus to approximately 5,250, an increase of 17 percent. In terms of reforming the apparatus through further cuts in personnel or increasing the capacity for detailed intervention in the economy, the option was obviously toward the latter course.

The turnover of department heads and deputies was far less extensive among the economic departments serving the union republics than among the departments for the Russian Republic. All but two of the heads of industrial departments of the non-Russian apparatus were appointed in 1961 or 1962. In 1963, only two department heads were identified for the first time: A. E. Biriukov replaced Abyzov as head of the Department for Construction, and P. I. Maksimov became head of the Department of Light, Food Industry, and Trade. Among first deputy and deputy department heads, turnover was heavier, with every department replacing a first deputy or deputy head. In the agricultural sector, M. G. Lukshin was identified as the head of the new department; and there was a clean sweep of deputies in the Agricultural Department. In the turnover for the Russian Republic, the expansion in the number of departments and appointment of new personnel was accompanied by a sweep of the Party Organs Department, a purge signaled by the departure of V. M. Churaev.

3

The New Republican Organization

Structural change in the republican Party organizations following the November plenum emphasized the increasing importance of the Party organs at the regional level. The new presidia and economic bureaus closely followed Khrushchev's prescriptions of September and November 1962. In forming a troika of Party organs from the former republican bureaus, the presidia were reduced in size from the usual eleven to nine members and an average of two or three candidate members. The latter figure varied, however, the Ukrainian committee electing five and the Lithuanian none. The reduction in size would increase the numerical strength of the professional apparatus on the new presidia. Among full members, decision-making became almost exclusively the prerogative of the Party secretariats, which increased from five to six members, including the chairman of the Party-State Control Committee. For the Ukraine, the number of secretaries was increased to seven. The most visible change in Party representation on the presidia was dropping republican department heads from membership and reducing the number of obkom and gorkom secretaries from twelve to three officials.[33]

The structural change in the presidial organs indicated a more dynamic operational role for the republican secretariats. Six-man secretariats were formed by adding a special secretary for control. In other respects, however, the November plenum would formalize the internal structure of the secretariats rather than create new relationships. The first and second secretaries remained generalists. The major change involved placing the two secretaries for industry and agriculture as chairmen of the newly formed Bureau for the Leadership of Industry and Construction and Bureau for the Leadership of Agriculture. The fifth secretary, as formerly, usually remained in charge of ideological questions. This underlying continuity suggests that rejuvenating the Party's decision-making organs at the republican level would depend heavily on the turnover of cadres.

Among first and second secretaries of republican committees, the changeover in 1963 and 1964 was moderate, greater among second than among first secretaries. During these two years, only two first secretaries were removed. In December 1962, D. A. Kunaev of Kazakhstan was replaced by I. Iu. Iusupov, a secretary of the republican committee. In July 1963, P. E. Shelest, then chairman of the Ukraine's Bureau for Industry and Construction, was promoted to replace Podgorny who had advanced into the Secretariat. The rate of turnover among second secretaries, however, was more thoroughgoing.[34]

The conservatism evident in the appointment of Party generalists to head the republican secretariats was likewise evident, although to a lesser degree, in the appointment of secretaries to head the new economic bureaus. Among industrial and agricultural secretaries, however, the pattern of appointment and turnover differed sharply. Among chairmen of the bureaus for industry and construction, eleven of fourteen industrial secretaries retained their positions. Seven were appointed in 1961 and 1962 and three in 1958, 1959, and 1960. Only one secretary had served as long as seven years. With the exception of four secretaries in the Central Asian republics and Kurilenko of Moldavia, all were nationals of the republics whose industrial economies they headed.

There were differences among them, however. In 1962, their ages ranged from thirty-eight to fifty-nine. While all with known education were credited with at least incomplete higher education, specialities differed and experience varied as well.[35] In 1963 and 1964, only one of the ten were replaced. N.

N. Kurilenko, sent to Moldavia in 1961 after serving for nine years as head of the Ukraine's Central Committee Department of Consumer Goods and Food Industry, was relieved by B. A. Steshov, also from the Ukrainian apparat, who had previously served as a secretary in the Simferopol Obkom.

Three new chairmen were appointed to the bureaus for industry and construction. The Ukrainian Party organization drew upon P. E. Shelest, fifty-four years of age, a Ukrainian with an evening degree in metallurgical engineering, whose career had been principally in the Kiev City and Oblast Party apparats. In Kazakhstan and Uzbekistan, however, the new chairmen of the bureaus for industry and construction were drawn from officials with training and experience predominantly in heavy industry. The new Kazakh Central Committee's Chairman was R. B. Baigaliev, fifty, also a metallurgical engineer, who had served a brief stint in 1962 as first secretary of the Alma-Ata Obkom. Since 1955, Baigaliev had served both as first deputy chairman of the Kazakh Gosplan and chairman of the Kazakh Sovnarkhoz. The pattern was similar in the appointment of N. V. Martinov in Uzbekistan.[36] The latter two appointments, however, appear to have been at best regional. When Shelest was promoted in July 1963, his replacement was A. P. Liashko, first secretary of the Donetsk Industrial Obkom. Liashko was forty-seven, an industrial engineer who had held minor posts in industry before rising within the Ukrainian apparat to become an obkom first secretary. Except for those officials brought in directly from industrial management, the renovation of industrial decision-making within the republican secretariats through the replacement of industrial secretaries was marginal.

Among agricultural secretariats, however, the situation was far different. Eleven of the fourteen agricultural secretaries were turned over in 1962. In Belorussia, the second and agricultural secretaries simply switched jobs. In the other ten republics new men were added. Averaging approximately fifty years of age, the new chairmen of the agricultural bureaus had had agricultural educations and had spent their careers within the republican agricultural sector. Three had headed the agricultural departments of their republican committees, and five had been either republican ministers of agriculture or deputy chairmen of the republic's council of ministers. Only one of these officials, Aliev of Tadzhikistan, had never served in the Party apparatus. In the Ukrainian and Kazakh republics, the new secretaries had followed the typical patterns of obkom first secretaries serving in agricultural oblasti, alternating their careers within the Party apparatuses with short stints as oblast executive committee chairmen. As a group, they were drawn from the republican establishments of which they were a part. Despite the heavy turnover, radical changes were few.

The Republican Economic Bureaus

The economic branch bureaus which Khrushchev emphasized in September and

November 1962 reflected a basic conservatism in the republican secretariats. The Ukraine and Belorussia did not publish membership lists; other lists were incomplete. Of the eight republican bureaus for the leadership of industry and construction which can be fully identified, the size ranged from six to nine members, including the chairman and his deputy. The full range of Party control can be seen in the appointment of their deputy chairmen—nine of twelve were taken from Party offices. No less than seven were heads of their republican departments of industry and transport, and two were former obkom and gorkom secretaries. Of the three remaining deputies, two were taken from the republican sovnarkhozy, and one was a former minister of construction.

The memberships of the new industrial bureaus were also traditional. In every republic, full time Party officials were an absolute majority. Further, the pattern of representation continued to emphasize heavy industry and production tasks. In all eight bureaus (for which complete data are available) the Department of Industry-Transport, or heavy industry, was either represented individually or through the deputy chairman. The importance of cadres was evident in placing the head of the Party Organs Department on the bureau in six of eight republics. The heads of other departments were represented less frequently. Only three heads of ideological departments were represented, and even fewer were represented for construction and light industry. Seven of the eight bureaus, however, included first secretaries of the capital city committee. Among state officials, every Bureau for Industry and Construction had a first deputy chairman of the Council of Ministers.[37]

The typical Bureau for Agriculture, like its industrial counterpart, normally contained six to nine members and was dominated by the Party apparatus. The seven-man Agricultural Bureau for the Kazakh Republic, for example, was composed of the chairman and the deputy chairman, who was also head of the Agricultural Department. Included as members of the bureau were the deputy heads of the Party Organs and Science, Higher Education, and Schools departments; among state agricultural officials, the bureau had as members the minister of agriculture, the chairman of the Virgin Lands Krai Soviet, and the deputy chairman for agriculture of the republican state planning commission.

Despite the evident stability of chairmen and deputy chairmen of both economic bureaus, turnover was heavy, an indication of the serious problems which arose in the dynamics of Party leadership during this period.[38]

The Republic's Administrative Apparatus

The structural change and regrouping of the republican departmental systems followed the pattern of the Russian Republic with one important exception. In establishing the troika pattern at the republican level, the normal division of individual departments would directly subordinate the staff departments to the presidia and assign the branch departments to their respective economic bureaus. Like the Russian Bureau's apparat, in all republican committees except one, the departments for Party organs and for ideology were initially split into departments for industry and agriculture. The expansion in the number of industrial departments, however, was minimal.[39] In the agricultural sector, new departments for industries processing agricultural products were set up in every republic; and, in three republics with extensive rural and irrigation construction, separate departments were established for rural construction. The initial structuring was changed in 1963 and 1964. In Belorussia and Moldavia, the troika pattern was abolished and all departments were placed under the direct control of the presidia; and in at least three republican committees, the experiment with divided Party organs and ideology departments was ended.

The departmental reorganization was accompanied by a heavy turnover in department heads. In the Ideological Department, every department head was replaced. For the Party organs and economic branch otdely, the figure was lower but substantial: in each, at least 50 percent of the department heads were changed. That such a high rate constituted a purge, however, is tempered by the fact that in ten republics in 1960 and 1961 the turnover of department heads of Party organs and propaganda and agitation otdely was 80 and 90 percent and a minimum of 70 percent for the branch otdely. In this respect, the heavy turnover, which indicated an underlying dissatisfaction with the performance of the apparatus, reinforced rather than initiated a trend.

4

The Oblast Party Organs

The most dramatic aspect of the November reorganization was the unprecedented division of the obkomy into industrial and agricultural divisions. But splitting the obkom structure along economic lines was simply the first and most drastic step toward reorienting and redefining the Party as a production apparatus. The changes in the size and composition of the bureaus, the role of the secretariat and particularly of the first secretary, the new departmental structures, and the renovation of cadres were equally important in the qualitative changes in the Party's *rukovodstvo* of the economy. While formal organizational change is limited in its capacity to produce new and creative bureaucratic structures, it does provide a key to the degree to which Khrushchev was practically able to redefine the nature of the Communist party in Soviet society.

The Oblast Administrative Structures

Enlarging oblast administrative boundaries, which had been among Khrushchev's basic policies, was a minor aspect of the reorganization. The changes were principally in Central Asia where six oblasti were disbanded. As partial compensation, however, two oblasti were formed in 1963 and 1964 in Uzbekistan. For the Soviet Union as a whole, on 1 April 1963 there were 113 territories and oblasti and twenty autonomous republics, of which sixteen were located in the Russian Republic.[40]

The selectivity exercised in restructuring the oblast Party organs was primarily, although perhaps not exclusively, for economic reasons. Of the 133 oblasti and autonomous republics, about 25 percent were in the industrial category, another 25 percent in the mixed industrial-agricultural economies, and 50 percent were agricultural oblasti. The obkomy which were not divided (with the exceptions of Astrakhan and Kaliningrad) were in agricultural areas. Significantly, the converse was not true. The most highly industrialized oblasti, such as Moscow and Leningrad, with comparatively unimportant agricultural sectors, were split, which suggests both the general importance of agriculture in the strategy of the reorganization and the attempt to enlarge the formal status of Party work in agriculture. While the economic factor predominated, an examination of the excluded republics and oblasti suggests that other factors were involved as well.

The decision to leave the autonomous republics alone may have been influenced by the fact that in the RSFSR their urban populations were largely Slavic and their rural populations indigenous. The decision to retain single committees in the Western Ukraine was probably political as well as economic. Geography seems to have influenced the decision to exclude six of the Far Eastern oblasti. The majority of excluded oblasti in the RSFSR and the Ukraine either bordered other republics or states or bordered an ocean or a sea. It is also possible that placing Kaliningrad under the Lithuanian Central Committee and the general supervision which the Leningrad Obkom exercised over the oblasti of Novgorod and Pskov contributed to the decision to retain single committees in these oblasti. But none of these reasons taken singly offers a sufficient explanation for retaining single committees.

The Oblast Executive Structures

Balancing the professional Party apparatus and the economic managers and technical experts was the fundamental problem in constructing the reformed oblast Party executive structure. The question was: Would "economics over politics" mean increasing the functional representation of the oblast's economic interest or changing the internal structure and composition of the Party organs themselves? The policy, begun in the late fifties, of not publishing the results of oblast Party elections in the republican press was continued in 1962–64. The relatively few completely identified bureaus inhibits generalization on this important point, but an analysis of the Moscow, Leningrad, and Kharkov industrial obkomy indicates that the latter policy was followed.

These bureaus continued to have eleven members and two or three candidates, and, unlike the regional organs at the republican level, secretarial dominance was reduced. Instead of five or six secretaries, each of the industrial bureaus was restricted to four men. The oblast Party apparatus, however, maintained its dominance by placing lower territorial officials or department heads of the oblast committee on the bureaus. In both the Moscow and Leningrad industrial obkomy, two gorkom secretaries and either the head of the Party Organs Department or the industrial-transport departments were added. On the Kharkov Obkom's industrial bureau, the number of apparatchiki was limited to six full members, including the first secretary of the Kharkov Gorkom and a Kharkov raikom first secretary. In all three bureaus, the chairmen of the industrial Soviet and regional sovnarkhoz were represented as formerly. Similarly, the oblast trade union chief was either retained or added. Among the fourth and fifth members, however, there was some variation. The Kharkov Obkom added the oblast's construction chief and a plant director; the Moscow Obkom, the head of the oblast KGB. The gain in functional representation, more substantial in the Kharkov example than in the other committees, was clearly insufficient to challenge the dominant role of the apparatus.

The major gain in functional representation at the oblast level was in agriculture, traditionally represented as a special interest by the chairman of the oblast Soviet executive committee. The new agricultural bureaus, which continued the work of the previous agricultural committees in raising agricultural interest, averaged nine members. The Moscow Bureau for Agriculture, for example, included four secretaries, the heads of the departments for ideology and Party organs, and the secretary of a territorial production committee. The two state officials on the Moscow agricultural obkom were the head of a territorial production administration and the chairman of the Moscow Rural Soviet. The Leningrad Bureau differed slightly. The head of the committee's Party Organs Department was made a candidate, with the three state offices filled by the chairman of the Rural Soviet, the head of the oblast's rural trade unions and, as an afterthought, the head of the Leningrad Military District. In both cases, the professional Party worker's role was unchallenged.

The secretariat, the core of the oblast's traditional power structure, was reduced by the reorganization but essentially unchanged internally. In response to Khrushchev's criticism that the internal division of labor permitted irresponsibility, more precise, formalized responsibilities and functions probably were adopted in 1963 and 1964. The most evident change was the assumption by the first secretary of the industrial or agricultural secretariat of the responsibilities formerly allocated to the industrial or agricultural secretaries. His responsibility for coordinating and integrating the oblast's economy ended with the divided committees, likewise his collateral responsibilities in the cultural and social areas of oblast life. The most dramatic change in the first secretary's role, however, was political.

For the first time since the establishment of tight centralized controls in the Party structure in the New Economic Policy period, an authentic political element was introduced at the oblast level in the competition of the two Party committees. Within the restricted areas of responsibility, the general authority of the industrial or agricultural first secretary, however, seems to have been undiminished. The second secretary appears to have continued as the counterpart of the first secretary, although his responsibilities were probably increased by absorbing the functions of the organizational secretary in those committees where this office was abolished.

The most precise formalization of functions was in the two remaining offices. One secretary continued as ideological secretary. In the Ukraine, the secretary was also usually in charge of the ideological otdel, but this practice seems to have varied in the Russian Republic. The new office in the secretariat was that of the secretary in charge of control, who was given charge of the oblast's Party-State Control Committee. In respect to the latter office, the subordination of this secretary to an authority outside of the oblast secretariat created a delicate and difficult problem.

The departmental changes at the oblast level resembled the patterns set in the central and republican committees, the major distinction being in the lack of a general Party coordinating body at this level. In nine autonomous republics, according to two Soviet writers,[41] two bureaus and a presidium were created, although this is difficult to substantiate. In the split committees, the typical industrial departmental structure included departments for Party organs and ideology, industrial-transport, construction and city economy, administrative-trade-financial organs, and a Party commission. An important aspect of the distribution of departments between committees was the decision to place the staff departments under the industrial obkomy.[42]

The Renovation of Party Cadres

The drastic reorganization of the oblast executive structure opened the way for an equally drastic purge of the apparatus at both the secretarial and departmental levels. Khrushchev's long and bitter struggle to replace the passive and unresponsive "administrators" with younger, more vigorous, more technically sophisticated "organizers" would be crucially tested in the final two years of his rule. This, too, was only partially realized. More discriminate at the secretarial level, the reorganization was felt in full force largely in the departmental structure.

The direct responsibility for daily direction of the oblast's industrial or agricultural economy made the office of first secretary even more important than it had been before. The available evidence clearly indicates that there was no purge. The overall turnover of obkom first secretaries between October 1962 and October 1964 was approximately 23 percent, well below the 1960–62 average.[43] The distribution of incumbent obkom first secretaries bespeaks the extent to which the Party was committed to the agricultural sector. In the assignment of obkom first secretaries to head industrial or agricultural oblasti, forty-three were placed in agricultural secretariats and only twelve went to industrial committees.[44]

The posting of a large majority of first secretaries to agriculture apparently opened the way for a new echelon of Party secretaries capable of dealing more effectively with the mounting problems of industrial administration. For the Soviet Union as a whole, twenty-nine new first secretaries were posted to agricultural and fifty-nine to industrial committees. The patterns of recruitment, however, indicate a high degree of conservatism. The industrial obkom secretaries were almost without exception recruited from the secretariats of the oblasti in which they worked before the reorganization.[45]

The political gain to Khrushchev in these new appointments does not seem to have outweighed the costs of the reorganization.[46] It was perhaps indicative of the political status of the new secretaries that only two were full and three were candidate members of the Central Committee. That the older obkom first secretaries remained in power after November, even though their power and status had been reduced by the reorganization, presumably intensified the antagonism between Khrushchev and the territorial Party apparatus. Recruiting relatively low status officials could not balance this hostility.

Whether the Party gained as an institution is more problematical. Virtually all of the 1963 obkom first secretaries had entered the Party during Stalin's lifetime. The majority of agricultural first secretaries, however, had entered the Party during or after the purges of the thirties; the newer secretaries, during the war or postwar years. The newer secretaries seem also to have escaped the full brunt of socialization within the Stalinist apparatus. According to Grey Hodnett, less than 5 percent of the 1963 and 1964 appointees had held a post as high as obkom secretary under Stalin.[47] The exact effect on these officials of reducing the influence of the Stalinist apparatus, however, is impossible to assess since in values and style, the Party continued to exhibit the conservatism of the Stalinist period.

In the literature justifying the reform, Soviet officials and writers stressed the gain in decision-making efficiency. A. P. Kirilenko reported to a conference on Russian Federation industry that of eighty-four first and second secretaries heading industrial obkomy, seventy-eight, or 93 percent, were engineers and in unified oblasts; all of the secretaries heading industry and construction were also engineers.[48] Among agricultural first and second secretaries, however, the figure was about 80 percent. By 1963 higher education had become prerequisite for an obkom secretary: 98.6 percent of all secretaries in industrial obkoms and 96.2 percent in agricultural secretariats had a higher education.[49] In the industrial secretariats there were 136 technical experts and engineers and twenty-seven candidates or doctors of a technical specialty.[50] There was also some effort to reduce the age levels of the secretariats.[51] The older and newer first secretaries had essentially similar social backgrounds. Those with peasant origins outnumbered those with worker and urban backgrounds by two to one.[52]

The changes in Party cadres at the secretarial level did not alter their essential continuity. While the new men were younger, better educated, and less exposed to the socialization of the Stalinist apparatus, they were drawn from the same cultural, social, and intellectual milieu as the older secretaries and had shared similar lives. Far more significant changes in the oblast Party apparatus occurred among heads of departments and instructors.

The data, while extremely limited, are suggestive. A number of industrial obkomy turned over all department heads, and "diploma specialists" were recruited directly into the obkom apparat to serve as instructors.[53] In the Perm industrial obkom, this resulted in 80 percent of the departments being staffed with industrial specialists with higher education.[54] The recruitment of technical specialists in the agricultural obkomy was clearly less successful.[55]

5

The Local Party Organs

The urban local Party organs, which had been a principal focus of reform during the preceding period, were essentially unchanged during the final two years of Khrushchev's rule. The decision to abolish gorkomy in oblast centers was implemented unevenly, and the size and composition of the gorkom and raikom bureaus and secretariats remained stable.[56] The gorkom departmental structures were changed, however, by the decision to reverse the 1957 trend toward abolishing special departments.[57] In Moscow, five special production-branch raikomy were set up for primary Party organs in the construction and building materials industries, transportation, trade, public transport, and communications.[58] In urban centers having both agricultural and industrial institutions, special Party organs were formed to unite Communists working in agricultural institutions.[59]

The major changes at the local Party level were in the agricultural sector. To guide industry in rural areas which were not turned over to the agricultural obkomy, industrial-production (zonal) committees were formed. Created on the basis of the revised administrative boundaries, these committees were small and poorly staffed. Their structure resembled that of the smaller urban raikomy: there was usually a secretary, one deputy secretary for organizational affairs and one for ideological questions, and from ten to fifteen instructors. Lacking a formal departmental structure, the zonal committees continued to assign instructors to enterprises according to branch of industry.[60]

The structure of the territorial production administration was essentially similar. Stretched over two to three of the abolished rural raiony, the Party apparatus usually consisted of a secretary, two deputies who were also usually heads of the organizational and ideological otdely, and was staffed by twenty to twenty-five inspector-Party organizers.[61] While their jurisdictional boundaries were smaller than in 1962, the areas covered were still so large that the inspector-Party organizer operated on a territorial rather than branch basis and often lived in the area he served.[62]

Party cadres was a major concern of the reorganization at this level as well, where the emphasis was on selecting technically trained officials with diplomas who were forty years of age or younger. In the elections held in the Ukraine, the number of gorkom and raikom first secretaries with higher education reached 85 percent.[63] Women were increasingly recruited; by 1963, 26.4 percent of all gorkom and raikom secretaries were women.[64] The number of gorkom officials under forty also increased.[65] In 1959, only 35.5 percent of the Leningrad raikomy secretaries were under forty, but by 1963 this figure had risen to 61.4 percent.[66]

"Economics over politics" appears to have been most concentrated at the local level in the heavy turnover of instructors. The policy of recruiting specialists directly from production as instructors was perhaps greater here than at the obkom level. Of twenty-six instructors in the Murmansk Gorkom, for example, twenty-one were taken directly into the apparatus without experience in the Party. Recruiting more women as instructors was also intensified. In the Moscow Gorkom and raikomy, undoubtedly an unusual case, the number of women instructors reached 50.4 percent.[67]

Party and Soviet workers released from the abolished rural raikomy and soviets staffed the new rural Party organs. In that respect, the reorganization did little to raise the technical levels of the rural Party cadres.

6

The Primary Party Organs

Although the November reorganization would affect the cadres and operational functions of the primary Party organs in a variety of ways, structural change was minimal.[68] A new form of industrial primary Party organization emerged in 1962 with the formation of branch production unions. In Leningrad, where fifty-five plants were combined into nine "firms," particularly difficult problems of coordination and direction of these committees arose since several of them were spread over three oblasti.[69] Within the individual plant committee, the most important change was the addition of another deputy secretary in charge of control. The handling of substantive economic and technical problems within the plant, however, remained the responsibility of the secretary.

At the primary Party level as at the local level, "economics over politics" meant raising the educational and technical qualifications of secretaries. The election-and-report meeting of 1963–64 witnessed a heavy turnover of secretaries despite the urgent protests of the gorkomy and raikomy.[70] Throughout the Soviet Union, the turnover was 56.5 percent,[71] in some cases as high as 70 percent, a significant rise from the usual turnover of 30–35 percent. Among secretaries in industrial and construction organs, 41.1 percent were engineering-technical workers.[72] The percentage varied widely, however. In Gorkii Oblast, which was highly industrialized, all secretaries of major primary Party organs had a higher education.[73] In Uzbekistan, however, only 38 percent of the secretaries at this level were credited with higher education. The introduction of specialists with diplomas but with no previous experience in Party work produced serious problems in political socialization at the mass level and increased the tensions in Party-state relations within the enterprises.[74]

7

The Party-State Control Committee

The attempt to reorganize bureaucratic controls into a complex structure of mass control to achieve economic efficiency and a disciplined, responsive economic bureaucracy reached its most intense phase with the November reorganization. Formed on 27 November 1962 by a joint decree of the Central Committee and the Council of Ministers,[75] the Party-State Control Committee was formally established on 20 December 1962 through a statute, summarized in *Pravda* and *Izvestiia* on 18 January 1963.[76] In 1964, the full text of the statute was published in the fifth edition of the *Spravochnik partiinogo rabotnika*.[77] In July 1964, a separate statute on groups and posts of assistance was published in *Partiinaia zhizn'*, presumably to clarify the rights and authority of the mass organs of control.[78]

The formal functions and authority of the new control organs were extensive. In addition to aiding in plan fulfillment and raising efficiency, they were given large powers over the administration.

The Party-state control agencies must give assistance to the Party in improving the work of the state and administrative managerial apparatus, furthering a reduction in its costs and perfecting its organization; they must put a decisive end to violations of Party and state discipline; to manifestations of localism, a narrow departmental attitude to matters; hood-winking; report padding; mismanagement and extravagance; they must wage a ruthless fight against bureaucratism and red-tape, bribe-taking, speculation, abuse of office, and any encroachment on socialist property; they must exercise control over the measure of labor and the measure of consumption, over the observation of the socialist principle "He who does not work, neither shall he eat," and they must oppose any other kind of action that brings harm to communist construction.[79]

Although theoretically no managerial act was exempt from public censure and criticism, the formal sanctions permitted the controllers were less extensive, modeled after the authority of the abolished Soviet Control Committee. The Committee on Party-State Control and its local organizations were empowered to issue instructions to heads of any state organization to eliminate shortcomings. The specific sanctions included requiring public reports of offending officials; the suspension of administrative orders; submitting individual cases to the comrades' courts; withholding an official's pay for damages; or the controllers could issue reprimands; impose disciplinary penalties, including suspension and fine; demote or fire the suspected officials; or, in extreme cases, they could turn the material over to the courts for criminal prosecution.[80] The Party-State Control Committee did not have the right to impose Party sanctions, including expulsion from the Party.

The formal authority structure was never fully defined. The question of whether these committees possessed the right to supervise the Soviets' elective bodies or to control the permanent commissions as an aktiv evoked sharply differing assessments.[81] In its final form, the Party-State Control Committee was a joint agency of the Party and the state, although its pervasive Party character was fully recognized. As one Soviet writer frankly admitted, "All work of Party-state control was conducted under the direct leadership of the KPSS."[82] It was ultimately structured as a collective organ and as a union republican agency. The degree of centralization and the resulting role of the territorial Party apparatus in terms of control were complex matters.

Some Soviet scholars, including M. B. Mitin, have discussed the Party-State Control Committee exclusively in centralist terms.[83] Other Soviet scholars, however, have called attention to distinctions in authority between the regional and local Party organs in relation to the control committees.[84] The republican, krai, and oblast committees were subordinate to both the regional Party committee and to the corresponding soviet. In practical terms, this meant that the regional committee was jointly controlled by the republican or central control committee and the regular Party organs. At the local level, however, with the exception of the Moscow and Leningrad city control committees,[85] neither the Party nor the soviet exercised formal authority. The control committees were directly subordinate to the oblast and higher control committees.

The separation of Party and control organs, justified as a necessary defense against localism, undoubtedly served as an informal check on the performance of local Party organs and, through the system of independent reporting, served to open both the regional and local agencies to more critical scrutiny. Formal disciplinary power, however, was the direct and indirect prerogative of the Party apparatus.

The structure designed to direct and organize such a massive penetration of the economic bureaucracy was stronger than the organs of state control. In 1964 throughout the Soviet Union, there were 3,280 control committees, with over sixteen thousand nonstaff departments and commissions, and 710 thousand groups and posts of assistance, with over four million activists.[86] From the center to the raion, the basic structure was essentially similar. Each control organ was composed of a committee and an apparatus for conducting the organization of control.

8

The Party-State Control Structure

The committees of Party-state control ranged from seven to fourteen members.[87] The union and Russian Republic committees remained unpublished, but they were presumably formed in general accordance with the statutes. The committees were composed of a chairman, deputy chairman, members of the committee's apparatus or lower control officials, representatives of the press, and individual workers, kolkhozniki, and members of the scientific or technical intelligentsia. Among those placed on the Union Party-State Control Committee were the chairman who was also a secretary of the Central Committee and a deputy chairman of the Council of Ministers, a first deputy chairman, two deputy chairmen, two secretaries of the All-Union Komsomols and Trade Union Council. The members of the central control apparatus and the representatives of society remained unidentified.[88]

The regional committees resembled the union committee. The republican committee was headed by a chairman who was simultaneously a secretary of the Central Committee, a deputy chairman of the Council of Ministers, and a member of the Presidium. The only exception to this was in the Ukraine where the chairman was a candidate of the Presidium. The Estonian Party-State Control Committee was representative. In addition to the chairman and two deputy chairmen, the committee was composed of the director of the Tallinn

Polytechnic Institute, a worker in the Tallinn Machine-Building Plant, a secretary of the Estonian Trades Union Council, a deputy editor of *Sovetskaia Estonia*, the head of a kolkhoz dairy farm, the deputy editor of the Estonian language newspaper *Rakhiva Khyayal*; and, finally, the second secretary of the Estonian Young Communist League.[89]

The oblast Committee of Party-State Control simply replicated the republican committees. Headed by an obkom secretary who was also a member of the oblast executive committee, the typical committee included a deputy chairman, the two secretaries of the oblast Komsomol and Trade Union Council, a representative of the oblast newspaper, one or two chairmen of lower control committees, and the representatives of various social groups. Divided committees normally reflected the industrial or agricultural character of the committee. The major break in the committee structure occurred at the local level where the committee chairman was not (except in Moscow and Leningrad) a secretary of the gorkom or raikom. The chairman was usually a prominent member of the aktiv, and the full-time members of the local committees were placed in charge of the apparatus and responsible to the oblast Party-State Control Committee. They were therefore under the direct control of the obkom or republican secretary.

The structures of the Party-state control committees, essentially similar from the union to local levels, were representative of their symbolic and general coordination functions. Their composition was broadly social rather than narrowly administrative and representative of neither the economic bureaucracy nor the professional controllers, including the police. The actual work of organizing the complex system of mass control, however, fell to the executive apparatus.

The administrative structure. Like the Party departmental system, the Party-State Control Committee's executive structure was designed on a production-branch basis; like the committees, the departments and commissions exhibited common structures from the central to local levels, the departments of the union Party-State Control Committee serving as a prototype for the lower committees. Among the departments identified in the Soviet press for the central Party-State Control Committee were two staff departments, the Department for Leading Cadres and Organizational Work and the Department for Administrative Organs. In addition, there were a series of production-branch departments: agriculture, chemical and oil industries; construction and building materials; educational institutions; science, culture, and health; machine building; heavy industry; coal industry; transportation; and probably a number of others, such as a Department for Light Industry.

The regional administrative systems were, of course, similar. Each republican apparatus had an organizational otdel responsible for complaints, processing information, and general coordination. The number and type of production-branch departments, however, varied with the republic or oblast. The Ukrainian apparatus, for example, consisted of departments for agriculture; chemical and oil refining industries; construction and building materials; heavy industry; light, food, and fish industries; machine building; and trade. In the smaller, less industrialized republics, industrial control was usually placed in a single department with a number of branch sections.

Among divided oblast control committees, the departments formed were normally more specialized than those in unified oblast or republican control committees. The Leningrad Gorkom, regarded as equal to an obkom, had thirteen departments, but others were smaller.[90] The average complement for nonstaff controllers at the oblast level was usually ten to fifteen per department. In a larger committee, however, such as Kharkov's, the number could rise to thirty-five or forty.[91]

The "mass" character of the Party-state control structure was most evident at the local level. Except for the larger cities, the formal departmental structures were less specialized and smaller in size. The regional committees were duplicated at the local level. All except the smallest city raikom and zonal committees had a bureau for workers' complaints and an organization department as well as three or four branch departments. Some local control committees also established permanent commissions for various industrial functions.[92] The smallest and least effective of the industrial control groups were found in the zonal committees, which were often composed of less than twenty inspectors in two or three otdely.[93]

In staffing these organs there was a clear effort to compromise the staff and volunteer principles on a hierarchical basis. At the union and republican levels, the departments were staffed with full-time control officials. At the oblast level, however, a directing core of full-time controllers was established around a large aktiv. While oblast control committees were nominally restricted to three to seven paid officials,[94] the operational rule was to head the most important departments with the paid staff. The Leningrad City Party-State Control Committee, for example, had a staff of nineteen full-time controllers.[95] At the local level, where the actual control operations were carried out under oblast or republican direction, the control committees were usually limited to a single paid official in charge of overall administration.

The total number of paid personnel in the control apparatus can be partially estimated by the size of the Ukrainian apparatus. In the Ukraine, and presumably for the Soviet Union as a whole, the ratio of staff to social controllers was one to thirty-four.[96] Since there were an estimated thirty thousand nonstaff inspectors in the Ukraine, there were approximately 900 full-time control officials for the republic.[97] Eighty of these officials were in the republican apparatus; another 484 were at the city and borough levels. The remaining 325 were assigned to the forty-four oblast committees, for an average of seven per committee. If these figures are extrapolated for the Soviet Union as a whole, on the basis of 130 thousand social inspectors, the total number of paid personnel in the control net would be approximately 4,000. This figure, however, should be approached cautiously. In Belorussia, there were a reported 2,515 social inspectors serving in twelve oblast and 125 local committees. At the ratio given for the Ukraine, this would constitute a paid apparatus of only seventy-five inspectors, which is clearly inadequate. To staff the smaller republics effectively, it seems evident that a ratio lower than one to thirty-four was required. In Belorussia, this figure would have been nearer one to ten or twelve. For Leningrad, the ratio would have been one to sixty-eight.

Recruiting personnel to staff the control net was placed under the Party Organs Department of the regional and central Party committees. The volunteer staff was recruited according to the criteria for selecting members of nonstaff organs of the regular Party committees. Principal reliance was placed on a mixture of pensioners and specialists drawn from active social and economic life. The number of pensioners varied from a relatively small number to over half the volunteer staff.[98] A special effort to recruit volunteers with higher education brought uneven results. The drawing of workers and kolkhozniki into the apparatus and the competition for manpower served to reduce the educational levels of these committees. In a heavily industrialized and urbanized area such as Leningrad, only half of the staff of the city's Party-State Control Committee had an incomplete higher or higher education.[99]

Recruiting paid officials to form the cadre core of the control net presented a more complex problem in terms of whether such officials would be selected from the local apparatus or sent in from the outside. The evidence, however incomplete, suggests that the cadres were Party apparatchiki, generally low-status officials selected primarily from the areas in which they were currently serving, thereby maximizing the possibilities of control by the local Party organs.

The key officials in the new control structure were the chairmen of the central, republican, and provincial committees and their deputies. The Chairman of the Party-State Control Committee, Shelepin, had had lengthy experience in the control structure under Khrushchev, as first secretary of Komsomols, a Central Committee department head, and before becoming a Central Committee secretary in 1961, as chairman of the Committee on State Security. His First Deputy Chairman, I. V. Shikin, had served as a Party official in the military apparatus and as deputy head of the Party Organs Department for the Union Republics before becoming ambassador to Albania in 1961. The deputy chairman was a close associate of Shelepin who had spent his entire career in the Komsomols except for a two-year tour as second secretary of the Kemerovo Obkom. Similar experience was evident in staffing the Russian Republic's control system. The chairman was G. V. Eniutin, a long-time Party official and chairman of the

USSR Soviet Control Committee. His deputy was V. M. Churaev, the former head of the Russian Bureau's Party Organs Department.

The officials selected to head the republican control committees showed more variety. Nine of the fourteen chairmen were currently serving as Party officials.[100] All but two were natives of the republics in which they served, and none were transferred from other republics to take the control post. Only one of the new chairmen had never served in the Party apparatus, in contrast to six chairmen whose careers were spent entirely within the Party structure. A number of others had spent most of their careers in the Party apparatus.[101]

The appointment of republican deputy chairmen revealed another pattern. Each committee normally had two deputies symbolically uniting the Party and state apparatuses; the usual arrangement was to match the chairman of the abolished Soviet Control Committee with a Party official. In the Ukraine, for example, A. S. Malenkin was joined with N. Kuznetsov, the head of the Administrative Organs Department. The pattern was not constant, however. In Belorussia, both deputy chairmen were drawn from the republican Central Committee.

In the appointment of the oblast secretaries for control lay a decisive victory for the regular Party organs. In the Ukraine, the large majority of new secretaries were selected from the oblast in which they were serving and had been either gorkom or raikom secretaries or heads of the oblast committees' Party Organs Department, a circumstance suggesting the strong influence of the obkom first secretary. In Belorussia, however, two of the new secretaries were sent down from the republican Party Organs Department.[102]

The explicit ties of the new Party-state control committees to the Party organs departments at the central and regional levels clearly pointed to a major concentration of the new committees on cadres and discipline.

The groups and posts of assistance. The mobilizing instruments of mass control were those groups and posts which blanketed the whole of the Soviet economy. The aktiv of over four millions, organized into 210 thousand groups and 500 thousand posts, was in theory a formidable force for moving the sluggish managerial bureaucracy toward the goals which Soviet leadership had placed upon it. The larger plants had a complex mass control structure. In the Minsk Tractor Plant, for example, there were a total of twenty-four assistance groups and 144 posts with 600 controllers. In the larger plants, such as the Minsk plant, the entire control net for the plant was directed by a general assistance group, usually comprising fifty members who were chairmen of subordinate groups and the larger posts. Where a general assistance group was formed, executive control work within the plant was transferred to a directing bureau of five to seven.[103]

Here, the primary Party organ was the central directing force. The chairman of the assistance group or bureau was a deputy secretary added for this purpose.

Under his purview, the activities of the plant's trade union and Komsomol controllers were integrated into the general structure and control. The communication flow between the mass control agencies and the central and territorial Party-state control committees was maintained through the nonstaff inspectors of the organizational otdely at each level of the apparatus. In relying on volunteers to service the internal operation and communication functions of the control apparatus, it seems clear that the advantages of social participation were offset by an extremely loose overall structure and serious difficulties in communication.[104]

The Dynamics of Party Reform

Khrushchev's ouster in October 1964, which closed a turbulent and complex chapter in the development of the Soviet political system, was largely the result of the political and administrative turmoil of the November reorganization. Among the major factors leading to his political isolation and defeat were his persistent struggle for power, his controversial policy initiatives, his relentless pursuit of the members of the Anti-Party Group, crowned by their expulsion from the Party,[1] and his increasingly bitter polemics with the Chinese.[2]

The compromises of the November plenum satisfied neither the liberals nor the conservatives of the Soviet elite. Its liberal and anti-Stalinist thrust was reversed in December 1962 with the crackdown on the cultural and literary intelligentsia,[3] and Khrushchev and his supporters were periodically required to defend his Stalinist apparatchik image.[4] At the same time, Khrushchev's advocacy of "economics over politics" raised conservative protest concerning the legitimate role of the Communist party as a political institution, a reflection, in part, of the failure to formulate an acceptable alternative to the traditional conceptions of Party authority, either within the Party or in Soviet society.

The political conflict surrounding Khrushchev's personal authority was linked to his economic and administrative policies. As the Togliatti memorandum indicated, economic policies constituted a major source of cleavage within the Soviet leadership.[5] Khrushchev's effort to reallocate investment and production priorities from steel to chemistry and the "progressive industries" and to shift the growth rates from heavy to light industry aroused deep controversy.[6] Moreover, the intensification of administrative controls over the managerial apparatus created complex new problems of industrial management without solving the most urgent of the old problems. The declining growth rate, the crisis in construction, and the mounting problems of consumer goods production—all revived public criticism by the advocates of economic methods of reform.[7] The permanence of the November resolution of the problems of economic management became more doubtful as the reform proceeded. The 1963 harvest failure led Khrushchev to critically reevaluate the administrative structures and the Party's role in agriculture.[8] In July 1964 and into the fall of the same year, the evidence pointed to a further reorganization of economic management.[9]

Establishing new economic priorities and restructuring the basis of economic administration were closely related to the role Khrushchev assigned the Party in 1963 and 1964. In general, the Party was limited to supervision and control of the construction and production plans of his chemical, consumer goods, and agricultural programs. If the Party's specific role in 1963–64 is viewed in terms of the November 1962 plenum and the preceding period, it will be seen that the policy of increasing the Party's economic leadership reached its most intense application during the final two years of Khrushchev's rule.

The attempts to broaden the Party's base, to recruit economic and technical specialists, to activate the Party committee as an economic aktiv, to increase the technical qualifications of Party officials and change their political style—all were aimed at increasing the Party's relevance as a social institution and at increasing growth rates and administrative efficiency. Extending the production principle in the Party structure and renovating cadres after the November plenum concentrated previous trends in addition to introducing new elements into Party life.

Although the purpose of the plenum was to strengthen the Party's role in economic administration, the Party apparatus did not win a simple or complete victory over the state economic administration in 1963 and 1964. In one respect, the Party appears to have reverted to the policies of 1957–60, when the territorial Party apparatus was supposed to penetrate the wall of conservative managerial resistance to economic innovation. In another respect, however, while the Party apparatus' direct administrative responsibilities increased rapidly under Khrushchev's economic policies and Party reform, the actual administrative power of the territorial apparatus experienced a further decline.

The direct substitution of Party agencies for the state administration at the production rather than at the higher levels of state administration reproduced many of the characteristics of Party *rukovodstvo* under the ministerial system. The atmosphere of tension and feverish activity in the Party and Party-state control agencies during the final years of Khrushchev's rule resembled the years of crisis and storm during the First Five-Year Plan.

The protests against the direct assumption of administrative power by the Party agencies, against the reform of the Party structure, and against "economics over politics" represented conventional Party wisdom as expressed in the traditional doctrine of the leading role. Khrushchev, who periodically affirmed his commitment to the traditional view, did so again in the spring of 1963. Evidently responding to the Party conservatives, he noted that the Party should become deeply involved in production but "that the Party organizations must not assume functions that do not belong to them, must not substitute for the economic agencies. Each is obligated to occupy itself with its own business. Party committees are agencies for the political and organizational leadership of the masses."[10]

Downgrading the functions of the Party apparatus in economic leadership was clearly tactical. In the summer of 1963, Khrushchev used the Party as the major instrument for translating the priorities of the Two-Year Plan into the new economic plans. As the urgency of his chemical program increased, Khrushchev directed the bureaus for industry and construction of the republican Party committees and the industrial obkomy to assume direct control over chemical construction.[11] Later, this was extended to such related industries as chemical machine-building.

As the massive problems in planning, construction, and supply emerged in the crash program of chemical construction, the Party became a general troubleshooter and *tolkach*, speeding up the construction and production processes as it attempted to ameliorate the severe tensions in the administrative structure which Khrushchev's policies produced. As in the pre–1962 period, Khrushchev concentrated on the practical consequences of the Party's role rather than on its normative boundaries. In his frequent complaints about the Party's intervention in administrative processes, particularly in agriculture, his fundamental criterion was the competence, rather than the existence, of substitution.

1

The Effect of Reform on the
Institutional Party

Institutionalized Party guidance within the Soviet economy has been conditioned by the structure of internal Party authority in relation to the distribution of decision-making power within the Soviet state. A centralized and monolithic structure has framed a rigidly inflexible system of internal authority which sharply reduced the initiative and the responsibility of the intermediate and lower levels of the hierarchy. The problem of supporting centralized direction and cohesion while simultaneously maintaining flexibility in the face of local and diverse circumstances has been noted by the Party's organizational specialists from Lenin to the present.

In practice, the internal Party authority structure has failed to achieve a delicate balance between centralized direction and local initiative. Tight centralization of authority and the transmission of power through the first secretaries at each level of the Party structure served to reduce the significance of those measures of decentralization and the emphasis upon collective leadership characteristic of Party reform following the Twentieth Party Congress. With respect to the problems of Party leadership arising from weaknesses of authority and structure, the November plenum indicated that the existing system of authority would not only be maintained but would undergo further centralization and specialization.

In general, the reform would weaken the Party structure and deeply disturb its internal life. Conflicts arising from its doubtful legitimacy and specific strains resulting directly from the reorganization weakened the internal authority structure. This, like other of Khrushchev's reforms, however, was far from thorough, and the threat to the Party's institutional cohesion evidently aroused conservative countervailing forces to maintain a measure of equilibrium. Continuity, rather than change, characterized 1963 and 1964. Further, the effect of the Party reform varied according to hierarchical level and functions. At the central, republican, and regional levels, the structural impact was primary. Cohesion was maintained through the continuity of Party cadres. At the local and primary Party levels, however, the situation was the reverse: structural reorganization was minimal, but the heavy turnover in Party cadres introduced serious problems of disequilibrium into the system.

2

The November Plenum and Internal
Party Authority

The November plenum was clearly intended to maximize centralized Party controls over the territorial Party apparatus; proliferating central Party organs and specializing the regional Party apparatus would limit the range and discretion of subordinate Party organs and increase the force of central Party directives. Khrushchev, who bitterly condemned the "localism" of the territorial Party structure in April 1963,[12] simply reverted to the traditional remedy of administrative centralism to increase compliance. In the spring of 1963, the centralist thrust was particularly marked. Both Khrushchev and Ilychev indicated that de-Stalinization did not mean a weakening of guidance or negation of authority. Khrushchev revived Lenin's metaphor of society as a gigantic mechanism requiring precise management and discipline;[13] Ilychev attacked anarchism and lack of discipline; both aimed at reinforcing the centralized controls of the reorganization.[14]

That the emphasis upon authoritarianism in the first half of 1963 was a reaction to the opposition of Party cadres and the liberal intelligentsia was pointedly suggested by V. V. Klochko, deputy head of the Faculty of Party Construction of the Higher Party School, who attacked the "view of some cadres that development of inner-Party democracy and volunteer principles has ended the need for centralization." Centralization "guarantees the unity and solidarity of the Party and helps it fight against localistic tendencies and violations of Party and state discipline." The November plenum, in his view, was directly related to the principle of centralization: "The production-based pattern of the Party's organizational structure ensures the necessary centralization of leadership."[15]

The emphasis upon centralism, even during 1963, was not unique. An editorial in *Partiinaia zhizn'* in the fall of 1963 reaffirmed the need to overcome stagnant, bureaucratic methods of Party leadership and to broaden the rights of local Party organs.[16] Articles by such prominent specialists as Shitarev and D. E. Bakhshiev stressing the development of Leninist norms in the post-Stalin period were part of a general trend toward blunting the centralizing force of the reorganization.[17] The forces within the Party favoring some degree of decentralization were undoubtedly aided by the Sino-Soviet polemics as well as by internal opposition from Soviet nationalists who resented the formation of interrepublican organs. Despite these factors, however, the net change in the distribution of authority would strengthen centralized Party controls over the territorial apparatus.

The actual distribution of power within the central Party structure is difficult to assess because of the differing authority and roles of the new central organs. The Party-State Control Committee added a major new element in Party decision-making. The three economic branch bureaus, on the other hand, remained largely empty forms exercising but marginal influence within the system of Party authority. In their two years of existence, the only published evidence of their activity was the disclosure by an obkom first secretary at the December 1963 plenum that the Bureau for the Chemical Industry and Light Industry had heard a report of the Severodonetsk Gorkom of the Ukraine on its leadership of chemical construction.[18] This, however, was a rare, if not a unique, event. When an all-union conference on consumer goods was held in the Central Committee, the sponsoring Party agency was the Department of Light, Food Industry, and Trade. And when the Sumgast Synthetic Rubber Plant's Party committee reported on the execution of the December 1963 plenum's decisions, the report was heard by the Commission for Organizational-Party Questions rather than by the Bureau for the Chemical Industry and Light Industry.[19]

More active were the two commissions for directing the Party's ideological and organizational affairs. Although their power in the system of internal authority was never revealed, the fact that they were commissions rather than bureaus or committees with independent administrative power may have been partially responsible for the greater scope and visibility of their activities. The more publicized of the two commissions, the Ideological Commission under L. F.

Ilychev, met frequently in the winter of 1963 and spring of 1964 to discuss a wide variety of topics, including the theatre and dramatic arts,[20] children's literature,[21] and the popularization of scientific and technical literature;[22] an important session on atheism repudiated a blatantly anti-Semitic book by T. Kichko.[23] But none of the published data on the work of the Ideological Commission were directly concerned with the ideological work of the regular Party organs.

The Commission for Organizational-Party Questions was, on the other hand, deeply involved in the Party's economic leadership. In 1963 and 1964, the commission held a session on the *rukovodstvo* of two production administrations in Volgograd and Poltava oblasti.[24] Sessions were also held on the work of the Karelian and L'vov industrial obkomy[25] as well as the primary Party organ of the State Committee for the Chemical and Petroleum Industries.[26] An investigation was conducted of the departments of Party organs of the union republics.[27] In conducting its investigations prior to formal hearings, the commission used independent investigators to gather material for the sessions. Although the number of public sessions was limited, the commission evidently operated on an all-union basis, investigating Party organs in the RSFSR as well as the union republics; and the scope of its activity was apparently directed toward controlling the economic functions of the territorial Party apparatus and the Moscow state apparatus. In this respect, its authority overlapped that of the economic bureaus and probably preempted them.

In their leadership of lower Party organs and in directing the economy, the three central territorial bureaus exhibited differing degrees of authority. As the activities of the Commission for Organizational-Party Questions reveal, the Party organs under the Russian Bureau were checked by a secretarial organ, although in other respects the Russian Bureau's authority was untouched. Decision-making power in the Russian Bureau remained within the bureau and was not delegated. The single public reference to a meeting of the Russian Bureau for the Leadership of Industry and Construction was to a session held on speeding up machine building. A. P. Kirilenko, who chaired the meeting, was identified as the first deputy vice-chairman of the bureau, and the resolution was issued in the bureau's name rather than that of its section for industrial guidance.[28]

The establishment of regional bureaus for Central Asia and the Transcaucasus ensnarled the definition of Party authority at a variety of levels. In respect to the central Party organs, their decision-making authority stemmed from the Presidium. Their administrative role, however, was more complex. Although each of the bureaus had a small permanent staff, there is no evidence that these were organized into formal departments. In guiding the republican Party committees within their jurisdictions, the regional bureaus evidently continued to share authority with the Department for Party Organs for the Union Republics.[29] It appears that the role of the regional bureaus was defined in terms of economic *rukovodstvo*, with the functions of internal organizational and ideological leadership remaining with the regular central staff, principally the Central Asian and the Transcaucasian sectors of the Party Organs Department. Such a clear division of functions, however, is not easily drawn. One of the functions exercised by the bureaus was ideological leadership, as indicated, for example, by the Transcaucasian Bureau's part in organizing a conference of historians in Tbilisi for the purpose of developing a regional approach to the writing of Transcaucasian history.[30]

Generally, the regional bureaus reduced the role of the republican organization. The formation of the Central Asian Bureau created such difficulties that Frol Kozlov was required to make several trips in the spring of 1963 to resolve them.[31] That the three Transcaucasian republics were sensitive is suggested by the joint report of the three republican secretaries in April 1963 declaring that sessions of the Transcaucasian Bureau would be held equally in all three capitals rather than in Tbilisi alone.[32] The status of the republican first secretaries in relation to their bureaus was far from equal, however. An interesting insight in this respect was provided by the one hundred fiftieth anniversary of Azerbaidzhan's annexation to Russia. While Bochkarev followed Podgorny and Mzhavanadze, the first secretary of Georgia, in the listing of notables he was placed ahead of Akhundov, the first secretary of Azerbaidzhan.[33]

The presence within Central Asia of a fully developed economic administrative apparatus clearly strengthened the role and authority of the Central Asian Bureau. The Transcaucasian Bureau, on the other hand, functioned primarily through the regional planning commission. Not limited to planning and coordination, it was also responsible for plan fulfillment in the individual republics. Although the Transcaucasian Bureau's precise degree of administrative authority is not clear, its position was manifestly weaker than that of its counterpart in Central Asia.

Whereas interrepublican systems in Central Asia were under the direct *rukovodstvo* of the Central Asian Bureau, the normal division of authority in such systems as the Transcaucasian Railroad involved the joint control of the Transcaucasian Bureau and the individual republican committees.[34] Issues of high central priority engaged the bureau's power directly and specifically. The bureau, for example, ordered the Georgian Industrial Bureau to take specific control over a chemical construction site and defined the concrete measures required to complete the job.[35] But the Transcaucasian Bureau was not the exclusive Moscow authority within its region. In 1963 and 1964, Central Committee commissions and brigades were sent into Azerbaidzhan to deal with problems of local significance.[36]

The opposition to the power of the regional bureaus was, in part, an extension of the more basic, continuous conflict created by the cleavages between the central and local Party and state leaderships. Central and republican officials recognized that the formation of interrepublican organs was a stage in the Party Program's long-range policy of eliminating existing national boundaries as definitive administrative units within the USSR.[37] The political struggle in 1963 and 1964 involved values of both cultural and economic nationalism. As part of the general campaign for ideological conformity,[38] republican leaders renewed emphasis on the positive role of the Russian peoples in the USSR and the Russian language as the language of "proletarian internationalism."[39] Cultural nationalism, however, was less important than economic nationalism.

Forming regional Party and state organs was, as noted previously, part of the more general policy of creating a rationalized administrative structure in which political boundaries and economic potential would coincide. In this respect, however, Khrushchev's reform policy ran afoul of that "fetishization of national sovereignty" and "narrow understanding of national interests" which actively fought to block the integration of the republics into a supranational organization.[40] Against the regionalizers' view that the Soviet economy was a single integrated organism, the defenders of the administrative status quo argued for "national equality" and the special characteristics of their *natsional'naia spetsifika*.[41] Each republican leader pressed for a policy of economic autarky and universal economic development against the policies of specialization and interdependence dictated by Moscow.

The policy, followed between 1955 and 1960, of decentralization and of broadening the rights of the union republics hindered Moscow in pressing for centralization.[42] Mutual jealousy and competition among the republics had been strengthened by the previous policy of emphasizing national equality and decentralization. By 1962, the demand for equal investment and equal distribution of economic and social benefits had become strongly entrenched in the psychology of republican leaders.[43] Moscow's aim in forming the Central Asian and Transcaucasian bureaus was directed toward establishing the proportions of Khrushchev's economic policy and toward breaking down national *mestnichestvo*.

The decision to penetrate the "closed" republican economies through increased centralized controls exercised through supranational political and administrative organs[44] was opposed in a variety of ways. Direct opposition was recorded by officials in both Central Asia and Transcaucasia.[45] Extending the Central Asian model to other economic regions was opposed in conferences held on the issue by the argument that the republican economies of Central Asia were exceptional, and that the regional institutions adopted for this area were not applicable to theirs.[46]

The most penetrating analysis of national localism was provided by G. Zimanas, a Lithuanian writer, who attributed localist opposition to the republican and local cadres' traditional distrust of the center.[47] Motivated by the view that "If we don't take care of ourselves, no one else will do it,"[48] the republican leaders struggled to defend and expand "their" short-term, limited interests against the longer-range interests of society as a whole. Securing officials willing to impose central policies in the localities was a complex problem. At the November plenum, Khrushchev advocated interchanging national cadres.[49] Zimanas, on the other hand, advocated interchanging higher and lower Party and state officials and frequent convocations of local officials in the center to reinforce the national point of view.[50]

The conflicts of interest between the center and the localities in relation to economic policy and administration provided one of the bases for the legitimacy of the Party's leading role. Providing the organizational mechanism for political and economic integration of Soviet society was a role assigned in theory and in practice as well.[51] The Party as an institution, however, is not an alien body transcending the particularities of society. The November plenum intensified nationalism by creating interrepublican institutions. At the regional level, localism was stimulated by the structural reform itself.

3

The Fissures in the Monolith

The November reforms of the system of Party authority most deeply disturbed the middle echelons of the Party structure, particularly those krai and oblast committees divided into industrial and rural sectors. The most concentrated post-Khrushchev criticism of the reorganization was directed against the division of the obkomy and the abolition of the rural raikomy. "The division," a recent critic of the reorganization has charged, "led to the lowering of the fighting capacities of the Party organizations, to lowering the role of Party committees as organs of collective political leadership, to the substitution of economic organs by Party committees, and in the final analysis caused harm to the union of the working class and peasantry."[52] While Soviet criticism was partly motivated by the political need to legitimate Khrushchev's ouster, the references to the changed roles of the divided obkomy in the general system of Party *rukovodstvo* contain a measure of truth. The changes, however, affected the various levels of the regional and local Party apparatus in different ways.

The effect of the production principle on the cohesion of the territorial apparatus was least evident in the republican Party committees. Khrushchev's fear that the new presidia would stifle the initiative of the branch bureaus seems to have been confirmed, although the amount of autonomy permitted the economic bureaus differed from republic to republic. In Estonia, for example, important economic decisions were usually issued by the Presidium. In Belorussia, however, basic decisions on industry and agriculture were issued by the branch bureau itself.

The potential for divisive jurisdictional conflicts at the republican level was reduced by the April 1963 decree of the Central Committee assigning fundamental responsibility for the republican economy to the Presidium.[53] Division of the republican apparatus, however, led to frequent conflicts at the republican level between the Party organs and ideological departments attached to each bureau. The reintegration of these departments under the Presidium, which began in July 1963, was a centralizing response to the problems of functional localism created by the reorganization. In the extreme case of Moldavia, the entire republican apparatus was removed from the control of the branch bureaus and placed directly under the Moldavian Presidium.[54]

The most important redistribution of authority and relationships within the regional Party apparatus was produced by creating two Party authorities within the same oblast and transferring the generalist and coordinating functions traditionally associated with the obkom first secretary to the republic or central Party apparatus. In one stroke, the reform created a political vacuum in the province, productive of subsequent instability and conflict, and undermined the institutional basis upon which the authority of the territorial apparatus had been built by Stalin and Molotov in the years following the Twelfth Congress in 1923. Although the strong continuity previously noted in secretarial cadres, political style, and traditional functions through 1963 and 1964 substantially blunted the more extreme implications of the division of Party power within the oblasti, evidence indicates that the reform did reduce the authority and blur the force of provincial Party power.

The novel relationship between the industrial and rural Party committees evinced much concern at the November plenum and during the period of the formation of the new Party organs. Although Khrushchev and Kozlov both warned that conflict between the two oblast organs would not be tolerated,[55] the establishment of working relationships between them nevertheless involved serious tensions throughout their two years of existence. Some of the ambiguity and conflict arose from the problem of geographical boundaries, a problem closely tied to the relationships between the industrial and rural soviety. In Tiumen Oblast, for example, the industrial obkom took over two national okruga and several cities in the southern part of the province. Cities in the central and northern parts of the oblast, however, were handed over to the agricultural obkom, and the overlap of functional and geographical authority caused continuous conflict.[56]

Local public services constituted a second area of jurisdictional conflict. To maintain a single Party authority over local construction, public health, education, communication, and everyday services, control was assigned to the industrial obkomy and sovety. The exact authority over the institutions assigned to industrial and agricultural obkomy and soviety, however, was never explicitly defined, with the result that major difficulties of direction and coordination arose in these areas.[57] These organs were then subordinated to two conflicting jurisdictions. At the oblast level they were subordinated to the industrial, and, at the local level, to the agricultural soviety and obkomy.[58]

In Poltava, for example, the enterprises and institutions connected with agriculture were placed in the jurisdiction of the agricultural Party organization at the same time that they were also attached to city soviety under the industrial obkom and soviet. Other institutions not connected with agriculture, such as auto parts, food combinaty, hospitals, and so forth, had Party organs under the agricultural obkom and guided by TPU, but the oblast administrations for these organs were subordinate to the industrial obkom. When the Poltava Industrial Obkom adopted decisions on industry situated on territory under the control of the rural obkom, the latter fought it, and when the "agrarniki" took joint obkom-oblispolkom decisions on industry, the industrial obkom reciprocated.[59]

These conflicts, however, were only part of the story. The primacy of the urban and industrial sectors over the agricultural and peasant sectors of Soviet society is a cardinal element in the ideological and modernizing values of the Party. "Weakening the union of workers and peasants" meant a slowdown or an absolute refusal of the industrial obkomy to extend the usual forms of *shefstvo* to the rural sectors. This was not true of all obkomy; instances of cooperation and of distributing ideological and industrial resources to agriculture were published in the Soviet press from time to time.[60] Among the majority of obkomy, however, isolation, localism, and lack of cooperation were characteristic.[61]

Rigidity and tension among the oblast committees were reflected in a variety of ways. In ideological work, dispatching such entertainment as theater groups, choruses, and circuses ceased in many oblasti.[62] In the Saratov Industrial Obkom, virtually every attempt to dispatch entertainers during the harvest of 1963 was held up until higher Party authorities intervened to change the obkom's policy.[63] The same relationship maintained where single committees and bureaus were retained but ideological departments were split. In the Bashkir Obkom, the industrial ideological otdel's strong resistance to sending urban resources to the countryside resulted in the reunion of the split otdely.[64] Dispatching urban cadres and workers to the countryside during harvest met a similar resistance.[65]

The extension by the industrial sector of various forms of industrial and construction aid to the rural areas was also adversely affected. "Recidivism" and the "narrow departmental approach to affairs" affected particularly the mobilization and above-plan production of spare parts for agriculture and the building of small but important rural projects. The control exercised by the industrial obkomy over the construction trusts resulted in a systematic discrimination against agricultural projects. In the most notable case, the conflicts between the Moscow industrial and agricultural obkomy on the construction of the high-priority poultry factories required Khrushchev's personal intervention to secure cooperation.[66]

The control of industrial resources by the industrial obkomy worked against the rural areas in other ways as well. A number of agricultural obkomy complained bitterly about their inability to secure supply and other materials from the sovnarkhozy or other economic agencies under the supervision of the industrial obkom.[67] It is apparent that the flow of consumer goods and services to the rural population declined with the reorganization. Denying these resources to the agricultural sector was indicative of the deep cleavages which plagued these organs in 1963 and 1964.

The struggle between the rural and industrial obkomy was clearly reflected in the relations between the territorial and zonal production committees in which the logic of the reorganization led in many instances to extremely awkward patterns of subordination and to complications of administration. In Kharkov Oblast, for example, three small industrial facilities were placed under a zonal committee which was eighty-five kilometers away when there was an agricultural committee in the same town.[68] The reverse situation, in which small agricultural installations were situated long distances away from the raion center, also occurred.

The abolition of the rural raikom, which created a vacuum among primary Party organs in the former raion centers, led to the creation of councils of secretaries which met regularly in the raion centers but possessed no statutory authority. The result was that these councils often began to assume the functions of the abolished raikomy and to challenge the authority of the production administrations in their jurisdictions.[69]

4

The Impact of the Party-State
Control Committee

The Party-State Control Committee and its local organs opened new dimensions in the basic structure of Party authority, principally the extension of the Party apparatus into economic management. The expansion in the Party's administrative power, however, was offset in some degree by the diminution of the discretionary authority over economic *rukovodstvo* of the regional and local Party organs.

Basically the new system of control would strengthen the central Party's leadership over the lower Party organs through the formation of a union-republic agency partially independent of the territorial Party apparatus. The union Party-State Control Committee's authority was sufficient to ensure that the control structure would be wholly dependent upon neither the central nor the territorial Party apparatus. The central control apparatus had a separate staff, conducted its own investigations, possessed its own communications net, and issued legally binding instructions under its own authority. It heard reports of lower control organs and issued formal decisions on the scope and methods of their operations. It also gave direct operating orders to the territorial control apparatus without the overt intervention of the regular Party organs.

The scope of authority extended to the central PGK indicates that its power greatly exceeded the narrow conducting of inspections to check up on compliance with central commands. The operational authority of the union control agency was that traditionally associated with *proverka*. Numerous examples in the Soviet press in 1963 and 1964 attest the active involvement of the central and republican control committees in economic decision-making and a situation which evoked a *Partiinaia zhizn'* editorial complaint that the local Party organs were handing over their checkup activities to the control committees.[70]

A typical example of the role of the union PGK is provided in a committee report, issued in June 1963, of an investigation of the Dnepropetrovsk Tire Plant. The investigation revealed major production problems delaying the fulfillment of the plant's production plan. In the resolution of the issue, the committee sharply criticized the Pridneprovskii Sovnarkhoz, the State Committee of the Oil and Gas Industry, as well as the plant's director and chief engineer. The Dnepropetrovsk Industrial Obkom, however, escaped criticism. To remedy the situation, the committee ordered the state committee, the sovnarkhoz, and the plant officials to renovate the plant by jointly elaborating a plan of reconstruction. The state committee was ordered to send specialists to supervise the work and the Council of National Economy to supply the materials needed to automate production. In this particular investigation, the Dnepropetrovsk Industrial Obkom would issue a Party penalty to the director and a strict reprimand to the chief engineer.[71]

The committee's penetration of the local economies was not confined to individual investigations. A series of mass checkups in both industry and agriculture represented further encroachments on the decision-making role of the territorial Party apparatus, and, to a lesser extent, of the central Party organs.

Establishing a parallel Party agency for control as part of the general proliferation of central Party agencies to bring the managerial apparatus under direct administrative control clearly contributed to the problems of centralized direction and coordination of the economy. The union committee overlapped with other secretarial organs, and instances of competitive decision-making were apparent.[72]

The competition for power extended beyond the limited sphere of economic decision-making. A major jurisdictional struggle developed between the Administrative Otdel and the Party-State Control Committee over the control of such agencies as the Procurator's Office, the courts, the Ministry for Safeguarding Public Order, and the commissions of Soviet executive organs. An article in *Pravda* in April 1963 by a deputy head of the Administrative Otdel indicated this department's strong intention of maintaining its jurisdiction over the regular administrative organs of state coercion.[73]

The issue of the PGK's role arose in the May 1964 session of the Administrative Otdel. In January, the Party-State Control Committee had unequivocally claimed control over the peoples' courts, the soviets, and the other administrative organs in a checkup conducted in Georgia, Armenia, Krasnodar, and Stavropol.[74] In the May meeting, N. N. Mironov, the head of the Administrative Otdel (who was dropped from his post in November 1964) indicated the need for cooperation between the PGK and the other agencies of social control but insisted adamantly that the PGK was only one method. He expressed deep concern about the Party agencies' weakened control over the security agencies, and he was disturbed by the Party and Party-State Control Committee competition for jurisdiction over these agencies.[75] While the underlying linkages between the Party-State Control Committee and the secret police were most likely strengthened during 1963 and 1964, countervailing power from the Party's staff organs and the state administrative apparatus seems to have confined the control commission's authority largely to economic questions.

The Party-State Control Committee's direct intervention in disciplining the individual Party official or member was explicitly denied the control committees. There were, however, misty areas in the control committees' relations with the individual Communist. The categorization of Party functions has never been so lucid that the jurisdictions of the Party-State Control Committee and the Party Control Commission could be absolutely distinguished. Communists and non-Communists alike were subjected to the sanctions of the committees for various economic shortcomings or crimes.

There was no single method for imposing sanctions on Party members. In some instances, as in the case cited above, the staff Party organ issued Party punishment to the offending economic officials. The reports of Party-state control checkups within the jurisdiction of an obkom were turned over to it for action. The checkups of the Belorussian PGK, for example, were regularly turned over to the obkom, and this undoubtedly applied in other cases as well.[76] In other situations, investigation and punishment were directly imposed by the control agency itself or turned over to the courts for action.[77]

The punishment of economic officials depended partially on the official's post and partially on the status of the investigating control committee. At the production level, both the plant director and chief engineer were normally open to sanctions from the oblast PGK and higher control agencies.[78] At the administrative level, the direct responsibility for economic shortcomings was usually placed on a deputy sovnarkhoz chairman or deputy chairman of a state committee.[79] The Party-State Control Committee's hierarchical level appears also to have been important. Lower committees had little effective power over central or republican officials. In every published case in which an economic official of the central managerial apparatus was brought to responsibility, the action was brought by the All-Union Party-State Control Committee.

The frequent direct intervention of the central and republican Party-state control committees in the guidance of local economic activity constituted the most obvious restraint on the authority of the lower Party apparatus. The regular Party staff organs possessed both statutory and informal resources to maintain control over the administrative environment. The structural relationships between the staff and control organs at the oblast level concentrated general authority in the secretariat and the Department for Party Organs. Formal controls included the affirmation of Party-State Control Committee staffs and the right to approve work plans, to receive reports of checkups conducted in their jurisdiction, to discuss control activities in the obkom or gorkom bureau, and to take formal action in relation to the control committees. These powers were not strong enough to permit total control by the regular Party organs over the activities of the control committees, and conflict and tension were apparent in their relations.

There was, in the first place, a clear reluctance on the part of the territorial apparatus to form the committee.[80] There were, secondly, complaints in the Soviet press of failure on the part of the obkomy and gorkomy to support the activities of the control committees.[81] The Ukrainian Party-State Control Committee, for example, investigated the Donetsk Industrial Obkom in 1964, charged the obkom with an unwillingness to support its control committee, and ordered it to increase its support to the committee.[82] The refusal by an obkom or gorkom to act on a complaint appears to have been the most common method of reducing the power of the control structure.

A case cited in the Soviet press indicates that such practices were not always successful, however. A plant director of a Derbent glass factory was accused by the group of assistants in his plant of lowering the quality of glass and juggling assortment figures. Prolonged conflict followed the accusation, but the gorkom and obkom refused to intervene. Finally, an appeal to the union PGK brought an independent investigation, and the obkom was forced to act. The obkom subsequently fired the chief engineer and bookkeeper and gave a strict warning to the plant director. Both the plant Party secretary and a gorkom secretary were "called to personal responsibility."[83] The number of cases in which the central control agency could intervene to support the local control apparatus in correcting the "localist" and "family group" tendencies of the Party apparatus, however, was limited by the staff resources of the union PGK.

In assessing the impact of the new control system on the authority and status of the lower Party organs, it is evident that at least three factors other than direct Moscow intervention worked to reduce the autonomy of the territorial Party apparatus. First, the Party organs were directly commanded by superior Party-state control committees to perform specific actions. The Chernigov Industrial Obkom, for example, was given a direct order by the Ukrainian Party-State Control Committee to restaff an unsatisfactory city soviet administration.[84] Secondly, the staff organs were subject to direct criticism by control organs on a higher level, the criticism often touching issues of internal Party life: The union PGK, for example, criticized both the Tallinn and Dushanbe gorkomy for their bureaucratic styles of leadership.[85] The Karaganda Party-State Control Committee charged the Dzhezkazgan Gorkom with a similar deficiency.[86]

The control apparatus' most important weapon, however, was the press. If the press organs under the given Party committee's jurisdiction were controlled, the central and republican press was less easily censored. Both the presidia of republican Party organs and the bureaus of obkomy were required to give a public account of their actions to correct deficiencies exposed in their jurisdictions. The Presidium of the Armenian Central Committee, for example, replied to a critical article in *Pravda* of 24 July 1964 by strictly reprimanding a plant director who refused to reinstate a worker he had fired despite the orders of the Erevan Gorkom and the Armenian Supreme Court.[87] The Presidium of Azerbaidzhan promised to improve the leadership of two gorkomy in guiding primary Party organs, and the Presidium of Latvia acknowledged its failure to support the Latvian press in publicizing the activities of its control agencies.[88] The Sverdlovsk Industrial Obkom was publicly required to account for the slow construction of an engineering shop in a plant in Cheliabinsk.[89] Similarly, the Kirov Industrial Obkom was required to justify its actions for permitting "disorder" in a lumber camp.[90]

5

The November Reorganization and the
Party's Political Style

Although one of the major purposes of the November 1962 reform, as V. I. Snastin has indicated, was "to break through the bureaucratic-administrative forms" associated with Stalin,[91] the Party's internal dynamics were too intricate to permit a simple or radical transformation of the style or authority of the territorial apparatus. Traditional *rukovodstvo* was intensified, which was to be expected in view of the opposition to the reform of the territorial Party apparatus and the continuity of cadres; and although the plenum also set in motion a number of liberalizing forces for altering the basic premises of the leading role in Soviet society, the breakthrough did not in fact occur. The essentially conservative leadership of the republican and oblast Party committees succeeded in containing, if not eliminating, the innovative forces.

The internal relationship between the territorial Party committees and bureaus and the apparatchik was least affected by the reform. In the criticism following the 1963 agricultural failures and Khrushchev's fall in 1964, the extent of apparatus control over the plena and conferences at the local level was seen to be unchanged. A *Sovetskaia Rossiia* editorial called attention to the irregularity of obkom meetings in Tomsk, Riazan, and "several others."[92]

Many obkomy were charged with indifference to preparing the agenda or to notifying the primary Party organs of the time, place, or substance of Party plenary sessions.[93] In addition, the meetings themselves remained carefully manipulated and tightly controlled. Speakers were selected and speeches censored in the gorkom or obkom prior to public discussion. "Staff orators" followed the empty form of reciting successes, shortcomings, and proposals for improvement.[94] At a gorkom conference on construction, several construction officials promised to institute more progressive construction methods. Two months later the construction officials, called back to the gorkom to report on the progress made, were at a loss since they could not remember what they had discussed at the plenum.[95] Exposed to more systematic criticism in 1963 and 1964 than in any period since Stalin's death, the Party apparatus fought to maintain its traditional control. The L'vov Industrial Obkom, for example, used the reorganization as an excuse for dumping its critics.[96]

Regional and local Party bureaus exhibited a strong continuity with past operational procedures. Four-man secretariats serving as the core of the apparatus-dominated bureau ensured the concentration of Party power at the middle and lower echelons. The practice of consultation on economic problems remained unchanged and may possibly have decreased. In other respects as well, the old authoritarian practices persisted and intensified.[97] Formal sessions of the bureaus of the oblast and city committees continued to be held on a weekly basis, usually with heavily loaded agendas and lengthy, time-consuming sessions. The central pressure for "concrete leadership" was reflected in a large number of narrow decisions on specific topics, usually of a production character.[98] While this held for both industrial and rural obkomy and local Party organs, it was particularly true of the agendas of the rural obkomy. Stylistic continuity was also reflected in the repeated bureau decisions on the same question.[99]

The Party apparat's increased role in economic decision-making was most immediately felt, however, in the informal sessions in the secretariat and departments where most of the day-to-day work of the apparatus was carried on. Holding informal sessions within the apparat has always been part of the administrative style of Party leadership, but central pressure and the Party's more detailed involvement in particularities increased their number. The virtually continuous round of conferences, some involving as many as eighty plant, Party, trade union, and administrative officials on a wide variety of specific issues, may have helped to coordinate the industrial activity of an oblast or city, but in conjunction with the related activities of the Party-state control committees it exacted a heavy toll on the time and energy of Party and state officials. Khrushchev, in short, had instituted a reform that intensified the bureaucratic style.

Various efforts, including a resolution by the Russian Bureau, were made to curb the "session fever,"[100] but they usually failed. The Omsk Industrial Obkom, for example, decreed that sessions would only be held three times per week and only after two in the afternoon, but pressures were such that this rule had to be abandoned.[101] Leading officials of the obkomy and gorkomy were not confined solely to holding sessions at headquarters. At the gorkom level in particular, the "production conference" often assumed abbreviated forms in the field. Rapid discussion and decisions concerning production problems through the *operativki*, *letuchki*, and *planerki* seem to have been extremely common.[102]

Inevitably, under conditions in which a large number of decisions were made rapidly and with insufficient investigation by political officials, conflicts arose which reduced administrative efficiency. Meetings on the same issue were often repeated in various Party and economic agencies and contradictory decisions made. For instance, the Astrakhan Obkom's Otdel of Construction and City Economy called a meeting to discuss the lag in the construction of a building for the music school. A week later a meeting on the same issue was called by the oblast executive committee. Shortly afterward, the Astrakhan Gorkom convened a third meeting on the school building. At each session, specific measures were adopted to speed up construction, and none of the measures agreed.[103]

The reorganization also increased the normal tensions and constraints on apparat department heads and instructors. There was some difficulty in placing instructors who had been released by the abolition of the rural raikomy.[104] The heavy turnover produced demoralization at this level of the apparat, and the disorientation in institutional relationships aroused the intense dissatisfaction of the old cadres, who charged that they were being mechanically eliminated solely because they lacked a diploma.[105] The wholesale recruitment of technical specialists into the oblast and local Party apparatuses, however, had much deeper implications for Party *rukovodstvo*. The cleavages in status were reinforced by a split that divided the institution along diametrically opposed lines.

"Economics over politics" pitted the "humanists" against the "technocrats." The "humanists" expressed the conservative view of the old cadres that Party work was primarily in the sphere of human relations and that its role should be defined in ideological and mobilizing terms. The "technocrats," on the other hand, defined the Party as an economic and technical managerial structure devoted to economic goals. As a group, the latter made up a major, politically unsocialized segment of the apparatus and brought an operational style developed in the state and economic managerial system. By training they tended to be indifferent to the forms and rituals of Party style, more pragmatic, and deeply involved in "narrow production questions" to the exclusion of other institutional values. If the trend initiated by the November reform was permitted to continue, a basic transformation, incremental and uncontrolled, in the nature of the Party as a political institution would have been inevitable.[106]

Despite the evident loss of cohesion of the regional and local Party apparatus through cleavages of structure, status, and value, the general Stalinist approach to *rukovodstvo* appears to have remained relatively unchanged. Since the early twenties, the major function of the instructor had been clerical—collecting data, preparing questions for bureau meetings, writing decrees and memoranda, and recording the results of Party decisions. The more detailed involvement of the territorial Party organs in economic management increased the already heavy demand for information by the central Party organs. In 1963, A. P. Kirilenko suggested curtailing the extremely detailed ten-day, monthly, and quarterly gorkom reports on industrial activity.[107] But intensifying the Party apparatus' direct administrative role only increased the paper work and red tape. Periodic efforts were made to control this phenomenon. For one notable example, the Kursk Industrial Obkom formed a commission to investigate "bureaucratism" in the local Party organs, with the sole result (so its critics charged) of increasing the already overwhelming amount of paper and red tape with which the gorkom had to cope.[108]

Increased administrative pressures appear to have been acute at the gorkom level. While the regional apparatus grew in proportion to its increased responsibilities, a similar expansion did not occur at the local level. Instructors rushed from task to task without plan or sufficient preparation, and the disorder and confusion were heightened by a host of minor inconveniences. In one gorkom, an instructor complained that he was not only required to deal with more paper but had to do his own typing as well. The shortage of typists was attributed to the fact that the city Party committee paid the lowest salaries for clerical help in the city.[109] The gorkom or raikom instructor had never had an enviable lot, and the November reorganization made this all the more so. Recruitment problems, which were partially the reason for setting up the nonstaff structure, may account for the rapid increase in the number of women instructors. Although there is little evidence to suggest that the Party's basically masculine image was revised, the potentiality was there.

The burdens on the gorkomy and raikomy were handled in a variety of ways. Some of the functions of checking, for example, were given to the Party-state control committees. There was a general deterioration in the guiding role of the local over the primary Party organs. But it was principally the nonstaff apparatus that bore the increased load on the administrative structure.[110] Expanding the social principle to democratize the Party bureaucracy and humanize its administrative and coercive methods of control continued in part to justify the nonstaff apparat, although the major thrust of the Party reform and the basic requirements of Party administration continued to restrict its decision-making role. That the professional Party apparatus maintained full control did not, however, eradicate the causes of conflict and inefficiency which had earlier plagued the volunteer concept. Relationships between staff and nonstaff structures were still formed on the basis of the role of the nonstaff apparat. Where volunteers served to ease the instructor corps of heavy clerical burdens, relationships were essentially cordial. Where the nonstaff organs impinged on the prerogatives of the regular staff, particularly in the preparation of bureau questions, there was conflict.

Reducing the nonstaff apparat to clerical auxiliaries of the professional Party organization did not increase the efficiency of the volunteers. In an extensive examination of the social principle in the Estonian apparat, a republican committee secretary listed ten problems limiting the volunteers' usefulness.[111] Much of their work was formalistic, for show. There was an excessive number of commissions and sectors. The nonstaff organs duplicated the work of numerous other Soviet and social groups formed to deal with the same institution or problem. There were too many checkups, and, in addition, a lack of responsibility on the part of the volunteers for the results of the checkups.

There was also a disturbing policy of appointing as heads of nonstaff commissions and departments the heads of institutions and enterprises over whom the groups exercised control. The recruitment of nonstaff officials left much to be desired. The general shortage of volunteers led to individuals being drafted into participation. The nonstaff commissions and sectors were also hampered by volunteers who belonged to too many groups and thus scattered their energies. Finally—sounding a theme to be heard throughout Party life in 1963 and 1964—the Party volunteers were accused of substituting their authority for the agencies they were called upon to supervise.[112] Despite its obvious shortcomings, however, this phase of Party activity would survive Khrushchev's fall.

The effect of the November reorganization on the Party's primary organs reflected the same ambiguities evident in the reform of the territorial apparatus. Their ideological and mobilizing functions in behalf of Khrushchev's economic policies continued, but concentration on "narrow production questions" limited their activity.[113] The general deterioration in the work of the primary Party organs seems to have had two major causes: (1) the large number of enterprises assigned to the instructor and his absorption in production issues reduced the status of these organs;[114] and (2) the tasks of guiding the primary Party organs were complicated by the wholesale turnover of secretaries in the election-and-report meetings of 1963 and 1964.

While the organizational departments of the city Party committees usually exposed these new secretaries to short courses to orient them to Party work, their training was insufficient to produce reliable officials with agitation and mobilization skills. As an example, a *Partiinaia zhizn'* editorial cited the Otdel for Party Organs' investigation of the Kirovgrad Industrial Obkom, which noted a sharp decline in the number and quality of the oblast's primary Party organs.[115] A number met only two or three times a year and then only on the agenda recommended by the gorkom.[116]

The reform's principal effect at the mass level in industry was to increase the secretary's power in relation to the plant administration. At the mass level, *Partiinaia zhizn'* complained in summary of the election-and-report meetings of 1963–64, the primary Party organs held too many production meetings, issued too many orders, substituted for the economic administration, and exercised little control over the execution of decisions.[117] One of the major objectives of the post-Khrushchev leadership was to reform and revive the ideological role of the primary Party organs in the system of *rukovodstvo*.[118]

6

The Political Style of Mass Control

The general limits of control have been well summarized by Grey Hodnett.

> The Soviet leadership has two major channels through which it may exercise 'control,' each with its own particular advantages and liabilities. It may choose to stress the role of 'public' (i.e., voluntary, nonpaid, party-led) organizations performing 'control' duties, thus maximizing the advantages of grassroots participation by people likely to be aware of what needs checking. This technique, however, sometimes leads to amateurish results, disrupts administrative routine, fails to overcome the resistance of local officials, and makes central direction difficult. Or the leadership may choose to exercise 'control' through various bureaucratic instruments legally authorized to conduct investigations. This approach helps overcome the defects of 'public' methods but it sacrifices coverage and ease of access to incriminating information. In practice, the leadership blends these techniques, varying the combination in response to specific circumstances.[119]

The territorial control apparatus followed the familiar institutional style of the territorial Party and Soviet organs. The basic decision-making unit of the control system was the committee, which convened periodically on an agenda of questions prepared by its departments. At the regional level, the fact that the committee chairman was also a secretary of the coordinate Party organ ensured some degree of Party control over the operation of the control organs. The existence of all-union and republican control activities and the fact that minutes of meetings were directed to both regular Party and superior Party-state control committees probably limited the capacity of the regular Party staff to dominate the committee meetings completely. The committee sessions, like the bureau meetings of the staff Party organs, were thoroughly bureaucratic. I. S. Grushetskii, summarizing the experience of the Ukrainian control apparatus, noted the numerous and lengthy sessions, the invitation of as many as 100 state and economic officials to attend, and the issuance of a large number of memoranda and decisions.[120]

The style of the organs of control was significantly affected by the conditions in which they operated. Recruiting competent volunteers to staff the control organs was a very difficult problem[121], and the competition at the local and mass levels appears to have been acute. Beyond this, however, were the problems inherent in using volunteers for mass control. Highly trained, competent specialists had little time or energy left from their own responsibilities to engage in extensive control work. Placed in control of their own specific enterprises, the goals of control were defeated. In committees staffed by workers and peasants, enthusiasm required tempering with technical training. Both the Party organs departments of the regular Party committees and the control committees themselves undertook to train volunteers in economics and law.[122] In at least one city Party-State Control Committee, the problem of cadres was handled by the chairman, who, by trying to do everything himself, failed to recruit a staff.[123] This practice, however, was not officially approved and seems to have been extremely rare.

The style of the control system was also conditioned by its resources for processing the informational inputs pouring into it. The number of complaints far exceeded the capacities of either the central or territorial organs to check and verify them. Into the central organs alone in 1963, some half-million letters and complaints were sent, with about 140 thousand receiving some form of processing.[124] The complaints themselves, however, presented additional difficulties, many of them being either inaccurate or slanderous, and deciding which complaints to investigate was often difficult to do.

The administrative style of the control organs compounded the difficulties of direction. The control apparatus was oriented toward statistical results. The Leningrad City Party-State Control Committee, for example, recorded over one million checkups of organs under its direction in 1963.[125] Emphasizing quantity often resulted in poor coordination and direction of control activities, repeated investigations, and a scattering of resources on trivial issues. The Sumy Oblast Party-State Control Committee, for example, investigated a plant which had failed to deliver nine meters of wood to a client.[126] Administrative coordination was additionally complicated by the jurisdictional conflicts which accompanied the efforts of the Party-State Control Committee to integrate the activities of the departmental controllers with mass control.[127]

The issues of style were perhaps most keenly felt among the groups and posts of assistance. Here, staffing presented particularly difficult problems, as they were frequently understaffed, drawn from a narrow circle, and technically incompetent.[128] It was decided in Minsk, for example, to check up on the expenditures of metal in a machine-building plant. Each controller was given a card stating how much metal was to be used in a given operation. But the norms were obsolete and the results questionable.[129]

The operational style of the groups and posts was sporadic and conducted in a campaign manner.[130] Intense activity alternated with passivity and indifference. Like the committees, the groups and posts suffered from poor administrative direction and communication. The often undefined specific obligations of individual controllers produced confusion and duplication of effort,[131] and the efficiency of the control structure in the individual plant was impaired by the vertical system of communication. Information and administrative direction passed up and down the structure, but there was no mechanism for horizontal coordination, which tended not only to centralize power within the given production unit but also to reduce the comprehensiveness of mass control.[132] Despite all these difficulties, however, the control apparatus was instrumental in the realization of Khrushchev's policy.

7

The Political Style of the Leading Role

The November plenum accelerated that realignment of functions which was basic to Khrushchev's policy of raising the Party's leading role in the economy. The final two years of his rule would test (within Soviet conditions) his thesis that the Party's relevance and social value as an institution lay in its assuming an entrepreneurial role. But conservatives opposed a primarily economic role for the Party for two reasons: (1) a fear that the Party's ideological and mobilizing roles were being sacrificed to expediency;[133] and (2) a fear that the radical alteration of its organizational role violated the traditional norms of Party *rukovodstvo*.[134]

In the criticism unleashed by Khrushchev's ouster, there was some complex truth in the view that restructuring the Party had led to a decline in its political role. But "economics over politics" did not mean simply abandoning Marxism-Leninism as social theory in favor of ideological neutrality; nor did the intensification of the Party's administrative role represent a fundamental break with existing practice. The shift in the style and substance of *rukovodstvo* in 1963 and 1964 was one of degree rather than kind.

The traditionalists' conviction that the propaganda and agitational apparatus would concentrate on economic and technical themes to the detriment of theory was not wholly founded. The reaction of the Party leadership to the liberal intelligentsia in the winter of 1962 and spring of 1963, the antinationalist campaign in the union republics in 1963 and 1964, and the intense effort in the spring and summer of 1964 to mobilize the Party in respect to the Sino-Soviet conflict indicated the continuing importance of political and moral themes in general propaganda. The November reorganization did not initiate a withdrawal of resources from ideological activity; on the contrary, it continued the massive upsurge in agitation begun in 1960 and 1961.

The political enlightenment net which enrolled over twenty-three million persons in 1962 and 1963 was expanded to twenty-six million in 1963 and 1964.[135] In 1963, almost 1.2 million were enrolled as propagandists and seminar leaders, two-thirds of them possessing at least an incomplete higher education and 650 thousand of them recruited from the economic and technical apparatus.[136] Finally, the November reorganization did not signal a decline in the mobilization functions traditionally associated with the Party's leading role. In 1963, for example, the Kemerovo Industrial Obkom enrolled over 700 thousand persons in various forms of socialist competition, with another seventy thousand in production conferences, some thirty-four thousand in the Party-state control net, and a large number in councils of rationalizers and innovators and other mass organizations.[137] The effort to intensify the indoctrinational program was perhaps even more concentrated because of the traditional ineffectiveness of propaganda and agitation in the countryside.[138]

The primacy of economics and technology in the indoctrinational effort of the Party apparatus, however, was the long-range goal of Khrushchev's policy, and in 1963 and 1964, economic and technical education was stressed at virtually every level of the Party structure. The Central Committee's Higher Party School and the four-year schools in the union republics underwent radical curriculum revision in March 1963. The permanence of the division of the oblast Party committees and the need for technically educated Party cadres were reflected by the curriculum, which devoted only 1,290 hours to political theory, Party history, and practice but used the remaining 1,910 hours for specialized financial, administrative, and technical training of industrial and agricultural cadres.[139] At the republican level, special Party schools were set up for the economic and technical training of cadres with shorter curricula emphasizing political economy, the spreading of leading experience, and the organization of work and norm-setting.[140] Similar schools, shorter and less intensive, were established at the city and oblast levels.

The ideological activity of the local and oblast Party organizations was clearly structured around economic themes. The ideological secretary of the Kiev Industrial Obkom considered himself primarily obligated to such activities as spreading leading experience, holding economic conferences, conducting semi-nars, and so on.[141] In some cases, such as that of the secretary of the Zaporozhe Industrial Obkom, the secretary actually undertook to teach technical subjects, including a course in welding.[142] Other ideological secretaries entered directly into production by undertaking such jobs as the organization of labor in the plant. The most impressive effort in behalf of "economics over politics," how-ever, was in the proliferation of vocational courses in the political enlightenment net.

Nevertheless, the general effect of the heightened ideological thrust was limited. In a lengthy and specific examination of the performance of the ideologi-cal cadres in Ivanovo, the Ivanovo Industrial Obkom's ideological secretary complained that long familiar problems were unchanged. Decisions on ideological questions were paper decisions. There was little observable change in the average worker's weltanschauung, as evidenced by his distaste for courses in political and social theory. Presentation remained abstract and formal, and lecturers were often poorly prepared. Moreover, the Party's mass agitational efforts on moral and technical themes were virtually worthless. Socialist competition was statistical and formal; there was a heavy turnover in labor in spite of ideological pressures to control it; and, finally, the production enterprises continued to be plagued by such phenomena as "storming" and other antisocial activities.[143] As a tool to increase the quantity and quality of production, ideology appears to have had little discernible effect.

The November plenum thus intensified the "administrative" style of Party leadership. In the agricultural sector, there was little apparent change in the scope of authority or the style of exercising Party power. The rural obkomy and territorial production administrations continued to issue production plans and harvesting schedules and to supervise the feeding of cows and the trans-portation and use of fertilizer. The high-pressure campaign style remained un-altered despite Khrushchev's policy of placing Soviet agriculture on a scientific basis.[144] In industry, the Party's expanded administrative role led to a fusion of functions around Party, Soviet, and economic organs and to charges of *kom-mandovaniia* and *administrirovaniia* in the Party's style of leadership.[145]

In 1963 and 1964, the thrust of the Party's administrative role was within the bounds of previous historical experience. The assumption by the territorial Party apparatus of direct responsibility for solving such problems as the production of milk-processing equipment, the production of electrodes for the shipbuilding industry, the use of lumber wastes in making cardboard, or the supply of bricks for construction was not new. Party involvement in operational decision-making was nevertheless more intense during 1963 and 1964 than it had been in any period after the Second World War, with predictable consequences.

The apparatus was severely burdened with petty administrative problems, internal Party discipline was weakened, and there was a loss of perspective and discrimination in guiding the state and economic mechanism.[146] The reorganization was said to have violated *edinonachalie*, weakened production discipline, and complicated the problem of accountability. Fusing the Party and state apparatuses not only reduced the internal cohesion and identity of the Party as an institution, but served also to aggravate the conflict and tension between Party and state.[147] In the reaction against the course undertaken in 1963 and 1964, the post-Khrushchev leadership reemphasized the traditional doctrine of *rukovodstvo*, stressing the Party's role in cadre selection, *proverka*, and mass mobilization.[148] And as the general debate on Party structure at the Twenty-third Congress suggests, at least part of the apparatus was interested in resurrecting the functional system of *rukovodstvo* through the formation of a cadres administration at the central level.[149]

The November plenum should also be judged empirically. The purpose of the reorganization was to advance Khrushchev's economic policies through the Party apparatus and to produce that economic growth and administrative efficiency which has preoccupied the Soviet leadership since Stalin's death. The reform raised the question of whether administrative methods of economic management, defined in terms of a tightly centralized system of planning and administration under close Party supervision, were sufficient to achieve Khrushchev's goals. In the economic context, the question was essentially whether the Party's leadership in economic decision-making was relevant under conditions of mature industrialization.

— 9 —

The Economic Impact of the November Plenum

The reorganization of the Party's administrative structure was accompanied by an equally basic reorganization of the state administrative mechanism. The thrust of decision-making in economic management generally paralleled the Party reform, particularly in terms of strengthening centralized and specific controls over enterprises and construction sites.[1] The reorganization of management in 1962 and 1963 proliferated central planning and executive organs designed to introduce administrative order into the structure of economic management and to produce a new economic efficiency within the perspectives of Khrushchev's priorities and goals.

The reform only succeeded, however, in intensifying the deep-rooted traditions of Soviet administrative experience and reinforcing those aspects of the Stalinist system which Khrushchev was formally committed to eliminate. Continuity in administrative authority and style produced an equally strong continuity in the *rukovodstvo* of the Party apparatus; and as the Party's role in economic decision-making developed during 1963 and 1964, the basic Party-state relationships, particularly at the territorial level, resembled those under the ministerial system.

As the massive problems in planning, construction, and supply emerged from the crash program in chemical construction, the Party's mobilizational role served dual and, in some respects, contradictory functions. On the one hand, the apparatus was an agent of pressure for accelerating construction and production; on the other hand, this pressure intensified the microimbalances of the command economy, which in turn induced further Party intervention in economic decision-making. The result was to promote internal disorganization within the Party and to reduce further the efficiency and rationality of the decision-making process.

213

1

The Reformed Structures of Industrial Administration

The new system of industrial administration evolved in two interrelated stages over a three-month period. From December 1962 to March 1963, Khrushchev's outline was translated into an organizational structure, and in January 1963, three new central organs were formed for the administration of planning and control over the industrial economy. In the new statute on planning, the central planning structure was reorganized by abolishing Gosekonomsovet and concentrating current and long-range planning in the State Planning Committee.[2] A new chairman, P. F. Lomako, was appointed to head Gosplan, and during 1963, four of five deputy chairmen were identified for the first time.[3] The committee of Gosplan was expanded to include the chairmen of the twelve state branch committees attached to Gosplan. To perform the altered functions of planning, five new departments were added.

The return of current and long-range planning to a single agency was accompanied by the creation of the Council of the National Economy of the USSR, an all-union sovnarkhoz, which was intended to place the republican Council of Ministers, the interrepublican agencies, and the union departments and ministries under a single operational control. Its chairman was V. E. Dymshits, a construction engineer who had supervised the construction of the Bhilai steel mill in India and had successively served as head of Gosplan's capital construction department and first deputy chairman of Gosplan. V. M. Riabikov, a defense industry specialist, and V. F. Zhigalin, a former chairman of the Russian Sovnarkhoz, were appointed first deputy chairmen. The council offered a complex representation of central and republican economic interests.[4]

Capital construction, so crucial to the realization of Khrushchev's economic policies, was centralized through a strengthened USSR State Construction Committee. In the new system, Gosstroi USSR became the single organ for conducting technical policy and for assuring new construction sites with technical estimates and projections.[5] The new chairman was I. T. Novikov, a former USSR minister of power plant construction. His first deputy chairmen were I. A. Grishmanov, one-time head of the Central Committee's Otdel of Construction, and A. A. Etmekhzhian, a construction official who served in 1962 and 1963 as a first deputy chairman of Gosplan. All five deputy chairmen had had extensive top-level experience in the various phases of heavy construction.

The role of the state committees, defined in November 1962 as the agencies primarily responsible for promoting technical progress in Soviet industry, was expanded. Their authority, however, fell far short of the power of the former ministries prior to 1957.[6] During 1963 and 1964, the structure of the ministries and state committees remained relatively stable; nine new state committees were formed, seven of them for economic functions. Changes among heads of ministries and state committees were also moderate. Only two ministers, one of them a replacement for Novikov, were changed; among chairmen of state committees, only Zverev, of the State Committee for Defense Technology, was replaced. As Khrushchev remarked in April 1963, virtually all of the state committee chairmen had been ministers under the old system.[7]

In the regional system of administration, the Central Asian Sovnarkhoz presented a complex organizational structure: some sixty officials of the Uzbek, Tadzhik, Kirgiz, and Turkmen republics were formed into a council, with a smaller collegium of fifteen, composed of the chairman, two first deputy chairmen, and the chairmen of the republican councils of ministers, Gosplans, and trade-union councils.[8] To organizationally integrate the republican administrative mechanism with the sovnarkhoz, the chairmen of the councils of ministers were made deputy chairmen of the sovnarkhoz.[9] The apparat was formed from the administrations of the existing republican sovnarkhozy.[10] The administrative system in Central Asia was additionally complicated by the formation of three specialized administrations for cotton growing, irrigation, and general construction, none of them subordinate to the sovnarkhoz. Their chairmen and the chairman of the Central Asian Sovnarkhoz were coordinated through their membership on the Central Asian Bureau.

The November plenum sharply altered the intermediate levels of industrial administration. Abolishing the four republican sovnarkhozy in Central Asia reduced their number to eleven. The reduction in the number of regional sovnarkhozy was more drastic. The sixty-seven sovnarkhozy of the RSFSR were cut to twenty-four enlarged sovnarkhozy. In the Ukraine, the fourteen regional councils were cut to seven. In Kazakhstan, however, the seven sovnarkhozy remained untouched.[11]

The new regional councils of national economy structurally resembled those they had replaced. Encompassing as many as six former oblast sovnarkhozy, the new sovnarkhozy were administered by a chairman, three to six vice-chairmen, and an apparatus of from thirty to forty branch and functional departments.[12] Enlarged sovnarkhozy permitted greater specialization among branch administrations, but the otdely of many councils were physically separated.[13] Where branch administrations were not moved to the new sovnarkhoz center, the internal administration of the sovnarkhoz was vastly complicated and the role of the oblast Party committees became problematical.

In 1963 and 1964, the changes in chairmen of the republican and regional sovnarkhozy were relatively moderate, however much the initial reduction in the number of sovnarkhozy constituted a purge of the intermediate levels of administrative leadership. In the eleven republican sovnarkhozy, six new chairmen were appointed. The succession, however, was orderly, with the appointment of first deputy chairmen to the vacant posts. The exception was in the Ukraine, where the new chairman was a former chairman of the Ukrainian Gosplan. In the Russian Republic, the abolition of forty-three oblast sovnarkhozy removed two-thirds of the administrative leadership. In the twenty-four new sovnarkhozy, seventeen had chairmen heading either existing or former oblast councils. The most prominent shift was the appointment of A. T. Shmarev, the former first deputy chairman of the Russian Sovnarkhoz and a prominent writer on economic administration, to head the Central Volga Sovnarkhoz in Kuibyshev. The stability of sovnarkhoz chairmen was more marked in the Ukraine. Six of the seven new chairmen had been chairmen of Ukrainian regional sovnarkhozy before the reorganization.

The second stage in the evolution of the system of industrial management occurred in March 1963. At a joint session of the Presidium of the Central Committee and the USSR Council of Ministers on 13 March, a new top-level agency, the Supreme Council of the National Economy, or Vesenkha,[14] was set up to direct and coordinate the work of Gosplan, Union Sovnarkhoz, and Gosstroi USSR. In addition, five ministries were changed into USSR State Production Committees,[15] of which three were placed under the direct jurisdiction of the Supreme Council and two others under Gosstroi USSR. The Supreme Council also took under its direct jurisdiction ten functional and branch committees concerned with technology. Finally—in a set of separate decrees issued by the Presidium of the Supreme Soviet—Gosplan, Union Sovnarkhoz, and Gosstroi USSR were transformed from all-union to union-republic agencies.[16]

Formal change at the enterprise level was largely reduced to the formation of "firms" and the addition of economists to the plant managerial staff.

The New System of Planning

In 1962, planning was further centralized and also further complicated by re-distributing planning functions and broadening participation in the planning process. The institutional base of the planning system continued to be the union and republican state planning committees, but Union Sovnarkhoz, Gosstroi USSR, and the state branch and production committees all had important planning functions. In addition, Khrushchev intensified the countercycle of "planning from below" and, in conformity with his conception of regionally planned and integrated economies, also established regional planning councils. And, as formerly, both the Ministry of Finance and the USSR State Bank were instrumental in establishing the financial structure of the annual plan.

The expectations of the reformed Gosplan were established in the enabling statute defining its powers and functions in January 1963.[17] Gosplan would correct problems of proportional development, material-technical supply, departmentalism and localism in the use of material and financial resources, violation of state discipline in assigning plan indicators to enterprises and construction sites, and put an end to parallelism and duplication in the work of the planning agencies.[18] The USSR Council of the National Economy would once again split the process of planning production from that of planning material-technical supply.[19] In January 1963, Union Sovnarkhoz was given the responsibility for elaborating the *nomenklatury* of products not designated in the plan, for the plan for interrepublican deliveries, and for all-union needs. In the crucial area of supply, Union Sovnarkhoz changed and affirmed supply plans, having the power to change delivery dates, assortments, standards of quality, and so forth. The interlocking and overlapping structures for planning and supply of current production and construction created serious administrative complications.

The planning and introduction of technical progress, which Khrushchev had identified as an acute problem at the November plenum, was given to Gosplan and the twelve state branch committees attached to it.[20] In contrast to the state production committees formed from former ministries in March 1963, the state branch committees lacked operational jurisdiction over the industrial enterprises within their branches. Nevertheless, they were expected to take full responsibility for introducing new technology and establishing technical policy for a given branch of industry independently of territorial jurisdiction.

The emphasis on branch planning was a logical result of Khrushchev's emphasis on investment and production in certain progressive branches of industry, particularly chemistry; but his concern for regional specialization and integration counteracted this emphasis. The regional planning commissions continued to operate, and, in the late spring of 1963, councils were set up for Coordination of Development of the National Economy.[21] The planning commissions, staffed with twenty to forty planners, were responsible for drawing up the regional balances for both industry and agriculture. They were specifically concerned during this period, however, with investment policy and specialization, although they appear to have played a minor role in establishing the current plan as well.[22]

While a planning commission existed for Transcaucasia, functions of regional planning for Transcaucasia and for Central Asia were the direct responsibility of the regional Party bureaus established for these regions. The councils for coordination usually included the first secretaries of the republican or oblast Party committees, the chairman of the regional sovnarkhoz, chairmen of regional soviety and production administrations, local planning and trade union officials, scholars, and specialists.[23] As a coordinating group for the major economic regions, the councils closely paralleled the planning commissions and were evidently intended to reinforce them. Their operational role, however, appears to have been minor.

The Central Asian Sovnarkhoz and the regional sovnarkhozy in the Russian and Ukrainian republics were important but not decisive in the new planning system. The Central Asian Sovnarkhoz, under the close operational control of the Central Asian Bureau, exercised direct guidance over the current planning structure of the four Central Asian republics. Its formal authority resembled that of the Union Sovnarkhoz, and its functions included the formation of current and long-range plans, the distribution of investment, the elaboration of a single technical policy, cooperative deliveries for other regions, and, most important, the distribution of material-technical supply. The Central Asian Sovnarkhoz was also empowered to change the republics' plans prior to submission to the central planning organs.[24]

The role of the regional sovnarkhozy, which had been steadily reduced under the previous system, was increasingly diminished in 1963 and 1964. In September 1964, V. V. Krotov complained at length about the rigid and detailed controls which the central planning organs continued to impose on the sovnarkhozy and enterprises. As they had previously, the central planners opposed any decentralization in planning authority or extension of the right of the sovnarkhozy to change centrally established indicators. The regional sovnarkhoz still lacked the right to dispose of above-plan production or to approve any sum above twenty thousand rubles for introducing new technology in the enterprises under its jurisdiction.[25]

The proliferation of central organs for a more comprehensive administrative control of planning was only one major aspect of the reform. Khrushchev's antibureaucratic and populist commitment, discussed below, was dramatically revealed in the summer of 1963 when he used the Party apparatus to mobilize mass pressure for breaking the institutional resistance of the managers to his priorities. The result of this new element was to introduce additional irrationalities into an already strenuously overburdened administrative structure.

The System of Industrial Administration

The Supreme Council of the National Economy held plenary power over all aspects of industry and construction, including operational control over plan fulfillment. Although the division of functions between Vesenkha and Union Sovnarkhoz was not explicitly established, the latter also exercised operational control over plan fulfillment and was a prime source of administrative pressure for technological development.

The centralization of operational control undoubtedly reduced further the authority and administrative discretion of the new sovnarkhozy in relation to Moscow. When the central organs were established as union-republic agencies in March 1963, the republican and regional sovnarkhozy were faced with more complex legal relationships than ever before. As a number of Soviet jurists pointed out, the sovnarkhozy were subject to two and three different subordinations, which led to a reduction in the role of republican institutions.[26] Scholars and sovnarkhoz officials both protested the detailed intervention of the central organs in the daily administration of the sovnarkhozy but to little practical effect.

The loss of autonomy by the intermediate layers of the industrial administration was partially compensated by their increasingly detailed control over the enterprises under their jurisdiction. The establishment of highly specialized branch administrations and the transfer of all local industry to sovnarkhoz jurisdiction enabled the sovnarkhoz to supervise the enterprises more tightly. It became clear during 1963 and 1964 that the developing administrative system directly opposed those economic methods which would enlarge the freedom and discretion of the plant managers.

After the November plenum, the administration of capital construction was extensively reorganized. Gosstroi USSR was administratively responsible for technical documentation, finance, establishing and maintaining investment priorities, and the distribution of supply.[27] The actual capital construction supply plan, however, was drafted by Union Sovnarkhoz, and the chief administrations for the supply of construction sites were under its control. The concrete operational decisions made by the central executive organs to fulfill the capital construction plan was a function of Gosstroi USSR rather than of Union Sovnarkhoz.

At the intermediate level of construction administration, the sovnarkhoz role was terminated. New, enlarged territorial construction trusts were formed whose relations with the sovnarkhozy were placed on a contractual basis. Despite the centralization of supply and executive control, however, the sovnarkhozy were still formally responsible for equipping the new construction sites and controlling the course of construction.[28] In capital construction and annual plan fulfillment, the traditional gap between power and responsibility, which had become acute under the ministerial system, returned in full measure during the final two years of Khrushchev's rule.

2

The Dynamics of Industrial Administration

The reorganization would bring the problems of power and efficiency inherent in the Stalinist system of management into sharp relief. Khrushchev revealed his lack of confidence in the industrial planners and managers by forcing his priorities on the managerial apparatus notwithstanding economic cost or calculation. But securing acceptable decisions on economic policy was only part of what he required from the administrative mechanism. To successfully change the structure of economic production and distribution also depended on the efficiency with which the administrative system met the challenges of implementing his priorities.

The return in 1963 and 1964 to tight central controls and administrative power resulted in a performance characteristic of the ministerial system. The system concentrated on selected, high-priority targets and marshalled the human and material resources required to implement them, but the costs were high. Unlike the earlier period of industrialization, the demands from such sectors as the military could not be radically suppressed. The intense central pressure, sifted through the channels of a complex administrative system, were diffused and productive of disequilibria and confusion. Although generalization is difficult at this level, the evidence suggests an intensification of the problems of microcoordination discussed in previous chapters. These conditions framed the dynamics of Party *rukovodstvo* at the territorial level.

The Administrative Process, 1963–64

Administrative centralism and the proliferation of central, interrelated planning and executive organs would increase the costs of coordination, intensify jurisdictional disputes, and increase administrative staffs.

In 1963 and 1964, Union Gosplan and Union Sovnarkhoz planned about 1,200 balances, and the chief administrations for interrepublic deliveries attached to Union Sovnarkhoz centrally planned about twenty thousand products by volume and nomenclature.[29] In addition, the assumption of direct operational control by Union Sovnarkhoz led to the bypassing of republican and regional organs of administration, which resulted in a large number of enterprises being directly controlled from Moscow.[30] For example, the otdely of Union Sovnarkhoz took over direct control of chemical plants producing synthetic ammonia, apatite concentrates, and other products required for mineral fertilizers. A smiliar direct control was placed over plants producing railroad and other types of equipment.

Three of the economic regions of the Russian Republic—Volga-Viatka, Central Black Earth, and the Northern Caucasus—were given all-union status and placed under central administration.[31] On the still critical issue of supply, one official complained that virtually every problem was resolved in Moscow, so that even Vesenkha, established to provide policy direction and overall coordination, was flooded with petty supply problems.[32]

The result was to slow down the decision-making process in both planning and execution. The time and energy expended to coordinate and secure approval of decisions undoubtedly increased in these years. A. P. Kirilenko estimated that some fourteen thousand to sixteen thousand officials arrived in Moscow daily to coordinate work, often remaining for lengthy periods to obtain results. In some cases, he noted that provincial officials made as many as eighteen visits to a single committee or organ to secure approval of the work or project of a single plant.[33] The chairman of Kazakhstan's Gosplan noted that 75 percent of his time was spent in Moscow.[34] Some plant directors estimated that as much as 50 percent of their time was spent in various decision-making centers, including Moscow.[35] Negotiating and affirming the current plan, always arduous and time consuming, were particularly difficult in 1963 and 1964. The plan for a machine-building plant, for example, was negotiated through regional sovnarkhozy, republican state planning committees and sovnarkhozy, and passed through Gosplan, Union Sovnarkhoz, and the relevant state branch committees under Gosplan, Gosstroi, or other organs. The director of the Vulcan Plant in Leningrad complained that it took four months to secure approval of his assortment plan at the republican and union levels.[36] Kosygin made a similar complaint about the affirmation of capital construction plans in the extreme centralization in this period.[37]

The proliferation of central organs and the absence of precise jurisdictional boundaries among them contributed to the general administrative confusion. The problem of overlapping and conflicting jurisdictions was particularly acute. A *Pravda* editorial noted:

It sometimes happened that they did not manage to implement in practice a particular reorganization of administration before new changes were introduced. This complicated economic and social processes. As an example we can cite the fact that in creating many committees of all-union and also republican significance, the statute which defined their rights and their authority was not considered. It turned out that a committee exists but it is not clear what questions it had a right to decide, who and in what degree it is responsible for checking and supervising and how its functions are differentiated from the functions of other departments and establishments.[38]

The inability to distinguish basic policy-making and allocative decisions from coordinative decisions produced frequent conflicts at all levels of the industrial administration. Even more serious, the complex interdependence and interlocking of functions, while inevitable in a large-scale organization, created a large number of veto-groups within the administration and frequently led to difficulties in assessing responsibility.[39] In a probably typical case, a machine-building plant in Barnaul produced presses for which there was no order. Five different agencies had passed on this decision; none of them, of course, would admit responsibility for the mistake.[40]

Forming interrepublican organs of administration lengthened the number of stages separating Moscow from the production units and carried its own administrative complexities as well. First, there was serious political opposition to large-scale specialization on a regional basis. Secondly, enforcing Khrushchev's policy of regional specialization and integration proved administratively difficult.[41] To compose a single coherent plan in Central Asia was particularly complex, for example. Its financial plan was constructed on a branch basis, so that in passing through the twenty departments of each republican planning agency, a gross plan was made filling five weighty volumes. To create a single plan, almost continuous coordination was required over distances of up to 2,000 kilometers. Moreover, each republic had its individual standards and procedures and opposed any effort to establish standardized norms or schedules. Also opposed was specialization which entailed moving a plant from the jurisdiction of one republic to another.[42]

The administrative difficulties of Central Asia were less acute in Transcaucasia and the Baltic. In the Baltic, the central thrust to produce specialized planning and executive organs for the region met intense opposition from the three republican gosplany and sovnarkhozy. The decision to place the Baltic fishing industry under a single administration subordinated to the Lithuanian and Russian sovnarkhozy as well as to Union Sovnarkhoz led to such jurisdictional conflicts that it was finally completely centralized and placed under the direct administration of the State Committee for the Fish Industry.[43]

An instructive example was the attempt by the Council for Coordination and Planning of the Western Economic Region to establish a long-range plan for the specialization of consumer goods. Each of the republics produced competing plans for 1963 which had to be ultimately compromised and adjusted in Union Gosplan.[44] Precisely the same condition developed in 1964 in regard to the regional plan for the production of consumer goods and machine tools. According to V. P. Lein, the chairman of the Latvian Bureau for the Leadership of Industry and Construction, the heads of the republican planning and administrative organs bargained to keep "advantageous" products for themselves and to unload "unadvantageous" products on their neighbors.[45] The "localist" pressure for republican autonomy was equally evident in the Transcaucasus. In some degree, both regions succeeded in blunting the tendency of the period toward tighter central controls.

Increasing the general administrative load, particularly at the center, did not improve the style of administrative leadership, solve the chronic and severe informational problems, or end the complaints about bureaucratism and red tape in decision-making.[46] The paper flow remained enormous between central and local organs of administration. Kirilenko complained that the Russian Sovnarkhoz was immersed in paper and the flood was increasing.[47] At the enterprise level, the paper flow produced maddening administrative strains. The Uralmashzavod alone processed some 137,405 different documents in 1963. Putting together the administrative paper and other types of documentary materials, some plants processed an estimated ton of documents per year.[48] The average machine-building plant handled some 120 thousand pages of blueprints, 200 thousand pages describing various technical processes, and 1.3 million *nariady* for different supply requirements.[49]

Much of the heavy correspondence on issues of supply was merely formal. In the East Siberian Sovnarkhoz, for example, it was estimated that 80 percent of the time of engineers in the apparatus was devoted to correspondence. Since requests for supply deliveries usually brought no immediate action, an elaborate game, fully understood by all participants, was played. A request by the Russian Sovnarkhoz to the Irkutsk Auto Tractor Plant for the delivery of drive shafts to a client plant was systematically checked out through several layers of the sovnarkhoz administration over several weeks even though the sovnarkhoz knew the reasons for the delay in deliveries.[50] The absorption of technical personnel into administrative activities removed such resources from research and production and contributed to the slowdown in technical progress.

The increase in red tape and paper brought an increase in the number of administrative workers, which reached over ten million by 1964. One Soviet specialist on administration attributed this to the low level of automation and mechanization of administrative work and the large number of centrally controlled indicators.[51] Whatever the gains in administrative rationalization between 1954 and 1962, they were largely lost in the final years of Khrushchev's rule. The alleged reduction of administrative workers from 13.8 to 9.2 percent was sharply challenged by F. Manoilo, a Ministry of Finance official, who held that the growth in administrative workers exceeded the growth in labor productivity and pointed to the large number of above-plan administrative workers concealed by plant administrations.[52] The new sovnarkhozy were charged with a similar growth in staff. In many sovnarkhozy, the ratio was as low as 1 to 4.2.[53] The growing number of links in the chain of command between the sovnarkhoz and the plant was most marked in the material-technical supply net.[54]

Increased administrative activity brought an epidemic of "session fever" in the state apparatus, a situation which an early 1964 *Kommunist* editorial described as approaching disastrous proportions.[55] Over half of the average administrator's time was spent in conferences and sessions, which were undoubtedly necessary to coordinate various activities and iron out chronic operational difficulties. The Moldavian Council of the National Economy, for example, held ninety-eight conferences in five months, each attended by seventy to 100 technical and economic officials. In October 1963, in Vladimir Oblast over 7,500 people were called into conferences of one sort or another, and it was not unusual for heads of construction trusts to be involved in lengthy, formal conferences every day of the week. At the enterprise level, the plant directors were subject to the additional headache of constant mass checkups by various control groups.[56] But this surge in energy did little to change the underlying, specific patterns of planning and plan fulfillment.

The Planning Process

One of Khrushchev's central purposes was to reorganize the planning process in such a way that the conventional process could be altered to the advantage of the progressive industries and chemistry. But the redistribution of control planning functions and increased centralization did little to change its substance. To alter the structure of current planning, in the summer of 1963 Khrushchev initiated a dramatic and decisive intervention by the center in the formulation of the new Two-Year Plan for 1964 and 1965. In June and July, some 300 central planning and Party officials joined with republican and oblast Party and state officials to construct the plan.[57] D. F. Ustinov, the head of Vesenkha, for example, flew to the Donbass, and Alexander Shelepin was dispatched to Moldavia to impose Khrushchev's priorities during the initial stages of plan construction.[58]

At the enterprise and sovnarkhoz levels, special commissions headed by Party officials pressed for the tightest possible plan.[59] The effort to break through the system of planning from historical indices, however, was not accompanied by a significant change in "success indicators," and the basic conflict of interest between national and enterprise plans was intensified. Plant officials continued to bargain for an "advantageous" plan and search for "reserves" of capital investment and supply, and the central planners continued to press for higher output quotas and lower planned inputs.[60]

The imposition through direct administrative and mass pressure of a new set of planning priorities produced an operational plan largely reflecting Khrushchev's personal policies. The Two-Year Plan outlined by P. F. Lomako before the December 1963 session of the Supreme Soviet targeted a rise of industrial production of 17.5 percent. Oil, paper, gas extraction and production, and electric power continued to receive priority. The most dramatic change was in chemical production, which was to rise by 36 percent over 1962 levels. To equip the expanded petrochemical industry, the production of machinery for the oil and chemical industries was scheduled to increase by a massive 50 percent. The severe strain on the machine-building industry produced by the voluntaristic approach to increasing chemical production was significant in generating the industrial administration crisis during 1963 and 1964.

Khrushchev was less successful in imposing his priorities for consumer goods. Group A industries were to outstrip the proposed growth rate of Group B by 18.6 percent to 14.5 percent. Planned growth in the consumer goods sector, moreover, was selective. The output of durable goods for which there was a heavy mass demand, such as refrigerators and transistor radios, was scheduled to double. Fibers for clothing had a planned increase of at least one-third. The increased production in clothing and footwear, however, was planned on the basis of substituting chemical for agricultural raw materials, which in turn depended upon the success of Khrushchev's investment and construction plans in the chemical industry.

The two-year investment plan which emerged from the perennial conflict over resource allocation indicated a moderate shift in the proportions devoted to chemistry, agriculture, and the light and food industries. Investment for 1964 and 1965 was planned for 36 and 39.5 billion rubles. The share of chemistry, agriculture, and light industry was to rise from 26 percent in 1963 to 33 percent in 1964 and 35 percent in 1965. The plan envisaged a gigantic expansion in chemical construction. The 1964 construction title list, cut to 960 approved projects for 1963, expanded dramatically to 5,800 projects, an increase of over 600 percent. Over the two-year period, fifty-seven new major chemical complexes were scheduled to go into construction and eighty-two chemical plants into operation. The underlying crisis in agriculture was revealed by the decision to pour 40 percent of the total investment in chemistry into mineral fertilizers and herbicides.[61]

The improved efficiency required to meet the ambitious 1963 and 1964 production and construction targets did not materialize. The deep-rooted problems of planning, so extensively explored since 1960 in the public press, continued in evidence and may have worsened as the result of increased centralization and the arbitrary suddenness with which Khrushchev launched his crash program in chemical construction. The division of planning responsibilities among different central and republican organs, jurisdictional disputes, the use of different indicators and standards by different planning organs, the lack of sufficient information in the central organs for accurate planning—all contributed to the planning organs' failure to achieve greater efficiency. Some machine-building plants experienced major difficulties, for example, because Gosplan planned instrument production by ruble and Union Sovnarkhoz by piece.[62] Because of a lack of accurate information, the Kazakh Sovnarkhoz was ordered to produce 21 percent more spare parts for tractors than the republic's plants had the physical capacity to produce. To correct the plan, the Kazakh planning officials had to press the issue through departments of Gosplan and Union Sovnarkhoz, the State Committee for Tractor and Agricultural Machine Building, and the Chief Administration of the Auto and Agricultural Machine Building.[63]

For the individual plant, the planning process was a complex and time-consuming chore. The final plan was centrally dictated, and the planning indicators remained numerous, complex, and calculated in physical and monetary terms. Plans were seldom internally consistent, and supply was a more critical issue in 1963 and 1964 than it had been in the preceding period. The pressure to raise and shift the balance of production induced further instability in the production plan. Production specialization was disrupted, and the enterprises were under continuous central pressure to increase production through supplemental planning by the supply organs.[64]

The most significant problem, however, was the lack of correspondence between the production and supply plans.[65] The imbalances arose in part from computational errors; in part, particularly in the chemical industry, from the imbalances in demand over supply. The supply problem was also attributable to serious administrative deficiencies. Planning organs continued to issue supply certificates on plants still in construction. Orders for supply were still affirmed before the production plan, and certificates for centrally distributed supply were usually not issued until after the first of the year. Input norms were often arbitrary or obsolescent, and frequent changes were made in the production plan without adjusting the supply plan.[66]

In addition, the increasingly cumbersome distribution net was not only excessively centralized but was also composed of supply organs which duplicated and overlapped each other at every stage of the process. Jurisdictional disputes and the fact that as many as eleven different stages separated supplier from client plants largely stimulated the demands, which Khrushchev endorsed, for direct ties between plants.[67] The complex distributional net permitted the draining off of supplies for "reserve" at each level, with the result that the ultimate client often failed to receive the full amount of his order. Irrational deliveries, excessive numbers of suppliers, inadequate warehousing, shortages of transportation, and a lack of spare parts and reserves multiplied the difficulties in supplying the enterprises and construction sites.[68] Because deliveries were late or incomplete, with the wrong assortment or quality, production costs were increased or disrupted.[69] Managers continued to hide reserves, practice *mestnichestvo*, and make extensive use of *tolkachi*.

The Process of Plan Fulfillment

The failure of the administrative reorganization to change existing systemic relationships was reflected in the processes of current plan fulfillment and capital construction. The falling growth rate in 1963 and 1964 was a fact of both political and economic significance. According to the most optimistic calculus, gross industrial rates fell from 9.5 percent in 1962 to 8.5 percent in 1963 and 7.1 percent in 1964.[70] The growth rates of major sectors of Soviet industry differed widely. Group A industries achieved steady rates between 10 and 11 percent. Despite their political importance, consumer goods dropped from 7 percent in 1962 to 2 percent in 1964. The capital construction program lagged as well. In the heavy industrial sector, the growth rates clearly indicated the responsiveness of the Party and state apparatus to Khrushchev's priorities. According to official Soviet statistics, the plan for 1963 resulted in increases of 16 percent for chemistry, 9 percent for metallurgy, and 10 percent for machine-building and metal-working industries. While machine-building for the chemical industry increased by 9 percent, for the oil industry it achieved only 95 percent of 1962 levels. The plan for 1964, the first of the new two-year plans, more clearly reflected Khrushchev's priorities. The production of mineral fertilizers increased 28 percent; herbicides, 35 percent. The industry growth rate for machine building declined to 9 percent, but equipment for the oil industry rose by 22 percent and for the chemical industry by 19 percent. The growth rates of the metal, fuel, and power industries declined.

The major problems were in consumer goods production and capital construction. During 1963 and 1964, soft goods and house construction also lagged behind projected 1965 goals. Part of the decline in Group B was undoubtedly attributable to the disastrous harvest of 1963. Grain production fell to levels below the poor harvest of 1957, and the Soviet leadership spent valuable foreign currency to purchase some 12 million tons of grain abroad. The best performance was in the durable goods sector, which recorded high growth rates in refrigerators, radios, and television sets. Even so, as Harry Schwartz has pointed out, the production of these goods fell far behind demand.[71]

The policy of concentrating capital investment on projects nearing completion was more successful in 1963 than in 1964. In 1963, 700 new construction projects were commissioned, and the Soviet industrial complex added 10 percent in fixed capital. In 1964, the number of new projects commissioned fell to 600, and the gain to the economy in fixed capital was cut almost in half to 6 percent. The general decline did not include chemical construction, however. Construction concerned with oil and gas facilities rose by 16 percent and chemical construction by 17 percent. The physical capacity for mineral fertilizer increased by some 8 million tons.

In general, the November reorganization of the administrative structure failed to bring about the expected upsurge in industrial growth and was undoubtedly responsible in some degree for its continuing slide. Although the application of direct administrative power in the chemical sector did produce a notable response by the administrative mechanism, the reorganization's positive achievements were flawed by a failure to deal with the underlying problems of operational *rukovodstvo* inherited from the past. In the criticism following the revival of the Liberman proposals in 1964, plant directors complained about "petty tutelage" by the central organs, the irrationality of the "success indicators," the counterproductive controls of the financial institutions, and supply.[72] In the high-priority industries such as chemical machine building, "storming" remained characteristic of plan fulfillment.[73] Labor turnover was high, and the increase in inexperienced workers raised production costs to such a degree that Khrushchev proposed introducing labor controls through a passport system.[74]

That managerial abuses were unabated was amply illustrated in the Soviet press. Plant directors responded indifferently to the leadership's demand to economize on raw material inputs or to improve the storage and use of raw materials or equipment.[75] The quality of production remained admittedly low in heavy industry and consumer goods.

Part of the low quality of production undoubtedly had technical causes: insufficient testing, inadequate inspection, and lack of quality control through the use of hand labor;[76] but it also reflected the problem of bonuses. Increasing the quality of production meant a rise in production costs, which in turn threatened managerial bonuses. Under pressure, the Iaroslavl Motor Plant increased the life of a motor by 150 percent and raised its horsepower while cutting fuel consumption. The new motor was 20 percent heavier than its predecessor, with the result that the increased costs brought a loss of premiums.[77] As in the past, normal managerial practice eschewed technical innovation in favor of reducing quality to fulfill the plan for costs. To meet its quota for costs, the Likhachev Plant substituted aluminum for steel in building a cooling system, reducing the life of the product by 50 percent.[78]

The conflict between the producer and the economy was also reflected in the issue of technical innovation. At the enterprise level, as one Soviet specialist pointed out, the sporadic and isolated introduction of new technology had little economic effect since the rhythm of production was necessarily geared to the obsolescent sector of production.[79] Another obstacle was the incompatibility of technical innovation with the existence of universal plants. Automation was considered to be economically viable only for long runs of serial production. The extension by the central organs of the plant's production profile, the lack of incentives of the sovnarkhozy for increasing output, the disruption and threat of breakdown from the introduction and use of new machinery—all evoked managerial resistance to the introduction of new technology.[80]

In this respect, the key measure of the November reform—centralizing technical policy and increasing the rights of the state committees—proved of marginal value. The lack of authority of these organs significantly reduced the capacity of the center to legislate technical innovation.[81] When these factors were added to such specific problems as long lead times for testing and installation, lengthy periods of time for affirming new models, late plans, and insufficient supply, the purely administrative obstacles to technical development appear formidable.

In the process of current plan fulfillment, other familiar managerial practices were frequently noted in the press. Enterprise officials continued to produce "advantageous" assortments, to include defective or incomplete production in shipments, to pad reports, to engage in bribery, and to send out large numbers of *tolkachi*.[82] In short, the most fundamental dynamics of current plan fulfillment were unchanged. Administrative power was sufficient to refocus administrative energies on Khrushchev's economic targets but not enough to induce a massive upsurge in performance.

The difficulty of translating Khrushchev's capital production program into operating production facilities lay in four specific problem areas: technical documentation, supply, construction and production cadres, and general administration. Supplying new construction sites with the proper design and technical documentation materials frequently lagged behind their needs. N. G. Egorychev admitted in reply to Khrushchev's criticism at the December 1963 plenum that the design institute simply could not cope with the suddenly increased volume of work.[83] The design institute's lack of legal responsibility for inadequate or incorrect designs, the poor coordination of research, the duplicated work, the slow, complex system of design approval—all contributed to holding up the construction process.[84]

The greatest bottleneck in the construction industry generally, and in the chemical industry in particular, was in supply, an acute problem in 1963 and critical in 1964. An investigation in Belorussia revealed that in 1964 only twenty of more than 200 major construction sites had the necessary equipment.[85] The problem was particularly acute in chemical machine building. Despite this industry's highest political priority, construction of chemical machine-building plants lagged in 1964, strong evidence of the large overcommitment of resources in this area. The delivery of defective equipment seems to have been unusually frequent. Of the apparatus for gas separators produced by the Sumy Machine-Building Plant, for example, 71 percent was considered defective and unusable.[86] Despite the decision of the collegium of Union Sovnarkhoz to directly control all deliveries of equipment to chemical construction sites, the situation remained critical.[87]

Providing human resources for the chemical industry presented an equally difficult problem. The surging demand for construction cadres and workers was partially met by sending thousands of young workers to the construction sites.[88] But low morale and a lack of adequate housing, schools, and recreational facilities resulted in a continuous turnover of cadres and workers, and the quality of construction suffered.[89]

The newly commissioned chemical plants also had problems of effective recruitment and staffing. In February 1964, *Pravda* estimated that 80 percent of the workers sent to the new chemical plants were technically unprepared and and that the shortage of qualified managerial and technical cadres was acute.[90]Recruited from various branches of industry, the managers usually lacked either the technical qualifications or the experience to manage chemical plants. Upon encountering serious difficulties in getting the plants into production, they responded by leaving.[91]

Other issues surfaced in the course of construction. The frequent complaint that the newly commissioned chemical plants were not reaching full utilization was attributable in part to the fact that water, heat, sanitary facilities, and sewers were either insufficient or nonexistent.[92] Again, the "success indicators" for the construction industry paid bonuses when the plant was placed in operation but not when it reached full production; and since plants were often put into operation before construction was completed, the construction trust officials had no material interest in finishing the job. Finally, it was clear that removing the construction trusts from sovnarkhoz jurisdiction did not end jurisdictional conflict. The average construction trust wasted much time haggling with the numerous subcontractors on a job. The most serious jurisdictional disputes arose between the contractors and the agencies in charge of installing equipment since the latter were outside the former's control. In capital construction as in the fulfillment of the annual plan, the administrative mechanism proved only partially viable.

3

The Party's Decision-Making Role in Industry

In 1963 and 1964, the Party apparatus and the new Party-state control organs were involved in establishing Khrushchev's chemical program and in evoking a maximum administrative effort to overcome its profoundly complex consequences. But the reorganization of industrial management served only to increase the traditional operational tensions of the Stalinist system of industrial management, so that this aspect of Party-state relations continued within traditional boundaries. The basic continuity in the Party's role, however, did not preclude short-run and often intense effects on the Party's decision-making power. Paradoxically, the reform simultaneously weakened and strengthened the power of the territorial Party apparatus over industrial administration.

Centralizing power and proliferating specialized central Party and state organs of administration had the effect of reducing the weight of the lower Party organs in the general process of decision-making. The flow of local, petty issues to Moscow further restricted the local Party organs' discretionary power, essentially recreating the conditions of Party *rukovodstvo* under the ministerial system. Tightening controls at the center undoubtedly cut the pluralist tendencies of the territorial Party apparatus but at the cost of further alienation and reduced efficiency. The territorial Party organs' loss of access to the central and intermediate levels of industrial administration was partially compensated by their increased power on the production line and at the construction site.

In translating "economics over politics" into organizational functions, the Party apparatus responded by energizing established channels rather than by creating new ones. Its absorption of economic and technical functions in 1963 and 1964 not only violated traditional norms governing the Party's administrative role but also generated such a massive involvement in specifics as to dissipate its resources and further threaten its cohesion, already strained by the divided oblast Party committees. Only the strong continuity of habitual response preserved the Party from further disintegration at this level.

The Central Party Organs

The central Party structure's expanded role in decision-making appears to have modified existing procedures only marginally. Holding joint sessions of the Presidium of the Central Committee and the USSR Council of Ministers undoubtedly bespoke a greater symbolic union of Party and state, but it also probably reflected political tensions within the Presidium.[93] Although the fusion of Party and state organs at the central level probably increased during this period, Khrushchev pointed out in April 1963 that the creation of the Supreme Council of the National Economy was not to be interpreted as a weakening of Party control over the economy; Vesenkha would operate under the direct supervision of the Central Committee.[94] It may also be assumed that expanding the number of secretaries and specializing and augmenting the central Party apparatus permitted more specific, detailed controls over their counterparts in the state administration.

The major failure at the center was the abortive role of the three secretarial branch bureaus. The three territorial Bureaus, on the other hand, were significant in decision-making at the central level. The Russian Bureau in particular continued to play a dominant and exclusive role within the Russian Republic; it exercised direct control over individual plants and intervened to raise production quotas or to resolve problems of supply.[95] As it was for the Party as a whole, the chemical program was likewise an urgent concern of the Russian Bureau, which was not only deeply involved in the details of construction but assumed operational responsibility for lagging construction as well. In February 1963, for example, it coordinated the efforts of Russian Gosplan, Russian Sovnarkhoz, and the republican Ministry of Installation and Construction in installing new equipment in the Novo Kramatorsk Chemical Combine.[96]

The Russian Bureau also responded to the demand for increasing technical innovation and raising the quality of production. In early 1963, it conducted a mass investigation within the republic to check on the introduction of new technology and held conferences on specific technical issues throughout the period.[97] It also undertook on specific occasions to break the managerial reluctance to improving the quality of production. A publicized case involving the Iaroslavl Motor Plant is interesting insofar as it indicates the capacities and limitations in the Party's use of administrative power to achieve technical development.

The bureau and the Iaroslavl Industrial Obkom forced the plant to produce a more durable, powerful motor.[98] But the plant management was bitterly critical of the experiment since it caused the plant to exceed the plan for costs and thereby suffer a loss of premiums.[99] Under tight Party supervision, changes could undoubtedly be made against the managers' will, but such an intensive application of administrative control was limited and selective. For each product so improved, there were probably hundreds of others within the same plant which either declined in quality or remained unimproved.

The two regional bureaus to emerge in early 1963 functioned with less authority and specific control than the well-established Russian Bureau. The Central Asian Bureau was the more important in decision-making, although problems of scale and the stubborn resistance of Party and state officials diminished the impact of direct central Party power. As Lomonosov noted in *Pravda* in May 1963, the four specific industrial priorities for Central Asia were developing the chemical industry, specializing machine building, concentrating capital investment, and placing special controls over cotton growing.[100] These priorities defined the bureau's role.

The Central Asian Bureau was instrumental in establishing the proportions of the Two-Year Plan, imposing a growth rate of 150 percent for chemistry for 1964–65, and it also ruthlessly forced the concentration of capital investment. When the four republics submitted a title list of 9,200 construction projects for affirmation, the bureau cut them by two-thirds.[101] The bureau's individual sessions also revealed its role in central policy-making. Its agenda included discussions of the chemical industry, the state of construction, the cotton harvest, the storage of cotton in Chimkent Oblast, the packaging and transport of mineral fertilizers, specialization of machine building and cable production, and undoubtedly other, more specific industrial concerns as well.[102] Like other Party agencies, the Central Asian Bureau closely monitored the fulfillment of the annual plan within each republic and showed particular concern over disruptions in plan discipline when they occurred.[103]

The Transcaucasian Bureau was less active. The priorities of the central leadership were pressed through the Transcaucasian Planning Commission, and planning seems to have been the bureau's paramount, if not its sole, responsibility. In the strategy of regionalization, it was explicitly instructed to press for specialization and integration of production, particularly in the food, textile, and electrotechnical industries.[104] In decision-making, the Transcaucasian Bureau differed markedly from either the Russian or Central Asian bureaus. Mass conferences rather than restricted bureau sessions appear to have been the principal vehicle for transmitting central instructions to the republics. In the numerous conferences reported in the press, 300 to 400 officials gathered to discuss such specific issues as vegetable production, chemistry, or construction.[105]

The bureau chairman and vice-chairman also exercised more concrete decision-making powers. The bureau was deeply involved in formulating the terms of compromise in the bargaining between the Transcaucasian Planning Commission and the three republics.[106] It established the investment proportions among the republics for the growth of the chemical industry for 1964–65, and it pressed for the specialization of such industries as agricultural machinery repair.[107] On the whole, however, the pressure exerted against the interrepublican organs was generally successful in blocking the scope and velocity of change which the bureau was able to achieve in planning.[108] The Transcaucasian Bureau was also responsible for the fulfillment of the annual and construction plans in a manner similar to that of the Central Asian Bureau, although supervision of the plan was more visibly shared here with the central Party apparatus. Twice in late 1963, Moscow dispatched investigating commissions to Azerbaidzhan to investigate the waste of gas and steel in individual plants and to examine the use of transport by the republican Ministry of Auto Transport.[109]

The Republican Organs

Although the discretionary authority of the republican and regional Party committees declined during the final years of Khrushchev's rule, they remained instrumental in realizing Party policy within their jurisdictional limits. Specializing the Party apparatus by economic sector provided the structural foundation for that close and continuous contact with the state industrial administration which was the essence of Khrushchev's concept of Party *rukovodstvo*. Expanding Party authority at the intermediate level, however, proved as complex and ambiguous in 1963 and 1964 as it had ever been.

The role of the republican Party apparatus at the republican level and below probably increased.[110] The republican committees, for example, spearheaded Khrushchev's drive to form the Two-Year Plan in accordance with his priorities.[111] The industrial and agricultural bureaus were a normal, although not final, stage within the republic for both the investment and the current plan.[112] The industrial and agricultural otdely of the Party apparatus continued to be responsible for the detailed breakdown of republican plans before they were sent on to the republican sovnarkhoz for distribution to the production agencies.[113]

The apparatus exercised extremely detailed control over those industries that fell within Khrushchev's priorities. In the Ukraine, for example, the Department of Machine Building took the republic's chemical machine-building industry under direct administration in response to the crisis in supply for new construction sites.[114] In another case, a sector head of the chemistry department extended his control downward to include instructing the head of the Western Ukrainian Gas and Oil Administration on the proper methods of drilling for oil.[115] In those industries directly administered by the republican departments, the decision-making role of the lower Party organs became marginal.

None of the functions assumed by the republican Party apparatus was new. The novel element in the system of Party *rukovodstvo* was the creation of specialized branch bureaus for guiding industry and agriculture. As noted in another context, the role of the new bureaus depended largely on the discretion afforded them by the presidia, which differed from one republic to another. In the Ukraine, the Bureau for the Leadership of Industry and Construction operated under the shadow of the Presidium, its public role confined to holding conferences on limited industrial issues, affirming plans and socialist obligations, and hearing reports from lower Party and state organs on production issues.[116] Other industrial bureaus were more active. The bureau in Georgia, for example, worked out the *grafik* for a chemical construction site.[117] The Belorussian bureau responded to the growing shortage in, and dissatisfaction with, consumer goods production by examining the situation in the republic in detail and meting Party punishment to the offending managers.[118]

In those industrial bureaus, such as Estonia's, that played an active organizational role, the addition of a new layer of decision-making added little to the efficiency of Party decision-making. Where problems were examined on an industry-wide basis, the bureau's leadership was said to be "declarative and formal." Where the bureau became operationally involved in a large number of specific industrial or construction problems, it was so swamped by petty issues that it lost perspective. Such cases not only dissipated time and resources on secondary matters but produced "doubling" of the work of other Party and state organs.

The Estonian bureau, for example, took charge of a chemical plant that was failing to meet the plan, and after three days of exhaustive investigation sent a resolution to the Estonian Presidium for affirmation. The same plant, however, had been subject to a similar intensive investigation by the Estonian Sovnarkhoz. When questioned, the chairman of the bureau replied that he was unaware of the other investigation.[119] In Estonia, where such incidents were frequent, the anticipated improvement in the direction and coordination of Party-state activities not only did not occur but may have worsened under the impact of another Party organ interfering in the administrative process.

The structural reorganization of the Party would most vividly affect the intermediate levels of the Party structure, particularly among the divided obkomy and kraikomy. The detailed functions of decision-making which the obkomy assumed in the industrial economy provides a clear picture of the extent to which the Party became an overseer of the economy.

The Oblast Industrial Committees

The November 1962 reorganization adversely affected the obkom's discretionary power in two fundamental ways: (1) dividing Party authority within the oblast reduced the status and resources and narrowed the jurisdiction of the obkom first secretary to an extent unique in Party history; and (2) the flow of decision-making power to Moscow diminished the number of issues within the obkom's control. Crucial decisions affecting the capacity of an oblast's industry to grow and fulfill current plans normally centered on the obkom's ability to obtain investment and supply from the center. In this respect, and even with respect to securing decisions from the Moscow agencies, the evidence indicates a sharp loss of power during 1963 and 1964.[120] In one notable case, after repeated failure to obtain a decision from the Supreme Council, the first secretary of the Tiumen Industrial Obkom publicly suggested forming a regional association of obkomy and sovnarkhozy to petition Vesenkha for decisions affecting their areas of responsibility.[121] The loss of power by regional Party organs undoubtedly curtailed their horizontal or "localist" tendencies but seriously reduced the industrial obkom's capacity for problem solving.

Centralization also weakened the authority of the obkomy over the intermediate organs of administration. The fact that the new, enlarged sovnarkhozy operated under close central controls limited the power of the regional Party authority as well. A more subtle problem arose with the joint obkom control over those new sovnarkhozy whose jurisdiction included several oblasti. General authority and control over the *nomenklatura* seems to have been placed in the oblast committee housing the headquarters of the new councils.[122] The perception that this obkom would dominate the others was largely responsible for the severe power struggle which developed among the committees to secure the new council headquarters within their jurisdictions.[123] The perception was correct; an *Izvestiia* article declared that the first secretary of the largest industrial obkom and the chairman of the sovnarkhoz were the leading industrial officials of the region.[124] The decision-making role of those obkomy whose sovnarkhozy had been abolished undoubtedly declined. On the issues of investment and supply—issues in which the obkom traditionally exerted the greatest pressure—the Kamchatka, Crimean, and Smolensk obkomy complained bitterly about the indifference of their regional councils to their requests for aid.[125]

Their responsibility for the fulfillment of plans within their jurisdictions, however, remained undiminished. Among divided committees, all industrial and construction sites (except for plants processing agricultural products) were assigned to the industrial committees. But it was the dominant obkom that decided the jurisdiction of the obkom over the administrations of the sovnarkhoz guiding these plants. Thus, on such issues of regional importance as specialization of production, the major obkom was basically responsible.[126] Sovnarkhoz branch administrations located in oblasti other than headquarters were controlled by the oblasti in which they were situated. The Zhitomir Industrial Obkom, for example, maintained close control over the three administrations located in Zhitomir Oblast but had no contact with those in either the Kirovgrad or Dnepropetrovsk oblasti.[127] While this new system seems to have worked reasonably well, tangling the lines of authority stimulated jurisdictional disputes and was a major factor leading to that general weakening of Party control over the sovnarkhozy which the Russian Bureau condemned in 1964.[128]

The specific functions of the obkomy in planning and administering the industrial economy were therefore conditioned by the context of authority and structure prevailing in 1963 and 1964. In the composition of the new current plan, the oblast Party committees were specifically responsible for maximizing production quotas and mobilizing mass opinion in favor of Khrushchev's priorities. The technique was simple: the individual enterprise was pressured into accepting production quotas which ran counter to its interests.

"Planning from below" meant holding open forums of workers, led by officials of the obkom, that indicated the "hidden reserves" of the enterprises.[129] Exposing these reserves normally led to a sharp increase in the production quotas, particularly in the chemical or auxiliary industries.[130] In virtually every case, the intervention of the obkom led to a raising of production indices and a tightening of the plan.[131] For the enterprise, however, the "voluntarist" approach to planning often produced severe tensions and losses. The Kemerovo Industrial Obkom, for example, pushed up the coal production quota of the Kuzbass Sovnarkhoz by 2.18 million tons. The pricing system had not been adjusted to cover the 30 percent rise in costs. The result was that the sovnarkhoz ended with a deficit and a loss of premiums.[132]

The obkom's role in investment planning fell as full centralization proceeded in capital construction. Despite Khrushchev's threat in April 1963 to remove the obkom from any consideration of the title list, the plan for capital construction passed through the industrial obkom's bureau. Nevertheless, as Tolstikov of Leningrad admitted, the obkom had little power in relation to investment planning or control over capital construction. In 1963 he declared that the obkom had been denied permission by Moscow to make a minor change in the jurisdictional boundaries of a construction site.[133]

The lack of power did not, of course, diminish the struggle of the oblast committees and sovnarkhozy for investment capital. To fulfill the new quotas, particularly in chemicals, required additional capital investment, and regional competition was intense. The normal pattern was to appeal the denial of funds at one level by taking it to the next higher stage, a process which often involved lengthy delays and ultimate rejection.[134] The regional Party apparatus could be quite bitter in instances of rejection. Having failed to secure a correction in the capital investment plan for his oblast, the first secretary of the Zaporozhe Industrial Obkom publicly attacked the centralists in Moscow who, he claimed, were still so imbued with the cult of personality "that they regarded any decentralization as a weakening of discipline and order."[135]

The obkom apparatus' deep involvement in the daily administration of the enterprise ranged over the spectrum of the oblast's industrial profile. The industrial and unified committees, however, concentrated their efforts on the chemical program and Khrushchev's other priorities. Reflecting the intense central pressure for results, the obkomy of the Russian Republic placed both chemical machine building and agricultural machinery production—Khrushchev's major priorities—under the direct supervision of the departments of the obkoms' apparatus.[136] Technical innovation was another major responsibility of the obkom during this period. The obkom continued to elaborate plans for technical progress in conjunction with the sovnarkhoz, to eliminate obsolescent products, to support the efforts of the technical and economic aktiv in working out specific proposals for various industries, to conduct seminars and give courses in advanced technology, to supervise the norming of inputs, and to press for specialization of production.[137]

Their various efforts to raise the quality of production or to promote technical progress, however, yielded meager results. Under special conditions, where the obkomy were firmly and extensively backed by the central Party organs, some technical innovation was achieved. Normally, though, the obkom was impotent in this respect. As the first secretary of the Kalinin Industrial Obkom pointed out, the most important resources for raising quality and introducing new technology were outside the obkom's power. The centralization of administrative power during 1963 and 1964 left the obkom powerless to influence investment, supply, pricing, documentation and blueprints, and the quality of raw materials and semimanufactures. Additionally, the planning agencies in Moscow continually expanded the production program of enterprises in direct violation of the policy of production specialization. Finally, technical innovation ran directly counter to managerial interests; and since the administrative settlement of 1962 did not alter the basic antagonism of central-local interests, the obkom's informal interests coincided in some degree with the oblast's managers.

The obkomy responded most intensely to Khrushchev's crash program of chemical construction, whose urgency induced a dynamism unknown at the regional level since the early phase of industrialization. Although the problems of capital construction were outside the obkom's control, strenuous efforts were nevertheless made to bridge the chasm between goals and resources.

Part of this thrust was undoubtedly declarative and designed for effect, the familiar complaint of *shablon*. The obkomy that took "direct control" over priority construction sites, however, also established special brigades or "staffs" on the construction sites. Usually headed by an obkom secretary, the staff was composed of instructors from the departments of Party organs, oil and chemistry, construction, and ideology to make on-the-spot decisions.[138] Lesser sites usually received an instructor permanently assigned to cut through red tape, resolve jurisdictional disputes, or to search for resources.[139] Few aspects of capital construction were outside the scope of the obkom's decision-making authority. Technical questions of construction, delivery and installation of equipment, project documentation, cadres, preparing the plant for entrance into production—all were absorbed by the Party apparatus.[140] In addition, the obkom, or more frequently the gorkom, mounted a massive campaign of agitation.

The activities of the Grodno Industrial Obkom in Belorussia typify this phase of *rukovodstvo*. The obkom took over direct control of a lagging chemical construction plant, its "staff" charged with maintaining the intense pace of construction and preventing bottlenecks. As troubleshooter, the obkom made strenuous efforts to mobilize resources for the construction site, which suffered from chronic shortages. Local building materials were used to supply the site, and the obkom was in continuous contact with suppliers and the obkomy and gorkomy that supervised them. The obkom took charge of the delivery of equipment, its storage, and its installation. To meet the critical shortage of cadres and workers for the new plant, the Grodno Obkom made an extensive search through the Russian Republic and the Ukraine and not only recruited workers for the new chemical plant but also undertook their training.[141]

The heavy recruitment of economic and technical officials into the obkom apparatus in 1963 undoubtedly contributed to the ease with which the average obkom absorbed economic and technical functions. Channeling the obkom's resources into direct control appears, expectedly, to have reduced the importance of the more traditional functions associated with the leading role. Systematic work with cadres was unevenly implemented. In a resolution that clearly applied to oblast committees throughout the Soviet Union, the Central Committee sharply attacked the Donetsk Industrial Obkom for drawing its cadres from a narrow circle, for high turnover, and particularly for holding some twenty-five thousand *praktiki* in executive positions within the plant while qualified engineers and technicians worked on the bench.[142] The Commission for Organizational-Party Questions criticized the L'vov Industrial Obkom for precisely the same defects in its work with cadres.[143]

The reorganization of the sovnarkhozy, on the other hand, permitted some improvement in the technical qualifications of workers at the intermediate level. The Perm Industrial Obkom, for example, succeeded in appointing to the West Urals Sovnarkhoz 87 percent of the responsible workers with at least a secondary education; it also conducted a purge of enterprise officials in technically lagging plants, and during 1963 every plant director appointed by the obkom had a higher education.[144] While it is difficult to generalize for the Soviet Union as a whole, cadres problems seem to have been generally acute, with particular strains felt in the Central Asian republics, Georgia, Moldavia, and the Ukraine.[145]

Intervening in daily administration increased the obkom apparatus' role as a service agency. It served as a "labor exchange" and helped to resolve the numerous disputes between lower Party organs and the state administrators and between organs of the industrial administration itself.[146] The most prominent obkom service function, however, continued to be supply. Obkom secretaries and heads of production-branch departments openly acted as *tolkachi* with the aid and encouragement of higher Party organs. The obkom not only flooded the central executive organs with petitions but operated extensively through the Party apparatus to meet the critical shortages of materials.[147] Members of the obkom apparatus would occasionally travel extensively through other parts of the country in support of plants within their jurisdictions, although much of this activity was wasted. A supply problem would be resolved within the central Party or state apparatus, over which the republican or oblast Party committee had only contingent influence.[148] In resolving the most vital industrial problems, the obkom moved like a spinning top: its motion was circular rather than linear.

The Local Party Organs

The November 1962 reorganization affected the city and borough committees much as it had affected the obkom, with the difference that centralization exerted only a minimal influence in the balance of authority between the local Party organs and the industrial apparatus. Local Party organs had had but marginal influence over the decision-making process under both the ministerial and sovnarkhoz systems. Like the obkomy, the gorkomy and raikomy directed themselves toward the production line and construction site. The case of the Kazan Gorkom is typical.

The chemical industry was the central focus of *rukovodstvo* of the Kazan City Committee. Each week the first secretary reserved four or five sessions for comprehensive discussion of chemical construction or production; the gorkom also concentrated on public utilities required for industrial purposes. The water shortage in Kazan required continuous gorkom sessions, and the gorkom took over direct supervision of the repair of damaged underground facilities. The gorkom also attended to the city's housing construction, working out the construction schedule for each building and supervising its construction. Like an obkom, the Kazan Gorkom was important in mobilizing resources. It was deeply involved in obtaining and distributing manpower, and its most important function was securing supplies.[149]

As it had in the past, the gorkom shared responsibility with the obkom for planning and implementing plans for technical progress. The power limitations of the gorkom or raikom in dealing with this issue, however, were even greater than those on the obkom. The experience of the Krivoi Rog Gorkom in introducing new technology into the coal mines under its control is illustrative. The Krivoi Rog Gorkom established a design institute for mining equipment under its direct control and attached an experimental plant to it. But the institute never achieved full efficiency since the gorkom was unable to staff it with competent technicians or to properly equip either the institute or the plant. Then a "scissors" developed between the institute and the plant as a result of their operating under different "success indicators." In its effort to secure resources for both, the gorkom repeatedly requested the aid of the Predneprovskii Sovnarkhoz and the Ukrainian Sovnarkhoz. Ignored by both of them, the gorkom insisted that it was powerless to cope with the problem.[150]

In capital construction, the roles of gorkom and obkom were often indistinguishable. On the less important sites, the gorkom established plans, shifted the leadership, mobilized the workers who were Party members into "shock forces," conducted training sessions, and engaged in mass mobilization. The gorkom became a prime instrument for maintaining the tempo of construction, setting up conferences to solve bottlenecks, and aiding in the search for cadres and supply.[151] To speed up construction, gorkomy decided where and how to erect buildings or where to install boilers.[152] On those projects under direct obkom control, the gorkom was essentially an auxiliary, concentrating on mass agitation and improving living conditions.

The functions normally associated with the gorkom underwent little discernible change under the new system of administration. The gorkom continued to control the *nomenklatura* of the smaller plants and especially attempted to improve the qualifications of foremen in the major production plants. The Kuibyshev Gorkom, for example, registered about six thousand shop foremen with an eye to replacing them with workers who had at least a secondary education.[154] The results, however, clearly failed to satisfy the Party leadership. *Partiinaia zhizn'* complained editorially that in many plants, half of the foremen lacked the proper educational qualifications and that improvement was imperative.[155]

Two traditional gorkom or raikom functions took on special significance during this period. First, as part of the more general function of mobilizing resources, the gorkom's role as a labor exchange undoubtedly increased. Continually searching for trained personnel, its success was limited since, as one gorkom official confessed, the city committee usually did not know where the specialists were.[156] Secondly, the raikom or gorkom had to resolve the increased number of personal and jurisdictional disputes which the reorganization had provoked. Expanding the power of the primary Party organs and control groups within the enterprise had aroused frequent and bitter conflicts with the plant management which the gorkom was often called upon to settle, usually in the latter's favor.[157]

The Party's deep involvement in the personal lives of Party members was occasionally reflected in cases handled initially by the gorkom. One such conflict involved a plant "family group." The director, chief engineer, and a third official periodically engaged in alcoholic binges. The wife of the third member finally persuaded her husband to stop drinking, and once withdrawn from the circle, he self-righteously criticized the director and chief engineer for their corruption. The conflict ended in the gorkom and, upon appeal, in the obkom. There, with something less than Solomon's wisdom, the obkom decided to condemn the wife for interfering. An appeal to the editors of *Sovetskaia Rossiia* was required to justify the good woman's persistence.[158]

As experience with the reform developed, it became increasingly clear that turning the local Party organs into "small sovnarkhozy" (as one gorkom official phrased it) was a dubious move. The most important phases of the industrial or construction process were well beyond their jurisdiction or influence. The continuous conferences and production sessions usually represented an unnecessary or incompetent intervention in the operational direction of the economy, or, at best, a primitive form of administrative pressure. At the same time, however, their absorption of economic and technical functions helped to maintain tempo, to mobilize resources, and to provide a valuable cutting edge in reducing the tangled administrative complexities and jurisdictional disputes which harrassed the operational levels of the industrial administration.

The Primary Party Organs

In 1963 and 1964 the primary Party organs turned decisively, like the higher Party organs, to the resolution of economic problems, serving as a mobilizing instrument for pressing Khrushchev's reforms on a recalcitrant plant management. Increasing the authority of the mass Party organs coincided with Khrushchev's strong commitment to social methods of economic management, but the confrontation of the primary Party organs and enterprise management raised the perennial problem of collective leadership and *edinonachalie* in an acute form. Warned by central Party officials not to substitute for enterprise officials, the primary Party organs were also urged to intervene decisively if management made the "wrong decision."[159] Such interventions were frequent, and the resulting conflict, probably intensified by the heavy turnover and the new secretaries' lack of Party experience, induced additional tension and administrative disorder.

The economic effect of the primary Party organs' role, of course, remained problematical. The reorganization reduced the influence of the mass organs on the higher levels of the Party and state administrations. Tightly controlled by the territorial Party apparatus, the primary Party organs were nevertheless significantly instrumental in establishing the structure of the current plan in the summer of 1963. At the priority construction sites, the mass organs were important in establishing a psychological climate of urgency and struggle. But increased administrative power did not resolve the traditional underlying ambiguity of the primary Party organs' role in enterprise administration. Active plant organs were accused of holding too many production meetings, issuing too many orders, holding too many checkups, and substituting for the administration.[160] Passive, they were charged with "lack of demandingness" to enterprise officials.[161] Both tendencies were present.

4

The Party and Control

To achieve Khrushchev's growth goals through an intensified application of centralized administrative power meant a strengthening control on the lower staff as well as on the mass levels of the Party, a traditional Soviet device for making the local sources of Party power more reliable channels of the central will. Shifting the balance of power between the central and local organs of administration would make the advancement of "localist" interests more difficult in 1963 and 1964 than at any period since the abolition of the ministerial system. The Soviet press indicates that the traditional weakness of the regional and local Party organs in the function of control was somewhat reduced during these years. Obkomy resorted to such "administrative" measures as firing plant directors who failed to meet the plan, extending various forms of Party punishment, and in extreme cases, giving the offender to the courts. The local Party organs resorted to similar types of sanctions.

The counterpressures generated by the specialized interests of the regional and local Party organs were, however, undiminished. The "success indicators" for the Party organs remained essentially local in character because they were still judged not by the performance of the economy as a whole but by statistics relevant to their own limited jurisdictions. Under the special conditions of 1963 and 1964, the lack of authority of the territorial Party apparatus, their dependence on central Party and state organs for resources and favorable decisions, the heavy overcommitment of resources—all increased the need for defense organs at the local level. There was therefore not only a general increase in administrative coercion exercised by the Party apparatus over the state and economic officials but also numerous examples of regional and local Party organs forming "family groups" and compromising with the informal, or illegal, managerial practices which continued under the administrative reform.

That the territorial Party apparatus failed to exercise enough control in view of the continuing decline in the growth rate in both industry and construction was revealed by P. E. Shelest. At a special plenum of the Ukrainian Central Committee in August 1964, he excoriated the apparatus for its passivity and willingness to compromise with the widespread managerial abuses.[162] In an intensive investigation of the L'vov Industrial Obkom, the Commission for Organizational-Party Questions declared that the obkom had "compromised" with the heads of the construction trusts and the head of the capital construction department of the sovnarkhoz despite the fact that of sixty-six construction trusts, over 50 percent had failed to meet the plan for the first five months of 1964. The commission charged that the obkom had also permitted widespread deception and fraud in the construction field.[163] In those jurisdictions where the problems of capital construction were particularly acute, the pressure for results undoubtedly impelled the obkomy toward various types of deception and report padding. In the Belorussian Republic, certifying defective or un-completed buildings as ready for commission seems to have been a regular practice of the industrial obkomy.[164]

The local Party committees received much criticism for tolerating the illegal managerial activities. A Moscow raikom, for example, not only refused to permit a raion procurator to arrest a *tolkachi* who had admitted bribing several plant officials to obtain needed supplies[165] but mounted a campaign of in-timidation and harassment against the investigators. In other cases, such as that involving the Kaunas City Committee, the gorkom refused to act despite persistent evidence of widespread graft, embezzlement, and deception within its jurisdiction.[166] In many cases where the obkom or gorkom protected managers engaged in such practices, the persons protected were unusually adept at meeting the demands of the Soviet administrative environment. Two such examples will suffice to clarify the basic relationship between Party officials and managers.

In the first case, a mine director in Rostov Oblast was repeatedly accused by the mine's Party committee of manipulating output figures and diverting state property for his personal use. Each effort by the mine committee to remedy this situation was repressed by the gorkom and probably by the Rostov Industrial Obkom as well. In July 1963, the primary Party organ finally succeeded in having the mine director removed, although the gorkom refused to take any action against him. In March 1964, to prevent criminal charges being brought against the director, the gorkom had his case investigated by the procurator's office, and the charges of criminal activity were dropped. The mine director was replaced by another official of the same stamp—equally competent and equally opportunistic. His conflict with the primary Party organs was also ignored by the gorkom until an appeal to the industrial obkom and possibly to the Central Committee forced the gorkom to act. To protect the accused mine director, he was removed from his post and the raikom *nomenklatura* and placed on the oblast committee's *nomenklatura* as the chief engineer of a construction trust.[167]

Such protection was often extended to the foremen, as a case involving the Krivoi Rog Gorkom illustrates. A shop foreman was accused of a variety of economic crimes, including pilfering state property, using plant labor for personal projects, and embezzling bonus premiums to finance his drinking debauches with the shop's Party secretary and a deputy director of the plant. After ignoring repeated complaints, the Krivoi Rog Gorkom was finally forced to turn the matter over to the oblast procurator. The shop foreman was expelled from the Party and ined, but he was not jailed because of the intervention of the local Party organs. During the investigatory phase, the raikom first secretary summoned both the chairman of the people's court and the raion procurator and warned them "to stop digging there." Two others involved in the case were simply transferred to equal jobs elsewhere. And despite complaints, the Dnepropetrovsk Industrial Obkom refused to act. Such incidents were frequent, and the Krivoi Rog Gorkom was invariably tolerant of them.[168]

The Decision-Making Role of the
Party-State Control Committee

The ambiguous role of the Party staff organs in relation to administrative control was less apparent among the central and local organs of Party-state control. Despite their weaknesses and complexities, the new agencies succeeded in penetrating the Soviet administration to an extent not experienced since the First Five-Year Plan. The PGK's basic role was defined in terms of Khrushchev's policy objectives. Its separate structure and local organs provided an alternative mechanism, not entirely controlled by the territorial Party apparatus, for exercising that mass pressure which Khrushchev considered essential for disciplining the industrial managers.

Assigning operational decision-making authority to the Party-State Control Committee necessarily led to some duplication and overlap with the staff organs, with the distinction that the Party staff organs continued to be judged in terms of overall industrial performance, whereas the control committees were judged within the much narrower bounds of control activity. The coexistence of general and special functions were compatible only up to a point. Intense pressure over the industrial managers by the control agencies could and did result in disrupting the informal equilibria which the administrative system had developed to counterbalance the irrationalities of the formal system. This was the source of that conflict of interest between staff organs and control agencies noted elsewhere.

The Party-State Control Committee's decision-making role was essentially operational. The committee took no public part in the planning process in the summer of 1963 nor in the discussions of the new perspective plan for 1964. The central PGK, however, engaged in establishing plans for individual enterprises, and the groups and posts within planning organs actively intervened in the planning process. The groups and posts within Russian Gosplan, for example, closely supervised the input-output norms; they ordered the working out of new plans for chemical machine building after the December 1963 plenum, reversed the plan for lowering the output of consumer goods for 1964, and acted as a troubleshooter in straightening out mistakes made by Russian Gosplan in the enterprise plans.[169] The control committees played no discernible role in the selection of cadres, although in other respects their concern with cadres was comprehensive. In the industrial activity of the Party-State Control Committee and its local organs, five major areas of decision-making predominated: the chemical construction program, the efficiency and quality of industrial output, supply, the control of informal or illegal managerial practices, and administrative rationalization.

PGK work in the construction industry generally, and in the chemical construction program in particular, precisely duplicated the work of the central and territorial staff organs. A conference on chemical construction convened by the Party-State Control Committee in October 1963 declared that the control agencies were required to enter deeply into every phase of the construction program. The decision-making axis of the Party-State Control Committee was its Otdel for the Chemical and Oil-Refining Industries which actively supervised the republican and oblast control apparatuses.[170] It was normal practice for the engaged control organs to establish nonstaff otdely for the chemical industry at the most important construction sites, where they either acted as auxiliaries of the local Party organs or assumed direct control.[171]

The Belorussian Party-State Control Committee, for example, managed the construction of the Soligorsk Chemical Combinat, a Mogilev artificial fiber plant, and several other high-priority sites.[172] The specific functions of the Party-state control committees in the localities included the techniques of construction, the uses of construction machinery, the mobilization of labor and its training, cadre procurement and training, and documentation. On some sites, the PGK was responsible for storing raw materials, securing supply, and for the living conditions of workers at the site.[173]

Such detailed and direct intervention in the administrative process was largely, although not exclusively, confined to the chemical program. When, for example, the construction plan for an important shop in the Moscow State Ball Bearing Plant No. 1 fell behind schedule, the Russian Republic Party-State Control Committee took the project under its direct supervision. It held a meeting of the plant administration, the Moscow Sovnarkhoz, the Russian Sovnarkhoz, and the Moscow Chief Administration for Construction to coordinate efforts and secure results. It then sent members of the control apparatus into the plant to resolve the various operational problems, particularly those involving material supply and labor.[174]

As part of the general concern with the chemical industry, the PGK was also active in the chemical machine building and related industries. The Russian Party-State Control Committee, for example, thoroughly investigated the Penza Chemical Machine-Building Plant and its output for the first ten months of 1963. The report stated that the plant was producing equipment of low quality, had little specialization of labor, was storming, and had failed to deliver critical supplies to twenty-nine construction sites. To correct these deficiencies, the Russian committee was given the task of supervising the concrete steps noted in a resolution of the Russian Republic Council of Ministers.[175]

Similarly, union Party-State Control Committee investigation of oil and gas drilling in the Northern Caucasus Sovnarkhoz and in the Kazakh, Uzbek, and Turkmen republics revealed poor technological methods of drilling and preserving oil and gas and indifference toward the training of workers. The committee ordered the Union Sovnarkhoz, State Geological Committee, and republican organs to improve the methods of drilling and training of workers. In neither these cases nor in others involving direct decision-making power by the Party-State Control Committee were the regular Party organs given a formal role in the decisions.

The control agencies' decision-making role in technical innovation overlapped that of the Party apparatus. In 1963, for example, the central committee undertook to raise the quality of production of the Saransk Lamp Plant, which used excessive raw materials, produced low-quality products, and had high levels of defective output.[176] The committee likewise investigated the state publishers of juridical literature, whose authors, it was claimed, were overpaid and drawn from an exclusive clique. Books lost money and were full of mistakes. Further, a species of informal managerial practice had developed in paying authors who had not fulfilled all the conditions of the production plan. The committee suggested specific remedies and fined one of the editors, the prestigious P. S. Romashkin, three months' pay for his part in the deception.[177]

Locally, the control agencies pursued a long list of specific activities designed to improve the economic efficiency of the enterprise. They were concerned with the expenditure of raw materials, the revision of obsolete norms, the quality of technology in producing artificial leather, the activities of research institutes, documentation, the substitution of plastics for metal, the economical use of electricity, the control of defective output, and the production of new automobiles and other products,[178] with special attention devoted to the output of consumer goods. The Ukrainian Party-State Control Committee ordered all oblast control agencies to bring to "strict material responsibility" those issuing defective consumer goods and provided an example by strictly reprimanding the deputy head of the Podolsk Sovnarkhoz and the head of the consumer goods administration.[179] Managers who included defective output as part of plan fulfillment were often fined. Although common practice among the staff Party organs, it was rare for the territorial control apparatus to assume responsibility for selecting technical variants or for directly supervising the installation of new equipment.

The Party-State Control Committee and its local organs functioned primarily in supply. Ironically, they became *tolkachi* notwithstanding that controlling this phenomenon was one of their functions. The committee secured and expedited supplies much as the regular Party organs did. Conferences were held on supply, and the union and republican committees often exercised their disciplinary and decision-making powers to solve bottlenecks and shortages. In March 1964, for example, the union committee investigated and heard reports on the supply of construction sites by Gosstroi and the republican ministries of construction and made specific recommendations to resolve the shortages.[180] In addition, the union and republican committees frequently intervened to secure supply for lagging chemical construction sites.[181]

The new control agencies also opened a third major channel to pressure suppliers for deliveries. The Krasnoiarsk Krai PGK received some two thousand letters in a six-month period requesting aid in securing supplies.[182] The more heavily industrialized oblast control committees were inundated with requests. The Cheliabinsk Industrial PGK reported an average of over forty letters a day on the issue of supply.[183] In responding to the requests for aid from plants within their own jurisdictions, the PGK usually sent a request to their counterparts in the republic or oblast where the supplier was situated and sought the influence of their own republican agency and the union Party-State Control Committee. When a Novo Kramatorsk plant sent defective equipment to a construction site in Cheliabinsk, the oblast PGK wired both the Ukrainian PGK and the union Committee to secure redress. These agencies responded by ordering the plant to send out specialists to remedy the deficiencies.[184] In another case, the Briansk PGK enlisted the Vladimir PGK to obtain its aid in getting a late delivery from a plant. The Briansk committee also tried to enlist the help of the Party-State Control Committee of the Russian Bureau and the Russian Sovnarkhoz—mute testimony to the inability of the local committees to deal with issues of this type. Finally, the PGK could often resolve supply problems within its own plants by ''raiding'' other plants to acquire the needed supplies.[185]

Rationalizing the administrative structure and processes was the final important sector of control activity.[186] Although an official of the control agency claimed that its activity had reduced the staff by 100,000, structural rationalization was not a high-priority goal of the Party-State Control Committee. Reducing the informal administrative practices of the managers, which Khrushchev once compared to squashing a bug, was considerably more important. The vision of a massive control effort from below pressuring the managers so that they were incapable of not conforming to central desires was chimerical. Yet, the mass control organs did exert greater control over the managers than previously under Khrushchev; and while these organs were occasionally repressed by the territorial Party apparatus and often met intense resistance among the managers themselves, they nevertheless succeeded in deeply penetrating the administrative system.

Although they themselves operated as *tolkachi*, they also attempted to control the whole effort of "pushing" for supplies and unnecessary travel.[187] Searching for hidden excess stocks was a more sensitive pursuit. Among the most important of the Party-State Control Committee's national raids was the dislodging of over 3 million tons of raw materials, including desperately needed ferrous and nonferrous metals. The checkup, conducted from 1 January 1964 to 1 March 1964, turned up several hundred thousand tons of hidden raw materials. In Gorkii Oblast, the PGK mobilized twelve thousand controllers who turned up some 8 tons of sheet metal, 33,000 tons of ferrous, and 1,900 tons of nonferrous metal.[188] In one plant in Novosibirsk, about 62 tons of copper were unearthed.[189] The control agencies were also active in controlling the enterprises' assortment plan and attempted to stop the diversion of investment from planned to unplanned tasks. The numerous strikes, raids, and checkups on the plant managers, however, disrupted the plant's routine and, in the case of exposing hidden reserves, were bitterly resented and opposed.

The Party-State Control Committee also attempted to control widespread managerial deceit, report padding, pilfering of state property, and diversion of public funds to private uses. Numerous examples in the Soviet press suggest the significance of the control agencies in this respect.[190] In one case, a Moscow plant director was forced to acknowledge his greed before his assembled plant for having both a house and an apartment in the city.[191] For diverting state resources to his own use and illegally accepting premiums, the chief engineer of another plant was punished by the PGK, although his fierce resistance to the local committee required the intervention of the union control committee.[192]

In cases of economic crime involving high-ranking officials, the control committees were more limited. A vast web of economic criminality was uncovered in the State Production Committee for Power and Electrification in which dozens of officials were implicated in distributing illegal premiums, certifying defective production as satisfactory, and plain swindling. Although many instances of diverting state materials for the private use of the construction executives were uncovered, the number of officials ultimately brought to trial was reduced to four by the personal intervention of the minister, P. S. Neporozhnii.[193] The agricultural control agencies, like the industrial, also participated in the effort to check pilfering, cheating, and deceiving the state in the harvesting and sale of agricultural products, a condition brought about by the poor harvest of 1963.[194]

The human cost of this assault was high, since exposing these practices often resulted in the persecution and ostracism of the informants. A worker in the capital construction department of the Russian Sovnarkhoz complained that bonuses paid to the workers were illegal, but the deputy head of the otdel refused to revoke the premiums. An investigation by the control group of the sovnarkhoz affirmed the facts; the head and deputy head of the otdel were fired; and in the aftermath, the resentful workers deprived of their premiums isolated him. His department superiors accused him of insubordination and drew up a series of minor charges against him; two special commissions were formed to investigate him and efforts were made to fire him and exclude him from the Party. Finally, his superiors did fire him; his appeal to the Leningrad Raikom was ignored; and for two months he searched fruitlessly for another job. But the organs of Party-state control took up his case and restored him to his job. Back in the department, open persecution apparently stopped, but he was assigned the most menial tasks; his career was plainly over; and as a commentator remarked, "The lesson was clear to all." [195]

Despite the massive quality and high costs of the movement for "control from below," the managerial practices which had become institutionalized under Stalin remained essentially intact during 1963 and 1964.

PART FOUR

AN EPILOGUE

The Leading Role since Khrushchev

The palace coup of October 1964 ended Khrushchev's political career as well as an important chapter in the history of the Party's leading role. Khrushchev's ouster was a direct consequence of the mounting economic and administrative disorganization which followed the reform of the Party and managerial bureaucracies in 1962 and 1963;[1] his proposals to correct the problems of management by further reorganizing the formal bureaucracy precipitated his major losing crisis. That his personal ambition, style, and policies alienated significant elements of the USSR governing elite was evident by the ease of his ouster and by the absence of clear opposition to the new regime.

Khrushchev's isolation in 1964 and the evident failure of his policies were largely owing to the difficulty of the problems he had attempted to resolve. His overthrow did not, of course, solve the power-efficiency dilemma, although it did offer an opportunity to engage the issue on the basis of a different set of definitions and policies. His specific experience in adjusting the Party's leading role to the exigencies of a relatively modernized industrial system provides a perspective by which to view the performance of his successors.

Overall, Khrushchev's reorganization introduced serious disorganization into the Party apparatus and lowered the Soviet economy's operational efficiency. Reorganizing the Party on a functional basis, of dubious legitimacy at best, engendered a multiplicity of complex organizational consequences which significantly affected the Party's internal dynamics, decision-making, and control functions. Centralization further reduced the initiative and power of the territorial Party apparatus, leading to frequent regional and national conflicts of interest. Internally, the reorganization promoted jurisdictional conflict, administrative disorganization, and disunity.

Proliferating central organs of industrial management and centralizing control only increased the microimbalance and bureaucratic inefficiency of the command economy. The economy could not absorb Khrushchev's crash program of chemical construction, which created further problems, and because of pressure and haste, industrial management became increasingly clogged with jurisdictional conflicts, slow and inefficient decision-making, red tape, and poor communication. Plans remained internally inconsistent; supply problems, critical. The chemical construction program was marred by deficiencies and shortages at every stage of the planning process. At the enterprise level, those managerial abuses associated with the planning and incentive systems were intensified.

The haste and compromise attending the Party apparatus' penetration into the industrial economy produced complex, spontaneous, and often unintended consequences. To advance Khrushchev's economic priorities and policies, the Party's managerial and mobilization functions increased dramatically, but the political and economic costs were high. The reorganization visibly disturbed Party *rukovodstvo* at the republican and oblast levels, disrupting the integrated leadership of industry, largely to the detriment of agriculture. Administrative pressure and a rapid shift in economic priorities increasingly engaged the apparatus in arbitration and in servicing the harassed managers. At the mass level, concentrating the primary Party organs on economic issues induced Party-state conflicts in the enterprise, a situation complicated by the large number of inexperienced secretaries recruited in 1963 and 1964.

The establishment of a distinct Party-State Control Committee compounded the Party's coordinative activity. The new committee expanded the information available to the center and in some degree inhibited the counterproductive practices of the managers, at the same time, however, that the new control agencies duplicated the coordination of the Party organs and provided still another source of administrative conflict and disorder. The intense effort to envelop the managers in a tight web of administrative and mass controls was thus itself counterproductive. The mixture of political pressure, centralized bureaucratic controls, and coercive mobilization, so successful for mobilizing resources in the initial stages of industrialization, had become functionally irrelevant at a more complex, differentiated stage of industrial development. In retrospect, the Khrushchev experience, particularly its final phase, convincingly demonstrated that the Stalinist organizational formula for economic development was exhausted. This is not to suggest that the system will one day explode or become a Western variant of political or economic pluralism. The evidence and analysis here indicate simply that the traditional monocratic, large-scale Soviet organization is incompatible with the further growth and development of the Soviet economy, a conclusion which does little more than acknowledge many of the judgments and policies of the post-Khrushchev leadership.

Since Khrushchev's fall, the current leadership has confronted the same power-efficiency dilemma, but has replaced the ebullient, personal, and agitational style with a conservative, bureaucratic, pragmatic approach. The basic task of maintaining monopolistic power for the Communist party and the system of central planning has not changed. What has changed is the definition of the problems and the time factor required to adjust the traditional organizational mechanisms to the environmental changes induced by industrialization and urbanization. These adjustments have included an effort to rationalize the Party's decision-making structure, an extensive implementation of the economic reform adopted in 1965, and a reordering of Party functions, partly in reaction against the Khrushchev experience in direct management, partly in response to the requirements of the new management structure.

1

The Rationalization of the Party

The virtually continuous reorganization of the Party's formal structure and disruption of its internal relationships generated a reaction against Khrushchev's "subjectivism" and "cap-throwing" in favor of a more stable, analytical approach. A *Pravda* editorial following the November 1964 plenum stating that traditional Party structure had not lost its force set the mood as well as the policy of internal Party rationalization.[2]

For Brezhnev as for Khrushchev, the most difficult and sensitive problems have undoubtedly involved (1) the vertical distribution of power between Moscow and the provinces, and (2) the horizontal allocation of power between the political generalists and specialists. These issues, inherent in any large-scale organization, have on the whole been conservatively approached in the post-Khrushchev period. The Party's monolithic authority structure and the claims of the central Party apparatus to comprehensive control over the lower Party organs have recently been authoritatively reaffirmed;[3] although increasing diversity of local conditions, the thrust of the reform in industrial management, and the protests of the lower Party apparatchiki against the extreme centralization of the previous period have induced some vertical decentralization.

Centralized Party controls were intensified over the lower apparatus during the two final years of Khrushchev's rule. In the wake of his fall, the immediate reaction of the territorial Party apparatus was to recover some of the authority that had been delegated in the first five years after Stalin's death. Between 1965 and 1967, decentralization within the apparatus proceeded cautiously. There was a formal affirmation of the legislation enacted between 1955 and 1958 granting the local Party organs greater organizational and financial control.[4] But the scope of these rights was extremely narrow, and even this limited policy of administrative decentralization appears to have been checked by the conservative antirevisionist campaign triggered by the events in Czechoslovakia.[5] Still, the defense of the centralized monocratic structure and the emphasis on discipline and control have not resulted to date in a withdrawal of local Party organs' rights over membership, structures, and cadres, delegated between 1965 and 1968.[6]

Collective leadership remains a complex, controversial issue. At the top, the idea has been to defend the oligarchic distribution of power which has prevailed since 1964. Through the Twenty-third Congress in March 1966, the acrimony concerning "voluntarism" and "strong-willed personalities" was clearly designed to justify the October 1964 coup.[7] Its persistence for almost six years after Khrushchev's fall suggests that those institutional elements intended to constrain and ultimately to depose him may have become permanent fixtures in the political system. Maintaining a stable oligarchy against an autocratic tradition and the pressures of urgent, complex issues has undoubtedly been difficult. That there is clear evidence of conflict within the Politburo on a wide variety of issues, including basic allocative policy and the Party's role in decision-making, is not surprising.[8]

With respect to local Party organs, the principle of conserving central Party power by applying internal and external checks and balances to the lower Party secretariats has been fundamental in central-local relations since the Civil War. Although there was growing recognition under Khrushchev that the first secretary's ascendancy as the dominant line official within the territory carried serious efficiency costs to the apparatus and to external control, the need for greater information, expertise, and integrated decision-making at the lower levels of the hierarchy is still an issue. The role of the first secretary (and by extension the secretariat) and the degree to which organizational dynamism requires free speech and free elections in the lower Party committees remain unresolved, and perhaps fundamentally unresolvable, questions within a monocratic organization.[9]

The development of the Party's formal structure has also been relatively conservative since Khrushchev. The primary thrust of the apparatus through the Twenty-third Congress was to restore the pre–1962 Party structure. Abolishing the Central Committee's bureaus and commissions, reuniting the divided oblast committees, and reestablishing the rural raion Party committee in November and December of 1964 were the first steps in a concentrated effort to eliminate virtually all of Khrushchev's significant structural innovations.[10] The relative conservatism of the policies on formal structure have been largely in response to the demands of territorial apparatus functionaries for greater stability and security of tenure.

The post-Khrushchev Party has therefore produced very little striking organizational innovation. The rate of membership expansion and the more careful methods of recruiting and checking have become matters of basic policy,[11] although the reaction against Khrushchev's liberal recruitment policies should not obscure the basic continuities within lines that he established. The recruitment of workers and economic specialists into the Party has intensified and administrative officials have declined under his successors.[12] The emphasis on recruiting workers since 1965 is a significant indication of the basic strategy of Brezhnev and the Party leadership toward the expected increase in the independence of the enterprise.

Adjustments in the elected Party committees have been moderate as well, taking into account the variations according to hierarchical level. The Central Committee elected in 1966 showed the least change. Membership expansion was moderate and turnover low, and there were only marginal shifts in the occupations represented. The representation of the Party apparatchiki declined to 42 percent, but those groups with the highest political visibility—the police, military, and economic reformers—showed no increase.[13] The Party's long-term adjustment to the complexities of modernization through co-optation remained unchanged. The most distinctive characteristic of the 1966 Central Committee was its collective age, which approached sixty in 1970.

The relative stability of the Central Committee indicated by its low turnover may have reflected political debts of the current Soviet leadership as well as an inability to secure a consensus on change. This may partially explain the significantly higher rates of turnover in the republican and, presumably, the lower Party organs as well. In six republican committees studied by a Western scholar, turnover ranged from 40 percent in the Ukraine to 55–60 percent in Moldavia. The heavy turnover seems to have particularly affected Party and Soviet officials, 40–50 percent of whom were dropped.[14] Although post-Khrushchev sources have not published turnover figures for the local level, authoritative Soviet writers make it clear that the proportionality of representation of various social and functional groups remained virtually unchanged in the 1967 and 1969 elections.[15]

In the fall of 1970, the Party's executive structure was still controlled at the top by those members of the Politburo who had engineered Khrushchev's ouster.[16] Four have been added since October 1964, one of whom, A. J. Pel'she, an Old Bolshevik and member of the 1917 Petrograd Soviet, was a largely symbolic appointment to replace the retired Old Bolsheviks Mikoian and Shvernik. The political basis of these appointments and their effect on the distribution of power within the Politburo is not clear.[17] In other respects, however, these appointments followed the practices of the Khrushchev period. The average age represented in the Politburo is currently fifty-seven, and all of the new Politburo members have had extensive experience as line officials within the Party apparatus. The appointment of K. T. Mazurov, a strong supporter of the economic reform and a former light industry official, may, however, have reflected an effort to strengthen the reform wing within the Politburo.

The change among Politburo candidates has been much greater. Only three of nine current candidate members are holdovers from the Khrushchev era. Major regional interests continue to dominate representation.[18] Functional representation, however, is expressed in the presence of two Central Committee secretaries (Demichev and Ustinov) and by the addition in 1968 of Iuri Andropov after his appointment as chairman of the Committee of State Security. The most unusual appointment was that of D. F. Ustinov, the long-time chief of the Soviet defense establishment, who had no experience in the Party apparatus before his dual appointment as a Politburo alternative and Central Committee secretary. The other eight members, whose collective age is approximately fifty-five, have career patterns generally resembling those of the full members of the Politburo.

It was Stalin's enduring contribution to Soviet government to bind together the distribution of political power and control over administrative machinery. In this respect, the post-Khrushchev leadership exhibits an underlying contradiction. While overlapping jurisdictions and some fluidity in administrative responsibilities and control seem basic to maintaining a balance of power within the Politburo, to develop cohesive policies and manage an increasingly complex system in the interests of efficiency and growth also requires some primary functional specialization within the leadership. The precise functional specialization within the Politburo, especially in the roles of the senior officials, cannot be fully determined. From Khrushchev's fall through 1967, the major initiatives in economic policy appear to have been divided between Brezhnev and Kosygin, the former formulating agricultural policy; the latter, industrial policy. Both Brezhnev and Kosygin have presumably needed a Politburo consensus to initiate policy.[19]

The functional and administrative responsibilities of the second echelon of the Politburo are somewhat clearer. A. P. Kirilenko and K. T. Mazurov are basically concerned with the operation of industry: Kirilenko as the secretary in charge of industry within the Party apparatus; Mazurov responsible for the managers. While Brezhnev himself appears to be the Politburo member most deeply involved with Soviet agriculture, D. S. Polianskii is the major agricultural figure in the Presidium of the Council of Ministers. The principal responsibilities of G. I. Voronov and P. E. Shelest are functionally more ambiguous since their fundamental roles appear to be regional representation. The most visible change in status in the Politburo has been the decline of A. N. Shelepin, whose trade-union responsibilities do not normally carry full Politburo status. A. J. Pel'she is the Politburo member in charge of Party control.[20]

The Politburo and Secretariat have political as well as functional relationships. The post-Khrushchev period has seen extensive change in the Secretariat. Only five members of Khrushchev's 1964 Secretariat remain in office. With the exception of Ustinov, the new additions are only slightly younger than the appointments to the Politburo and exhibit the same general career patterns in the Party and state bureaucracies.[21] In contrast to the political appointments to the Politburo, the additions to the Secretariat indicate a clearer, more differentiated relationship to the decision-making process, another reaction against the administrative melee of Khrushchev's 1962 reorganization.

I. V. Kapitonov, the organizational secretary with primary responsibility for cadres, had spent most of his career as a line official in the Party apparatus. Both M. S. Solomentsev and Ustinov, the secretaries in charge of the civilian and defense industrial establishments functioning under Kirilenko, were co-opted after extensive industrial management experience. Similarly, F. D. Kulakov, the agricultural secretary, had passed his entire career as a Party and state official in agricultural management. The political aspect of appointments to the Secretariat, however, is illustrated in the case of K. F. Katushev, an engineer and former obkom first secretary, who replaced Iuri Andropov in 1968 as secretary for Party relations within the bloc. Moving Demichev in 1965 from industrial supervision to ideological work illustrates the generalist qualities still expected of appointments to the current Secretariat.

The traditional approach to formal structure guiding the Party leadership in administrative change has ruled out any significant alteration in the Central Committee departmental system. There is some slight evidence to suggest that, in the period of most intense reaction against Khrushchev's *administrirovanie i reformatorstvo*, there was discussion of proposing an administration for cadres resembling the Zhdanov model of Party structure.[22] Eliminating the branch departments paralleling the agencies of industrial management would have followed the logic of the Party's functional role projected under the 1965 economic reform, but this was not done. Abolishing the Russian Bureau in 1966 and consolidating the dual system of departments has, in fact, restored the Party's central executive structure to its configuration under the ministerial system. Khrushchev's ouster and the merging of the departments for the union republics and the Russian Republic have resulted in an intensive turnover of department heads, the great majority of whom were Khrushchev appointees.[23]

Traditionalism also characterized the reformation of the territorial Party apparatus after 1964. From the republican to the borough levels of the hierarchy, the bureaus continue to be numerically dominated by the apparatchiki.[24] The republican and obkom secretariats are now normally composed of five secretaries, including the first and second secretaries and specialized secretaries for industry, agriculture, and ideology. The urban and borough secretariats remain fixed at three: a first secretary, and secretaries for organization and ideology. With the separation of Party and state control, the major change has been to release the special secretary for control from the secretariat. The chairman of the Committee of Popular Control, however, has remained a member of the bureau.

Rationalizing the departmental structure of the territorial apparatus (to which the Party press has given considerable attention) has involved little innovation. The one clear response to the requirements of economic reform was to raise the section for economic-financial affairs to departmental status in 1967. Since the Twenty-third Congress, there has been a notable effort to increase the dynamism of the Party commissions.[25] Since Khrushchev, the full-time Party apparatus has been reemphasized and the staff expanded.[26] Reversing Khrushchev's policy of the "withering away of the apparatus" has been accompanied by an extensive reorganization of the nonstaff Party apparatus that developed so rapidly after 1959. The volunteer apparatus has been too useful, particularly at the lower levels of Party structure, to be eliminated entirely. Reducing the numbers and status of the volunteers has largely removed the political competition and administrative burden which the expansion entailed, although complaints continue to appear in the Party press concerning the direction and coordination of their activity and their interference in the economic and technical functions of the managers.[27]

Separating Party from state and social control in December 1965 was an important concession to the Party apparatus. But while the competition from the Party-State Control Committee and the problems of jurisdiction and internal conflict engendered by the system of joint control have been largely eliminated, the activation of Party control and the subjection of Party members to a dual system of control have raised new problems of the same type. The formation of the Committee of Popular Control, with the same formal structure and rights as the former Party-State Control Committee, indicates the continuing importance of control in the relationship between the Party and the managers under conditions of economic reform.[28]

Although since 1964 the patterns of recruitment and socialization of Party cadres have emphasized the Party's traditional values and structures, a major effort has nevertheless been made to frame recruitment and socialization policies that will meet new environmental challenges and the Party's new role under the conditions of economic reform. Turnover, for example, has been highly selective. Among republican and obkom first secretaries, the relatively conservative rate of turnover has ranged from 45 to 64 percent.[29] The turnover among secretaries of primary organs has been cut to half of 1964.[30] In contrast, among republican and obkom department heads and instructors and within the secretariats and departments of local Party organs, turnover has been extensive.[31] The latter, of course, were most heavily recruited in 1963 and 1964.

Replacing these officials has for the most part involved clearly defined policies. Youth and higher technical education continue to be emphasized,[32] but the wholesale drafting of economic and technical specialists into the Party as department heads, instructors, and gorkom secretaries has virtually ended. Closely related to this policy is an emphasis on promotion from within the apparatus, with particular emphasis on advancing second secretaries.[33] The bitter conflict between the "humanists" and "technocrats" of 1962–64 has been resolved. The present determination is to combine technical education and experience with intensive indoctrination and experience in the Party apparatus as means of preserving the Party's institutional integrity along with its enhanced decision-making capacity.[34]

Tightening internal organization has not constituted the sole change in the post-Khrushchev apparatus; it has also been recognized that the Party bureaucracy's operational efficiency must be improved. To that end, the mass principle has been deemphasized in favor of a more moderate, pragmatic method of bureaucratic rationalization. Like Khrushchev, his successors have attempted to raise Party efficiency without making fundamental change in the monocratic structure. Their approach, however, has been more sophisticated, undoubtedly reflecting lessons learned during the Khrushchev period.[35]

Specific measures adopted since 1964 to improve the decision-making processes have stressed an analytical approach, structural rationalization, a heavy emphasis on comprehensive in-service training, and, not least, more effective methods of internal and external communication. This pragmatic, objectivistic thrust has implications for the future legitimacy and control of the apparatus, although there is little concrete evidence to suggest either a significant erosion of power or growth in efficiency during the past six years as a result of policies which have been implemented. Most of the measures to improve bureaucratic coordination and control have been traditional. Emphasizing differentiated, rather than stereotyped, approaches to concrete problems, stressing basic issues rather than administrative details, broadening the decision-making base by means of more systematic consultation and discussion—all of these were continually pressed under Khrushchev.[36] Reducing the number of issues decided, attempting a deeper, more thorough analysis of questions and a more rational distribution of authority among various levels of the Party hierarchy are likewise part of the conventional wisdom of organizational reform.[37] Continuity is also evident in the determination to implement an organizational, rather than administrative, style of *rukovodstvo*.[38]

Other developments since 1964 have been more important and controversial. The expanded use of experts and the spread of sociological methods represent serious efforts to meet the challenges of increased complexity.[39] The more extensive reliance on experts outside the apparatus is connected with the reassessment of the Party's decision-making role under the 1965 reform, although its implications extend to more fundamental political issues. Party officials recognize that the apparatus lacks the personnel and resources for direct economic and technical decision-making.[40] One obkom first secretary noted that however qualified the Party apparatchik may be, he must still rely on specialists and technicians to run the economy.[41] The recognition that economic and technical decision-making exceeded the Party's competence and strained its structure is significant, although the ultimate cost of this recognition to the managerial apparatus remains to be seen.

The acknowledgment of structural differentiation and functional specialization has been extended to social life and behavior as well as to the economy. Sociological methods of investigation and analysis have been adopted to define problems and test the effectiveness of decisions, particularly in ideology, communication, and mass attitudes. The practice has been to establish special research institutes on social principles under a Party committee. In two years, for example, the Gorkii Gorkom researched twelve problems related to such topics as religion, labor turnover, and the Communist movement for labor.[42] The collected and processed data are undoubtedly valuable in expanding the apparatus' consciousness and eliminating those sociological stereotypes which arise from ideological predisposition and obsolescent definitions.[43] But the validity of the results is questionable because of the shortage of trained researchers and facilities, and the scope and uses of sociology has also triggered a prolonged conflict between opponents and advocates of the role of social science in Party decision-making.[44]

Efforts to rationalize the dynamics of the apparatus since 1964 have been addressed to familiar problems, evident in the apparatus since NEP, arising from the Party's monocratic structure. The principal measures have once again concentrated on the lower Party organs, where the internal strains are greatest. Recognizing that the number of specific Party directives that are executed or even effectively communicated is low has undoubtedly been significant in renewing emphasis on improving the apparatus' efficiency.[45] The more basic policies have emphasized planning within the apparatus, generally for two years; improving internal communication through mechanization and by expanding the clerical staff; establishing closer, more regularized procedures for internal reporting and communication; and generally humanizing relationships within the apparatus as a means of, among other things, reducing the heavy turnover at the gorkom and raikom levels.[46]

Efforts to rationalize the internal dynamics of the lower Party apparatus have centered on reconsidering the role and functions of the instructor under conditions of economic reform, an especially important aspect of the strategy of *rukovodstvo* since the reform emphasizes an increased role for the primary Party organs. Rationalizing the instructor's role has involved reducing his purely clerical functions to place him in the field[47] and extensively debating the merits of functional specialization below the obkom level,[48] the latter expressive of the inherent conflict between the apparat's general political functions and the specialized controls it has long striven to achieve. Retaining branch departments at the gorkom level through the middle of 1970 indicates the persistence of this problem.

Alternating intensive in-service training with practical experience has been traditional; the expansion of Party schooling since 1965, however, has added a new dimension reflecting a need to strengthen Party institutionalization after its decline in Khrushchev's final years.[49] This conservative emphasis has been reinforced by the desire to indoctrinate officials recruited into the apparatus since 1964 and to retrain older apparatchiki whose skills and knowledge have not been wholly relevant to modern conditions. A new note has been introduced into Party training since 1968, following the antiapparatus emphasis of the Czech reform.[50] *Partiinoe stroitel'stvo* and the doctrines associated with the leading role have been concerned with creating a common outlook toward structure and with combatting attacks on the Leninist Party structure.[51]

The emphasis on economic and technical training has been partially reversed in the post-Khrushchev Party. Although the revised curriculum of the Higher Party School is not yet published, the heavily specialized curricula accompanying the 1962 reform has very likely been altered to include more ideological, political, and managerial subjects.[52] The short courses set up in 1968 at the intermediate level were probably ineffective; the month-long courses for repreparation of cadres were hastily put together and over-ambitious in terms of available resources.[53] However weak the massive program of continuous in-service cadre training may be, however, the policy bespeaks the current Soviet leadership's determination to maintain the Party's traditional structure and improve its efficiency.

Bureaucratic rationalization has presupposed an effective reform of internal communication. Informational problems, while less severe than in the structures of industrial management, have significantly reduced the apparatus' efficiency. Many communication difficulties result from the vertical stratification of authority, among them the complaint about *shablon* in reporting to higher Party organs—i.e., deliberately distorting information to avoid the bad opinion of higher Party officials.[54] But organizational theory would seem to ensure the continuation of this particular deficiency in communication. Cross-checking and multiple channels of reporting—the traditional Stalinist defense against distortion—have probably increased with the activation of the Party Control Committee and the Committee of Popular Control.

Certain limited efforts have been made to improve reporting and communication in the post-Khrushchev years. Reducing the local Party apparatus' involvement in the details of economic decision-making has been accompanied by an effort to reduce the amount of economic reporting and to emphasize political reporting, particularly in relation to mass attitudes.[55] The use of sociology, social psychology, and learning techniques, and such innovations as press conferences and daily press coverage of various types of official and Party communication are part of a general policy to broaden Party influence.[56] Of special interest has been the development of *politinformatory*, educated and specialized agitators who communicate with those normally outside the mass agitational net.[57] But these measures are still too new to evaluate. The *politinformator*, a direct threat to long established, relatively ineffective methods of mass agitation, however, has been seriously opposed by conservatives within the apparatus and has begun to decline in importance.[58]

A survey of the post-Khrushchev Party bureaucracy indicates that the monocratic system is very deep-rooted, and that any change that would significantly alter the apparatus' status or power will be seriously challenged. The Khrushchev experience may have strengthened this trend; certainly, the post–1964 apparatus has reverted to a highly conservative form of authority and formal structure. In any event, efforts to improve the decision-making processes of the Party bureaucracy are not without merit and may be of future importance. The leadership's determination to emphasize the authority of the line official and the bureaucratic opposition to innovation in the interests of greater efficiency suggest that the power-efficiency dilemma is in many respects more complex and difficult in 1970 than it was in 1953.

2

Economic Reform and the Bureaucracy

Although the policies of bureaucratic rationalization and the structure of economic reform adopted in the fall of 1965 have both been concerned with reducing the dysfunctional consequences of monocratic structure, the rationalization of the two structures has differed. Except for some experimentation and absorption of new techniques and methods, the reform of the Party apparatus has followed traditional lines. The reform of industrial management, however, has gone much farther. At its base, it has envisioned a partial replacement of classical bureaucracy to direct and coordinate the vastly complex Soviet economy. The 1965 shift to economic methods, the subject of intense public debate after 1960, carries profound, if abstract, implications for Party *rukovodstvo*.

The issues and rationale of Soviet allocative policy so prominent in the post-Stalin period have persisted under Khrushchev's successors. Khrushchev's determination to develop the regime's political legitimacy through increased welfare has been retained as policy, although the reversion to political and ideological repression in 1965 indicates that basic political trust between leaders and led is still weak.[59] Theoretically, welfare relates to the necessity of providing sufficient material incentives to make the economic reform work. The shift to new economic priorities and allocative policies after 1964, however, has produced a politics as profoundly complex as it was under Khrushchev. Under a political oligarchy, resource allocation will inevitably be the object of competition and conflict. The result, however, has been to produce an intricately balanced set of compromises subject to marginal change over time. Moreover, despite the emphasis on scientific planning, the economy has been under significant political pressure for growth, particularly since 1967.

Although space does not permit a detailed account of the changes in Soviet economic priorities, some indication of the scale and intensity of the shifts among defense, investment, and welfare goals is required to judge the effectiveness of the reform and the Party's role in decision-making. The 1965 plan, the last prepared under Khrushchev, emphasized the growing importance of consumer goods and agriculture at the expense of heavy industry and defense.[60] There was a significant conflict over priorities in 1965. In March, Brezhnev announced a massive transfer to agriculture of some seventy-one billion rubles, which the draft proposals of the new Five-Year Plan publicly affirmed in February 1966.[61]

The symbolic cut in defense was not maintained after 1965.[62] The increase in public commitments to defense from 13.4 billions to 17.7 billions in 1969 has strained the Soviet economy as it did under Khrushchev. On the whole, Khrushchev's successors have attempted to maintain more balance in setting allocative policy. There have, nonetheless, been sharp vacillations in projecting growth rates and in sectoral allocations, reflecting underlying political pressures and the continuing shortages of resources.[63] Allocative policy has shifted most dramatically toward increasing the proportion of consumer goods in the annual plans. Whereas the plans for 1966 and 1967 maintained the traditional priority of Group A industrials, the plans for 1968–70 narrowly reversed this bitterly contested aspect of Stalinist economic policy.[64] Investment priorities have wavered, although power, fuels, the progressive branches of machine building, and investment in machinery for light industry have been consistently favored. Allocations to agriculture have been continuously challenged, and the familiar conflict between the "metal eaters" attacked by Khrushchev and the chemical investment program remains in evidence.[65]

At each point where significant choices of economic policy have had to be made, there has been disagreement within the Soviet Politburo. The March 1965 decision to shift resources into agriculture was challenged, and the cuts in the military budget were restored.[66] The publication of the control figures for the Five-Year Plan initiated a lengthy debate among resource claimants on economic policy, which resulted in the expanded plan of 1968–70. The ongoing debate in the Politburo to give precision to the investment and production goals of the Five-Year Plan after the Twenty-third Congress evoked open disagreements among the top leadership. Kosygin frankly asserted the need to increase the products of light industry to meet the rising demand.[67] Ustinov, who had been co-opted into the Secretariat from defense, defended increased allocations to the military;[68] and Podgorny, in 1965 an advocate of consumer goods and a year later a supporter of heavy industry and defense, favored increased investments in agriculture.[69]

The conflict resulted in increased allocations to all the major claimants. To satisfy the advocates of both consumer goods and defense, increases in production were to be achieved through increased efficiency and cutbacks in less favored sectors.[70] In 1967 the major upward revision in the Five-Year Plan in heavy industry, defense, and consumer goods culminated a lengthy debate evident as early as March 1967.[71] That neither Brezhnev nor Kosygin could hold military expenditures at existing levels after the Arab-Israeli War of June 1967 is indicated by the major increases in metallurgical investment in August.[72] D. S. Polianskii indicated that these reallocations were to be achieved at the expense of agriculture when, in an article in *Kommunist* on the fiftieth anniversary of the Revolution, he called for a principle of equivalency between industry and agriculture and protested the siphoning off of investment from agriculture into the priority industrial sectors.[73]

That there were serious pressures on the Soviet economy through the middle of 1970 is evident from Brezhnev's repeated attempts to assert the primacy of agriculture and his failure to reorient his own priorities decisively. At the agricultural plenum in October 1968, he sharply criticized the decline in agricultural investment. Of the 41 billions to be invested from the central budget, only 21.2 billions have in fact been allocated. Brezhnev complained that in every republic substantial cuts in the production of agricultural machinery and fertilizers had been reallocated to housing and public services.[74] In 1969, needless to say, the familiar tug-of-war for resources was repeated.[75]

The conflict over basic economic policy should now be considered central in the dynamics of the political system. Brezhnev's decision to push the priority of agriculture and heavy industry and the announcement that new decisions would be made at the forthcoming Party Congress indicate a new round in the battle.[76] As these lines are being written, there is little to suggest that these issues will be soon resolved without restructuring political control at the top.

Basic economic decisions have been affected by the war in Vietnam, the bitter struggle with the Chinese, and the Arab-Israeli War. Poor harvests in 1965, 1967, and 1969 have indicated Soviet agriculture's vulnerability to natural contingencies and unsatisfactory social organization. Basic policy and the Party's leading role have been conditioned by the efficiency and technical progress of the coordinative factor in the decision-making process. Growth and efficiency have been as securely linked since 1964 as they were under Khrushchev.

The reforms in economic management introduced at the September 1965 Plenum of the Central Committee were clearly the result of the intense economic criticism of 1961 and 1962 that had been revived in 1964. Kosygin attributed the growing stagnation and inefficiency in industry to the excessive centralization of coordinative decision-making and to an ineffective technical policy administered through a regional rather than industrial branch structure.[77]

In converting from administrative to economic methods of management, the reform envisaged two basic measures. First, Kosygin advocated separating general economic decision-making from operational supervision and coordination to overcome the chronic microimbalance characteristic of the Stalinist system. Secondly, to reduce the overload of information and centralized direction in the new structures of industrial management, he proposed a significant degree of decentralization to permit self-coordination of the enterprise through the use of indices that would integrate the interests of the national and enterprise economies.

The reform aimed at establishing a workable compromise between the traditional structures of bureaucratic planning and management and the limited use of market principles.[78] Advocates of reform assumed that the fifty thousand industrial enterprises in the Soviet Union would find it in their economic interest to intensify the exploitation of existing technologies, to promote technical development and to eliminate managerial deviance. Major gains in economic and administrative efficiency would be achieved through a rationalization of planning and the legislation of economic stimulants designed to optimize microeconomic decision-making.

The key features of the complex reform enacted in the legislation of 4 October 1965, analyzed in detail elsewhere, need only be noted here:[79] (1) planning would be restructured by expanding direct contracts between enterprises, with the aggregate orders forming the basis of the production plan within the reduced central indicators; (2) new success indicators would be adopted for the large majority of products based on sales or profit and profitability, the latter conceived as a percentage of capital; (3) three incentive funds would be formed for bonuses, improving enterprise services, and funding enterprise capital investment; (4) interest and rent would be adopted; (5) the supply system would be rationalized with the eventual adoption of wholesale trade and placing the supply agencies on economic accountability; (6) the sovnarkhozy would be abolished and replaced by twenty-three industrial ministries; and (7) the system of prices would be reformed. In the revised planning system, Gosplan again controlled the important planning functions which it had surrendered in 1963. Supply was placed in a separate agency, the State Committee on Material Technical Supplies (Gossnab), and the formal planning rights of the restored industrial ministries and enterprises were coded in separate statutes. There was special emphasis on expanding the production associations, *firmy* or *obedineniia*, which had begun to form before the 1962 reorganization.[80] As in the case of the Party, returning to a conservative formal managerial structure was accompanied by measures designed to produce significantly altered functional relationships.

The measures summarized in the legislation of October 1965 to improve the efficiency of industrial decision-making were conscious efforts of debureaucratization to improve the processes of microcoordination.[81] Decentralizing planning and coordination would allow central officials to concentrate on more fundamental developmental decisions. In addition, the increased, though still limited, authority of the enterprise would provide operational flexibility by correcting the existing weaknesses in horizontal communication and regional coordination.

The identification of economic incentives with efficiency went beyond Khrushchev's mixture of moral and economic factors. An important step in this respect was reorienting Soviet management toward a pattern of decision-making which frankly recognized the primacy of economic incentives in the enterprise and the conflicting interests between national economic goals and the subgoals of the enterprise. Emphasizing qualitative indicators based largely on commercial principles was logically related to an increase in managerial incentive, risk-bearing, and concern for efficiency absent from the earlier system. The possibilities for encouraging ideological secularization and political pluralism were, of course, equally evident.

The issue of increasing the efficiency of Soviet management has not been exhausted by the aggregate measures adopted in October 1965 and later. The earlier alternatives, based on the conservative view that the problems of management were primarily structural and informational, have brought about a continuing effort to incorporate into Soviet organizational structure the classical mechanistic principles of scientific management, an approach which not only accepts but strengthens monocratic structure.

In theory and in practice, bureaucratic rationalization has aimed at improving the mechanisms of planning and administration and incorporating new managerial technologies. The latter has included economic and social forecasting, cybernetics and operations research, the application of social science techniques to industrial relations, the introduction of NOT, or Taylorism, in management, and the training of Soviet managers in the techniques and skills of business administration. In addition, staffs have been cut, formal structure reorganized, and production specialized and concentrated through the emergence of such structures as *firmy* or *obedinenniia*.[82]

Since 1965 there have been significant efforts to rationalize the heavily overloaded system of vertical communication and to improve its informational and analytical quality by means of decentralization, reduced reporting, and the extension of lateral communication through an expanded scope of enterprise decision-making. Similar implications were involved in the increased reliance on value categories, particularly in the light of a reformed price structure.[83]

The use of mathematical methods and computers in working out the fifteen thousand partial balances in Gosplan and Gossnab and in processing the fifty million indicators in the annual draft plans submitted from below is a significant step forward. Similarly, the expansion of empirical sociological research on economic problems and the introduction of automated systems of information processing and management in a series of branches and plants have been important in dealing with severe substantive and computational problems.[84]

Five years are not enough to judge the reform's effect on the distribution of power or managerial efficiency. The original measures have been revised in many respects and, as a result of Brezhnev's comprehensive criticism of industrial management at the December 1969 Central Committee Plenum, further discussion and change will undoubtedly occur. The transfer of enterprises to the new system was not completed in the main until 1969 when some thirty-six thousand enterprises passed over.[85] Nonetheless, the experience of the reform has been sufficiently extensive to permit several conclusions on the structures which have developed.

Soviet economic performance has been only marginally affected by the reform. In his defense of the reform in the spring of 1970, following the December plenum, a prominent liberal economist argued that the quality and consistency of plans have improved; supply has increased in reliability; and a new consciousness of economic knowledge and values has emerged. But the return on assets has been slow; there has been no upsurge in technical progress; labor productivity is increasing slowly; and wages have been rising faster than productivity.[86] These assessments are confirmed by a recent study of Soviet growth under the reform.

In 1968 and 1969, the years when the bulk of the enterprises transferred over to the new system, Soviet growth vacillated considerably. In 1968, a good year for agriculture, the economy showed a growth rate of 5.8 percent. The poor harvests in 1969 undoubtedly contributed to the drop in the growth rate to an estimated 2.3 percent, the lowest since World War II.[87] In both 1968 and 1969, industry showed a decline in every sector. Construction materials and the paper and pulp industries dropped by almost two-thirds in comparison with 1966–67, metals and chemicals by one-third, the drop in chemicals following the investment cuts of 1965–67. Despite a favorable allocative policy, steel grew by only 2.8 percent in 1969. Civilian machinery dropped only slightly, thanks to the rapid growth (15 percent) in refrigerators, washing machines, and television receivers. Nondurable consumer goods fell sharply, however, due to the short falls in agriculture.[88]

Many of the short-term variations are transitional. In the past, long-term Soviet growth has been largely a matter of quantitative increases in capital and labor inputs. The basic relationship between these factors of production appear little changed under the reform, as Birman has indicated. Stanley H. Cohn has calculated that productivity growth rates, which were zero between 1960 and 1963, have been only 2 percent between 1963 and 1967.[89] Moreover, the steady rise in capital-output ratios, which has been so dramatic since 1960, has continued its upward course, one sign that the expected gains in productivity from new technology have not yet been achieved.[90] This can be attributed in part to the chronic deficiencies of the capital investment program which continued to be felt under the reform.[91]

Whether such problems of static and dynamic efficiency can be relieved in the near term is questionable. Many of the command economy's operational problems will be transformed only with great difficulty over a long period of time. The aggregate measures of the reform, as Robert Campbell noted in 1968, have not added up to a coherent system.[92] The reform's lack of coherence has stemmed not only from the inherent technical difficulties of an enterprise of this scale but also from the complex set of compromises to emerge from the year-long consideration of the issue in the Central Committee and the Presidium.[93] The reform has been only a short step toward resolving the chronic problems of bureaucratic management through the development of a market mechanism.[94] The anomalies of the current system of management cannot be attributed to the bureaucratic factor alone, although, as it is argued here, the effect of the monocratic structure is still decisive.

The price system, for example, reformed in 1966 and 1967 and annually revised since, has remained an administered price structure based upon average rather than marginal values, providing little information in relation either to costs or to scarcities.[95] Moreover, the influence of the new success indicators and the incentive funds on economic choice has proved disappointing. The revised success indicators have been internally inconsistent and have failed to redirect managerial decision-making toward qualitative factors.[96] Calculations for deductions into the incentive funds have been complex, their utility lowered by the small percentage of the material incentive fund contributing to wages. The incentive value of the social and production funds has been reduced by the inability of the enterprises to secure the necessary construction resources for expanding facilities.[97]

The persistence of the administrative factor can be seen in virtually every aspect of plan construction and implementation. There has been continuous conservative opposition to the reform, and its implementation, as some Western analysts have pointed out, has been cautious and less liberal than the experiments of 1964.[98] On the redistribution of planning authority, the earlier processes of routine plan construction have retained their most important operational characteristics. The determination to achieve greater flexibility of planning by making the five-year plan the basic planning instrument has not been achieved through 1970. As one Gosplan official succinctly summarized the situation, "The most important indices of such plans are not confirmed for the individual enterprise, do not have the force of directives, and are not an organic part of its economically accountable activity."[99]

The extent to which planning authority has actually been decentralized under the reform is difficult to estimate, although it has evidently been less than expected in 1965. To date there has been little decentralization in the most important types of industrial products. In late 1968, physical balances for 2,000 products were still planned in Gosplan and another 13,000 planned in Gossnab or the supply committees attached to it.[100] Continued tight controls over supply and wages constitutes part of that "invisible centralization" which liberal critics have charged with hampering the progress of the reform.[101] In this respect, two major aspects of the reform in planning and supply have developed very slowly. Through the first half of 1969, direct contracts were established between only 500 supplier and 6,000 client plants.[102] More significantly, the transfer to wholesale trade in the means of production has been slow.[103]

There was evidence in 1966 and 1967, when the most productive plants were transferred to the new system, that the reform would stimulate efficiency in Soviet industry. As Academician Federenko warned in early 1967, however, these early successes were temporary and deceptive because they were based upon existing reserves.[104] The failure of the new system to stimulate large-scale change in either managerial practice or the efficient use of resources was revealed in an investigation by the Central Statistical Administration of 580 plants which had gone over to the new system. The failure of the enterprises to accept tight plans, to fulfill established assignments, or to deliver planned assortments had cost the economy some three billion rubles.[105] The plant officials' lack of confidence in the planning and supply structures as well as the much publicized "psychological barriers" were major factors in the failure of the enterprise generally to respond to the reform.

The plant continues to restrict output goals and to maximize the increment of investment and material and human resources, despite the effect of such practices on profitability.[106] On the whole, operational relationships among the various levels of the planning and administrative hierarchy are still characterized by mutual distrust, bargaining, and compromise.[107] The search for reserves, for example, is undiminished. As a Gosplan official has complained, "When the plan for 1969 was worked out, the growth rate for output, sales, and profits envisaged for the majority of enterprises going over to the new working conditions in 1966 were not only lower than those actually attained but even lower than those established at the time of the changeover to the new system."[108]

Maintaining the essential monocratic structure of the pre-reform period has, of course, profoundly affected the general power and efficiency dilemmas and the Party's leading role. Western analysts and Soviet critics alike see bureaucratic inertia and resistance as the chief obstacle to implementing the reform, a condition as common since 1965 as under Khrushchev.[109] The intervention by the ministries and glavki in planning and supply has been particularly counterproductive.[110] Sending down late plans, changing plans without prior consultation or changes in other indicators, changing suppliers, and other policies have not only restricted the scope of the reform but have contributed to the microimbalance as well.[111]

The pervasive jurisdictional conflicts and bureaucratic politics which have accompanied the reestablishment of the ministerial system are likewise productive of microimbalance. That the predominant proportion of production is concentrated in all-union or union republican ministries has restricted regional planning and administration and brought a rise of ministerial autarky, a condition Khrushchev attacked in the 1957 reorganization.[112] There has been acute struggle at the center for control over the functions and resources of industrial management among the planners, supply agencies, and ministries. Gosplan's distrust of the ministries has been such as to attempt bypassing them and dealing directly with the plants.[113] In addition, the struggle between central and territorial administrative organs continues to be interwoven with the conflict of nationalities.[114]

The central managers' success in maintaining a high degree of routine coordination of the industrial economy in Moscow has had its usual effect on the efficiency of the structure. In 1968 and 1969, years of declining growth and increasing problems in the coordination of capital construction and development of new technology, the efficiency of the industrial bureaucracy was increasingly questioned. A *Partiinaia zhizn'* editorial on the Ninth Five-Year Plan noted the excessive number of linkages, the high costs of coordination, and the slow decision-making of the managerial apparatus.[115] The ministries have been criticized for their "bureaucratic-chancery" methods of leadership.[116] But the most significant developments in formal structure have been at the enterprise level, where the apparatus, unexpectedly, has rapidly expanded.[117] Expenditures on *tolkachi* remain particularly heavy.[118]

Informational processes and computation have not yet been sufficiently improved to resolve the increasingly severe problems of vertical and horizontal communication. This is partly due to the continued use of multiple vertical channels of reporting as a control device. The higher administrative organs' restless search for data from the enterprises is undoubtedly an effort to maintain detailed operational leadership and to subvert the reform.[119] The growth of ministerial autarky has clearly reduced the degree of local communication and coordination.

The reform itself, nonetheless, has increased the generation and flow of information to the point where the indicators of even small plants may exceed one million per month.[120] The principal problem remains the inability to digest this massive flow of data. An investigation of the Central Statistical Administration reveals that only about 4 percent of the available information is actually used. Furthermore, the quality of data employed by the central decision-makers is low. Accurate and timely information is usually unavailable on production potential or needs,[121] and, despite the growth in communications technology, the management system still lacks the instruments, models, and trained manpower required to develop an efficient system.[122]

3

Toward a New Role for the Party

Historically, close, interacting relationships have been central in determining the Party's leading role. First, the monocratic character of the Party bureaucracy has set the boundaries of apparatus decision-making. Monolithism has, to be sure, never been fully achieved since informal cleavages of interest and value have traditionally influenced Party operations at all levels. Structural limits have induced sharp policy conflicts, endless reorganization of the formal structure, and periodic efforts to reduce bureaucratization and routinization.

There have been environmental boundaries as well. In the initial phase of industrialization, the command economy's system of centralized planning and implementation was valuable in maintaining the leadership's operational priorities and mobilizing scarce human and material resources; but it became routinized in time to the point of rigidity and stagnation. The routinization of growth and the microimbalance induced by bureaucratic controls produced a series of problems in coordinative decision-making which have structured the Party's administrative involvement in the economy.

The October 1965 reforms were designed to maintain political control of the macroeconomy while permitting greater flexibility and efficiency in coordinating the microeconomy. But their conservatism, principally the result of bureaucratic resistance and inertia, has so far failed to achieve the desired integration of the macro- and microeconomies. The persistence of the bureaucratic system with its resulting imbalances in coordinating planning, supply, and plan implementation has meant a general failure to utilize existing technologies or to develop new technology. It has also created grave problems in the functional definition of the Party's proper role.

Redefining the Party's decision-making role since 1965 has been strikingly complex, partly the result of mixing innovation with large doses of organizational conservatism. In general, Party policy has reemphasized legitimating and integrating social processes by separating and reordering Party and managerial functions. Neither the conception of the reform nor the specific definition of the Party's role, however, has indicated a significant withdrawal of the Party from economic decision-making.

Insofar as this can be determined from the Soviet press, the Party's role in establishing fundamental economic policy or in determining allocations has not been directly challenged. Judgments at this level are, of course, difficult to make or sustain. While the presence of interest group activity at the top of the structure is virtually certain, the processes of articulation and aggregation remain even more elusive under Khrushchev's successors than before. Still, there is little doubt that conservatives have perceived an indirect threat to a system of leadership based upon bureaucratic controls both within the Party and outside.

Anxiety may have fed the strong undertow of opposition which accompanied the legislation of October 1965. "Politically immature" intensity was compared by one prominent ideologist to the situation that had confronted Lenin in introducing NEP.[123] It required the antirevisionist campaign connected with the developments in Czechoslovakia to reveal the deep fears of political pluralism, managerial autonomy, and market socialism for the political future of the Communist party. The massive defense of Soviet intervention made clear the Soviet leadership's hostility to any form of "automatism" in economic regulation. The preservation of central planning and the categorical denial of full managerial autonomy were closely associated with the defense of traditional methods of *rukovodstvo*.[124] Brezhnev made it clear that there would be no weakening of the Party's organizational base through pluralism or "separation" of the leading role from economic management.[125]

The redefinition of the leading role has focused on microcoordination; i.e., the type and degree of supervision that the territorial Party apparatus may undertake. The problem has been familiar since the Zhdanov-Malenkov conflict of the middle thirties on the relative importance of politics and economics in defining the leading role. On the one hand, it is feared that without active apparatus supervision, the managers will not carry out Party policy. On the other hand, there may be too much involvement in the details of economic administration, as in 1963 and 1964. "The Party's purity and dynamism are threatened if, the state having been reduced, it must itself attend to microeconomic administration. The State bureaucracy will then reproduce itself inside the Party, with corrupting consequences, as Zhdanov foresaw."[126]

The November 1964 plenum, which restored the pre–1962 Party structure, indicated how far Khrushchev's reform had reduced the state's role in microadministration and the absorption of these functions by the Party apparatus. The *Pravda* editorial which rather intemperately demanded an end to intervention in the details of coordination, however, also noted that the apparatus' involvement in economic decision-making would remain fundamentally unchanged: "The Party will in the future as well strive to see to it that all Party organizations delve more deeply into production, study economics, technology and advanced experience, solve practical tasks knowledgeably, utilize internal reserves, increase the output of products, raise their quality, and lower their production tasks."[127]

Reorienting the apparatus toward economic efficiency and development and withdrawing from the mass of petty administrative problems was a conscious return to Zhdanov's position and a revival of traditional *rukovodstvo*.[128] Once again, the literature stresses a selective, developmental approach to economic decision-making, primary concentration on the recruitment and socialization of cadres, *proverka*, mass mobilization, and an increased role for the primary Party organs.[129] Returning to a broad functional approach also served to emphasize ideological orthodoxy and the importance of guidance through the Party's "own methods." As in previous periods, of course, a primary political responsibility has been enforcing Moscow's directives against "localism," particularly in its growing nationalist manifestations.[130]

The territorial Party apparatus has recognized the significant limitations of the Party apparatus in economic decision-making. Shitarev has noted that, by its nature, personnel, and methods, the Party lacks the resources for direct administration.[131] It was also recognized that by relying solely on its own resources to resolve economic questions, the Party apparat lowered the utility and efficiency of economic decisions. In the wake of the reform, there was recognition that the Party simply could not function without the managers.[132] There was an additional frank recognition of the close relationship between the problems of microeconomic coordination and the Party's role. A. J. Pel'se pointed out that Party intervention compensated for shortcomings in planning, management, and incentives. "The new system," he predicted, "will lead to the disappearance of these ill-starred methods of guidance alien to Party agencies."[133] Ideologists opposed to the secularization implied in the reform nonetheless welcomed the traditionalist redefinition of *rukovodstvo* because it promised a better balance between politics and economics.[134]

A recognition of the realism of the Zhdanov approach to decision-making did not preclude certain reservations. The shift to economic methods made new demands on the knowledge and skills of the middle-level apparatchik and complicated his status and authority in relation to the presumably liberated plant managers.[135] At the middle and lower levels of the apparatus, there was some anxiety concerning the effect of the reform on the Party's ideological functions.[136] There was also conflict over the necessity for active intervention by the apparatus. Some held, like Malenkov at the Eighteenth Conference in 1941, that without close and dynamic Party involvement, economic decisions would not be made or implemented.[137]

Another question concerned how to distinguish between politics and economics. A perplexed gorkom first secretary asked, "Where does the border separating Party work from economic work lie? In fact does such a border exist?"[138] Underlying everything else was the crucial dilemma which has persistently structured the response of the Party apparatus to problems of microcoordination: Can the local Party organ stand aside when the success of the plan is threatened? The evidence suggests strongly that pressures inherent in both the reform and in Party policy have pressed the local Party organs toward intervention.

The concentration of local Party organs on economic issues, however, has apparently varied. The Irkutsk Party organization responded to the reform in three, perhaps typical, distinct stages. From the September plenum until the middle of 1966, the Party was deeply involved in implementing the reform. Attention then slackened until the beginning of 1968 when the apparatus returned to industrial and construction problems.[139] The resurgence of Party involvement in the industrial economy in 1968, exemplified in the Irkutsk experience and clearly decided at the highest levels of the Party structure, involved the ascendancy of the status and prestige of Brezhnev and the Party apparatus over the industrial managers.[140] It also involved broader factors whose more important aspects remain obscure. The conservative thrust of the Czech events, the pressures on allocation, the operational difficulties of the reform, the insufficient response of the planners to Brezhnev's priorities, and the need to maintain the morale of the lower Party apparatus—all were reasons for the turn in policy.

The Party's greater engagement in economic decision-making after 1968 is related to the reform's failure to meet the leadership's expectations for efficiency. The operational characteristics associated with the command economy have thus permitted some shift in the balance of power between the Party and state bureaucracies at the same time that they have provided the environment framing the problems and strategies of Party *rukovodstvo*. To what extent the central Party apparatus has changed its scope of control over the ministries and glavki is not clear, although the large number of secretaries suggests close administrative integration of Party and state agencies at the top.

At intermediate and lower levels of the hierarchy, the effect of the reform is more marked. The actual exercise of power by the territorial apparatus depends upon the extent to which planning, allocation, and coordination have been centralized within the structure of industrial management. The return to the ministerial system in October 1965 did not in itself signify a loss of power for the Party apparatus; but the return to a branch system of management together with the retention by the planners and ministries of major controls over the enterprise has revived the conditions of the earlier ministerial system and shaped *rukovodstvo* in customary ways.

In addition to Party apparatus' opposition to abolishing the sovnarkhozy, conflict and competition have arisen between the local Party organs and Moscow since 1965 over a wide range of issues and functions. The loss by the lower Party apparatus of authority over planning and allocative decisions should not be exaggerated. The centralized coordination during the two final years of Khrushchev's rule exceeded anything that has occurred since. Nonetheless, centering major control over investment, current planning, and supply in Moscow has evoked frequent complaints by the lower Party apparatus on its inability to influence these types of decisions.[141] The chief new element here is the reduced capacity of local Party organs to coordinate on a regional basis the activities of enterprises of union or union-republican subordination.[142] The dominance of branch over regional planning and the emergence of ministerial autarky have had expected effects.

Centralizing power within the state apparatus has reopened the yawning gap between power and responsibility in the Party apparatus. Responsible for developing and promoting efficiency, the Party still lacks the authority or ability to carry out its mandate, notwithstanding that the revolution in economic theory under Khrushchev increased the apparatus' awareness of greater economic efficiency. Under Stalin and Khrushchev, the apparatchiki accepted the norms of extensive growth through increasing investment and inputs of human and material resources.

The labor shortage, however, has forced some reconsideration of intensive growth through increased labor productivity and technical innovation.[143] The reform's failure to date to have interested the managers in technical development has reduced the apparatus' efficiency. Lack of authority, bureaucratic inertia, and managerial resistance based upon still deficient success indicators have confined the Party to small-scale technical change and to improving operational efficiency by such measures as loading up shifts, organizing work flows more rationally, and improving the social environment of the plant.[144]

However reluctant its involvement, the local Party apparatus assumed major responsibilities in the transition from the old system. The republican and oblast Party committees were actively involved in the initial selection of plants going over to the new system, setting up incentive funds, reorganizing the enterprise, propagandizing the reform, and advancing new cadres. These functions, however, they shared with the ministries in a context of sharp friction.[145] In the aftermath of the reform, the territorial apparatus retains formal responsibility for the effective conduct of the reform. Intensive investigations reveal the relative ineffectiveness of the regional Party apparatus in promoting qualitative improvement in managerial efficiency or stimulating interest in the longer-range problems of industrial management.[146]

The territorial Party apparatus' control functions in the bureaucratic management system were related less to technical development or increasing productivity than to dealing with the microimbalance produced by the command economy. Withdrawing the apparatus from microadministration was, of course, the key element in adopting the political variant of *rukovodstvo* which developed in 1964 and 1965. If the success of this strategy depends on the degree to which the reform has corrected the problem, then the Party's intervention in this phase of industrial management is an important aspect of the leading role.

What norms should be used in judging the effectiveness of the apparatus? From 1965 through 1967, there was discussion within the Party of applying noneconomic criteria to evaluate the apparatus' performance, a logical result of increasing the separation of Party and state.[147] But Brezhnev's announcement that the apparatus would be judged primarily by economic criteria has temporarily stilled this issue.[148] The practice of evaluating Party performance by the same operational criteria as the enterprises under their jurisdictions, however, has preserved that community of interest which has traditionally influenced the strategy of *rukovodstvo*, particularly in control.

The Party's role in microcoordination reflects continuing preoccupations as well as new problems that have arisen since 1965. The coordination of material supply, a major concern of the local Party apparatus, has improved but is still chronically defective, due largely to the policy of centralized allocation.[149] The labor shortage has involved the local Party organs in the recruitment, distribution, and control of labor.[150] The Party still arbitrates disputes and represents the interests of enterprises within their jurisdictions, a condition which has probably increased as a result of the reform. The settlement of numerous contractual disputes, including the disposal of output refused by client plants, is among the more important problems pressed upon the lower Party apparatus by the reform.[151] The most difficult and important problems of microcoordination in the post-Khrushchev period, however, are in capital construction.

Although the political, or Zhdanov, approach has been consistently maintained in industrial decision-making, since 1968 official Party policy has encouraged an active coordinating role for the territorial apparatus in construction.[152] The practices so abundantly present during Khrushchev's later years have persisted under his successors, as the experience of the Vologda Obkom illustrates. In August 1967, the obkom undertook the supervision of the construction of the largest ball bearing plant in the Soviet Union; it has served as the coordinating center for the activities of two ministries, several glavki and construction trusts, design and supply organs, and the plant officials of the future plant. In the process, the obkom apparatus has been turned into *tolkachi* and dispatchers, spending its time securing labor, cement, and documentation, establishing construction schedules, and holding numerous *operativki* and *planerki*. Not unexpectedly, this has led to the serious neglect of its political and ideological functions.[153]

The recruitment and socialization of cadres has been a particularly important function in the political variant of *rukovodstvo* because the reform not only projected greater managerial autonomy but also made more complex demands on the skills and resources of the *khoziaistvenniki*. In this respect, cadre policy carries a potential challenge to Party direction of the economy and to the efficiency with which the reform has been implemented as well. Party leadership has been sensitive to the power implications of the reform with respect to cadre control. As one Soviet writer (quoting Lenin) has remarked, "If the Central Committee loses the right to distribute cadres, then it cannot direct policy."[154]

The *nomenklatura* remains the basic method for cadre control under the reform, although it has undergone a degree of rationalization since 1965. There has been additional decentralization and redistribution of offices from the secretariats to the departments; economic and other cadres tend to be confirmed rather than designated.[155] The central question of the reform on cadre policy has involved the authority of the local Party organs in relation to the new ministries. Under the earlier ministerial system, the territorial Party apparatus had highly restricted authority in appointing and dismissing plant managers and chief engineers of union and union-republican ministries.

Whether reestablishing the ministerial system has produced a relationship like the earlier one is difficult to determine by the available evidence. It is probable, however, that the local Party organs' dominance over personnel has declined. Primary responsibility for appointing and dismissing intermediate and lower level managers has been transferred to the ministries with the provision that personnel activity by the ministries be "coordinated" with the local Party organs,[156] a shift consistent with the trend toward affirmation rather than designation in the role of local Party organs. Reduced authority may account for the frequent complaints about a superficial, formal approach to appointments by Party committees, their generally low priority, and the demand that the ministries and glavki increase their attention to cadres in the production enterprises.[157]

The Party's decreased control over enterprise officials should not be over-interpreted. Local Party organs still participate in preliminary selection, recommendation, and (perhaps) nomination, and they may initiate dismissals as well. In cases of joint responsibility, the *nomenklatura* provides a well-established formal lever for vetoing ministerial appointments. In the case of special appointments and dismissals, principally where the Central Committee apparatus actively intervenes in a high-priority industrial sector, the Party apparatus has expanded authority. The Volgograd Obkom, for example, under the direction of the Department for the Chemical Industry, advanced some 2,500 new specialists to leading posts in the chemical and petrochemical industries.[158]

However blurred the details in the shifted balance of power concerning the appointment and selection of economic cadres, Party policy continues to emphasize the line posts in industrial management. The turnover of economic cadres has been generally heavy but the results are uneven.[159] In a heavy industrial oblast such as Gorkii, the formal educational qualifications have improved for directors of larger enterprises and construction trusts.[160] In the less industrialized and less accessible regions, in such formerly low-priority industries as light and food, in the medium and smaller plants, improving the formal qualifications of economic cadres has lagged. Young specialists and women have not been advanced rapidly enough. The ministries and the local Party organs still prefer to appoint "experienced specialists" over the untried and unknown.[161]

Appointment and promotion policies have influenced the enthusiasm with which the managerial apparatus has implemented the reform. It was expected that the older generation of *khoziaistvenniki*, traditionally oriented toward engineering, production, and monocratic administrative structures, would have psychological difficulty adjusting to the demand for primary attention to economic calculation. Repreparing and retraining the managers was initially the job of the Party apparatus. But the burden was heavy, and in 1966 the responsibility was transferred to the ministries and higher educational institutions. In 1967 the apparatus concentrated its schooling responsibilities on ideological and political indoctrination, although economic and technical issues remain important aspects of the Party's total propaganda effort.[162]

Perhaps the most fundamental continuity in socialization since 1965 has been in the assumptions under which the Party's ideological enterprise has been carried out. The basic purpose of indoctrination, a *Partiinaia zhizn'* editorial declared, was to inculcate a sense of moral responsibility in the managers.[163] This distrust of the managers, expressed in Pareto's terms, is clearly a residue of the earlier revolutionary commitment. The economic reform has little changed the long-held conviction that the managers have not sufficiently internalized the rules of the system to function independently of Party tutelage.

Distrust of the managers by the Party apparatchiki, evident at every stage in the exercise of *rukovodstvo*, may be a rationalized defense mechanism in behalf of Party superiority since it supports the Party's moral and political ascendance in the face of the managers' greater technical expertise.[164] This has been expressed in each of the functional aspects of the leading role but nowhere more pointedly than in relation to the Party's right of control.[165] The right and necessity to *proverka* has been defined traditionally: active Party supervision in the implementation of decisions and in behavioral control. The determination to keep this function, however, has not resolved the power-efficiency dilemma; indeed, it may have sharpened it.

For the Party leadership, the dilemma is only too familiar. Trusting cadres was acknowledged to be a necessary condition for raising their initiative and willingness to bear risks in the interests of efficiency and growth. Without close Party control, however, the reform aroused conservative qualms of slackened effort, a striving for lower plans and "advantageous" orders, violations of Party and state discipline, *mestnichestvo*, and all the rest. Balancing a "trust" in cadres (*doverie*) with a "demandingness" toward them (*trebovatel'nost*) has reflected both the political exigencies within the collective leadership and the pressures of longer-range institutional factors.

It is strongly believed that the control structure headed by A. N. Shelepin increased in power and scope after Khrushchev's fall, and that its dissolution in December 1965 was linked to Shelepin's subsequent loss in status.[166] The creation of separate control structures after the reform, however, can be otherwise viewed. Khrushchev's proposal to merge Party and state control was a strongly contested issue even before the Twenty-second Congress, and the structure's dissolution was consistent with both the opposition to Khrushchev's 1962 reorganization and with the larger policy of withdrawing the Party apparatus from the details of administrative coordination.[167] Within the context of the reform, the formation of the Committee of Popular Control was widely interpreted as a reduction of the functions of control and the status of the organs of control.[168] The assumption, however, was premature, because the importance of control and of the Party Control Committee were emphasized at the Twenty-third Congress.[169] The subsequent expansion of the control function has been largely a response to the reform's failure to reach its projected goals, the mounting pressures on allocation, and the political conservatism accompanying the antirevisionist campaign of 1968. In 1967 and 1968, the structures of both Party and state control were strengthened.

In 1967 the Central Committee ordered the Party commissions of the republican and oblast Party committees to expand their control activities.[170] The controversial Party commissions for the control of the administrations formed by Khrushchev in June 1959 were revived in 1968.[171] Intensifying control has even included activizing the Central Revision Commission.[172] The climax was reached with the publication after three years of the Statute on Popular Control, which was followed in the first half of 1969 by a thorough Party reorganization of its apparatus.[173]

Party and state control functions have little changed under the reform from the Khrushchev period. The Party apparatus has been responsible for maintaining leadership priorities in the face of local pressures, a condition most dramatically illustrated by Brezhnev's repeated calls to the Party apparatus to enforce his agricultural priorities.[174] The Party apparatus and the KNK have been expected to promote technical innovation and to increase the efficient uses of production facilities by monitoring plan fulfillment, economizing on the use of material and labor inputs, raising labor productivity, rationalizing administration, and, not least, controlling those managerial illegalities that have adjusted to new conditions. As formerly, control has included both bureaucratic and mass methods.[175] Since the December 1965 plenum, however, mass methods have declined in intensity.

The increased prominence of the Party Control Committee, and to a lesser extent the Central Revision Commission, indicates the top leadership's determination to discipline the lower Party apparatus and curb its propensity for elevating local over central priorities and, more frequently, for interpreting control directives in terms of local interests.[176] All the same, the new management system has brought little apparent change in the actual performance of Party control, whose weakness has been a traditional problem of *rukovodstvo*.

The reform itself was initially responsible since the slogan "confidence in cadres" was widely interpreted within the Party to mean reduced control.[177] This is not to suggest, even in 1966 and 1967, that Party and state control has been ineffective in the post-Khrushchev period, particularly in microcoordination. Numerous examples in the Soviet press report local Party organs directly supervising the introduction of new technology, tightening plans, conducting mass raids and *smotry* to uncover above-norm stocks, and disciplining enterprise officials.[178] The Party Control Committee, of course, has been noticeably active in this respect. As under Khrushchev, the Committee of Popular Control has conducted thousands of mass raids and checkups at every level of the industrial bureaucracy, often uncovering significant quantities of frozen resources, opening up alternate channels of communication, and heightening discipline.[179]

Brezhnev's intensified control effort in 1967 and 1968, however, appears to be no more successful than Khrushchev's more concentrated effort to control managerial behavior or to improve efficiency.[180] The reasons for this lie in the basic ambiguities of the leading role. After five years of the new system, the reform has only modified the Stalinist structure of political pressure and centralized bureaucratic controls. The modifications are important insofar as they indicate further change; in the short run, however, chronic and persistent microimbalance, in part the result of distrust of the new system at every level of the managerial hierarchy, has evoked deeply routinized responses from the industrial bureaucracy. As it has in the past this structural continuity defines the approach and sets the limits to control by the lower Party organs.

Control limitations are linked with the more general boundaries which frame the Party's decision-making role. Although Soviet theory makes no theoretical distinction between policy-making and implementation (a distinction which Lenin frequently rejected), the Communist party apparatus shares with most human organizations a greater capacity to accept decisions than to implement them. Like decision-making on policy issues, the control function has created uncertainty concerning the legitimate boundaries of Party intervention. The centralization of power, the lack of technical and human resources in the apparatus, and the significant limitations imposed by the Party's monocratic organization provide other administrative restraints. In the post-Khrushchev period as previously, the Party apparatus has lacked the resources for the span and intensity of control revived by the policy of 1967.

Finally, the economic reform has not disturbed the underlying community of interest binding local Party and managerial officials together against the center. In no period during the history of the Soviet regime, even in times of crisis, have national and local interests fully coincided, and the reform's failure to reduce significantly the gap between the macro- and microeconomies has perpetuated this condition. Since local Party organs are still judged by the same criteria as the enterprises they are required to control, their tolerance of "localism" and illegal and counterproductive practices (which are in some respects positive responses to the defects of the system) is understandable.[181] Managerial opposition to increased demands from the Party and continuous managerial search for support in carrying out its production and investment programs produce responses consistent with the relatively narrow interests of the local Party organ itself.[182]

Mass control functions have been closely linked in the practice of *rukovodstvo* with the Party's mobilization function. The return to mass mobilization and control over the industrial apparatus suggests the tenacity of the conception of the Party as an agency of mass mobilization and direction. That the Party leadership revived a political strategy less than three years after Khrushchev's fall indicates, on the one hand, the continuity of Khrushchev's problems. On the other hand, the ideological significance of mass participation is so deeply rooted in the Leninist tradition of the Party as a vanguard that redefinition would seriously alter the Party's institutional self-image. However anachronistic or ritualized the function has become in contemporary Soviet conditions, the return to traditionalism in October 1964 served not only to preserve but to emphasize mobilization as a primary means of rebuilding the Party's identity and cohesion.

The return to political *rukovodstvo* and the adoption of the reform placed the primary Party organs at the center of attention. At the September 1965 Central Committee Plenum, Brezhnev emphasized the role of the Party's mass organs as the first line of defense against the increased independence of the enterprise.[183] The intensive discussion and rationalization of the Party apparatus was largely directed toward increasing the effectiveness of the primary Party organs. Informational and agitational activities, concern with problems of entrance into the Party, the proper conduct of meetings, and similar preoccupations have received more attention in the past few years. But the emphasis on Party methods of leadership has not obscured the priority of economic issues. Mobilizing resources to fulfill the state plan remains the primary function of the Party's mass structures.[184]

Enlarging the rights of the enterprise in 1965 evoked a particularly complex manifestation of the traditional problem of bureaucratic authority and community or mass control, a conflict of authority chronic in Soviet administrative experience. While *edinonachalie* and *kontrol* have experienced little theoretical development, liberals and conservatives give differing weights to managerial autonomy and Party control. A. F. Rumiantsev, speaking for advocates of the reform, stressed that control did not mean the right to interfere in the operational activity of the enterprise because a fusion of functions led to the violation of *edinonachalie*.[185] In September 1965, Kosygin, more subtly, emphasized the primary Party organ as a moral force, presumably as an antidote to the commercial atmosphere which economic priorities were expected to heighten.[186]

Reducing the Party to an ideological force, of course, runs counter to the Party's activist and power-oriented traditions. Whatever the drift in this direction discernible early in the reform, the antirevisionist campaign of 1968 has clearly rechanneled Party energies toward organization. The primary Party organs have sought greater efficiency and output through thoroughly orthodox methods of mobilization and control. Plans have been tightened and inputs reduced through socialist obligations and various forms of socialist competition.[187] Production mobilization in search of higher output or hidden reserves continues to be generated through a constant round of meetings, criticism, inspections, *smotry*, raids, and conferences.[188] A particular feature of the reform has been integrating agitation with the new incentive system over which the primary Party organs have been given substantial power.[189]

The Party's mass organs have traditionally been weak in overcoming the limits on industrial efficiency imposed by the system of management. The multiplication of external controls in 1967 and 1968 indicates that the original emphasis on the primary Party organ as the principal instrument of Party *rukovodstvo* has been quietly reduced. The failure to mobilize the resources of the Soviet enterprise is primarily, of course, a failure of the reform itself. Technical deficiencies in the formation of the enterprise funds or an arbitrary action by a ministry or glavki can adversely affect mobilization. On 31 December 1969, for example, the Miass Steel Combine received a congratulatory telegram for its preschedule fulfillment of the plan. The next day a second telegram arrived from the ministry rescinding the previous one, revising the plan upward, and announcing that all bonuses were cancelled, an action seriously damaging the credibility of the mobilization effort at this particular plant.[190]

The average primary Party organ's inability to control the enterprise effectively is attributable less to the new system of management itself than to its continuities. As in the lower Party apparatus, a combination of restricted authority, extended span of control, lack of technical resources, managerial opposition, and a community of interest dilute the control effort. There is little reason to assume that multiplying control agencies will be more successful now than under Khrushchev. An investigation of mass control in Estonia in the early phase of the reform attributed the ineffectiveness of public control to excessive duplication, scattering of forces, disruption of the work of the enterprises, poor coordination, and its episodic character.[191] A similar review by the Yaroslavl Obkom in January 1969 reached essentially the same conclusions.[192]

Maintaining a functional balance between conflict and cooperation in the relationships between the Party and plant management has never been simple. During the initial phase of the reform when the emphasis on cadres was paramount, the Party made a determined effort to take over the hiring and firing of plant officials, including plant directors. But this was cut short by a brisk reminder to the primary organs that they have only traditional rights of consultation, not the rights conferred by *nomenklatura* over enterprise personnel.[193] Since the primary Party organs depend for political support on the higher Party organs and enterprise management, they evidently still lend passive or active support to counterproductive managerial practices. As under Stalin and Khrushchev, *podmena*, or "substitution," should be interpreted primarily as a service function which the primary Party organ renders management, particularly in the manner of supply.[194]

4

The Leading Role in 1970

In 1970, the dramatic expectations aroused by the October 1965 reforms of industrial management still remain to be seen. The past five years have provided abundant evidence of the difficulty of achieving rapid or fundamental change in the dynamics of these highly institutionalized, complex organizations. To be sure, the degree to which spontaneous and informal change has in fact occurred since 1965 may have been misperceived. The complex, transitional quality of current Soviet conditions and the particular problems of the structural-functional approach may obscure the emergence of new structures and relationships which may be dominant in the future. Nevertheless, both Soviet and Western analysts agree that the fundamental structures and problems of Stalin's command economy have remained.

This book has focused primarily on an issue of middle-range theoretical concern, namely the functional relationships of the Party apparatus with the decision-making processes of the industrial economy. The analyst does not directly observe the processes by which basic and allocative economic policy is made; the administrative and coordinative decisions which flow from decisions on allocation are more open to systematic study. It has been assumed that all decision-making occurs within a political context and that specific decisions are formalized and transmitted through large-scale bureaucracies which have become institutionalized and have acquired a degree of legitimacy over the course of time. If there is a discernible conflict between politics and administration in the Soviet Union, it lies in the political leadership's commitment to develop and otherwise change an administrative structure which, through institutionalization, has become highly change-proof.

For the Soviet political leadership the basic dilemma has increasingly become a choice between power and efficiency as competing values. The proliferation of functions and roles which has accompanied systemic modernization has burdened the large-scale bureaucracies that arose as the major organizational instruments of Soviet industrial decision-making under simpler conditions. The tension has been persuasively analyzed by Victor Thompson. The distribution of authority within and between the Party and structures of industrial management has become dysfunctional. Khrushchev and his successors have wrestled with the problem of maintaining the existing power structure without paying the heavy price in routinization and rigidity which monocratic organization seems to entail.

Consistent with his own power position and the Bolshevik tradition, Khrushchev attempted to resolve the dilemma by reducing the alternatives to a single issue: expanding the Party's role was prerequisite to raising the efficiency and the technical development of the Soviet economy. But this approach was insufficiently sensitive to resource shortages and to the complex of interests that would ultimately blunt or frustrate his initiatives. As the consequences of his failure grew, Khrushchev turned increasingly to bureaucratic reorganization and mass mobilization. His dramatic November 1962 thrust in this direction must be accounted among the principal reasons for his ouster two years later.

Khrushchev's successors have brought a more sophisticated approach to the power-efficiency dilemma; their central trends of adjustment and reform have reflected the lessons of the immediate past. Khrushchev had attempted a limited but nonetheless real ideological and structural adaptation of the Party to modern conditions. The current Soviet leadership has, on the other hand, moved to consolidate the Party's monocratic structure by a traditional approach to ideology and formal structure. While recognizing the inefficiencies of the Party apparatus, their efforts to overcome the consequences of large-scale organization have been to date quite modest, principally involving the appropriation of more efficient technologies, in computation and communications especially. The most evident continuity with the Khrushchev era lies in recruiting to line posts cadres with technical training, managerial experience, and intensive training and experience within the Party apparatus.

These modest measures have gone together with the reform of industrial management. From the perspective of Party leadership, the dominant problems of the command economy arose from the microeconomic imbalance which impelled the Party to intervene in the details of enterprise administration. The reform proposals adopted in October 1965 were intended to maintain centralized political control over Soviet basic and allocative policy, reduce the incidence of imbalance through decentralizing microadministrative decisions to the enterprise, and restructure the incentive system to correspond with existing Soviet conditions. But these proposals—the outcome of a year of debate and compromise within the Politburo—have not been fully implemented. The legislation of October 1965 has run into strong bureaucratic resistance and inertia, and the reform itself has exhibited technical difficulties. Microeconomic balance continues to characterize the Soviet economy; and despite the official policy of withdrawal, microadministration has been dominant in Party activity, particularly since 1968.

That the Party has once again become an agency of mobilization and control should not obscure the fact that this return to traditional methods of *rukovodstvo* has hitherto failed to satisfactorily resolve the power-efficiency dilemma. The Khrushchev experience indicated that the Party apparatus is inherently limited in inducing economic efficiency and technological growth. Increased administrative pressure and mobilization has the advantage of promoting the power dimension in the short run, but at a cost to efficiency in the long run.

Consistently choosing power over efficiency, a routine pattern under Stalin, is probably no longer possible, however, even if the current Soviet leadership wished to restore it. Political pressures on economic resources have gained a momentum which no Soviet political leader can ignore. "No other matter," said Brezhnev in August 1970, "is more important to the economy than carrying through the scientific and technological revolution. The solution of many problems of our society depends upon and will stem from this."[195] The slow growth in labor productivity and technological innovation under the existing structures of management is producing serious political pressures for change.

Yet there is little evidence of a consensus within the Soviet elite on the specific directions which such change should take. Certain Soviet economists, such as G. Lisichkin, would extend the reform to a full market socialism; but the intense conservative reaction to the economic and political reforms in Czechoslovakia has produced a political climate hostile to significant change in a pluralist direction. The return to a Stalinist type of centralized bureaucratic management reinforced by a system of computers seems only slightly less likely. In this respect, the uncertainty of the leadership was summarized by Brezhnev's declaration, "Past experience is a poor counselor here, but the elaboration of new things calls for persistent efforts and searches."[196]

The Soviet picture in 1970 projects neither radical contingency nor total necessity. Human institutions are fragile bridges for the working out of human purposes over the troubled water of dissolution and ossification. Potential change in either direction is possible. This study suggests that such change will be moderate and incremental and as the vector of conflicting forces. The crucial question for the Party as an institution involves function more than power. Its role as an agent of industrialization and modernization appears to have ended. The gradual evolution of *rukovodstvo* into a conservative, limiting force is a brake on further Soviet economic development. Whether the Party apparatus can articulate new social and economic functions in place of industrialization in an environment radically different from the one in which it seized power is the crucial issue for the future of the leading role. If the Party cannot redefine itself and its role in Soviet society, the leading role and the monocratic political instrument which Lenin created to carry it out may gradually wither away.

Notes

Introduction

1. Alfred Meyer, "Authority in Communist Political Systems," in Lewis J. Edinger, ed., *Political Leadership in Industrialized Societies* (New York, 1967), p. 85.

2. Zbigniew Brzezinski and Samuel P. Huntington, *Political Power: USA/USSR* (New York, 1964), pp. 202–3.

3. Talcott Parsons, "Suggestions for a Sociological Approach to the Theory of Organizations," *Administrative Science Quarterly*, no. 1 (1956), 63—85; reprinted in Amitai Etzioni, ed., *Complex Organizations: A Sociological Reader* (New York, 1962), p. 32 ff.

4. For a comprehensive critique of decision-making rationality, see James G. March and Herbert A. Simon, *Organizations* (New York, 1958), pp. 137 ff.

5. Cf., for example, Felix A. Nigro, *Modern Public Administration*, 2nd ed. (New York, 1970), pp. 83–105.

6. Victor A. Thompson, *Modern Organization* (New York, 1961), p. 19.

7. Nigro, *op. cit*; Daniel Katz and Robert L. Kahn, *The Social Psychology of Organizations* (New York, 1966), pp. 71 ff.

8. Thompson, *op. cit.*, chap. 2.

9. Robert K. Merton, "Bureaucratic Structure and Personality," in Robert K. Merton, *Social Theory and Social Structure*, rev. and enl. ed. (Glencoe, Ill.: Free Press, 1957), pp. 195–206; reprinted in Etzioni, *op. cit.*, pp. 48–61.

10. Katz and Kahn, *op. cit.*, pp. 223 ff.; Peter M. Blau and W. Richard Scott, *Formal Organizations: A Comparative Approach* (San Francisco, 1962), pp. 116–39.

11. Samuel P. Huntington, *Political Order in Changing Societies* (New Haven, 1968), pp. 344–46.

12. Michel Crozier, *The Bureaucratic Phenomenon*, trans. by the author (Chicago, 1964), pp. 145–49.

13. Victor A. Thompson, *Bureaucracy and Innovation* (University, Ala., 1969), chap. 3.

14. Gregory Grossman, "Notes for a Theory of the Command Economy," *Soviet Studies* 15, no. 2 (1963): 101–23; P.J.D. Wiles, *The Political Economy of Communism*, (Cambridge, Mass., 1964), particularly pt. 2.

15. Gregory Grossman, "Soviet Growth: Routine, Inertia, and Pressure," *American Economic Review* 50, no. 2 (1960): 62–72.

16. For an interesting discussion of this conception, see T.H. Rigby, *Communist Party Membership in the USSR, 1917–1967* (Princeton, N.J., 1968), pp. 6 ff.

17. Among the most valuable of the numerous critiques of the totalitarian model are the three essays in Carl J. Friedrich, Michael Curtis, and Benjamin R. Barber, *Totalitarianism in Perspective: Three Views* (New York, 1969).

18. Paul Hollander, "Observations on Bureaucracy, Totalitarianism, and the Comparative Study of Communism," *Slavic Review* 26, no. 2 (1967): 302–7; reprinted in Frederick J. Fleron, Jr., ed., *Communist Studies and the Social Sciences: Essays on Methodology and Empirical Theory* (Chicago, 1969), p. 219.

19. As a general problem of the one-party system, this issue has been brilliantly analyzed in Samuel P. Huntington, "Social and Institutional Dynamics of One-Party Systems," in Samuel P. Huntington and Clement H. Moore, eds., *Authoritarian Politics in Modern Society* (New York, 1970), pp. 3–20.

20. The second issue is the basic focus of an excellent set of essays in Zbigniew Brzezinski, ed., *Dilemmas of Change in Soviet Politics* (New York, 1969).

21. Significant efforts to conceptualize this process have been made by Robert Conquest, *Power and Policy in the USSR* (New York, 1961); Carl A. Linden, *Khrushchev and the Soviet Leadership, 1957–1964* (Baltimore, 1966); and H. Gordon Skilling, "Interest Groups and Communist Politics," *World Politics* 18, no. 3 (1966): 435–51. The conceptions of political change are well treated in Frederick J. Fleron, Jr., "Toward a Reconceptualization of Political Change in the Soviet Union: The Political Leadership System," *Comparative Politics* 1, no. 2 (1969): 228–44; reprinted in Fleron, *op. cit.*, pp. 222 ff.

22. B. M. Volin and D. N. Ushakov, eds., *Tolkovyi slovar' russkogo iazyka*, 4 vols. (Moscow: sovetskaia entsiklopediia, 1939), 3: 1402.

23. Leopold Haimson, in Margaret Mead, ed., *Soviet Attitudes toward Authority* (New York: McGraw-Hill, 1951), app. B, p. 115.

24. O. V. Kuusinen, ed., *Fundamentals of Marxism-Leninism*, 2nd ed. rev. (Moscow, 1963), p. 686.

25. *Ibid.*, p. 687.

26. E. I. Bugaev and V. M. Leibson, *Besedy ob ustave KPSS* (Moscow, 1964), p. 23.

27. L. Slepov, *Vysshie i mestnye organy partii* (Moscow, 1958), [Higher and lower Party organs] (New York, 1959), p. 31.

28. L. Slepov and G. Shitarev, *Leninskie normy partiinoi zhizni i printsipy partiinogo rukovodstva* (Moscow, 1956), p. 19 (hereafter cited as *Leninskie normy*).

29. See, for example, William Kornhauser, *The Politics of Mass Society* (Glencoe, Ill., 1959). The literature on totalitarianism is extensive. See also Hannah Arendt, *The Origins of Totalitarianism* (New York, 1960); Zbigniew Brzezinski, *Ideology and Power in Soviet Politics* (New York, 1962); Carl J. Friedrich and Z. K. Brzezinski, *Totalitarian Dictatorship and Autocracy* (New York, 1960).

30. Ivo Lapenna, "Party and State in the Programme," in Leonard Schapiro, ed., *The USSR and the Future: An Analysis of the New Program of the CPSU* (New York, 1963), pp. 150–1. This issue is also raised by Boris Meissner, "Party Supremacy: Some Legal Questions," *Problems of Communism* 14, no. 2 (1963): 32 ff.

31. V. A. Vlasov and S. S. Studenikin, *Sovetskoe administrativnoe pravo* (Moscow: Gosudarstvennoe Izdatel'stvo Iuridicheskoi Literatury, 1959), p. 34.

32. A. Denisov and M. Kirichenko, *Soviet State Law* (Moscow, 1960), p. 190.

33. Kuusinen, *op. cit.*, p. 526.

34. This problem is discussed by Alfred Meyer, *The Soviet Political System* (New York, 1965), pp. 197–201. Meyer holds to the reality of the distinction in contrast to Leonard Schapiro who questions the separation of Party and Soviet apparatuses at the highest levels (see Schapiro, "The Party's New Rules," *Problems of Communism* 11, no. 1 (1962): 31–32.

35. See G. Glezerman, *KPSS—rukovodiashchaia sila sotsialisticheskogo gosudarstva* (Moscow, 1954), p. 54.

36. V. M. Lesnoi, *Rukovodiashchaia rol'KPSS v sovetskom gosudarstve* (Moscow, 1961), p. 25.

37. This clear premise for total politicization was recently affirmed by the first secretary of the Georgian Communist party at the Twenty-third Congress (*XXIII S"ezd KPSS, 29 marta–8 aprelia 1966, stenograficheskii otchet* (Moscow, 1966), 1 :184 [hereafter cited as *XXIII S"ezd, otchet*]).

38. This is the normal sense in which political guidance is used. See, for example, Ia. V. Storozheva, ed., *Voprosy partiinoi raboty* (Moscow, 1959), p. 44 (hereafter cited as *Voprosy partiinoi raboty* (1959).

39. Slepov and Shitarev, *Leninskie normy*, p. 48.

40. Slepov, *Higher and lower Party organs*, pp. 42–43.

41. L. Slepov, *Mestnye partiinye organy* (Moscow, 1954), pp. 9—10.

42. *Ibid.*, p. 9.

43. P. F. Pigalev, *Mestnye partiinye organy–organy politiches kogo i organizatsionnogo rukovodstva* (Moscow, 1962), p. 15.

44. The economic responsibilities of the local Party organs are heavily emphasized by Slepov, *Mestnye partiinye organy*, p. 10.

45. Glezerman, *op. cit.*, p. 246; Denisov and Kirichenko, *op. cit.*, p. 205.

46. Lesnoi, *op. cit.*, p. 30.

47. Glezerman, *op. cit.*, p. 246.

48. The ideal Communist leader who functions as a guide and teacher is depicted in G. Krivoshein, *Partiinaia zhizn'*, no. 8 (1961): 11—17; and G. Shitarev, *Kommunist*, no. 9 (1960): 48–60.

49. A. M. Dimitrev, in A. P. Fillipov, ed., *Voprosy partiinogo stroitel'stva* (Leningrad, 1962), pp. 159–61 (hereafter cited as *Voprosy partiinogo stroitel'stva*); for a detailed and frank discussion of the problems of technically handling a large *nomenklatura*, see the essay by N. N. Popov, *ibid.*, pp. 329–30.

50. V. I. Gorev, in K. I. Suvorov, ed., *Nekotorye voprosy organizatsionno-partiinoi raboty v sovremennykh usloviiakh* (Moscow, 1961), p. 289.

51. John A. Armstrong, *The Soviet Bureaucratic Elite: A Case Study of the Ukrainian Apparatus* (New York, 1959), p. 35.

52. *Ibid.*, p. 37; quoted in Brzezinski and Huntington, *op. cit.*, p. 144.

53. *Voprosy partiinoi raboty* (1959), pp. 33–36.

54. *Ibid.*

55. David Granick, *The Red Executive* (Garden City, N. Y., 1960), pp. 144–48.

56. *Ibid.*, chap. 3. For an analysis of the social background of Party executives, see Brzezinski and Huntington, *op. cit.*, pp. 129–40, and Armstrong, *op. cit.*, chap. 2.

57. Granick, *op. cit.*, pp. 173, 108–9; also Joseph Berliner, "Managerial Incentives and Decision-Making: A Comparison of the United States and the Soviet Union," in U. S., Congress, Joint Economic Committee, *Comparisons of the United States and Soviet Economics*, pt. 1 (Washington, D. C., 1959), pp. 355–56.

58. A. Malyshev, *Partiinyi kontrol'deiatel'nosti administratsii predpriiatii* (Moscow, 1959), p. 64.

59. Leopold Haimson, "Decision-Making and Communication in Soviet Industry," in Margaret Mead, ed., *Studies in Soviet Communication*, vol. 2, pt. 5 (Cambridge, Mass., 1952), p. 348.

60. The active and organizational character of *proverka* is emphasized by Jerry F. Hough, "The Soviet Concept of the Relationship between the Lower Party Organs and the State Administration," *Slavic Review* 24, no. 2 (1965): 228–29. This is the most reasonable interpretation of such writers as Slepov and Shitarev, *Leninskie normy*, p. 52.

61. *Voprosy partiinoi raboty* (1955), pp. 56–57.

62. See, for example, *ibid.*, p. 128.

63. V. N. Bazovskii, in *Voprosy partiinogo stroitel'stvo* (1960), p. 138.

Chapter 1

1. V. I. Lenin, *Collected Works*, 4th ed., 45 vols. (Moscow, 1960–70), 33: 51.

2. *Ibid.*, p. 52.

3. *Ibid.*, 32: 334.

4. V. I. Lenin, *Sochineniia*, 4th ed., 37 vols. (Moscow, 1941–57), 25: 376.

5. *Ibid.*, 17: 23.

6. Lenin, *Collected Works*, 33: 480.

7. *VIII S"ezd RKP (b), mart 1919*, (Moscow, 1959), p. 19 (hereafter cited as *VIII S"ezd, protokoly*).

8. Alfred Meyer, *Leninism* (Cambridge, Mass., 1957), p. 69.

9. The conflict of authoritarian and bureaucratic means versus the humane and democratic goals of Marxism is the major theme of the Barrington Moore, Jr., *Soviet Politics: The Dilemma of Power*; The Role of Ideas in Social Change (Cambridge, Mass., 1950), pp. 59–60.

10. Lenin, *Sochineniia*, 5: 410.

11. *Ibid.*, pp. 437–38.

12. The charge of "organized distrust" implicit in Lenin's centralism was brought by Lieber, the leader of the Jewish Bund, following the Second Congress. For Lenin's rebuttal, see *ibid.*, 7: 231–32.

13. Moore, *op. cit.*, p. 66.

14. Lenin, *Sochineniia*, 11: 402–3.

15. Moore, *op. cit.*, pp. 68–70.

16. Meyer, *op. cit.*, p. 187.

17. Lenin, *Collected Works*, 27: 274.

18. *Ibid.*, 30: 470 ff.

19. *Ibid.*, p. 48 ff.

20. *VIII S"ezd, protokoly*, pp. 160–1.

21. *Ibid.*, pp. 25–26.

22. Lenin, *Sochineniia*, 31: 185.

23. Lenin, *Collected Works*, 31: 44.

24. Edward H. Carr, *The Bolshevik Revolution, 1917–1923*, 3 vols. (New York, 1950–1953), 2: 187.

25. Lenin, *Collected Works*, 27: 250–75.

26. Lenin, *Sochineniia*, 30: 286.
27. V. I. Lenin, *Polnoe sobranie sochinenii*, 5th ed., 55 vols. (Moscow, 1958–65), 37: 245.
28. Lenin, *Sochineniia*, 31: 44–45.
29. *Ibid.*, 30: 400–1.
30. Leonard Schapiro, *The Origins of the Communist Autocracy: Political Opposition in the Soviet State; The First Phase, 1917–1922* (Cambridge, Mass., 1956), pp. 221 ff.
31. *Ibid.*, p. 223.
32. *Ibid.*, p. 224. Detailed accounts of both Oppositions have been given in Robert V. Daniels, *The Conscience of the Revolution: Communist Opposition in Soviet Russia* (Cambridge, Mass., 1960), V; Carr, *op. cit.*, 2: 198–227; and Louis Fischer, *The Life of Lenin* (New York, 1964), pp. 438 ff.
33. Lenin, *Sochineniia*, 30: 401.
34. Schapiro, *op. cit.*, pp. 224–34; Daniels, *op. cit.*, pp. 125–27.
35. Lenin, *Collected Works*, 32: 50.
36. *Kommunisticheskaia partiia Sovetskogo Soiuza v rezoliutsiiakh i resheniiakh s''ezdov, konferentsii i plenumov Tsk*, pt. 1 (Moscow, 1954), pp. 530–33 (hereafter cited as *KPSS v rezoliutsiiakh*).
37. See Lenin, *Sochineniia*, 26: 91–92.
38. Carr, *op. cit.*, 1: 234.
39. Lenin, *Collected Works*, 31: 47–48.
40. *Ibid.*, p. 48.
41. *VII Ekstrennyi S''ezd, RKP (b), mart, 1918, Protokoly* (Moscow, 1962), pp. 171–2.
42. *VIII S''ezd, Protokoly*, p. 292.
43. *Ibid.* For the remarks of Sapronov, pp. 169–71; for those of Osinskii, pp. 164–7.
44. *Ibid.*, pp. 181–2.
45. *Ibid.*, p. 289.
46. *Ibid.*, p. 292.
47. *Ibid.*, p. 429.
48. Krestinskii, *X S''ezd, RKP (b), mart 1921, stenograficheskii otchet* (Moscow, 1963), p. 56 (hereafter cited as *X S''ezd, otchet*).
49. *Ibid.*, pp. 311–12.
50. See Leonard Schapiro, *The Communist Party of the Soviet Union* (New York, 1960), chap. 13 (hereafter cited as *History CPSU*).
51. *Izvestiia tsentral'nogo komiteta*, no. 21 (1920): 7 (hereafter cited as *Izvestiia TsK*).
52. *IX S''ezd RKP (b), mart–aprel' 1920, protokoly* (Moscow, 1960), pp. 62–63.
53. *VIII S''ezd, protokoly*, p. 22.
54. Merle Fainsod, *Smolensk Under Soviet Rule* (Cambridge, Mass., 1958), p. 37.
55. *X S''ezd, otchet*, pp. 83–84.
56. *VIII S''ezd, protokoly*, p. 294.
57. *X S''ezd, otchet*, pp. 57–66.
58. A. V. Venediktov, *Organizatsiia gosudarstvennoi promyshlennosti v SSSR*, 2 vols. (Leningrad, 1957, 1961), 1: 435–39.
59. *Ibid.*, 440.
60. P. J. D. Wiles, *The Political Economy of Communism*, pp. 29—30.
61. Alexander Baykov, *The Development of the Soviet Economic System* (Cambridge, Eng., 1946), pp. 7—8. For other essentially similar evaluations, see Wiles, *op. cit.*; Maurice Dobb, *Soviet Economic Development since 1917*, (New York, 1948), pp. 97 ff.

62. Jeremy R. Azrael, *Managerial Power and Soviet Politics* (Cambridge, Mass., 1966), chap. 2.
63. *Ibid.*; Carr, *op. cit.*, 2: 184–85.
64. Carr, *op. cit.*, 183–84.
65. Lenin, *Sochineniia*, 30: 108.
66. Venediktov, *op. cit.*, 1: 441–42.
67. Simon Liberman, *Building Lenin's Russia* (Chicago, 1945), pp. 37–38.
68. *Ibid.*
69. Lenin, *Sochineniia*, 28: 303.
70. Carr, *op. cit.*, 1: 224–26.
71. Fainsod, *op. cit.*, pp. 36–42.
72. A. A. Dobrodemov and A. N. Ponomarev, *Ocherki istorii moskovskoi organizatsii KPSS* (Moscow, 1966), pp. 309 ff.
73. V. P. Antonov-Saratovskii, *Sovety v epokhu voennogo kommunizma, 1918–1921*, 2 vols. (Moscow, 1928–29), 1: 117, 172, 406–7, 436–37.
74. *Ibid.*, 2:375.
75. Lenin, *Polnoe sobranie*, 45: 88–89.
76. *Ibid.*, 43: 210.
77. *Ibid.*, 45: 112.
78. *Ibid.*, 43: 230.
79. *Ibid.*, 45: 122–23; see remarks at Eleventh Congress.
80. *Ibid.*, pp. 114 ff.
81. Lenin, *Sochineniia*, 33: 356–58.
82. *Ibid.*, pp. 326 ff. Lenin, however, was inconsistent since he held at other times for the greatest possible scope for the localities (*Sochineniia*, 32: 415).
83. Lenin, *Polnoe sobranie*, 45: 86.
84. Lenin, *Sochineniia*, 43: 391.
85. Lenin, *Polnoe sobranie*, 45: 81–82.
86. Lenin, *Sochineniia*, 33: 440–4.
87. Moore, *op. cit.*, pp. 131 ff.
88. Azrael, *op. cit.*, pp. 76 ff.
89. L. Krasin, *XII S"ezd RKP (b), 17–25 aprelia 1923, Stenograficheskii otchet* (Moscow, 1968), pp. 124–27.
90. *Ibid.*, pp. 142–45.
91. *Ibid.*, p. 47.
92. J. V. Stalin, *Works*, 13 vols. (Moscow, 1952–1955), 10: 106 ff.
93. Edward H. Carr, *Socialism in One Country, 1924–1926*, vol. 1 (New York, 1959), p. 201.
94. *Ibid.*
95. Robert V. Daniels, "The Secretariat and the Local Organizations in the Russian Communist Party, 1921–1925," *American Slavic and East European Review* 16, no. 1 (1957): 35 ff.
96. *X S"ezd, otchet*, p. 56.
97. *XIV S"ezd VKP (b), 18–31 dekabria 1925, stenograficheskii otchet* (Moscow, 1926), p. 67 (hereafter cited as *XIV S"ezd, otchet*).
98. *XV S"ezd VKP (b), dekabr' 1927, stenograficheskii otchet*, I (Moscow, 1961), 123 (hereafter cited as *XV S"ezd, otchet*).
99. *XI S"ezd, RKP (b), mart–aprel' 1922, stenograficheskii otchet* (Moscow, 1961), pp. 60–63 (hereafter cited as *XI S"ezd, otchet*).

100. *XV S"ezd, otchet*, 1: 123.

101. *Ibid.*

102. *XIII S"ezd, RKP (b), stenograficheskii otchet* (Moscow, 1963), p. 132.

103. *XI S"ezd, otchet*, p. 53.

104. *Spravochnik partiinogo rabotnika*, (Moscow, 1927), pp. 509–10 (hereafter cited as *Spravochnik* (1927).

105. *XV S"ezd, otchet*, I: 115.

106. Schapiro, *History CPSU*, p. 311.

107. Aleksandrov [pseud.], *Kto upravliaet Rossiei?* (Berlin, 1933), chap. 4.

108. *XIV S"ezd, otchet*, pp. 526, 535.

109. *Saratovskaia partiinaia organizatsiia, 1921–1925*, 2 vols. (Saratov, 1957), pp. 230, 303, 317.

110. *Izvestiia TsK*, no. 20 (1928): 14–16.

111. *Ibid.*, no. 4 (1927): 4–5.

112. *Ibid.*, no. 20 (1928): 16.

113. *XI S"ezd, otchet*, p. 51.

114. *Spravochnik* (1927), pp. 555–57.

115. *Izvestiia TsK*, nos. 16–17 (1928): 20–21; for additional information on the instructor's role: *Spravochnik* (1927), p. 247; *Izvestiia TsK*, no. 18 (1926): 5—6; nos. 7–8 (1927): 1–3.

116. *KPSS v rezoliutsiiakh*, I: 771–72.

117. *XV S"ezd, otchet*, I: 115.

118. *Izvestiia TsK*, no. 15 (1928): 17–18.

119. *Ibid.*, nos. 16–17 (1928): 6.

120. Aaron Yugow, *Economic Trends in Soviet Russia* (London, 1930), p. 72.

121. Venediktov, *op. cit.*, 2: 56 ff.

122. *Ibid.*, pp. 41–42, 51–52.

123. Baykov, *op. cit.*, pp. 113—15.

124. *Ibid.*, pp. 114–15.

125. *Ibid.*, p. 116.

126. *Ibid.*

127. *XV S"ezd, otchet*, I: 447. As an example, Ordzhonikidze cited the Vesenkha decision approving an expenditure of 266 rubles for repairing a plant in a sugar trust.

128. *Ibid.*, pp. 459–60, 551–52.

129. *Direktivy KPSS i Sovetskogo Pravitel'stva po khoziaistvennym voprosam*, 4 vols. (Moscow, 1957–1959), 1: 501–2 (hereafter cited as *Direktivy KPSS*).

130. *Izvestiia TsK*, no. 13 (1927): 2; *ibid.*, nos. 12–13 (1926): 8 and 9.

131. *IX S"ezd, protokoly*, pp. 307–9.

132. *Izvestiia TsK*, no. 3 (1923): 33–37.

133. *Ibid.*, no. 5 (1923): 26–27.

134. *Ibid.*, nos. 22–23 (1925): 6–7.

135. *Bol'shevik*, no. 8 (1928): 64–65.

136. *Izvestiia TsK*, no. 1 (1926): 2–3.

137. *Saratovskaia partiinaia organizatsiia*, pp. 39, 128–29, 142, 295.

138. *XV S"ezd, otchet*, 1: 77.

139. *Izvestiia TsK*, nos. 33–34 (1926): 4.

140. *Bol'shevik*, no. 7 (1925): 60–71.

141. *Izvestiia TsK*, nos. 45–46 (1926): 3–4.

142. *Ibid.*, nos. 24–25 (1926): 11–12.

143. *Ibid.*, nos. 5–6 (1927): 4.
144. *Ibid.*, nos. 3–4 (1926): 2–3.
145. See Kossior's remarks, *XV S''ezd, otchet*, I: 107.
146. *Bol'shevik*, no. 7 (1925): 60–71.
147. *Izvestiia TsK*, no. 1 (1923): 31.
148. Schapiro, *History CPSU*, p. 313.
149. *Izvestiia TsK*, no. 8 (1925): 2.
150. *KPSS v rezoliutsiiakh*, 1: 627–28.
151. *Izvestiia TsK*, no. 39 (1925): 1–2.
152. *Spravochnik* (1927), pp. 570–73.
153. *Direktivy KPSS*, I: 442–43.

Chapter 2

1. Alexander Ehrlich, *The Soviet Industrialization Debate, 1924–1928* (Cambridge, Mass.: Harvard University Press, 1960), particularly chaps. 1 and 2.

2. The positions of Left and Right and Stalin's position in the debate are neatly summarized in Alexander Ehrlich, "Stalin's Views on Economic Development," in E. J. Simmons, ed., *Continuity and Change in Russian and Soviet Thought* (Cambridge, Mass., 1955), pp. 81–99.

3. For an excellent historical review of the changing policies, see Edward H. Carr and R. W. Davies, *Foundations of a Planned Economy, 1926–1929*, vol. I, pt. 1 (London, 1969), pp. 271 ff.

4. Cf. Boris Nicolaevsky, "The Letter of an Old Bolshevik," in Janet D. Zagoria, ed., *Power and the Soviet Elite* (New York: Praeger, 1965), pp. 26–65.

5. The literature on the command economy is extensive. Among notable recent contributions, in addition to those cited, are Alexander Ehrlich, "Development Strategy and Planning: The Soviet Experience," in Max F. Millikan, ed., *National Economic Planning* (New York, 1967), pp. 233–78; Z. M. Fallenbuchl, "The Communist Pattern of Industrialization," *Soviet Studies* 21, no. 4 (1970): 458–84; Gregory Grossman, *Economic Systems* (Englewood Cliffs, N. J., 1967), pp. 75 ff.

6. Herbert S. Levine, "Pressure and Planning in the Soviet Economy," in Henry Rosovsky, ed., *Industrialization in Two Systems* (New York, 1966), p. 270.

7. Stalin, however, was prepared to sacrifice growth for power when circumstances demanded it. During the 1937 purges of the Party and apparatus, industrial growth slipped to under 3 percent for the years 1937–40. See Naum Jasny, *Soviet Industrialization 1928–1952* (Chicago, 1961), pp. 181–98.

8. *Ibid.*, pp. 6 ff.

9. *Ibid.*, pp. 7–8.

10. Abram Bergson, *The Real National Income of Soviet Russia since 1928* (Cambridge, Mass., 1961), p. 25. As Professor Bergson points out, "Contrary to common supposition, the industrial worker fared no better than the peasants under Stalin's five year plans."

11. Jasny, *op. cit.*, pp. 72–78.

12. *Ibid.*, pp. 181–98; 236–45.

13. Abram Bergson, *Planning and Productivity under Soviet Socialism* (New York, 1968), pp. 22, table 1.

14. Abram Bergson, *The Economics of Soviet Planning*, (New Haven, 1965), pp. 327 ff.

15. Bergson, *Planning and Productivity*, p. 33.

16. Samuel P. Huntington, *Political Order in Changing Societies*, pp. 26–27.

17. Leonard Schapiro, *History CPSU*, pp. 397–98.

18. See Robert Conquest, *Power and Policy in the USSR*, pp. 31–37.

19. Jeremy R. Azrael, *Managerial Power and Soviet Politics*, pp. 104 ff.

20. Merle Fainsod, in Joseph La Palombara, ed., *Bureaucracy and Political Development* (Princeton, N. J.: 1963), p. 256.

21. Jeremy R. Azrael, "The Internal Dynamics of the CPSU, 1917–1967," in Samuel P. Huntington and Clement H. Moore, eds., *Authoritarian Politics in Modern Society*, pp. 268 ff.

22. J. V. Stalin, *Works*, 2: 114–15.

23. For an early indication of Stalin's authoritarianism, see his attack on Martov, *ibid.*, 1: 63 ff.

24. *Ibid.*, 1: 56, 125 ff.

25. *Ibid.*, 2: 198.

26. *Ibid.*, 1: 258.

27. *Ibid.*, 1: 65–70.

28. *Ibid.*

29. *Ibid.*, 2: 301, 359–61.

30. *Ibid.*, 1: 37–38, 44–48.

31. *Ibid.*, 3: 55.

32. *Ibid.*, 6: 181–82.

33. *Ibid.*

34. *Ibid.*

35. *Ibid.*, 8: 34–35.

36. *Ibid.*, 10: 106 ff.

37. Leon Trotskii, *The New Course*, trans. by Max Schachtman (New York, 1943), p. 22.

38. *KPSS v rezoliutsiiakh*, I: 780.

39. Stalin, *op. cit.*, 9: 3–155 for his detailed attack on Trotskii.

40. J. V. Stalin, *Problems of Leninism*, 11th ed. (Moscow, 1954), pp. 172–73.

41. *Ibid.*

42. Nikolai Bukharin, *The Path to Socialism and the Worker-Peasant Bond*, trans. by Eugene Hardy (Moscow-Leningrad, 1925), pp. 48–59.

43. Stalin, *Works*, 12: 349, 363.

44. Stalin, *Problems of Leninism*, p. 194.

45. Stalin, *Works*, 13: 41.

46. *Ibid.*, p. 112.

47. Herbert Marcuse, *Soviet Marxism, a Critical Analysis* (New York: Columbia University Press, 1958, Vintage, 1961), p. 90.

48. *XVIII S''ezd VKP (b), 10–21 marta 1939, stenograficheskii otchet* (Moscow, 1939), p. 33 (hereafter cited as *XVIII S''ezd, otchet*).

49. *XVII S''ezd VKP (b), 26 ianvaria–10 fevralia 1934, stenograficheskii otchet* (Moscow, 1934), p. 30 (hereafter cited as *XVII S''ezd, otchet*).

50. *Bol'shevik*, no. 3 (1946): 1–9.

51. For examples of a stubborn, if guarded, defense of the traditional notion of the leading role, see the following articles in *Bol'shevik:* K. Ostrovitianov, no. 21 (1947):

33–48; Ts. Stepanian, no. 14 (1949): 10–26; M. Zhuravkov, no. 17 (1949): 60–61; D. Chesnokov, no. 18 (1950): 9–21; L. Slepov, no. 2 (1951): 47.

52. P. Pospelov, *Bol'shevik*, no. 20 (1947): 27–39; M. A. Suslov, *Bol'shevik*, no. 2 (1948): 1–11.

53. *Izvestiia TsK*, no. 27 (1928): 1–3.

54. *XVI S''ezd VKP (b)*, 26 iiunia–13 iiulia 1930, stenograficheskii otchet (Moscow, 1935), pp. 93–94 (hereafter cited as *XVI S''ezd, otchet*).

55. *Ibid.*

56. *Izvestiia TsK*, no. 4 (1929): 2–4; nos. 5–6 (1929): 8–10.

57. *XVII S''ezd, otchet*, pp. 527–28.

58. For a discussion by Stalin of the apparat, see *Works*, 12: 345–46.

59. *Partiinoe stroitel'stvo*, no. 5 (1931), 12. Also, Leonard Schapiro, *History CPSU* pp. 447–48.

60. *Partiinoe stroitel'stvo*, no. 24 (1931): 12.

61. *Ibid.*, nos. 13–14 (1933): 11–13.

62. *XVII S''ezd, otchet*, pp. 38–39.

63. *Ibid.*

64. *Partiinoe stroitel'stvo*, nos. 9–10 (1931): 40–42.

65. *Ibid.*, nos. 11–12 (1930): 30–36.

66. *Ibid.*, no. 6 (1932): 18 ff.

67. *Ibid.* Fifty percent of the oblast and 65 percent of the okrug secretaries were in their jobs less than a year, and only 20 percent of obkom secretaries were in the same post for over two years.

68. *Ibid.*, nos. 1–2 (1933): 9.

69. An excellent account of the change in formal structure can be found in A. V. Venediktov, *Organizatsiia gosudarstvennoi promyshlennosti v SSSR*, 2: 249–98.

70. *Ibid.*

71. For the relevant decrees, see *Direktivy KPSS*, 2: 333, 343–44.

72. F. V. Samokhvalov, *Sovety narodnogo khoziaistva, 1917–1932* (Moscow, 1964), pp. 266–301.

73. *Direktivy KPSS*, 2: 117–19, 120–21.

74. L. Kaganovich, *XVII S''ezd, otchet*, p. 538.

75. *XVI Konferentsiia VKP (b), aprel' 1929, stenograficheskii otchet* (Moscow, 1962), pp. 492–95.

76. *Ibid.*, p. 495.

77. *XVI S''ezd, otchet*, p. 317.

78. *XVII S''ezd, otchet*, p. 534.

79. *XVI S''ezd, otchet*, p. 317.

80. *XVII S''ezd, otchet*, p. 535.

81. *Ibid.*, p. 537; see also the series of decrees of the Central Committee of 8 August 1929, 5 February 1930, 5 March 1930, in *Direktivy KPSS*, 2: 97–106.

82. *Partiinoe stroitel'stvo*, no. 2 (1931): 15.

83. Zbigniew K. Brzezinski, *The Permanent Purge* (Cambridge, Mass., 1956), pp. 52–56.

84. *Bol'shevik*, no. 3 (1931): 15–16.

85. Merle Fainsod, *How Russia Is Ruled*, 1st and rev. eds. (Cambridge, Mass., 1953, 1963), pp. 360–63; also Robert Conquest, *The Great Terror* (New York, 1968), pp. 549–56. The attack on the non-Party industrialists was clearly pressed both to provide scapegoats for the industrial failures of the plan as well as to eliminate opponents of the bacchanalian plans of the period.

86. For Stalin's views of the purge, see *Works*, 13: 74, as well as his report to the Sixteenth Congress, *ibid.*, 13: 352–53.
87. *XVI S''ezd, otchet*, p. 96.
88. *Bol'shevik*, no. 3 (1931): 12.
89. In 1931, the Politburo heard progress reports every five days on the construction of the Stalingrad Tractor Plant.
90. Alexander Barmine, *One Who Survived* (New York, 1945), pp. 211–13.
91. *Partiinoe stroitel'stvo*, no. 5 (1931): 14 ff.
92. *XVI S''ezd, otchet*, p. 96.
93. *Bol'shevik*, no. 3 (1931): 24.
94. *Direktivy KPSS*, 2: 19.
95. *Ibid.*, p. 378.
96. Merle Fainsod, *Smolensk under Soviet Rule*, pp. 51–53; S. P. Kniazev, ed., *Ocherki istorii leningradskoi organizatsii KPSS*, 2 vols., (Leningrad, 1968), 2: 373 ff.
97. A. A. Dobrodemov and A. N. Ponomarev, *Ocherki istorii moskovskoi organizatsii KPSS*, p. 475.
98. *Partiinoe stroitel'stvo*, no. 10 (1932): 15 ff.
99. Dobrodemov and Ponomarev, *op. cit.*, pp. 478–79.
100. *Bol'shevik*, nos. 5–6 (1932): 4–6.
101. Fainsod, *Smolensk under Soviet Rule*, pp. 318–19.
102. *Partiinoe stroitel'stvo*, no. 17 (1933): 19–21.
103. Stalin, *Works*, 12: 116.
104. *Ibid.*
105. *XVI S''ezd, otchet*, p. 51.
106. B. N. Ponomarev, ed., *Istoriia Kommunisticheskoi Partii Sovetskogo Soiuza* (Moscow, 1959), p. 408.
107. *XVI S''ezd, otchet*, p. 51.

Chapter 3

1. Alexander Barmine, *One Who Survived*, p. 199.
2. J. V. Stalin, *Problems of Leninism*, p. 783.
3. Leonard Schapiro, *History CPSU*, pp. 438–40. The new policy of recruiting line officials in the state and industrial apparatus began as early as May 1930. Recruiting the "best people," as T. H. Rigby has pointed out, integrated the new power groups created by industrialization but at the cost of divorcing the Party from the average Soviet citizen. T. H. Rigby, *Communist Party Membership in the USSR, 1917–1967* pp. 410–11, 426 ff.
4. *KPSS v rezoliutsiiakh*, 3: 230–31.
5. *Partiinoe stroitel'stvo*, no. 17 (1935): 73–74 for the 1935 structure of Leading Party Organs.
6. *Ibid.*, no. 7 (1935): 47.
7. Merle Fainsod, *Smolensk Under Soviet Rule*, p. 114.
8. *KPSS v rezoliutsiiakh*, 3: 371–73.
9. *Ibid.*, 433–34.
10. Merle Fainsod, *How Russia Is Ruled*, 1st ed., chart 5, p. 175.
11. *Bol'shevik*, no. 7 (1937): 16.

12. Fainsod, *How Russia Is Ruled*, p. 178; see also Schapiro, *History CPSU*, p. 525 and n. 1.

13. Schapiro, *op. cit.*

14. George Fischer, "The Number of Soviet Party Executives: A Research Note," *Soviet Studies* 16, no. 3 (1965): 330–33.

15. *XVIII S"ezd, otchet*, p. 529; also *Bol'shevik*, nos. 15–16 (1939): pp. 60–61.

16. John Armstrong, *The Soviet Bureaucratic Elite*, pp. 21–22.

17. *Ibid.*, pp. 31 ff.

18. *Ibid.*, pp. 22–23.

19. *Bol'shevik*, no. 7 (1937): 20; for Zhdanov's remarks, nos. 5–6 (1937): 6 ff.

20. G. Malenkov, *Current Soviet Policies*, Leo Gruliow, ed. (New York, 1952), 1: 118–20 (hereafter cited as *CSP* and volume).

21. Fainsod, *Smolensk Under Soviet Rule*, p. 86.

22. B. N. Ponomarev, ed., *Istoriia kommunisticheskoi partii sovetskogo soiuza*, p. 600.

23. The arbitrary and only partially controlled power of the territorial first secretary was a major theme of the February–March 1937 plenum and a principal issue in Khrushchev's organization report to the Nineteenth Congress (for the latter, see *CSP*, 1: 135).

24. B. Deriugin, in *Partiinaia rabota v promyshlennosti* (Moscow, 1956), p. 255; other examples can be found in *Partiinoe stroitel'stvo*, no. 10 (1941): 38–39; *Partiinaia zhizn'* no. 5 (1947): 34.

25. *Bol'shevik*, no. 23 (1948): 32–41.

26. For specific accounts of the continuing low status of the instructor at the local level, see L. Slepov, *Mestnye partiinye organy*, pp. 56 ff.; *Voprosy partiinoi raboty* (1955), p. 117; *Partiinaia zhizn'*, no. 5 (1947), 42–43; *ibid.*, no. 15 (1947) 47 ff.

27. Slepov, *op. cit.*, p. 58.

28. Bazovskii, in *Voprosy partiinogo stroitel'stva*, p. 144.

29. *Ibid.*, pp. 143–44. The problem of smooth coordination and operation was related to each department's effort to create its own closed and inviolate structure, or *polochka* (L. Slepov, *Higher and lower Party organs*, p. 105).

30. Stalin, *op. cit.*, pp. 787–88.

31. *Ibid.*

32. *CSP*, 1: 120–21.

33. *XVIII S'ezd, otchet*, pp. 528–29.

34. *Partiinoe stroitel'stvo*, nos. 4–5 (1941): 28 ff.

35. For a frank consideration of this problem, see *Bol'shevik*, no. 12 (1948): 8, and *ibid.*, no. 20 (1947): 27–39, particularly p. 33.

36. *Direktivy KPSS*, 2: 414–47.

37. *Ibid.*, p. 512.

38. Fainsod, *How Russia Is Ruled*, pp. 333–34.

39. V. A. Vlasov, *Osnovy sovetskogo gosudarstvennogo upravleniia* (Moscow, 1960), p. 147.

40. S. S. Studenikin, *Sovetskoe administrativnoe pravo*, p. 212.

41. A. Arakelian, *Industrial Management in the USSR* (Washington, D. C., 1950), pp. 123–36.

42. *Partiinoe stroitel'stvo*, no. 10 (1937): 24.

43. Zibigniew Brzezinski, *The Permanent Purge*, p. 52. For a recent analysis of the purge of the Red directors, see Jeremy R. Azrael, *Managerial Power and Soviet Politics*, pp. 96–100.

44. John A. Armstrong, *The Politics of Totalitarianism: The Communist Party of the Soviet Union from 1934 to the Present* (New York, 1961), pp. 93–94; also Azrael, *op. cit.*, chap. 8.

45. *Partiinoe stroitel'stvo*, nos. 11–12 (1940): 18–19.

46. For general assessments of the economic and managerial problems of the Soviet economy, see Gregory Grossman, "The Structure and Organization of the Soviet Economy," *Slavic Review* 21, no. 2 (1962): 203–22; Barry Richman, *Soviet Management* (Englewood Cliffs, N. J., 1965), pp. 108–11.

47. *Bol'shevik*, nos. 3–4 (1941): 13–17.

48. *Direktivy KPSS*, 2: 311–17.

49. *CSP*, 2: 154.

50. *Sovetskoe gosudarstvo i pravo*, no. 6 (1954): 11.

51. *Kommunist*, no. 7 (1954): 72. In 1956, about 80 percent of all accounting personnel were at the enterprise level. A. Efimov, *Perestroika upravleniia promyshlennostiu i stroitel'stvom v SSSR* (Moscow, 1957), p. 26.

52. N. A. Bulganin, *Current Digest of the Soviet Press* 7, no. 28 (1955): 13 ff. (hereafter cited as *CDSP* with volume and date).

53. An excellent description of the pressures and politics of Soviet economic administration can be found in Joseph Berliner, *Factory and Manager in the USSR* (Cambridge, Mass., 1957), particularly pp. 21–41; Ralf Dahrendorf, *Class and Class Conflict in Industrial Society* (Stanford, Calif., 1957), pp. 314–17; Fainsod, *How Russia Is Ruled*, pp. 417–19; and Leopold Haimson, in Margaret Mead, ed., *Soviet Attitudes toward Authority*, pp. 393–406.

54. A detailed catalog of the informal and illegal managerial practices developed under the ministerial system can be found in *Bol'shevik*, no. 14 (1951): 11–17; Alec Nove, "The Problem of 'Success Indicators' in Soviet Industry," *Economica* (February 1958): 1–13; Richman, *op. cit.*, pp. 109 ff.

55. *CSP*, 2: 161.

56. Bulganin, *op. cit.*, pp. 15–16.

57. A comprehensive review of the serious problems of capital construction is contained in *Kommunist*, no. 8 (1954): 41–55.

58. Bulganin, *op. cit.*, p. 9. For other commentary on the problem of technical progress, see the following issues of *Promyshlenno-ekonomicheskaia gazeta:* no. 3 (1956): 5; no. 11 (1956): 3; no. 20 (1956): 2; no. 34 (1956): 2; and no. 51 (1956): 1.

59. Bulganin, *op. cit.*, p. 15: *Kommunist*, no. 7 (1953): 37–53; also, *Promyshlenno-ekonomicheskaia gazeta*, no. 14 (1956): 1.

60. *Kommunist*, no. 10 (1955): 3; Efimov, *op. cit.*, pp. 23–24.

61. *CSP*, 2: 39.

62. Alf Edeen, "The Civil Service: Its Composition and Status," in Cyril E. Black, ed., *The Transformation of Russian Society: Aspects of Social Change since 1861* (Cambridge, Mass.: Harvard University Press, 1960), p. 290.

63. Ponomarev, *op. cit.*, p. 483.

64. *CSP*, 2: 187.

65. Much of the following data is drawn from the excellent summary of the work of the central Party apparatus in Louis Nemzer, "The Kremlin's Professional Staff, the 'Apparatus' of the Central Committee, Communist Party of the Soviet Union," *American Political Science Review* 44, no. 1, (1950): 85.

66. *Ibid.*, pp. 70–72.

67. F. Titov, *Kommunist*, no. 1 (1958): 61; L. Slepov and D. Shumsky, *Pravda*, 20 June 1960, p. 2; see also A. Viatkin, *Partiinaia zhizn'*, no. 22 (1955): 16–17.

68. Titov, *op. cit.*; V. Churaev in *Partiinaia rabota v promyshlennosti*, p. 191; P. F. Pigalev, *Mestnye partiinye organy*, p. 12.

69. *Partiinoe stroitel'stvo*, no. 6 (1937): 27–28; *ibid.*, no. 9 (1934): 7; *Bol'shevik*, no. 21 (1934): 8–11. For the role of local Party organs during the war, see Arakelian, *op. cit.*, p. 157; *Bol'shevik*, no. 14 (1941): 2; *Direktivy KPSS*, 2: 406–7.

70. Armstrong, *The Politics of Totalitarianism*, p. 97; David Granick, *Management of the Industrial Firm in the USSR: A Study in Soviet Economic Planning* (New York, 1959), p. 205.

71. Slepov, *Mestnye partiinye organy*, pp. 25–26.

72. *Ibid.*

73. *Voprosy partiinoi raboty* (1955), pp. 131–33.

74. *CDSP*, 7, no. 36 (1955): 22.

75. *Pravda*, 31 May 1955, p. 2.

76. See V. Churaev, *Partiinaia zhizn'*, no. 15 (1955): 10–11; for specific examples, see *Pravda*, 29 December 1946, p. 2; *Pravda*, 7 October 1948, p. 2.

77. Bulganin, *op. cit.*, p. 19.

78. Slepov and Shumskii, *op. cit.*, p. 2; for a general discussion of "localism" in the Party apparatus, see K. Zhukov, *Bol'shevik*, no. 20 (1952): 83 ff.; Slepov, *Bol'shevik*, no. 21 (1952): 66–71.

79. Iakolev, *Partiinaia rabota v promyshlennosti*, pp. 70–71; *Pravda*, 10 October 1955, p. 2.

80. Slepov and Ilinskii, *Pravda*, 10 May 1955, p. 2.

81. Iakolev, *op. cit.*

82. V. K. Klimenko, *CSP*, 1: 218–19.

83. Slepov, *Bol'shevik*, no. 2 (1951): 51; *Pravda*, 2 November 1955, p. 2.

84. *Pravda*, 26 May 1953, p. 2; *Pravda*, 2 November 1955, p. 2; *Partiinaia rabota v promyshlennosti*, pp. 247 ff; Slepov, *Bol'shevik*, no. 2 (1951): 51; *Partiinaia zhizn'* no. 9 (1956): 7.

85. The complex authority relationships among the different levels of the Party apparatus are thoroughly discussed by Jerry F. Hough, *The Soviet Prefects: The Role of Local Party Organs in Industrial Decision-Making* (Cambridge, Mass., 1969), pp. 28 ff.

86. *Partiinaia zhizn'*, no. 17 (1955): 23 ff.; *Pravda*, 16 October 1948, p. 2.

87. L. Martynev, *Instruktor gorkoma i raikoma* (Moscow, 1956), passim.

88. Slepov, *Mestnye partiinye organy*, p. 37.

89. Armstrong, *The Politics of Totalitarianism*, p. 96.

90. *Ibid.*; cf. *Pravda*, 8 May 1946, p. 2.

91. *Pravda*, 23 December 1946, p. 1.

92. For an extensive analysis of the causes of the relative passivity of the local Party's role in industrial decision-making, see *Partiinaia zhizn'*, no. 17 (1955): 19–27. Other complaints can be found in numerous articles preceding the Nineteenth Party Congress; for examples, *Pravda* editorial, 7 February 1952, p. 2; *Pravda*, 16 April 1952, p. 2.

Chapter 4

1. The rationalization processes of Party control under Khrushchev are covered in part in Paul Cocks, "The Rationalization of Party Control," in Chalmers Johnson, ed., *Change in Communist Systems* (Stanford, Calif., 1970), pp. 166 ff. As Cocks

points out, rationalization concerns perfecting existing machinery rather than systemic change.

2. The effect on the political system of the decline of terror is discussed in Alexander Dallin and George W. Breslauer, "Political Terror in the Post-Mobilization Stage," in Johnson, *op. cit.*, pp. 191–214.

3. Zbigniew Brzezinski, "The Soviet Political System: Transformation or Degeneration," in Zbigniew Brzezinski, ed., *Dilemmas of Change in Soviet Politics*, pp. 13–14.

4. Edward Crankshaw, *Khrushchev: A Career* (New York, 1966), p. 225.

5. *Ibid.*, p. 235.

6. Merle Fainsod, "Khrushchevism," in Milorad M. Drachkovitch, ed., *Marxism in the Modern World* (Stanford, Calif., 1965), pp. 111 ff.

7. See R. V. Burks, "Technology and Political Change in Eastern Europe," in Johnson, *op. cit.*, pp. 266–67. Burks traces very clearly the close relationship between legitimation of the regime, economic development, and technical progress.

8. This point is persuasively made by Jeremy R. Azrael, *Managerial Power and Soviet Politics*, p. 144.

9. Gregory Grossman, in Donald W. Treadgold, ed., *Soviet and Chinese Communism, Similarities and Differences* (Seattle, Wash.: University of Washington Press, 1967), p. 294.

10. Robert Conquest, "Immobilism and Decay," in Brzezinski, *op. cit.*, p. 68.

11. There are several good biographies and perceptive appraisals of Khrushchev. Among the most useful, in addition to Crankshaw, are Mark Franklund, *Khrushchev* (New York, 1967); Konrad Kellen, *Khrushchev—A Political Portrait* (New York, 1961); Lazar Pistrak, *The Grand Tactician: Khrushchev's Rise to Power* (New York, 1961).

12. Crankshaw, *op. cit.*, p. 86.

13. Walter Lippmann, *The Communist World and Ours* (Boston, 1958), p. 27.

14. N. S. Khrushchev, *O kommunisticheskom vospitanii* (Moscow, 1964), p. 111 (hereafter cited as *O kom. vosp.*).

15. *Ibid.*

16. *CSP*, 2: 59.

17. *Ibid.*, 3: 41.

18. *Ibid.*, p. 66.

19. *Ibid.*, 2: 174.

20. *Ibid.*, pp. 174 ff.

21. *Ibid.*, p. 172.

22. *Ibid.*, p. 186.

23. *Ibid.*, p. 187.

24. *Ibid.*, p. 186.

25. *Ibid.*, p. 173.

26. *Ibid.*, p. 186.

27. *Ibid.*, p. 186.

28. George Lukacs, "Reflections on the Cult of Stalin," *Survey*, no. 47 (1963): 105.

29. Richard Lowenthal, "Development vs. Utopia in Communist Policy," in Johnson, *op. cit.*, p. 54.

30. Robert C. Tucker, "A Credo of Conservatism," in *Problems of Communism* 10, no. 5 (1961): 3 ff.

31. *Ibid.*; see also Khrushchev, *CDSP*, 13, no. 44 (1961): 8.

32. *CSP*, 2: 60.

33. *Ibid.*, 2: 57; *CDSP*, 13, no. 45 (1961): 51.

34. *CSP*, 2: 56; *O kom. vosp.*, p. 22; *CDSP*, 13, no. 17 (1960): 3.

35. *CSP*, 2: 56.

36. *Ibid.*, p. 55.

37. *Ibid.*, p. 175.

38. *Voprosy partiinoi raboty* (1959), pp. 345–46.

39. *Spravochnik partiinogo rabotnika* (Moscow, 1957), pp. 405, 408, 436.

40. *Ibid.*, p. 429.

41. *Ibid.*, p. 440.

42. *Ibid.*, pp. 441–42.

43. *Spravochnik partiinogo rabotnika* (Moscow, 1959), pp. 555–56. This emphasis on the degree of decentralization in the formal structure is not intended to be comprehensive. Informal delegation may have gone much further, particularly in economic decision-making. The evidence for such a contention, however, with the possible exception of the *nomenklatura*, is ambiguous.

44. *CDSP*, 13, no. 46 (1961): 31.

45. *CSP*, 2: 56.

46. Zbigniew Brzezinski and Samuel P. Huntington, *Political Power*, pp. 200–1.

47. G. Shitarev, *Voprosy istorii KPSS*, no. 7 (1964): 37.

48. John N. Hazard, "Has the Soviet State a New Function?" *Political Quarterly* 24, no. 4 (1962): 382 ff.; Donald D. Berry, "The Specialist in Soviet Decision-Making: The Adoption of a Law," *Soviet Studies* 16, no. 2 (1964): 154–65. The use of expert opinion to buttress competing positions also seems to have been frequent.

49. *CSP*, 1: 135.

50. *Ibid.*, 2: 78.

51. *Ibid.*, p. 58. These points are reiterated in L. Slepov and G. Shitarev, *Leninskie normy*, pp. 19 ff.

52. *CSP*, 1: 138.

53. *CSP*, 2: 195, for the change in the Party rules.

54. *CSP*, 1: 117.

55. N. S. Khrushchev, *Stroitel'stvo kommunizma v SSSR i razvitie sel'skogo khoziaistva*, 8 vols. (Moscow: 1963–1964), 5: 350.

56. *Ibid.*, p. 97; see also *O kom. vosp.*, p. 22. On the elitist character of the Party, see D. I. Tiurin, *Chlenstvo v KPSS* (Moscow, 1962), p. 6; P. F. Pigalev, *Mestnye partiinye organy*, pp. 11–13.

57. T. H. Rigby, "Social Orientation of Recruitment and Distribution of Membership in the Communist party of the Soviet Union," *American Slavic and East European Review* 16, no. 3 (1957): 277 ff.

58. *Ibid.* According to V. Gorin and V. Vasiliev, *Partiinaia zhizn'*, no. 5 (1960): 8, the normal recruitment of workers prior to the Twentieth Congress was 30–32 percent but for collective farmers only 10–11 percent.

59. Rigby, *op. cit.*, p. 279.

60. *Partiinaia zhizn'*, no. 1 (1962): 45–46.

61. *Ibid.*, p. 50.

62. *Ibid.*, p. 45.

63. *Ibid.*, pp. 47–48.

64. *Ibid.*, p. 48.

65. *Ibid.*, p. 49. In 1962, however, the Party was still dominated by men recruited during the Stalin era. Those who joined the Party prior to 1950 were an absolute majority of 60 percent in 1961, and the percentage of Communists with less than ten years membership actually declined from 60 percent in 1952 to 40 percent in 1961. As a

counterbalance, only 15.6 percent of the Party membership was over fifty years of age.

66. T. H. Rigby, *Communist Party Membership in the USSR, 1917–1967*, chap. 9 summarizes these conclusions.

67. Article 25 of the 1961 Party Rules; translated in John N. Hazard, *The Soviet System of Government*, 3rd ed. (Chicago, 1964), p. 151.

68. For an extensive analysis of the dynamics of Central Committee changeover, see Michael P. Gehlen, *The Communist Party of the Soviet Union* (Bloomington, 1969), pp. 50–57. Data on change within the territorial Party committees is contained in A. M. Bardinova, *Voprosy partiinogo stroitel'stva* (1962), pp. 152 ff.

69. Gehlen, *op. cit.* These data are derived from Frederick Fleron, "Representation of Career Types in the Soviet Political Leadership," in R. Barry Farrell, ed., *Political Leadership in Eastern Europe and the Soviet Union* (Chicago, 1970), table 6.1, p. 113.

70. Fleron, *op. cit.*, table 6.8, p. 125. The theoretical basis for Fleron's position as a systemic development is contained in Fleron, "Co-optation as a Mechanism of Adaptation to Change. The Soviet Political System," *Polity* 2, no. 2 (1969): 177–201.

71. A. D. Moshchevitin, *Podbor i vospitanie rukovodiashchikh kadrov* (Moscow 1962), p. 5; the data for the 1961 committees at the local level is in *Partiinaia zhizn'*, no. 1 (1962): 53.

72. Philip D. Stewart, *Political Power in the Soviet Union* (Indianapolis and New York, 1968), table 6, pp. 43 and 46.

73. For a sociological analysis of the Presidium, see Brzezinski and Huntington, *op. cit.*, p. 151; also table 9, p. 178.

74. Between March 1953 and February 1955, the Secretariat wavered between four and six; in 1956, the Secretariat expanded to eight and in July 1957 to ten. In May and July 1960, the Secretariat was cut in half. At the Twenty-second Congress, it rose again to eight.

75. For an analysis of the political implications of the 1961 changes in the Secretariat, see Michel Tatu, *Power in the Kremlin*, trans. by Helen Katal (New York, 1968), pp. 195–204.

76. At the republican and province levels, the secretariats were from five to seven; all secretaries were normally included in the nine to eleven-man bureaus. For a detailed study of change in the Stalingrad Obkom, see Stewart, *op. cit.*, pp. 83–133.

77. *CSP*, 2: 58; also *CDSP*, 13, no. 43 (1961), 7.

78. See, for example, Khrushchev's complaint about resistance to this notion in *Stroitel'stvo kommunizma*, 2: 126.

79. *CSP*, 2: 58.

80. *Spravochnik partiinogo rabotnika* (1957), pp. 410–15. For an extensive analysis of this issue, see Wolfgang Leonhard, *The Kremlin since Stalin*, trans. by Elizabeth Wiskemann (New York, 1962), pp. 280–82; Frederick C. Barghoorn, *Politics in the USSR* (Boston, 1966), chap. 4.

81. Churaev, *World Marxist Review*, 27.

82. Frol Kozlov, *World Marxist Review*, no. 6 (1962): 7, 9.

83. *Ibid.*

84. *Partiinaia zhizn'*, no. 3 (1962): 4.

85. M. Polekhin and F. Iakolev, *Partiinaia zhizn'*, no. 13 (1960): 13.

86. *Pravda*, 14 January 1962, p. 2.

87. See John A. Armstrong, *The Soviet Bureaucratic Elite*, pp. 88 ff. The importance of these general distinctions should be modified in terms of the effect of bureaucracy

on behavior. The effect of hierarchy and status on the work of ideological specialists is analyzed by Erik P. Hoffman, "Communication Theory and the Study of Soviet Politics," in Frederick J. Fleron, Jr., *Communist Studies and the Social Sciences*, pp. 379–96.

88. Among the most relevant studies are George Fischer, *The Soviet System and Modern Society* (New York, 1968); Michael P. Gehlen, "The Soviet Apparatchiki," in Farrell, *op. cit.*, pp. 140–56; Jerry F. Hough, *The Soviet Prefects*, chap. 3; and Stewart, *op. cit.*, chap. 7.

89. Gehlen, *op. cit.*, pp. 142 ff.; Hough, *op. cit.*, pp. 65 ff.

90. Fischer, *op. cit.*, pp. 25–26. His group includes Central Committee secretaries and department heads; first and second secretaries of republican committees; first secretaries of gorkomy of republican capital cities; and oblast first secretaries.

91. *Ibid.*, particularly pp. 39 ff and 74 ff.

92. Jerry Hough has pointed out in his important study that the systematic recruitment of Party officials with technical training and industrial experience actually began after the Great Purge. Khrushchev's expanded policy however, indicates a qualitatively new policy (Hough, *op. cit.*, pp. 43–47).

93. Armstrong, *op. cit.*, pp. 49 ff.

94. U.S., Congress, Senate, Committee on Governmental Operations, *National Policy Machinery in the Soviet Union* (Washington, D. C., 1960), chart 1, p. 25.

95. George Fischer, "The Number of Soviet Party Executives: A Research Note" *Soviet Studies* 16, no. 3 (1965): 330–33.

96. B. F. Shilov, *Voprosy partiinogo stroitel'stva* (1962), p. 255. The Perm Obkom was composed of nine departments and sixty-four instructors. In industrial oblasti, the departmental structure usually contained two or more specialized otdely.

97. Fischer, "The Number of Soviet Party Executives," *op. cit.*; this followed a Central Committee decree of 24 March 1956 ordering a 25–30 percent cut in regional Party organs (*Spravochnik partiinogo rabotnika* [1957], p. 406).

98. For a detailed examination of the evolution of the rural Party structures, see Howard Swearer, "Agricultural Administration under Khrushchev," in Roy D. Laird, ed., *Soviet Agricultural and Peasant Affairs* (Lawrence, Kansas, 1963), chap. 2.

99. *Spravochnik partiinogo rabotnika* (1957), p. 406.

100. *Sovetskaia Rossia*, 3 September 1959, p. 2; also *Spravochnik partiinogo rabotnika* (1957), p. 406.

101. Pigalev, *op. cit.*, p. 60.

102. Fischer, "The Number of Soviet Party Executives," *op. cit.*

103. G. I. Kliushing, *Partiinaia organizatsiia v borbe za pod''em promyshlennosti v gody semiletki* (Moscow, 1963), p. 81.

104. G. Shitarev, *Partiinaia zhizn'*, no. 11 (1961): 12.

105. Cocks, *op. cit.*

106. Kliushing, *op. cit.*, p. 72.

107. *Voprosy partiinoi raboty* (1959), p. 346.

108. G. Shitarev, *Partiinaia zhizn'*, no. 11 (1961): 15.

109. Kliushing, *op. cit.*, p. 72.

110. *Pravda*, 27 January 1962, p. 2.

111. P. Pigalev, *Kommunist*, no. 7 (1962): 61 ff. (hereafter cited as *Kommunist*).

112. V. Tsybul'ko, *Obshchestvennye nachala v partiinoi rabote* (Kiev, 1962), p. 75. In a Donetsk gorkom, for example, thirty-five engineers and technicians, seventeen steel specialists, and seventeen professors were added to the twelve engineers and technicians serving as staff instructors.

113. P. Pigalev, *Partiinaia zhizn'*, no. 24 (1961): 12–13.

114. Pigalev, *Kommunist*: 64.

115. I. Sytnik and M. Mizhnik, *Obshchestvennye nachala v partiinoi rabote*, pp. 123–24; G. Shitarev, *Partiinaia zhizn'*, no. 11 (1961): 14–15.

116. Khrushchev, *CDSP*, no. 43 (1961), 7.

117. *Partiinaia zhizn'*, no. 1 (1962): 53–54.

118. *Ibid.*

119. Hazard, *op. cit.*, p. 251.

120. For an indication of the opposition in the Ukraine to the new change in the Party Rules, see the remarks of Kazanets, *CDSP* 14, no. 7 (1962): 5.

121. *Partiinaia zhizn'*, no. 15 (1962): 9.

122. I. I. Petrovskii, in V. A. Smyshliaev, ed., *KPSS v period stroitel'stva kommunizma* (Leningrad: Izdatel'stvo Leningradskogo Universiteta, 1967) pp. 47–48.

123. *Spravochnik partiinogo rabotnika* (1961), pp. 555–61.

124. P. F. Pigalev, *Partiinaia zhizn'*, no. 24 (1961): 13.

125. V. V. Skriabin, *Novoe v rabote partorganizatsii po rukovodstvu promyshlennostiu* (Kiev, 1960), pp. 34 ff.

126. *Pravda*, 2 July 1961, p. 1.

127. *Spravochnik partiinogo rabotnika* (1961), pp. 564–65.

128. Skriabin, *op. cit.*

129. *XXII S''ezd KPSS, 17–31 oktiabria 1961, stenograficheskii otchet*, vol. 1 (Moscow, 1962), p. 237.

130. R. S. Sikov, in K. I. Suvorov, ed., *Partiia i massy* (Moscow, 1966), p. 101.

131. E. I. Bugaev and V. H. Leibson, *Besedy ob ustave KPSS*, p. 144.

132. *Sovetskaia Rossiia*, 2 February 1958, p. 1; *ibid.*, 1 November 1959, p. 1.

133. *Pravda*, 14 August 1961, p. 2; *ibid.*, 15 August 1961, p. 4.

134. *Partiinaia zhizn'*, no. 15 (1960): 29–31.

135. *Kommunist*, no. 13 (1964): 82.

136. *Partiinaia zhizn'*, no. 11 (1963): 8.

137. These familiar complaints are summarized in *Voprosy partiinoi raboty* (1959), pp. 364 ff.

138. I. Vivdychenko, in *Partiinaia rabota v promyshlennosti*, p. 9.

139. *Sovetskaia Rossiia*, 7 October 1958, p. 2.

140. V. Bazovskii, *Voprosy partiinogo stroitel'stva*, pp. 142–44.

141. For an indication of the deep resistance of the apparatus to the public principle, see Pigalev, *Kommunist*: 67–68.

142. S. A. Smirnov, *Demokraticheskii tsentralizm* (Moscow, 1966), p. 37.

143. *Partiinaia zhizn'*, no. 3 (1962): 9.

144. Tsybul'ko, *op. cit.*, pp. 85 ff.

145. Shitarev, *Partiinaia zhizn'*, no. 11 (1961): 13.

146. I. Vivdychenko, *Obshchestvennye nachala v partiinoi rabote*, p. 10.

147. *Partiinaia zhizn'*, no. 3 (1962): 11–12.

148. Pigalev, *Kommunist*: p. 63.

149. Vivdychenko, *Obshchestvennye nachala*, p. 10.

150. Pigalev, *Kommunist*: pp. 67–68.

151. *Ibid.*

152. *Kommunist Belorussii*, no. 1 (1960): 62.

153. Robert Conquest has calculated that during and after Malenkov's fall, ten officials from the Ukrainian apparat were appointed to major posts outside the republic and that thirty-one obkom first secretaries connected with Malenkov were purged (Robert

Conquest, *Power and Policy in the USSR*, p. 285). T. H. Rigby's estimate for the two and one-half year period is slightly higher: forty-five of eighty-four obkom first secretaries turned over (T. H. Rigby, "Khrushchev and the Resuscitation of the Central Committee," *Australian Outlook* 13, no. 13 [1959]: 174; cited in Howard R. Swearer, *The Politics of Succession in the USSR* [Boston: Little, Brown, 1964], p. 139).

154. Khrushchev, *Stroitel'stvo Kommunizma*, 1: 405.

155. See Sidney Ploss, *Conflict and Decision-Making in Soviet Russia: A Case Study of Agricultural Policy, 1953–1963* (Princeton, 1965), pp. 249, 253 ff. For the political relations between Khrushchev and Voronov, see Tatu, *op. cit.*, pp. 132–34.

Chapter 5

1. *Pravda*, 3 February 1955, pp. 1–5; for a translation, *CDSP* 7, no. 6 (1955): 3.

2. *CSP*, 2: 177.

3. Robert Conquest, *Power and Policy in the USSR*, p. 320. The charge of opposing politics to economics, of course, went to the very heart of Khrushchev's strategy.

4. *Pravda*, 9 May 1958, pp. 3–4. An authoritative Soviet criticism of the Yugoslav Program is contained in P. Fedoseev, I. Pomelov, and V. Chepralov, *Kommunist*, no. 6 (1958): 16–39.

5. *Sovetskaia Rossiia*, 5 May 1958, pp. 2—3.

6. *Partiinaia zhizn'*, no. 22 (1958): 74 ff.

7. *Pravda*, 7 November 1957, pp. 2–4; *CDSP* 9, no. 45 (1957): 13–14.

8. *Pravda*, 19 November 1957, pp. 1–2; *CDSP* 9, no. 46 (1957): 3–4.

9. *Pravda*, 22 December 1957, pp. 3–4; *CDSP* 10, no. 1 (1958): 3.

10. *Pravda*, 4 June 1958, pp. 1–3; *CDSP* 10, no. 28 (1958): 8 ff.

11. *Pravda*, 19 November 1957, pp. 1–2; *CDSP* 9, no. 26 (1957): 3.

12. *Pravda*, 16 February 1958, pp. 1–2; *CDSP* 10, no. 7 (1958): 20.

13. N. S. Khrushchev, *Vneocherednoi XXI S''ezd KPSS, 27 ianvaria–5 fevralia 1959, stenograficheskii otchet*, 2 vols. (Moscow, 1959), 1: 93—100 (hereafter cited as *XXI S''ezd, otchet*).

14. For a penetrating discussion of this conflict, see Solomon Schwartz, *Sotsialisticheskii vestnik*, nos. 8/9 (1961): 137–38, no. 12 (1961): 213 ff.; also in Solomon M. Schwartz, "Is the State Withering Away in the USSR?" in Leonard Schapiro, ed., *The USSR and the Future: An Analysis of the New Program of the CPSU* (New York, 1963), pp. 161–68.

15. *XXII S''ezd KPSS, 17–31 oktiabria 1961, stenograficheskii otchet*, 3 vols. (Moscow, 1962), 3: 308–10 (hereafter cited as *XXII S''ezd, otchet*).

16. O. V. Kuusinen, ed., *Fundamentals of Marxism-Leninism*, pp. 674–75.

17. *Ibid.*, pp. 685–88.

18. *XXII S''ezd, otchet*, 1: 209–15.

19. *Ibid.*, pp. 117–18.

20. The 1961 Program, pt. 7, in Schapiro, *op. cit.*, pp. 310 ff.

21. For Khrushchev's emphasis upon the Party's political and ideological role, see *XXII S''ezd, otchet*, 1: 255. At the Twentieth Congress, he noted the necessity for *proverka*: "Check-up is also necessary on the work of conscientious people because check-up is first of all a system; it disciplines officials and prevents them from making mistakes and heightens their responsibility for the job entrusted to them" (*CSP*, 2: 54).

22. There have been a number of excellent Kremlinological studies of the power struggle following Stalin's death. See John A. Armstrong, *The Politics of Totalitarianism*; G. Boffa, *Inside the Khrushchev Era* (London, 1959); Conquest, *op. cit.*; Wolfgang Leonhard, *The Kremlin since Stalin*; Carl A. Linden, *Khrushchev and the Soviet Leadership; 1957–1964*; Roger Pethybridge, *A Key to Soviet Politics: The Crisis of the Anti-Party Group* (New York, 1962); Sidney Ploss, *Conflict and Decision-Making in Soviet Russia*; Myron Rush, *The Rise of Khrushchev* (Washington, D. C., 1958); Michel Tatu, *Power in the Kremlin*.

23. Jeremy R. Azrael, *Managerial Power and Soviet Politics*, pp. 111 ff.

24. Ploss, *op. cit.*, pp. 60–61.

25. For a recent study of the policy process by which Khrushchev maneuvered the Presidium's acceptance of the Virgin Lands project, see Richard M. Mills, "The Formation of the Virgin Lands Policy," *Slavic Review* 29, no. 1 (1970): 58–69.

26. Bulganin, *CDSP* 7, no. 28 (1955): 19.

27. Khrushchev, *CSP*, 2: 52–54.

28. *Pravda*, 4 September 1956, p. 1.

29. *Ibid.*, 22 November 1956, p. 1.

30. *Ibid.*, 25 December 1956, p. 1.

31. *Ibid.*, 26 December 1956, p. 1.

32. *Ibid.*, 6 February 1957, p. 1.

33. *Ibid.*, 16 February 1957, pp. 1–2.

34. Azrael, *op. cit.*, pp. 132–33.

35. The most intensive full-length study is that by Pethybridge, *op. cit.* Shorter, but equally intensive, analysis can be found in Armstrong, *op. cit.*, and Conquest, chap. 23, *op. cit.*, chap. 12.

36. An extensive treatment of this phase of the assertion of Party control can be found in Roman Kolkowicz, *The Soviet Military and the Communist Party* (Princeton, 1967), pp. 130–34; also Conquest, *op. cit.*, chap. 13.

37. Conquest, *op. cit.*, p. 304.

38. In his close study of the fate of these officials, Jerry F. Hough has noted that "nearly all of the twenty-four ministers whose ministries were abolished were given strategic industrial positions in the sovnarkhoz period." In addition, 85 percent of 105 identified deputy ministers were given high posts during this period (Jerry F. Hough, *The Soviet Prefects*, p. 56).

39. Ploss, *op. cit.*, particularly chaps. 3–6.

40. See Tatu, *op. cit.*, pp. 67 ff.

41. The most cohesive case for the ascendancy of Khrushchev's personal ambition is made by Jeremy R. Azrael, "The Internal Dynamics of the CPSU, 1917–1967," in Samuel P. Huntington and Clement H. Moore, eds., *Authoritorian Politics in Modern Society*, pp. 273 ff.

42. *Ibid.*

43. Cf. N. S. Khrushchev, *Stroitel'stvo kommunizma v SSSR razvitie sel'skogo khoziaistva*, 5: 19, 187, 349–50.

44. *CDSP* 13, no. 43 (1961): 7.

45. Tatu, *op. cit.*, p. 121, has stressed, rightly in our view, the continuous conflict between centralizers and regionalists after 1957. Gregory Grossman has also pointed out that the process of recentralization was an expected organizational response to a partially reformed structure. These explanations do not necessarily conflict (Gregory Grossman, "The Soviet Economy, 1960–1962," in *Problems of Communism* 12, no. 2 (1963): 39).

46. *Spravochnik partiinogo rabotnika* (1961), pp. 36–37.

47. *Pravda*, 2 July 1959, pp. 1–3; there is a complete translation of Khrushchev's speech in *CDSP* 11, no. 28 (1959): 7.

48. Linden, *op. cit.*, pp. 94 ff.

49. *Spravochnik partiinogo rabotnika* (1961): pp. 93–94.

50. *Ibid.*, p. 87.

51. The precise relationship of specifics of the reform to the power struggle is not always clear. Some measures, such as the cutting of staffs, which began even before Stalin's death, were in full swing in 1954. Others, such as decentralization, were politically more sensitive and apparently began only with Malenkov's fall.

52. Decree of 11 April 1953, *Direktivy KPSS*, 4: 7–18.

53. The early phase of the administrative reform is examined by Elton Rogers, "Recent Trends of Reform in Soviet Constitutional and Administrative Practice," *Saint Antony's Papers* (Oxford: St. Antony's College 1956), pp. 10–12.

54. M. I. Chistiakov, *Osnovye voprosy metodiki planirovaniia promyshlennosti* (Moscow: gosplanizdat 1958), p. 36.

55. *Direktivy KPSS*, 4: 444–50.

56. *Ibid.*, pp. 155–56, 311–17.

57. *Ibid.*; see also Rogers, *op. cit.*, p. 10; M. V. Kharlamov, *Deiatel'nost' KPSS po dal'neishemu ukrepleniiu sovetskogo sotsialisticheskogo gosudarstva* (Moscow, 1956), p. 4.

58. For instances in the central press of this resistance, see *Izvestiia*, 1 June 1955, p. 2; *ibid.*, 6 September 1956, p. 1; *ibid.*, 26 October 1956, p. 2.

59. *Current Soviet Policies*, 2: 140–41.

60. *Ibid.*, p. 161.

61. A. Zverev, *Kommunist*, no. 16 (1954): 31.

62. K. Furtseva, *Izvestiia*, 28 February 1956, p. 1.

63. N. S. Khrushchev, Theses, *Pravda*, 30 March 1957, pp. 1–4; *CDSP* 9, no. 13 (1957): 3–9.

64. *Ibid.*, pp. 9–10.

65. A detailed report of the reform is contained in A. Efimov, *Perestroika upravleniia promyshlennostiu i stroitel'stvom v SSSR*.

66. A number of valuable studies on the sovnarkhoz reform which still read well appeared in the West. See, among others, Oleg Hoeffding, "The Soviet Industrial Reorganization of 1957," *American Economic Review*, 49, no. 2 (1959): 49–65; Nicholas Laskorsky, "Reflections on Soviet Industrial Reorganization," *American Slavic and Eastern European Review*, 17, no. 1 (1958): 47–58; Michael Kaser, "The Reorganization of Soviet Industry and Its Effects on Decision-Making," in Gregory Grossman, ed., *Value and Plan* (Berkeley, 1960), pp. 213–34; and the "Comment" by Grossman, *op. cit.*, pp. 235–40; J. Miller, "The Decentralization of Industry," *Soviet Studies*, 9, no. 1 (1957): 65–83; Alec Nove, "The Soviet Industrial Reorganization," *Problems of Communism*, 6, no. 6 (1957): 19–25.

67. Of these, seventy were in the Russian Republic; eleven in the Ukraine; nine in Kazakhstan; and eight in the Uzbek Republic (N. F. Kolbenkov, in P. I. Kotel'nikov, ed., *Voprosy istorii KPSS* [Moscow: VPSh pri Tsk KPSS, 1959], pp. 59 ff.).

68. *Ibid.*, pp. 64 ff.

69. *Sovetskaia Rossiia*, 10 May 1959, p. 2; Kolbenkov, *op. cit.*, p. 59.

70. The decrees can be found in *Sovetskaia Rossiia*, 19 June 1960, p. 1; *Kazakhstanskaia pravda*, 24 June 1960, p. 1; *Rabochaia gazeta*, 7 July 1960, p. 1.

71. V. G. Vishniakov and A. I. Zavgorodenko, *Sovetskoe gosudarstvo i pravo*, no. 3 (1964): 92–93.

72. Herbert R. Levine, in U.S., Congress, Joint Economic Committee, "Recent

Developments in Soviet Planning," *Dimensions of Soviet Power* (Washington, D. C., 1962), pt. 1, p. 171.

73. I. Berlovich, *Finansy SSR*, no. 11 (1962): 39.

74. P. Veronina, *Partiinaia zhizn'*, no. 2 (1962): 11; *Pravda*, 25 January 1960, p. 2; *Sovetskaia Rossiia*, 13 May 1959, p. 2.

75. A. Birman, *Ekonomicheskaia gazeta*, no. 13 (1963), 7.

76. *Pravda*, 4 September 1961, p. 3.

77. Decree of 22 January 1959, *Spravochnik partiinogo rabotnika* (1959), pp. 374 ff.

78. Ye. Frolov, *Kommunist*, no. 2 (1958): 49–63.

79. For accounts of specific aspects of these conflicts, see A. T. Shmarev, *Sovetskoe gosudarstvo i pravo*, no. 1 (1961): 86–94; V. V. Razorenova, *Planovoe khoziaistvo*, no. 1 (1961): 16; Vishniakov and Zavgorodenko, *op. cit.*, p. 90.

80. A. I. Menabde, *Sovetskii gosudarstvennyi apparat i voprosy ego dal'neishego sovershenstvovaniia* (Tbilisi, 1965), pp. 90 ff. For a discussion of this problem, see Leon Smolinski and Peter Wiles, "The Soviet Planning Pendulum," *Problems of Communism* 12, no. 6 (1963): 21–34.

81. Abram Bergson, *The Economics of Soviet Planning*, pp. 87–88.

82. This complaint was one of the reasons for Khrushchev's radical reordering of the planning process in 1962–63. For specific data on this problem: *Ekonomicheskaia gazeta*, no. 119 (1960): 2; D. Zherebin, *Pravda*, 8 May 1958; p. 2; A. Tolkachevana and others, *Planovoe khoziaistvo*, no. 5 (1961): 4–13. The changes in the planning system are clearly described in M. C. Kaser, "Changes in Planning Methods During the Preparation of the Soviet Seven-Year Plan," *Soviet Studies* 10, no. 4 (1959): 321–38; Herbert S. Levine, "Input-Output Analysis and Soviet Planning," *American Economic Review* 52, no. 2 (1962): 127–37; Barry M. Richman, "Formulation of Enterprise Operating Plans in Soviet Industry," *Soviet Studies* 15, no. 1 (1963): 58–71.

83. *Izvestiia*, 17 May 1962, p. 3. There is little doubt that the processes of negotiation analyzed in Joseph Berliner, *Factory and Manager in the USSR*, were basically untouched by the reorganization.

84. *Izvestiia*, 4 August 1962, p. 3.

85. O. Soich, *Pravda Ukrainy*, 24 January 1962, p. 3; Z. Zibadullaev, *Planovoe khoziaistvo*, no. 2 (1963): 32.

86. Alec Nove, "The Industrial Planning System: Reforms in Prospect," *Soviet Studies* 14, no. 1 (1962): 4.

87. M. Liashko, *Izvestiia*, 1 June 1961, p. 3.

88. *Ibid.*

89. *Pravda*, 1 July 1961, p. 4; M. Alekseev, *Planovoe khoziaistvo*, no. 1 (1963): 70–72.

90. On the overcommitment of resources, see the letters and declarations of the Central Committee of 26 November 1959, on the use of electricity; of 17 November 1959 on the use of nonferrous metals; and of 27 April 1962, on the use of ferrous metals. The documents are assembled in *Spravochnik partiinogo rabotnika* (1961), pp. 225, 236, 281. The pressure on resources from overcommitment was inherent in Khrushchev's policies. (see Gregory Grossman, "Communism in a Hurry: The 'Time Factor' in Soviet Economics," *Problems of Communism* 8, no. 3 (1959): 1–7; Oleg Hoeffding, "State Planning and Forced Industrialization," *Problems of Communism* 8, no. 6 (1959): 38–46). A specific study of time as an investment determinant is in John P. Hardt, "Investment Policy in the Soviet Electric-Power Industry," in Grossman, *Value and Plan*, pp. 295—311.

91. *Pravda*, 23 September 1961, p. 2.

92. *Izvestiia*, 23 October 1963, p. 3.

93. On the localist issue, see Nove, "The Industrial Planning System," *op. cit.*, p. 3; *Izvestiia*, 9 September 1962, p. 3; *Planovoe khoziaistvo*, no. 4 (1960): 79–80.

94. For example, *Pravda*, 2 September 1961, p. 4; *Ekonomicheskaia gazeta*, no. 50 (1958): 2; V. V. Laptev, *Sovetskoe gosudarstvo i pravo*, no. 11 (1962): 52 ff.

95. *Pravda Ukrainy*, 2 December 1961, p. 3; *Ekonomicheskaia gazeta*, no. 37 (1960): 3; *Pravda*, 25 January 1960, p. 2.

96. *Ekonomicheskaia gazeta*, no. 1 (1961): 2; *Sovetskaia Rossiia*, 6 September 1958, pp. 2–3.

97. Kolbenkov, *op. cit.*, pp. 92–93; *Sovetskaia Rossiia*, 6 September 1958, pp. 2–3.

98. Alekseev, *op. cit.*, p. 70.

99. *Izvestiia*, 6 July 1961, p. 3; *Sovetskaia Rossiia*, 15 June 1960, p. 2.

100. For a thorough survey, see editorial, *Planovoe khoziaistvo*, no. 7 (1961): 3 ff.

101. *Izvestiia*, 23 November 1961, p. 1.

102. *Ibid.*, 29 May 1962, p. 3.

103. *Sovetskaia Rossiia*, 1 June 1959, p. 2; *ibid.*, 9 June 1959, p. 2; *Pravda Ukrainy*, 23 July 1959, p. 2.

104. V. I. Snastin, *V edinstve teorii i praktiki—zalog pobedy kommunizma* (Moscow, 1963), pp. 63 ff.

105. *Izvestiia*, 29 May 1962, p. 3.

106. V. Garbuzov, *Zasedaniia Verkhovnogo Soveta SSR, 6-aia sessiia, otchet* (Moscow, 1961), p. 46.

107. *CSP*, 4: 148.

108. I. V. Maevskii, in I. A. Gladkov, ed., *Razvitie sotsialisticheskoi ekonomiki SSR v poslevoennyi period* (Moscow, 1965), p. 98.

109. *Izvestiia*, 7 July 1961, p. 5.

110. *CSP*, 4: 148.

111. *Ibid.*

112. Khrushchev, *CSP*, 4: 56.

113. For examples of this, see *Izvestiia*, 7 July 1961, p. 5; Editorial, *Pravda*, 29 July 1958, p. 1.

114. *CSP*, 4: 148.

115. P. N. Demichev, *Plenum Tsentral'nogo Komiteta KPSS, 19–23 noiabria 1962, stenograficheskii otchet* (Moscow, 1963), pp. 127–28.

116. For this and other logical and circumstantial factors influencing the strategy and orientation of the local Party organs, see Hough, *op. cit.*, pp. 199–209.

117. K. Gerasimov, *Pravda*, 14 July 1960, p. 2.

118. For an excellent indication of the degree of detail to which the Presidium and Russian Bureau entered into the specifics of operational management, See Averki Aristov, *CSP*, 3: 124–25.

119. *Promyshlenno-ekonomicheskaia gazeta*, no. 1 (1960): 2.

120. *Pravda*, 17 July 1962, p. 2.

121. Iu. N. Nikoforov, *Voprosy istorii KPSS*, no. 10 (1963): 19.

122. *Sovetskaia Rossiia*, 16 February 1958, p. 3.

123. *Partiinaia zhizn'*, no. 1 (1959): 10.

124. *Ibid.*, p. 12.

125. *Promyshlenno-ekonomicheskaia gazeta*, no. 5 (1959): 2; K. N. Popov, *Voprosy partiinogo stroitel'stva* (1962), p. 326.

126. *Voprosy partiinoi raboty* (1959), pp. 388–91; *Partiinaia zhizn'*, no. 15 (1962): 4; *ibid.*, no. 1 (1959): 12–13.

127. See the joint protest against excessive plans of, for example, the head of the industrial-transport of the Orenburg Obkom and the head of the oil administration otdel of the Orenburg Sovnarkhoz. (*Sovetskaia Rossiia*, 2 December 1958, p. 2).

128. *Partiinaia zhizn'*, no. 20 (1958): 22.

129. V. Skriabin, *Novoe v rabote partorganizatsii po rukovodstvu promyshlennostiu*, p. 17.

130. When the local Party organs did order above-plan production not decreed by the center, they were subject to sharp criticism (see *Partiinaia zhizn'*, no. 15 (1958): 24).

131. *Izvestiia*, 14 June 1960, p. 2.

132. *Sovetskaia Rossiia*, 16 April 1958, p. 2.

133. *Promyshlenno-ekonomicheskaia gazeta*, no. 29 (1959): 2; V. M. Churaev, *World Marxist Review*, no. 6 (1959): 23.

134. *Partiinaia zhizn'*, no. 15 (1958): 22–24.

135. For Khrushchev's severe criticism of Party *rukovodstvo* in capital construction: *XXII S''ezd, otchet*, 1: 64–66.

136. See, for example, *Izvestiia*, 12 February 1960, p. 4.

137. A. Titarenko, *Partiinaia rabota v promyshlennosti* (Kiev: Gospolitizdat USSR, 1959), pp. 92–93.

138. V. V. Gorev, in K. I. Suvorov, ed., *Nekotorye voprosy organizatsionno-partiinoi raboty v sovremennykh usloviakh*, pp. 279–331.

139. For examples of this conflict, see *Pravda*, 30 May 1959, p. 2; *Pravda Ukrainy*, 28 November 1959, p. 2.

140. Skriabin, *op. cit.*, pp. 32–33.

141. *Ibid.*

142. *Pravda Ukrainy*, 14 February 1962, p. 2; *ibid.*, 17 October 1957, p. 3.

143. *Partiinaia zhizn' Kazakhstana*, no. 5 (1962): 5.

144. *Pravda*, 28 July 1958, p. 2.

145. *Pravda Ukrainy*, 11 June 1959, p. 2.

146. The Party Control Commission, in contravention of the Party statutes, appears to have been deeply involved in control over Party guidance (see the remarks of N. M. Shvernik, *XXII S''ezd, otchet*, 2: 220 ff.

147. *Pravda*, 20 June 1960, p. 2.

148. Gorev, *op. cit.*, p. 322.

149. Skriabin, *op. cit.*, pp. 28–29.

150. A. Bulgakov, *Partiinaia rabota v promyshlennosti*, pp. 58 ff.

151. *Promyshlenno-ekonomicheskaia gazeta*, no. 98 (1958): 2; *Ekonomicheskaia gazeta*, no. 14 (1960): 2.

152. *Spravochnik partiinogo rabotnika* (1961), p. 35.

153. *Ibid.*, p. 93.

154. *Sovetskaia Rossiia*, 8 April 1960, p. 2.

155. *Ekonomicheskaia gazeta*, no. 81 (1961): 3.

Chapter 6

1. Alec Nove, "Some Thoughts on Agricultural Production," *Studies on the Soviet Union* 3, no. 4 (1964): 1.

2. *Ibid.*

3. Central Intelligence Agency, Office of Research and Reports (August, 1962), p. 7.

4. An excellent review of the changes in agricultural administration between 1953 and 1962 is contained in Howard Swearer, "Agricultural Administration under Khrushchev," in Roy D. Laird, ed., *Soviet Agricultural and Peasant Affairs*, chap. 2.

5. Nove, *op. cit.*, pp. 6–7; Swearer, *op. cit.*, pp. 24–28.

6. The opposition to the abolition of the machine tractor stations is traced by Carl A. Linden, *Khrushchev and the Soviet Leadership, 1957–1964*, pp. 61–69.

7. Swearer, *op. cit.*, p. 27; an excellent institutional description of agricultural management by a Soviet source is in V. K. Grigorev, *Gosudarstvennoe rukovodstvo kolkhozami* (Moscow: Izdatel'stvo Moskovskogo Universiteta, 1961), pp. 22–30.

8. N. S. Khrushchev, *Plenum Tsentral'nogo Komiteta Kommunisticheskoi Partii Sovetskogo Soiuza, 5–9 marta 1962, stenograficheskii otchet* (Moscow, 1962), p. 60 (hereafter cited as *March 1962 plenum, otchet*).

9. Swearer, *op. cit.*, p. 29.

10. A. I. Menabde, *Sovetskii gosudarstvennyi apparat i voprosy ego dal'neishego sovershenstvo-vaniia*, p. 61.

11. Swearer, *op. cit.*, p. 30.

12. Simon Kalbysh, "The Reorganization of Party Leadership in Agriculture," *Bulletin of the Institute for the Study of the USSR* 10, no. 5 (1963): 46–47.

13. The Stalinist system of agricultural management is thoroughly discussed in Merle Fainsod, *Smolensk Under Soviet Rule*.

14. A comprehensive statement of the duties of the Party organizer was formally defined in *Partiinaia zhizn'*, no. 5 (1962): 24–25.

15. In 1953, the secretariats of the rural raikomy were reorganized. Raikom Secretaries were assigned with two or three instructors to each MTS. The system came under serious criticism in 1955 and 1956. Khrushchev acknowledged the criticism at the Twentieth Congress but declined to introduce a change. The system was finally abolished in the fall of 1957 (for Khrushchev's remarks, see *CSP*, 2: 59.

16. *March 1962 plenum, otchet*, p. 70. The politics of the plenum is discussed by Sidney Ploss, *Conflict and Decision-Making in Soviet Russia*, pp. 247 ff.

17. The deep opposition to the changes announced at the March plenum is evident in the speeches of G. I. Voronov, *March 1962 plenum, otchet*, pp. 99–100; N. V. Podgorny, *ibid.*, pp. 111–12; V. P. Mzhavanadze, *ibid.*, p. 217; L. V. Florentev, *ibid.*, pp. 342–43.

18. *March 1962 plenum, otchet*, pp. 313–14.

19. *Ibid.*, p. 76.

20. *Ibid.*, pp. 104–5.

21. For some of these conflicts, see N. Petrovich, *Partiinaia zhizn'*, no. 13 (1962): 12.

22. *Pravda*, 30 June 1962, pp. 1–4; a condensed text is in *CDSP* 14, no. 26 (1962): 6–12, 29.

23. *Ibid.*, p. 8.

24. *Ibid.*

25. *Ibid.*, pp. 8–9.

26. *Ibid.*

27. The decree of 7 October 1961 on construction is in *Spravochnik partiinogo rabotnika* (1963), pp. 253 ff.

28. Decree of 13 October 1961, *ibid.*, pp. 277 ff.

29. *Ibid.*, pp. 525 and 533.

30. S. Strumilin, *Kommunist*, no. 13 (1961): 25–26.

31. Rush Greenslade, "The Soviet Economic System in Transition," in U.S., Congress, Joint Economic Committee, *New Directions in the Soviet Economy*, pt. 1 (Washington, D. C., 1966), p. 3.

32. *Ibid.*, p. 9.

33. Editorial, *Planovoe khoziaistvo*, no. 10 (1962): 7 ff.

34. B. Goncharenko and I. Maevskii, *Voprosy ekonomiki*, no. 3 (1962): 22.

35. This conference is fully covered in *Voprosy ekonomiki*, no. 8 (1964): 63 ff.

36. A. Birman, *Planovoe khoziaistvo*, no. 3 (1963): 11–21. A much fuller and more critical amplification of industrial administration is to be found in his *Nekotorye problemy nauki ob upravlenii narodnym khoziaistvom* (Moscow, 1966) (hereafter cited as *Nekotorye problemy*).

37. R. Belousov, *Pravda*, 13 November 1964, p. 2.

38. Birman, *Nekotorye problemy*, pp. 68–74.

39. Belousov, *op. cit.*; Birman, *Nekotorye problemy*, pp. 52–54.

40. For an excellent discussion of the progress of the debate on cybernetics, see John J. Ford, "Soviet Cybernetics and International Development," in Charles R. Dechert, ed., *The Social Impact of Cybernetics* (New York, 1967), pp. 161–92. The March 1964 round table is reported by L. Gatovskii in *Voprosy ekonomiki*, no. 8 (1964): 63 ff.

41. B. M. Kedrov, *Voprosy ekonomiki*, no. 8 (1964): 68.

42. Iu. Oblomskii, *Voprosy ekonomiki*, no. 8 (1964): 69–70; S. Strumilin, *ibid.*, pp. 88–89.

43. A. Kochubei, *Planovoe khoziaistvo*, no. 11 (1962): 8–16.

44. The administrative reform of the enterprise is thoroughly analyzed in N. Drogichinskii, *Planovoe khoziaistvo*, no. 5 (1962): 16–17; also in I. Ivonin, *ibid.*, no. 11 (1962): 17–27; N. Baikov, *ibid.*, no. 5 (1962): 16–23; A. Soich, *Pravda Ukrainy*, 24 January 1962, p. 3.

45. *Pravda*, 9 September 1962, p. 2. To attribute economic methods to Liberman alone is, of course, a serious oversimplification. Economic methods were advocated by a number of senior Soviet economists, including Nemchinov and Trapeznikov. It is because of Liberman's early prominence in pressing for an alternative to purely bureaucratic management that the popular association of his name with the movement for reform is deserved.

46. *Ibid.*

47. Birman, *Nekotorye problemy*, pp. 4–5.

48. This problem is reviewed in John F. Hardt, Dmitri M. Gallek, and Vladimir G. Treml, "Institutional Stagnation and Changing Economic Strategy in the Soviet Union," in *New Directions in the Soviet Economy*, pt. 2, pp. 58 ff.

49. Grey Hodnett, "Khrushchev and Party-State Control," in Alexander Dallin and Alan F. Westin, eds., *Politics in the Soviet Union: 7 Cases* (New York, 1966), p. 119, n. 2.

50. *CSP*, 1: 30.

51. *Ibid.*, 2: 59.

52. *Ibid.*, p. 54; see also the remarks of N. G. Pervukhin, *ibid.*, p. 154.

53. *Pravda*, 30 March 1957, pp. 1 ff; the complete text is translated in *CDSP* 9, no. 13 (1957): 12.

54. *Pravda*, 28 August 1957, p. 1.

55. Hodnett, *op. cit.*, pp. 127–28.

56. *Izvestiia*, 14 August 1959, p. 1.

57. *Partiinaia zhizn'*, no. 17 (1959): 23–25.

58. *Pravda*, 23 July 1961, p. 1; also A. E. Lunev, *Obespechenie zakonnosti v SSSR* (Moscow, 1963), pp. 88 ff.

59. G. Eniutin, *Izvestiia*, 7 September 1961, p. 3.

60. *Izvestiia*, 16 February 1962, p. 4.

61. The leadership debate on the Party's role in mass control is thoroughly analyzed in Hodnett, *op. cit.*, pp. 139–42.

62. *Ibid.*

63. A. I. Boliasnyi, *Kommunist*, no. 15 (1961): 89–91.

64. Khrushchev, *XXII S''ezd, otchet*, 1: 117.

65. N. Khrushchev, Zapiska of 10 September 1962, in N. S. Khrushchev, *Stroitel'stvo kommunizma v SSSR i razvitie sel'skogo khoziaistva*, 7: 166 (hereafter cited as *September 1962 zapiska*). Essentially the same proposition is found in N. S. Khrushchev, *Plenum Tsentral'nogo Komiteta KPSS, 19–23 noiabria 1962, stenograficheskii otchet* (Moscow 1963), pp. 13–14 (hereafter cited as *November 1962 plenum, otchet*).

66. *November 1962 plenum, otchet*, pp. 13–14.

67. *Ibid.*, p. 14.

68. *Ibid.*, pp. 14–15.

69. *Ibid.*, pp. 19–20.

70. *Ibid.*

71. *Ibid.*, pp. 171–72.

72. *Ibid.*, pp. 19–20.

73. *Ibid.*

74. *Ibid.*

75. *Ibid.*

76. *Ibid.*, p. 23.

77. *Ibid.*

78. *Ibid.*

79. *Ibid.*, p. 449. The resolution of the plenum mentioned only two bureaus for industry and agriculture.

80. *Ibid.*, pp. 26–33.

81. *Ibid.*, pp. 37–42.

82. *Ibid.*, pp. 42–43.

83. Rush Greenslade, "Khrushchev and the Economists," *Problems of Communism* 12, no. 3 (1963): 29.

84. *November 1962 plenum, otchet*, pp. 60–61.

85. *Ibid.*, pp. 34–37.

86. *Ibid.*, p. 38.

87. *Ibid.*, p. 61.

88. *Ibid.*, pp. 65–66.

89. *Ibid.*

90. *Ibid.*, pp. 57–58.

91. *Ibid.*, p. 59.

92. *Ibid.*

93. *Ibid.*, p. 60.

94. *Ibid.*, p. 46.

95. *Ibid.*, pp. 65–66.

96. *Ibid.*, p. 84.

97. *Ibid.*, p. 83.

98. *Ibid.*, p. 86.

99. *Ibid.*

100. *Ibid.*, pp. 86–87.
101. *Ibid.*
102. *Ibid.*, pp. 90–92.
103. *Ibid.*, p. 93.
104. *Ibid.*, p. 94.
105. *Ibid.*
106. *Ibid.*
107. Priscilla Blake, "Freedom and Control in Literature, 1962–63," in Dallin and Westin, *op. cit.*, p. 173.
108. The prosecution of economic crimes, heralded by the legislation and events of 1961 and 1962, was reflected in 1962 and 1963. For analyses of specific trials, see *New York Times*, 13 September 1962, p. 5; *ibid.*, 28 March 1963, p. 3; *ibid.*, 12 June 1963, p. 3.
109. *Pravda Ukrainy*, 27 November 1962, p. 1.
110. *September 1962 zapiska*, p. 177.
111. *Pravda*, 28 September 1962, pp. 1–2.
112. *Pravda*, 21 October 1962, p. 1. Priscilla Blake suggests that the lines: "No wonder Stalin's heirs seem stricken/ with heart attacks these days...." indicate that Frol Kozlov was among the foremost of Khrushchev's opponents in the Presidium; Blake, *op. cit.*, p. 168.
113. The evaluation of the degree of support for Khrushchev revealed in statements made at the plenum is, of course, subjective. There is, however, an unmistakable indication of degree of social distance in the forms used by Voronov and Rashidov, on the one hand, and those used by D. A. Kunaev and others in their references to Khrushchev (see *November 1962 plenum, otchet*, pp. 102, 173, and 183).
114. V. Ia. Akhundov, *November 1962 plenum, otchet*, p. 192; V. F. Mzhavanadze, *ibid.*, pp. 213 ff.; Ia. N. Zarobian, *ibid.*, pp. 280 ff.
115. *Ibid.*, p. 168.
116. *Ibid.*, p. 118.
117. *Ibid.*, pp. 358–63.
118. *Ibid.*, pp. 219–20.
119. *Ibid.*, p. 582.
120. *Ibid.*, pp. 242–49.
121. *Ibid.*, pp. 127, 128–29.
122. Cf., Lazar Slepov, *Sovetskaia Rossiia*, 29 November 1962, p. 1.
123. *Pravda Ukrainy*, 27 November 1962, p. 2.
124. P. Fedoseev, *Pravda*, 9 December 1962, p. 1.
125. Slepov, *op. cit.*
126. E. Bugaev, *Pravda*, 19 December 1962, p. 1.
127. D. Chesnokov, *Kommunist*, no. 2 (1963): 11–20.
128. *Izvestiia*, 19 December 1962, p. 4.
129. Michel Tatu has noted the doubts in Soviet ideological circles concerning the authenticity of the document. Iuri Frantsev and E. I. Bugaev, for example, ignored the document. Only three members of the Presidium—Brezhnev, Kosygin, and Podgorny—cited the document in defense of the new arrangements within the Party (Michel Tatu, *Power in the Kremlin*, pp. 258–60). Other writers replied to the charge of pragmatism levelled against Khrushchev by asserting that Marx had no dogma for building the material base of communism, and therefore his remarks were relevant only for his time and place (see N. G. Kristosturian, *Voprosy istorii KPSS*, no. 6 (1963): 41–42).

130. E. Ligachev, *Ekonomicheskaia gazeta*, no. 4 (1963): 3.
131. G. Glezerman, *Kommunist*, no. 7 (1963): 30–40.
132. Ligachev, *op. cit.*
133. *Pravda*, 11 May 1962, pp. 1–3; *CDSP* 14, no. 19 (1963): 10.
134. Academician V. S. Nemchinov, *Pravda*, 21 September 1962, p. 2.
135. *Izvestiia*, 1 June 1962, p. 1.
136. Khrushchev discussed the scissors between wages and supply in his speech to the Cubans (*Pravda*, 3 June 1962, pp. 1–2).
137. *Ibid.*, 28 July 1962, p. 1.
138. See the revealing account of I. S. Grushetskii, then first secretary of the Lvov Obkom, who complained that the July conference had decided to expand the concept of the firm but that the legislation formalizing this decision had not been passed (*November 1962 plenum, otchet*, p. 486).
139. This decision, like the decision on the firm, was not publicized. The first indication of the reform was made by Tabeev, the first secretary of the Tatar Republic, in *Izvestiia*, 24 August 1962, p. 3.
140. *Pravda Ukrainy*, 15 December 1962, p. 1; Tatu, *op. cit.*, pp. 285–86, has suggested a major defeat for Kosygin in a presidial meeting on 8 November on the day preceding the announcement of the convocation of the November plenum. If the account pieced together here is valid, it would appear that the specific issue on the agenda of the Presidium was not a major enactment of the Liberman proposals but rather a limited experiment. The Presidium's authorization had apparently been given in September, held up, and then reauthorized in early November. Its fate indicates that the release order of November was subsequently withdrawn.
141. V. S. Tolstikov, *November 1962 plenum, otchet*, p. 147.
142. Liashko, *ibid.*, p. 247.
143. Podgorny, *ibid.*, p. 122; Mzhavanadze, *ibid.*, p. 214.
144. Demichev, *ibid.*, p. 133.
145. Podgorny, *ibid.*, p. 121.
146. Mazurov, *ibid.*, p. 161.
147. Komiakov, *ibid.*, pp. 532 ff.
148. Dymshits, *ibid.*, p. 413.
149. Krotov, *ibid.*, pp. 241–42.
150. Kostousov, *ibid.*, pp. 138–40.
151. Grafov, *ibid.*, p. 355.
152. L. Gatovskii, *Kommunist*, no. 18 (1962): 61.
153. *Ibid.*
154. *Pravda*, 1 December 1962, p. 1.
155. *Ekonomicheskaia gazeta*, no. 1 (1963): 8–13; *ibid.*, no. 2 (1963): 11.
156. *Pravda Ukrainy*, 15 December 1962, p. 1.
157. Linden, *Khrushchev and the Soviet Leadership*, pp. 166–67.
158. *Ibid.*, pp. 159 ff.
159. *Pravda*, 26 April 1963, pp. 1–6; *CDSP* 15, no. 17 (1963): 5.
160. *Ibid.*, pp. 1–4.
161. Demichev, *November 1962 plenum, otchet*, pp. 134–35.
162. Voronov, *ibid.*, p. 102.
163. The expressions of support at the November plenum are catalogued by Hodnett, *op. cit.*, p. 146. The establishment of attitudes derived from formal declarations is, of course, open to varied interpretation.
164. *Pravda*, 18 January 1963, p. 1.
165. The Party-State Control Committee's authority, particularly in relation to the Party, is discussed in chap. 7.

Chapter 7

1. This data is taken from *Partiinaia zhizn'*, no. 10 (1965): 8–17; the complete text is in *CDSP* 17, no. 29 (1965): 14–15.

2. *Ibid.*

3. *Ibid.*, p. 16.

4. *Ibid.*, p. 15. The 1963 and 1964 changes were sociologically insignificant. Those with higher education increased from 13.7 to 15 percent. The percentage of Great Russians reached 61 percent, but the increase of women amounted to less than one-half of 1 percent of 1961.

5. M. Karpov, Yu. Mel'kov, *Kommunist*, no. 5 (1965): 47–51; see also, V. Zasorin, *Partiinaia zhizn'*, no. 8 (1963): 14–15.

6. The practice of extending Party membership for achievement, while compatible with Khrushchev's basic policy, was sharply at variance with the Leninist tradition of Party membership. Cf., John N. Hazard in Alexander Balinky et al., *Planning and the Market in the USSR* (New Brunswick, N. J., 1967), p. 69.

7. In Belorussia, all six city committees were abolished. In the Ukraine, the original ten city committees scheduled were reduced to eight. In Central Asia, relatively few committees were finally eliminated.

8. G. I. Voronov, *November 1962 plenum, otchet*, p. 103.

9. V. S. Tolstikov, *November 1962 plenum, otchet*, p. 144.

10. The gorkomy of Novosibirsk, Volgograd, Omsk, and Kalinin oblasti were among those abolished. But city committees in Sverdlovsk, Gorkii, Astrakhan, and Irkutsk, for example, were retained. Whether the oblast Party committee was divided appears to have been irrelevant.

11. The figures are those of V. Karlov and V. Zasorin, *Po proizvodstvennomu prinfsipu* (Moscow, 1963), p. 18.

12. P. Pigalev, *Partiinaia zhizn'*, no. 15 (1963): 22.

13. *Ibid.*

14. P. A. Rodionov, *Kollektivnost'—vysshii printsip partiinogo rukovodostva* (Moscow, 1967), p. 226.

15. E. I. Bugaev and V. M. Leibson, *Besedy ob ustave KPSS*, p. 124.

16. Editorial, *Kommunist Ukrainy*, no. 3 (1963): 5.

17. Karlov and Zasorin, *op. cit.*, p. 22.

18. Editorial, *Partiinaia zhizn'*, no. 6 (1964): 10.

19. Karlov and Zasorin, *op. cit.*, p. 22.

20. *Partiinaia zhizn'*, no. 1 (1962): 52.

21. V. Sevriakov, *Partiinaia zhizn'*, no. 12 (1964): 8.

22. *November 1962 plenum, otchet*, p. 443.

23. Bugaev and Leibson, *op. cit.*, p. 148.

24. The data used in identifying the structures of the central and territorial apparatuses has been largely drawn from the U. S., Department of State, Division of Biographic Registry; *Directory of Soviet Officials*, vols. 1 (November 1963) and 2 (August 1964). Biographical data has been obtained from *Who's Who in the USSR, 1960/1961* and *Who's Who in the USSR, 1965/1966*. Valuable biographical data can also be found in the *Ezhegodniki bolshoi sovetskoi entsiklopedii 1963* and *1966* and the sketches in the *Deputaty Verkhovnogo Soveta SSSR* for the Sixth (1962) and Seventh (1966) Sessions. Useful as well are the earlier *Biographical Directory of the USSR*, 1958 and *5000 Sowjetkopfe*. More extensive biographical analyses of major Soviet leaders have been recently published in George W. Simmonds, ed., *Soviet Leaders* (New York, 1967).

25. Michel Tatu has pointed out the conflict between Efremov and Voronov in his *Power in the Kremlin*, p. 288.

26. The replacement of V. V. Shcherbitskii as a candidate member of the Presidium in December 1963 appears to have been an essentially regional affair. In this connection, however, it is interesting to note that Shcherbitskii was replaced by P. E. Shelest, one of the most vocal critics of the 1962 agricultural reorganization.

27. See chap. 5.

28. This was particularly true of agriculture (see G. I. Voronov, *November 1962 plenum, otchet*, p. 105).

29. John N. Hazard, *The Soviet System of Government*, p. 77.

30. T. Daveletin, "The Reorganization of Administration in Turkestan," *Bulletin of the Institute for the Study of the USSR* 10, no. 5 (1963): 28 ff.

31. I. F. Ilychev, *Pravda*, 19 June 1963, pp. 1–6; *CDSP* 15, no. 24 (1963): 10.

32. U. S., Congress, Subcommittee on National Security, *Staffing Procedures and Problems in the Soviet Union* (Washington, D. C., 1963), charts 3 and 4.

33. The changes in the presidia of the union republic committees are conveniently catalogued by Jerry F. Hough, "The Soviet Elite: I," *Problems of Communism* 16, no. 1 (1967): 30.

While the representation of lower Party officials was reduced on the new presidia, the major loss was to the state apparatus. In the new organs, the number of state officials was cut from fifty-six to thirty-three. In partial compensation, however, the number of candidates increased from eight to eleven. The most stable and uniform representation in this category continued to be the chairman of the Council of Ministers and the chairman of the Presidium of the Supreme Soviet. While these were represented on every presidia, the third office varied from republic to republic. The Kirgiz and Turkmen presidia elected the chairmen of the republican KGB. Armenia added the chairmen of the republican sovnarkhoz; the Ukraine, the first deputy chairman of the Council of Ministers in charge of industry. In five other republics, the heads of military districts were elected; in two other republics, the republican Komsomol and Trade Union Council chairmen.

34. A. Lebed, "Extension of the Powers of Republican Second Secretaries," *Bulletin of the Institute for the Study of the USSR* 10, no. 8 (1963): 34–37.

Of the six republics that received new second secretaries during this period, Latvia, Georgia, Turkmenia, and Kazakhstan received their secretaries from the Russian Republic. All five officials were posted directly from the Department of Party Organs of the Moscow City Committee. Georgia was the only republic to turn over two second secretaries. D. S. Zemlianskii, appointed in November 1962, died in 1964 and was replaced by P. N. Rodionov, an ideological specialist from the Moscow Gorkom. In Kazakhstan, the replacement of N. N. Rodionov, whose career had been in the Leningrad apparatus prior to his appointment in 1960, was M. S. Solomentsev, an engineer who had served as both an obkom first secretary and as chairman of the Cheliabinsk Sovnarkhoz. In the Ukraine as well, the appointment of I. P. Kazanets opened the way for N. A. Sobol, first secretary of Kharkov, an official with heavy industrial experience. The new Belorussian Second Secretary, P. M. Masherov, whose entire career had been spent in leading work in the republican Komsomol and Party apparatuses, replaced F. A. Surganov, an agriculturist, who became chairman of the Agricultural Bureau.

35. Only one secretary whose career pattern is available in detail spent his career entirely within the Party apparatus. Two of the secretaries, Maniushies of Lithuania and Vakulov of Kirgiz, were former republican ministers of construction drafted directly into the apparatus. For four other secretaries, experience in the territorial Party apparatus was combined with state executive tours. Three had been at least department heads

in the republican sovnarkhozy or gosplany, and one, G. A. Gogeshidze of Georgia, had served as a deputy minister of State Security.

36. A Russian, Martinov was fifty-two and a power engineer. Serving as a deputy minister prior to the sovnarkhoz reform, he became successively chairman of the Tashkent and Uzbek sovnarkhozy. There is no evidence of his having served for any period in the Party apparatus.

37. Five were represented by either chairmen or deputy chairmen of the republican sovnarkhozy, with Lithuania represented by both. Three republican planners were added as were three trade union council chairmen. Only a few bureaus reflected specifically local conditions. One was Latvia which placed the chief of the Main Administration of Fish Industry in the Western Basin on the Bureau for Industry and Construction.

38. In Latvia and Moldavia, virtually the whole bureau was turned over. The average turnover, experienced by eight republics, however, was between two and three members. An essentially similar pattern was evident in the agricultural bureaus. The Uzbek Bureau remained unchanged. In Kazakhstan, however, the chairman and the full bureau were completely changed in March 1963. In Turkmena and Latvia, all ordinary members and one deputy were turned over. Less drastic changes of two to four members were made in four other republics. With the exception of Latvia, there was evidently no correspondence between the rates of turnover in the separate bureaus within each republic; and it seems evident that the turnover reflected replacement of republican Party committee department heads rather than of the state officials.

39. The emphasis on chemistry in 1963 and 1964 resulted in the formation of new chemical departments in Belorussia, Kazakhstan, and Kirgiz and the reorganization in 1963 of the former Department of the Oil Industry in Azerbaidzhan to the new Department of the Petroleum and Chemical Industries. In some republics, the trade section of the Department of Administrative, Financial Organs, and Trade was divided between the industrial and agricultural bureaus.

40. Grey Hodnett, "The Obkom First Secretaries," Slavic Review 24, no. 4 (1965): 637–38; primary data is in Narodnoe khoziastvo SSSR v 1962 goda (Moscow: Gosudarstvennoe Statistnicheskoe Izdatel'stvo, 1963), p. 33. In the distribution of oblasti and kraia, fifty-five were in the Russian Republic, twenty-five in the Ukraine, eighteen in Kazakhstan, six in Belorussia, and eight in Uzbekistan. The Kirgiz Republic retained a single oblast. Not all oblast committees were divided. The autonomous republics retained their single committees. Among oblasti and kraia, seventy-five of 113 Party committees, or approximately 66 percent, were divided. The reorganizations seem clearly to have been directed toward the Russian, Ukrainian, and Belorussian republics. In the RSFSR, five of six territories and thirty-seven of forty-nine oblasti were divided. In the Ukraine, nineteen of twenty-five obkomy were split, and in Belorussia all six oblasti were divided. The major variations were in the Central Asian republics. In Kirgiz, the Osh Oblast was divided, but in Kazakhstan, the most developed of the Central Asian republics and specifically excluded from the control of the Central Asian Bureau, only three of eighteen kraia and oblasti were split. In Uzbekistan, the figure was only four of ten.

41. Karlov and Zasorin, op. cit., p. 15.

42. Ibid., p. 19. The oblast structure is discussed in detail in this excellent study. The reorganization was also accompanied by the creation of numerous special otdely for heavy industry, coal, chemical, oil, and other branches of industry where these departments were not present. There was thus an evident change in policy toward enlarging the obkom apparatus, a structural reflection of the policy of increased Party intervention in the details of economic decision-making. Under the agricultural bureaus, each apparatus

had sections for party organs, ideology, agriculture, an otdel for industries processing agricultural products, and, in some committees, special otdely for agricultural construction, water economy, and presumably others as well.

43. John A. Armstrong, "Party Bifurcation and Elite Interests." *Soviet Studies* 17, no. 2 (1966): 417–30.

44. Hodnett, *op. cit.*, table 2, p. 641. The patterns were not identical in each republic. In the Russian Federation, of thirty obkom first secretaries who were also full members of the Central Committee, twenty were posted to agricultural, and only nine to industrial, committees. Among candidate members, generally holding office in the more agricultural oblasti, fourteen were sent to agricultural, but only three to industrial, committees. In Belorussia, four of six first secretaries were assigned to agricultural obkomy, with no first secretaries assigned to industry. The major deviation from the pattern was in the Ukraine. While eight of the nineteen first secretaries were sent to agricultural committees, nine were to head industrial obkomy. In respect to full and candidate members of the Central Committee, this deviation was even more marked. Five full members and one candidate became industrial first secretaries, but only one full member and two candidates were assigned to agriculture.

45. *Ibid.*, p. 651. In the Russian Republic, of the thirty-two first secretaries advanced in November, fifteen were virtually unknown. Of the remaining seventeen first secretaries, six had been obkom secretaries; four were obkom second secretaries; and two, gorkom first secretaries. Only three were chairmen or deputy chairmen of Soviet ispolkomy, and only one chairman of an abolished oblast sovnarkhoz was recruited to head an industrial obkom. In the Ukraine, only one sovnarkhoz chairman and one chairman of an oblast soviet were recruited as industrial first secretaries. In Belorussia, all except one obkom first secretary were appointed from the local Party apparatus. Among agricultural first secretaries, the pattern of recruitment was more usual. In the Russian Republic, for example, nine of twelve were from the oblast apparat or the oblast agricultural administration, including chairmen of oblast Soviet executive committees.

46. There is some dispute on this issue. Armstrong, *op. cit.*, p. 418, holds that the objective of the reform was to strengthen the role of the older obkom first secretaries. This view, however, is inconsistently applied since the author indicates that the reorganization was deeply resented by the most influential body of older secretaries, the members of the Central Committee.

47. Hodnett, *op. cit.*, p. 648.

48. A. P. Kirilenko, *Sovetskaia Rossiia*, 24 April 1963, p. 3.

49. *Kommunist*, no. 16 (1963): 14.

50. Karlov and Zasorin, *op. cit.*, p. 22.

51. M. Polekhin, *Partiinaia zhizn'*, no. 1 (1964): 26; Hodnett, *op. cit.*, table 3, p. 642; Armstrong, *op. cit.*, p. 429. This was particularly true of second secretaries. Prior to the reform, Polekhin reported, only two obkom or kraikom secretaries in the Russian Republic were under forty. In 1963, the number rose to fourteen in industry and twenty in agriculture. While the average age for second secretaries is not known, the average age of obkom first secretaries before the reform was 49.2 years. In 1964, the average age was reduced to 47.7 years, with the industrial first secretaries an average of two years younger than the agricultural.

52. Hodnett, *op. cit.*, table 4, p. 643; Armstrong, *op. cit.*, p. 423.

53. Both the Leningrad and Moscow industrial and agricultural obkomy changed over 90 percent of their department heads between 1962 and 1964. The Kalinin industrial obkom substituted the purged department heads with officials having higher education and experience in industry (*Partiinaia zhizn'*, no. 5 (1963): 14).

54. B. Vladimirov and V. Nakoriakov, *Kommunist*, no. 14 (1964): 88.

55. *Partiinaia zhizn'*, no. 1 (1964): 25.

56. The Moscow City Bureau retained six secretaries during the period; the Leningrad City Bureau, five. There was also little change in representation. Eight of eleven full members of the Moscow Gorkom were from the Party apparatus.

57. G. Shitarev, *Kommunist*, no. 18 (1963): 66. Industrial-transport, trade and financial, or construction departments were reestablished or expanded in gorkomy or raikomy where they had been eliminated. The Sverdlovsk Gorkom, for example, added a special otdel for construction and city economy, and industrial-transport otdely were restored in all of its raikomy.

58. *Pravda*, 27 December 1963, p. 2.

59. Karlov and Zasorin, *op. cit.*, p. 19.

60. G. Krivoshein, *Partiinaia zhizn'*, no. 5 (1963): 30–33; B. Smirnov, *Partiinaia zhizn'*, no. 6 (1964): 26–30.

61. Karpov and Zasorin, *op. cit.*, p. 17; see also, *Partiinaia zhizn'*, no. 11 (1963): 3–7.

62. *Partiinaia zhizn'*, no. 3 (1963): 21–26.

63. V. Serdiuk, *Kommunist Ukrainy*, no. 4 (1963): 38; *Ekonomicheskaia gazeta*, no. 8 (1963): 15; I. I. Petrovskii, in V. A. Smyshliaev, ed., *KPSS v period stroitel'stva kommunizma*, pp. 47–48. Although the number of technically trained secretaries was lower at the local than at the regional levels, serious efforts were made to recruit technicians. In Primorskii Krai, all gorkom and raikom first secretaries were engineers or technicians. In the Leningrad raikomy, all secretaries were reported to have had higher education, and all secretaries dealing with industry and construction were engineers with extensive experience in economic management.

64. Polekhin, *op. cit.*, p. 26.

65. In Georgia, two-thirds of all secretaries above the primary Party level were under forty in 1963. In Perm Oblast, the absolute majority of gorkom and raikom first secretaries were under forty.

66. Petrovskii, *op. cit.*

67. Polekhin, *op. cit.*

68. The number of primary Party organs in 1963 and 1964 increased but only by some 5,500 units (*Partiinaia zhizn'*, no. 10 (1965); cf. *CDSP* 17, no. 29 (1965): 17).

69. V. Beriozov, *Partiinaia zhizn'*, no. 6 (1964): 36.

70. Rodionov, *op. cit.*, p. 225.

71. *Partiinaia zhizn'*, no. 1 (1964): 10.

72. *Ibid.*, no. 2 (1964): 10.

73. *Ekonomicheskaia gazeta*, no. 45 (1963): 13.

74. *Partiinaia zhizn'*, no. 16 (1965): 34.

75. *Pravda*, 28 November 1962, p. 1.

76. *Ibid.*, 18 January 1963, p. 1.

77. *Spravochnik partiinogo rabotnika* (1964), pp. 303–9.

78. *Partiinaia zhizn'*, no. 14 (1964): 31–34.

79. *Pravda*, 18 January 1963, p. 1.

80. *Ibid.* For Soviet commentaries on the scope and authority of the control agency, see L. M. Bubnova, ed., *Partiino-gosudarstvennyi kontrol' v deistvii* (Moscow, 1964), pp. 15–17; M. B. Mitin, *Sovetskaia sotsialisticheskaia demokratiia* (Moscow, 1964), pp. 180–82; N. A. Shipoleva and A. I. Nedavnii, *Osnovy sovetskogo gosudarstvennogo stroitel'stva i prava* (Moscow, 1965), pp. 352–55; V. I. Turovtsev, ed., *Narodnyi kontrol' v SSSR* (Moscow, 1967), pp. 87–90.

81. Turovtsev, *op. cit.*, p. 85; the contrary view is expressed in L. Karapetian and V. Razin, *Sovety obshchenarodnogo gosudarstva* (Moscow, 1964), p. 150.

82. Turovtsev, *op. cit.*, p. 89.

83. Mitin, *op. cit.*, p. 180.

84. Shipoleva and Nedavnii, *op. cit.*, pp. 352–53.

85. For the purposes of control, the Moscow and Leningrad city committees were considered to be equal to oblast committees.

86. V. Gorin, Yu. Polenov, *Kommunist*, no. 6 (1964): 68–69.

87. Turovtsev, *op. cit.*, p. 85.

88. This data can be found in the *Directory of Soviet Officials*, vol. 2.

89. While the Estonian Committee did not include members of the republican control apparatus, the Kirgiz Committee added the heads of the Department for Organizational Work and the Department for Agriculture, Water Economy, and Procurement. The Ukrainian Committee had as representatives the heads of the Heavy Industry Department and the Light, Food, and Fish Department.

90. The Kharkov Industrial Party-State Control Committee had a single industrial department with sections for machine building, chemicals, instruments, and scientific institutes, a department for transport and communications, and departments for construction and urban economy; schools, science, culture, health; light and food industries; trade and everyday services. In contrast, the Lipetsk agricultural PGK had four nonstaff branch otdely: a Poultry and Agronomy Service; Animal Husbandry and External Service; Trade and Daily Services to the Population; and an Otdel for Enlightenment, Culture, and Health Preservation.

91. The Briansk Oblast PGK, for example, had eight nonstaff otdely and three commissions with seventy-five nonstaff controllers (*Partiinaia zhizn'*, no. 11 (1963): 45–46). The Iaroslavl industrial obkom PGK had nine external staff otdely with 100 men (*ibid.*, no. 24 (1964): 15–16).

92. *Sovetskaia Rossiia*, 18 May 1963, p. 2. The Serpukhov Committee, for example, formed departments for industry, construction, transport, trade and public catering, a bureau for workers' complaints, and a revizor group of supervising and coordinating all control activities within the city. Another city committee, the Noginsk Party-State Control Committee, in addition to the usual departments, established a number of commissions for controlling such industrial activities as labor productivity, technical safety, supply, progressive methods of construction, and so on.

93. *Pravda*, 10 May 1963, p. 2.

94. Turovtsev, *op. cit.*, p. 84. In both the divided and unified obkom control committees, the full-time staff was from five to seven men.

95. L. G. Krapunev, in Smyshliaev, *op. cit.*, p. 166.

96. A. Malenkin, *Kommunist*, no. 6 (1964): 75.

97. I. S. Grushetskii, *Partiinaia zhizn'*, no. 19 (1964): 16.

98. *Sovetskaia Belorussia*, 27 November 1963, p. 1. In Belorussia, for example, only 15 percent of the social controllers were pensioners, but the proportion was higher in the more heavily industrialized regions where the labor supply was tighter. In a typical Leningrad raikom forty-seven of sixty controllers were pensioners.

99. Krapunov, *op. cit.*, p. 166.

100. Among republican chairmen, at the time of appointment rwo were republican Party secretaries, three were obkom first secretaries, one was an obkom second secretary, two more were heads of republican Party organs departments, and one headed an ideological department. Of the five officials from the republican state apparatus, one was serving as a sovnarkhoz chairman, one was a first deputy, and two were deputy chairmen of republican council of ministers. One was a minister of education.

NOTES 325

101. Only one official, Kerimov of Azerbaidzhan, had experience in a republican security agency, and only E. T. Astsatrian of Armenia and N. M. Murakhanov of the Uzbek Republic had extensive experience in industrial administration.

102. This judgment is based principally upon data for the Ukrainian and Belorussian republics. The full oblast secretariats for the Russian Republic were not published, in contrast to the usual custom. The number of new obkom secretaries identified for Belorussia was 50 percent; in the Ukraine, 20 percent. The sample, particularly for the Ukraine, is small, but the high degree of consistency seems to support the tentative judgments concerning the predominantly local and low status quality of the obkom control secretaries.

103. *Partiinaia zhizn'*, no. 14 (1964): 32.

104. *Sovetskaia Belorussia*, 14 September 1963, p. 2.

Chapter 8

1. The alleged reasons for the ouster are in Henry Tanner's dispatches, *New York Times*, 30 October 1964, p. 13, and *ibid.*, 1 November 1964, p. 4. The expulsion of the Anti-Party Group was announced by Suslov at the February 1964 Central Committee Plenum but not published until April 1964.

2. The polemics with the Chinese were thoroughly discussed by M. A. Suslov, *Pravda*, 3 April 1964, pp. 1–8. For running commentary, see *Pravda*, 20 July 1964; *Sovetskaia Rossiia*, 17 January 1963; *Pravda*, 22 September 1964. Khrushchev's grand design for Soviet development was central in the polemics. He reacted bitterly to the Chinese charge that his emphasis upon consumer goods was bourgeois and would lead to the decline of revolutionary élan in Soviet society (see, for example, *Pravda*, 17 August 1964).

3. For an excellent account of the conservative reaction against the literary and cultural intelligentsia, see Priscilla Blake, "Freedom and Control in Literature, 1962–1963," in Alexander Dallin and Alan F. Westin, eds., *Politics in the Soviet Union*, pp. 165–205.

4. For various efforts of Khrushchev's supporters to clear him of any complicity in the Purges of the thirties, see *Pravda*, 10 March 1963, pp. 1–4; *ibid.*, 20 June 1963, p. 2; *ibid.*, 28 March 1964, p. 2; and V. P. Grigoriev, M. I. Popkova, and A. F. Sleshina, *Voprosy istorii KPSS*, no. 10 (1963): 1–4.

5. An excellent summary of the memorandum in the context of elite conflict is contained in Carl A. Linden, *Khrushchev and the Soviet Leadership, 1957–1964*, p. 204.

6. Evidence of the struggle over resource allocation and Group B products was extensive during 1963 and 1964. In February 1963, Khrushchev publicly admitted the pressures over investment policy (*Sovetskaia Rossiia*, 28 February 1963, p. 3). The decision to cut back on the production of strategic bombers and surface warships and signing the Test Ban Treaty were evidence of this capital shortage. The conflict over investment policy and the validity of Khrushchev's economic priorities was concentrated on the composition of the Two-Year Plan for 1964 and 1965 and the proportions of the Five-Year Plan (for the latter, see *Pravda*, 5 June 1963, p. 1; G. Sorokin, *ibid.*, 1 December 1963, p. 1; V. Kolotov, *Literaturnaia gazeta*, 30 November 1963, p. 2; N. S. Khrushchev, *Plenum Tsentral'nogo Komiteta KPSS, 9–13 dekabria 1963, stenograficheskii otchet* [Moscow, 1964], pp. 15–17 [hereafter cited as *December 1964 plenum, otchet*]; A. A. Arzumanian, *Pravda*, 24 February 1964; *ibid.*, 25 July 1964, p. 1; *ibid.*, 2 October 1964, p. 1).

7. The Liberman experiments, stillborn in Kharkov in 1963, were instituted in Moscow and Gorkii in 1964 as a result of the continuing pile-up of consumer goods on retail shelves. Conflict between the Ministry of Finance and the managers of the two experimental plants was in clear evidence (*Pravda*, 2 October 1964, p. 1; *ibid.*, 4 October 1964, p. 4; *ibid.*, 8 October 1964, p. 1). For the assault by the liberals on the existing structure of industrial management, see the articles by Academician Trapeznikov, *ibid.*, 17 August 1964, p. 2; L. Leontiev, *ibid.*, 7 September 1964, p. 2; Liberman, *ibid.*, 7 September 1964, p. 2; and O. Volkov, *ibid.*, 23 August 1964, p. 2.

8. For a Soviet discussion of the problematic efficiency of the TPU, see Khrushchev, zapiska of 2 November 1963, in Khrushchev, *Stroitel'stvo kommunizma*, 8: 243. There was little evidence, however, that the controversial November 1964 plenum contemplated any abolition of the TPU (see the purported agenda: *Pravda*, 12 August 1964, p. 1).

9. The most controversial aspect of Khrushchev's reform of agricultural management was his scheme for centralized, large-scale management of animal husbandry through "factories." The scheme, approved in early 1963, was strongly pressed by Khrushchev during 1964 (see Khrushchev, *Stroitel'stvo kommunizma*, 8: 516 ff.; *Pravda*, 14 July 1964, pp. 1–5; *ibid.*, 12 August 1964, p. 1).

10. *Pravda*, 26 April 1963, pp. 1–6; *CDSP* 15, no. 17 (1963), 5.

11. *Pravda*, 10 December 1963, pp. 1–6; *CDSP* 15, no. 48 (1963), 22.

12. *Pravda*, 26 April 1963, pp. 1–6; *CDSP* 15, no. 17 (1963): 12–13.

13. *CDSP* 15, no. 17 (1963): 12–13.

14. L. F. Ilychev, *Pravda*, 19 June 1963, pp. 1–6; *CDSP* 15, no. 2 (1963): 10–11.

15. V. V. Klochko, *Partiinaia zhizn'*, no. 14 (1963): 22–28; *CDSP* 15, no. 38 (1963): 25–26; Editorial, *Kommunist*, no. 7 (1963): 3 ff.

16. Editorial, *Partiinaia zhizn'*, no. 19 (1963): 3 ff.

17. G. Shitarev, *Voprosy istorii KPSS*, no. 6 (1963): 3–5; D. E. Bakhshiev, *ibid.*, no. 2 (1964): 30–41.

18. V. V. Shevchenko, *Pravda*, 13 December 1963, p. 3.

19. *Pravda*, 21 May 1964, p. 2.

20. *Sovetskaia Rossiia*, 1 December 1963, p. 1.

21. *Izvestiia*, 6 February 1964, p. 1.

22. *Sovetskaia Rossiia*, 28 February 1964, p. 2.

23. *Pravda Ukrainy*, 5 April 1964, p. 3.

24. *Pravda*, 7 June 1963, p. 2.

25. *Ibid.*, 21 May 1964, p. 2.

26. *Partiinaia zhizn'*, no. 19 (1963): 38–42.

27. *Pravda*, 21 May 1964, p. 2. See also Rashidov's report to the June 1963 plenum of the Uzbekistan Communist party, *ibid.*, 17 July 1963, p. 2.

28. *Sovetskaia Rossiia*, 5 February 1964, p. 1.

29. *Bakinskii rabochii*, 12 September 1964, p. 1. Titov's presence was noted in *Pravda*, 29 May 1964, p. 2. In the order of listing, N. N. Mironov, the head of the Administrative Otdel, was placed before Lomonosov.

30. *Bakinskii rabochii*, 20 April 1963, p. 1; *Kommunist* (Erevan), 26 November 1963, p. 2.

31. *Pravda*, 22 February 1963, p. 2, and *ibid.*, 26 March 1963, p. 2.

32. *Bakinskii rabochii*, 6 April 1963, p. 1.

33. *Ibid.*, 31 May 1964, p. 1.

34. *Ibid.*, 19 April 1963, p. 2.

35. *Izvestiia*, 10 October 1963, p. 1.

36. *Bakinskii rabochii*, 10 January 1964, p. 1.

37. P. Rogachev and N. Sverdlin, *Kommunist*, no. 9 (1963): 14. This is explicitly stressed in two articles by E. V. Tadevosian, *Voprosy istorii KPSS*, no. 4 (1964): 54–62 and *Voprosy filosofii*, no. 4 (1964): 21–37.

38. Rogachev and Sverdlin, *op. cit.*, pp. 18–19.

39. For examples of the campaign against "nationalist survivals" and "anti-Russian feeling": D. A. Kunaev, *Kazakhstanskaia pravda*, 26 December 1962, p. 1; Sh. Rashidov, *Pravda*, 23 May 1963, p. 2; O. Bagdasarian, *ibid.*, 25 September 1963, p. 2; V. Akhundov, *Kommunist*, no. 8 (1964): 18–19.

40. T. Usubaliev, *Kommunist*, no. 2 (1964): 17. The same complaint was registered by Secretary Lein of Latvia in *Pravda*, 27 May 1964, p. 2.

41. G. Zimanas, *Kommunist*, no. 2 (1963): 81.

42. The abuses of the policy of broadening the rights of the union republics is scored by M. O. Mnatsakanian, *Voprosy istorii KPSS*, no. 10 (1963): 14–15.

43. Usubaliev, *op. cit.*, pp. 18–19.

44. This aspect of the policy is discussed by V. Snastin, *Kommunist*, no. 6 (1963): 36–37.

45. *Izvestiia*, 3 April 1964, p. 3; see also the remarks of Bochkarev at the 1964 Azerbaidzhan Party Congress, *Bakinskii rabochii*, 28 January 1964, p. 2.

46. Usubaliev, *op. cit.*, pp. 14–15.

47. Zimanas, *op. cit.*, p. 84.

48. *Ibid.*, p. 85.

49. N. S. Khrushchev, *November 1962 plenum, otchet*, p. 25.

50. Zimanas, *op. cit.*, p. 83.

51. A. G. Gindin and S. G. Markin, *Voprosy istorii KPSS*, no. 2 (1965): 22; Usubaliev, *op. cit.*, p. 20.

52. P. A. Rodionov, *Kollektivnost'—vysshii printsip partiinogo rukovodstva*, p. 232.

53. Decree of the Central Committee of 9 April 1963 (*Spravochnik partiinogo rabotnika* [1964]: pp. 263 ff.).

54. I. I. Bodiul, *Sovetskaia Moldaviia*, 20 October 1963, pp. 2 ff.

55. *Pravda*, 26 April 1963, pp. 5; *Leningradskaia pravda*, 27 February 1963, p. 2.

56. L. A. Smoredinakov, ed., *Ocherki istorii partiinoi organizatsii Tiumenskoi oblasti* (Sverdlovsk, 1965), pp. 323–24.

57. K. Trusov, *Izvestiia*, 22 August 1964, p. 2.

58. P. Shelest, *Pravda*, 6 February 1965, p. 2.

59. P. Rukabetz, *Partiinaia zhizn'*, no. 22 (1964): 41–42.

60. See *Sovetskaia Rossiia*, 13 July 1963, p. 2; *Izvestiia*, 16 April 1963, p. 1; *Pravda Ukrainy*, 15 October 1963, p. 2.

61. A *Kommunist* editorial, no. 16 (1963): 11, warns explicitly against this situation.

62. *Ibid.*, p. 12.

63. *Sovetskaia Rossiia*, 18 August 1963, p. 1.

64. Z. Nuriev, *Kommunist*, no. 18 (1964): 38.

65. *Sovetskaia Rossiia*, 13 July 1963, p. 2.

66. *Izvestiia*, 11 September 1964, p. 5.

67. See *Partiinaia zhizn'*, no. 14 (1964): 46.

68. Shelest, *op. cit.*, p. 2.

69. *Partiinaia zhizn'*, no. 3 (1964): 38 ff.

70. Editorial, *ibid.*, p. 5.

71. *Izvestiia*, 29 June 1963, p. 6.

72. A major area of responsibility of the Party-State Control Committee was in executing Khrushchev's chemical policy (See *Pravda*, 10 May 1963, p. 3; *ibid.*, 11 October 1963, p. 2; *ibid.*, 8 July 1963, p. 3).

73. *Ibid.*, 27 April 1963, p. 4.

74. *Ibid.*, 25 January 1964, p. 4.

75. *Ibid.*, 8 May 1964, pp. 2–3.

76. *Izvestiia*, 6 December 1963, p. 3.

77. A. S. Malenkin, *Kommunist*, no. 6 (1964): 75–79.

78. The party members who were punished by the Party-State Control Committee could, and did, appeal to the corresponding Party committee for relief. The degree to which the regular Party organs reversed the committees is difficult to judge, but it appears that the regular Party organs acted to moderate the "administrative" approach of the control agencies (see the interesting article of N. Egorychev, *Pravda*, 9 October 1964, p. 3).

79. The deputy chairman of the Central Asian Sovnarkhoz was attacked in *Pravda*, 11 October 1963, p. 2; *Pravda Ukrainy*, 24 July 1963, p. 2 and *Pravda*, 1 November 1963, p. 3, offer other examples.

80. *Pravda Ukrainy*, 6 March 1963, p. 1.

81. Cf., I. S. Grushetskii, *ibid.*, 1 March 1964, p. 2; for other examples, *ibid.*, 10 September 1963, p. 1; *Sovetskaia Belorussia*, 24 September 1963, p. 2.

82. *Rabochaia gazeta*, 28 July 1964, p. 1.

83. *Pravda*, 29 January 1965, p. 2.

84. *Rabochaia gazeta*, 15 November 1964, p. 1.

85. *Pravda*, 24 May 1965, p. 2.

86. *Ibid.*, 25 May 1963, p. 3.

87. *Ibid.*, 9 October 1964, p. 4.

88. *Ibid.*, 15 January 1965, p. 3.

89. *Sovetskaia Rossiia*, 2 July 1963, p. 2.

90. *Ibid.*, 6 August 1963, p. 3.

91. V. I. Snastin, *V edinstve teorii i pratiki—zalog pobody kommunizma*, p. 55.

92. *Sovetskaia Rossiia*, 8 May 1964, p. 1.

93. P. Polozov, *Partiinaia zhizn'*, no. 13 (1964): 14–20; also K. Gorushin, *Pravda*, 16 November 1964, p. 1.

94. *Sovetskaia Rossiia*, 8 April 1964, p. 2; *Pravda*, 15 April 1965, p. 1.

95. *Partiinaia zhizn'*, no. 19 (1965): 37.

96. D. Shumskii, *Pravda*, 6 July 1964, p. 2.

97. *Sovetskaia Rossiia*, 22 February 1964, p. 2; *ibid.*, 8 May 1964, p. 1; also, A. P. Kirilenko, *ibid.*, 24 April 1963, p. 1.

98. *Pravda*, 18 November 1964, p. 1.

99. See *Kommunist*, no. 16 (1963): 10.

100. Decree of 27 December 1963 (*Spravochnik partiinogo rabotnika* [1964], p. 300 ff.).

101. *Pravda*, 15 August 1963, p. 2.

102. *Sovetskaia Rossiia*, 1 September 1964, p. 2.

103. V. Antonov, *Partiinaia zhizn'*, no. 8 (1965): 34.

104. L. B. Ermin, *Partiinaia zhizn'*, no. 1 (1963): 24.

105. *Ibid.*, no. 16 (1965): 34.

106. *Kommunist*, no. 13 (1964): 89. This article gives an excellent analysis of the "technicizing" of the Party apparatus.

107. *Sovetskaia Rossiia*, 24 April 1963, p. 3.

108. *Partiinaia zhizn'*, no. 1 (1965): 26.

109. *Ibid.*, no. 22 (1965): 35.

110. P. Pigalev, *Partiinaia zhizn'*, no. 15 (1963): passim.

111. *Ibid.*, no. 19 (1964): 23.

112. *Ibid.*, pp. 23–24.

113. I. Pronin, *Partiinaia zhizn'*, no. 12 (1963): 41.

114. For example, see *Pravda Ukrainy*, 26 December 1964, p. 3; *Pravda*, 21 October 1964, p. 2; *Partiinaia zhizn'*, no. 5 (1965): 5.

115. Editorial, *Partiinaia zhizn'*, no. 19 (1964): 5.

116. *Ibid.*, p. 6.

117. Editorial, *ibid.*, no. 6 (1964): 8–11.

118. *Ibid.*, no. 2 (1965): 13.

119. Grey Hodnett, "Khrushchev and Party State Control," in Dallin and Westin, *op. cit.*, p. 114.

120. *Pravda Ukrainy*, 1 March 1964, p. 2; also, A. S. Malenkin, *Kommunist*, no. 6 (1964): 75–76.

121. *Pravda*, 10 May 1964, p. 2; see also the complaint of the Russian Bureau on the low quality of information (*Sovetskaia Rossiia*, 5 June 1964, p. 2).

122. *Izvestiia*, 15 November 1963, p. 3; *Pravda*, 23 August 1963, p. 4; A. I. Kostenko, *Partiino-gosudarstvennyi kontrol' v deistvii* (Moscow: "Sovetskaia Rossiia," 1964), pp. 8–9.

123. A. Prazdnikov, *Partiinaia zhizn'*, no. 4 (1964): 38.

124. V. Gorin and Iu Polenov, *Kommunist*, no. 4 (1964).

125. G. Krapunova, *Partiino-gosudarstvennyi kontrol' v deistvii*, p. 59.

126. Grushetskii, *op. cit.*, p. 2.

127. H. Minich, *Izvestiia*, 17 July 1963, p. 4; *ibid.*, 4 February 1964, p. 3; *Pravda*, 15 April 1965, p. 4.

128. Prazdnikov, *op. cit.*, p. 38; editorial, *Sovetskaia Belorussia*, 9 March 1963, p. 1; *Bakinskii rabochii*, 7 August 1963, p. 2.

129. V. Zaluzhnyi, *Partiinaia zhizn'*, no. 5 (1964): 12.

130. *Bakinskii rabochii*, 7 August 1963, p. 2; Zaluzhnyi, *op. cit.*, p. 13.

131. Zaluzhnyi, *op. cit.*, pp. 12 ff.

132. *Sovetskaia Belorussiia*, 30 August 1963, p. 2.

133. Yu. I. Tarasov, in V. A. Smyshliaev, ed., *KPSS v period stroitel'stva kommunizma*, p. 82.

134. Editorial, *Kommunist*, no. 16 (1964): 3.

135. *Pravda*, 13 January 1964, p. 2.

136. *Ibid.*, 11 June 1963, p. 2.

137. *Partiinaia zhizn'*, no. 24 (1963): 16.

138. See Iu. Fishevskii, *Partiinaia zhizn'*, no. 12 (1963): 52–56.

139. *Spravochnik partiinogo rabotnika* (1964), pp. 257–60.

140. Editorial, *Pravda*, 10 January 1964, p. 2.

141. *Rabochaia gazeta*, 24 April 1963, p. 2.

142. *Ibid.*, 18 April 1963, p. 2.

143. I. Gladnev, *Partiinaia zhizn'*, no. 8 (1964): 54 ff.

144. E. Bugaev, *Partiinaia zhizn'*, no. 15 (1964): 47; V. Kozlov, *Pravda*, 4 November 1964, p. 2.

145. Editorial, *Partiinaia zhizn'*, no. 2 (1965): 4–6.

146. *Ibid.*, no. 23 (1964): 6.

147. For examples of the conflict between the Party, Party-state control, and the managerial apparatuses at the production level, see L. Rudenko, *Partiinaia zhizn'*, no. 23 (1964): 33–34; *Pravda*, 25 January 1964, p. 4; *Sovetskaia Rossiia*, 31 January 1964, p. 2.

148. Editorial, *Partiinaia zhizn'*, no. 23 (1964): 6.

149. See, for example, the illuminating remarks of Kebin, the first secretary of Estonia and a strong advocate of close Party control over the economic administrators (*Pravda*, 3 April 1966, p. 4; a partial translation is in *CDSP* 18, no. 17 [1966]: 16).

Chapter 9

1. For an evaluation and justification of the intensified administrative centralism, cf. M. Piskotin, *Kommunist*, no. 17 (1963): 30–31; also Ts. Iampol'skaia, *Sovetskoe gosudarstvo i pravo*, no. 6 (1964): 39–40.

2. An excellent description of the structural change is in M. V. Breev, *Planirovanie narodnogo khoziaistva SSSR* (Moscow, 1963), pp. 117–18.

3. The data on personnel are from the U. S., Department of State, *Directory of Soviet Officials* (1963).

4. A good description of the structure of Union Sovnarkhoz is contained in T. I. Ponizov, *Upravlenie promyshlennym proizvodstvom v SSSR* (Moscow, 1963), pp. 118–21. The council consisted of officials drawn from the sovnarkhoz, the chairmen of state committees subordinate to the council, the deputy chairmen of committees subordinate to Gosplan, and the chairmen of interrepublican and republican sovnarkhozy. An apparatus similar to the republican and regional sovnarkhozy was set up to exercise systematic control over production. In the reorganization, the chief administrations for interrepublican deliveries was transferred to the Union Sovnarkhoz from Gosplan.

5. M. I. Baryshev, *Sovetskoe gosudarstvo i pravo*, no. 8 (1963): 81, 87–89; see also *Spravochnik partiinogo rabotnika* (1964), pp. 80–85.

For the purposes of daily administration, an apparatus was formed of twenty-two administrations, employing about 700 officials and workers. In January 1963, three state committees were placed under the jurisdiction of the new Gosstroi; in March, three state production committees were added.

6. V. S. Prochina, *Sovetskoe gosudarstvo i pravo*, no. 11 (1963): 35ff.; G. Ivanov, *Planovoe khoziaistvo*, no. 11 (1963): 86–87.

7. N. S. Khrushchev, *Pravda*, 26 April 1963, p. 1; *CDSP* 15, no. 17 (1963): 3.

8. *Izvestiia*, 3 April 1964, p. 3.

9. Iu. M. Bagdabarov, *Sovetskoe gosudarstvo i pravo*, no. 6 (1963): 50–51.

10. This *apparat* is discussed in detail by B. N. Moralev, *Turkmenskaia iskra*, 13 February 1963, p. 1; see also T. Daveletin, "The Reorganization of Administration in Turkestan," *Bulletin of the Institute for the Study of the USSR* 10, no. 5 (1963): 28 ff. There were eight chief branch administrations and a number of functional departments. In addition, some chief administrations formed subsidiary administrations in each of the four republics. The subsidiary administrations, however, had a dual subordination to the sovnarkhoz and to the individual republics.

11. Ponizov, *op. cit.*, pp. 128 ff.

12. *Ibid.*

13. The Northern Caucasus Sovnarkhoz had only thirteen of twenty-nine branch administrations in Rostov; five were in the Kuban and others elsewhere (*Sovetskaia Rossiia*, 19 February 1963, p. 1).

14. According to the enabling statute of Vesenkha, the council was composed of chairman, first deputy chairman, the chairmen of Gosplan USSR, Gosstroi USSR, Sovnarkhoz USSR, the chairmen of the State Committee for Coordinating Scientific Research, State Committee for Labor and Wages, and the chairmen of the state branch and production committees subordinate to the Supreme Council. A bureau of eleven was headed by D. F. Ustinov, head of the Defense Industry. The first deputy chairmen were A. M. Taranov, who had been chairman of the Belorussian Sovnarkhoz and S. A. Tikhomeriv, a chemical specialist, who had been minister of the chemical industry until 1958 and then head of the State Committee for Chemistry (the joint decree is found in *Spravochnik partiinogo rabotnika* [1964], pp. 96–98).

15. *Pravda*, 14 March 1963, p. 1. The five ministries were: the Ministry of Medium Machine Building, Ministry of Transport Construction, USSR Ministry of Power and Electrification, USSR Ministry for Construction in Central Asia, and the USSR Ministry of Geology and Preservation of Mineral Resources.

16. *Ibid.*

17. The powers and functions accorded to Gosplan USSR can be found in the Law of 11 January 1963, in *Spravochnik partiinogo rabotnika* (1964), pp. 75–80.

18. Gosplan continued to be responsible for laying down the key indicators of the plan and for producing a single integrated plan with the participation of Union Sovnarkhoz and Gosstroi USSR. Gosplan was also expected to monitor production and plan fulfillment of the progressive branches and the output of new products. Planning for capital construction was placed under the direct jurisdiction of Gosstroi USSR. The capital construction plan, however, was subject to cross-checking by Gosplan, Union Sovnarkhoz, and in critically important projects of chemical construction, by the Supreme Council of the National Economy.

19. *Spravochnik partiinogo rabotnika* (1964), pp. 65–70. Sovnarkhoz USSR also took direct control over cooperative deliveries for special parts required by the machine-building industry. The Union Sovnarkhoz, with Gosplan, had the right to introduce changes in the plans of the union republics and the Central Asian Sovnarkhoz. It was given control over the distribution of above-plan production and also had the important function of assigning supplemental plans to the lower organs.

20. The statute is contained in *Spravochnik partiinogo rabotnika* (1964), pp. 70–75; see also, Ivanov, *op. cit.*; pp. 86–87 and Prochina, *op. cit.*, pp. 35 ff. Within the planning process, their function was to dovetail the regional plans of the republics with branch requirements into a single national plan. The process of coordinating plans compiled from below was to be combined with the active selection by the state committees of the volume and assortment of products, to establish new technical processes, and to remove obsolete products from production. Finally, the state committees were to participate in establishing the qualitative plan indicators, particularly for labor productivity and for cost reduction.

21. *Spravochnik partiinogo rabotnika* (1964), pp. 109–12. The councils for coordination of development of the national economy were established in twenty-one economic regions of the Russian Republic, in seven economic regions of the Ukraine, and in three regions of the Kazakh Republic.

22. V. Pavlenko, *Ekonomicheskaia gazeta*, no. 42 (1963): 12–13; *CDSP* 15, no. 42 (1963): 3–5.

23. *Ibid.*

24. B. N. Moravlev, *Turkmenskaia iskra*, 13 February 1963, p. 1. However, the sovnarkhoz lacked the power to introduce changes in the approved central plan for the region.

25. *Izvestiia*, 27 September 1964, p. 2.

26. Cf., A. A. Rashkin and I. E. Kras'ko, *Sovetskoe gosudarstvo i pravo*, no. 7 (1963): 99–105. These scholars insisted that from the juridical point of view the regional sovnarkhozy could no longer be considered local organs of administration (p. 100); see also L. M. Shor, *ibid.*, no. 6 (1963): 55–63. Botli articles protest the detailed intervention of the center in local decisions.

27. *Spravochnik partiinogo rabotnika* (1964), pp. 80–85.

28. A. Kuzmich, *Kommunist Ukrainy*, no. 1 (1963): 15–16; also Baryshev, *op. cit.*, 89.

29. *Planovoe khoziaistvo*, no. 4 (1965): 70; *Pravda*, 14 September 1964, pp. 2–3.

30. *Ekonomicheskaia gazeta*, no. 47 (1963): 2.

31. Pavlenko, *op. cit.*

32. *Ekonomicheskaia gazeta*, no. 47 (1963): 2.

33. A. P. Kirilenko, *Sovetskaia Rossiia*, 24 April 1963, pp. 2–3.

34. *Izvestiia*, 4 February 1964, p. 2.

35. *Pravda*, 2 June 1964, p. 2.

36. *Ibid.*, 1 December 1964, p. 3.

37. *Ibid.*, 10 December 1964, p. 1.

38. *Ibid.*, 6 December 1964, p. 1.

39. For a good discussion of this problem, see Iu. Tikhomirov, *Sovetskoe gosudarstvo i pravo*, no. 1 (1964): 26 ff. The role of veto-groups described here refers to limited technical and product innovation.

40. *Ekonomicheskaia gazeta*, no. 47 (1963): 2.

41. V. Akulintsev, *ibid.*, no. 20 (1963): 40–41.

42. *Ekonomicheskaia gazeta*, no. 32 (1964): 10.

43. *Izvestiia*, 10 September 1964, p. 3.

44. O. Latsis, *Ekonomicheskaia gazeta*, no. 7 (1963): 14.

45. *Pravda*, 21 May 1964, p. 2.

46. See L. Kalchina, *Kommunist*, no. 15 (1964): 39–46 for a general discussion of administrative practice during this period.

47. *Sovetskaia Rossiia*, 22 May 1964, p. 3.

48. *Ibid.*, 24 July 1964, p. 2.

49. *Ibid.*, 23 September 1964, p. 2.

50. *Izvestiia*, 4 August 1964, p. 4.

51. Kalchina, *op. cit.*, pp. 39–46.

52. *Izvestiia*, 1 August 1963, p. 3; A. Korovkin, *Planove khoziaistvo*, no. 1 (1965): 80–82.

A study of a machine-building plant in Moscow indicated that while production workers grew by 15 percent, the number of administrative workers was 47 percent greater in 1963 than in 1960. In a Stavropol machine-building plant, the same study indicated, the percentage over the same period of time was 23 percent and 71 percent.

53. M. I. Piskotin *et al.*, *Sovetskoe gosudarstvo i pravo*, no. 9 (1964): 24.

54. N. Koshelov, *Izvestiia*, 27 November 1963, p. 3.

55. Editorial, *Kommunist*, no. 3 (1964): 11–18.

56. *Ibid.*

57. Iu. Chadaev, *Planovoe khoziaistvo*, no. 11 (1963): 3.

58. *Pravda*, 16 July 1963, p. 2.

59. *Izvestiia*, 13 August 1963, p. 2.

60. *Pravda*, 25 July 1963, p. 2.
61. P. Lomako, *Pravda*, 17 December 1963, pp. 2–4.
62. A. Venzovskii and M. Stoliarova, *Planovoe khoziaistvo*, no. 7 (1965): 45.
63. *Ibid.*
64. Revived criticism of the advocates of economic methods of management reflected, of course, the continuation of the most problematic aspects of the traditional administration of planning (for a specific example, see *Pravda*, 9 July 1964, p. 2).
65. *Planovoe khoziaistvo*, no. 12 (1963): 74–75.
66. *Ekonomicheskaia gazeta*, no. 7 (1963): 9; M. Alexeev, *Planovoe khoziaistvo*, no. 4 (1965): 67; *Pravda*, 28 August 1964, p. 2; *Ekonomicheskaia gazeta*, no. 38 (1964): 7, 8; *Sovetskaia Rossiia*, 7 September 1963, p. 1.
67. See *Ekonomicheskaia gazeta*, no. 28 (1963): 14–15.
68. *Ibid.*, no. 38 (1964): 7–8.
69. Alexeev, *op. cit.*, pp. 64 ff.; *Sovetskaia Rossiia*, 6 September 1963, p. 2; *Ekonomicheskaia gazeta*, no. 23 (1964): 2.
70. Data released by the Central Statistical Administration and found in *Pravda*, 24 January 1964, pp. 1–2 and *ibid.*, 30 January 1965, pp. 1–2. The results of the Soviet performance in industry and agriculture are well summarized in Harry Schwartz, *The Soviet Economy since Stalin* (Philadelphia, 1965), pp. 128–33. A close student of the Soviet economy, Rush Greenslade, however, estimated the Soviet growth rate to be as low as 4 percent for the 1961–65 period (Rush Greenslade, "The Soviet Economy in Transition," in U. S., Congress, Joint Economic Committee, *New Directions in the Soviet Economy*, pt. I, p. 4).
71. *Ibid.*
72. M. Alexeev, *Pravda*, 7 December 1964, p. 2; I. Manvelov, *ibid.*, 19 September 1964, p. 3.
73. *Pravda Ukrainy*, 10 June 1964, p. 2; *Sovetskaia Rossiia*, 7 July 1964, p. 2.
74. *Pravda*, 8 March 1964, p. 1; G. Fedorov, *Partiinaia zhizn'*, no. 17 (1963): 22–23.
75. In his summary of managerial practices, V. Zaluzhnyi listed eight points of criticism; among them, the desire of managers to fulfill the plan at any cost or deception in the reporting of plan fulfillment. In the vital area of managerial response, it is clear that the reform made no appreciable improvement over the past (V. Zaluzhnyi, *Partiinaia zhizn'*, no. 1 [1965]: 13–16; for similar complaints, *Ekonomicheskaia gazeta*, no. 3 [1964]: 2; *Izvestiia*, 9 May 1963, p. 3; *Pravda*, 9 July 1964, p. 2).
76. P. Solomonov, *Pravda*, 2 October 1963, p. 4.
77. *Ekonomicheskaia gazeta*, no. 47 (1963): 13.
78. Solomonov, *op. cit.*
79. *Izvestiia*, 19 July 1963, p. 2.
80. See the remarks of the chairman of the Black Sea Sovnarkhoz, *ibid.*, 5 September 1963, p. 3.
81. V. V. Krotov, *ibid.*, 14 June 1963, p. 3.
82. Zaluzhnyi, *op. cit.*; *Pravda Ukrainy*, 10 June 1964, p. 2.
83. *December 1963 plenum, otchet*, pp. 105–6.
84. N. Ia. Cherniak, *Sovetskoe gosudarstvo i pravo*, no. 2 (1964): 56 ff.
85. *Izvestiia*, 13 September 1964, p. 2.
86. *Pravda*, 17 July 1963, p. 1.
87. *Pravda Ukrainy*, 3 June 1964, p. 1.
88. According to the figures released by S. P. Pavlov, some 160 thousand Komsomols were mobilized for the chemical construction industry (*December 1963 plenum, otchet*, p. 264).

89. *Pravda Ukrainy*, 5 July 1964, p. 2.

90. *Pravda*, 3 February 1964, p. 2.

91. *Izvestiia*, 11 November 1963, p. 2.

92. *Ibid.*, 13 September 1964, p. 2; *Pravda*, 4 March 1964, p. 2.

93. The joint sessions of 13 March 1964 and at the end of September 1964 were both held to deal with Khrushchev's controversial economic policy.

94. Khrushchev, *Pravda*, 26 April 1963, pp. 1–6; *CDSP* 15, no. 17 (1963): 4.

95. See, for example, *Pravda*, 26 August 1964, p. 2.

96. *Sovetskaia Rossiia*, 13 February 1963, p. 1; for other examples see *ibid.*, 2 April 1963, p. 1; 13 August 1963, p. 1; 31 May 1964, p. 1.

97. *Ibid.*, 14 February 1963, p. 1; *ibid.*, 9 January 1964, p. 2.

98. *Ibid.*, 29 February 1964, p. 1.

99. See the remarks of the first secretary of the Iarostavl Obkom, *ibid.*, 11 March 1964, p. 2.

100. *Pravda*, 8 May 1963, p. 2.

101. *Kommunist Tadzhikistana*, 27 August 1963, p. 1.

102. *Ekonomicheskaia gazeta*, no. 27 (1963): 3.

103. *Ibid.*, no. 20 (1963): 40–41.

104. *Kommunist* (Erevan), 11 January 1964, p. 1.

105. For a report on these conferences, see *Bakinskii rabochii*, 28 August 1963, p. 1; *ibid.*, 29 May 1964, p. 2.

106. *Ibid.*, 4 February 1963, pp. 1–2.

107. *Ibid.*, 28 January 1964, p. 2.

108. E. N. Alikhanov, *Izvestiia*, 27 May 1964, p. 3.

109. *Bakinskii rabochii*, 10 January 1964, pp. 1 and 3.

110. The increased power of the republican apparatus was confined, however, to republican agencies and below. With respect to the central State organs, this rule was reduced.

111. *Ekonomicheskaia gazeta*, no. 32 (1963): 4.

112. *Ibid.*, no. 39 (1963): 3.

113. O. Latsis, *ibid.*, no. 7 (1963): 7.

114. *Ekonomicheskaia gazeta*, no. 45 (1963): 12.

115. *Rabochaia gazeta*, 21 July 1964, p. 2.

116. *Pravda Ukrainy*, 7 March 1963, p. 1; *ibid.*, 16 November 1963, p. 1.

117. *Izvestiia*, 10 October 1963, p. 1.

118. *Sovetskaia Belorussiia*, 5 August 1963, p. 1; *ibid.*, 16 September 1963, pp. 1–2.

119. *Pravda*, 12 November 1963, p. 2.

120. *Ekonomicheskaia gazeta*, no. 45 (1963): 13; *Sovetskaia Rossiia*, 7 August 1963, p. 2; *Pravda*, 18 August 1964, p. 2.

121. A. Protozanov, *Izvestiia*, 23 October 1963, p. 3.

122. *Ekonomicheskaia gazeta*, no. 8 (1963): 15.

123. L. B. Ermin, *Partiinaia zhizn'*, no. 1 (1963): 24.

124. *Izvestiia*, 22 October 1963, p. 3.

125. *Pravda*, 7 February 1964, p. 2; *ibid.*, 9 September 1963, p. 2; *Sovetskaia Rossiia*, 7 August 1964, p. 2.

126. Decree of the Central Committee of 6 March 1963, *Spravochnik partiinogo rabotnika* (1964), pp. 252–57.

127. *Pravda Ukrainy*, 27 August 1964, p. 2.

128. *Sovetskaia Rossiia*, 11 March 1964, p. 2.

129. *Pravda*, 25 July 1963, p. 2; see also *Ekonomicheskaia gazeta*, no. 40 (1963): 3, and *ibid.*, no. 41 (1963): 3.

130. Editorial, *Pravda*, 14 August 1963, p. 1; editorial, *Sovetskaia Rossiia*, 1 August 1963, p. 1.

131. *Partiinaia zhizn'*, no. 5 (1963): 15; *Ekonomicheskaia gazeta*, no. 45 (1963): 12.

132. *Pravda*, 4 March 1965, p. 2.

133. *Izvestiia*, 16 November 1963, p. 3.

134. K. I. Galanshin, *December 1963 plenum, otchet*, pp. 235 ff.; *Pravda*, 10 September 1964, p. 2.

135. *Pravda Ukrainy*, 8 May 1963, p. 3.

136. *Partiinaia zhizn'*, no. 24 (1963): 28.

137. For examples, see *Ekonomicheskaia gazeta*, no. 27 (1964): 4; editorial, *Kommunist*, no. 16 (1963), 3–16; *Ekonomicheskaia gazeta*, no. 38 (1963): 3; *Pravda*, 26 August 1964, p. 2; *Sovetskaia Rossiia*, 24 April 1963, p. 2.

138. B. Vladimirov and V. Nikolaev, *Kommunist*, no. 13 (1964): 85–87.

139. *Partiinaia zhizn'*, no. 19 (1963): 8–10.

140. P. Sivanov, *Sovetskaia Belorussiia*, 3 December 1963, p. 1.

141. *Ibid.*

142. *Partiinaia zhizn'*, no. 11 (1963): 22–23.

143. D. Shumskii, *Pravda*, 6 July 1964, p. 2.

144. *Partiinaia zhizn'*, no. 15 (1964): 35–36.

145. *Pravda*, 15 October 1963, p. 2; *ibid.*, 26 December 1963, p. 2; *Sovetskaia Moldaviia*, 20 October 1963, p. 3; *Pravda Ukrainy*, 14 June 1964, pp. 1–2.

146. For examples of the latter point, see *Partiinaia zhizn'*, no. 24 (1963): 30; *Izvestiia*, 28 March 1964, p. 3; and *ibid.*, 20 February 1965, p. 3.

147. *Izvestiia*, 23 October 1963, p. 3; *Sovetskaia Rossiia*, 8 August 1963, p. 3; *Kommunist Belorussii*, no. 10 (1963): 31.

148. Complaints concerning their inability to influence the center on vital issues frequently appeared in the press (*Izvestiia*, 13 November 1963, p. 3; *Pravda Ukrainy*, 26 May 1964, p. 2; *Pravda*, 20 August 1963, p. 2).

149. *Pravda*, 16 January 1965, p. 2.

150. *Ibid.*, 27 February 1963, p. 3.

151. M. Shul'gin, *Kommunist Ukrainy*, no. 8 (1964): 56–59; *Pravda Ukrainy*, 8 January 1964, p. 2; *Rabochaia gazeta*, 12 September 1963, p. 1; *Pravda*, 24 February 1965, p. 2.

152. *Pravda*, 24 February 1965, p. 2.

153. *Partiinaia zhizn'*, no. 24 (1963): 31–32; *Sovetskaia Rossiia*, 19 June 1964, p. 2.

154. V. Vetlitskii, *Partiinaia zhizn'*, no. 11 (1964): 55.

155. *Ibid.*, no. 3 (1964): 5.

156. *Ibid.*, no. 22 (1965): 37 ff.

157. For examples, see L. Rudenko, *ibid.*, no. 23 (1964): 33–34; *Sovetskaia Rossiia*, 12 November 1963, p. 2; *Pravda*, 9 March 1963, p. 2.

158. *Sovetskaia Rossiia*, 12 March 1964, p. 2.

159. I. Pronin, *Partiinaia zhizn'*, no. 12 (1963): 40 ff.

160. Editorial, *ibid.*, no. 6 (1964): 8–11.

161. For complaints about poor control see, *Pravda Ukrainy*, 26 December 1964, p. 3; *Pravda*, 25 May 1963, p. 4; *ibid.*, 26 November 1964, p. 3; *ibid.*, 21 October 1964, p. 2.

162. *Pravda Ukrainy*, 21 August 1964, p. 3.

163. Shumskii, *op. cit.*; for other examples: *Izvestiia*, 6 October 1963, p. 2; *Pravda Ukrainy*, 13 July 1963, p. 3; *ibid.*, 5 July 1964, p. 8.

164. *Sovetskaia Belorussiia*, 6 August 1963, p. 2.

165. *Ekonomicheskaia gazeta*, no. 9 (1963): 42.

166. *Pravda*, 6 May 1963, p. 2; *Sovetskaia Rossiia*, 4 January 1964, p. 2.

167. *Pravda*, 8 January 1965, p. 2.

168. *Rabochaia gazeta*, 13 July 1963, p. 2.

169. N. Zenchenko, *Partiinaia zhizn'*, no. 22 (1964): 43–44.

170. *Pravda*, 11 October 1963, p. 2.

171. *Izvestiia*, 7 January 1964, p. 3.

172. See A. S. Malenkin, *Kommunist*, no. 6 (1964): 75–79; *Pravda*, 6 July 1963, p. 2; *Izvestiia*, 6 December 1963, p. 3.

173. *Sovetskaia Rossiia*, 25 April 1963, p. 2.

174. *Pravda*, 28 December 1963, p. 3.

175. *Izvestiia*, 23 February 1965, p. 3.

176. *Ibid.*, 2 November 1963, p. 3.

177. *Ibid.*, p. 4.

178. *Ibid.*, 7 January 1964, p. 3; *Pravda*, 28 December 1963, p. 2; *ibid.*, 26 March 1964, p. 2; *Rabochaia gazeta*, 30 September 1964, p. 2; *Sovetskaia Rossiia*, 2 July 1963, p. 2.

179. *Pravda Ukrainy*, 20 May 1963, p. 2.

180. *Pravda*, 3 April 1964, p. 3.

181. *Ibid.*, 25 January 1964, p. 4; *Pravda Ukrainy*, 4 June 1963, p. 2; *Pravda*, 18 April 1965, p. 4.

182. *Pravda*, 23 August 1963, p. 4.

183. *Sovetskaia Rossiia*, 25 September 1963, p. 2.

184. *Ibid.*, 15 August 1963, p. 2.

185. I. Mitin, *Partiinaia zhizn'*, no. 11 (1963): 46–47.

186. V. Gorin and Iu. Polenov, *Kommunist*, no. 6 (1964): 72.

187. Decree of the PGK of 19 July 1963, *Spravochnik partiinogo rabotnika (1964)*, pp. 317–18; *Kommunist Estonii*, no. 5 (1964): 95–98; *Sovetskaia Belorussiia*, 1 November 1963, p. 2.

188. *Sovetskaia Rossiia*, 31 January 1964, p. 2.

189. *Ibid.*, 17 April 1963, p. 2.

190. For an account of the general role, see A. E. Lunev, *Obespechenie zakonnosti v SSSR*, pp. 105 ff. Specific examples were given in profusion in the various *listki* of the Party-State Control Committees: *Pravda*, 8 April 1963, p. 4; *Pravda Ukrainy*, 30 June 1964, p. 4; *Pravda*, 23 January 1964, p. 3; *Rabochaia gazeta*, 14 March 1964, p. 1.

191. V. Zaluzhnyi, *Partiinaia zhizn'*, no. 5 (1964): 10.

192. *Pravda*, 28 December 1963, p. 4.

193. *Izvestiia*, 20 August 1963, p. 4.

194. For examples of the specific control activities of the agricultural PGK, see L. Korniiets, *Pravda*, 8 June 1963, p. 3; *Pravda Ukrainy*, 28 September 1963, p. 2; *Sovetskaia Kirghiziia*, 11 October 1963, p. 2; *Kommunist Tadzhikistana*, 31 October 1963, p. 2.

195. *Pravda*, 11 February 1965, p. 2.

Chapter 10

1. Michel Tatu, *Power in the Kremlin*, pp. 387 ff.
2. *Pravda*, 18 November 1964, p. 1.
3. I. Pronin and S. A. Smirnov, comps., *Zhiznennaia sila leninskikh printsipov partiinogo stroitel'stva* (Moscow, 1970), pp. 75—77.
4. The reaffirmation of the legislation of 1955–58 is in *Spravochnik partiinogo rabotnika* , 7th ed. (Moscow, 1967), pp. 405–55. A description of additional rights delegated but not published, such as the republican Party committees' control over their presses, can be found in B. N. Moralev, *Respublikanskie, kraevye, oblastnye, okruzhnye, gorodskie, i raionnye organizatsii partii* (Moscow, 1967), pp. 38–41.
5. There was an extensive outpouring in the Party press in defense of the Party's role and authority structure. Cf. S. A. Kovalev, *Pravda*, 25 April 1968, pp. 2–3; N. Lomakin, *Pravda*, 19 September 1968, pp. 3–4; F. Petrenko, *Partiinaia zhizn'*, no. 20 (1968): 12 ff.
6. Cf. V. Zasorin, *Partiinaia zhizn'*, no. 3 (1969): 14–15.
7. The attacks on Khrushchev and his personal style were, of course, also directed at the heavy economic and administrative costs produced by the November 1962 reorganization (see, among others, N. Lomakin, *Partiinaia zhizn'*, no. 21 (1965): 10–11, and P. Rodionov, *Partiinaia zhizn'*, no. 19 (1965): 37 ff.).
8. An excellent review of the major issues of conflict in the post-Khrushchev leadership is to be found in Sidney I. Ploss, "Politics in the Kremlin," *Problems of Communism* 14, no. 3 (1970): 6–7. As these lines are written in the fall of 1970, there is cumulative evidence that Brezhnev is reaching, or has reached, a hegemonic position in the Soviet leadership. The fact that he was required to postpone the convocation of the Twenty-fourth Party Congress until 1971, despite his public advocacy for holding it in 1970, is evidence that he still operates under significant political restraints. The argument for continuing stability in the collective leadership is well developed in Jerome M. Gilison, "New Factors of Stability in Soviet Collective Leadership," *World Politics* 19, no. 4 (1967): 563–81; see also Tibor Szamuely, "The USSR since Khrushchev," *Survey*, no. 72 (1969): 51–69; and, most recently, an excellent analysis by T. H. Rigby, "The Soviet Leadership: Towards A Self-stabilizing Oligarchy," *Soviet Studies* 22, no. 2 (1970): 167–91.
9. The most extreme view of the liberal position on collective leadership known to the author is that of F. Petrenko, *Pravda*, 20 July 1966, pp. 2–3, who declared, "The Secretary of the Party committee is not a boss; he is not empowered with the right to command." The antirevisionist literature dominant since 1968 has either ignored the issue or indirectly supported the role of the line official.
10. *Pravda*, 17 November 1964, p. 1. The Twenty-third Congress completed the job of tightening admission policies, abolishing the Russian Bureau, renaming the Presidium the Politburo, renaming the first secretary as general secretary, and retaining the principle but abolishing mandatory quotas of turnover (*Pravda*, 9 April 1966, p. 4).
11. The most pointed criticism was offered by I. V. Kapitonov, the Central Committee's organizational secretary, who noted that "new members were needed not for advertising purposes but for serious work" and that "some comrades, living as they do in an environment marked by increasing social homogeneity and moral and political

unity of the people, at times tended to the view that matters such as those enumerated should not be raised in admitting new members'' (I. V. Kapitonov, "The CPSU after the 23rd Congress," *World Marxist Review* 9, no. 9 (1966): 6). Kapitonov's reference to the growing sense of consensus has, of course, basic implications for the political system.

12. The Party's overall composition through 1969 has changed only moderately. In 1969, workers rose to 39.3 percent; kolkhozniki dropped to 15.6 percent; and 45.1 percent were employees (Pronin, in Pronin and Smirnov, *op. cit.*, p. 85).

13. Extensive sociological and quantitative analyses of the 1966 Central Committee are provided by Michael P. Gehlen and Michael McBride, "The Soviet Central Committee: An Elite Analysis," *American Political Science Review* 62, no. 4 (1968): 1232–41; Jerry F. Hough, "In Whose Hands the Future?" *Problems of Communism* 16, no. 2 (1967): 19; A. Lebed, "The Party Oligarchy after the Twenty-third Congress," *Bulletin of the Institute for the Study of the U.S.S.R.* 13, no. 7 (1966): 36–42.

14. Hough, "In Whose Hands," p. 21; for an extended analysis of the six committees, see Jerry F. Hough, *The Soviet Prefects*, table A. 1, p. 322.

15. Pronin, in Pronin and Smirnov, *op. cit.*, p. 80; see also V. Zasorin, *Partiinaia zhizn'*, no. 3 (1969): 10–18. In conformity with long established practice, the post-Khrushchev leadership has continued to reduce the proportion of apparat representation the lower the committee in the hierarchy.

16. The holdovers are Brezhnev, Kosygin, Podgorny, Polianskii, Suslov, and Voronov. In addition to Khrushchev, Frol Kozlov, Mikoian, Shvernik, and Kuusinen have left the 1962 Presidium.

17. A. N. Shelepin and P. E. Shelest were added in November 1964; K. T. Mazurov in March 1965; and A. J. Pel'she at the Twenty-third Congress. The appointment of Shelepin and Shelest apparently reflected their part in Khrushchev's ouster. Pel'she was a student with Boris Ponomarev at the Institute of Red Professors in the early thirties and may therefore be associated with Suslov. Mazurov was associated with the Komsomols and with light industry, thus providing possible linkages with Shelepin and Kosygin. The case for linking the Belorussian apparatus with Shelepin is made by Robert M. Slusser, "America, China, and the Hydra-Headed Opposition," in Peter H. Juviler and Henry W. Morton, eds., *Soviet Policy-Making: Studies of Communism in Transition* (New York, 1967), pp. 190 ff.

18. The regional representation includes: V. V. Grishin (Moscow); P. M. Masherov (Belorussia); V. P. Mzhavanadze (Georgia); D. A. Kunaev (Kazakhstan); V. V. Shcherbitskii (Ukraine); and Sh. R. Rashidov (Uzbek Republic).

19. Even during the reformist phase of the post-Khrushchev era, the lines of authority were not fully or clearly drawn. The evidence since 1968 indicates a definite upsurge in the role of Brezhnev and the Party apparatus. Brezhnev's effort to control industrial policy and management climaxed in his severe criticism of the managers at the December 1969 Plenum of the Central Committee.

20. The interpenetration and struggle for control within the Politburo over the key functional areas of Soviet life was suggested by a number of appointments in 1967 and 1968, particularly in relation to the international Communist movement and the police. Appointing K. F. Katushev as a Central Committee secretary in April 1968 to replace Andropov, in charge of Bloc Communist Parties, suggested a challenge by Brezhnev to Suslov's position in the international Communist movement. The appointments of Pel'she in 1966 and Andropov in 1967 as chairmen of the Party Control Committee and the KGB suggested a strong role for Suslov in domestic affairs. Jerry F. Hough in "Reforms in Government and Administration," Alexander Dallin and

Thomas B. Larson, eds., *Soviet Politics since Khrushchev* (Englewood Cliffs, N.J.: Prentice-Hall, 1968), p. 30, has indicated the probability of Suslov's taking over the Administrative Organs Department.

That this move has been countered by Brezhnev and probably others as well is indicated by the reorganization and renaming of the Ministry for Safeguarding Public Order as the Ministry of Internal Affairs and the reappointment of N. A. Shchelokov as its head. Shchelokov had been a close associate of Brezhnev in Dnepropetrovsk and Moldavia. That neither Brezhnev nor Suslov is totally dominant, however, is indicated by the fact that in addition to Kirilenko and Andropov, Voronov and Mazurov participated in an all-union police conference of the MVD in December 1968. Rigby, *op. cit.*, p. 189, has pointed to the trouble of the MVD and KGB as well as to the distribution of plural centers in appointments and holding office.

21. The appointment in 1968 of K. F. Katushev, forty-one, to the Secretariat lowered the average age of the Secretariat to below that of the Politburo. Without Katushev, the average age differential between the two bodies would be insignificant.

22. The call to place all cadre work in the same hands was made by F. S. Goriachev, first secretary of Novosibirsk, *Pravda*, 31 March 1966, p. 5. The argument against a special cadres department is made by I. G. Kebin, the Estonian first secretary (*Pravda*, 5 April 1966, p. 4).

23. Hough, "In Whose Hands," p. 21. The most active structural change in the Party apparatus occurred between the October 1964 plenum and the Twenty-third Congress. The adjustments since mid-1966 have been minimal.

24. Quite inexplicably, the republican bureaus were cut back to nine full members in 1965 although the obkom bureau usually numbered eleven. In fourteen republican bureaus, of 123 full members, seventy-five were republican secretaries and department heads. The pattern has been similar in the usual obkom, except that at least one gorkom first secretary has been added to the bureau. While the gorkom bureau presumably shows a somewhat more diverse composition, the structure of the Rostov City Committee may be typical. It included three secretaries, one department head, two urban raikom secretaries, a newspaper editor, an enterprise director, the chairmen of the city soviet and Committee of Popular Control, and the first secretary of the Komsomol (for the relevant data see Hough, *The Soviet Prefects*, pp. 332–33, and Pronin, in Pronin and Smirnov, *op. cit.*, pp. 32–33).

25. Moravlev, *op. cit.*, pp. 36 ff.

26. A Soviet source has indicated a significant expansion since 1965 in the size of the apparatus, now apparently at the 1953 levels. The expansion of the general membership and increase in the number of primary Party organs, however, has maintained the heavy pressure on the local Party organs (see F. L. Chusovikin, in A. F. Iudenkov, ed., *Voprosy partiinogo rukovodstva na sovremennom etape* [Moscow, 1969], p. 38).

27. For an extensive survey of the nonstaff Party organization, see the unsigned editorial article in *Partiinaia zhizn'*, no. 22 (1968): 8–13. While aggregate figures are not revealed in this article, the extent of the reduction is evident from a survey of eleven oblasti in the RSFSR which had a total of only fifteen-hundred instructors.

28. At the beginning of 1969, the Committee of Popular Control had about seven million in 900 thousand groups and posts (I. Shikin, *Partiinaia zhizn'*, no. 2 (1969): 8–15). A comprehensive discussion of the structure and functions of the committee is contained in V. I. Turovtsev, ed., *Narodnyi kontrol' v SSSR*, chap. 4).

29. Through the 1970 elections to the Supreme Soviet, six of fourteen republican first secretaries had been removed. In the Russian Republic, twenty-eight of fifty-five oblast committees changed first secretaries. Sixteen of twenty-five first secretaries in

the Ukraine turned over as well as half those in Belorussia. The most distinctive change in the post-Khrushchev period has been the appointment of sixteen former first secretaries in the Russian Republic who moved into the state apparatus as deputy ministers, ministers, or members of the republican or Union Council of Ministers, an evident reversal of Khrushchev's policy.

30. The redu⸰ed turnover has been accompanied by an increase in the number of full-time secretaries and a steady increase in the number of committees and Party groups (cf. *Partiinaia zhizn'*, no. 3 (1968): 27; *ibid.*, no. 5 (1969): 8). In 1970, elections were held in 363 thousand primary Party organs; 87 percent of the secretaries had at least a secondary education (*ibid.*, no. 6 (1970): 9–11).

31. In 1967, at the obkom level (excluding first secretaries), 63.9 percent of the secretaries and ⸰ 2.8 percent of department heads had been in office less than three years. Among gorkom first secretaries, 57.5 percent were in office the same length of time. The "overwhelming number" of officials at the local level, including instructors, were also removed after 1964 (Moralev, *op. cit.*, p. 48).

32. Chusovikin, *op. cit.*, pp. 19–20. In 1947, only 41.3 percent of the regional and 12.7 percent of local Party secretaries had higher education. In 1967, 97.6 percent of the republican and oblast secretaries had higher (63 percent with specialized) education; and 91.1 percent of city and raion secretaries had higher education, although only 51 percent were specialized. The emphasis on youth is evident in the data released on their age. Among regional secretaries in 1967, 25 percent were under forty; 52 percent were from forty to fifty; and only 23 percent were over fifty. Among local Party secretaries, 54 percent were under forty and 3 percent were fifty (I. Pronin and M. Stepichev, *Leninskie normy partiinoi zhizni* (Moscow, 1969), p. 153). The same emphasis is found in the appointments of obkom department heads. In 1967, 96.7 percent had a higher education, of whom 38.3 percent were engineers and economists, and another 10.6 percent agronomists. (Moralev, *op. cit.*, pp. 45–46).

33. G. Krivoshein, *Kommunist*, no. 5 (1968): 53; see also, F. Tabeev, *Pravda*, 12 December 1966, p. 2. In the Tatar Republic, 109 of 123 gorkom secretaries had served as secretaries of primary Party organs. Technical specialists without Party training or experience are still promoted, however (V. Tolstikov, *Pravda*, 29 March 1967, pp. 2–3; K. F. Katushev, *Partiinaia zhizn'*, no. 10 (1967): 29).

34. One important change has been an emphasis on training in a Higher Party School in addition to technical training in a higher educational institution (Moralev, *op. cit.*, p. 48). In the 1967 obkomy, 40 percent of the secretaries and 32 percent of the department heads had some form of higher Party schooling.

35. I. V. Kapitonov's career declined abruptly in 1959 under Khrushchev. While his criticism of Khrushchev's style may be somewhat exaggerated, it typifies the reaction against intuition as a major mode of decision-making: "There were cases when conceited and none too competent functionaries, though possessing only a smattering of the knowledge required, or displaying little interest in the subject, were guided solely by considerations of the moment, and did not even trouble to verify the soundness of their opinions. At times the most primitive calculations were used. But, where people are concerned, knowledge of the four rules of arithmetic are not enough" (Kapitonov, *op. cit.*, p. 10).

36. Cf. *Pravda*, 8 October 1966, p. 2; V. Mazyrin, *Partiinaia zhizn'*, no. 20 (1966): 38–42; A. Vatchenko, *Partiinaia zhizn'*, no. 13 (1968), 18–22.

37. The most recent efforts are discussed in detail by G. Kolbin, *Pravda*, 6 February 1967, pp. 2–3, and Pronin, in Pronin and Smirnov, *op. cit.*, p. 83.

38. As many Soviet commentators note, however, the habits of the apparatus are extremely tenacious. The current Party leadership's success in changing the organizational

style of the Party bureaucracy has presumably been quite limited (cf. Kolbin, *op. cit.*
and F. Tabeev, *Kommunist*, no. 1 (1967): 41; Moravlev, *op. cit.*, pp. 29 ff.). Moravlev
notes that the Fergana Obkom planned 119 questions for 1965 and 1966 but actually
decided 568 questions, not counting the consideration of appeals, affirmations of the
nomenklatura, and other business normally transacted.

39. N. Rodionov, *Kommunist*, no. 9 (1967): 58–59.

40. G. Shitarev, *Partiinaia zhizn'*, no. 18 (1965): 28–37; Vatchenko, *op. cit.*, pp.
18–22.

41. Z. Nuriev, *Kommunist*, no. 16 (1965): 59–67.

42. V. Smirnov gives an extensively detailed description of the structure and operation
of the Gorki Institute, connected with Gorki University, in P. N. Andreev, ed., *Partiinyi
komitet i ekonomicheskaia reforma* (Moscow: Politizdat, 1968), p. 51.

43. It was assumed in Gorki, for example, that labor turnover was greater among
younger, inexperienced, and poorly trained workers. In fact, movement was greater
among those over thirty who worked over six years in a plant. Hard manual work
and routinized jobs principally accounted for the heavy turnover (Smirnov, *op. cit.*,
p. 53). The Gorkii Gorkom, however, was cited for its shortage of sociologists
(Chusovikin, *op. cit.*, p. 11).

44. The use of the social sciences was approved by the Central Committee in September
1967 (cf. *Partiinaia zhizn'*, no. 17 (1967): 3–12). For the argument stressing the need
of social research for scientific Party leadership, see E. Lisavtsev, V. Naslin, and N.
Ovchinnikov, *Pravda*, 11 May 1965, p. 2. The conservative Party view is expressed
by S. Trapeznikov, head of the Department of Science and Educational Institutions,
Pravda, 8 October 1965, pp. 3–4. The continuing conflict between the ideologists and
sociologists is evident from the report of the conference held in November 1969 at
the Academy of Social Sciences of the CPSU. Burlatskii and Glezerman attacked Levada
for his apoliticism as well as for the influence of Western sociology on his thought
(for the report, see V. E. Koslovskii and Ia. A. Sychev, *Filosofskie nauki*, no. 3 (1970):
173 ff.).

45. F. L. Chusovikin cites a study conducted in Leningrad which estimated that
only 25–30 percent of the decisions adopted were actually executed. Communication
problems were equally serious. Among the apparatchiki from the Leningrad Obkom
to the primary Party organs, between 56 percent and 77 percent knew nothing about
a series of Party decrees (Chusovikin, *op. cit.*, p. 30).

46. *Ibid.*, pp. 35–40. The Soviet press has provided a great deal of specific information
on the application of NOT (Scientific Organization of Labor) to the Party bureaucracy
(cf. G. Popov, *Partiinaia zhizn'*, no. 16 (1966): 9–10; M. Gavrilov, *Partiinaia zhizn'*,
no. 12 (1966): 43 ff.; P. Golovchenko, *Pravda*, 22 January 1967, p. 2; *Partiinaia
zhizn'*, no. 17 (1968): 35–39.

47. After Khrushchev's fall, a number of time-motion studies were made on the
division of time spent by instructors. One gorkom secretary noted that over fifty-six
days, approximately 70 percent of the instructors' time, was spent in preparation of
materials, collection of data, and "*rukovodstvo*" by telephone. The instructors of the
agitprop otdel were frequently shunted off to collecting data on purely production tasks,
and the instructors of the industrial transport otdel spent an average of thirteen days
per month collecting data on production (M. Kolesnikov, *Partiinaia zhizn'*, no. 10 (1968):
31 ff.). For similar analyses, see N. Rodionov, *Kommunist*, no. 9 (1968): 61, and
G. Popov, *Kommunist*, no. 13 (1968): 73.

48. The argument against specialization is summarized by Chusovikin, *op. cit.*, pp.
39–40. The isolation and red tape in the apparatus and the inability of the instructor
to develop the proper degree of functional specialization have been cited as reasons

for abolishing branch departments of this level (cf. *Partiinaia zhizn'*, no. 15 (1968): 41 ff.).

49. Two new two-year divisions of the Higher Party School have been formed in Gorkii and Kharkov. In addition, in 1968, 120 republican and oblast centers were formed for retraining local Party, Soviet, and journalist cadres (*Partiinaia zhizn'*, no. 17 (1968): 22–26; see also M. Nazarov, *Kommunist*, no. 1 (1970): 78). Through 1969, approximately 140 thousand Party and other cadres had passed through the new courses.

50. To increase the capacity to fight revisionism, the Institute of Marxism-Leninism was reorganized and expanded in 1968. Whether a similar reorganization of the Academy of Social Sciences occurred is not clear (*Partiinaia zhizn'*, no. 16 (1968): 20–21).

51. For the need to develop courses as a defense against revisionism, see *Partiinaia zhizn'*, no. 15 (1968): 37–40. The curriculum and organizational problems of the new courses are discussed in *ibid.*, no. 22 (1969): 32–39.

52. The Higher Party Schools may be undergoing a shift in function. The emphasis upon higher Party education in the recruitment of secretaries as an addition to civilian training rather than as a substitute for it may indicate a new strategy in which the principal concentration of the net of Party schools is on political, ideological, and organizational training rather than, as under Khrushchev, a major source for the technical training of Party cadres (for the recruitment figures, see Moralev, *op. cit.*, p. 48).

53. With some variation, the short courses include Party history, the ideology of Communist construction, the economy and organization of production, and the practice of Party organization and leadership. The first several course cycles were characterized as disorganized and poorly prepared (*Partiinaia zhizn'*, no. 17 (1968): 22–26).

54. A. Liashko, *Partiinaia zhizn'*, no. 15 (1968): 19–20; A. Beliakov, *Partiinaia zhizn'*, no. 14 (1969): 35–38.

55. M. Ponomarev, *Ekonomicheskaia gazeta*, no. 26 (1968): 6.

56. M. Khaldeev, *Partiinaia zhizn'*, no. 9 (1969): 24–25; S. Sabanev, *Pravda*, 21 June 1969, p. 2; editorial article, *Partiinaia zhizn'*, no. 7 (1969): 3 ff.

57. The development of *politinformatory* as a means of reaching educated audiences with the Party view is authoritatively discussed in V. I. Brovikov and I. M. Popovich, *Sovremennye problemy politicheskoi informatsii i agitatsii* (Moscow: "Mysl," 1969). The book, the result of a survey of the Sociological Laboratory of the Academy of Social Sciences, gives interesting and valuable data on the degree of penetration of the Party press.

58. The conflict between conservatives favoring traditional methods of agitation over the newer form of agitation is convincingly discussed by Aryeh L. Unger, "Politinformator or Agitator: A Decision Blocked," *Problems of Communism* 19, no. 5 (1970): 30–43.

59. The reversal of the initial policies of de-Stalinization is dated by Wolfgang Leonhard in the spring of 1965. The political conservatism of Khrushchev's successors is closely related, but not identical, with the organizational traditionalism discussed above (cf. Leonhard, "Politics and Ideology in the Post-Khrushchev Era," in Dallin and Larson, *op. cit.*, pp. 44–45).

60. *Pravda*, 10 December 1964, pp. 1–3. The growth rate of heavy industry was held steady at 8.2 percent and consumer goods were raised from 6.5 percent in 1964 to 7.7 percent in 1965. Agricultural investment was raised by 18 percent over 1964 and the defense budget cut by one-half million rubles. In the conflict between metallurgy and chemicals, Kosygin opted for chemicals (*ibid.*).

61. *Pravda*, 20 February 1966, pp. 1–6. The draft proposed doubling chemical production, a 40 percent rise in Group B, and a major increase in the production of passenger automobiles. Steel was to be held to a growth rate of slightly over 10 percent. The

final draft directives in April made major new commitments to welfare. A basic shift in priorities was indicated by the decision to increase allocations to steel (*ibid.*, 10 April 1966, pp. 2–7).

62. In 1970, token planned increases in the public defense budget were made for the first time since 1965. The budget was held at 17.9 billion rubles (cf. V. F. Garbuzov, *Pravda*, 17 December 1969, pp. 4–5).

63. An excellent example of the collective leadership's difficulties in meeting the claims on resources is provided by the upward revision of the Directives of the Five-Year Plan in 1967. The rate of industrial growth was increased from 47 to 50 to 53 percent; Group A was to increase to 55 percent, B to 49 percent (N. K. Baibakov, *Izvestiia*, 11 October 1967, pp. 2–3). In part this stemmed from the new welfare proposals which committed the leadership to an additional six billion rubles. The subsequent annual plans for 1969 and 1970, however, had reduced targets and Group B was given priority. Actual assignments still greatly favor heavy industry.

64. In 1968, the rates for B outstripped A 8.6 to 7.9 percent; in 1969, 7.5 to 7.2 percent; and in 1970, 6.8 to 6.1 percent (cf. *Izvestiia*, 11 October 1967, pp. 2–3; *Pravda*, 11 December 1968, pp. 1–3; and *Pravda*, 17 December 1969, pp. 1–3).

65. Despite the 1967 committments to metallurgy, the 1969 and 1970 annual plans have again given majority priority to a chemical program.

66. In late May, Podgorny announced in Baku the new priority given to consumer goods at the expense of heavy industry and defense. In June, however, Suslov declared the desire to improve consumption but added that sacrifices were required to maintain defense (*Pravda*, 22 May 1965, pp. 1–2; *ibid.*, 5 June 1965, pp. 3–4). Brezhnev bowed to the military priorities in July, as did Kosygin (*ibid.*, 4 July 1965, pp. 1–2, and *ibid.*, 12 July 1965, pp. 1–2). About a month earlier, Brezhnev had proposed an increase in allocations for agricultural reclamation (*ibid.*, 28 May 1966, pp. 1–2).

67. *Ibid.*, 9 June 1966, pp. 1–2.

68. *Ibid.*, 5 June 1966, pp. 2–3.

69. *Ibid.*, 10 June 1966, pp. 1–2.

70. *Izvestiia*, 25 September 1966, p. 2. The major formal cutback was in the production of passenger automobiles, a personal priority with Kosygin.

71. Cf. Kosygin's remarks, *Izvestiia*, 7 March 1967, pp. 1–2; Podgorny, *Pravda*, 19 March 1967, pp. 1–2; Brezhnev, *Pravda*, 11 March 1967, pp. 1–3.

72. Brezhnev, *Pravda*, 6 July 1967, p. 2; for the decree on metallurgy, see *Izvestiia*, 6 August 1967, p. 2.

73. D. S. Polianskii, *Kommunist*, no. 15 (1967): 27–28.

74. *Pravda*, 30 October 1968, pp. 1–3.

75. In April, Kapitonov publicly advocated increasing allocations to defense prior to the announcement that additional production and delivery of 119 million rubles of consumer goods would be produced (*Pravda*, 23 April 1969, p. 2, and *Izvestiia*, 26 April 1969, p. 2). In June, Brezhnev noted that substantial funds had to be allocated to defense (*Pravda*, 8 June 1969, pp. 1–4).

76. In July 1970, Brezhnev proposed an increase of 70 percent in agricultural allocations over existing levels (*Pravda*, 3 July 1970, pp. 1–3). At the same plenum he indicated that his priorities would be affirmed at the Twenty-fourth Congress later in the year. Two weeks later, the congress was postponed (*Pravda*, 14 July 1970, p. 1).

77. A. N. Kosygin, *Pravda*, 28 September 1965, pp. 1–4; a full translation is contained in *CDSP* 17, no. 38 (1965): 4.

78. There are a number of excellent commentaries on the reform by Western economists. See, among many others, Theodore Frankel, "Economic Reform: A Tentative

344 Notes

Appraisal," *Problems of Communism* 16, no. 3 (1967): 29–41; Keith Bush, "The Reforms: A Balance Sheet," *ibid.*, no. 4 (1967): 30–41; Gertrude E. Schroeder, "Soviet Economic Reforms: A Study in Contradictions," *Soviet Studies* 20, no. 1 (1968): 1–21.

79. The Law of 4 October 1965 is reprinted in *Spravochnik partiinogo rabotnika*, 6th ed. (Moscow, 1966), pp. 281–332.

80. For an excellent description of the structural changes in 1965, see Alec Nove, *The Soviet Economy: An Introduction*, 2nd rev. ed. (New York, 1969), pp. 82 ff. A full Soviet account of the planning structure at all levels of the hierarchy can be found in G. A. Ivanov and A. Sh. Pribluda, *Planovye organy v SSSR* (Moscow: Ekonomika, 1967), particularly pp. 55 following.

81. On the general theory of the reform, cf. Frankel, *op. cit.*, and Bush, *op. cit.* A precise, clear account of the transitional period from 1962 to 1966 is contained in Eugene Zaleski, *Planning Reforms in the Soviet Union, 1962–1966*, trans. Marie-Christine MacAndrew and G. Warren Nutler (Chapel Hill: University of North Carolina Press, 1967).

82. Cf. A. Aleksandrov, *Pravda*, 19 March 1968, p. 3; V. Lisitsyn and G. Popov, *Pravda*, 19 January 1968, p. 2; Lisitsyn and Popov, *Kommunist*, no. 1 (1970): 56–61; A. Berg and I. Novik, *Kommunist*, no. 2 (1965): 19–29. Two particularly interesting efforts to resolve the dilemmas of power and functional specialization can be found Iu. Tikhomirov, *Sovetskoe gosudarstvo i pravo*, no. 1 (1967): 14–22 and V. G. Visniakov, *Sovetskoe gosudarstvo i pravo*, no. 11 (1966): 30–38.

83. A. Berg, V. Belkin, and A. Birman, *Izvestiia*, 9 September 1966, p. 2.

84. An excellent discussion of the development of information processing is contained in N. Kovalov, *Voprosy ekonomiki*, no. 2 (1970): 120–31; see also, A. Burmistrov, *Ekonomicheskaia gazeta*, no. 38 (1970): 5 ff; *Ekonomicheskaia gazeta*, no. 39 (1970): 10; A. I. Berg, *Trud*, 17 December 1967, p. 2; F. A. Savenkov, *Sovetskoe gosudarstvo i pravo*, no. 3 (1967): 23–30; K. Sergeichuk, *Ekonomicheskaia gazeta*, no. 28, (1969): 22–23.

85. *Pravda*, 25 January 1970, p. 1. In 1968, the number of enterprises on the new system increased from 7,000 to 27,000 enterprises.

86. A. Birman, *Literaturnaia gazeta*, 14 February 1970, p. 10.

87. The calculations are those of Stanley H. Cohn, in "General Growth Performance in the Soviet Economy," U. S., Congress, Joint Economic Committee, *Economic Performance and the Military Burden in the Soviet Union* (Washington, D. C., 1970), p. 9.

88. Robert A. Dockstader, "Developments in Soviet Industry," in *Economic Performance and the Military Burden*, pp. 18–20. Of special political interest have been the short falls in deliveries of industrial products to agriculture; with the exception of mineral fertilizers, the goals of the March 1965 plenum will not be met.

89. Cohn, *op. cit.*, p. 14.

90. *Ibid.*, p. 12. For an excellent analysis, see Gertrude E. Schroeder, "Soviet Technology: System vs. Progress," *Problems of Communism* 19, no. 5 (1970): 19–30. For a lengthy Soviet analysis of the technical lag, see O. Sitnikov, *Planovoe khoziaistvo*, no. 9 (1969): 31–42.

91. These include high labor turnover, shortages of skills and construction materials; underutilization of equipment; jurisdictional disputes; revisions in plans; mismanagement in supply; and confusion arising from too many competing projects; Scot Butler, "The Soviet Capital Investment Program," *Economic Performance and the Military Burden*, pp. 44–45.

92. Robert W. Campbell, "Economic Reform in the USSR," *American Economic Review* 58, no. 2 (1968): 550.

93. Tatu, *op. cit.*, pp. 437–60, traces in close detail the struggle of liberals and conservatives on the reform of the economy. The opposition of the Party apparat to the abolition of the sovnarkhozy was particularly evident.

94. Abram Bergson, *Planning and Productivity under Soviet Socialism*, pp. 69–70.

95. Gertrude E. Schroeder, "The 1966–1967 Soviet Industrial Price Reform: A Study in Complications," *Soviet Studies* 20, no. 4 (1969): 462–77.

96. V. Trapeznikov, *Izvestiia*, 18 January 1970, pp. 1, 3.

97. Schroeder, "Soviet Economic Reforms," pp. 12–14; see also O. Latis and G. Ustinov, *Izvestiia*, 27 November 1968, p. 2.

98. Schroeder, "Soviet Economic Reforms," p. 6; see also Bush, "The Reforms," p. 31.

99. V. Ivanchenko, *Pravda*, 14 January 1969, p. 1.

100. *Economicheskaia gazeta*, no. 40 (1968): 11 ff.

101. E. Liberman and L. Zhitnitskii, *Planovoe khoziaistvo*, no. 1 (1968): 19–28.

102. V. Ivanov, *Voprosy ekonomiki*, no. 5 (1969): 40. Direct ties encompassed about 21.5 percent of the delivery of ferrous metals, 29 percent of cement deliveries, but only 11 percent of chemical products (see also V. Dymshits, *Economicheskaia gazeta*, no. 36 (1969): 4–5).

103. P. Krasnobaev and V. Ivanchenko, *Planovoe khoziaistvo*, no. 7 (1970): 1–11; also *Ekonomicheskaia gazeta*, no. 9 (1968): 14–15. There were, however, a number of experiments in "free" (*bezfondy*) trade (see *Ekonomicheskaia gazeta*, no. 46 (1967): 9).

104. N. Federenko, *Planovoe khoziaistvo*, no. 4 (1970): 6 ff.

105. L. Volodarskii, *Pravda*, 8 July 1968, p. 3.

106. Academician Federenko, in favor of reform but critical of the existing system, has suggested the following reasons for the priority of security as a basic value in enterprise decision-making: (1) higher plans lead to higher normatives which, in turn, threaten lower profits; (2) uneven supply and lack of effective sanctions for suppliers in default; (3) unfulfilled plans are still more disadvantageous than lower fulfilled plans since in the former, the bonus is lost; (4) the wide variety of success indicators leads to manipulation of targets; (5) the frequency of plan changes upward in the original targets without compensating changes in resource allocation requires reserves; (6) all moral and political stimuli stress plan fulfillment; (7) a new form of "plan dogmatism" has developed. During the implementation of the plan, all unplanned economic effects are routinely postponed to receive the bonus in the following year (N. Federenko, *Voprosy ekonomiki*, no. 3 (1970): 60).

107. Cf. N. Baibakov, *Pravda*, 1 October 1968, pp. 2–3; K. N. Rudnev, *Ekonomicheskaia gazeta*, no. 23 (1968): 10; V. Karpov, *Izvestiia*, 7 August 1969, p. 2.

108. Ivanchenko, *op. cit.* One should note, of course, that the emphasis upon current planning and output has its logical effects on implementing technical innovation.

109. Cf. Bush, "The Reforms," pp. 32–33; Karl W. Ryavec, "Soviet Industrial Managers, Their Superiors, and the Economic Reform: A Study of An Attempt at Planned Behavioral Change," *Soviet Studies* 21, no. 2 (1969): 208–29. A Soviet spokesman has noted: "Many people reasoned and still reason today as follows: The whole trouble lies in the bureaucratic habits of the apparatus, in the inability and unwillingness of the employees of the ministries and departments to adjust to the new conditions and to understand the "spirit of the reform." I shall not dispute this; in part, it is true. But is this the only thing that explains the lack of coordination in the activities of chief administrations and plants?" (A. Pevzner, *Komsomolskaia pravda*, 20 December 1968, p. 2).

110. There was, of course, full recognition of the dangers to the reform: implementation

346

Notes

in resurrecting the ministerial system (cf., among many others, K. T. Mazurov, *Pravda*, 3 October 1965, p. 2; Liberman and Z. Zhitnitskii, *op. cit.*; Birman, *op. cit.*).

111. A Central Committee checkup on ministerial-enterprise relations in 1966 noted the tenacity of ministerial efforts to control the enterprise (*Partiinaia zhizn'*, no. 24 (1966): 25–26; see also, I. A. Tanchuk, *Sovetskoe gosudarstvo i pravo*, no. 1 (1967): 96–100; *Izvestiia*, 12 May 1968, p. 1; K. Voronov, *Ekonomicheskaia gazeta*, no. 1 (1970): 7).

112. A. Sh. Tuganbaev, *Sovetskoe gosudarstvo i pravo*, no. 6 (1969): 60–64; K. M. Gerasimov, *Ekonomicheskaia gazeta*, no. 24 (1968): 10–11. Increased departmentalism at this level has produced serious problems in supply and area coordination of cooperative action among ministries (*Ekonomicheskaia gazeta*, no. 35 (1969): 3).

113. M. S. Solomentsev, *Ekonomicheskaia gazeta*, no. 9 (1968): 5; V. Dymshits, *Pravda*, 5 January 1968, 2–3.

114. A. I. Lepeshkin, *Sovetskoe gosudarstvo i pravo*, no. 6 (1966): 3–11. The resurrection of the ministerial system was closely linked with the growing struggle against nationalism and regionalism (cf. *Pravda*, 16 December 1965), p. 2; *Pravda* editorial, 24 January 1966, p. 1; editorial, *Kommunist*, no. 16 (1965): 8–13).

115. *Partiinaia zhizn'*, no. 19 (1970): 3 ff.

116. A Central Committee investigation of the Ministry of the Meat and Dairy Industry charged the ministry with a continuous flow of administrative orders and paper work, a massive concern with collecting data, and superficial decision-making; internally, the ministry was criticized for excessive structure, poorly defined functions, lengthy and excessive consultation and coordination (*Partiinaia zhizn'*, no. 4 (1970): 4; see also the editorial article, *Izvestiia*, 13 March 1968, p. 1).

117. M. Simanok, *Ekonomicheskaia gazeta*, no. 36 (1969): 8; S. Smirnov, *Planovoe khoziaistvo*, no. 8 (1970): 46; Savenkov, *op. cit.*; K. Novikov, *Kommunist*, no. 13 (1969): 99–108.

118. V. Garbuzov, *Ekonomicheskaia gazeta*, no. 48 (1969): 7–8.

119. B. Kolpakov, *Kommunist*, no. 7 (1966): 66–72. Two observers believe that the ministries' search for data approaches absurdity (P. Bogatyrev and V. Shterev, *Pravda*, 20 March 1969, p. 3). This is an especially deeply ingrained tradition of Soviet industrial administration.

120. *Pravda*, 28 August 1969, p. 2.

121. Federenko, *Voprosy ekonomiki*, *op. cit.*, pp. 63 ff.

122. Kovalov, *op. cit.*, p. 125; S. Volkov, *Izvestiia*, 31 July 1968, p. 3; P. Bosikh, *Izvestiia*, 24 August 1969, p. 3; *Izvestiia*, 13 March 1968, p. 1; Simanok, *op. cit.*, p. 8.

123. Lomakin, *Partiinaia zhizn'*, *op. cit.*, pp. 9–10. For a vigorous defense of the reform against those who predicted the "collapse" of central planning, see also editorial, *Ekonomicheskaia gazeta*, no. 37 (1965): 2–3.

124. S. Titarenko, *Pravda*, 4 March 1969, pp. 4–5; G. Glezerman, *Pravda*, 29 January 1969, pp. 3–4. The relevance of the antirevisionist campaign is indicated by P. Ignatovskii, *Izvestiia*, 1 December 1968, p. 2, who pointed to the decline in the use of agricultural machinery when the MTS were abolished in 1958 and the kolkhoz took over control of machinery.

125. L. Brezhnev, *Pravda*, 13 November 1968, pp. 1–2.

126. P. J. D. Wiles, "Rationality, the Market, Decentralization, and the Territorial Principle," in Gregory Grossman, ed., *Value and Plan*, p. 202.

127. *Pravda*, 18 November 1964, p. 1.

128. At the celebration of the seventieth anniversary of Zhdanov's birth, *Pravda* lauded his report on the Party Statutes at the Eighteenth Congress (*Pravda*, 26 February 1966, p. 4).

129. See, among others, editorial, *Partiinaia zhizn'*, no. 2 (1965): 3–7; Shitarev, *op. cit.*, pp. 28–37; Kaldeev, *op. cit.*, pp. 18 ff. A lengthy essay on *rukovodstvo* is in A. A. Khromova, in K. L. Illiuminkarskii, *Voprosy partiinogo stroitel'stva* (Leningrad: Lenizdat, 1968), pp. 22–46.

130. Cf. E. Bugaev, *Partiinaia zhizn'*, no. 9 (1967): 12 ff.; *Pravda*, 9 April 1966, pp. 3–4; editorial, *Partiinaia zhizn'*, no. 1 (1966): 3–7. On the close relationship between nationalism and Party control, see G. Zimanas, *Pravda*, 24 January 1969, pp. 2–3. As Zimanas points out, the identification of Party and local interests is as often self-deception as it is conscious deception.

131. Shitarev, *op. cit.*, pp. 32–33.

132. Rodionov, *Kommunist, op. cit.*, pp. 53–64; Nuriev, *op. cit.*, p. 59 ff.

133. *Pravda*, 25 March 1966, p. 2.

134. V. Stepanov, *Pravda*, 28 December 1967, pp. 2–3.

135. S. Karnaukov, in Andreev, *op. cit.*, p. 132.

136. Despite repeated reassurances by the top Party leadership concerning the growing importance of these functions, the underlying anxiety of ideological erosion, particularly during 1966 and 1967, was clearly manifest (cf. *Partiinaia zhizn'*, no. 21 (1966): 9–18; I. Pomelov, *Pravda*, 20 February 1967, pp. 2–3).

137. L. Liaporev, *Pravda*, 23 August 1967, p. 2.

138. G. Kolbin, *Pravda*, 6 February 1967, pp. 2–3.

139. S. S. Karnaukov, *Ekonomicheskaia gazeta*, no. 47 (1968): 8. The lack of enthusiasm of the Party apparatus for the reform, even during its initial phase, was evident in the complaints voiced at the republican Party congresses preceding the Twenty-third Congress, where the republican organizations were accused of dragging their feet in implementing the reform (cf. S. Kovalev and G. Lebanidze, *Pravda*, 9 March 1966, p. 2; K. Zarodov, M. Odinets and V. Fomin, *Pravda*, 20 March 1966, p. 2).

140. The reemphasis on the Party's role in economic decision-making with its conservative emphasis upon discipline and control was announced by Brezhnev in his speech to the Moscow City Party Conference (*Pravda*, 30 March 1968, pp. 1–2). The close relationship between the Czech events and raising the role of the Party in economic decision-making was stressed in the commentary in the Party press on the April 1968 plenum (cf. editorial, *Partiinaia zhizn'*, no. 9 (1968): 7–8).

141. Cf., among many reports, P. Afansiev, *Partiinaia zhizn'*, no. 5 (1966): 16–22; G. Romanov, *Partiinaia zhizn'*, no. 11 (1967): 22–23; K. Gerasimov, *Ekonomicheskaia gazeta*, no. 22 (1968): 10–11; N. Nikolaev, *Ekonomicheskaia gazeta*, no. 35 (1969): 3.

142. An example of the type of conflict between the local political organs and the ministries has been the siting of plants by the ministries. Committed to improving the quality of urban life, the territorial Party apparatus has unsuccessfully fought the placing of new construction in industrially concentrated areas because of the pressure on labor and public services (cf. *Pravda*, 27 August 1969, p. 3, and *ibid.*, 7 January 1970, p. 2).

143. A. Tokarev, *Ekonomicheskaia gazeta*, no. 7 (1965): 4–5; G. Vashchenko, *Kommunist*, no. 13 (1967): 95–96. The latter reported that his reply to managers seeking more investment to cope with higher plans was that even if additional shops were built, no workers were available.

144. M. Sergeev, *Partiinaia zhizn'*, no. 12 (1966): 23–31; editorial, *ibid.*, no. 2 (1969): 3–7; cf. also, the roundup of 1968 local Party conferences, *ibid.*, no. 6 (1968): 18–21.

145. I. Savchuk, *Partiinaia zhizn'*, no. 22 (1966): 12–18; Golovchenko, *op. cit.*, p. 2; Tabeev, *Kommunist, op. cit.*, pp. 95–96.

146. See the Resolutions on the Omsk Obkom, *Partiinaia zhizn'*, no. 10 (1967): 3–9, and on the Rostov Obkom, *ibid.*, no. 21 (1968): 24–26. The former noted that Omsk Obkom still operated on the basis of statistical averages, was weakly concerned with efficiency, permitted a lag in capital construction, and reduced the importance of ideology and work with lower Party organs. The Rostov Obkom was criticized principally for the slow tempo of technical innovation and weak control over the enterprise funds.

147. N. Rodionov, *Kommunist*, no. 9 (1967): 63; Vatchenko, *op. cit.*, p. 18.

148. At the 1968 Moscow City Party Conference, Brezhnev declared, "The level of work done by Party organizations and the level of ideological work must be judged first and foremost by how production assignments are fulfilled, by how labor productivity is increasing, by the state of labor discipline and by how implacably the struggle against all manifestations of lack of organization and slackness is being waged" (*Pravda*, 30 March 1968, pp. 1–2). This call for more active penetration by the Party was affirmed in a *Pravda* editorial, 2 April 1968, p. 1.

149. Cf. I. Strelkov, *Pravda*, 9 March 1968, p. 2; *Partiinaia zhizn'*, no. 14 (1968): 41–42; Moralev, *op. cit.*, pp. 20–21; *Sovetskaia Belorussiia*, 2 February 1969, p. 2. At the December 1969 plenum, it was reported the Bryansk Obkom had received 1,898 requests for supply in one year (editorial, *Partiinaia zhizn'*, no. 5 (1970): 7).

150. I. Iunak, *Pravda*, 8 April 1967, p. 2; V. Mukhin, *Partiinaia zhizn'*, no. 3 (1968): 41–44. The shortage of labor has created an active competition among enterprises for personnel, largely through wage and salary inducements. In at least one case, a gorkom has intervened to stabilize wage and salary levels (M. Bogachev, *Pravda*, 21 August 1970, p. 2).

151. L. Melitski, *Pravda*, 19 March 1967, p. 2; *Pravda*, 9 March 1968, p. 2; I. Strelkov, *Pravda*, 8 April 1968, p. 2; *Izvestiia*, 19 August 1970, p. 3.

152. *Partiinaia zhizn'*, no. 5 (1968): 17–19.

153. *Pravda*, 22 September 1970, p. 2; see also editorial, *Partiinaia zhizn'*, no. 5 (1970): 9. The criticism expressed at the December 1969 plenum was largely confined to the city and raion Party committees.

154. Nazarov, *op. cit.*, p. 68.

155. For a comprehensive analysis of the *nomenklatura* but using materials largely from the pre-reform period, see Bodhan Harasymiw, "*Nomenklatura:* The Soviet Communist Party's Leadership Recruitment System," *Canadian Journal of Political Science* 2, no. 4 (1969): 496 ff, 505–7. The trend toward decentralization began, of course, under Khrushchev. In an interview, Professor Hough was informed that in Minsk about ten plant directorships were on the Central Committee *nomenklatura* and another forty to fifty on that of the republican committee (Hough, *The Soviet Prefects*, p. 152). A 1969 Soviet source indicates, however, that a medium-sized gorkom is still large. The *osnovnaia nomenklatura*, affirmed by the bureau, of the Kalinin Gorkom had 750 posts and another 180 on the *uchetno-kontrol'naia nomenklatura*, which lists the less important posts cleared in the departments. A basic concern since 1965 has been with the latter lists since it has traditionally been a source of cadre reserves (Pronin and Stepichev, *op. cit.*, pp. 170–71).

156. G. Sotnikov, *Pravda*, 10 September 1970, p. 2; see also F. Frolov, *Partiinaia zhizn'*, no. 19 (1967): 28–29. As the Central Committee decree on the work of the Estonian Central Committee on cadres pointed out, however, the responsibility for cadres is a joint one (*Partiinaia zhizn'*, no. 6 (1967): 8–12). The control over political posts and of enterprise officials subordinate to local soviets, however, has not changed (cf. Iu. Zavarukhin, *Partiinaia zhizn'*, no. 5 (1970): 12 ff.).

157. Frolov, *op. cit.*, pp. 26–31; *Partiinaia zhizn'*, no. 19 (1968): 3–5; *Pravda*, 5 June 1966, p. 3.

158. L. Morozov, *Ekonomicheskaia gazeta*, no. 40 (1968): 3–4.

159. In Volgograd Oblast, according to a Central Committee decree, 25 percent of the directorships on the obkom *nomenklatura* turned over in two years (*Partiinaia zhizn'*, no. 19 (1968): 4). Morozov notes that some 43.5 percent of the enterprise directors in the oblast turned over in the same period (Morozov, *op. cit.*, p. 4). In virtually every oblast reporting, turnover involved hundreds of positions.

160. In the Leningrad Gorkom's *osnovnaia nomenklatura* 81.5 percent of those listed had higher education and 17.7 percent had at least a secondary education; 34.4 percent in 1970 were in their jobs longer than five years in contrast to the 27.4 percent of 1965 (Zavarukhin, *op. cit.*, p. 11). In Gorki, K. F. Katushev reported 84 percent of the directors of large enterprises were engineers and technicians, and all heads of construction trusts had at least a secondary education (*Partiinaia zhizn'*, no. 10 (1967): 21–29).

161. The Irkutsk Obkom, for example, was severely criticized for the fact that only half of the chief engineers and heads of design bureaus had higher specialized education (*Partiinaia zhizn'*, no. 21 (1969): 10–12; see also Morozov, *op. cit.*, pp. 3–4; on cadres in the service and trade net, the Central Committee decree, *Partiinaia zhizn'*, no. 9 (1968): 18–20).

162. An order to reform the preparation and repreparation of economic cadres is contained in *Spravochnik partiinogo rabotnika*, 7th ed., pp. 260–70. The Central Committee decree stressing the Party's political role is in *Partiinaia zhizn'*, no. 2 (1967): 23. The Party's still important role in technical education is discussed in N. Rodionov, *Partiinaia zhizn'*, no. 14 (1968): 11–14; A. Shibaev, *Partiinaia zhizn'*, no. 10 (1967): 26 ff.

163. Editorial, *Partiinaia zhizn'*, no. 2 (1969): 4–5.

164. Perhaps the bluntest statement of the Party's need to exercise control over the managers was made by Nuriev, the first secretary of the Bashkir Obkom, who feared the managers might try to cheat on the reform (*Kommunist*, no. 16 (1965): 59–67). Similarly, the first secretary of Cheliabinsk declared he would not stand aside waiting for the ministries and glavki to resolve enterprise problems (N. Rodionov, *Kommunist*, no. 9 (1967): 54–56).

165. Editorial, *Partiinaia zhizn'*, no. 14 (1965): 5–10; editorial, *ibid.*, no. 14 (1966): 3–7; E. Bugaev, *ibid.*, no. 1 (1967): 12.

166. The evidence suggesting a basic conflict between the Party apparatus and Brezhnev and Shelepin and the Party-State Control Committee is gathered by Christian Duevel, "The Dismantling of Party and State Control as an Independent Pillar of Soviet Power," *Bulletin of the Institute for the Study of the USSR* 13, no. 3 (1966): 3–18.

167. A major objection of the Party-State Control Committee was the potentiality of control over the Party organs themselves. In December 1965 Brezhnev noted explicitly that the organs of popular control did not have the right to control the Party's apparatus (*Pravda*, 7 December 1965, p. 1).

168. V. I. Zaluzhnyi, *Narodnyi kontrol' v sovremennykh usloviiakh* (Moscow, 1970), p. 27.

169. *Pravda*, 9 April 1966, pp. 3–4.

170. Central Committee Decree of 30 June 1967, *Spravochnik partiinogo rabotnika*, 8th ed., pp. 297–98. The strengthening of the Party commissions indicated not only the strengthening of control over the lower Party apparatus but also the determination to maintain the primacy of Party control in the ongoing competition between the Party and state under Khrushchev's successors (cf. *Partiinaia zhizn'*, no. 9 (1967): 13–14).

171. Vatchenko, *op. cit.*, p. 24; an extensive discussion of the revived agencies is in A. Agapova, *Kommunist*, no. 4 (1969): 65–74.

172. *Partiinaia zhizn'*, no. 21 (1968): 9; *Ekonomicheskaia gazeta*, no. 45 (1968): 2.

173. *Spravochnik partiinogo rabotnika*, 9th ed., pp. 184–93. The general reorganization is described in Zaluzhnyi, *op. cit.*, pp. 30–32.

174. *Pravda*, 28 May 1966, p. 1; *ibid.*, 31 October 1968, pp. 1 ff. The control organs in 1967 and 1968 were directed to public services as well as to the construction of enterprises of the metallurgical, chemical, food, meat and dairy, and light industries (Zaluzhnyi, *op. cit.*, pp. 34, 130–1).

175. Zaluzhnyi, *op. cit.*, pp. 34–39; Shikin, *op. cit.*, pp. 11–14; editorial, *Partiinaia zhizn'*, no. 19 (1965): 5–10.

176. *Partiinaia zhizn'*, no. 9 (1967): 13.

177. *Ibid.*, no. 2 (1969): 5–6.

178. S. Sdabet, *Partiinaia zhizn'*, no. 3 (1967): 30–31; D. Dmitriev, *Partiinaia zhizn'*, no. 10 (1969): 15–19. A. Georgiev, *Partiinaia zhizn'*, no. 19 (1968): 38–43.

179. The work of the Party Control Committee has been periodically reported since 1966 in *Partiinaia zhizn'*; cf., as examples, the following issues: no. 21 (1966): 50; no. 9 (1967): 13; no. 17 (1968): 45.

180. P. Kovanov, *Izvestiia*, 24 November 1966, p. 15; P. Kovanov, *Kommunist*, no. 7 (1967): 49–56; I. Shikin, *Izvestiia*, 13 February 1968, p. 1.

181. On the toleration of local Party organs to violations of state discipline, see editorial, *Pravda*, 2 April 1968, p. 1; editorial, *Partiinaia zhizn'*, no. 2 (1969): 4–5; *ibid.*, no. 9 (1969): 69; *ibid.*, no. 11 (1967): 43, and many others. The role of the Party organs is not only one of passive toleration, however. In 1968, in accordance with the directives of the reform toward decentralized investments, complaints were received of the siphoning off of large sums of investment from centrally approved projects to public buildings, stadiums, swimming pools, and so forth. A Soviet writer complained that the local Party organs not only compromised with the situation but actually "pushed them on the path" (editorial, *ibid.*, no. 4 (1970): 35).

182. For examples of the opposition to increased plans by the managers, largely because of fears of supply failure, see G. Krivoshein, *Partiinaia zhizn'*, no. 3 (1968): 37–40; Vashchenko, *op. cit.*, pp. 95–96; Mukhin, *op. cit.*, pp. 41–44. The managers' assumption that they have a moral right to support from the Party apparat has been stressed in the literature discussing the opposition of the managers to Party withdrawal from the problems of microcoordination (see *Pravda*, 9 March 1968, p. 2; V. Fedenin, *Kommunist*, no. 17 (1969): 99–108; A. Eshtokin, *Pravda*, 26 February 1967, p. 2).

183. L. Brezhnev, *Pravda*, 30 September 1965, pp. 1–3.

184. V. Ososkov, *Partiinaia zhizn'*, no. 19 (1965): 25–28; K. Sergeev, *Partiinaia zhizn'*, no. 2 (1967): 42; editorial, *Partiinaia zhizn'*, no. 3 (1968): 26.

185. A. F. Rumiantsev, *Partiinaia zhizn'*, no. 2 (1965): 37 ff.

186. A. Kosygin, *Pravda*, 28 September 1965, pp. 1–4. It should be pointed out that neither Rumiantsev nor Kosygin denied the right of Party control under the new conditions. The distinctions, while those of degree, have been, and undoubtedly will be, significant.

187. Golovchenko, *op. cit.*, p. 2; editorial, *Partiinaia zhizn'*, no. 10 (1967): 8–9; I. Zaitsev and I. Pronin, *Partiinaia zhizn'*, no. 14 (1967): 30–35.

188. A. Putria, *Partiinaia zhizn'*, no. 1 (1969): 44–49; P. Pavliukevich, *Partiinaia zhizn'*, no. 3 (1968): 28 ff.

189. V. Shrivrinskii, *Partiinaia zhizn'*, no. 21 (1968): 35–37.

190. Bogachev, *op. cit.*, p. 2.

191. I. Kh. Kallion and Kh. Kh. Shneider, *Sovetskoe gosudarstvo i pravo*, no. 3 (1967): 65–72.

192. Zaluzhnyi, *op. cit.*, p. 178. For an assessment of the duplication and conflict between the groups and posts of popular control and the Party's commissions for control over the administration, see Agapova, *op. cit.*, pp. 65–74.

193. *Spravochnik sekretariia pervichnoi partiinoi organizatsii* (Moscow, 1965), p. 29; see also, F. Kozyrev, *Partiinaia zhizn'*, no. 4 (1968): 39. On occasion, where a primary Party organ has the support of the Party apparatus in a conflict with a director, it can force ministry to replace him, as in the case of the Nikolaev Building Materials Plant (editorial, *Partiinaia zhizn'*, no. 2 (1969): 7).

194. V. Provotorov, *Pravda*, 29 May 1969, p. 2.

195. *Pravda*, 29 August 1970, pp. 3–4.

196. *Ibid.*, 14 April 1970, pp. 1–2.

Glossary

chinovnik	A bureaucrat.
edinonachalie	One-man management; the assignment of responsibility for the operation of an institution to one man.
glavk	A chief or main administration; an intermediate organ of administration with specialized responsibilities.
gorkom	A city party committee.
Gosbank	The central bank of the Soviet Union.
Gosekonomsovet	The State Scientific-Economic Council which assumed responsibility for long-range planning in 1960 and was abolished at the November 1962 plenum.
Goskontrol'	The system of controls carried out by the Soviet state apparatus; the specialized ministries, committees, and commissions of state control exercising control.
Gosplan	The State Planning Committee.
Gossnab	The State Committee for Material-Technical Supply.
Gosstroi U.S.S.R.	The State Committee for Construction; the specialized committee for coordinating construction.
guberniia	A province; replaced in 1929–30 by the oblast, krai, and autonomous republic.
gubkom	A provincial Party committee.
ispolkom	An executive committee; usually a local Soviet (state) organ.
khozrashchët	The system of economic accountability by which an enterprise is legally and financially responsible for its economic transactions and is, theoretically, financially autonomous.
KNK	The Committee of Popular or People's Control.
krai	A territory; legally, it is similar to an oblast or autonomous republic.
kraikom	A territorial Party committee.

kto kogo	A Bolshevik term expressing the need to eliminate rivals in the struggle for power.
kustarnichestvo	Lack of professionalism in revolutionary work.
letuchka, letuchii kontrol'	A form of mass control characterized by sudden, rapid, or unannounced visits.
mestnichestvo	The violation of state discipline by placing local or regional interests above national priorities.
nomenklatura	A list of products centrally planned or supplied; a list of offices requiring party approval or designation.
nachal'nik	Head or superior of an organization; in industry, the head of a shop.
Narkomfin	The People's Commissariat of Finance; in 1946 it became the Ministry of Finance.
natsional'naia spetsifika	Cultural and other characteristics defining a community or a people.
obkom	A provincial Party committee.
oblast'	The administrative designation of a province.
oblispolkom	The executive committee of the provincial soviet.
operativka	A short production conference.
Orgburo	The Organizational Bureau of the Central Committee, formed in 1919, abolished in 1952.
Orgotdel	The organizational department of city and rural Party committees.
otdel	Department or division of the Party or state apparatus.
Partorg	A Party organizer; Party official placed in one of the more important industrial enterprises who reported to the Central Committee; the job was abolished in 1956.
PGK	Party-State Control Committee; an administrative organ which merged Party and state control in November 1962 and was abolished in December 1965.
planërka	A short conference, usually related to planning or supply.
politotdel	A department within the Party apparatus for strengthening political control over an economic sector.
praktiki	Administrative and industrial officials who lack the formal educational credentials associated with a post.
promfinplan, tekhpromfinplan	The basic technical, industrial, and financial plan of the enterprise.
Prompartiia	Political designation for a group of Soviet industrial specialists who were tried in December 1930 for espionage and sabotage.
proverka i kontrol'	Checkup and control; supervision of the execution of decisions by the Party apparat.
rabkor	Volunteer press correspondent at an industrial plant or construction site.
raikom	Rural or urban district Party committee.

raion	Small administrative territorial division in the U.S.S.R. in oblasti and large cities.
RKI	Raboche-krest'ianskaia inspektsiia, or rabkrin; The Workers' and Peasants' Inspectorate organized in 1920 which merged with the Central Control Commission in 1923 to form a joint Party-state control system.
rukovodstvo	The leadership functions of the Soviet Communist Party.
shablon	A routine or stereotyped approach to decision-making.
shefstvo	The patronage or aid extended by an urban or industrial group to an agricultural enterprise.
shturmovshchina	The rush to fulfill the plan by an industrial enterprise.
Soiuzsel'khoztekhnika	All-Union Farm Machinery Association formed in 1961 to supply agriculture with industrial products.
sovnarkhoz	A council of the national economy; the system of regional industrial boards which directed Soviet industry during the Civil War and NEP. In 1957, they were reorganized in a different form to replace the ministerial system and were abolished in 1965.
Sovnarkom	The Council of People's Commissars; the leading executive organ of the Soviet state between 1917 and 1946 when it became the present Council of Ministers.
tolkach	Literally, a "pusher"; a go-between who informally coordinates supply with the production needs of an enterprise.
TPU	A territorial production administration; formed in 1962 to manage agriculture on an interdistrict basis and abolished in 1965.
tsekh	A shop; the basic production or service subdivision within an enterprise.
Tsentrosoiuz	The Central Union of Consumers' Societies in the U.S.S.R.; a prerevolutionary group of cooperatives taken over by the Bolsheviks and used extensively during NEP.
uchastok	A subdivision within a shop.
Uchraspred	The Account-Assignment Division of the Central Committee. Formed in 1920 for the listing and distribution of cadres, it merged in 1924 with the Organizational-Instruction Department to form the Organizational-Assignment Division (Orgaspred).
udarnik	A shock worker.
uezd	A district prior to 1929–30.
Vesenkha	The Supreme Council of the National Economy; from 1917 to 1932, the central organ for industrial administration. Reinstituted in 1963 to coordinate the economy, Vesenkha was abolished in 1965.
vospitanie	Upbringing, or more broadly, training or education.

A Bibliographic Note

The primary Soviet sources for this study have been the central and republican press and the specialized Party and economic journals cited in the text. Since Stalin's death, the monographic literature published in the Soviet Union by specialists on the Party apparatus, economic policy, and industrial management, while hampered by political caution and rigid methodology, is nonetheless extremely useful for gaining the contemporary Soviet perspective on the issues under investigation. Any serious effort to probe systematically any aspect of the Soviet political system will rely on the important Western empirical and theoretical studies on Soviet politics and economics, many of which are listed below and which the author gratefully acknowledges.

The Western literature which examines the relationship of the Communist party to economic decision-making is still unfortunately limited. For the student interested in the formulation of industrial and agricultural policy within the Soviet leadership, there is only the hazardous path of Kremlinology, the course of which has been impressively charted in the work of Robert Conquest, Carl Linden, Wolfgang Leonhard, Boris Nicolaevsky, Roger Pethybridge, Sidney Ploss, and Michel Tatu. Problems of the structural relationships between the Communist party and the Soviet economy have received intensive analysis in the work of John Armstrong, Jeremy Azrael, Merle Fainsod, Carl Friedrich and Zbigniew Brzezinski, Michael Gehlen, Leopold Haimson, Jerry Hough, Barrington Moore, and Leonard Schapiro. Of particular importance in this respect is the work of Jerry Hough, which surveys much the same terrain as this study but from different perspectives.

The trans-disciplinary character of this study has made the distinguished work of Western students of the Soviet economy of major importance. In addition to the theoretical work of Gregory Grossman and Peter Wiles, the author has drawn heavily upon the work of Abram Bergson, Joseph Berliner, Alexander Ehrlich, David Granick, Naum Jasny, Alec Nove, Herbert Levine, Barry Richman, and Harry Schwartz.

357

Bibliography

A Selected Bibliography

Congresses of the CPSU and Plena of the Central Committee, CPSU

VII Ekstrennyi S''ezd, RKP (b). mart, 1918. Stenograficheskii otchet. Moscow: Gosudarstvennoe Izdatel'stvo Politicheskoi Literatury, 1962.

VIII S''ezd, RKP (b). mart, 1919. Protokoly. Moscow: Gosudarstvennoe Izdatel'stvo Politicheskoi Literatury, 1959.

IX S''ezd, RKP (b). mart-aprel, 1920. Protokoly. Moscow: Gosudarstvennoe Izdatel'stvo Politicheskoi Literatury, 1960.

X S''ezd, RKP (b). mart, 1921. Stenograficheskii otchet. Moscow: Gosudarstvennoe Izdatel'stvo Politcheskoi Literatury, 1963.

XI S''ezd RKP (b). mart-aprel', 1922. Stenograficheskii otchet. Moscow: Gosudarstvennoe Izdatel'stvo Politicheskoi Literatury, 1961.

XII S''ezd RKP (b). 17–25 aprelia, 1923. Stenograficheskii otchet. Moscow: Izdatel'stvo Politicheskoi Literatury, 1968.

XIII S''ezd RKP (b). Stenograficheskii otchet. Moscow: Gosudarstvennoe Izdatel'stvo Politicheskoi Literatury, 1963.

XIV S''ezd VKP (b). 18–31 dekabria, 1925. Stenograficheskii otchet. Moscow: Gosudarstvennoe Izdatel'stvo, 1926.

XV S''ezd VKP (b). dekabr', 1927. Stenograficheskii otchet. 2 vols. Moscow: Gosudarstvennoe Izdatel'stvo Politicheskoi Literatury, 1961.

XVI Konferentsiia, VKP (b). aprel', 1929. Stenograficheskii otchet. Moscow: Gosudarstvennoe Izdatel'stvo Politicheskoi Literatury, 1962.

XVI S''ezd VKP (b). 26 iiunia–13 iiulia, 1930. Stenograficheskii otchet. 2 vols. Moscow: Partizdat TsK VKP (b), 1935.

XVII S''ezd VKP (b). 26 ianvaria–10 fevralia, 1934. Stenograficheskii otchet. Moscow: Partizdat, 1934.

XVIII S''ezd VKP (b). 10–21 marta, 1939. Stenograficheskii otchet. Moscow: Gosudarstvennoe Izdatel'stvo Politicheskoi Literatury, 1939.

Gruliow, Leo, ed. *Current Soviet Policies: The Documentary Record of the Nineteenth Communist Party Congress and the Reorganization After Stalin's Death.* New York: Frederick A. Praeger, Inc., 1953.

XX S''ezd KPSS. 14–25 fevralia, 1956. Stenograficheskii otchet. 2 vols. Moscow: Gosudarstvennoe Izdatel'stvo Politicheskoi Literatury, 1956.

Gruliow, Leo, ed. *Current Soviet Policies. Vol. II: The Documentary Record of the 20th Communist Party Congress and Its Aftermath.* New York: Frederick A. Praeger, 1956.

Vneocherednoi XXI S''ezd KPSS. 27 ianvaria–5 fevralia, 1959. Stenograficheskii otchet. 2 vols. Moscow: Gosudarstvennoe Izdatel'stvo Politicheskoi Literatury, 1959.
Gruliow, Leo, ed. *Current Soviet Policies. Vol. III: The Documentary Record of the Extraordinary 21st Communist Party Congress.* New York: Columbia University Press, 1960.
XXII S''ezd KPSS. 17–31 oktiabria, 1961. Stenograficheskii otchet. 3 vols. Moscow: Gosudarstvennoe Izdatel'stvo Politicheskoi Literatury, 1962.
Saikowski, Charlotte, and Leo Gruliow, eds. *Current Soviet Policies. Vol. IV. The Documentary Record of the 22nd Congress of the Communist Party of the Soviet Union.* New York: Columbia University Press, 1962.
XXIII S''ezd KPSS. 29 marta–8 aprelia, 1966. Stenograficheskii otchet. 2 vols. Moscow: Izdatel'stvo Politicheskoi Literatury, 1966.
Plenum Tsentral'nogo Komiteta KPSS. 24–29 iiunia, 1959. Stenograficheskii otchet. Moscow: Gosudarstvennoe Izdatel'stvo Politicheskoi Literatury, 1959.
Plenum Tsentral'nogo Komiteta KPSS. 13–16 iiulia, 1960. Stenograficheskii otchet. Moscow: Gosudarstvennoe Izdatel'stvo Politicheskoi Literatury, 1960.
Plenum Tsentral'nogo Komiteta KPSS. 10–18 ianvaria, 1961. Stenograficheskii otchet. Moscow: Gosudarstvennoe Izdatel'stvo Politicheskoi Literatury, 1961.
Plenum Tsentral'nogo Komiteta KPSS. 5–9 marta, 1962. Stenograficheskii otchet. Moscow: Gosudarstvennoe Izdatel'stvo Politicheskoi Literatury, 1962.
Plenum Tsentral'nogo Komiteta KPSS. 19–23 noiabria, 1962. Stenograficheskii otchet. Moscow: Gosudarstvennoe Izdatel'stvo Politicheskoi Literatury, 1963.
Plenum Tsentral'nogo Komiteta KPSS. 9–13 dekabria, 1963. Stenograficheskii otchet. Moscow: Izdatel'stvo Politicheskoi Literatury, 1964.
Plenum Tsentral'nogo Komiteta KPSS. 10–15 fevralia, 1964. Stenograficheskii otchet.

Books and Pamphlets

Arakelian, A. *Industrial Management in the U.S.S.R.* Translated by Ellsworth Raymond. Washington, D.C.: Public Affairs Press, 1950.
Aleksandrov, pseud. *Kto upravliaet Rossiei?* Berlin: Parabola, 1933.
Antonov-Saratovski, V. P. *Socety v epokhu voennogo kommunizma, 1918–1921.* 2 vols. Moscow: Izdatel'stvo Kommunisticheskoi Akademii, 1928–1929.
Arendt, Hannah. *The Origins of Totalitarianism.* New York: Meridian Books, 1960.
Armstrong, John A. *The Politics of Totalitarianism: The Communist Party of the Soviet Union from 1934 to the Present.* New York: Random House, 1961.
_____. *The Soviet Bureaucratic Elite: A Case Study of the Ukrainian Apparatus.* New York: Praeger, 1959.
Azrael, Jeremy R. *Managerial Power and Soviet Politics.* Cambridge, Mass.: Harvard University Press, 1966.
Balinky, Alexander, Abram Bergson, John N. Hazard, and Peter Wiles. *Planning and the Market in the U.S.S.R.* New Brunswick, N. J.: Rutgers University Press, 1967.
Barmine, Alexander. *One Who Survived.* New York: Putnam, 1945.
Barghoorn, Frederick C. *Politics in the USSR* Boston: Little, Brown, 1966.
Baykov, Alexander. *The Development of the Soviet Economic System.* Cambridge, Eng.: Cambridge University Press, 1946.
Bergson, Abram. *The Economics of Soviet Planning.* New Haven: Yale University Press, 1965.

_____. *Planning and Productivity under Soviet Socialism*. New York: Columbia University Press, 1968.

_____. *The Real National Income of Soviet Russia since 1928*. Cambridge, Mass.: Harvard University Press, 1961.

_____, and Simon Kuznets, eds. *Economic Trends in the Soviet Union*. Cambridge, Mass.: Harvard University Press, 1963.

Berliner, Joseph. *Factory and Manager in the U.S.S.R*. Cambridge, Mass.: Harvard University Press, 1957.

Bienstock, Gregory, Solomon Schwarz, and Aaron Yugow. *Management in Russian Industry and Agriculture*. New York: Oxford University Press, 1944.

Biographical Directory of the U.S.S.R. New York: Scarecrow Press, 1958.

Birman, A. *Nekotorye problemy nauki ob upravlenii narodnym khoziaistvom*. Moscow: "Ekonomika," 1966.

Bishaev, M. A., and M. Fedorovich. *Organizatsiia upravleniia promyshlennym proizvodstvom*. Moscow: Gosudarstvennoe Izdatel'stvo Planovoekonomicheskoi Literatury, 1961.

Blau, Peter M., and W. Richard Scott. *Formal Organizations: A Comparative Approach*. San Francisco: Chandler, 1962.

Boffa, G. *Inside the Khrushchev Era*. London: Marzani and Munsell, 1959.

Breev, M.V. *Planirovanie narodnogo khoziaistva*. Moscow: Izdatel'stvo Ekonomicheskoi Literatury, 1963.

Brzezinski, Zbigniew. *Alternative to Partition: For a Broader Conception of America's Role in Europe*. New York: McGraw-Hill, 1965.

_____. *Ideology and Power in Soviet Politics*. New York: Praeger, 1962.

_____. *The Permanent Purge*. Cambridge, Mass.: Harvard University Press, 1956.

_____, and Samuel P. Huntington. *Political Power: USA/USSR*. New York: Viking, 1964.

_____, ed. *Dilemmas of Change in Soviet Politics*. New York: Columbia University Press, 1969.

Bubnova, L. M., ed. *Partiino-gosudarstvennyi kontrol' v deistvii*. Moscow: "Sovetskaia Rossiia," 1964.

Bugaev, E. I., and V. M. Leibson. *Besedy ob ustave KPSS*. Moscow: Gospolitizdat, 1964.

Bukharin, Nikolai. *The Path to Socialism and the Worker-Peasant Bond*. Translated by Eugene Hardy. Moscow-Leningrad, 1925.

Carr, Edward H. *The Bolshevik Revolution, 1917–1922*. 3 vols. New York: Macmillan, 1950–1953.

_____. *Socialism in One Country, 1924–1926*. Vol. I. New York: Macmillan, 1959.

_____, and R. W. Davies. *Foundations of a Planned Economy, 1926–1929*. Vol. I, Part I. London: Macmillan, 1969.

Conquest, Robert. *The Great Terror*. New York: Macmillan, 1968.

_____. *Power and Policy in the USSR*. London and New York: St. Martin's Press, 1961.

_____. *Russia after Khrushchev*. New York: Frederick A. Praeger, 1965.

Crankshaw, Edward. *Khrushchev: A Career*. New York: Viking Press, 1966.

Crozier, Michel. *The Bureaucratic Phenomenon*. Translated by the author. Chicago: University of Chicago Press, 1964.

Dahrendorf, Ralf. *Class and Class Conflict in Industrial Society*. Stanford, Calif.: Stanford University Press, 1957.

Dallin, Alexander, and Alan F. Westin, eds. *Politics in the Soviet Union: 7 Cases.* New York: Harcourt, Brace and World, 1966.
Daniels, Robert V. *The Conscience of the Revolution: Communist Opposition in Soviet Russia.* Cambridge, Mass.: Harvard University Press, 1960.
_____. *The Nature of Communism.* New York: Vintage, 1963.
Dechert, Charles R., ed. *The Social Impact of Cybernetics.* New York: Simon and Schuster, 1967.
Denisov, A., and M. Kirichenko. *Soviet State Law.* Moscow: Foreign Languages Publishing House, 1960.
Direktivy KPSS i Sovetskogo Pravitel'stva po khoziaistvennym voprosam. 4 vols. Moscow: Gosudarstvennoe Izdatel'stvo Politicheskoi Literatury, 1957–1959.
Dobb, Maurice H. *Soviet Economic Development since 1917.* New York: International Publishers, 1948.
Dobrodemov, A. A., and A. N. Ponomarev. *Ocherki istorii moskovskoi organizatsii KPSS.* Moscow: Moskovskii Rabochii, 1966.
Drachkovitch, Milorad M., ed. *Marxism in the Modern World.* Stanford, Calif.: Hoover Institution on War, Revolution, and Peace, 1965.
Edinger, Lewis J. *Political Leadership in Industrialized Societies.* New York: Wiley, 1967.
Efimov, A. *Perestroika upravleniia promyshlennostiu i stroitel'stvom v SSSR.* Moscow: Gosudarstvennoe Izdatel'stvo Politicheskoi Literatury, 1957.
Etzioni, Amitai, ed. *Complex Organizations: A Sociological Reader.* New York: Holt, Rinehart and Winston, 1962.
Fainsod, Merle. *How Russia Is Ruled.* 1st and rev. eds. Cambridge, Mass.: Harvard University Press, 1953, 1963.
_____. *Smolensk Under Soviet Rule.* Cambridge, Mass.: Harvard University Press, 1958.
Farrell, R. Barry, ed. *Political Leadership in Eastern Europe and the Soviet Union.* Chicago: Aldine, 1970.
Fedoseev, A. F. and N. M. Keizerov. *Politicheskaia organizatsiia obshchestva pri perekhode k kommunizma.* Leningrad: Izdatel'stvo Leningradskogo Universiteta, 1968.
Fillipov, A. P., ed. *Voprosy partiinogo stroitel'stva.* 2 vols. Leningrad: Lenizdat, 1960, 1962.
Fischer, George. *The Soviet System and Modern Society.* New York: Atherton Press, 1968.
Fischer, Louis. *The Life of Lenin.* New York: Harper and Row, 1964.
Fleron, Frederick J., Jr., ed. *Communist Studies and the Social Sciences: Essays on Methodology and Empirical Theory.* Chicago: Rand McNally, 1969.
Franklund, Mark. *Khrushchev.* New York: Stein and Day, 1967.
Friedrich, Carl J., and Z.K. Brzezinski. *Totalitarian Dictatorship and Autocracy.* New York: Praeger, 1960.
_____, Michael Curtis, and Benjamin R. Barber. *Totalitarianism in Perspective: Three Views.* New York: Praeger, 1969.
Gehlen, Michael P. *The Communist Party of the Soviet Union.* Bloomington: University of Indiana Press, 1969.
Gladkov, I. A., ed. *Razvitie sotsialisticheskoi ekonomiki SSSR v poslevoennyi period.* Moscow: Izdatel'stvo "Nauka," 1965.
Glezerman, G. *KPSS—rukovodiashchaia sila sotsialisticheskogo gosudarstva.* Moscow: Gosudarstvennoe Izdatel'stvo Politicheskoi Literatury, 1954.

Granick, David. *Management of the Industrial Firm in the U.S.S.R.: A Study in Soviet Economic Planning.* New York: Columbia University Press, 1959.
_____. *The Red Executive.* Garden City, N. Y.: Doubleday, 1960.
Grigorev, V. K. *Gosudarstvennoe rukovodstvo kolkhozami.* Moscow: Moskovskii Gosudarstvennyi Universitet, 1961.
Grossman, Gregory. *Economic Systems.* Englewood Cliffs, N. J.: Prentice-Hall, 1967.
_____, ed. *Value and Plan.* Berkeley: University of California Press, 1960.
Haimson, Leopold. "Decision-Making and Communication in Soviet Industry." In Margaret Mead, ed., *Studies in Soviet Communication,* Vol. III, Part V. Cambridge, Mass.: CENIS, 1952.
Hardt, John P., Marvin Hoffenberg, Norman Kaplan, and Herbert S. Levine. *Mathematics and Computers in Soviet Economic Planning.* New Haven: Yale University Press, 1967.
Hazard, John N. *The Soviet System of Government.* 3rd ed. Chicago: University of Chicago Press, 1964.
Hough, Jerry F. *The Soviet Prefects: The Role of Local Party Organs in Industrial Decision-Making.* Cambridge, Mass.: Harvard University Press, 1969.
Huntington, Samuel P. *Political Order in Changing Societies.* New Haven: Yale University Press, 1968.
_____, and Clement H. Moore, eds. *Authoritarian Politics in Modern Society.* New York: Basic Books, 1970.
Hutchinson, John D. *Organizations: Theories and Classical Concepts.* New York: Holt, Rinehart and Winston, 1967.
Iudenkov, A. F., ed. *Voprosy partiinogo rukovodstva na sovremennom etape.* Moscow: AON, 1969.
Jasny, Naum. *Soviet Industrialization 1928–1952.* Chicago: University of Chicago Press, 1961.
Johnson, Chalmers, ed. *Change in Communist Systems.* Stanford, Calif.: Stanford University Press, 1970.
Juviler, Peter H., and Henry M. Morton, eds. *Soviet Policy-Making: Studies of Communism in Transition.* New York: Praeger, 1967.
Karlov, V., and V. Zasorin. *Po proizvodstvennomu printsipu.* Moscow: Znanie, 1963.
Karapetian, L., and V. Razin. *Sovety obshchenarodnogo gosudarstva.* Moscow: Politizdat, 1964.
Katz, Daniel, and Robert L. Kahn. *The Social Psychology of Organizations.* New York: Wiley, 1966.
Kellen, Konrad. *Khrushchev—A Political Portrait.* New York: Praeger, 1961.
Kharlamov, M. V. *Deiatel'nost' KPSS po dal'neishemu ukrepleniiu sovetskogo sotsialisticheskogo gosudarstva.* Moscow: Znanie, 1956.
Khrushchev, N. S. *O kommunisticheskom vospitanii.* Moscow: Izdatel'stvo Politicheskoi Literatury, 1964.
_____. *Stroitel'stvo kommunizma v SSSR i razvitie sel'skogo khoziaistva.* 8 vols. Moscow: Gosudarstvennoe Izdatel'stvo Politicheskoi Literatury, 1963–1964.
Kommunisticheskaia partiia Sovetskogo Soiuza v rezoliutsiiakh i resheniiakh, s"ezdov. konferentsii i plenumov TsK. 4 vols. Moscow: Gosudarstvennoe Izdatel'stvo Politicheskoi Literatury, 1961.
Kolkowicz, Roman. *The Soviet Military and the Communist Party.* Princeton: Princeton University Press, 1967.
Korelev, A., M. Nazarev, and B. Tulepbaev. *Partiinuiu rabotu na uroven' novykh zadach.* Moscow: Politizdat, 1968.

Kornhauser, William. *The Politics of Mass Society.* Glencoe, Ill.: Free Press, 1959.
Kuusinen, O. V., ed. *Fundamentals of Marxism-Leninism,* 2nd ed. rev. Moscow: Foreign Languages Publishing House, 1963.
Laird, Roy D., ed., *Soviet Agricultural and Peasant Affairs.* Lawrence, Kans.: University of Kansas Press, 1963.
Leites, Nathan A. *A Study of Bolshevism.* Glencoe, Ill.: Free Press, 1953.
Lenin, V. I. *Collected Works,* 4th ed., 45 vols. Moscow: Foreign Languages Publishing House, 1960–1970.
——————. *O sovetskom stroitel'stve.* Moscow: Gosudarstvennoe Izdatel'stvo Iuridicheskoi Literatury, 1957.
——————. *Polnoe sobranie sochinenii.* 5th ed. 55 vols. Moscow: Gosudarstvennoe Izdatel'stvo Politicheskoi Literatury, 1958–1965.
——————. *Sochineniia.* 4th ed. 37 vols. Moscow: Gosudarstvennoe Izdatel'stvo Politicheskoi Literatury, 1941–1957.
Leonhard, Wolfgang. *The Kremlin since Stalin.* Trans. by Elizabeth Wiskemann. New York: Praeger, 1962.
Lesnoi, V. M. *Rukovodiashchaia rol' KPSS v sovetskom gosudarstve.* Moscow: Izdatel-'stvo Moskovskogo Universiteta, 1961.
Liberman, Simon. *Building Lenin's Russia.* Chicago: University of Chicago Press, 1945.
Linden, Carl A. *Khrushchev and the Societ Leadership, 1957-1964.* Baltimore: Johns Hopkins University Press, 1966.
Lippmann, Walter. *The Communist World and Ours.* Boston: Little, Brown, 1958.
Lunev, A. E. *Obespechenie zakonnosti v SSSR.* Moscow: Iuridicheskaia Literatura, 1963.
Malyshev, A. *Partiinyi kontrol' deiatel'nosti administratsii predpriiatii.* Moscow: Moskovskii Rabochii, 1959.
March, James G., and Herbert A. Simon. *Organizations.* New York: Wiley, 1958.
Martynev, L. *Instruktor gorkoma i raikoma.* Moscow: Moskovskii Rabochii, 1956.
Menabde, A. I. *Sovetskii gosudarstvennyi apparat i voprosy ego dal'neishego sovershenstvovaniia.* Tbilisi: Metsniereba, 1965.
Meyer, Alfred. *Leninism.* Cambridge, Mass.: Harvard University Press, 1957.
——————. *The Soviet Political System.* New York: Random House, 1965.
Millikan, Max F., ed. *National Economic Planning.* New York: National Bureau of Economic Research, 1967.
Mitin, M. B., *Sovetskaia sotsialisticheskaia demokratiia.* Moscow: Nauka, 1964.
Moore, Barrington, Jr. *Soviet Politics: The Dilemma of Power; The Role of Ideas in Social Change.* Cambridge, Mass.: Harvard University Press, 1950.
——————. *Terror and Progress, USSR: Some Sources of Change and Stability in the Soviet Dictatorship.* Cambridge, Mass.: Harvard University Press, 1954.
Moralev, B. N. *Respublikanskie, kraevye, oblastnye, okruzhnye, gorodskie i raionnye organizatsii partii.* Moscow: "Mysl'," 1967.
Moshchevitin, A. D. *Podbor i vospitanie rukovodiashchikh kadrov.* Moscow: "Moskovskii Rabochii," 1962.
Nicolaevsky, Boris. *The Crimes of the Stalin Era.* New York: The New Leader, 1956.
——————. *Power and the Soviet Elite.* Edited by Janet Zagoria. New York: Praeger, 1965.
Nigro, Felix A. *Modern Public Administration.* 2nd ed. New York: Harper and Row, 1970.
Nove, Alec. *Economic Rationality and Soviet Politics; or, Was Stalin Really Necessary?* New York: Praeger, 1964.

_____. *The Soviet Economy: An Introduction.* 1st and 2nd rev. eds. New York: Praeger, 1961, 1969.

Obshchestvennye nachala v partiinoi rabote. Kiev: Gosudarstvennoe Izdatel'stvo Politicheskoi Literatury SSSR, 1962.

La Palombara, Joseph, ed. *Bureaucracy and Political Development.* Princeton, N.J.: Princeton University Press, 1963.

Partiinaia organizatsiia v borbe za pod''em promyshlennosti v gody semiletki. Moscow: Izdatel'stvo VPSh i AON, 1963.

Partiinaia rabota v promyshlennosti. Moscow: Gosudarstvennoe Izdatel'stvo Politicheskoi Literatury, 1956.

Partito Communista Italiano. *Problemy e realta dell'URSS.* Rome: Editorial Riuniti, 1958.

Pethybridge, Roger. *A Key to Soviet Politics: The Crisis of the Anti-Party Group.* New York: Praeger, 1962.

Pigalev, P. F. *Mestnye partiinye organy—organy politicheskoi i organizatsionnogo rukovodstva.* Moscow: Izdatel'stvo VPSh i AON, 1962.

Pistrak, Lazar. *The Grand Tactician: Khrushchev's Rise to Power.* New York: Praeger, 1961.

Ploss, Sidney I. *Conflict and Decision-Making in Soviet Russia: A Case Study of Agricultural Policy, 1953–1963.* Princeton, N. J.: Princeton University Press, 1965.

Ponomarev, B. N., ed. *Istoriia Kommunisticheskoi partii Sovetskogo Soiuza.* Moscow: Gospolitizdat, 1959.

Ponizov, T. I. *Upravlenie promyshlennym proizvodstvom v SSSR.* Moscow: Izdatel'stvo Ekonomicheskoi Literatury, 1963.

Pronin, I., and S. A. Smirnov, comps. *Zhiznennaia sila leninskikh printsipov partiinogo stroitel'stva.* Moscow: Izdatel'stvo Politicheskoi Literatury, 1970.

_____, and M. Stepichev. *Leninskie normy partiinoi zhizni.* Moscow: Izdatel'stvo Politicheskoi Literatury, 1969.

Richman, Barry. *Soviet Management.* Englewood Cliffs, N. J.: Prentice-Hall, 1965.

Rigby, T.H. *Communist Party Membership in the USSR, 1917–1967.* Princeton: Princeton University Press, 1968.

Rodionov, P. A. *Kollektivnost'—vysshii printsip partiinogo rukovodstva.* Moscow: Izdatel'stvo Politicheskoi Literatury, 1967.

Rosovsky, Henry, ed. *Industrialization in Two Systems.* New York: Wiley, 1966.

Rush, Myron. *Political Succession in the USSR.* New York: Columbia University Press, 1965.

_____. *The Rise of Khrushchev.* Washington, D. C.: Public Affairs Press, 1958.

Samokhvalov, F. V. *Sovety narodnogo khoziaistva, 1917–1932.* Moscow: Izdatel'stvo "Nauka," 1964.

Saratovskaia partiinaia organizatsiia, 1921–1925. 2 vols. Saratov: Izdatel'stvo Saratovskogo Universiteta, 1957.

Schapiro, Leonard. *The Communist Party of the Soviet Union.* New York: Random House, 1960.

_____. *The Origins of the Communist Autocracy: Political Opposition in the Soviet State; The First Phase, 1917–1922.* Cambridge, Mass.: Harvard University Press, 1956.

_____, ed. *The USSR and the Future: An Analysis of the New Program of the CPSU.* New York: Praeger, 1963.

Schwartz, Harry. *The Soviet Economy since Stalin.* Philadelphia: Lippincott, 1965.

Shchegolev, A. I. *O leninskom stile v rabote.* Riga: Latgozizdat, 1963.

Shipoleva, N. A., and A. I. Nedavnii. *Osnovy sovetskogo gosudarstvennogo stroitel'stva i prava*. Moscow: "Mysl'," 1965.

Shitarev, G., ed. *Partiinoe stroitel'stvo*. Moscow: "Mysl'," 1968.

Simon, Herbert A. *Administrative Behavior*. 2nd ed. New York: Macmillan, 1957.

Simmons, E. J., ed. *Continuity and Change in Russian and Soviet Thought*. Cambridge, Mass.: Harvard University Press, 1955.

Simmonds, George W., ed. *Soviet Leaders*. New York: Thomas Y. Crowell, 1967.

Skriabin, V. *Novoe v rabote partorganizatsii po rukovodstvu promyshlennostiu*. Kiev: Gosudarstvennoe Izdatel'stvo Politicheskoi Literatury, 1960.

Slepov, L., and G. Shitarev. *Leninskie normy partiinoi zhizni i printsipy partiinogo rukovodstva*. Moscow: Znanie, 1956.

Slepov, L. *Mestnye partiinye organy*. Moscow: VPSh pri TsK KPSS, 1954.

_____. *Vysshie i mestnye organy partii*. Translated as *Higher and Lower Party Organs*. New York: U. S. Joint Publications Research Service, 1959.

Smirnov, S. A. *Demokraticheskii tsentralizm*. Moscow: VPSH pri TsK KPSS, 1966.

_____. *Partiinoe rukovodstvo khoziaistvennym stroitel' stvom*. Moscow: "Mysl'," 1967.

Smoredinakov, L. A., ed. *Ocherki istorii partiinoi organizatsii Tiumskoi oblasti*. Sverdlovsk: Sredne-Ural'skoe Knizhnoe Izdatel'stvo, 1965.

Smyshliaev, V. A. *KPSS v period stroitel'stva kommunizma*. Leningrad: Izdatel'stvo Leningradskogo Universiteta, 1967.

Snastin, V. I. *V edinstve teorii i praktiki—zalog pobedy kommunizma*. Moscow: Gosudarstvennoe Izdatel'stvo Politicheskoi Literatury, 1963.

Spravochnik partiinogo rabotnika. 10 vols. Moscow: Gosudarstvennoe Izdatel'stvo Politicheskoi Literatury, 1927, 1955–1969.

Spravochnik sekretaraia pervichnoi partiinoi organizatsii. Moscow: Izdatel'stvo Politicheskoi Literatury, 1965.

Stalin, J. V. *Problems of Leninism*. 11th ed. Moscow: Foreign Languages Publishing House, 1954.

_____. *Works*. 13 vols. Moscow: Foreign Languages Publishing House, 1952–1955.

Stewart, Philip D. *Political Power in the Soviet Union*. Indianapolis and New York: Bobbs-Merrill, 1968.

Storozheva, Ia. V., ed. *Voprosy partiinoi raboty*. 3 vols. Moscow: Gosudarstvennoe Izdatel'stvo Politicheskoi Literatury, 1955–1959.

Suvorov, K. I., ed. *Nekotorye voprosy organizatsionno-partiinoi raboty v sovremennykh usloviiakh*. Moscow: Izdatel'stvo VPSh i AON, 1961.

_____, ed. *Partiia i massy*. Moscow: "Mysl'," 1966.

Tatu, Michel. *Power in the Kremlin*. Translated by Helen Katal. New York: Viking, 1968.

Thompson, Victor A. *Bureaucracy and Innovation*. University, Ala.: University of Alabama Press, 1969.

_____. *Modern Organization*. New York: Knopf, 1961.

Tiurin, D. I. *Chlenstvo v KPSS*. Moscow: "Mysl'," 1962.

Trotsky, Leon. *The New Course*. Translated by Max Schachtman. New York: Pioneer Publishing Co., 1943.

Tucker, Robert. *The Soviet Political Mind: Studies in Stalinism and Post-Stalin Change*. New York: Praeger, 1963.

Turovtsev, V. I., ed. *Narodnyi kontrol' v SSSR*. Moscow: Nauka, 1967.

Ulam, Adam. *The Bolsheviks: The Intellectual and Political History of the Triumph of Communism in Russia*. New York: Macmillan, 1965.

_____. *The Unfinished Revolution: An Essay on the Sources of Influence of Marxism and Communism*. New York: Random House, 1960.

U.S. Congress. Joint Economic Committee. *Comparisons of the United States and Soviet Economies*. Washington, D.C.: Government Printing Office, 1959.

U.S. Congress. Joint Economic Committee. *Dimensions of Soviet Power*. Washington, D. C.: Government Printing Office, 1962.

U.S. Congress. Joint Economic Committee. *Economic Performance and the Military Burden in the Soviet Union*. Washington, D. C.: Government Printing Office, 1970.

U.S. Congress. Joint Economic Committee. *New Directions in the Soviet Economy*. Washington, D. C.: Government Printing Office, 1966.

U.S. Congress. Senate. Committee on Governmental Operations. *National Policy Machinery in the Soviet Union*. Washington, D. C.: The Government Printing Office, 1960.

U.S. Congress. Subcommittee on National Security. *Staffing Procedures and Problems in the Soviet Union*. Washington, D. C.: Government Printing Office, 1963.

U.S. Department of State. *Division of Biographic Registry; Directory of Soviet Officials*. 5 vols. Washington, D. C., 1960–1966.

Venediktov, A. V. *Organizatsiia gosudarstvennoi promyshlennosti v SSSR*. 2 vols. Leningrad: Izdatel'stvo Leningradskogo Universiteta, 1957, 1961.

Vlasov, V. A. *Osnovy sovetskogo gosudarstvennogo upravleniia*. Moscow: VPSh pri TsK KPSS, 1960.

_____. and Studenikin, S. S. Sovetskoe administrativnoe pravo. Moscow: Gosudarstvennoe Izdatel'stvo Iuridicheskoi Literatury, 1959.

Yugow, Aaron. *Economic Trends in Soviet Russia*. London: Allen and Unwin, 1930.

Who's Who in the USSR, 1960/1961. New York: Scarecrow Press, 1962.

Who's Who in the USSR, 1965/1966. New York: Scarecrow Press, 1966.

Wiles, P. J. D. *The Political Economy of Communism*. Cambridge, Mass.: Harvard University Press, 1964.

Wolfe, Bertram D. *Communist Totalitarianism: Six Keys to the Soviet System*. Boston: Beacon, 1961.

Zaluzhnyi, V. I. *Narodnyi kontrol' v sovremennykh usloviiakh*. Moscow: "Mysl'," 1970.

INDEX

Academy of Sciences, Economic Division of, 153

Administration, Agricultural: agricultural councils formed, 125-126; formation of Territorial Production Administrations (TPU), 126; July 1962 conference, 127-128; structural evolution under Khrushchev, 124-128; territorial production administration, 1962-1964, structure of, 178

Administration, Industrial: authority and structure during NEP, 20; and bureaucratism, 222-224, bureaucratism under NEP, 21; Central Asian Sovnarkhoz: functions of, 218, structure of, n. 10 p. 330; centralization during Civil War, 12, during 1963-1964, 218-219, 220; civil war structure, 11-13; cleavages within, 96; conflict and controls during civil war, 12-13; coordinative problems during 1963-1964, 220-222; councils of the national economy, 12; and cybernetics, 130; functions during civil war, 11-14; informational and communicational problems, 272; Law on the Socialist Enterprise, 154; liberal-conservative conflicts about, 130; "machine-school" theory, xxii-xxiii; managerial resistance to reform, 103-104; monocratic organization, xxiii; November 1962 criticism of, 139-143; politics of reform, 150-154; post-Stalin decentralization, 103-104; problems of coordination, 271-272; problems during First Five Year Plan, 37-38; rationalization of, 268; rise of economic reformers, 129-131; shortage of technicians during First Five Year Plan, 37; stages of industrial reform, 102-109; State Committees: structure of (1963-1964), 215, and technological progress, 217; structural change during First Five Year Plan, 36-37; structural evolution of (1962-1964), 214-219; Supreme Council of the National Economy, 154, role of, 218, structure of, n. 14 p. 331; trust system under NEP, 20; USSR Council of the National Economy: planning role of, 217, structure of, n. 4 p. 330, and supply, n. 19 p. 331; Vesenkha, 11-13, under NEP, 20. *See also* Gosplan (State Planning Committee); Khrushchev; Ministerial system; November 1962 Plenum; Plant directors; Sovnarkhozy

Agriculture. *See* Administration, Agricultural

Andropov, Iuri, 162, 257

Anti-party group, 97; role of Party and Military, 98-99

Antonov-Saratovskii, V. P., 14

Armstrong, John A., xxxiv, 61, n. 87 p. 305, n. 43 p. 322; on Ukrainian apparat, 46, 51

Azrael, 13; on Anti-party group, 98

Barmine, Alexander, quoted, 39-40, 43

Baykov, Alexander, 12

Bedny, Demian, 33
Bergson, Abram, 106
Birman, A., 269; and economic reform, 130
Blake, Priscilla, 145, n. 112 p. 317
Brezhnev, L. N., 164, 258; appointment to Secretariat, 163; and economic policy, 266; and intensified Party Control, 282-283; quoted, 287
Brzezinski, Z. K., xxi
Bukharin, N., ideological defense of NEP, 32
Bulganin, N., 54, 97, 103
Bureaucracy: communication within, xxiv; pluralism, xxiii-xxiv; reform of, xxiv-xxvii

Campbell, Robert, 270
Carr, Edward Hallett, 13, 17
Central Asian Sovnarkhoz, structure of, 215
Central Control Commission, Workers' and Peasants' Inspectorate, 13, 18, 23, 38, 39; and November 1962 Plenum, 143
Central Revision Commission, activated, 281
Cheka, as agent of industrial control, 13
Chesnokov, D., 149
City Party Committee: functions of, 239-241; increased burden of (1962-1964), 205-206; relations with enterprise, 60; relations with ministries, 60; role under sovnarkhozy, 114-115; structure and personnel of, 178; and supply, 115-116; and technical progress, 116-117
Cocks, Paul, n. 1 p. 302
Cohn, Stanley H., 269
Command economy: administrative problems of, 52-55; characteristics of, xxv-xxvi; defined, xxv-xxvi; Stalin's formula for, 26-27
Committee on Popular Control: and control, 281-282; formation of, 260
Communist Party
  as agent of industrialization, 26-29
  bureaucratism under ministerial system, 46-49
  cadre policy, 278-279
  Central Asian Bureau: functions of, 192-194; 1963-1964, 232; structure of, 165-166
  Central Committee departments: dual structure of, 82; under ministerial system, 56-57; reorganization of, 167-168
  Central Committee: September 1953 Plenum, 97; July 1955 Plenum, 97, 103; December 1956 Plenum, 98; February 1957 Plenum, 98; June 1959 Plenum, 100, 116; July 1960 Plenum, 129, on role of Party, 100-101; January 1961 Plenum, 107, 124; November 1962 Plenum, 138, 144-145; September 1965 Plenum, 266
  central departments: formed, 10-11; role during First Five Year Plan, 35
  and collective leadership, 256; under Khrushchev, 75; after Stalin, 74-75
  Commission for Organizational-Party Questions, 138
  Composition of Committees (1962-1964), 159-160

Conferences: Ninth, 6; Seventeenth, 41; Eighteenth, 52

Congresses: Eighth, 8, 9, 10, 11; Ninth, 21; Tenth, 8, 11; Eleventh, 16; Twelfth, 16; Fourteenth, 21; Seventeenth, 41, 42, 43, 44; Eighteenth, 45, 48, 49; Nineteenth, 49, 65, 75; Twentieth, 54, 70, 75, 77, 103; Twenty-first, 65, 70, 75; Twenty-second, 79,117

control, xxiv-xxvi

co-option of officials under Khrushchev, 78, 80-81, 89

decentralization, after Khrushchev, 255-256; under Khrushchev, 73-74

development of functional system, 35-36

disorganization during First Five Year Plan, 35-36

"economics and politics," (1962-1964), 209-212

economic and technical training, 262-263

evolution of Party committees under Khrushchev, 77-78

formal authority of, xxx

functional problems during NEP, 17

functioning of, under Khrushchev, 87-88

as "general staff", 8

growth under First Five Year Plan, 34-36

internal communication, 262-263

leading role. *See Rukovodstvo*

Local Party organs: control over personnel, 279; and economic decisions, 275-276; under First Five Year Plan, 40-41; and *Rukovodstvo*, 277-278

membership (1962-1964), 158-159

opposition to agricultural reforms, 127

Orgburo: established, 10; personnel and control, 10-11; role during First Five Year Plan, 40; role during NEP, 32

Party and non-staff relations of, 87-89

personnel, xxxiii-xxxv; cadre training under Khrushchev, 80; changes in secretarial appointments, 80-81; problems during First Five Year Plan, 36; turnover of Party cadres under Khrushchev, 80. *See Nomenklatura*

Politburo, 15; commissions under Stalin, 56; conflicts over allocation, 265-266; established, 10; post-Khrushchev composition of, 257-258; Presidium, 99, characteristics of under Khrushchev, 79; role under First Five Year Plan, 39-40; role during NEP, 21; role after Stalin, 74; specialization within, 258

political limits on reform, 66

post-Khrushchev rationalization of, 255-264; structural innovation, 256-257

post-1965 role in decision-making, 261

rationalization during NEP, 19-20

recentralization of power, 276-277

recruitment and turnover, 260

reform of general membership under Khrushchev, 76-77

role of local party organs under the ministerial system, 57

role of local party organs during NEP, 22. *See also* Guberniia Party Committee; Uezd Party Committee

role of under reform, 277-278

Russian Bureau, 138; authority in, 192; creation of, 79; functions of (1963-1964), 231-232; new departments of 167-168; reform proposals, 137; reorganization of, 164-165; role of, 110; structure of, 82
search for viable structure under ministerial system, 44-46
Secretariat, 17-18, 99; abortive role of new economic bureaus, 231; appointments to, 161-162; Bureau for Agriculture, 161, 162; Bureau for the Chemical Industry and Light Industry, 161, 162, 191; Bureau for Industry and Construction, 161, 162; changes in, 161-164; Commission for Organizational-Party Questions, 161-162, activity of, 192, established, 10; evolution under Khrushchev, 79; Ideological Commission, 138, activity of, 191-192, structure of, 161-162; under ministerial system, 56-57; post-Khrushchev role of, 256; post-Khrushchev structure and composition of, 258-259
Structure: development of non-staff apparatus under Khrushchev, 83-84; local Party organs, structural rationalization of, 82-83; Party organs and non-staff apparatus, 206; politotdely, 10; Primary Party organs under Khrushchev, 84-86; September 1962 proposals for reform, 136-138
Transcaucasian Bureau: functions of, 192-194; role of (1963-1964), 232-233; structure of, 166-167
use of sociological methods, 261-262
vertical communication during Civil War, 10-11
volunteer principle, 260.
See also Anti-Party Group; Guberniia Party Committee; Industrialization; November 1962 Plenum; Primary Party organs; Uezd Party Committee
Conquest, Robert, 99; on Khrushchev as reformer, 68, n. 153 p. 307
Constitution, Soviet, 8
Control: mass, decline under ministerial system, 61; during First Five Year Plan, 37-38; *letuchii kontrol'*, 13; party: ambiguity of, 116-117, control over managers, 242-244, under ministerial system, 59, Party Control Commission, 85-86, and supply, 115, Party Control Committee, 133; purge of specialists, 38-39; State, State Control Commission, strengthening of, 133-134; *udaanichestvo*, 41. See also Khrushchev; Oblast Party Committee; Party-State Control Committee
Councils of National Economy. See Sovnarkhozy
Crankshaw, Edward, on post-Stalin reform, 66
Crozier, Michel, xxiv
Czechoslovakia, impact of economic reforms, 274

Demichev, P.N., 79, 109, 152, 153, 155, 161, 162, 164, 257, 259
Democratic Centralists, 7-8, 75
Dymshits, V.E., 214; defense of central planners, 152
Dymshits, V.N., replacement of V.N. Novikov as head of Gosplan, 150

Economic Policy: allocative policy, 264-266; conflict over resources, n. 6 p. 325; conflicts over allocation, 225
Economic Reform: adverse reactions to, 274; and the bureaucracy, 264-272; bureaucratic resistance to, 271; decentralized planning, 270-271; general

results of, 269-272; growth under, 269-270; incentive funds, 270; managerial response to, 271-272; and mass control, 283; planning under, 270-271; of the price system, 270; and *rukovodstvo* 273

Edeen, Alf, on czarist and Soviet bureaucracies, 55
Edinonachalie 41, 212; and *Kontrol*, 283
Efremov, L.N., 162, 163, 165
Eniutin, G., 133
Evtushenko, E., "Stalin's Heirs," 146

Fainsod, Merle, 45, n. 85 p. 298
Federenko, 271
Fischer, George, 45, 81, 82, 83
Fundamentals of Marxism-Leninism, quoted, 93-94

Gosplan (State Planning Committee), 22, 104, 139, 140; criticism of, 139-140, *see also* November 1962 Plenum; functions of (1963-1964), 216-217, n. 18 p. 331; problems of planning under reorganized sovnarkhozy, 224-226; problems of planning under sovnarkhozy, 106-107; reorganization of, 98; structure and composition of (1962-1964), 214; and technological progress, 217

Glexerman, G., 149
Gosstroi U.S.S.R. *See* State Construction Affairs Committee
Greenslade, Rush 129; on Khrushchev approach to reform, 140
Grossman, Gregory, xxv, n. 45 p. 309
Guberniia Party Committee (Gubkom), structure of, 18-19

Haimson, Leopold, xxxv
Hazard, John N., and constitutional reform, 164
Higher Party School, 80, 93, 263; 1962-1964, curriculum of, 210. *See also* Communist Party, personnel
Hodnett, Grey, n. 40 p. 321, n. 44 p. 322, n. 49 p. 315, n. 163 p. 318; quoted, 207
Hoffmann, Erik P., n. 87 p. 306
Hollander, Paul, xxvi
Hough, Jerry F., n.85 p. 302, n. 88 p. 306, n. 92 p. 306, n. 38 p. 309
Huntington, Samuel P., xxi, xxiv

Ignatov, E.N., 9
Ilychev, L.F., 79, 161, 162, 164, 192
Industrialization: and collectivization, 26; debate during NEP, 25; processes of, 27-28
Industrial—production (zonal) committees. *See* Raion Party Committees

Kaganovich, Lazar, 17, 34, 69, 97
Kamenev, L.B., 10, 16; at Ninth Congress, 21
Kapitonov, I.V., 259

Katushev, K.F., 259

Kautski, Karl, 7

Khoziaistvenniki. See Managers

Khozrashchët, under NEP, 20

Khrushchev, Nikita S., xxvii-xxviii; advantages of apparat specialization, 135-136; on advantages of sovnarkhozy, 104-105; and agriculture, 124-128; on bonuses for party officials, 79; on building Communism, 72, *see also* Party Program, 1961; cleavages with the Party apparatus; conflict with G.I. Voronov, 159; de-Stalinization, 70-71; on dogma, 69-70; and economic specialization of Party, 127; effects of reform, 96-102; ideological commitment 69-70; impact of Stalinism on Party, 70-72; interview with Iverach McDonald, 92; interview with Henry Shapiro, 92; and Liberman reforms, 131-132, 141-142; limitations as reformer, 95-102; on managerial initiative, 54-55; and managers, 97; on managers, 98, 101-102; and mass control, 132-134, 140-141, 143-145; on monolithism of Party, 73; and November, 1962 Plenum, 137-143; ouster of, 187-188; on Party-State relations, 72-73, 90-94; personality and style, 68-69; populism of, 94-95; on reduced role of Party under Stalin, 56; revisionism and Party reform, 92-93; struggle with Malenkov, 96-97; struggle for power, 99-100; struggle to reform, 65-66; on withering of Party apparatus, 94-95; on withering away of state, 92-94; *zapiska* (memorandum) of 10 September 1962: proposals for structural reform, 136-138

Kirilenko, A.P., 150, 165, 176, 192, 205, 220-221, 258, 259

Klochko, V.V., quoted, 190-191

Kollegial nost' and *edinonachalie,* 6-7

KNK. *See* Committee on Popular Control

Kosygin, A.N., 79, 98, 101, 108, 221, 258, 265, 283; and bureaucratic reform, 266-267; as reformer, xxvii

Kozlov, Frol, 80, 115, 150, 163, 193, 196

Krasin, Leonid, on Party's role, 16

Kulakov, F.D., 259

Lenin, V.I.: on bureaupathology, 15; centralism of discipline, 5-6; conceptions of authority, 5-8; on decision-making at 11th Congress, 15; *Immediate Tasks of Soviet Government,* 6; new version of, 146; *Leftwing Communism, an Infantile Disorder,* 6; on modernization, 3; and NEP, 14-17; *One Step Forward, Two Steps Back,* 4; Opposition to Democratic Centralists and Workers' Opposition, 7-8; on Party-state control, 16; on Party-state relationship, 8-11, *see also Rukovodstvo;* primacy of organization, 5; on proletarian dictatorship, 7; on revolutionary flexibility, 4; on the revolutionary vanguard, 4; role of mass participation in management, 6-7, 13; on Russian backwardness, 15; *State and Revolution* 8, 92; *Tax in Kind,* 3; on Taylorism, 6-7; on weak control of bureaucracy, 15-16; *What is to Be Done,* 4

Liberman, Evsei, xxvii, n. 7 p. 326, n. 45 p. 315; controversy over, 150-154; proposals for reform, 130-132

Liberman, Simon, 13

Lippmann, Walter, 69

Lisichkin, G., 287
Lowenthal, Richard, 72
Ludwig, Emil, 33
Lukacs, George, quoted, 71

Malenkov, G., 47, 48, 49, 52, 96-97, 274-275; and managers, 103
Management, Industrial. *See* Administration, Industrial
Marcuse, Herbert, on role of Soviet state, 33
Mazurov, K.T., 152, 257-258
Meyer, Alfred, xxi
Mikoian, 257
Ministerial system, administrative characteristics of, 51-55
Ministerial system: centralization under, 50; evolution of, 49-51; personnel
    under, 50-51; planning and production under, 53-54; problems of capital
    construction, 52-54; role of enterprise, 50-51; and technical progress, 54
Molotov, V., 17, 40, 97-98, 133
Moore, Barrington, n. 9 p. 292

Nemzer, Louis, n. 65 p. 301
Nogin, V.P., 17
Nomenklatura, xxxiv, 35, 41, 127, 278, 279; development of, 22-23; ministerial
    dominance, 58; under ministerial system, 57; under sovnarkhozy, 111
November 1962 Plenum: evolution of Party reform proposals, 136-138;
    ideological defense of, 148-149; industrial administration: administrative
    centralism of, 140; Central Asian Sovnarkhoz, 140, *see also* Central Asian
    Sovnarkhoz, criticism of, 138-143, proposed sovnarkhoz reforms, 139-140,
    142, *see also* sovnarkhozy; and Liberman proposals, 141-142; and mass
    control, 143-145, response of Party apparatus to, 155-156; and nationalism,
    194-195; response of Party apparat to, 145-149; response of Party apparat to
    economic reform, 151; summary of results, 253-255
Novikov, I.T., 214-215

Oblast Party Committee: ambiguity toward managerial controls, 117-118;
    expanded role under sovnarkhozy, 111-112; impact of November reorganiza-
    tion, 235; industrial, as agent of Moscow, 236-237; industrial and construc-
    tion, 237-238; industrial, planning role of, 236-237, relations with sovnar-
    khozy (1963-1964), 235-239; industrial and supply, 238-239; industrial and
    technical progress, 237; ministerial relations, 59-60; and personnel changes,
    175-177; and plan fulfillment, 113-114; planning role of, 112-113; relations
    with enterprise under ministerial system, 60; relations between industrial and
    agricultural Party committees, 195-198; as spokesman for regional interests,
    118; structure of, n. 40 p. 321, n. 44 p. 322, n. 45 p. 322; structures of
    divided committees, 172-175; and supply, 60, 115-116; and technical progress,
    116-117
Ordzhonikidze, Sergo, 21
Orgburo. *See* Communist Party

Osinskii, V. V., 6, 7

Parsons, Talcott, on decision-making process, xxii
Party Program, 1961, 93-94; on dictatorship of proletariat, 94; discussion of, 86-87; political uses of, 72; provisions of, 72-73
Party-State Control Committee: and administrative rationalization, 247; authority of, 198-199; authority and functions of, 179-181; competition with Party organs, 200-202; conflict with regular Party organs, 244; conflicts about, 134; control over managers, n. 78 p. 328; and control over plant directors, 247-249; elimination of 259-260; emergence of, 125-126; and managers, 145-146; personnel of n. 98 p. 324, n. 100 p. 324, n. 101 p. 325, n. 102 p. 325; political uses of, 143-145; role in construction, 245-246; and role in technical progress, 246-247; and selection of cadres, 245; staffing of, 183-186; structure of, 181-183, n. 89 p. 324, n. 90 p. 324, n. 91 p. 324, n. 92 p. 324; style of, 207-209; subordination of, 161; and supply, 247
Party-State Relations. *See Rukovodstvo*
Pel'she, A.J., 257, 258, 275
Planning Commissions: local, 232-233; establishment, 217
Plant directors: Communists among during NEP, 22; *edinonachalie*, 142; managerial practices under sovnarkhozy, 107-108; under ministerial system, 50-51; under NEP, 20; response to conditions under ministerial system, 54-55; response to imbalance, 1962-1964, 225, 226; and technical progress, 227-228
Ploss, Sidney, 99
Podgorny, N., 146, 152, 265; appointment to Secretariat, 163
Polianskii, D.S., 165, 258, 266
Politburo (Presidium). *See* Communist Party, Politburo
politinformatov, 263
Ponomarev, B., 79
Poselov, P., 34
Preobrazhenskii, E., on Party's role, 16
Primary Party organs: functions during NEP, 23-24; impact of November reorganization on, 206-207; mobilization under ministerial system, 61; relations with enterprise administration, 61; role during 1963-1964, 241-242; structure and personnel of (1962-1964), 178-179
Prompartiia (Industrial Party) Trial, 38
Proverka. *See* Communist Party, control

Raion Party Committee: abolition of (November 1962), 159; formation of industrial-production (zonal) committees, 178; problems of industrial-production committees, 197-198
Republican Party Committee: new structures of, 168-172, n. 33 p. 320, n. 34 p. 320, n. 35 p. 320-21, n. 36 p. 321, n. 37 p. 321, n. 38 p. 321; role of economic bureaus, 233-235
Rigby, T.H., 77, n. 153 p. 308
RKI. *See* Central Control Commission, Workers' and Peasants' Inspectorate
Romashkin, P.S., 93

Rudakov, A.P., 161, 162

Rukovodstvo: ambiguity of, xxxi; as an application of machine model, xxix; centralization during Civil War, 12-13; changes in Party's role with industrialization, 28-29; defined, xxvi, xxviii-xxxvi; defined at Eighth Congress, 9-10; development in 1961-1962, 128; economic reform and Party control, 132; evaluation of November reorganization 209-212; evolution under Lenin, 5-6; functions of in industrial administration, xxxii-xxxiii; "Humanists" and "technocrats," 204-205; impact of November 1962 reorganization on internal party life, 202-204; legitimacy of November 1962 Reforms, 149, *see also* November 1962 Plenum; limitations of, 275; and party control over managers, 280; party role during Civil War, 13-14; Party-state conflicts during Civil War, 9-11; and Party-state relations, xxix-xxxii; Party-state relations under Khrushchev, 94-95, under ministerial system, 57, during NEP, 21-22; politics and economics, xxxii; "politics and economics" under ministerial system, 47-49; problems of, xxxii-xxxiii; redefinition of, 274-275; redefinition under Khrushchev, 72; role of local Party organs, xxxi-xxxii; role of Party under sovnarkhozy, 109-110; role of primary Party organs, 283-284; role under reforms, 274-276; role and strains, 1962-1964, 188-190; routinization under ministerial system, 56; scope of application, xxx-xxxi; stress in a developed society, xxvii

Rumiantsev, A.F., 283

Russian Bureau, abolition of, 259

Schapiro, Leonard, 7, 45

Schwartz, Harry, 227

September 1965 Plenum, Kosygin and reform, 266-267

Shakhty Trial, 38

Shelepin, A.N., 79, 161, 162, 258, 280

Shelest, P.E., 127, 258

Shitarev, 275

Shliapnikov, A.M., 7

Shvernik, 257

Slepov, Lazar, xxix

Smirnov, Vladimir, 7

Solomentsev, M.S., 259

Sol'ts, A.A., 11

Sovnarkom (Council of Peoples' Commissars), 10

Sovnarkhozy, 139-140, 142; administrative evolution of 105-106; developments of mestnichestvo (localism), 111-112; establishment of, 99, 104-105; industrial enterprise under, 107; and mestnichestvo (localism), 226; problems of capital construction, 108-109, (1962-1964), 229-230; recentralization of, 105; structure of (1963-1964), 215-216; supply under, 106-107; supply problems (1962-1964), 225-226. *See also* Administration, Industrial; November 1962 Plenum; Plant directors

Stakhanovite movement, 61

Stalin, J.V., xxxiii; administrative centralism under, 39-40; appointed General

Secretary of CPSU, 17; appointed head of RKI, 13; *Economic Problems of Socialism*, 52; on equality, 33; on "family groups," 23; *Foundations of Leninism*, 30, 34; on ideological indoctrination of specialists, 48-49; and Lenin, 26, 29-30; and the Oppositions, 32; on Party-state relationship, 16-17, *see also Rukovodstvo; Questions Concerning Leninism*, 30, 34; struggle with Trotskii, 16; on unity and centralism, 31; and Zinoviev, 31. *See also* Command economy

State Construction Affairs Committee, 140; functions of, 219; structure and functions of, 214

State Scientific-Economic Commission, abolition of, 139, 214

Strumilin, S., 129

Supreme Council of the National Economy. *See* Administration, Industrial, Vesenkha

Suslov, M., 34, 75, 163

Sverdlov, Jakob, 9

Swearer, Howard, 125

Tatu, Michel, n. 22 p. 309, n. 45 p. 309, n. 129 p. 317, n. 140 p. 318

Territorial Party apparatus. *See* City Party Committee; Communist Party, Local Party organs; Oblast Party Committee; Raion Party Committee raion Party committees

Thompson, Victor, 285; on bureaucratic reform, xxiv-xxv; on deficiencies of monocratic organization, xxiii

Titov, V.N., 162

Totalitarianism: defined, xxvi; as mobilization, xxix

Trotskii, Leon, bureaucratic degeneration of the Party, 31

TsKK-RKI. *See* Central Control Commission, Workers' and Peasants' Inspectorate

Tucker, Robert, 72

Uezd Party Committee, (Ukom) structure of, 19

Ustinov, D.F., 257, 258, 259, 265

Vesenkha. *See* Administration, Industrial

Voronov, G.I., 127, 146, 155, 159, 165, 258; career of, 89

Wiles, Peter, xxv

Workers' Opposition, 7-8, 75

Zhdanov, A., 46, 48, 274, 275

Zhukov, G., 99

Zinoviev, G., 6, 9, 11, 16